They Didn't Listen,
They Didn't Know How

They Didn't Listen, They Didn't Know How

Olwen Davies

authorHOUSE®

AuthorHouse™ UK Ltd.
1663 Liberty Drive
Bloomington, IN 47403 USA
www.authorhouse.co.uk
Phone: 0800.197.4150

Published by AuthorHouse   08/31/2013

ISBN: 978-1-4918-7539-1 (sc)
ISBN: 978-1-4817-9764-1 (hc)
ISBN: 978-1-4918-7540-7 (e)

Contents

Acknowledgement xi
About the Author xiii
This book is dedicated to Llewela xvii
Who inspired me to become a story teller? xix

Where did Julian's journey begin? 1
His Big accident 19
Other early Hospital episodes.. 26
The Day we both said "I do" 36
Llewela Jane 54
The Eve of the millennium.. 99
Julian's life changing news 106
Julian's first obstacle.. 128
Julian's first Ambulance Journey 131
Julian's second Ambulance Journey 133
Someone's listening 135
The visitor.. 139
He Conformed to the end 142
His second encounter with Insulin Crisis 149
The beginning of the end 157
Julian's Third Ambulance trip 159
His big plan... 166
Julian's Forth Ambulance trip 169
The worst night ever 174
The day the Solicitor came to visit.................................. 179
Julian's days of dehydration 181
Julian's fifth Ambulance transfer 186
Teaching Tibetan Chant 187
Julian's Claustrophobia 190
Rejection.. 194
No time to say Goodbye... 197
Julian's sixth Ambulance journey 199
Good bye Papa 206
The blindness 210
Julian's final negotiation with the Doctors 218

Putting things in order 223
To much for to long 226
Julian's 8th and final journey by Ambulance 233
Tuesday 11th of November 238
Final Goodbye's 242
What next 254
Friday 21st November 2008 258
My Coming home 262
Julian's coming home 266
The day of the funeral 270
16th December 2008 281
Our first Christmas without Julian 283
Winter of 2008 292
Spring 2009 295
 Summer of 2009 298
My Longed for Letters 300
The Law on Consent 308
Post Mortem Report 311
Pathologist Conclusion 318
Preparing for the Inquest 320
The morning of the Inquest 326
The Crossroads in my life 340
Living with regrets 343
All those learned people! 344
All my coincidences 353
Guilt's? 363
Dealing with them 366
Confrontation 367
The head stone 370
Trying to let go 375
Adult Abuse 385
The man with a will of iron 391
Question of Diabetes 395
History of Diabetes 400
What tests were available 417
'Did Julian have an Adrenal Tumour'? 425
Pandora's Box 449
Hydrogenated oil 451

Processed food and Additives.. 465
Exposure to toxic substance.. 474
Environmental Factors 485
Artificial Sweeteners 499
Genetic Engineered Food 508
Organic Food... 520
Genetically Engineered Medicine 531
Black Box warning label 538
Balance of Acid and Alkaline.. 570
My Conclusion 580
I understand... 589
Disappearing Bees 607
Thank you 638
My fund raising days after Julian 655
I have no bow to my bundle.. 664
Organised Crime.. 717
Raising Concerns 765
My Affidavit... 779

References 781

Preface

They say "Don't judge a book by its cover" but it's human nature, we instinctively do it. On the cover I've placed a picture of my husband framed, indicting from where he is, he can see a bigger picture with a message "They Didn't Listen, they Didn't Know How" The Back cover has a selection of photographs of him enjoying life, against a background of yellow Honeycombe with the inscription ". . . life became too sweet for me"

Please, I invite you to read on.

To view the coloured photographs within this book please go to:-

http://www.olliedavies.org/

Acknowledgement

I would like to express my sincerest gratitude to all my family and friends who have supported me through the years, especially the ones who have shown support and concern towards me since my husband's death. I would like to thank Llewela our daughter first of all for being so strong and setting me an example on how to conduct myself in public. My sister for being my life line every hour of every day, especially when I needed her most and of course my parents for being such down to earth people and giving me such good grounding in my early years. Glyn my brother, who I didn't realise, was so close to my husband until after his death. I later discovered they used to communicate late into the night on the computer. Alwyn, my younger brother, who I think of as the strong silent member of the family, I can always rely on at a moment's notice to help me out mechanically.

Gill who only came into our life four weeks before my husband died, who has now become a very valued friend of the family. A big thank you to Steve Ward who supported me at my hour of need at the inquest and of course all my long standing colleagues at Kidderminster Hospital. Also to my friends at Max Spielmann, Matthew, Shirley and Kevin who have helped me with all my photography problems. Not forgetting my special friends Joanna and Michael Butera, who also happen to be my daughters God Parents. Joanna has become my private overseer, who watches me like a hawk and is always ready to report back to my mother.

The worry is, when you start mentioning names you are bound to leave some one out.

Forgive me if I have offended anyone.

About the Author

I was born at Welshpool cottage Hospital, in mid Wales on 28th June 1957; I boast of a twin sister, called Gwenfron fondly known as Gwenn to her friends and Gweno to her family. I also have two younger brothers named Glyn who lives in Oswestry and Alwyn who lives in Elsmere, Shropshire.

Born to Welsh speaking parents, who always speak Welsh in the family home but are not Welsh Nationalist, but we haven't forgotten our roots either. My parents are Eirlys and Elfyn Jones, fondly known of Mynydd Dwlan, Llwydiarth, near Lake Vernwy.

'Mynydd—Dwlan' being the name of the farm where we were raised, that's how they operate in Wales. In fact the name of the farm is often placed on their Headstone. I found the absence of this practice in England strange when I migrated over the boarder to England. I was known then as 'Olwen Mynydd-Dwlan' rather than Olwen Jones.

The four of us were brought up on a farm, with country values. My twin and I left school at the age of 15 to attend Newtown College of Further Education, in mid Wales. We studied for our pre-nursing certificate and we both started our nurse training together at Wrexham War Memorial Hospital in North Wales and qualified on 23rd August 1977 as State Enrolled Nurses in our 'Emergency ward 10'look a-like uniforms. This is the day we exchanged our striped uniform for a bottle green dress, with our frilly cuffs, nursing buckle, starched aprons and a black and red lined cape. We also exchanged our second year striped paper hat for an elaborate frilly cotton one. I remember I wore my badges with pride, but the 'no makeup, perfume or jewellery' policy remained even after we qualified.

Still in tandem with our career we both seek employment at The Robert Jones and Agnes Hunt Orthopaedic Hospital in Gobowen near Oswestry where we obtained our Diploma in Orthopaedic Nursing. Our first post after qualifying was on the Spinal Injury Unit where we both learnt much valued life lessons. After 18 months on the unit we parted company and I moved to Golders Green, Hampstead heath, North London where I took up a post on yet another Orthopaedic ward, I stayed there for twelve months. Although I'd met Julian my future husband a few years previously we rekindled our friendship in the summer of 1980. Twelve months later on 3rd of October 1981 Julian and I were married at St Ambrose Church, Kidderminster where I took up yet another post on an orthopaedic ward, we were blessed with 28years of happy married life. After some years at Kidderminster as a State Enrolled Nurse I was told I had to complete a further course to convert to a State Registered Nurse or alternatively become a Nursing Auxiliary. I was more than happy to do just that, but then Julian reminded me how hard I'd worked for my qualifications and was I prepared to dis-regard my efforts? Recapping on my struggles I agreed to complete the last lap. I qualified as a Staff Nurse, to date I have 36 years of nursing experience under my belt as it were.

I also did Girl Guides as a hobby for about 11 Years, and was a Brown Owl for about 4 of those years, in charge of 24 Brownies, which I took on camp once a year. That also required an additional qualification and constant training days.

My studying days are now coming to an end I hope, but you never know what the future has in store for any of us, but this is my journey so far. For someone who could only read and speak Welsh until she went to secondary school, I haven't done too badly. No harm done, except may be for my poor spelling, knowing another language is no burden to anyone.

Sadly after 28 years of marriage our partnership came to a sudden end and I became a widow at the age of 51. The content of this book will be about Julian's life before we met our married life together, and sadly my life without him.

Photograph of myself, just before we met.

This book is dedicated to Llewela

This book is dedicated to Llewela our daughter, who incidentally does not need a book to remind her how good a Father he was to her. He had dedicated his adult life to teaching her life surviving skills, which are now paying dividend. The two of them used to make fun of me, compare me to David Bailey the famous photographer because I was constantly clicking away with my camera.

I use to remind them both, how else can I capture the moment! If I don't go click, click?

Llewela has since thanked me for taking so many photographs, over the years, and how now she has 'little snippets of time' captured on card to remind her of what happy times we had together"

Who inspired me to become a story teller?

Going back to my own childhood, I remember when I lived on the farm, I've mentioned before called Mynydd-Dwlan. Our Nain, which is Welsh for grandmother in Mid Wales used to come to stay with us during school term usually around June time, and she would stay for about six weeks. We looked forward to her visits, it always entailed going to bed early, not because we had too but because we wanted to. The bedrooms seemed large in those days or maybe they appeared large because we were so small. Going back to the story, Gweno and I slept in a double bed in our bedroom, and our two brothers slept in single beds in the second bedroom, Mum and Dad of course had a double bed in the third bedroom. When Nain came to stay she slept in a double bed on her own in the corner of our bedroom. That's shows how big the bedrooms were.

Nain was a great story teller, I have recollection of repeatedly asking her in Welsh of course after having our evening meal "Can we go to bed now Nain?" she would answer "No, it's only six o'clock"

The four of us would repeatedly ask the same question, until she gave in. We'd all scramble up that wooden stair case and with soap filled eyes jump into bed eagerly awaiting our bed time stories. The boys would get changed into their pyjamas hurriedly in their own bed room, while Nain, my sister and I would change into our night wear in our bed room. Once the three of us were in our nightgowns and 'cwched' up in bed, (a name we use in Welsh for hugging the bedclothes up to your chin) Nain would call out, "Ok boys the coast is clear you can come in now." Glyn and Alwyn would be allowed to sneak into her double bed in the corner while Nain would snuggle into to our bed, ready for our story telling. Then the story telling would begin in earnest. At the end of each story we'd all say in unison, "Tell us another story Nain, please tell us another" She would start off by telling us about her true life stories, of when she was a little girl, they were simple stories but interesting and funny. When her personal stories dried up she would start on the Bible. Those stories were just as colourful; she always managed to bring the

Bible to life somehow. She had such great faith, and I think it is to her I owe her my gratitude for such good grounding in the Christian faith. (Thank you, Nain.)

I used to lie in that bed as a child watching her in awe, thinking I hope one day I would be able to tell stories like my Nain.

Ironically Nain also became a widow at a young age too; she was only 54 when our Taid died.

She was only three years older than myself, when my husband and I were so abruptly parted.

I wonder if storytelling to children has all but died out in our modern day computer age.

Well! This is it; this is my one and only chance to prove my story telling skills. The trouble is, it's not a fairy tale it's based on my husband's life, his suffering and the journey I have travelled since his death, to find out why and how his life came to such a sudden abrupt and a sad end.

It's important for me to tell the truth at all cost, in case there is someone out there who can take this true story seriously enough to help me make a change in the world. My only fear is, if my theory is ridiculed and the book is discredited, then I will have let both Julian and others like him down.

I don't want people to think I'm writing a story at Julian's expense, many people over the years tried to coax him into writing his own biography, he used to say to them "And where do you think I can find time?." It was true what he used to say, he was always too busy living his dream to write about it. But in his memory I'm going to attempt to do it on his behalf.

Instead of Julian Paul Davies's 'Biography' I will write his 'Autobiography'

Maybe everybody should write their own memoirs, when its either, hard to let go of loved ones, frightened you might forget the past, want something to be handed over to future generations or simply to explain something when you feel 'someone has been wronged' I'm doing it for the latter reason.

Where did Julian's journey begin?

Julian's life began on the 16th September 1953; this bundle of joy must have seemed like a living doll to his mother who was only 16 when she married his father. Imagine someone so young being blessed with such a live wire for a first born, meddling in everything crawling at the speed of lightening, tottering as fast as a whippet, progressing to running faster and faster as a child. Then at the tender age of five he channelled all his energy into trying to think and doing any task better and faster than anyone else. I'm exhausted just thinking about his whirl wind upbringing, it felt as if his whole life was in 'fast forward' with no pause button at hand. This high speed life he led reflected in what others might consider as an accident prone childhood.

It was as if he was living by, 'You can't win, if you don't take risks' the competitiveness in him was great, but not in a boastful way, you were just drawn into his energy and wanted to run the race of life with him.

His first family home was at Cherry View Cottage, Knighton-on-Teme, near Tenbury Wells, a small market town in the heart of Worcestershire. He was born into a farming back ground, although one of his grandfathers was a black smith.

Two more boys followed a middle brother 5 years after Julian, then a third son 5 years later. Having 3 boys in the house must have been quite hair rising at times as these three boys did not lack boisterousness. Julian in particular had oodles of energy, which got him into more trouble than most. The family used to joke, that Tenbury Cottage Hospital survived mostly because of Julian's attendances. There was one instance which required a hospital visit, when his mother trundled off with young Julian in tow to the local Hospital. This time however the visit seemed different more hostile, because the Matron had taken an interest in young Julian's frequent visitations, and had requested to speak to his mother in her office.

The Matron suggested that she should go home and return later, and on her return a Social worker would be waiting to speak to her. Off she went; I don't know what must have been going through this young mothers mind while she waited her fate later that afternoon.

As she approached the Matrons office, one of the other Mothers called out "Matron wants to speak to you, in the office." Knowing this, she must have felt furious that the Matron had discussed her plight with this other Mother. Bravely she approached the office door, only to be greeted by kindness itself, all barriers down, and the tea and biscuits were flowing. There was definitely a change of attitude here, what was going on?

Matron greeted her with. "Well! Mrs Davies young Julian's a very naughty boy isn't he, I don't know how you manage him, as soon as you left, young Julian fell off his bed and unfortunately he's now got a lump the size of an egg on his forehead. I got one of the porters to get a cot from the store room, we placed it upside down and tied it over Julian's bed, so he's safe now in-effect he's in a cage."

And needless to say, she had already cancelled the Social Worker.

So from a very young age it was hard to keep this young man down. He had to be tied down as a child and did not fare much better as a grown man either.

Photograph of Julian pre-school age on his trike.

He looks as if he's been in some mischief here and is harbouring an exciting secret.

When his parents first got married they both worked for a milk delivery company, which they later owned and as time progressed they had a supermarket built, first one of its kind in the town from what I'm told. I must say his father was ahead of his time, they sold all sorts by the sound of it. One day when his father was buzzy cutting ham off the bone in his white grocery coat, a customer in the shop noticed some one passing the window. He remarked, "Oh! I just see young Julian just passed the window" Julian's father not paying much attention replied, "Yes, I expect you did"

The customer was a bit perturbed that his father seemed disinterested and informed him, "No, I don't mean walking past, I mean from top to bottom"

They all rushed out, and sure enough, Julian had stepped out of the bed room window on to a bit of a balcony then jumped off attached to a bed sheet, attempting to fly like Batman. I can't remember anyone saying if there was a trip to the local Hospital on that occasion, but I expect there was. And I don't suppose he was the first to attempt flying at such a young age and he probably won't be the last. Although most children these days probably have never heard of Batman, never mind who Robin is.

When Julian was about nine the story goes that his Father had asked his Mother to choose a place to go on holiday before he returned home from work that evening. As the three boys were notorious for been little rascals, she hadn't had time to study the map. So when she heard the car pull up the drive, she quickly got the map out and stuck a pin on one of the pages. As he entered the house, he promptly asked, "Have you chosen a place to go on holiday then." She replied "Yes, Pendine Sands." "Pendine Sands!" he repeated. She said, "Yes, it's no good you trying to change my mind"

And that's exactly where the family went for their fortnight's holiday. On their return his mother sent Julian's Father to the garage for a pint of milk; Julian went along for the ride. They were some time at the garage, and on their return voices were raised as to what took them so long. His Father explained he thought the caravan holiday was enjoyable, but felt the rental was a bit expensive so while he was out purchasing a pint of milk he also bought a caravan and would be taking it down

3

the following week end. And here started Julian's love affair with Pendine Sands. The caravan was taken down as promised the following weekend and then revisited nearly every week end, summer holidays, bank holidays, Easter and Whitson with the exception of the Christmas break. It didn't stop there, from what I can recall from the family, his Aunty then bought a caravan on the same site, as did his widowed grandmother on his mother's side. Julian's father's family then joined in with his grandmother, uncles, aunts bringing with them their children. So from an early age Julian spent all his growing up years with his cousins from both sides of the family running riot on sunny Pendine Beach. How many other cousins can boast of such fun and closeness, getting up to all sorts of boisterous antics, this is probably why this second generation were as close as adults? They were always reminiscing at such functions as Weddings, Christenings and Funerals hankering for the good old days spent on their sunny Pendine Beach. It must have felt as if Tenbury itself had arrived at Pendine, when all the Davies's invaded the site each season. He often use to retell tales about his child hood days to me during the first eight years of our marriage about the time he spent at Pendine, talking about old fashion beach entertainments such as kite flying, beach ball games, beach cricket, rock climbing, rock pooling with their buckets and fishing nets, cliff walking, cave exploring, with fancy dress and sand castle competitions on various bank holidays. You can almost smell the atmosphere, the wafting smell of fish and chip lingering in the street, the sweet smell of candy floss. The sea breeze, leaving your lips tasting of salt and off course the famous 1960s sunburnt bodies tingling in the evening after the hot sun bearing down on them for hours on end, the aggravating grains of sand grinding between the toes.

The magnitude of different ice creams of all shapes and flavours dripping under the heat of the sun. Not forgetting the defining screeching sea gulls flying overhead and the loud pop music, blaring out of passing 'boy racer' cars in the evening.

Topped up with the excitement of rushing off the beach at the end of each day, to beat the tide from devouring your pressures transport, many a vehicle were lost to the raging sea at this little cove over the years, not covered by insurance of course because it was a private beach. The secret was to ask the beach attendant at the ticket booth what time the tide was due in that afternoon. That way you were sure to be off the beach in time to save your car for another day's adventure. He used to say, the sea wasn't fussy whether it took an old banger or a spanking new car; it didn't recognise its value or its number plates. The mangled remains could be seen all smashed up in the bay the next day. Back at Tenbury, this was no sleepy hollow in the back of beyond either, there was often some live entertainment going on here too. They had a very active amateur dramatics society which Julian's parents were members of as well as being involved in arranging outside entertainers to entertain the locals. A lady by the name of Pat Lambert and her husband were among these like-minded people who got together to see what they could do to entertain the young people of Tenbury. The largest ballroom at Tenbury Wells at that time was at the Bridge Hotel, this society called them-selves, 'The Riverside Club' and in 1962 they booked a virtually unknown Liverpool group to play the following year for £100. As time approached for the live group to attend, their Agent contacted the society to ask if they could pull out of the agreement. The committee replied with a good farming reply "No, a contract is a contract" so they had to attend. By the time they were due to perform at little old Tenbury they were in the charts with, "Please, Please me"

The group was none other than the famous "Beetles" they still honoured their original agreement to play at this tiny Worcestershire venue. The tickets were soon snapped up at three shillings and six pence each. A local hair dresser remembers the exiting day and you can find her story on the web. Her clients with no inhibitions about their hair being wet or in rollers got up from their chairs and stood single file in the street to watch them walk by. The hair dresser remembers Ringo Star eating an ice cream and sure enough he had got one in his hand in the picture taken in Team Street.

This sounds like an unlikely story but next time you're in Tenbury, ask one of the locals. Julian's cousin Carol Vernalls was one who had their autograph on the back of a Beatles record. Last time I spoke to her she said she wouldn't part with it for the world, well not just yet any way.

Photograph of the Beetles walking down Team Street,
in Tenbury Wells.

He often spoke of other claims to fame in his home town too, such as when Queen Victoria visited Tenbury. This sounds like an another unlikely story, but he used to say she had affectionately nicked named the town, "My little town in the orchard" In Victorian days all the surrounding fields would have been heaving with orchard crops of all kind, mainly apples, pears and hops.

Worried that I may be caught out retelling an inaccurate story, I wrote to our present reigning Queen Elizabeth ll for confirmation of this tale. The Assistant Archivist at Windsor Castle wrote back apologising for the delay but they were in the process of digitalizing all of Victoria's Journals in their entirety, and to my surprise there was a reference to Princess Victoria stopping at 'The Swan Hotel' in Tenbury Wells whilst she waited for her horses to be exchanged for fresh ones and the Worcestershire troops to take over her protection from the Shropshire troops. This piece of journal was dated October 1832 stating she was on her way to Whitley Court traveling from Downham Court. The Christmas tree at Whitley Court is said to be decorated with real crystals, and would have been a grand affair. I wondered was it possible she spent Christmas there that year? Unfortunately this magnificent house was burnt down in 1937. I'm only surmising she may of spent Christmas at Whitley Court because a month later in the same year in

November 1832 it is documented while en route through Tenbury Wells she visited 'Hewell Grange' another grand stately home, I calculated the young Princess would have been 13 years of age at the time. I don't know if she ever visited the Malvern Hills on her travels to the county of Worcestershire, but Queen Victoria refused to travel without her bottled Malvern Water, and it is also known to be Queen Elizabeth's favourite drinking water too. I'm only mentioning this Royal visit to Tenbury because Julian was often thought to be telling tales of grandeur only to be discovered to be telling the truth later.

Another fondness he had for Tenbury was the long tradition of a century and a half old Mistletoe Fare, which started in 1854. The mistletoe is supplied by locals and gypsies from far afield; the fare is regarded as the Head Quarters in Britain for its unique sale. Proud of this annual event the town folk were worried that this age old tradition might diminish, to rejuvenate the interest they included the crowning of a Mistletoe Queen and a Holly Prince. The crowning is followed by a Santa Parade, dressed of course in his traditional green suit followed by a trail of children carrying lanterns, the morning then concluding on a more serious note with the Mistletoe Auction. To cap it all in 2005 Parliament endorsed a fixture of 'National Mistletoe day' to be held on the first Saturday in December. With a little incentive from the locals, it sounds to me as if the old tradition is safe for a few more years yet! To boost attendance a few years ago the BBC film crew brought the 'Country File' program to Tenbury to highlight the Mistletoe market, it was hosted by John Craven. In my opinion, any local hype is good if it's saving an ancient old tradition of 'kissing under the mistletoe' which is largely unknown in the rest of the world.

Julian and his family moved from Tenbury in or around 1963, but he remained faithful to his accident and emergency department where ever he went especially when I read such entries in his medical notes dated as far back in 1964, 'hit on forehead'. I wonder which brother did that. Later in 1967 records showed he was being treated for a boil, which sounds as if his immune system was already on the decline.

As the years rolled on, Julian and his family were still spending time at their lovely Pendine. When he was 14, although still loving the beach life style, he started to develop another interest in life which was fashionable clothes, to impress the girls. I would say most boys his age, didn't bother about trying to attract the opposite sex, but always advanced for his years Julian did.

Still in this race for life he decided to get himself a summer job, off he went in search of one. He didn't have to go far, he asked a gentleman on the beach if he had a summer job, and within minutes he'd landed himself a job as a deck chair boy. He used to repeat to me often that summers, in those days were long and hot, he recalled that he was only rained off the beach once that particular summer. In other words he only had one day off because of bad weather. So it wasn't our memories playing tricks with us, we really did have proper seasons then.

The following summer on 11th June 1969 age 15 he underwent a right knee operation, I don't think Julian was keen about the surgery but he was told if he didn't have the surgery he could be in a wheel chair for the rest of his life. As he wanted to continue with contact sport, he took fright and had the operation. The operation he undertook was called 'Medial Meniscectomy' I don't know why he was given such a grim outcome it's only removing some meniscus cartilage from around the knee joint. He often used to repeat the story in a humorous way, saying it was the most painful operation he'd ever endured and if he'd known he really was going to be in a wheelchair for the rest of his life because of another reason he wouldn't have bothered with the painful knee procedure.

Later that summer, he went to see his previous employer to see if he could get back his old deck chair job for another season. Unfortunately the gentleman explained he didn't have the deck chairs any more but he did however have a spare Ice cream van he could drive for him.

Julian hesitated for a moment, remembering he had lied the previous year about his age. The gentleman quickly reminded him "Your 17 this year aren't you." Julian just as quick said "Yes" he thought no harm done the Ice cream Company was only situated across the road from the beach; all he had to do was carefully drive across the road. What he said next panicked him, "Come early tomorrow, your patch is on the next seaside resort at Saundersfoot"!

Driving licence was apparently not a requirement for a driving job in 1969, well not for this particular interview anyway. How things have changed!

Julian keen to start his new job, turned up early.

His new boss was impressed with his punctuality, and informed him "You will have to wait until your partner turns up, because he will have to drive in front of you because your van has no brakes, you will use his van as your brakes."

Julian thought he was jesting at first, and laughingly repeated "What no brakes at all?" Sure enough the other van was his brakes. Going up the steep hill to his place of work was no trouble but coming home was hair-raising. If any of you have ever visited Pendine beach you will know about the very steep hill at the back of the village that ascends to heaven, but coming down must of felt like descending down to hell, especially if you didn't have any brakes. A bus did come down this hill once some years later when the brakes had failed; he called to his passengers to quickly get to the back of the bus while the driver took his chances in the front awaiting his fate. Every one survived except for the driver. There is a memorial plaque placed on the wall in his memory, where the bus collided with the sea defence wall, explaining how he gave up his life for others.

I only mentioned this incident to emphasise how treacherous the steep hill was, and even worse without brakes as the bus driver found out as his demise.

After a few days at his new job Julian asked his boss if he could help himself to the odd ice cream every now and then, as he didn't want to risk losing his summer job over a single ice cream.

To his amazement his boss said, "Help yourself to as much ice cream as you like" Julian thought he had gone to heaven. The first day he ate about 20 ice creams, the second day he ate about 16 and so on until the numbers decreased each day until he didn't fancy one at all in the end. In fact the very thought of them made him feel ill. In all the years I knew him, I cannot recall him ever having soft whip ice cream. I suppose you can have too much of a good thing. What a clever employer, it cost him a buck or two at the beginning but the expense was soon cured.

The following year he was 16, and still a boarder at a local private school, incidentally there was no need for him to live in but he loved the life style. It's not for everybody; his brother for one disliked the boarding way of life intensely and chose to live at home. As the boarding school took in boys from all over the world, lots of the boys could not get home for the shorter holiday breaks like Easter. Julian was famous for befriending any one and every one, because he could see the good in all.

He often took one of the boys home with him during these short school holidays.

One particular holiday Julian's family were getting ready to traipse down to South Wales in droves to their lovely Pendine. This poor young man was sucked up in the usual Davies exciting jaunt which was fine, but don't forget that Julian had been blessed with an abundance of energy when he was born. His friend may have thought of a restful holiday but Julian had other plans, Julian intended to find both of them a seasonal job.

This time Julian had to go further afield to find temporary work. Word of mouth guided him to the top of the hill that same treacherous hill, to work for a local builder. Both of them were given a chance as long as they worked hard. Their new job was to be a 'plasterer's mate'.

Julian's friend came from a wealthy family, and had never come across hard work in his life before. The two of them would arrive back at the caravan each evening so dusty they looked like a couple of lads dipped in flour, they would have a 'strip wash' outside the caravan in their shorts in case the plaster dust clogged up the shower drains.

The two of them would then in turn have a shower, and then join the family for their evening meal. After the hot shower, hot food and total exhaustion his poor friend would be too tired to even say good night and would be found collapsed on the bed spread eagled and fast asleep, and there he would stay until the following morning ready for another days work. But not Julian Oh! No he'd get his glad rags on all dressed up with his dancing shoes and stay out late into the night.

The two of them did this routine every night throughout the summer holidays. Unlike Julian, his friend didn't need the money; he only wanted Julian's company. Julian use to say, I expect it gave him a good insight into how hard his father's labourer worked. I hope he took that experience home with him in preparation for taking over his Fathers Company. So the time he spent with Julian wasn't all bad.

That same summer Julian would sit on the wall with his back to the sea in his trendy cloths eyeing up the local and visiting talent wolf whistling in his teasing way, and watching all the crazy teenage drivers showing off in their super cars, skidding and tooting as they drove a thousand times backwards and forwards through the village from early evening into the late of the night to impress the girls.

He used to say it wasn't just him on the wall; all the local young men would congregate there too.

After returning to school, I think it was the following Easter break he decided to tour as much of Europe as he could. Off he went with a rucksack on his back, hitch hiking on his own with nothing but a thumb for a lift. It must have been an experience of a life time, a lot of people did it in the early 70`s with all that flower power mania.

On one occasion, he was sat on his own in a cafe in the south of France having lunch, when a young man approached his table asking, "Is it ok if I share your table" Julian said that was fine and they made small talk, as they munched through their lunch. When they had both finished, the stranger asked, "Do you know who I am?"

Julian quickly replied, "Yes, Mungo Gerry" He was puzzled that Julian hadn't mentioned it earlier. Julian explained, "I thought even Mungo Jerry deserves peace and quiet while he's eating, but now you have mentioned it do you mind if I ask you for your autograph".

He laughed and thanked him for showing such respect. As his hitch hiking tour came to an end so did Julian's money. He took a chance and rang home hoping his Father would send him some money for his return journey. The answer was, "No, it can teach you a lesson to manage your money better" maybe fathers are stricter towards their sons, but I can't imagine us leaving our daughter stranded in a strange country to make her way home without a penny, just to teach her a lesson. There must have been an Angel watching over Julian that day because as he sat on the embankment of a motor way pondering on how to get home, I don't know if he prayed, but how often do we all say, silently in our heads "Please God, can you help me" not realising we've actually asked for help.

When all of a sudden he saw this huge lorry in the distance and he recognised the logo on the side, as fast as he could he gathered up his ruck sack and ran like mad down the embankment to herald this massive articulated lorry for a lift. He did this by standing in its path with his legs apart and his arms out stretched waving above his head, in a distressed manner. The lorry pulled up onto the hard shoulder, with Julian racing along its side. Before Julian had a chance to say anything, the lorry diver verbally laid into him, with raised voice "You stupid boy, I could have killed you; do you know how dangerous it is to try and stop

11

a lorry, travelling at high speed down the motorway?" Julian apologised, and flippantly asked if there was any chance of a lift?

The driver enquired, "Where are you going". Julian replied "Kidderminster". He said, "Jump in then." You see the lorry was bound for Kidderminster returning from the South of France empty after delivering carpets. The company he was driving for was "Brintons" Carpets of Kidderminster

As they approached Kidderminster, Julian asked this already kind driver to do him yet another favour, could he possible detour down Sutton Park Road? That way he could drop him off just outside his front door. The driver said, "You've got the cheek of the devil kid, but yes ok then"

Imagine the shock on his father face when he walked in to the kitchen less than 24 hours after the pleading phone call to say he was stranded penniless in the South of France.

At the end of his last Autumn half term holiday, spent at Pendine as a teenager, most of the caravans had closed up for the winter, the hustle and bustle had left the streets, the beach was motionless, and the cafes were empty, nothing left but quietness and stillness. He decided to take himself up the cliffs just one last time before he returned back home to the midlands and he sat and look into the distance over the 7 miles of golden sandy beach reminiscing about the fun he'd had over the last decade and the realisation that this would never be recaptured. For one thing he would never have seven weeks holiday again; life would be very different from now on.

This idyllic childhood must have put him in good stead for his adult life, if there was one thing Julian was good at it was having fun and always making the best of every situation. I don't mean every now and then, I mean every waking moment of his life.

There must have been unpleasant moments in his past, we can all find those if we dig deep enough, but if there were any such moments Julian never mentioned them.

The only two things he did mention about his past were from his school days which he considered outstanding, and had the most profound effect on his adult life. One was when a teacher was giving one of those off the cuff lectures. He asked the class did they feel privileged that they were lucky enough to receive private education. There was mixed answers, most of the boys came from very wealthy backgrounds.

The next question he asked was, did any of them feel that some occupations such as a mechanic would be beneath their stations in life, most of the boys said yes immediately.

He then he went round the class asking what sort of car could they visualise buying.

By this time Julian was wondering where this sort of teaching was leading. His last question forced the classroom into silence when he asked, "When you're out in your posh sports cars and it happens to break down, who would they ask to repair it"? The boys became dumbfounded; the answer of course, was a mechanic. After pausing, the teacher then asked, "Who's the clever one now then"?

The moral of that lesson was, we're all important in our own way. I never heard Julian boasting about his education or belittling other people's capability, maybe that story kept his feet firmly on the ground. He certainly didn't mind getting his hands dirty.

The other tale he often told me, was, he never confessed to being an Angel at school. The posh and the rich had to take their punishment like the rest. As Julian was more mischievous than most it stands to reason he had more punishment than most. He claims all the canings he had on a daily basis never hurt him once until one day he was called into the Head masters office for his almost daily dose of caning. This time was different, this time he was having a caning for something he hadn't done. He said it was the most painful experience he ever had to endure. On completion the Head Master asked him if he had anything to say, meaning apology I expect. In retaliation Julian again denied the crime, for this he had another six of the best.

He used to say there is nothing more painful in life, than serving a sentence for a crime you have not committed. And because of this experience he always tried to listen to both side of the story before making a decision. I think these were his two biggest lessons in life, and he lived by them.

Sometime before leaving school, Julian asked his Father if he could go on an Outward Bound course. I could not tell you if he asked or begged to go, but permission was granted by his father. His bags were packed and to be fair his Father did travel to the boarders of Scotland to drop him off at the appointed Moor, I cannot be more specific than that.

Once Julian was dropped off, rucksack and all, off his father sped into the distance heading back towards the horizon of Worcestershire. Sometime later when organisation was taking place the young men were been grouped together, most of them professionals such as Policemen, Ambulance men even off duty Soldiers. A young Policeman became very disgruntled with this little whippet called Julian Davies who had been assigned to his party. So he went to complain about him and said they didn't want him in their group. When the Superior came to smooth things over, he stared at Julian and asked, "How old are you?" Julian replied, "16 Sir". He explained, "This course was specifically for people of an older age group, how, did you get here?"

Julian innocently said, his father had brought him. He replied, "Get you father to take you home straight away" Julian replied, "I can't Sir he's long gone"

"Very well, you'll just have to tag along with your group, but don't hinder them"

The Policeman complained again before they despatched, that Julian was trying to take over the group but they wouldn't listen.

Julian over heard what the Superior said, "You know what to do with little pip squeaks who think they know it all, put them in charge, when they fail miserably, takeover"

"Right Sir" he said.

The plan was they had to start walking Friday night, camp overnight, and pick up instructions or clues on the way, avoid being seen or caught by their superiors with the aim to arrive back at camp late Sunday afternoon.

With Julian in charge, off they went. When they were out of the Supervisors sight, Julian instructed his group to start running. They thought he was mad to start to run at this early stage, but run they did. They ran and ran until they arrived back at camp on Saturday afternoon 4pm. There was no welcoming party to greet them so they had to search the ground to find someone to check their cards. The military tall men with their posh accent said, "It's impossible that you could have completed the course Davies". The young Policeman said breathlessly in no uncertain terms, "Oh! yes we did Sir, he made us run right through the night and all day today without any sleep" He spoke to the Policeman with his back to Julian and said in a whispering voice, "I thought I told you to take over" The Policeman said, "And I told you Sir, he wouldn't listen"

He then turned to Julian and said, "Why did you drive these men like this?"

Julian's reasoning was, "I worked it out Sir, I assumed you had already planted the instructions, so all we had to do was beat you by speed, and as you had trucks out looking for us and we only had our legs, I figured you would be taking it easy until Saturday afternoon, Sir. The men can rest now while they wait for the others to come in tomorrow. I don't know what they are belly aching about Sir, they were the first back weren't they."

So you see, Julian was already a grown man at the young age of 16. Now can you understand the force I was dealing with during our married life? He truly was a wise man you could almost imagine he'd been here before. In fact he must have been, to pick up as much knowledge as he did. You know the old sayings, "He's been here before or he's got an old head on young shoulders"

Incidentally I still receive Christmas cards and updates from "The Outward Bound Trust" I also have his certificate and tie framed and hanging up in the lounge.

In May 1972 Julian had a pain in one of his back teeth. A quick visit to the dentist confirmed that his wisdom tooth needed extracting, he was advised to return the following day. He returned the next day as instructed on his own, a fearless young man ignoring comments from his friends such as, "You're not going to him, he's a butcher" Julian didn't take any notice of the provocation and turned up the following morning.

After the dentist had been struggling for some time to extract his troublesome tooth, he called the receptionist to assist him; she held his head whilst the dentist wedged his knee into Julian's lap. The tooth did eventually give way and it was extracted. Later that evening when his mother came home, she started to lecture him on how she disliked fighting. Julian tried to protest with a slurred speech that he hadn't been fighting. She wanted to know how he got two black eyes! He eventually made himself understood and that he'd been to the dentist. She was shocked and insisted he went back the following morning; he did as he was told and returned. On entering the surgery the receptionist put her head round the door informing the dentist, "It's that boy who was making a fuss yesterday". He came out full of rage shouting, "Get

15

out of my surgery I don't want you upsetting my patients like you did yesterday" Barely able to talk never mind make a fuss, he returned home. On hearing what he had to say his mother was furious and immediately drove him to the local casualty department. The greeting they both got off the on call doctor was, "Oh! Who's been fighting then?" When Julian's mother protested on his behalf explaining it was the result of dental treatment, an x-ray was arranged and the horror was revealed. The dentist had broken his bottom jaw in two places and the four prongs to his wisdom tooth were still left in his jaw. Unfortunately Julian's roots had hooks on, if the dentist had x-rayed him when he was first having difficulty, he would have foreseen the problem. When Julian tried to speak, the middle part of his bottom jaw stayed dropped. No wonder he couldn't talk, eat, drink or sleep. I don't know if dentists can set up a practice in their own private homes because, on this occasion he didn't have x-ray facilities. He told me, he had no idea what was ahead of him, he thought the plan entailed going to theatre for root extraction then go home late in the day, but as he was recovering from the anaesthetic he felt he couldn't breathe, his nose was blocked with dry blood and his top and bottom jaw had been wired together. He was not prepared for this otherwise he would have warned them he always breathed through his mouth. They had however removed one tooth so he could pass a straw through for liquids.

Next day when Julian was recovering from his procedure, an irate visitor stormed on to the ward demanding to see a Julian Davies. As he was being escorted off the ward he could be heard shouting, "You've ruined my career, and who do you think you are reporting me like this"? In actual fact it wasn't any of Julian's doing; it evidently turned out to be the Doctor in casualty who had reported him.

Not surprisingly, Julian's fear of the dentist stemmed from this experience it would have sent his Adrenal Function into disarray, affecting his fight fear and flight. Not to mention he had to endure this wired brace for two months.

Anyone who knew Julian in later years would have thought he needed to visit his dentist, but I've never seen anyone so obsessed with brushing their teeth as Julian, anything to avoid any dental visits. Luckily for us, dentists don't behave like butchers any more.

Just before leaving school Julian's form master took him to one side and said, "I'm worried about you Davies; you have such an abundance of energy I just don't know which direction you'll take in life. Whichever way it will be, it will be full on, not sparing the horses" Julian smiled; the form master was trying to warn him to slow down. He tried again, "I can usually foresee what positions in life my pupils take up, but not you Davies. You will either be a high flyer or in prison, unless something stops you in your tracks"

Julian retold this pep talk so many times; it must have made a lasting impression on him to recall it as often as he did.

After finishing school he set about finding himself a permanent job, it was not too long before he found one. I cannot for the life of me remember what the name of the company was, except that it was an American company. It entailed working in the office and he often told me he loved the job. He had been told that if he worked hard he could go far with this company. With his determination I'm sure he would of, he probably would have run the show.

He'd already passed his driving test before starting this job and like most young men at the beginning of their career he was strapped for cash. Because of the lack of capital he only possessed a banger of a Mini for transport. When the manager was looking out of the office window one day he noticed this 'substandard car' parked in the staff car park. The manager was horrified to see this clapped out old Mini, and demanded the owner should be brought up to his office immediately. That owner was none other than young Julian Davies, when Julian explained his financial situation, his boss explained that it looked bad for the company's image to have one of his employees driving such a thing.

Julian bewilderedly asked, "What shall I do". His boss must have been confident that Julian was going to stay with the company for some time, because he advised Julian to go and sort some finance out with the wages department. Consequently Julian went out and bought something flash a "Bond Bug" for £629:00 bearing in mind a brand new Mini only cost £620:00 in those days, so for £9 extra he could get a sportier looking car. Why not he thought, it certainly went with his nick name, "Flash"

Bond Bugs were a wedge shape micro-car. A fun two seater, British made sports car. Only 143 were ever produced all finished a bright tangerine colour, with the exception of six cars which were finished in white for a cigarette promotion. The design was a fashion statement, aimed at the younger driver in the early 1970`s. It boasted of twin mud flaps, rubber front bumper, a spare wheel and a must for the 70`s an ashtray. Entry was gained by swinging the lift up canopy forward, on to two front hinges, suspending on what was left of the bonnet. They were only produced from 1970 to 1974.

He must of bought one as soon as it produced, I saw one on E-Bay recently number 74 apparently they were numbered as they came off the production line, and it fetched a grand total of £2,000-00? (What a shame Julian smashed his up.)

Photograph of a "Bond Bug" identical to the car Julian had in the early 1970`s

When I showed Llewela this picture recently, she couldn't stop laughing. She wasn't making fun of her Dads choice, but this was not the image she had carried round in her head all those years of her Fathers sports car. But Julian had to be different; he was never your normal run of the mill man.

His Big accident

On the eve of his big accident, his Grandmother was staying at the family home as she often did in those days. This particular night, she was in bed when she heard Julian's car screech to a halt outside the house. She then heard him running down the back path, into the house up the stairs and into his bed room. His Grandmother told me years later she had called out, "What are you looking for Julian?" his reply was, "More money Nan, my friends are going on to another disco and I've run out of cash" At that he ran down the stairs, through the house down the path then into his car and left at high speed. No wonder he'd earned himself the nick name 'Flash' amongst his friends.

His Grandmother can remember lying in bed that night thinking, if that boy does not slow down soon he's going to come to a sad end.

The word 'soon' being the operative word

The very next day Julian had what he called his, "Big accident" meaning he had many mishaps and near misses but this was the big one.

He was rushing from his work in Cannock to his home in Kingswinford, calling at the shops on the way to buy new cloths for his much 'longed for' holiday at his lovely Pendine. Do you remember in the pre-1970`s workers had to work for 12 months before they received any holidays. The first year you were entitled to one week, and then it would increase with the years of services.

Julian had served his first 12 months with no holiday (another punishment as he called it) and was now entitled to one week holiday. The excitement might have got the better of him because in the added rush of beating the five thirty shop shutting times, he needed to buy these 'must have cloths' for his holiday. The shops in those days weren't like they are today open all hours; there were no Granville shops about then. The accident happened on a roundabout between Cannock and Kingswinford, incidentally the roundabout has long since given way to a dual carriage way. On the afternoon in question his front wheel caught the kerb on the roundabout, at high speed. He used to confess this to youngsters years later in an attempt to frighten them, hoping they would ditch their high speed in exchange for a walking life.

On impact the car started to spin in the air, at that the door which I mentioned acted as the roof burst forward onto the bonnet, and of course as Julian's body was not strapped in by a seat belt, he was catapulted out like a cannon ball up in the air and then landing on to the Tarmac diagonally on the central white line, bearing in mind, this was in the days before seat belt laws were enforced.

He used to say the car burst into flames, in that case maybe on this one occasion it was a blessing in disguise that he was catapulted out away from the burning flames, otherwise he may well have suffered severe burns as well as his other injuries. The emergency services were summoned the Ambulance men attending to him was getting ready to manoeuvre him off the road on to a stretcher the Police man was heard shouting from a distance, "Get that lad off the road". The Ambulance men shouted back, "He's complaining of pain in his back." The reply was, "I don't care what he's complaining of, get him off the road it will soon be rush hour." Julian remembers this dialogue going back and forth, and then the Ambulance men asked him, "Can you feel your legs mate"? His reply was, "Yes, but I beg you, can you do something about this excruciating pain in my back" The last thing Julian remembers hearing is the Ambulance men saying

"He must be alright" and they continued to lift him, one at his ankles and the other at his shoulders, then he blacked out. One can only assume at this point his spinal cord was intact when he demonstrated he could move his legs, but when he was lifted in a bow fashion the fractured vertebras must have severed his spinal cord. Julian was taken that hot summer's afternoon 1ˢᵗ August 1972 not to Pendine as he had planned, but to "The Birmingham Accident Hospital" Julian was 18 years old when this devastating accident happened. He used to tell our daughter "I don't remember my 19ᵗʰ birthday darling, I spent it in Hospital and I was out of it, I can't remember a single thing."

It states in the medical notes, that Julian was transferred from the Birmingham Hospital by Ambulance to the famous "Robert Jones and Agnes Hunt Orthopaedic Hospital" near Oswestry, Shropshire on the 10ᵗʰ August 1972 this was nine days after his accident.

As far as Julian could remember it was a very hot summers day, but when he regained consciousness he used to re-tell the tale of those waking moments, as being upside down and tied down to a bed by his head. In actual fact he was not far wrong, the tied down feeling he was describing was the skull callipers attached to traction at the head of the bed. The callipers do appear a bit gruesome when you first encounter them as they are screwed into the skull then attached a considerable amount of weights and the head is shaven prior to the insertion of the metal work. The head of the bed was then tilted down giving him that upside down feeling, in other words the foot of the bed was elevated in an effort to counter act the traction. This sensation I would imagine would have been frightening if you were unconscious when the procedure first took place.

He used to say, "I woke up upside down, with only a view of a window behind my head, and that view was upside down too" which confused him even more. That was not all it was now snowing, his orientation of time and space was up the shoot as they say.

He was struggling with these thoughts, how could it be snowing? it was boiling hot on an August afternoon a few minutes ago, and why wasn't he on Pendine Beach! The explanation was, he had been in a coma since August, and it was now November.

As the days passed, he had private thoughts that when he was released from these skull callipers he would not be like these other youngsters paralysed and in wheelchairs. But bit by bit he started to have serious thoughts that maybe he might be permanently paralysed because he still couldn't feel his legs. Once he had accepted that his body may be paralysed, he then courageously asked one of the nurses the dreaded question, "Will I ever walk again"? at the same time not wanting a negative answer.

The ward policy at the time was, nurses were not allowed to part with that sort of information and rightly so. This sort of delicate conversation if not handled properly could either make this already low in mood patient, look at life in a negative or a positive light. If the subject was dealt with badly then society could have a permanently depressive and disabled human being on their hands. Who wants to be in the company of someone who is permanently feeling sorry for themselves?

So depending on how the next few minutes of this person's life was dealt with, it would set the tone for the rest of his natural life. It has to be done by a highly competent person, in Julian's case it was done by the ward Physician who also had some psychiatric back ground which certainly paid dividend in how Julian moulded his life from here on. The Doctor would sit with the patient for hours in some cases until "their head was sorted," as Julian used to say. This technique appeared to turn out level headed young adults. I don't know if the same protocol is used to day.

As soon as the physician finished discussing Julian's possibilities, with his now different life, Julian asked if he could use the portable phone, he said, "I need to ring a Solicitor, I need to put my property on the market. So although Julian had been in the fast lane from birth, he realised he had been resting in a lay by for the last few weeks, it was time to get back on the road again.

His battle for survival started that day and it was fought and won in his more than able mind.

After 10 weeks following his injury, Julian was allowed to sit up in bed. Then rehabilitation commenced but Christmas was approaching fast and Julian had other ideas, he begged the medical staff to allow him home for a few days over the festive season.

Once he was home there was no going back to finish his rehabilitation.

The history I got off Julian spanning from his accident until Christmas was very murky. Once I obtained his medical notes, I got a clearer picture of the events that took place.

I found a discharge letter in Julian's medical notes describing Julian's recovery, the letter was sent to Julian's GP it started by informing him of the consequences of Julian's accident it then went on to say, "Julian had sustained a fracture to his 4th cervical vertebra resulting in Tetraplegia with loss of power to both hands trunk and limbs. He also sustained a fracture of his 7th cervical vertebra which was referred to as a complete sever of the spinal cord. He arrived at Oswestry on the 10th August 1972 with skull traction in place" When I worked on the Spinal Injury Unit the boys from the Black country usually required more weight on their traction as they had stockier necks, I wondered why and asked the physician. His theory was the men from the midlands were great chain makers for ship yards, chains for the Titanic being one of them. It was felt because of the heavy industrial work that took place in the midlands their necks had evolved to withstand the heavy duty work. The letter went on to say, "An early complication was a chest infection with a complete collapse of his right lung. Fourteen days after his accident on the 15th August 1972 it became necessary to perform a tracheotomy and a repeat bronchial suction". (It is referred to, as an under water drainage seal bottle these days, where they insert thick tube into the lower chest cavity to inflate the lung and drain any excess fluid out)

"The first few weeks of his treatment were anxious as he not only had these two problems he also developed a severe paralytic ileum". This is when the intestine decides to go to sleep as it were; survival is a bit of touch and go. The only treatment for this is to rest the gut by withholding diet and introduce nasogastric tube to drain gastric juices from the stomach and wait for recovery. This was probably made easier for Julian as he couldn't eat any way, because of the Tracheotomy. This is a tube surgically inserted in to the throat below the Adams apple to gain air entry into his lungs.

After 10 days following his injury things started to settle down, and after two weeks he managed without his tracheotomy.

"At 10 weeks he was able to sit up in bed and rehabilitation could then begin more strenuously, and he made remarkable progress. His neurological level was now at Cervical 7, with good power in both hands and fingers. There is however, no power in his lower limbs and trunk below his sternum level. Despite this, this young man is independent in every daily activity, including dressing himself, getting in and out of the bath, coping with getting on and off the toilet. He has also taught himself to drive a car." Although Julian had passed his driving test before his accident, he arranged for the driver instructor to pick him up from the Hospital while he was an in-patient to go for driving lessons in and around Oswestry. Consequently he passed his driving test for the second time, before leaving the Hospital. The physician gave in and allowed Julian to go home for a short spell over Christmas, it is documented by the Doctor, "Once Julian scented home there was no keeping him". (I don't feel this was a spelling mistake. I know Julian, once he tasted freedom, he was not going back to be locked up again.)

Julian was formally discharged in his absence, on the 15th January 1973, with the rehabilitation documented as "was as far as we can take it." Evidently, they could not teach him anymore.

From admission to discharge Julian was back out in society with in five months.

From been unconsciousness for 10 weeks on traction, suffering a heart attack, insertion of tracheotomy, chest infection, collapsed lung, paralytic ileum, passing his driving test, and rehabilitation of daily activities. All his rehabilitation was done in 6 weeks because the rest of the time he was unconscious.

His achievements sounds impossible but certainly an inspiration to all newly injured patient at the unit today.

The Physician at Oswestry did however manage to get Julian to agree to attend Portland College after his discharge, in Nottinghamshire where he agreed to study Accountancy. He had a good head for numbers, but disliked figures intensely. From what I recollect, Julian told me that after he sold his property he moved into a bungalow in Chase Terrace, Burnt wood, Staffordshire.

While he was waiting to go to Portland College he had difficulties obtaining a tax disc for his car. He'd tried all sort of ways, then one evening in the local pub he mentioned his predicament to a costumer who happened to be the local MP. He, assured him someone would ring him the next day, Julian did not hold his breath because he'd had so many disappointments. However the next day the phone did ring, Julian answered repeating his number when the caller said, "This is Barbra Castle speaking" Julian replied with, "Yes and my name is Micky Mouse" and put the receiver down. The phone rang again, and again the same voice said, "No really I am Barbara Castle the New Minister of Transport, I hear you are having a problem getting a tax disc"? He realised the caller was genuine and apologised for his rudeness. He explained the car had been parked on his drive for eight months collecting moss, unable to be driven. She asked, "Could the hold-up be because you need to pass your driving test again, following your accident"? Julian explained he'd already done that.

The following morning the appropriate papers were on the doormat delivered by post.

He appreciated her help, because in September arrangements had been made for him to start at Portland College and getting there would have proved difficult without his own transport. As it was, he had to accept living in accommodation Monday to Friday. Julian learnt a lot of deep life psychological skills here. One lesson in particular he learnt was to be grateful for what he had. He used to tell me of a young girl who used to sit opposite him every day for her meals, but he never knew what she looked like because she wore a bag over her head with holes for her eyes and her mouth of course. He once said to her, "Take off the bag, were all disabled here" her reply was, "If I take off this bag, you will never eat again." He accepted her refusal, and never asked her again. She had suffered burns to her face which she did not think was acceptable for people to see.

He said once, "I might be disabled but I can show my face in public, that poor girl couldn't".

I digress, the discharge letter concluded, "Despite Julian's brilliant rehabilitation, much of this is due to his own qualities. I am anxious, as he is a bit of a "FREE THINKER" and may not be taking seriously all we tell him in self-care for his paralysis.

I thought, what a lovely discharge letter, but there was no mistaking who he was talking about, it was definitely-Julian Paul Davies.

Sadly in the summer of 1976 his youngest brother died at the tender young age of 13. He was found hanging in a tree by his 16 year old adopted sister. He used to like swinging like Tarzan on a rope at the bottom of the garden.

I was told years later that an open verdict was passed, as it was unclear how the accident happened. The rope was found tucked under one armpit, stretching across his upper chest like a seat belt, but tucked close to his neck on the other side. One can only summarise that the rope had slipped causing his fatality. It affected all the family including Julian very badly, and his name was rarely mentioned, not in my presents any way. He died on the 28th of June 1976 I know and remember this date as it is also my birthday. The circumstances of his death used to leave ever body wondering, was it an accident, or did he feel sad that day. In the end I used to tell Julian, "We won't know the truth until we join him, and when we do it won't matter one iota"

Other early Hospital episodes

Three years later Julian was readmitted on New Year's Day in 1978 six years after his big accident, this time with multiple burns to both legs as a result of sitting too near a portable gas fire.

He admitted he may have had a small drink or two the night before, which contributed to his carelessness after all it was it was New Year's Eve. This is how he described the incident to me. He had returned home late on New Year's Eve, this particular winter was very cold. For a quick warm up before going to bed he turned on the portable gas fire, and then in his tiredness feel asleep leaning on the surface. On waking in the morning he felt hot, and sweaty thinking it was the heater causing him to feel hot, he decided to have a quick bath then grab a few hours of 'catch up sleep' As he was removing his trousers, he could hear a ripping noise and thinking it was his brand new trousers he was damaging he stopped and on inspection he realised he was skinning himself. He abandoned the bath went in to the bedroom and rang the Doctor.

His GP said, "Julian! Do you know what day it is?" Julian acknowledged he knew it was New Year's Day, but he would still like him to visit. The Doctor then pointed out to him, "Julian this had better be important" by the time the Doctor arrived Julian was drifting in and out of consciousness.

Fever and delirium had already set in and an ambulance was summoned immediately. It was documented in the Hospital notes that on arrival at the Spinal Injury Unit he was vomiting, he had a fever, accompanied with rigors, and emergency blood test results indicated he was suffering from Streptococcal Septicaemia. So his immune system was considerably hampered for the Septicaemia to set in so quickly. It was necessary, due to his multiple third degree burns to nurse him on a water bed. Julian had to have several units of blood transfusion and heavy doses of Antibiotics but was home and back in circulation within two months. This proves what fantastic healing skin Julian had in those days. The Consultant wrote to Julian's GP, the discharge letter explained about this hospital episode.

"My anxieties about this young man are chiefly on the social side for he proposes returning to living alone, and it is difficult to get him to accept any help. I hope he will shortly be able to take up work again as a book keeper." He also wrote, "He declined Phenol block to his flexor muscle, but one does not use the 'Hard sell' when there is any ambulatory treatment in view"

The medical staff could not convince Julian that these injections were harmless, on those grounds he refused. The physician informs his GP by letter saying, "I would not dream of pressing him, although I believe it would give him much relief."

In those days, Doctors respected patient's wishes, and spoke to them with great respect, wrote about them with integrity and in return they were held in high regard. The old saying, you have to earn respect, still stands in my book.

What's gone wrong? We appear to have gone backwards, this is not true of all Doctors of course, but shouldn't we all be of the same high standard?

On yet another occasion the same physician wrote to his GP saying, "It is remarkable how Julian bounces from one complication to another, but still retains his spirit."

(What a lovely epitaph.)

After he finished his stint at Portland College and qualified as an Accountant he returned to live in the Black Country. From there he worked for a friend of his father as an accountant, his company manufactured handbags. When he used to reminisce about this factory, I used to conger up the under wear factory in the soap series 'Coronation Street'. Although Julian's position was clerical, he did have an added interest in making sure the work force was kept going. To increase profit, he used to say to me that it didn't make economic sense to employ someone to repair the sewing machines if he could do the job himself, so Julian the 'Accountant' did just that. He said you couldn't afford to have a machinist with 'hands idle'.

That was another skill Julian picked up, he was a self-taught sewing machines maintenance man.

In 1978 he picked up sticks and moved to a ground floor flat in Kidderminster, at the same time making a bit of a career change by decided to go free-lance still working as an accountant. The only difference was he had to let his customers know beforehand that he was a 'Para', (short for Paraplegic) and they would make provisions for him by clearing a corner on ground floor for him. A couple of his customers were two brothers, they weren't too keen on accountants prying in to their personal affairs, so to win their confidence Julian used to speak to them with a Black Country accent and always made a point of joining the workers for lunch at the local pub.

Julian found favour with these two brothers and they offered him a permanent post. Julian declined, and there closed one of his windows of opportunity. The two brothers were none other than the Richardson twins called Don and Roy. The two revamped the steel works site in 1982, and today it is better known as The Merry Hill Shopping Centre.

Following this poor judgment he remained a poor man all his life, but he survived living independently, for another couple of years.

As he was labelled by the physician at Oswestry a free thinker, Julian did have friends staying with him from time to time. When they were 'down on their luck' as he called it, but they wouldn't stay long he'd soon knock them back into shape. Hard work was a good antidote for plucking someone out of feeling sorry for themselves he used to say. They would either get sorted or leave because they couldn't keep up with Julian's pace. They weren't all young men either, there were some young ladies along the way too.

To recap a little, just before Julian's accident he had developed an interest in a new style of music called Northern Soul Music, mostly Motown label. These events were held in more northerly side of England, as the name suggests. Also referred to as "All-nighters" because that's what they were. The young people just danced all night at night clubs such as "Wigan Casino" in Wigan, "The Torch" in Manchester, "Turning Wheel" in Stoke, and the "Tower Ballroom" in Blackpool. Sadly they have all closed down now, except for the Tower Ballroom. It certainly kept young people off the streets in those days. This style of dancing was so fast, accurate and energetic one could even describe it as athletic. To achieve this high standard of performance they would have to practice every evening in order to perform on the dance floor at the weekend. What was so amazing was that it was all self-taught; there were no classes to teach those moves.

To get a flavour of this type of dancing, look it up on the web there are original old clips for you to understand what I mean. The clubs would be jammed packed full of nonstop solid dancing, it was compelling to watch and would last the whole weekend day and night.

Like most young people in the 70`s Julian was skinny, and of course not happy being a wall flower in these Night Clubs, he had to be the centre of attention like so many others there. He would practice his back flip drops, front drops, splits and spinning on his forehead each evening then perform each weekend, showing off his fancy foot work in his high waist and flared trousers, all this energising would result in hot sweaty bodies. Because of this, all the dancers carried a sports bag with several change of clothes along with a wash bag. It was a good job there was no alcohol sold on the premises otherwise it would soon travel to their heads. Fizzy drinks were the only beverage available. He use to tell me how he won cups for the best dancing, but he often wondered in later years what had become of them. Well never mind, one man's treasure is another man's rubbish.

After his paralysing accident his love for the 'Northern Soul' music continued. His Mother was then living at the 'Freemasons' pub, it later became known as the 'The Barrel'.

Julian, still hooked on his music realised he could not join in the dancing anymore, so he did the next best thing. He increased his record collection and purchased disco equipment and became a DJ. I use to jokingly say, 'J.D. by name, D.J by hobby'.

Julian was given the free range of his mother's pub to attract punters with his disco skills. The place was often heaving. The ground floor was off course the Bar, the second floor was a large room so Julian used to tell me, with a long oak boardroom table running up the centre of the room with chairs all around and a fascinating <u>little</u> open and shut sliding door in the centre of the door. Evidently this is where the Freemasons use to have their secret meetings, hence how the pub got its name. The living quarters were on the top floor.

It was from this pub Julian used to organise lifts to attend these "All-nighters" as they were referred to. Willing drivers would take three or four passengers in their cars on most Friday nights and form a convoy traveling north.

Sometimes Julian would take his disco equipment with him as well as his records in the hope one of the DJs would let him have a turn while they went for a break. He considered it a big honour when they did invite him up.

Julian became known as one of the trust worthy fillers. Then one Friday night as Julian was about to enter the Night club he was refused entrance on the account the club had been refurbished bringing with it new fire regulations. The new ruling was, 'no wheel chair users were allowed above ground floor, it was considered a fire hazard to other punters in the event of evacuating people in an emergency.

Other young people heard of this, they slipped pass Julian informed the DJ who then announced it on the speakers. Out they all came, Julian bewilderingly asking, "What's going on?" His friends said, they have all done a mass walk out in protest against your denial of entry they're protesting 'one out all out'. Soon there were about 500 strong on the street cascading on to the main road bringing the traffic to a standstill. The police arrived, to investigate the traffic holdup. The spoke person explained the situation, the police then went to clarify the denial of entry, after some time they both re-emerged outside to negotiate with the crowd, the police explaining he could arrest them all for kerb obstruction. The crowd were not budging on this one, saying he didn't ask to be in a wheel chair and it was discrimination. The Night club owner argued rules were rules. The police concluded in the end that if the chap in the wheelchair could find four men to be held responsible for his safety by carrying him up and down the stairs in his wheel chair and not cause harm to others he would be allowed in. The additional agreement was in the event of a fire then the four chosen and the wheel chair had to leave last in case the chair got dropped then cause obstruction on the stairway.

Everybody was happy, just in case Julian didn't get the chance to thank the chosen four for their bravery and support and all who walked out to protest on Julian behalf that night.

I will thank you all myself.

I don't know if his brother was present that knight but this lifting up and down stairs was a regular occurrence, as most public buildings did not have lifts. Most disabled people would have given up with the attitude 'Oh Well no lifts no access' Not Julian his motto was 'No lifts, I will still gain access' he used to say "There is more than one way to skin a cat"

If his brother was out socialising with him and Julian needed one of these lifts, the two of them would burst out into their usual song, 'he ain't heavy, he's my brother.'

This song was released in 1969 by the Hollies. The lyrics went like this—

The road is long
With many a winding turn
That leads to who knows where.
But I'm strong.
Strong enough to carry him.
He ain't heavy, he's my brother.
The load doesn't weigh me down at all,
He ain't heavy he's my brother.

Others helping to carry him would often join in with the singing.

It's nice that Northern Soul is making a big comeback in 2011 they say it's bigger than ever.

At one of these weekends Julian stupidly shared a can of pop with another, on his return he heard a knock at the door, and to his surprise it was a Policeman that was filling his door frame asking if he knew of a certain young man. Julian acknowledged he did, and was he all right? They explained he was in casualty receiving treatment and he needed to go with them right away to be tested as well. Julian said, "Tell them I'll come in the morning" The police said, "I don't think you realise the seriousness of the situation, you need to be tested first then treated and educated on how not to contaminate others after. You have to come right now, we have been sent to fetch you"

His friend had been diagnosed with Hepatitis C, and sure enough Julian was tested positive too.

Apparently your more lightly of contracting Hep C via blood cross contamination, but contracting it through saliva is not totally impossible either.

He told me years later he took two medications for nearly twelve months. I remember asking him was it antibiotics, but he replied "No but something similar". The two tablets he was referring to were antivirals drugs called Ribavirin and Interferon and the course lasts for 48 weeks. He boosted he was cured because the treatment was started as soon as it was.

Julian use to tell me about lots of other crazy incidents after his accident. In December 1978 a year before we met, a friend of his asked him if he fancied a ride on the back of his motor bike. Julian always game for a laugh said, "Yes why not!" This I fancy must have taken a lot of man power, because it entailed transferring a chap who was paralysed from high chest down from a wheel chair on to the back of the motor bike. His skinny body would have been floppy like a puppet from the sternum down. The only support he would have had was holding on to the rider.

Off they sped into the winter sun set, it must have been exhilarating, but the price he paid was to last him a life time. Because unbeknown to him, his shoe fell off as soon as he got on the bike. The rider was oblivious to the lack of attention his friends were paying on the pavement. As soon as they rode off a short distance Julian's sock obviously did not have the griping power to stay in position consequently the foot slipped off and made contact with the tarmac for miles on end. As the rider pulled up to a slow stop, his friends laughingly said, "Did you know you left your shoe behind, as you took off?"

Julian said in horror, "You're joking" They thought it was funny but Julian didn't, after the transfer back into his wheel chair Julian immediately inspected his foot not only did he find a hole in his sock, but more serious than that a big chunk of flesh out of his heel. After weeks of dressings, it healed of a fashion but the heel always brook down depending on what shoes he wore. Was the ride worth it? Julian would probably say yes.

Julian and I met for the first time on New Year's Day in 1979. Although I feel absolutely and besotitley in love with him the minute I set eyes on him. It rally was love at first sight but knowing he was in a wheel chair, I restrained my feelings thinking it's easy to start a relationship but it's difficult to end one but more than that, what would people think of me if I broke a disable man's heart. So I decided to stay focus on my career instead and continued with further training.

I went on to complete my Diploma in Orthopaedic training which took another 12 months, I then returned to the Spinal Injury Unit to work for a further six months.

I thought I would venture further afield now I had my Diploma under my belt so I thought I'd take a chance and make my fortune as they say in London. A private agency found me work and accommodation in North London. It was a nice part of London with plenty of public parks about, the district was called Golders Green I worked there for 12 months, but in the summer of 1980 I offered to take two Dutch nurses home to stay at my parents for a week. After I waved them goodbye at Gobowen train station I walked over to the Hospital to visit a colleague I used to work with twelve months previously, but unbeknown to me she was now working on the Spinal Injury Unit. As I approached the ward, who do you think was the first person I met?

Your right, Julian Paul Davies, my feelings hadn't changed at all for this man.

Butterflies came back as strong as ever, my stomach started to churn. I was aware I was blushing and worst of all I felt as if I was going to faint. Although it was a pleasant feeling, I didn't like being out of control. I felt like a silly teenager who had a crush on a school friend.

After chatting to my friend in the office she informed me Julian was being discharged later that afternoon after been hospitalised with a Trochanteric sinus for the last couple of months. I can remember thinking at the time; his immune system must be really shot to develop a sinus.

As I was leaving he called over and said, "They're discharging me this afternoon, I'll pick you up tomorrow morning I'll take you to the sea side, be sure to bring a picnic, and I'll just bring my springer spaniel" The golden rule of nursing was, never befriend a patient you were nursing. But this time was different I was not nursing him; I was employed elsewhere at a London Hospital.

Inside my head I intended to say no, but my heart called out Ok, what time.

The following morning as I was waiting on my parent's lawn with my picnic basket, I started wondering or more likely worrying of how we could all fit in his vehicle? There would be Julian, myself the picnic basket the wheel chair and the big Springer Spaniel! I needn't have worried because he turned up in a Sunbeam Talbot car, with plenty of room in the boot for everything including the dog. You see I assumed wrong, I assumed he was going to turn up in one of those light blue Robin Reliant cars. This was my first mistake, I underestimated this man's capability I presumptuously labelled him Dis-abled instead of 'More-able-than-most'.

It was a gorgeous hot summer's day; I remember we drove all the way with the side windows down. He took me to Porthmadog beach and later we had our picnic on Black rock sands calling at Portmerion on the way back. I also remember thinking I was so happy, I never thought of it before but it was actually our first date. What I do remember is we didn't stop for a drink on the way back because it happened to be a Sunday, and they were dry counties in Wales in those days. Sunday drinking ban wasn't lifted in some parts of Wales until 1996.

Photograph of me waiting for Julian to take me on
my first date.

After rekindling our friendship I started to commute from London to Kidderminster by train visiting him on my days off. The first manly project Julian got me involved with, was renovating an early 1920 Alvis Boat tail car. Our courting days were spent sanding down the body, and then painting the underneath with red oxide paint. Nine months later he asked me to marry him. But before I accepted he jokingly said, don't worry this might not be a long term contract as he had been told by physicians at the time of his accident not to despair he still had 10 years of life left in him. He was told this when he was 18 years of age, he was 27 when he proposed. But I didn't want a short term contract I wanted to capture as much happiness as I could with this man.

After he proposed he said, "Arrange it quick, before I lose my bottle" He had a bit of a phobia about going down the aisle in a wheelchair. I was so excited, and accepted instantly I never thought love could be this exiting.Money was tight, so I bought some white velvet material hoping I could get someone to make this once in a life time wedding gown for me. I knew of a wedding shop in my home town, so I asked Julian to take me home to go and see this lady. I didn't drive in those days and had to rely on him to chauffer me about. Luckily the lady who owned the wedding shop did wedding dress alterations. But I was hoping she could make one from scratch, my plan was to stay there for the remainder of the day then sleep over at my parents and Julian was going to pick me up the following morning.I arrived at the bridal shop promptly at nine o'clock armed only with the material, and a library book with a picture of a lady on horseback in a riding suit, which entailed her wearing a jacket and a long skirt. The dressmaker was amazed that I didn't have as much as a zip a button or at least a pattern not to mention the lining for the outfit. She was marvellous and very patient with me every time she needed anything she would send me out to the appropriate shop to get whatever was needed. The fittings went on all day; I don't recall either of us having as much as a cup of coffee never mind lunch. When the last fitting was done at five o'clock precisely, I can recall saying to Christine, "Thank you, now Cinderella can go to the ball" then I curtsied. The only disappointment I had about the whole outfit was the hat, I had envisaged in my mind a small Edwardian riding hat not a big Victorian one otherwise I was over the moon with my antique two peace wedding gown.

The Day we both said "I do"

The photograph of Julian and I on our wedding day,
with Julian saying, "I do" on the 3rd of October 1981,
at precisely 3pm.

Lots have asked me over the years, why I chose this style of wedding dress. To me the Edwardian style dress sense seem to be the most elegant in history, so if I could just escape into history for one day, what better day to choose to escape to this era, than on my wedding day.

Pure magic!

When I was growing up trying to make sense of the English language, I found the words fascinating. If I didn't understand what they meant I would break them up and try and find their origin. Asking such questions, why do we call our elbow funny bone only to realise in biology class later it was called the humorous bone. Why we call a stiff shoulder a frozen shoulder when in fact due to altered nerve supply it is actually freezing cold!

So when I came across the word bridesmaid, I broke the words down and landed up with Brides-Maid and that's exactly what I intended my bridesmaid to look like so there they were, they were dressed in delicate pink cotton dresses with Victorian/Edwardian style apron and pinafore. The older bridesmaid wore a lace rosette attached to some ribbon in her hair and the younger one wore a white mop cap, needless to say the romance flourished and it was the start of a beautiful love story. We had our differences, who doesn't? Male and female don't always think the same and definitely don't have the same idea about life.

I always think of the example I was once told about a mother and a father discovering their son balancing on a roof top. The mother gasped in horror saying, "My boy, my boy what if you should fall to your death" But the father puffed out his chest with pride and says, "That's my boy, how brave is he"! Both loved him equally, they just thought differently.

Just like the imaginary couple, we both loved the same things in our own male/female ways. I believe if couples never disagree then just may be one of them is giving in too much!

Once I decided to take the plunge and step into this exciting new world that belonged to Julian Davies, my life just became intertwined with his and my feet never touch the ground for 29 years. It was like living on a helter-skelter. He was right when he warned me that he could not offer me a world of wealth but it would be exiting. As promised it turned out to be fun, fast and furious. The question was, did I have the stamina to keep up with him? The answer to that was "Barely"

I took up residence with my new husband in a ground floor flat in Kidderminster. I loved my new life, and I was excited for the future.

I started off married life by being the dutiful house proud wife. This didn't last long, when Julian tackled me saying "This is not what I wanted from our marriage, I can keep a house squeaky clean on my own, but I can't make memories on my own." So it was agreed whoever was left on their own in years to come at the end of this marriage, would spend their free time making the house squeaky clean, but until then we were destined to make memories together.

Every single minute we had together we spent helping each other in some way. I would rely on his genius and spontaneous ideas and he would rely on my physical help. A good partnership you might say. Because of this, we became extremely close and off course we became to rely on each other greatly. In fact our life became so synchronized that both of us knew the other's needs, above all, telling each other, we loved each other every day. He was naughty he would say it when I least expected it, often in a middle of a row. How can you continue then? The wind would be taken straight out of my sails, accompanied by his cheeky smile; I couldn't help but make it up.

So began this marital journey which was only enjoyed at three addresses, our first marital home started in the ground floor flat where he had forbidden "house proud" to be part of our partnership, instead we converted his rambled over grown garden into a little organic haven. Apart from enjoying our own home grown vegetables we also had free range chickens; we were self-sufficient except for meat and milk. I took pride in watering the garden morning and night, but not half as much pride in gathering my home grown crop and gracing our table with wholesome home grown vegetables. Parked at the top of this over grown bramble was a Ford Poplar car otherwise known as a 'Sit-up-and-beg' car, believing the old car belonged to a neighbour (by the way my neighbour then was Helen Bethel who also became a widow the same month as me) they say you could buy these cars in any colour during and after the war as long as it was black. Apparently the car turned out to belong to Julian himself. To make more room for my vegetable patch Julian paid a scrap dealer, £25 to have it towed away. I was absolutely distraught when I discovered the car belonged to Julian. It was my fault that I didn't let him know it was my long life ambition to own a black Ford Poplar car. I'm still grieving for that decision he made those 30 years ago.

Under Julian's supervision I built some wide paving slab steps into the garden, wide enough to accept a wheelchair; I could lower him one step at a time to help me cultivate our garden. While I continued to care for our garden Julian had other projects in mind. He started to convert a transit van into a Fish and Chip van, it used to worry me dreadful that he was going to be dealing with boiling fat, out there wherever he was, while I was working shifts.

He had a will of iron, so there was no point fussing or trying to stop him.

In the meantime in the winter of 1981 Julian decided to take up weight lifting, at the local gym. He would sit in his wheel chair and pull on those weights for all his might. I recall him telling me he pulled so hard the one night he stood up and was heading for the ceiling. The trainer had to haul him down by pulling on his legs. Imagining this hilarious scene, suggested to me he was lifting his own body weight, and that can't be good for anybody's joints. Needless to say he didn't go the following week or ever again because he'd developed a right olecranon Bursitis, sometimes referred to as 'Popeye's elbow' usually caused by a Repetitive injury but it can also be brought on by a compromised immune system.

Luckily the Fish and Chip project came to a sudden halt when he discovered an Off Licence was going for sale just down the road from us. I can remember thinking, "Goodness gracious me, how will we ever manage" the phrase out of the frying pan into the fire came to mind. His idea was that I would continue with my full time job and he would take care of the shop. I did go along with the idea thinking it might work, even against my better judgment.

I didn't want to land up in old age thinking we nearly did all sorts, but I put a stop to all of his hair raising ideas. In the spring of 1982 while we were waiting for the contracts to be signed Julian went to see his GP to see if anything could be done about his abdominal pain, profuse sweating and headache which had lasted more than eight weeks. No cause could be found so he plodded on with every day activities.

Just as I imagined this shop business turned out to be very hard work, not just for him but for me to. I was working full time unsociable hours at the Hospital, and then I would walk home at 9:30pm in time to shut up shop at 10pm. After shutting shop we would balance the till, stock up the shelves, wash the floor, and make a list of stock that was required from the cash and carry run the following morning. Once the shop was ship-shape we would ascend to our living quarters above the shop. I say ascend because the two of us would have to muster up all our strength to get Julian up the stairs physically, as we didn't have a lift from the shop floor to the living quarters above the shop. Although, Julian had built a shaft with the aid of a young lad called Ricky Pooler, but because the shaft was from the shop area to our living quarters upstairs, there was no financial help to be got from the social services to install a lift.

Hence this back breaking job of lifting poor Julian up and down those treacherous curving stair case had to be done twice daily once in the morning and again at night before retiring to our bed. To be fair Julian did take most of his own weight while I lifted his legs, and negotiating the curve in the stair case was our biggest dread.

In those days he was only issued one wheelchair, so once we arrived at the top of the stairs I then had to run back down for the chair. Taking care not to over balance him in case he fell down the stairs, I would gingerly raise the collapsed chair over his head. Then I'd run back down again for his cushion, detached foot plates and arm rests. The chair would be re-assembled at the top once more making sure the brakes were off so that I could bend over the back of the chair and get hold of the back of his trousers, then lift with an almighty lift. Julian helping by using his arms on both sides of the banister, and I from his waist band from the back, we would both on the count of three lift and I would with perfect timing and precision push this wheelchair, with no brakes I may add under his butt for a safe landing. Once safely in his chariot they two of us would start cooking our evening meal, we rarely got into bed before twelve midnight and that was every night. Up again every morning at five o'clock allowing time for both of us to get in and out of the bath before our descent down those wooden stairs again. I started work at seven thirty in those days, and as I didn't drive I had a half hour walk before my shift started.

I call this tale, 'We all come tumbling down'

Going back, to the top of the stairs as I lifted Julian up I misjudged the edge of the top step and the front wheels went over. The phrase practice makes perfect is a load of rubbish, because down we all went, Julian first, wheelchair second then thirdly myself holding on to poor Jus waist band for all my might and fourthly, Sami the Alsatian dog, who had decided to join us to add a little excitement to her life.

As usual when my life takes on an emergency situation something weird happens, my life seems to slow down in speed, I mean real slow, even my thoughts slow down as well as the environment around me. I can remember thinking as we all tumbled down; "Please-God-don't-let-him-bump-his-head, I couldn't-bare-it-if-he-had-a-head-injury"

When we arrived at the bottom I called, "Ju, Ju are you all right?"

He said, "Off course not, I have to do it all over again now" Luckily all three of us, chair included were fine.

In June 1983 Julian attended New Cross Hospital Wolverhampton to have Keyhole surgery to crush some bladder stones. He begged the Consultant not to cut him if he could help it because he was self-employed and would not be able to abide by any restrictions on how he shouldn't life any heavy objects not to mention going up and down stars on his bottom. The procedure proved to be very difficult, the surgeon said he'd never come across such hard stones and crushing them was nearly impossible especially when one of them got away and was lodge in the neck of the bladder. Back on the ward the Consultant made a Beeline for him saying sternly, "Don't you ever put me under pressure like that again, if it was anyone else I would have surgically removed the little blighters" Luckily for Julian, because the Consultants had honoured Julian's request he was back in action the very next day serving behind his counter. Julian was always good at making deals.

I call this story, 'Nature is always in control'
After two years we left the shop and bought his mother's house off her, that first summer I recall going on holiday to the south of France with my brother and his girlfriend in the early 1980`s. As organised as ever, Julian had by his steering wheel a cascading long narrow list of road numbers, motorways, coffee breaks, lunch breaks and tea breaks, and this orderly list was matched up to a time schedule. When Glyn my brother all of a sudden said on the journey "I need to go to the toilet." Julian said "NO", because it was not on the list of scheduled stops. But reluctantly he did stop at a service station.

While Glyn was in the toilet, suddenly, Julian decided he now needed to go the toilet as well. So, all stations go, all had to pile out, first the wheel chair, then the cushion, the transfer board then lastly transfer Julian himself out. I push like mad to make up time to try and catch Glyn up. As Julian was going towards the toilet Glyn was coming back. Glyn looked puzzled at us and said, "What's going on, this stop is unscheduled" Julian replied with his arms in the air, "When needs must" and off we both buzzed. We laughed such a lot over this incidence. The bottom line is, man can try to be a 'control freak' over everything, but in the end nature always has the last word.

This next tale I call, 'Frozen Fingers' tale.
After returning from this holiday Julian took it into his head he wanted a jeep like buggy, as he couldn't afford one he did what he always did, built one of his own. So that's exactly what he did, he went out and bought an old mini, once he got it home he took metal cutters and a grinder to it. I wish I'd taken photographs of him cutting it down; by

the time he'd finished all that was left was a base on a chassis with four wheels one to each corner, an engine and a steering column attached to a steering wheel. Then the welding began in earnest, it took months. When it was finished, passers-by would stop to chat and congregate with him outside the garage, boastfully informing Julian that he would not be able to legally drive it on the road. Of course they had under estimated Julian's constant over engineering habit which he did with all his projects. To prove them all wrong he took it to the Police for them to scrutinise it with high Tec testing equipment making sure it was totally road worthy. And of course it passed with flying colours. I remember that Christmas our regular car was off the road, and as Julian had made a promise to attend my family Christmas gathering, he intended to keep it. So in thick snow Julian and I ventured in our home made Mini-Moke Jeep with no sides, doors or roof for shelter. We started our sixty mile journey, stacked high with Christmas presents to my parents' home in Oswestry.

He was keen to deliver something else he'd made with his own hands, it was a five foot tall, handmade wooden 'shop front' for the only child in the family at the time, her name is Cerys. We were frozen; we both had a hot water bottle each under our coats to keep us warm, two pairs of gloves, two coats and scarfs. What you'll do when you're young and mad. The only thing we nearly lost on our journey was his wheel chair; we must have looked like Mother and Father Christmas to passing motorists. We should have dressed in red to look the part. I can still feel the pain of my frozen fingers just thinking about it.

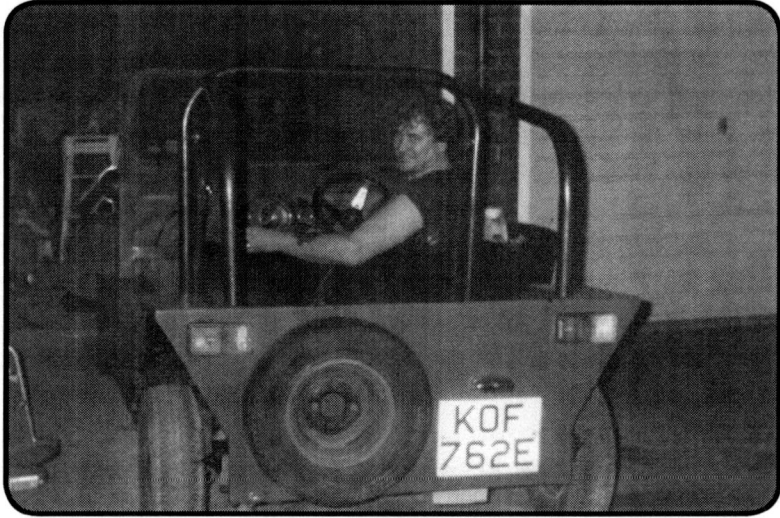

Photograph of Julian looking very proud of his finished
master piece, his Mini-Moke.

It was about this time Julian's started to complain of his Epigastria pain again, he paid his GP another visit, this time blood samples were taken and this was the first time it was recorded that he had raised Gama GT results, this was in February 1996 we didn't know why at the time but evidently there was something wrong with his liver! The pains came and went, but Julian persevered and carried on with life.

I call this next story, 'Julian's Cornish fire'.

Some years later Julian's Grandmother came to stay with us and she lived with us for over two years. Her oldest daughter lived in Cornwall and she invited her to go and stay with her for a month. She asked Julian to take her all the way to Cornwall, Julian agreed to take her. I was working that day and unable to accompany them. On his return journey he pulled into a garage to fill up with petrol. While he was at the pump he leaned out of his window to press a button for assistance. He had been using this facility for some time; I didn't even know it existed. While he was waiting for assistants a local gentleman strolled over to talk to Julian, saying in a broad yokel accent referring to Julian's van he said, "Herr's very warm isn't her" pointing to the van. Julian replied "I expect she is, she's done a long journey".

He said, "No! I mean Herr's very warm, herr's on fire, there's flames coming from underneath her." Julian shocked by his comments opened the door and leaned out of the driver's side to glimpse underneath the van, and sure enough there was flames gushing from underneath. A lorry driver parked behind him, jumped out of his cab and asked Julian to release the handle of the bonnet. This hero spontaneously sprayed the whole of the engine with white foam, but was struggling to douse the remaining few flames. He ran round and then asked, "Have you got an engine hub in the cab?" Julian replied, "Yes" as he opened the cover out reached these tall flames. The quick acting lorry driver soon leaned over Julian and sprayed the engine from the inside and within minutes the cab was soon cocooned in foam.

The whole time the lorry driver was shouting, "Jump out, for God sake man jump out" Julian kept telling him, "I can't without my wheelchair" the wheelchair was in the back of the van. He explained afterwards to the lorry driver "I got someone to put it in the back of the van in Cornwall thinking my wife was going to lift it out for me in Kidderminster when I got back home, I didn't know this was going to happen"

The lorry driver had a bit of a job getting the wheel chair out of the back of the van, because Sam our Alsatian was growling in the back he wasn't going to let go of the chair that easy. They eventually managed to get Julian out into his wheel chair, but do you think they could get the dog out. No way, Hozay! The dog was not budging. When the kafuffle settled, so did the dog, and he was coaxed out of the back by Julian. As Julian raised his gaze into the distance, and to his amazement he saw huge crowds of people looking in his direction, all standing behind a red and white tape. He wondered what was going on; the ribbon was in a semicircle holding back the crowd. Slowly but surely he thought these people are spectators, they appeared to be staring at him. He asked the petrol pump attendant why are they gathered there? He replied, "They were customers in the café and restaurant on either side of the motorway, the Fire Brigade had them evacuated for safety when you drove your vehicle engulfed in flames into the forecourt and then parked it next to the petrol pump." Julian apologised explaining, he would not have done such a thing had he known.

This confirmed the attendants opinion, because an onlooker shouted, "You idiot what possessed you to pull into the garage engulfed in flames?" Julian couldn't resist retaliating back, "Do you think I would have done it if I'd known it was on fire?"

The traffic on both side of the motor way was held to ransom at Julian's embarrassment. Looking back it had to be done, when you consider how many thousands of gallons of petrol and diesel there is underground supplying all the pumps. I don't know how much damage would have been done if the inevitable had happened, but I don't know how much help a thin red and white tape would have done to save them.

When Julian came home that evening in the break down truck, I casually asked "What's happened then, did the van broken down?" Julian said, "Break down, I brought two sides of the motorway to a standstill, evacuated two cafés, two restaurants and nearly blew up a petrol station"

A likely story I thought, but I never caught him out lying before. I could feel a long story coming. Looking back I'm amazed he had the courage and stamina to do the long journey there and back in one day on his own anyway, but at the same time I had total faith in him because he was capable. The point of telling you about this story is that he then needed a new engine. And that leads me on to another story.

I call this next story my 'Yorkshire tales', not dales. This is a long tale so if you want to make a cup of tea first, this is a good time to stop.

A few days later Julian found just the engine he wanted for his Daihatsu van up in "The last of the summer wine" country. He happened to mention this to his brother during a telephone conversation the evening before he was going to fetch it the following morning. His brother offered to go with him to keep him company, good job he did otherwise I don't know what sort of a tale I'd be telling you right now.

Julian also had a mini at the time and luckily he had a tow hook and a trailer. So off they went in the early hours of the morning to Yorkshire to pick up this engine. I however decided to rearrange the lounge while he was away for the day. He picked up his brother on route, and then continued on their long journey north. Just before they got to their destination Julian suddenly felt the car sway, he said to his brother, "Oh! Bother I think we've got a puncture." As it happened there was the famous mile upon mile of our traditional orange bollards that we expect to see all over Britain.

I don't know why we don't exchange the symbol of the English rose for the orange bollard for our National Emblem; it would be more fitting I think. (Actually this was about 1983 and nothing's changed) Any way back to the story, his brother got out and changed the wheel, while he was mid task a Policeman stopped his car and said, "You can't stop here!" They explained the situation, and luckily the Policeman appreciated their predicament and advised them not to be long.

Onward they ventured up and down dales mile after mile then at last they arrived at the farm house. Julian must have struck up a bit of a comradeship with this Yorkshire man, because he mentioned that his Grandmother was from Yorkshire. As a result of that he offered Julian four spare Daihatsu wheels free of charge in the deal. Julian accepted them gratefully, not knowing how helpful they would be on his return journey. Off they set homeward bound up and down these dales again, and would you believe it at almost the exact spot again Julian said, "I don't believe it, I think we've got another puncture". His brother asked, "What are we going to do, you've already used the spare wheel?" Julian then remembered the four extra spare wheels the kind Yorkshire man had given him. His brothers face lit up, things were not so grim after all. Yet again they pulled in between some orange bollards. His brother went to inspect the damage, he called out to Julian "It's not the car this time it's the trailer" Hardly having time to start the job when the very same Policeman pulled over again saying, "Haven't I told you two lads before you're not allowed to stop here?"

They explained they knew that, but they had a different puncture this time. "Ok, but don't be long about it," was the request. So as quick as he could he changed the tyre. Off they went; they hadn't travelled far when Julian said, "Something is not right, the trailer is pulling to one side." Over they pulled between the orange bollards again. Again the same Policeman pulled over and said, "Are you two taking the Mickey, what's the matter now?" They explained when they changed the tyre on the trailer they didn't realise that the spare Daihatsu van wheels were not quite the same size as the trailer tyre and it was pulling to one side, they wouldn't be long they would just swap the good tyre for the same size. The police man was getting a bit irritated now. "Just be quick, ok?" They travelled about five miles down the road when a lorry in the opposite direction spins a tiny chipping in to Julian's windscreen. Needless to say it shattered into a thousand pieces, but it remained intact. Julian remained optimistic as ever and said, "Don't worry; it appears there is some sort of a safety device. Although the windscreen was like a glass mosque, there was a small patch of un-cracked glass at eye level the size of a dinner plate. Julian continued to drive on the motor way in this state. I don't know how legal this was, but it didn't last for long because the petrol light came on. Julian said, "I don't believe it, I need to come off the motor way to get some petrol its urgent" Off they came and soon found a garage, Julian's last words to his brother was, "Whatever you do don't slam the door shut when you get out, the air vacuum will pull the windscreen in" he agreed he wouldn't. But, its human nature to slam a car door isn't it! So that's exactly what he did, he slammed the door shut. In came all this glass, thousands of pieces. He opened the door and said sorry. I don't know what for he could have said it through the empty windscreen. Julian reassured him by saying, "Never mind it's done now" They purchased their petrol and continued on their journey down the motor way. The noise must have been horrendous, but the worst thing he complained of was his eye lashes being blown into his eyes. He shouted to his brother, "It's no good my eyes are hurting, I need to pull over" So that's what they did. His brother said, "I know, I'll take off my shirt and wrap it round your head leaving little slits for your eyes" Julian agrees to this, and off they went again. I don't know what other drivers must have thought of them, a car with no windscreen, a driver with a shirt wrapped round his head and a passenger with no shirt on at all, on a cold day.

Would you believe it, it started to rain but Julian pressed on with his journey, but had to give in the end because he shouted, "The rain is coming at my eye balls like daggers, it's no good it's too painful I need to pull over again".

This time he came up with another idea! A few days earlier there was a documentary on the TV about how dangerous using cling film was over hot food when placed in the microwave. Hence that's why every catering department was ditching all their cling film by making a fast buck. Julian bought one of these catering rolls, I can remember asking him at the time, "If it's not good enough for others, how can it be good enough for us"? Any way the roll of cling film never made it into the house and lucky for them it was still in the boot of the car. His brother did as Julian suggested, and wrap the windscreen in cling film in an attempt to keep the rain out of his eyes. He pulled over quite soon again because this time he shouted, "It's no good I can't see clearly enough" This time Julian suggested that his brother should wrap the cling film round his eyes instead of the windscreen. Reluctantly his brother agreed, off they trekked again. This time he shouted, "It's no good, my breath is steaming up the cling film, we need to buy an emergency windscreen, and we need to come off the motor way."

By a fluke chance they found a small garage run by an elderly gentleman, and when they enquired about an emergency windscreen, the elderly gentleman pondered a while saying I've got one somewhere. He eventually found one at the very back of the garage all covered in dust. He explained he could not let them have it because he could not convert the old currency to modern sterling.

The price was seven shillings and six pence. How many youngsters could convert that sum today? In the end Julian said, "Please I beg you, take the tenner, I can't drive home without a windscreen" The old man eventually gave in and accepted the tenner.

So when I heard Julian's mini pull up into the car park that evening, one half of me was excited to show him the new lay out of the lounge the other half of me wanted to shout at him for being so late. As you can imagine my greeting was "Where have you been Julian, I expected you home hours ago". All he could say was, "You won't believe the day we've had" He was right, I couldn't believe it, and I couldn't match it either. The Moral of the story is, don't assume anything until you've heard the other side of the story first. Certainly don't shout at anyone before you do, you could find yourself apologising. Looking back on this bizarre journey most of us would have screamed, why does everything always happen to me? But not Julian he used to say, "Why not me, it happens to others why not me!" But I used to think, not as much as you Julian!

Needless to say soon after this escapade he joined one of the Breakdown Services.

Julian was one for the women before I met him, but to be fair once he had made a commitment to our marriage chivalry was definitely not dead. Although he was not one for showering me with flowers on a weekly basis, he did have a funny romantic side to him. On a daily basis he would catch me unaware and wink at me, maybe across a packed room. Always kissed me before I went to work, and again as I arrived home and as many times as he cared for as a thank you in between. No matter how bad the row was, he would always take the leading role of making it up before we went to sleep, even if I was in the wrong. He would often say to me "Come here, you can say sorry first if you like" and squeeze me tight. A slap on the bottom was an often occurrence, he even slapped my twin sisters bottom by mistake once.

He never made that mistake again.

Birthday presents was never your traditional bunch of roses, or an expensive silk scarf. They were however always practical and always something I needed at that moment in time. I remember once he drove up the slope towards the house tooting his horn, which he knew made me thumping mad, neighbours are always doing it. I consider it the height of laziness, not to mention rudeness for intruding on some ones tranquillity. On top of his mini he had asked the local DIY warehouse assistant to carefully assemble, balance and secure a garden table and chairs to the roof giving the impression it was a 'mobile dinner' he was giving me. As he pulled outside the front door he tooted like mad while unwinding the passengers window shouting, "I couldn't wrap it, so save you guessing I thought I'd make a grand entrance instead, can you guess what it is?" grinning from ear to ear. I loved that spontaneity about him. I had other non-romantic birthday presents like a watering can, fork and a spade, but I treasure them more because they were my birthday presents.

I can't remember what year Julian started with this hobby, but it was one of those hobbies one could stop and start any time. In other words if there was nothing else to do he could always do jobs on his Porsche! Sounds posh doesn't it, well it wasn't he had it imported from Miami Beach.

I remember when I was vacuuming it for the first time, I froze as I saw the sand being sucked up the nozzle realizing this may well have been sand from Miami Beach. After he set about renovating this Porsche, I remember came home from work one day hearing a lot of tinkering going on in the garage and to my horror this is what I found. He'd suspended the rear end of the car on a couple of beer barrels so he could weld a new petrol tank in place.

Wow! Health and safety at work comes to mind!

Sometime in the spring of 1989 Julian needed to inspect something under his car, instead of waiting for me to either have a look or get prepared by getting a large five foot long and four inch deep sponge he normally used from the garage to lie on, he impatiently jumped out of the driver's seat on to the tarmac surface landing on his hip.

When I arrived you can imagine the nag, nag, nag that went on. That evening Julian started to perspire profusely for no apparent reason. He confessed before going to bed that when he landed on his hip he did hear a bit of a crunch. The decision to jump out of the car that day was not one of his better moves in life. Because it later cost him nine months freedom, and had to be hospitalised back in Oswestry and instructed to stay on bed rest. That thud had progressed to osteomyelitis in his right hip again, which means infection of the bone and the only treatment for this is to remove the bone. They performed what they call a Gerdalstone operation which entailed removing the head of his femur, the ball that fits in the socket in other words. Unfortunately the first operation wasn't successful in removing all of the osteomyelitis, so four operations later they had gnawed away four inches of his upper shaft. His balance was never the same again. Before and during this hospitalisation I happened to be pregnant, and at the same time I was living and working in Kidderminster. Trying to get to Oswestry was proving to be very difficult as I didn't drive and the train connections were impossible. The days were long for Julian, but refusing to let boredom rote his brain he struck up a friendship with a patient in the next bed. He was an Indian gentleman who lived in Birmingham, Julian spoke to everybody like an open book, to him no subject was untouchable. Most of us would not even approach this next personal subject, but not Julian. He would get in there, to see if he could learn something or be enlightened. Have you guessed the topic, well yes it was Religion. With time on his hands he asked if he could borrow his Qur'an he would like to read it. Nervous about handing over this precious book, he did allow Julian to have a look at it. From early morning until late into the night he would read, then one day he handed the Holy Book back and said, "Thank you, but it's really very similar to our Christian Bible, there is no reason why we can't all live peacefully together." There are parts in there, if you took them literally could cause a fanatic to create war. For example it says, "Whoever then acts aggressively against you, inflict injury he has inflicted on you" Julian explained in the Old Christian Testament it also says, "An eye for an eye, and a tooth for a tooth" this is similar teachings, but of course in the new Christian Testament however it says, "Forgive one another, and turn the other cheek" In the Koran it also gives similar guide lines, "Pardon the wrongdoer" Julian liked the word Salaam which carried the same meaning to Shalom, he said it's so versatile and thought we should use it more often when we greet and leave people, it can mean hello, goodbye, peace be with you, and much more but he liked this one the best "Mighty blessings be upon you"

When I visited Julian later that night he said, "I think Judaism, Christianity and Islam have a lot in common although they practice in different holy buildings such as Synagogues, Churches and Mosques. To think they then read from different holy books called the Qur'an, Bible and Torah it's fascinating that they have such similar teachings. They all seem to carry similar mysteries of their scriptures and as the old saying goes, these holy books are 'simple enough for a child to understand but too difficult for scholar to grasp' how versatile; these three books suits all ages.

Unfortunately it appears that all Nations of all beliefs in the past have gone beyond the rules of religion and used their faith as an excuse for war, how sad it's the extremists that spoil religion by destroying personal faith for most, leaving the majority with no faith at all—existing as atheists. Why I'm mentioning this is because, I don't know how Julian and I could have managed without our quiet faith. I thought we were supposed to be tolerant of all faiths, but sadly the innocent are often paying with their lives in the name of religion. Julian and I had a homily or a sermon once when the Priest compared a Pizza to faith, how you could go to lots of different Pizza parlours in Rome and ask for a Margarita Pizza and they would all be slightly different the base is the same but the topping is slightly different.

You chose the topping yourself, like we choose which faith to follow. On the other hand you might decide to go without altogether.

I appear to have digressed, but I was just explaining how Julian got to read the Qur'an and how he never missed an opportunity to learn something new every day so that he could always have a balanced and knowledgeable contribution to any topic that arose. On a previous occasion he had looked into the roots of Methodism, Baptise, Presbyterian, Church of England, and lots more but he always came to the same conclusion that they all had something good to offer.

He confessed once, his one regret in life was he had never attended a Gospel singing service. He always loved those happy clippie hymns we used to sing at our church years ago, when a young at heart Priest used to bring his guitar to the evening Mass.

Once Julian had finished reading the Qur'an he was wondering what he could do next, his brain had been taxed mentally, but now he fancied doing something more physical. The very next day he asked if his bed could be pushed down to the Occupational Therapy department to do something more recreational. Knowing the baby was due any day, but not knowing what sex it was, he thought of making something out of wood that would be suitable for either a boy or a girl. That afternoon he started his first "Must make for my baby" project, it was a wooden rocking horse.

The seed 'I want to be a good father' was planted that afternoon. He built this rocking horse lying on his side, still on bed rest as he was not allowed to sit up on his butt. How many of us could conduct such carpentry lying down on our side?

I'm sure we all wish we could stay in bed longer each morning when that alarm goes off. But it's not until your forced to stay in bed for months on end and not just stay in bed but lying on your side for a long period not allowed to roll over in bed yourself, but had to be dependent on others to turn you from side to side every two hours. That's when you learn to appreciate the beauty in the freedom of getting out of bed of you own accord. Have you ever tried to drink lying down, have you ever tried to eat three meals a day for nine months lying on your side?

He was always an early riser because of these restrictions he'd endured; he used to say as soon as a spark of light entered the bed room "Got to get up, people die in bed" and his other favourite saying was, "Come on let's get up, people rot in bed"

Llewela Jane

Although we resided in Kidderminster and all my antenatal preparation had been done in my home town and Julian was a patient at Oswestry I found myself flitting backwards and forwards between Worcestershire and Shropshire Counties. Then one night after visiting Julian and staying at my parents I was caught short, half way through Coronation Street. I mean I went into labour and was taken by Ambulance to Shrewsbury Maternity unit. As Julian was hospitalised at another hospital, brilliant as he was he could not be in two places at once, and I still wanted him to be the first to hear whether he was a proud father to a baby boy or a baby girl. We plotted a scheme, as soon as I knew what I'd had I would ring Julian's ward and ask the 'nurse in charge' to relay a message to Julian. The arrangement was if it was a boy I would tell the nurse, "Tell Julian, he needs to buy an eternity ring" but if I'd had a girl, I was to tell the nurse, "Tell Julian, there was no need to buy a ring". As Julian was quite convinced I was having a boy he was quite sure he would be buying a ring. That night there happened to be some celebration on at the Hospital Social Club where patients from the Spinal Injury Unit had been invited to attend.

It may have been a long service member of staff leaving. Functions like this used to encouraged Paraplegics and Tetraplegia patients who were close to discharge to attend, to help build up their confidence with socialising skills. As Julian was an old timer, he was biting at the bit to go but staff put their foot down and said, "NO! You're on bed rest Julian; you're not going to any party on a bed."

Incidentally this social club has been demolished since, a great loss to the confidence booster of the patients, not to mention all the staff special birthday celebrations, weddings and christenings and Christmas parties. I fear it was short sightedness of some high power hospital administrator who saw fit to give permission to build a car park instead! Disgruntled about being forced to be a party pooper, he settled down to watch the telly.

Baring in mind the ward was running on skeletal staff that night, Julian soon realised the program that was about to begin was about babies born with physical deformities, some with brain damage, learning difficulties and Down syndrome. Julian at this stage was now begging for mercy, he started shouting, "Sister, Sister, Sister" In the end he gave up and settled down to watch the most insensitive program at that point in his life. The television hand control evidently was out of reach on another patient who was paralysed from the neck down. The poor lad kept shouting to Julian, "I'm so sorry Ju, I just can't do anything about it"

The ward sister eventually emerged from the side room shouting "What's the matter out here, who's creating all that din?"

Julian replied, "It doesn't matter anymore the programs finished, I don't care what she has now I just want the baby to be born well"

The following day the same Sister was on duty, I made my phone call as promised and asked for the message to be relayed to Julian as planed, "Tell him he's safe, he doesn't have to spend his money"

She hollered this message down the long ward, like a fish wife on market day.

Julian shouted, "It's a girl, it's a girl, ask if they're both alright?"

At 2:29pm on the 16th December 1989 Julian became the proud parent to a baby girl.

The following morning when I woke, I peered at this tiny little face in the cot beside me and I truly felt I had received a gift from God. How could anyone be so unkind as to inflict harm on such a defenceless little thing? Besides they are a small part of you, so why would anyone want to harm parts of them-selves? When I read this quote by Elizabeth Stone it just reiterates how I felt, "Making a decision to have a child is momentous. It is to decide forever to have your heart go walking outside your body" What a lovely way of putting it.

I digress, later that morning I was transferred from Shrewsbury to the Oswestry Cottage Hospital by hospital car. The driver bless him was kind enough to do a small detour on my behalf and stopped the car for two minutes outside the Orthopaedic Hospital for Julian to have a quick peak at his new baby daughter. Lying on his back in his Hospital bed, he held her up above his face and said, "Please God, let me see her come of age, let me teach her all I know and please God teach me how to be a good Father to her"

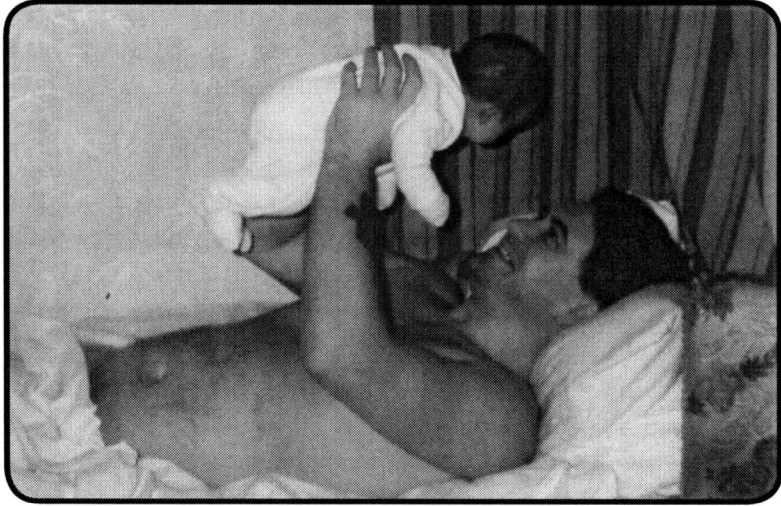

Photograph of Julian making a Devine deal.

On settling into my new abode at the cottage hospital, I learnt the food at the cottage Hospital came from the Orthopaedic Hospital, I had a sudden brain wave after each meal, three times a day I would place a note sealed in an envelope addressed to Julian Davies, care of the spinal Ward. Then Julian in turn would do the same and leave his reply on his tray to go via the kitchen addressed to me at the cottage Hospital. This way we both kept in touch, I updating him on how Baby Davies was doing and he on how he was frantically trying to negotiate on how to gain access to the Occupational Therapy flat that was normally used for patient rehabilitation in preparation for home life. Those letter writings proved to be better than the modern mobile phones. I still have the romantic letters safely stored in the attic, we exchanged all those years ago. Baring in mind her birth was seven days before Christmas day, time was of the essence. Once he got permission off the Occupational Therapist, he then had to convince his Consultant that it would be a good idea for us to have some family time together. God was good to us, as luck would have it, the Doctor and his wife had also just become proud parents to a baby girl the same week. Julian must have touched a soft spot when he begged for this unusual request. Permission was granted as long as he agreed to return back to the ward every night to sleep. The journey was not long, just up the corridor, back to his ward. Julian did give into this, but the deal still wasn't sealed yet, there were further obstacles he had to get over, the ward staff still had to agree and be willing to bring him down to the department each morning then take him back each night. He asked the ward Sister and she agreed as long as the Male Orderlies were willing to take him. Now he had to find out himself, who was working on which shift each morning and each . evening to see if they would agree to these extra duty's, morning and night. Bless them all, they all agreed but I don't know if they realised how special they were making our first Christmas as a family together. Little did the kitchen staff and the food trolley porters know how much they were contributing towards the best Christmas present ever, the three of us were wishing for? This is a twenty three year 'belated thank you' to all the hospital staff who were involved. "Thank you everybody" Julian eventually managed to get word to me on Christmas Eve that he was officially in possession of the keys to the flat, and luckily I too was discharged by the skin of my teeth from the cottage Hospital around four o'clock on Christmas eve. Historically I was amongst one of the last patients to leave this Cottage Hospital as it never re-opened again, but was later demolished to make room for a housing estate, how sad.

As the hour was late I asked my mother to look after the baby so that my father could take me food shopping for the festive season. The rush was on before the shops closed on Christmas Eve.

On Christmas morning Julian was pushed as arranged on his hospital bed down the long corridor after he'd finished his ablutions. Unfortunately his bed was too wide for the door of the Occupational flat, so they had to man handle him through the door then plant him safely onto another bed inside the flat. The nursing staff had kindly found a spare Christmas tree and had decorated it to make it extra special for baby Davies, not to mention a portable black and white Television with only one channel; I'm not complaining I was grateful. Thank God for 'Only Fools and Horses' I say. Christmas's wouldn't be the same without them. This was the start of many wonderful Christmas's together. Christmas happens to be our daughter's favourite time of the year. I sometimes wonder if it was because she subconsciously picked up on the vibes of excitement we both felt that Christmas and did she sense how much effort her Father had gone to, to make her first Christmas so special. I would like to extend another thank you to Steve Roberts one of the Orderlies who came down to the flat in his own time, armed with an elaborate camera and took lots of photographs of the three of us together, and very professional they look too.

Taking care of this new baby and visiting Julian twice a day as well as getting wrapped up in the Christmas festive spirit didn't leave me much time to think of a name. The agreement was if the baby was a boy, Julian would choose the name but if it was a girl, it was my call. As he'd totally convinced me it was going to be a boy there was no need for me to think of a girl's name. But six weeks down the line Julian frightened me with "If you don't register this baby's birth tomorrow the police will take her away" Struggling with my hormones I got upset, thinking Id waited so long for her, only to see her being whipped away.

That same evening as we were watching Central news together, Julian suggested the name Llewela, after Llewela Bailey the news reader? So Baby Davies was eventually given her first name six weeks and one day after her birth. The following morning in fear she may be taken from me I left the baby with my mother, I then went into town to proudly register the birth of our baby daughter, Llewela Jane Davies, at last she was given her own identity.

You may wonder why have I gone into such detail about this private part of our family life, well most people who have a new arrival take the baby home and the rest just merges into a mist?

Julian had to struggle to make life seam normal for us.

It was about this time when Julian was diagnosed with something called MRSA! Neither of us had heard of it before but we realised it must be something unusual, because every day the Infection Control Nurse was whispering at the bottom of his bed discussing different treatments with the Doctors and Ward Sisters. Worried that it might be contagious Julian asked me to buy him a nail brush, and I was to make sure it was a robust one. Which I did, that evening when I went to visit I couldn't understand why he was so red, his face, arms his whole body in fact. At first glance I thought it might have been the result of this MRSA they were talking about. The scrubbing brush turned out to be, the culprit, he had spent all afternoon scrubbing his body clean in case the baby caught this new bug! As well as having this new bug Julian's Albumin levels were noticed to be in his boots, his Consultant wanted Julian to be on a high Protein diet. To increase his Albumin level I went to a health shop in Oswestry to buy some awful powder to mix with water, it looked and smelt quite revolting but Julian was so desperate to come home, he would take anything. Coupled with his wound devouring his protein levels he was discarding much needed protein in his urine.

Realising his immune system was shot; I thought the best place for him was home where I could feed him any amount of protein.

His protein intake from the hospital food was miniscule, on the account that the kitchen had run out of money to feed the patients, so they were being fed on a bank overdraught.

On hearing this he spontaneously asked the Consultant if he could be discharged due to what he felt was special circumstances, he simply said, "No, he had months of bed rest ahead of him" Julian wasn't wearing that, he had responsibilities now. Julian was constantly been told that Ambulance services won't take patients over county borders, Julian then set about his own discharge plan. After only one week of passing my driving test, he sent me on some hair raising journeys with a shopping list in search of different warehouses in and around Oswesrty to buy x number lengths of aluminium tubing, then to a wood yard for some four ply wood, then to a Saddler for some leather strap, Velcro and strong needle and cotton, then to an upholstery shop for a long length piece of four inch deep sponge and to a haberdashery for some canvas. Then he ordered a £1,000 wheelchair with detachable wheels, brakes and cross bars for this new project.

You're probably thinking, 'what was he building'?

He was setting about building himself a 'Homemade Ambulance' and an Ambulance trolley. After spending hours carefully designing the Prone trolley he then asked to be pushed each afternoon on his bed down the corridor to the Occupational Therapy department to cut and pop rivet this Prone trolley together.

Once he cut the wood to size and the sponge, he then covered the sponge with the canvas, it started to take shape. The sewing of the leather straps he did in the evening back on the ward while watching TV, he didn't mind the ribbing off the male Orderlies about taking up sewing. The wheel chair arrived by post on the ward from Sweden, he soon set about striping it down only using the bits he wanted mainly the wheels, brakes and the chassis. In the meantime he had asked his brother to detach some garden fencing in our back garden at home, and then re-assemble it by fixing hinges on one end of the fence panel and a sliding bolt on the other side. The idea was, with these hinged panels the trolley could take a wide sweep round the corner to gain access into the house.

When this Monster of a Homemade Ambulance trolley was completed, it would take the place of a professional Ambulance trolley transporting Julian from his Hospital bed down the corridor on to the hospital car park then carefully roll him into the back of our pretend Ambulance. Luckily at the time the only transport we possessed was a small Daihatsu van, which consisted of two front seats and nothing in the back. At least it made it easy for him to plan his bedding facility for the journey home. My work wasn't finished yet, I was then sent off to purchase long lengths of 2x2 inch wood to make the four legs required for the bed. At the same time I was to pick up a four ply piece of wood for the base of the bed, calling in town for another four inch thick sponge to act as a mattress.

Once permission was given the rest of the journey should be a doddle after Id driven him the 60 mile journey home. The plan was Id transfer him out of the van at the other end on to his new trolley then push him along the back path, then down the garden slope, through the conservatory and the kitchen and finally into the lounge where we could triumphantly transfer him on to a bed in the lounge. But first he had to convince the Doctor what he proposed was safe and practical.

When everything was set in place, he bravely re-appealed to the Doctors better nature. He felt he may have blown it the previous time by being clumsy with his verbal request, this time he wasn't taking any chances so he decided to write a letter and be more sensitive with his wording. The following morning the Doctor had returned from his fortnight's holiday, and after reading the letter, stormed out of his office and made a bee line for Julian's bed, asking in a raised voice, "What's the meaning of this, leaving letters on my desk the answer is still NO Julian" Julian pleaded saying, "Since you've been away on holiday I've built myself an Ambulance trolley down in the Occupational Therapy department, and I've made a make-shift Ambulance bed in our van, and I asked my brother to hinge the fence panel at home to gain better access into the house, and I've rung the social services to deliver an electric hospital bed downstairs, and that was delivered yesterday. I've rung the GP to see if he's happy to accept me home, I've rung the District Nurse to see if she can do the dressings in case you don't want Olwen to touch it, and I think that's it really."

This time permission was granted.

He must have been impressed with Julian's 100% effort, it always pays off.

At last we were all going home together, although during all this engineering of the home coming, I had returned back to full time employment, although Llewela was only three months old. Circumstances had forced me to leave her with my parents who lived 10 min walk from the Hospital. It pulled at my heart strings to leave her, but I thought Mum could at least take her to see Julian every day in my absence.

That way she would at least be in contact with one of her parents on a daily basis.

Excited about the home coming I felt I wanted to kill the fattest calf.

As the three of us were reunited we soon settled down to becoming "The Three of us."

I continued to work full time doing unsociable shifts that nurses are expected to do, while Julian was left holding the baby as it were. He enjoyed being left to his own devices to bond and care for this vulnerable little bundle. This is where he started to practice at being the perfect father. Before going to work I had to bed bath Julian, wash his hair, leave him hot water to shave, tumbler for his teeth, dress his wounds, change his bed sheets and help him get into his clean cloths Then I would bath Llewela, change her into day cloths and give her breakfast before kissing them both goodbye.

As Julian was still on strict bed rest and Llewela was still only a tiny baby in the pram next to him, he soon devised a routine. For nappy changes he would roll over onto his side in bed, change her nappy while she was still in her pram, this way he felt she was safe. To feed her he would do all the dangerous stuff first, on the writing desk on the other side of the bed. Once he made the area safe, he would pick her up and feed her. My biggest problem was trying to remember to leave him everything he needed for himself and Llewela while I was at work all day. I had to try and remembering everything including making sure the telephone was in reach, the television remote control and his computer were at hand. I also had to make sure his lunch was in reach, tea bags, milk, water and the kettle, for the baby I had to remember to leave the baby milk, baby food, baby wipes and nappies including many changes of clothes. I remember one day coming home exited to see the two of them, only to find Julian in a terrible mood. I asked, is everything ok. He replied "No, you forgot the tea bags"

"S-o-r-r-y" There was another occasion I forgot to leave the electric kettle lead.

You'd think the Health Visitor would have a field day with this set up. The last time I recall Julian telling me when the Health Visitor called, I was at work and Julian was still on bed rest. She had to let herself in through the back door. Julian had just finished feeding her when she visited. He informed her he was about to change her nappy, and she would not find a blemish on her. To his surprise she said, "Inspection won't be necessary Mr Davies, she's obviously very well cared for."

Julian being Julian said, "You're going to inspect her any way, I want you to write the truth about how you found her" The visit ended with her informing Julian she will not be calling again. You call me if there is a problem" That was reassuring to know, that she, like me, totally trusted him. Julian's hip eventually healed and he was allowed to resume normal activities from his wheelchair.

Photograph of how Julian took care of Llewela while
I was work.

Julian continued to be a protective Father, very strict but fair with lots of treats when she did well and because of this, their bond grew. Although Julian had been blessed with Llewela's company his way ward ways did not cease to exist, these are just a few true stories of Llewela's growing up years I would like to share with you. Strict as he was, Julian did not always having the upper hand, some times Llewela did.

I remember when Llewela was about two, while I was at work one day a friend of mine Tracy Berry said to me, "I think I saw Julian with Llewela yesterday." As she knew Julian very well, I couldn't understand why she said she thought she saw him. I asked, "Well you either saw him or you didn't" She said, "I couldn't be sure I couldn't see his face he was wearing a pram on his head." Wanting to get to the bottom of this I couldn't wait to get home to ask him that night. On enquiring he pondered a while then remembered, "Oh! Yes I remember, I thought for a bit of exercise I'd push myself to the shop with Llewela on my lap. The shopping I thought could go in a bag on the handle bars at the back of the wheel chair. We were just about to leave the house when 'madam here' decided she wanted to walk herself and take the dolls pram with her. We argued for ages, in the end to prove a point I let her push the pram, she walked there alright, but as soon as we got out of the shop she started, 'Carry me Daddy, carry me, please Daddy carry me'. She nearly drove me mad, it was very hot and I couldn't be bothered to argue any more. I put the shopping on the handle bars as planned, and disgruntled, I allowed her to climb up on to my lap which left the wretched pram on the pavement? There was nothing for it, I just had to turned it upside down and put it on my head. It was awful Olwen, I couldn't see where I was going, so to add insult to injury I had to rely on her telling me where to wheel. Little monkey, so I suppose they're all laughing at me at your work place now are they"?

I still don't know who met their match when Llewela met Julian.

Llewela must have known he had tons of love for her, because she pushed her boundaries as far as she could, if any one did the same with Julian, I'm sure he would have knocked their block off.

Moral of this story is, just like the old saying 'Works good, if you can get it', it's the same with a Fathers love, 'It's good if you can get it'. Llewela got lucky and had plenty.

The two of them understood each other perfectly, on one occasion as I was leaving the house to go shopping, Llewela wanted to come along for the ride. As she ran ahead of me I called after her, "Stay at the top of the path Llewela" but she didn't listen, she carried on running to the car park. On this particular day I decided to address the situation. I asked her sternly to return into the house, and sit on the settee immediately. She knew she was in for a good talking too, when the 'settee' was mentioned. I asked her, why she always ran away when I asked her not too but when her father asked her to stay at the top of the path she did. She replied in a childish voice, "Daddy can't run after me like you can" She was barely able to talk but she had worked that out for herself.

Soon after this incident I needed to use the settee treatment again. This time she had a pair of scissors in her hands and my heart nearly stopped as I took a sharp intake of breath. I thought I need to get those scissors off her, but calmly. I explained to her when she sat down clenching the scissors, "Llewela what if you were to run and fall and the scissors point went into your cheek, people would say when you grow up, she seems like a nice girl, pity about the scars on her face" She calmly presented me the scissors on two open tiny palms. And as she climbed off the settee she half turned to face me with her eyes to the floor and her hands behind her back, "Mummy there so dangerous, you shouldn't have them either"

As she walked away I wanted to react, but I calmly said, "Your right darling, I'll put them away straight away" It was just as if she wanted to have the last word!

At about this age Julian introduced Llewela to his lovely Pendine.

Photograph of Julian giving Llewela a
"I love my baby' hug on Pendine beach.

When Llewela was about three I accidentally dropped a toy of hers on the floor.

To my surprise she didn't waver at all, she just carrying on doing what she was doing then said without flinching or looking at me, "Don't worry Mummy, Daddy will fix it" I immediately took it to Julian and said, "You've just got to fix this" He said, "Throw it away its cheap tack, I'm not mending that" I pleaded with him, "It's your reputation at stake, she thinks you can fix everything"

So later that evening he stayed up late gluing this cheap toy together, mumbling under his breath, I can't believe I'm mending this. Early next morning Llewela got up and hurriedly brought me the toy saying, "See Mummy, I told you Daddy would fix it, he can fix everything"

Julian winked and mimed to me, "I see what you mean"

There was another time when Llewela was about three, Julian's Uncle Frank saw them both in a supermarket, Julian had the shopping list and Llewela was running and fetching and carrying the groceries to him as if it was a game. His Uncle Frank returned home to tell his wife Aunty Barbara that he'd seen Julian in the supermarket. His wife asked how Julian was; and did he manage to speak to him? He said, "No I couldn't it nearly made me cry to see the two of them struggling to do the shopping".

I can relate to this scene, I would sometimes join them after work to help them with the remainder of the shopping, I would catch a glimpse of Llewela standing on tip toe on the very verge of his knees with total faith he would save her if she slipped. Her arms would be out stretched trying to reach something of the top shelf.

On another occasion I recall coming home from work to hear banging inside our brand new campervan. Julian had gutted the new interior and put it in the attic because the lay out wasn't wheel chair friendly. I asked him, "What's going on, what's that noise in the van"?

I looked inside the van and to my horror I found Llewela bending over some wood, banging away with a hammer. I asked again, "What's is she doing, she'll destroy the van"

Julian got cross, and in a stern voice shouted, "Leave her be, she's only just got the hang of it after practising all day" In an irate tone I then retaliated, "Practising what"? He replied, "Hammering a nail in straight". I said, "Julian, for goodness sake she's only four years old" With pride and puffed out chest he replied, "Yep! Well she may only be four years old, but she can now hammer a nail in straight"

He needn't have worried about wishing for a boy when she was born. He had an all-rounder in our Wella, as they say in cricket. She can turn her hand to anything, just like her Father.

Now she's grown up, and head strong like a man, but every bit a woman.

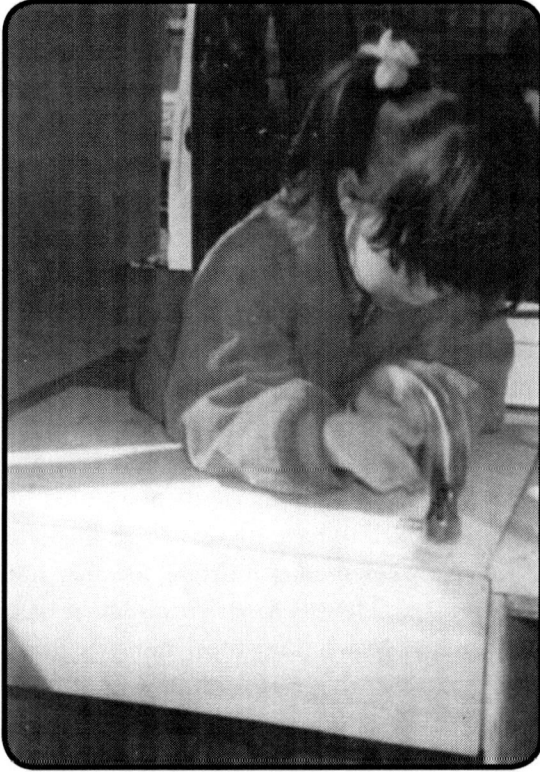

Photograph of Llewela hammering a nail in straight in our
brand new Camper van.

When Llewela was nearly five, one of Julian's friends (Mick Westwood) said to Llewela "Would you like a pup of your own?" The bread of dogs he owned at the time was Chihuahua. Julian and I were shocked he'd mentioned such a thing to a child without first discussing it with her parents. Worried we couldn't afford to make her dream come true if she said yes. How were we going to say to her "No honey we can't afford it".

As the time for the expectant bitch to give birth came closer Julian approached the subject of the cost. Mick said, Oh! No she can have one free of charge, you do plenty for me."

One night quite soon after, we were all fast asleep in bed when the phone rang. It was two o'clock in the morning. I immediately jumped out of bed to answer it, thinking it might have been an emergency. Mick was on the phone informing the house hold that the pups were just about to be born. Half-awake and yawning I returned upstairs I whispered the message to Julian, then suddenly the whole bed room lit up and Julian noisily scrambled out of bed, hurriedly putting his cloths on any which way, at the same time shouting, "Quick Wella, you need to get up now, the pups are just about to be born, were going to Mick's this minute quick get your coat on" I could not grasp the excitement, why would you drag a child on a school day in the middle of the night to watch pups being born. I said "You don't mind if I don't come, I'm working in the morning." Apparently Julian and Mick had discussed being there at the birth previously and Llewela was obviously involved in this conversation and the decision making to.

So off the two of them went into the night air to see nature at its best, her best friend was just about to be born. Her new friend was to be called 'Domino' some readers might think, was this man mad or how many of you would secretly have liked to have someone like Julian for a Father?

Because of Julian's spontaneous attitude towards life, grab it with both hands as it happened, Llewela experienced life at its best. While she had Julian as her teacher, growing up must have seemed like being in a maze garden never knowing what was coming next.

This is another true story, this time when Llewela was about six years old.

Julian and his Grandmother were very close, let's say they had a fiery relationship, that's what happens when you get two intellectuals together. His Grandmother was an ex-headmistress and Julian was heading for a degree.

Some years previously, Julian's Grandmother who had been living with us for two years decided to go and visit her daughter in Cornwall. Her other daughter who lived in South Wales had just returned from the South of France. This is Julian's mother I'm talking about. She and her husband did not fly in those days but preferred to drive.

Consequently they intended to travel from the south of France the day before, then sleep at their home in South Wales and the following morning she planed to drive up to the midlands to collect Julian's Grandmother, then do an about turn and journey down to Cornwall on the same day. Julian reflecting on her plans, and mentally clocked up the miles she was covering in those two days, he offered to meet her half way. He suggested, "Why don't I bring Nana down to meet you half way down to the Giordano Service Station on the motorway. Nana can exchange transport and you can then do a u turn and complete the remainder of your journey down to Cornwall"

His mother was very grateful for the offer; it was cutting down on her mileage considerably. So that's what we did, it became a family affair. Julian drove Nana, with her luggage in our Campervan with Llewela and I in tow to meet his mother.

Funnily enough both Julian and his mother pulled up into the car park at exactly the same time.

We thought it would be a good idea to have a cup of tea at the services, but as the queue turned out to be so long we decided to use our own facilities on board. Once the cab seats were turned round it was comfortable to seat eight people round the table. As our time to say goodbyes came round, Julian's Grandmother squeezed Julian's arm and said to Julian, "If I need to come home Julian, you will come for me, won't you? Julian knowing how his Mother, Auntie and Grandmother fell out frequently with each other, always short term may I add said, "Nana I don't want to hear, that you have fallen out with Mum and Aunty, just have a good time". She kept insisting, "You will come for me, won't you if I need to come home?" She said this several times, in the end I said, "Julian, for goodness sake just promise" so he did. We parted company; the plan was she was going for a month.

A few days later his mum rang to say that while out visiting a seaside resort, Nana appeared to be choking, so his mother drove to the nearest Accident and Emergency department to see what could be done. It appeared that poor Nan had, had a stroke, after been admitted she had several strokes and was eventually left unconscious. Days passed with her two daughters by her bed side, in her lovely Cornwall. My mother in law rang Julian and asked him to come down to be with them. Julian, Llewela and I travelled down in our camper van to be with them. I had time off work and Llewela had time off school. She died quite soon after we arrived. Llewela and I went to say our goodbye even though Llewela was only 6 she managed to stand on tip toes and gave her Great-Nan a kiss on her forehead as if it was quite normal. While Julian on the other hand could not, he said, "Oh no, I'd rather remember her as she was" The whole family then congregated on this very hot summer's afternoon outside the caravan the three of them had hired. Over a cup of tea the family started to discuss such things as hymns and readings whilst all together.

Later on that evening I recall after we had just had finished our evening meal with a lovely evening sunset outside the caravan, Julian leaned over towards me and whispered a question in my ear, he said "Olwen, ask my Aunty if it would be ok for me to take Nana back to Kidderminster myself ?"

I was shocked at his request, and did a double take and asked why?

He explained, "I'm having trouble living with my last words to Nana, what I promised her I'd do for her" I then recalled the promise. He had promised to bring her back to Kidderminster, if she needed to come home, and now she needs to come home. What had I done, I felt a sudden pang of guilt because I had made him promise to go to fetch her if she needed to come home.

Julian's theory was if his Auntie saw no harm in his request may be his mother might be ok about it to, so this is what we did, I then he asked his Aunt to ask his Mum. When the question was asked of his Mother there was a deathly silence inside the caravan. We all held our breath for poor Julian, then suddenly the caravan kitchen window burst open, and his Mother curiously asked, "Are you sure, you couldn't even go in to kiss her good bye at the end?"

Julian said, "I know, but I promised"

Still stunned at his request, we all respected his wishes. If you had never met Julian you could not help but respect him. His mother had no objection but her brother in Canada had to be consulted in case he considered the idea offensive. He was called and he had no objections either, the plans could go ahead. Unbeknown to us, Julian had, had several conversations with Nana regarding her funeral arrangements while I was at work. She had saved for years for her funeral expenses, and did not want the funeral cost to be a burden to anyone. So she made Julian promise that there should not be any additional expense.

Of course Nana had not taken into account that she may die hundreds of miles away from home.

So, poor Julian was struggling with two promises now.

We had to make serious investigation as to whether it was legal and above board to transport a deceased relative half way across England.

Julian made some phone calls and right enough it was possible to do so. The other option was to get the funeral directors to come for her. The quote was £1,000 to bring her back; their reasoning was that a driver and an escort would have to be accommodated in a Hotel overnight. The family agreed for Julian to take Nana on her last journey home like he promised.

The instructions we were given was to pick up a coffin from the funeral director in Kidderminster, then travel down to Cornwall to the mortuary, then place his Grandmother in the casket and then make arrangements to be back in Kidderminster at a certain time. We had to remember to pick up the death certificate at the same time from the hospital in Cornwall; otherwise they may not allow us to pick up the casket from Kidderminster. The next day we travelled back to Kidderminster and that evening I cleaned the camper van inside and out, out of respect for Nan. I assembled the bed, and then I covered the mattress with a maroon blanket. I put away all the clutter to make it look reverent. That evening we picked up the coffin so that we could make an early start the following morning. The three of us, that is, Julian, Llewela and I made our early morning start to head back down once more to the tip of Cornwall. We arrived there at eleven o'clock in the morning, called at his mother's and his Auntie for a cup of coffee before going on to the Hospital mortuary.

When we arrived there, the mortician invited me in to identify his Grandmother before the casket was sealed. Then she was glided into the back of the camper, I then drew all the curtains round, so when we travelled down the motor way passers-by would not be shocked by what we had on board. We spent the next 5 hours talking and reminiscing about Nana how she loved the camper and probably would be pleased that Julian was keeping his promises.

The other thing I can remember saying was, "It was a good job I came with you Julian, because how would you have coped with identifying her!" As he originally intended to bring her back on his own. As the funeral director was closing at 4 o'clock in Kidderminster, we had a schedule to keep to. It was very difficult, on the one had we we had a rush on to get there before the doors were locked and on the other hand we wanted to show Nana respect by travelling leisurely.

Poor Julian didn't know what to do for the best, one minute I'd say, "You need to speed up we're not going to make in time" so he would speed up, then I would say, "Slow down Julian, show a bit of respect".

Julian got cross at one stage by saying, "Look here Olwen, if I keep up this slow, fast slow speed a Policeman is going to pull me over and then they will want to see what we've got in the back, if they hinder us goodness knows what time we'll get back. Then poor Nan will have to sleep in the car park" I said, "Oh! Don't say that Julian" he replied "I'm not making fun I'm just being practical" I said, "We'll take her into the house over night before we leave her in the car park"

We eventually arrived outside the funeral directors ten minutes late and as we feared the doors were locked, but luckily there was a mobile number attached to the door. So we rang that and about half an hour later two helpful gentlemen came to help us and take Nana into their Parlour.

The reason I have included this part of Julian life in this book is for those who knew Julian, they knew Julian's word was his bond. For those who did not know him, maybe they can take a leaf out of his book. The moral of the story is, if you promise to do something for someone, you should do it to the best of your ability at any cost. Even if you don't know how to set about it, be like Julian and just ask. Nothing was ever impossible to him it was just a question of mind over matter.

Most people were shocked that Julian insisted that Llewela attended her Great grandmother's funeral. He said I don't want her to be traumatised when one of us goes, I want her to feel familiar with the setting of a funeral, the way people dress in black, the way they conduct themselves, and how it's perfectly ok to cry in public when you have lost someone you love. As we stood outside the Church and they were pushing the coffin into the back of the hearse. Llewela whispered to me, "Is Nana inside that box?" I said, "Yes, honey"

Llewela said, "Mm. She must be really dead then" Julian leaned towards me in his wheel chair and whispered, "You see she had to come, she understands now"!

Another one of Julian's little 'life preparations' for Llewela.

As Llewela was growing up Julian was always reminiscing about his time spent on Pendine sands, until one day I said, "Instead of constantly talking about it Julian, why don't you show us how good it was" So the very next sunny day Julian drove us down to his lovely Pendine Beach, where I'm glad to say Llewela develop the same passion Julian had for the place years before. From then on whenever we had free time we always made a beeline to our favourite beach. Somehow we always managed to get our regular camping spot across the road from the beach, with only a wall to part us from either the beautiful beach or the raging sea, depending on the weather of course. During Julian's growing up years at Pendine he'd made lots of local friends, most of them in later years became fishermen. On rekindling their friendship they would often at the end of the day sling some of their catch onto the wall for us, calling "Some more fish for you Julian"

It was a regular occurrence to see Llewela and Julian gutting and tailing the fish before cooking them while they were fresh. As Llewela had been taught from a young age how to cut and gut the fish, it became second nature to her.

We often took a companion for Llewela on our jaunts and they weren't always familiar with this gruesome technique, and to start with often found the process a bit squeamish. Passers-by would stop to watch and often either strike up a conversation or show their grandchildren how a fish is prepared for the pan. It must have been some sight, a man in a wheelchair and a girl aged about seven behaving like a fish wife chop, chop then the gutting into one bucket then dunking the fish in blood red cold water swoosh, swoosh to finish off the task before proudly handing it over to me to cook on the gas burner outside. Julian insisted on doing everything out side, weather permitting. Outdoor life was meant to be lived out of doors. Moral of this story was, he wasn't planning on raising a squeamish wimp.

Photograph of Llewela and her cousin Wyn, preparing the catch of the day.

I remember on another occasion at Pendine Julian took a gang of boys with him to show them how to catch a fish with only homemade equipment for their tools, a stick for a rod, string for a line and left over ham for bate, there may have been a hook involved from the fishing tackle shop next door. As they were about to leave the camp site, Llewela called to Julian, "Dad can I come"? One of the boys replied "No you can't, it's not sissy stuff you know" Julian overrode his suppressive comment and said, "Off course darling, do you think you'd like fishing"?

I don't know if she did enjoy the adventure, but she was the only one who returned with a fish!

Moral of that story was, have a go you don't know what you can achieve until you try!

Julian was still full of his wayward ideas trying to help others, to teach, or just simply to have fun. When Julian found himself as a patient at Oswestry Hospital yet again, out of boredom he asked for his bed to be pushed down to the Occupational Therapy Department. While he was there he noticed a box full of mechanical bits and asked about its content, the reply was it was that it was parts of a Trike. Julian then asked why hadn't anyone bothered to put it together. The second reply was, "It can't be done Julian, because there isn't an instruction book with it". They should never have said, "Can't" The word 'can' derives from 'cant' in Julian's reckoning, which meant it could be done and the phrase 'watch this space' came to mind. You guessed it, on his discharge from hospital the box containing the Trike in bits was placed in the boot of the car and made its journey home with us. This box then became Julian's new project, his 'jigsaw project' as I use to call it.

Within the year the Trike was up and running, I confess it had lots of teething problems but not enough to spoil our fun. So how did we manage to get it to Pendine you may ask? You need to put your imagination head on for this one.

First we pushed the red Trike up some ramps onto a small trailer. Luckily the Campervan had a tow hook and he had just paid for a tow-hook to be fitted one to the Trike, the trailer was then towed on the back of the campervan all the way to Pendine, with the Trike as its cargo in the trailer. Once down on the beach the trailer was then unhooked from the camper and the cargo being the Trike was rolled onto the sand, then roll reversal took place. The Trike would then tow the trailer, simple don't you think 'one favour deserves another'.

Julian was then transferred from his wheel chair onto the Trike. He loved it, to feel the wind in his hair once more was great he said. Julian would then ferry Llewela and her friends including myself to the edge of the sea some distance away, and then at a wave of our hands he would come back to pick us up. Off course other children would think it was a service that was laid on for holiday makers, and would shout to Julian, "Hoi Mister! How much for a ride?" He would reply, "No charge, but I need to speak to your parents first, then we'll see".

He just wanted permission off them to give them a lift, and not get accused of kidnaping or even sued from some safety aspect.

The moral to this story this time was, if you want to see something happen badly enough you'll find a way.

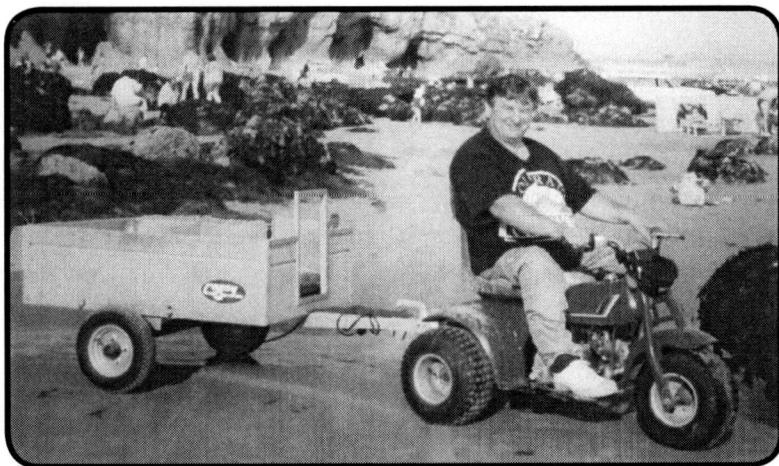

Photograph of Julian on his Trike, tugging the little trailer.

Notice the attention to detail, the cushions for comfort in the back.

This trekking down to Pendine wasn't always confined to the three of us, we once took the 'Italians' as we called them, for a long weekend away. On this occasion we stayed at a different location which could accommodate all of us. We chose an 'out of bound' site, high above Pendine village, Julian and I stayed in our Camper van as normal while the others slept in bunk beds in a wooden barracks type accommodation.

Our first priority was to rearrange the dining area to create a long banqueting table, so we could all join in the communal jolliness of eating drinking and being merry together. It was lovely being part of this big family, while the women cooked Julian was plotting the next adventure. The weekend entailed collecting mussels, caving, rock pooling, kite flying, coast walking, and of course a ride in Julian's trailer was a must which he towed behind his three wheeler Trike up and down the beach for hours on end. Julian even allowed the 'nearly old enough teenagers' to drive his camper on the seven mile long hard sandy beach, may I add he allowed this lesson to take place away from the danger of harming other humanoids. They loved it, but most of all they felt honoured he'd entrusted them with his vehicle. Other visits included driving out to Laugharne a nearby village to see the 'Boat house' where Dylan Thomas had lived, and also to see his 'Writing Shed' where he did all his writing and composed his poetry. A visit to the beach museum was also standard requirements of the holiday, to view the famous vintage land speed record car of Parry Thomas called 'Babs' which is exhibited on the beach each summer in a glass dome. In February 1927 Malcolm Campbell broke the land speed record on this very beech, traveling at 174 miles an hour. The following month in March Parry Thomas died attempting to beat his record, while traveling at 170 miles an hour when his 'drive chain' snapped and partially decapitated him. Saddened by this dreadful event, the crew and spectators buried the car in the dunes on Pendine beach. Another claim to fame the beach possess is, in 1933 Amy Johnson and her husband took off from this beach attempting to fly non-stop to New York.

Anyway I digress; the high light of our 'Italian week end' was when Julian arranged for an ex-army trainer at the camp site to take any willing parties on a proper out of bound circuit. What a mess, but what fun. Lucky for us they loaned the participants an all-in-one suit to save our outer garments but it did not account for the fact that our under wear, socks and trainers had to be thrown away. The smell and the brown stain from the mud simply could not be removed. Happy memories, if only we could bottle laughter, how rich we'd all be!

On the strength of the success of this weekend my Brownie leader and I took 24 brownies on a camp, to this camp site, using Pocahontas as our theme.

Photograph of the Italians and the
Davies's dinning together at Pendine.

Years later we used to ask Llewela what she thought of the beaches we took her to when we travelled abroad, she'd always have the same answer, "There all right, but there not like Pendine beach" It was true; you can't make sand castles anywhere in the world like you can with Pendine sand. Moral of this story is, sometimes you need to use your imagination to have a good time, it's not always necessary to spend a lot of money.

As well as taking part in the general running of the home, Julian also adored cooking, it seemed he could and would conjure up dishes out of nothing.

He also loved entertaining, but he had to be the 'King in the kitchen' Llewela and I being his 'run-a-rounds'. He taught Llewela how to cook, bake and even make homemade wine. I came home one day to find Llewela in this big plastic bucket treading grapes with her skirt tucked into her knickers. I shouted, "Julian that does not look hygienic to me" "Oh! Its hygienic all right, she's had a bath, clean cloths, washed her hair, and I've cut her toe nails short" Llewela joined in, supporting her father's claims by making no eye contact with me saying, "Yep Mum he has, he's cut my toe nails <u>really short</u>, and he wheeled me in on his lap so my feet wouldn't touch the ground"

77

I wish I'd taken a photo with her hair scuffed up, into a 'man-made' bun on top of her head.

To be fair, the wine they made from the old Black Roman grape in our back garden tasted like Port, and between them they produced 33 litres every year. I personally used to try and keep the stock down as much as I could. Then one day I came home from work to find the old vine cut level with the ground, Llewela greeted me with a smile by saying, "Dad said we had to do it Mum, to put a stop to your drinking" consequently as a result of their severe pruning there was never any more wine produced on our premises after that day. Moral of this story was, 'you can have too much of a good thing'!

Photograph of Llewela harvesting the old black Roman grape from the Pagoda Julian built, can you see her best friend the dog in tow! He was never far away.

Money was never plentiful in our house so if one of us needed anything which was too expensive he'd make it himself, from wood, metal, cardboard or fibreglass. He was a great engineer, he taught himself to weld, grind, carpentry and floor and wall tiling.

He once designed and welded a homemade hoist to transfer engines in and out of cars; neighbours would walk over from their houses to borrow it.

This came about after I came home from work one day to find what I thought was a twisted piece of metal on the kitchen table, I was about to throw it away when Julian shouted, "Don't throw that away that's my wedding ring" An engine in the garage had evidently landed on his hand, he claimed the ring saved his finger. One of the lads that was helping him that day had to quickly use metal cutters to cut off the ring and that's how it became to look so chewed up. Hence that's how the idea of a hoist came about. He made Llewela a sturdy wooden sledge, a wooden slide, two long church pews for the conservatory for Llewela to store her toys in. House rule was when both pews were full then she knew she had to find them a new home. He also made large wooden games to help raise money for different charities.

Photograph of the fundraising games
Julian made from scraps of wood.

I call this next tale, 'Parade of Nations'.

For the first ten years of our married life I periodically begged Julian to take me to see the Llangollen International Musical Eisteddfod, in North Wales. Each time I mentioned it, Julian would say the same old answer, "Olwen, it's not my scene please stop asking" Then one day he said, "I'm going to give you one chance, I'll take you once, but don't ever ask me again" I agreed to the deal, once we arrived at Llangollen, after only ten minutes into the Pavilion grounds I could see he was in awe. He turned to me and said, "Why haven't you brought me here before this is fantastic" This was the only time I ever felt like rolling my eyes and shout "Men" The festival is always held the first week in July and people have been coming in droves from all over the world dressed in their National Costume since 1947. It started in 1943 when a certain person called Harold Tudor an Officer of the British Council invited Government-in-exile to attend the Welsh National Eisteddfod, known to a Welsh person as the Eisteddfod Genedleithol, that particular year it was held in Bangor.

Following the event a Czechoslovakian wrote to Harold praising the value of music and wondered if it could act as a way of healing the effects of war. Inspired by this letter he found favour with Gwyn Williams a Welsh composer and they proposed an 'Independent Musical Festival' together they attracted energy from a George Northing a teacher from Dinas Bran on the out skirts of Llangollen and between them they pressed for this festival to take place at Llangollen after the war ended. The story goes, a soldier invited comrades in arms to attend this festival when the war finished.

Baring in mind the locals would be expected to supply accommodation to these over-seas friends if and when it did take place. It was arranged that some would stay in Churches and School halls but mainly people gave up their own beds. Feeding them might have been a problem, as rations were still in place so ration coupons had to be saved. Added to these difficulties there was a railway strike in France but against all odds coachloads arrived in droves. Amongst these choirs, came one solitary group of Spanish Dancers and to the delight of the audiences, it inspired other 'Folk Dancers' to attend and perform at Llangollen in their National Costume and they have been coming ever since. I love this additional story of how far peace was extended in 1949 when Peace

Promotion Mission was amplified, only three and a half years after the war had ended.

On this particular Sunday, the last choir to be announced begged forgiveness from deep within every spectator's soul who was present in the pavilion that night. The commentator Hywel Roberts nervously asked the audience to put their hands together and give a worm welcome to our friends from across the water. He then hurriedly left the stage for the choir from West Germany to make their entrance. Silence fell as the audience went in to shock, because every person in the audience would have experienced a loss of someone special during those five years of turmoil. Then one isolated person started to clap really slowly, and then another and another until the whole Pavilion was applauding. That was true forgiveness and welcome extended to fellow man following such an ugly war. That is why the annual event is often referred to as a 'The Musical Festival born from Peace'.

It became known as "The International Musical Eisteddfod", traditionally since 1947 on the opening day, the public are entertained by dancers in their traditional costume performing folk dancing in both the pavilion and weather permitting in the grounds at random. The day ends with an hour of spectacular array of colourful costumes parading through the town and is referred to as 'The Parade of Nations' starting at four thirty in the grounds near the Pavilion. For such an event the Town is closed to traffic and the pavements are packed shoulder to shoulder, with spectators heaving from bedroom windows, the young and old waving their flags and cheering. It's a sight to behold to see so many people from around the world enjoying music and dancing, proudly wearing their National costumes parading their flag in the name of peace.

Performers are asked to remain in their costume at all times during the week which is a long time, as the grounds with their stalls selling local crafts and souvenirs are open from 8:30am until 11pm at night. The week finishes with a Sunday evening Gala Concert held in the Pavilion, which incidentally seats 4,100 listeners? They have hosted such names as Kennedy the violist, Rick Astley, Kiki Dee, Katherine Jenkins, Shirley Bassey, Bryn Terfel, Michael Ball, Lulu and many more. Even Luciano Pavarotti confessed when he re-visited Llangollen in 1995 that he had performed at Llangollen in his youth 40 years previously in 1955 with a choir. At the time he was at a cross roads in his life, pondering whether to continue teaching or go solo and become a professional singer. His decision was made at this event, as he soaked up the love the world had for music. Another famous person who has attended this venue in recent years is Terry Waite former President 'Peace envoy', who was held hostage in Kuwait for five years. Apart from his family the other profound thing he missed in captivity was the sound of music. After attending this festival he felt the Eisteddfod still had the power to heal divisions between Nations through the power of music and because of this in 2004 he nominated the Eisteddfod for the Nobel Peace Prize!

On 5th July 2012 at twelve noon the organisers took peace a step further by requesting that the ground fell silent when everyone was asked to link arms for a moment of reflection as the 'Llangollen Message of Peace' was broadcast to the world. In the hope the world would witness the 'moving sound of silence' for one minute in both the Marquee and in the field. Over the years 500,000 overseas performers have attended this field. Not to discredit other performers Julian, Llewela and I over the years found it hard to better the Cossacks and the Irish dancers; with their outstanding stamina and energy on stage.

Getting back to my original tale of Julian and Llewela's first experience of this musical festival, Llewela said after a while, "Where are all the Welsh costumes Dad" Julian noticing there wasn't anyone representing the hosting country and quickly replied, "Your right darling, there isn't any! Don't worry, we'll come back next year, and you can dress up in a Welsh costume" And that's exactly what happened, and Llewela was splashed all over most of the local newspapers. The year after that, Llewela expressed a cringe at the publicity and said, "Dad I don't want to dress up this year, I don't like all those camera men." Julian said, "Quite right too darling, I'll get your Mother to dress up as well this time" Because Julian always paid such attention to detail; he made sure the tweed that was used had the traditional Montgomeryshire stripes for both the skirt and the long coat or 'Goban' as it's called in Welsh. The third year Julian bought my Mother a Welsh costume for her birthday. The fourth year he bought my sister one. Each year the 'Jones Tribe' grew until we were six strong. When Llewela was about six the organiser's head hunted us and asked us to lead the parade. We explained we weren't competitors but he didn't seem to mind he just wanted the Welsh costume to be represented in the parade. Llewela was appointed to carry the flag but just before we started she commented to Julian, "Dad this flag pole is too heavy for me" He said, "Come here, what you need to do is to tighten up your belt" Poor Llewela, she still had to carry the flag through the streets of Llangollen in an hour long parade. The moral of this story is, Julian wasn't being unkind, he was trying to teach her it's important to be proud of her roots.

Photograph of our Celtic Clan in National Costume,
demonstrating we were proud of our roots.

When Llewela was about eight I came home from work to hear a din in the conservatory and Julian's voice getting louder and louder, "No Llewela, look, not like this, like this, straight up." I thought whatever is going on behind those closed doors it defiantly warrants a photo I thought, so I opened the door suddenly and snapped a shot. Julian was not so much teaching her this time, but seeking assistance from Llewela to act as an extension to his arms, he just couldn't reach far enough into the corner to do that last screw up. The pair of them had obviously did a good job that day assembling this work top with no legs because when it came to dismantling it thirteen years later it proved to be quite a job.

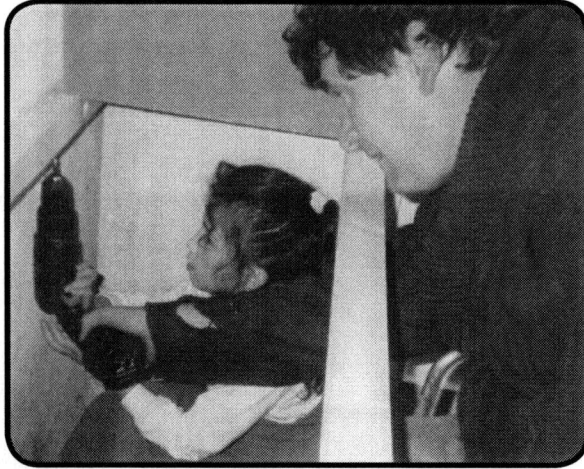

A Photo of Llewela and Julian, assembling a sturdy work top,
which was used for all sorts.

I used to stand on it with no reservation, that it would hold my weight.

In the summer of 1997 Julian was hospitalised once more, this time
he underwent a Cholecystectomy procedure, this is a medical name given
for removing the gallbladder with the gall stones intact if they can. But
in Julian's case the Consultant informed him that his loaded gallbladder
ruptured as soon as it was touched. The Peritoneal Cavity was irrigated
with normal Saline to flush out the spillage of bile and the escaped gall
stones. Julian was quite poorly after this procedure, I suspect it was for
this reason he produced Glucose and Protein in his urine at the time.

It was no wonder his gall bladder burst, Julian had been long
suffering with this pain and these offending little pebbles for 11 years.
He first complained of epigastria pain way back in 1986 accompanied
with elevated Gamma GT as high as 165 on some occasions.

When I first started nursing, this procedure was conducted under
the knife, today it is often conducted under laparoscopic procedure or
key-hole surgery and in even more modern procedure called lithotripsy
entailing laser to blast them.

I don't recall Julian having several follow up after this surgical
procedure, but one of the things one should be on the lookout for, is
one of these little stones migrating into the Pancreas, but rest assured we
would all have known about it if it had.

After he was discharged I often wondered how or why he suffered with Gall stones, evidently there are several causes, Hereditary, Hepatitis or prolonged Antibiotic abuse and Julian qualified for all three.

Life soon returned to normal and Julian took into his head to do some outside living after been cooped up indoors recovering. I call this next story, 'Teaching Survival skills'.

I've already mentioned Julian going on his Out of Bound course and how much he enjoyed it, having three nephews in the family and Lewela all of similar age inspired him to buy them all a two man tent for their Christmas present. He then asked Gweno if he could set up camp in her orchard one spring weekend. The idea being, Julian and I would sleep in the Camper van and the children would pitch up camp in a semi-circle in close proximity to the Camper. The expedition was to last from Friday night to Sunday evening. First he was going to teach them how to erect their own tent soundly, and then have a pow-wow on what the week-end entailed. They had to devise a rota of who was going to wash up after each meal time, and who was going to dry. He then taught them how to make a camp fire in an old oil drum, they weren't keen on matches but he taught them, "It's when you're silly with them that they become dangerous" As they weren't allowed into Gwenos farm house they huddled round the camp fire cooking their own sausages and beans. We also had two other children from the neighbouring farm join us for part of the weekend, that made six in total, they all sat at the table wolfing their 'own cooked' meal. Luckily for us, Gweno had an outside toilet, so none of us needed to trundle through her house with dirty shoes so we could be totally self-sufficient outdoors? The following morning everyone was expected to make their own beds, Julian inspecting each tent for their tidiness. Again they cooked their own bacon and eggs and after breakfast they all had to make their own pack lunch to take with them on a trek up Cregion Mountain. That day's lesson was about taking care of them-selves and watching out for others. Julian gave them all a bit of a pep-talk on first aid and what to do if they had an accident. Once the washing up was done, we all piled into the camper and he drove us all to the base of the chosen Mountain where he awaited all alone for our return with the comfort of plenty of tea and a good book. We started our long climb, each taking small individual pots of sloppy plaster of Paris. Julian had instructed them to watch out for animal foot prints on the way up, and if they were to see any to pour their sloppy plaster of Paris into the paw prints. Then, on their return journey they were to collect the hardened plaster with the imprint and bring it back to base.

In the meantime at the peak of the mountain we enjoyed our much needed packed lunch and drink before we descended down the mountain collecting the set foot prints on the way. This expedition took all afternoon, with my sister and I in tow to supervise.

Once back at 'Jus Camp' as we called it, they had to make their own evening meal and again wash up. That evening he taught them how to improvise, Gweno had an old disused wooden railway carriage in the orchard, so for shelter and warmth we congregated in there for the evening. He'd taken with him this big ball of rope, he gave them two long pieces each, then set about teaching them how to tie different knots, once they'd grasped that he then asked them to show him the plaster foot prints they'd collected earlier. Julian pulled out the book he'd been studying all afternoon while they were on their trek. They all seemed enthusiastic about sharing their finds and to be honest I couldn't believe how many species were roaming the hills late at night. That evening about ten of us huddled up in this carriage, playing cards and sipping drinking chocolate. The following morning they woke up with the larks, it was Easter Sunday; after their chores were finished we all went for a long walk and played 'Poo sticks' over a nearby brook in the morning sun. After lunch they decorated the inside of the carriage in preparation for the afternoon guests. Two more nephews were coming later, Molly aged 4 and George aged 3, for an outdoor Easter party. They all joined in colouring boiled eggs then using them in an egg and spoon race, jumping bunny race and finally Easter egg hunt. After hand washing they made their own tea of boiled egg sandwiches and decorated cup-cakes.

Moral of this story is, don't let your children grow up saying, 'I didn't know how to survive'

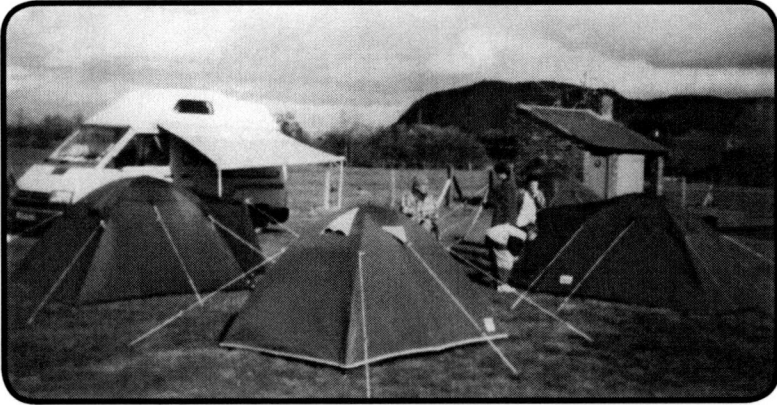

Photograph of 'Julian's Camp' with the outside toilet at hand,
and our Mountain in the distance.

I call this the story of the 'Birth place of Modern Olympics'

Before Julian started to take a deep interest in Llewelas education, he was already trying to help Gweno's son with his homework. What you might call distance learning, she mentioned one day that Wyn was studying the Olympics at school. Julian got excited and made arrangements to meet Gweno and Wyn one weekend at Much Wenlock in Shropshire. Julian was trying to convince all of us where modern day Olympics started. Yep! Well another likely story we thought, but we would go along for the ride any way. Julian led the five of us through the town in search of this Museum, he asked a passer-by and sure enough he was able to point us in the right direction, they said just follow the trail on the pavement. The museum attendant informed us that a man by the name of Doctor William Penny Brooks a local surgeon born in 1809, had spent some time in the 1830's with some French men excavating a site of ancient Olympics in Greece. He was so moved by how physical fitness and the mental strength made fine humans.

On his return he started a 'Class' studying ancient games, and in 1850 Much Wenlock rekindled the Olympic flames once more and 'The Wenlock Olympian Games' began. Humour was not excluded from these games, 'Old woman's race' was included as well as a 'Blind-folded wheel barrow race' To me it appears this gentlemen has become the missing link in our modern day Olympics and his contributions to the games have been forgotten. Although the President of the International Olympic Committee did visit Much Wenlock in 1994 to pay homage to

Doctor William Penny Brooks the founder of the Modern day Olympic Games, and laid a wreath on his grave. The name Baron Pirrie de Coubertin is sometimes associated with the beginning of the games but in fact in 1890 Doctor Brooks invited the Barron to watch the games at Much Wenlock, the Barron became so inspired that in 1896 he began the International Olympic Games which were first held in Athens. So because of Julian, Wyn returned home that night a wiser boy, and excited to tell his teacher what his Uncle Ju had taught him about the roots of the Olympic Games.

Moral of this story is without the origin of every topic, we can only know half of what we have been taught.

Photograph of Wyn taken with Doctor William Penny Brooks
in the back ground, the man history forgot.

Llewelas childhood revolved round Education and looking back she probably had a more colourful education than most. Julian had this lovely way of bringing History to life by making learning fun. Our weekends would involve trekking across the country in our campervan to see whatever was appropriate to her school curriculum.

Our first encounter with the past in the form of re-enactment was in Wroxeter, Shropshire. We were greeted by Romans Soldiers, they mulled round all day talking to us and educating us on all aspects of Roman life from clothes, religion, medicine, food, engineering, warfare, weapons, artillery and military drills.

I think the most spectacular thing I witnessed that day was the shield formation. The drill commands and songs were in Latin even the names of the legionnaires and civilians were exchanged on the field as their 'pretend' birth name. Go on line, their videos clips give you a better insight, but to attend these days is even more spectacular.

Some schools do go on such field trips, Llewela never had the opportunity but it didn't matter, Julian saw to all her field trips.

Another weekend we witnessed was 'Battle Stations' this was a re-enactment at Kenilworth Castle, on these days the Castle was transformed into a medieval encampment and brought to life, the period of the War of the Roses. Here we saw Crossbow-men and Archers demonstrating their skills. Afterwards visitors could walk amongst the men and study and feel the armour and garments and sometimes have the opportunity of trying part of the garments on. To feel how heavy the shields and swords were. Children love it, girls as well.

At Tewkesbury we saw Knights troop into battle, this year they boasted of 2,000 strong all in period costume, this was a noisy event clashing of swords, cannons sounding off in the distance and whistling arrows. Tewkesbury laid claim to the biggest re-enactment in Europe to date.

Our next venture took us to Welshpool, mid Wales. Where, the Royalists and the Parliamentarians gathered to battle it out. This time they were dressed as 'Cavaliers and Roundheads' to sort out the civil war. It isn't just the battle and smell of the gun powder in the air and the noise, it's all the women, children and very tiny babies in bonnets, we got to see the type of food they ate and how their families lived in tents. While on location some of them sleep in their home made tents made from animal hides I'm sure it was goat skin they used.

The last one I can recall attending was at Goodridge castle, near Ross-on-Wye. That particular time we witnessed English versus the French, the Anglo-Saxons fighting the Normans.

The aims of these societies are not to glorify war but to honour those who died in battle for what they believe and to educate the public, young and old about wars, how they dressed and lived.

I'm glad Julian took Llewela on such field trips because I got educated in her shadow too.

My advice is, take a picnic and go into battle for the sake of your children's education. If the man of the house says, "It's not my scene" then grab your Sat Nav and let your children live and breathe history. Julian believed the greatest gift we can ever give our children is Education. Once they're given it, it can't be taken away and consequently that's one place they can be rich.

The authenticity of these costumes is very important to them. They only have to have one learned spectator as an onlooker to discredit one small detail in the costume to cause unrest. Some of these costumes can cost as much as £7,000 or more. Due to the cost, people often made their own.

On the strength of these days out, Julian took it into his head to make his own chain mail armour. Julian could be seen most evenings making the links first, and then linking them together to form the armour. I remember Llewela once saying to him, "Dad why don't you buy a box of links off the internet, that job looks so boring" He replied, "It's the most boring thing I've ever done in my life, but if I buy them I will not have done the whole costume myself, will I?"

She then said, "Dad why on earth are you making it anyway, you're never going to go into battle with it are you?" He said, "No, but it's symbolic, you never know when you need protection in life"

Still on the subject of education, in addition to two state schools and one private school, Llewela was then blessed with another type of schooling, one to one private tuition as it were off Julian in the 'school of life'. He believed that it was the teachers responsibility to teach them the three 'R's' (**A**rithmetic, **W**riting, and **R**eading) any additional lessons should be up to the parents. He sometimes felt the teacher's concentrate too much on fun instead of teaching, the teachers are paid to teach, and parents should be responsible for teaching them how to have fun.

Teenagers have been leaving schools for many years unable to tell the time from a numeric clock, they only recognise the digital clock. I also fear that modern day phones teach children bad habits with spelling with all their abbreviations and mixing numbers in their sentences.

I was shocked to discover that a fifth of all school leavers in Europe, leave school illiterate. My mother age 83, left school all those years ago (up in the mountains I might add) knowing her three 'R's' in both Welsh and English language, and wrote in beautiful hand writing. She still boasts of a prize she was once presented for the best handwriting. What's gone wrong with education? Julian was adamant that he was not going to raise an illiterate daughter.

If everybody took as much interest in their children's education as Julian did, maybe children would have more pride in themselves and do better, especially if they had more enthusiasm and encouragement from the home front. He used to get so excited about her homework, from the age of five each day when returning home from school, dragging her school bag behind, as if she had the world on her shoulders, he would greet her at the back door rubbing his hands together and saying, "Come on Wella, what homework have we got tonight.?"

He never scorned her and told her to go to her bedroom to do her homework he even once said to me, "How children can produce good work under those circumstances, is beyond me!"

To set an example of how important he felt education was, Julian started a Distance learning course and on August 5th 1998 he successfully archived a Diploma in Personal Computer Repairs.

One morning before the summer holidays that year, when Llewela was only ten years old, Julian took Llewela to school, he then impulsively drove us both to attend an open day at our local Private School to gauge the cost of tuition fees, and also to compare Private Education with state schools. He wanted to find out if private school was still as good as it used to be, after all he was once a Boarder himself receiving Private Education which had been good to him.

As we chatted to the Head Mistress, she was keen to speak to Llewela herself; after all it was her that she would be dealing with over the next few years. We agreed we would bring her back the very next morning, I loved the way the conversation included Llewela, how she treated Llewela with such respect and spoke to her as an adult. One of the questions she asked Llewela was, "What do you think you're good at Llewela?" Llewela pondered for a while then said in a shy voice, "Nothing really" My heart was crushed, I wanted to sprout tears but to console me the head mistress then said, "Don't worry my dear, may be the right buttons haven't been pressed yet"

She then informed us, that she could not guarantee a place for her the following year but she could secure a place for her that September. Julian's reply was, "You'd better have her now then."

The sentence reminded me of the Biblical story of the boy called Samuel who was taken to the Temple to be given up to do Gods work.

Except in this case Julian was handing her over for what he felt was best for her, a good education.

You will be glad to hear that Llewela did go on to be good at a lot of things, which I will tell you about later. I did worry at the time that we might not be able to bear the brunt of the fees, but we learnt to make sacrifices in other places, it depends how bad you want something in life, doesn't it.

We should be good to our children after all we chose to have them. Although it says in the 10 commandments to honour your Mother and Father it also says in Proverbs 22 verse 6 Train a child in the way he should go, and when you are old he will not turn from you.

In another book in the Bible called Ephesians chapter 6, verse 4 it says, "Parents do not treat your children in such a way to make them angry"

This is not a quotation from the Bible, but I was once told, you can tease a child once but after the second tease it becomes bullying. I see people do this with animals all the time, they tease and tease and tease then wonder why the animal bites. It's the same with children, when they are teased they get cheeky or aggressive. There is nothing worse than seeing a child showing disrespect towards an adult in public, at the same token it's just as bad to see adults showing disrespect towards a child in public.

I recall a story of a mother who was fed up with her child screaming each week when she tried to do the weekly shopping. Her husband trying to belittle the situation, he dismissed the ordeal. The wife then offered the husband to do the weekly shopping with the child in tow. Sure enough the child started to scream. The father feeling embarrassed decided to match like for like and lay on the floor with his hands and feet in the air screaming. The child feeling ashamed of his father's behaviour pulled at his father's arm and said "Stop it Dad, your embarrassing me" The bad behaviour ceased from thereon.

Raising children sounds like a 50/50 partnership to me, maybe we should make a binding contract with children when they are about 5 for both parties to sign, "Don't embarrass us in public and we won't embarrass you in front of others"

Why have I mentioned all this about education and raising children? I mentioned it because I want to emphasise how seriously Julian considered the raising of children, from education to public behaviour including introducing her to faith, which all helps to differentiate right and wrong?

Although most of us strive to be good parents we don't always get it right. I remember one such incidence when we went on holiday to France with my parents, we three in the campervan and my parents in their caravan. While dining one evening outside our vans at the communal dinner table, Julian and I were having a marital disagreement. The atmosphere was not good, Llewela got up from the table and with her small soft hands she got hold of her father's face, squiggling his cheeks and said, "Dad, say sorry to Mum." With a strong neck he shook his head from side to side. Llewela was not having any of it; she then changed tactics and moved the position of her hands, one on top of his head and the other under his chin. On tip toes she then said, "Look Mum, Dad is saying sorry, aren't you Dad" squeezing her nose on his cheeks and rocking his head in an up and down movement in a 'yes' gesture. Try as we might the rest of us couldn't help but laugh. Llewela wasn't finished yet as she made her way over to me, she turned to my parents rolled her eyes saying, "They're always doing this, Nain" as if she was conducting a regular ritual.

Her idea was to force me to apologise in the same manner to her father, but I could see what was coming and quickly retrieved the situation by saying, "Ok, ok I apologise to your father"

For those of you who didn't know Julian, it was a courageous thing Llewela did because Julian was not only a strict Father but quick tempered too. May be Llewela knew how far to push him.

Moral of this story is, adults should not let their guard down in public, in case your children end up behaving more like grownups than them.

Remembering this tale it brings to mind another episode while on holiday with my parents again, I sometimes wonder what my parents must have first thought about having a chap in a wheel chair for a son in law. They were probably like me, forgot he was in a wheel chair the minute they met him, to such a degree my Mother was so at ease with him they both called a spade a spade in each other's company. Another tiff arose this time between my mother and Julian, the atmosphere was a bit strained. While out walking after lunch this particular afternoon, Julian asked me to stop pushing the wheel chair and reached out to break a branch off a tree. He then called Llewela over and said, "Give this to Nain and tell her it's off your Dad" off she skipped shouting, "Nain, Nain I've got something for you, off Dad" When Mum accepted it she burst out laughing, and started to walk back then proceeded to whip him teasingly with the branch saying, "You are naughty Julian, don't forget you're not too old to have a good hiding off me" The branch was an olive branch, a sign of peace. And there ended the row.

Photograph of my Mum holding the
Peace offering 'Olive branch'

Although Julian always put Llewela first he did have a life of his own, he was on a committee involved in fund raising for pilgrims to go to the South of France. Then one year he was asked if he would like to lead a Jumbulance, he wasn't sure at first because he knew how much work it entailed, it wasn't just the fund raising and organising events, it was trying to have brain storms for different entertainment evenings. It was also about interviewing helpers, visiting the sick, choosing a house mother, finding four nurses a Doctor and a Priest to accompany them on the trip, not forgetting deciding who the VIPs were going to be. It was a name they gave the walking wounded, (very important people) who also wanted to go on the Pilgrimage to Lourdes in the Pyrenees.

As Julian started to visit the sick, he could not get them to understand what a Jumbulance was. In his frustrations one evening as he came buzzing down the back path at high speed, calling to me "I've got to make one, I can't get them to understand" Make what I asked. "A Jumbulance" So that was his first project; to build one to an exact scale in miniature 'like for like'. In reality it's a purpose built half coach half Ambulance, hence the name 'Jumbo-ambulance' It contained eight Ambulance stretchers down the one side of the coach and fourteen coach seats down the other side. It had a large disabled toilet at the back with a sliding door to facilitate wheelchair access. The house mother would be in charge of the spacious kitchen at the rear of the coach. No detail was too small in this replica Jumbulance, he placed high heel shoes a miniature Bible dishes in the sink and even newspaper on the seat. He made the stretchers out of coat hanger wire and chose identical colour material for the curtains, not to mention the precision of the art work on the outside of the coach. The point of telling you about this miniature engineering project was, if there was ever a need for a project to envisage a complicated explanation then no detail was to be spared. His reasoning for his constant perfection was he never knew who would one day inspect his workmanship! The Jumbulance went everywhere with him, when he was fundraising for this trip. People used to marvel at the details in this three foot long coach, 'hand made by a cripple' as Agnes Hunt would say and with those big thick fingers of too.

It was on this trip in 2001while traveling down the motorway through France, Maureen Brewer our house mother for the trip spotted someone offering homemade cake out of a cake tin without as much as a doily or a serviette. She was so alarmed she shouted, "No, no, no they have to have the trimmings, its etiquette" Needless to say the sandwiches were cut into neat triangles, not door steps that would be served to working navies.

Julian responded to her reaction by attracting every body's attention saying aloud, "Listen up every body, can I have a bit of attention here I want everybody to know that when I die I want Maureen to do my funeral food she pays such attention to detail don't you think" everybody just howled with Laughter.

Photograph of the miniature 'Jumbulance' Julian built for the
Pilgrims he led to Lourdes.

Incidentally on this trip Julian was approached, to see if he was interested in becoming a Eucharistic Minister when he returned home. Julian declined several times during the trip.

He knew what it involved, taking turns in giving Communion in church and after Mass taking the host out into the community to the sick and house bound.

On his return the Priest paid him a visit to ask why Julian kept refusing to serve the church. Julian tried to explain he couldn't, he didn't think he was Holy enough. The Priest smiled and said he hadn't asked because of his Holiness but because he wanted Julian to help him be a messenger, none of us are probably holy enough we just have to strive to be Holy. Julian said, "Well when you put it like that, I will be honoured to serve and be a messenger" This conversation happened to take place about twelve months before Llewela's First Holy Communion.

As Julian took his new post seriously, Llewela's time was spent preparing for her First Holy Communion. She wondered if it was Julian's turn to be the Eucharistic minister that particular Sunday. His reply was

"I don't know darling but if it's not my turn I'm not going to ask anyone to change the rota, what will be will be" and she respected her father's decision on the matter. But Julian went on to say, "If it does happen to be my turn, I want you to promise me you will go to whoever is free at the time. I mean don't push past everybody to get to me" She promised, but as it happened it was Julian's turn that Sunday. Considering there were ten children taking their first Holy Communion that morning, Llewela's chance of receiving wine off her own father was pretty slim. After Llewela had received the host from the Priest, she genuflected and gracefully walked over to receive a goblet from one of the six ministers who were dispensing wine that morning. And would you believe it, the only Eucharistic minister available at that exact moment in time was Julian. Llewela behaved as reverent as she could as she accepted the goblet off her own father in order to complete the second half of her 'First Holy Communion.

The second miracle that took place that morning was Llewela's Godmother who happened to be sitting near to Julian, managed to capture the moment on camera. Do you think that both incidences were divine intervention or simply a case of coincidence? We will never know, but Julian did take Llewela to one side later to point out that it wasn't <u>who</u> offered her the goblet that mattered, but what the act represented.

But the photograph became a treasured image which captured a moment of memory in time.

Photograph of Llewela receiving part of her first Holy Communion from her Father.

The Eve of the millennium

Before the eve of the millennium Llewela then aged10, asked Julian if we could do something other than touring France to mark the millennium.

Julian tried to reason with her, "We can't darling, you know we have to go in the camper, I can't risk going in to Hotels." Llewela replied "I mean, we can still go in the camper but go to somewhere like Italy for a change" Julian thought for a minute and then said, "That's feasible" so the exiting plans began to mark the beginning of the millennium.

This is a photograph taken by Llewela of
Llewela's God Parents, Joanna, Michael with Julian and I on
New Year's Eve 2000.

We used the Italian holiday to commemorate more than one celebration that year, the millennium itself, Llewela's First Holy Communion, Julian gained his Higher National Diploma in Computing and my passing my conversion examination and becoming a Registered Nurse four months before on September the 1st 1999. I can remember thinking what was this 2000 year celebration all about? Then realising it was 2000 years since the death of Jesus. Whether we are religious or not, our life still revolves round this man's death. We refer to our time as BC Before Christ or AD Anno Domini which means after Christ's death. For example I was born one thousand nine hundred and fifty seven years after his death. Llewela was right to say, let's celebrate not his death but his life.

In that case our visit to Rome was not only appropriate but turned out to be very memorable too, the site seeing was endless, that is to say we did not see everything. Some readers will have very strong views about the wealth that is lavished on these buildings. I once voiced the same opinion to someone less fortunate than myself and to my embarrassment it was pointed out to me that someone had donated these gifts to these holy places and had I ever given someone a gift only to discover that person had given it away and hoe insulting it is when we find out!

The very same person then said, "I hope they never get rid of the riches in holy places, in my poverty stricken life it's the only time I ever get to see splendour at its best. To me it represents the riches of heaven."

It was the poor I was thinking of when I thought we should strip the churches bare and give the money to the poor, but some of them want to witness splendour. Who are we to deny them of this momentary pleasure? Our highlight was probably having Mass in St Peters square in front of the Vatican. My biggest regret was Julian declined to join Llewela and I in tossing a coin over our left shoulder into the 'Trevi Fountain' ensuring a safe return visit to Rome one day.

A few days later we travelled much further south to Pompeii, not far from Mount Vesuvius.

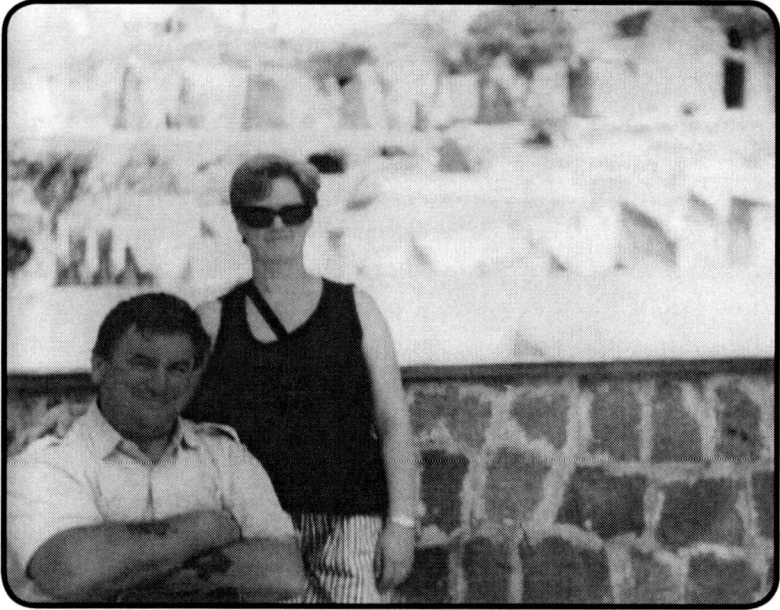

This is a photograph of Julian and I
at the entrance of Pompeii City ruins.
The photo does not give the heat of the day any justice.

As we arrived in Pompeii at 12 noon, it was an extremely hot day in mid-August. The three of us suddenly became "Mad dogs and English men, who ventured out in the mid-day sun" Had we engaged in more common sense, the two of us should of said let the heat of the day cool down. But Julian was so excited about going to see the ruins of Pompeii, he could hardly contain himself. I suspect he thought it was a place he would never visit in his life time.

We paid our money, but getting through the turn stile proved to be more troublesome.

The delay of the gate keeper with his keys should have raised our suspicion that it may not be as wheelchair friendly as we were hoping it to be. Once through the gate, we turned the corner and to our horror, our hearts slumped in disbelief that the ticket collector had taken Julian's money knowing the root the three of us had to take with a wheelchair, with only one woman and a young girl to help him. For the first time in my life I saw Julian's face depict defeat. Julian said, "Leave it Olwen, you two go ahead. I can't expect you two to push me up and down that crazy path". If you have never been to Pompeii I cannot start to describe the sharp decent down and even steeper ascent up. It reminded me of the Great Wall of China with all its ups and downs, the footpath was laid with thin wooden slats that ran diagonally, making wheelchair pushing extremely difficult. That was not our only obstacle, every so often there were two large protruding stones on either side of the path, about one and a half foot high. These were obviously the base of some ruined pillars of bygone age. The stumps of columns were in pairs, to close together to wheel through and too close to the edge to wheel round. Julian's practical mind could see it was going to be impossible and repeated his concerns, "Please Olwen, leave it" I pleaded, "You haven't put yourself through hell driving down here to the south of Italy to see the ruins of Pompeii, just to turn back at its gate. Please, this is your birthday treat, Ju please try." We started our journey, he was right Llewela and I could hardly hold him from going back down this very, very steep hill. Luckily for us, some very polite Polish young men appeared from nowhere and offered their assistance. As they approached the columns, the four of them lifted Julian and his wheelchair clear of every obstacle until at last Julian reached level ground. I was so grateful to our four helpers, and thanked them repeatedly for their kindness but Julian offered no such gratitude but remained silent, which I found odd. After their departure I turned to Julian to see what had offended him, to my horror he'd taken on the look of a frightened rabbit, his eyes were huge, shifting franticly from side to side as if he was disorientated. I asked him if he was feeling alright, he shook his head and said "No I don't feel well at all, and I'm really frightened about how am I going to get back to the van"

Apart from his abnormal behaviour he also looked physically different, his face was extremely pale he appeared breathless and was sweating profusely. This didn't look like heat exhaustion to me, there was some wrong! He then became verbally aggressive, telling Llewela and I to leave him alone. Worried that he'd become ill, I insisted on staying thinking we were in a foreign land unable to speak the language. But Julian detested 'fussing' so Llewela and I had to do as he instructed. Feeling guilty that I was abandoning him, I begged Llewela to return to her father to check on him. After about 15 minutes we both ventured back after purchasing a couple of cans of cold orange pop from a pop-seller who was meandering round with a cool box. Julian was so glad to see us, even gladder when we produced these two cans of pop.

After he'd drunk them in the shade of a tumbled down ancient wall, he confessed he felt so much better especially now his vision was returning. I was absolutely furious inside that he'd insisted that we left him in that state. I had no idea he'd lost his sight, but thankfully his colour was coming back. After a short rest I asked him if he felt well enough for me to push him round the sights in the shade, he agreed and he thoroughly enjoyed the excavation site and strangely enough, once we were up there it was actually very wheelchair friendly. Coincidence or not the week before we went to Pompeii, we'd both watched a documentary about the Volcano Vesuvius that had engulfed poor Pompeii on 24 August 79AD. The comments we both remembered from the documentary was, the commentator pointing out that the beautiful paintings of the lovely slim young ladies with their flowing chiffon gowns might have been a figment of the artist imagination. As most of the female skeletons that were examined following excavation were found to have an enlarged pituitary fosse, which indicate they would of had endocrine problems. These women may have had other appearance or characteristics, hair thinning on their head, round plump bodies, facial hair, large hands and feet, weight gain across upper back and round face.

With these images in mind, and looking at these elegant lady's paintings on the wall I can remember commenting how sad that we know why they looked and felt like they did 1,921 years after they died, but at that time they could not correct their condition.

From time to time Julian and I often went back to this scene, thinking this is where Julian's funny turns first started, but what started I don't know?

What made us both sigh with disbelief after we'd finished our sightseeing that afternoon was the fact we'd discovered a small side gate at the top, which enabled us to exit onto the main street into the city. Why didn't the gatekeeper direct us to this side gate in the first place, instead of causing both of us to nearly have a heart attack, not to mention inflicting unnecessary physical strain on those poor Polish boys?

The next day still in Pompeii, an Italian family befriended us by invited us into their family home for something to eat. We had homemade Pizza and home grown salad from their gardens; it was like visiting our Italian friends at home. One of the children could speak a little English so Julian asked if there was a way he could go up Mount Vesuvius to get closer to the volcano. When he translated the request to his family, they all howled in fits of laughter explaining that the lava dust was far too hot. When walking visitors go up, they are given special protective footwear over their shoes. They were laughing because of Julian's rubber tyres, they said they would melt. Julian resigned to the fact that this little mission might be just beyond his calculation, but he still had the pluck to ask even after the escapade the day before. Moral of that story, always ask they can only say "No"

Julian always made sure every journey he planned was as exciting going as it was homeward bound. Before our millennium holiday, Llewela had mentioned to him that she would one day like to visit the Leaning Tower of Pisa. While Llewela was fast asleep in the back of the camper, Julian included me in on his intension to surprise Llewela. As we pulled up to this attraction Julian called out in a panicky state, "Llewela, quick Wella, it's time to wake up, you need to help your Mother make dinner" Llewela stood up, stretched her arms yawned and glanced out of the window only to see the Leaning Tower of Pisa to the side of her. She screamed, "Dad, dad you won't believe where you've just stopped, look Dad, through the window" with her two hands from behind him she cupped his face in her hands and directed it towards the tower. "Look Dad it's the Leaning Tower of Pisa, I just can't believe it, it's my dream come true"

You could see his heart puffing up with pride that he had pleased his little girl.

He kept up this pretence, that this stop was a co-incidence for a long time just to retain the magic in both their hearts. The journey home was not yet complete, not without first popping into Euro Disney, Julian used to insist it was a family ritual which had to be done every time we went to France in case the complex closed before our next visit to France. Is this a measure of a father's love, when each time he would endure a long and boring day year in year out waiting for her to queue for every ride then patiently await her return to listen to the excitement in her voice only to watch her queue again for another ride? He used to tell me, the boredom was worth the excitement he saw in her face. He knew she adored Disney, especially when she used to say, "Dad, when I grow up I'm going to come here for my honey moon and stay in the pink Hotel". He used to say every year, "We'll see darling".

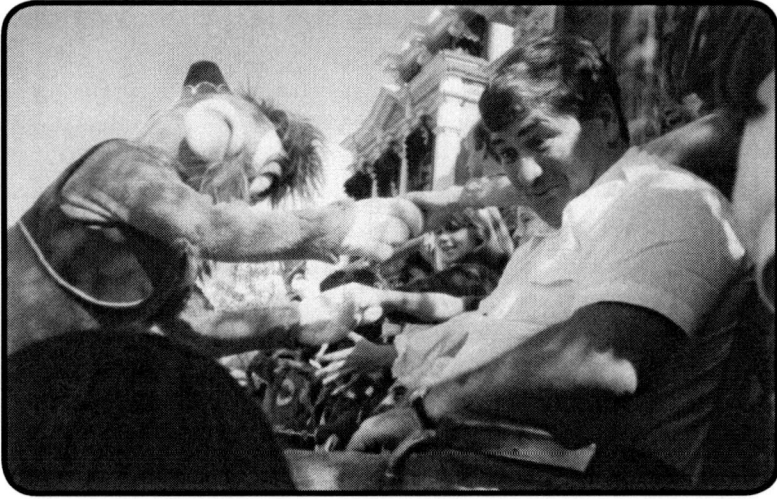

Photograph of Julian in Disney, who's the most
exited Julian or Llewela?

Following this memorable holiday in Italy, on the morning of the 4th
December 2000, as Julian was trying to get out of bed he complained
that his vision was not right; he said "It's just like when I was in Pompeii
in August; it feels as if I'm looking through rippling water". I knew he
was worried, because he squeezed my waist and buried his head in my
side and said, Oh! Olwen, how will I manage in a wheelchair, coping
with blindness?" I had no answer; I just squeezed him back and we both
held tight for a very long time saying nothing.

Later that morning I managed to get an appointment with the
GP, who referred him to an eye specialist. I applaud who ever got him
the appointment so soon, his appointment was 4 days later on the 8th
December 2000. The Ophthalmologist could not find anything wrong
except that there could be a vitreous detachment, but felt the eye
disturbance was probably due to dehydration. He confessed as it was four
days after the event that it was difficult to give an accurate diagnosis.
Incidentally the vision disturbance lasted 24hrs.

The only other illness he was suffering from at the time was a bad
bought of urine infection, which on reflection did affect his drinking
because he felt so nauseas with it. Would it be plausible to assume it was
caused by his dehydrated body?

Julian's life changing news

Less than two months later after the visual disturbance, Julian attended his GP surgery on the 29th January 2001 with a minor infection thinking he would be prescribed antibiotics. It came as a shock to him when the GP decided instead to run some blood tests instead, this being a Thursday evening he thought he'd have to wait until at least the following Monday for the results, but on Friday evening he received a phone call from his GP informing him he was Diabetic and he needed to return to the surgery first thing Monday morning. For the first time in all our married life we didn't do anything that weekend, all tasks stopped and we both went into shock we just pondered over our new way of life. Julian had no family history of Diabetes so it was not at the forefront of our mind that he could possibly be a Diabetic, but considering modern trend we both realised that half the population was fast becoming Diabetics.

Following his visit to the Doctor, he tried to control his glucose levels himself with a diabetic diet, controlled being the operative word. Food that you thought might raise his blood sugars often didn't, and food that should not have often did! It didn't make any sense to Julian at all, but much less sense to me; in fact it was fast becoming a growing nightmare. Within two weeks of been diagnosed Diabetic on St Valentine's day the 14th February 2001 he was prescribed his first diabetic tablet, Glycoside 80 mg which did very little to lower his blood sugar readings.

The raised glucose readings I started to take personally, what sort of a nurse was I who could not control her own husband's sugar levels?

He was, I must say a very good patient because he took his new diagnosis very serious. He recorded his own blood sugar readings religiously before most meals, and then kept to his diet including sugar free beer. As you might have gathered once he made his mind up about something, he became focused and was determined to conquer his difficulties in life. He used to say "I'm definitely going to master this Olwen before our next trip to France" The more he tried the worse the blood reading became. So every now and then he would break the rules and have some thing he knew he wasn't allowed. On returning home one evening from a Buffalo function he confessed his sins to me, saying he

106

had eaten white bread and drank normal beer. Out of interest he did his BM (blood monitoring) reading to see how much higher the glucose levels had gone up after committing this terrible sin. To both our dismay his readings had gone down! This did not make sense to me, Julian or to his non-medical friends. The only thing that he did different on those nights was to take a couple of extra analgesic tablets before going out. He normally took two first things in the morning for his so called irritable bowel. Because of these peculiarities I started to record what he ate on a food chart to see if I could detect a pattern, but to no avail there didn't seem to be a connection with low carb diet and low sugar readings and vice versa with high. The only pattern that was apparent was his glucose readings went down when he took analgesia!

It should have rung alarm bells then; analgesia should not reduce glucose levels.

In reality the bells did ring but I chose to ignore them!!!!!!!!

The following Easter, in 2001 Julian decided he wasn't going to let these high sugar readings put his life on hold so the three of us took off to France in our campervan, this time with a box full of tablets touring as usual, then one afternoon while sitting under the shade of the canopy. Julian said, "Olwen get me out of this heat push me inside the van" I did as he asked, a few minutes later he said, "Olwen can you get me out, its boiling inside this van" Again I did as he asked and a few minutes later he said, "I'm sorry Olwen but I can't take this heat, can you push me in again".

By now I expressed my own opinion and said, "Wait a minute Julian, now I'm getting hot with all this in-out-in-out". With a loud sigh he apologised then suddenly said, "You're right, quick the two of you lets pack up were off to find somewhere cool. So that's exactly what we did, he took us to a local supermarket where we loitered in the freezer isle until we cooled off.

He said, "I'm too old for these 'tin can' holidays Olwen, after last summer in Pompeii I just can't take the heat like I used to" at that we met a French couple who we'd met a few days previously. They invited us to their home that night for a drink. Julian accepted their hospitality immediately, mainly because he was determined to improve his French.

As we entered their house that evening Julian said, "Wow! This is what we need, a cool French house." They explained they did not have air conditioning because the house had thick walls which kept it warm in the winter and cool in the summer.

On returning back to our 'hot tin can' as he called it, we spent the remainder of the evening talking about the possibility of buying a house in France.

This was the first time I ever lay down the law in our marriage, I told him "Don't mess with my head Julian, either we do it or we don't. But don't get me all excited about getting a place abroad and then not go through with it" He explained he was serious; he could not go through that heat wave he suffered the day before again.

It was not beyond our means, the mortgage had been paid off on the house in England and we were thinking of moving into a bungalow ready for retirement which would involve another mortgage and the houses were still cheap in France. While we were munching over our breakfast he held a family Pow-Wow. We were all in agreement to go ahead with this dream villa in the South of France. All he asked was before we started our search was that we all agree on the same house. What he meant was he didn't want to buy a house one of us did not want to return to, has usual he was always thinking ahead. First of all we had to find an equivalent to an estate agent first, and one who could speak English. Luckily we found an 'Agent Immobilier' in the next village who could speak English, her accent proved to be a bit difficult to understand at first but we were grateful for any English. You see the estate agent lady had spent her teenage years working in a cider factory in Scotland to improve her English. In other words we were dealing with a French lady who spoke broken English with a Scottish accent. She told us she normally chose three houses for her clients, which she considered suitable for viewing.

The first house we were shown Llewela loved and adored, it had a balcony from what would be her bed room window, but not practical because the house was on a very steep slope. The next house was a one up one down which Julian loved and adored because of the fire place, but not practical because it had a spiral stair case. The third house I loved and adored, because it had 10 bed rooms every room was on different level but I agree not at all disabled friendly and in addition to that it didn't have running water or electricity. Julian's reaction to this one was, "No, no, no, I don't speak French fluent enough to get permission off different authorities to dig up half their road system just to get those amenities into the house. And on top of that, we'll want the work done during our holiday; I don't think they'll wear that do you?" Point taken, which meant we hadn't had any joy with the house hunting at all. But she surprised us by saying she had one trump card; she wanted to show us one more house. This house was only a mile away from our camp site; Julian was shocked when we pulled up in front of her trumped card house. Leading from the road to the front door was three steps, and they were on a slant. Viewing this house was impossible for Julian, it was totally inaccessible. He said, "Ok girls, out you get don't appear rude you two go and view the house, I'll stop in the van"

As I entered the house there was a wash room to my left with no window which I found strange, but I thought it would make a splendid ground floor bed room. The kitchen-come-dining room was spacious enough to have a wheelchair party in if we wished. Upstairs there were only two rooms, one with a bed and one with a settee and both possessed the very best view of the village square. On a clear day the lady translated, you could see the sea in the distance. We thanked the owner for her time, but access would prove a problem with the wheel chair.

For the remainder of the day I must have appeared quiet to Julian, but not intentionally. That evening while eating our evening meal, Julian asked, "Are you still pondering over that last house, I am not buying a house that I cannot gain entry Olwen." I said, "I know" He paused and then said, "Ok, let me just sleep on it, I might come up with something by morning." He often went to bed troubled, and would dream the answer. The following morning I could not restrain myself from asking, "Did you dream last night?"

Deciphering dreams is nothing new; it's been going on since Biblical times.

Half way through breakfast he confessed he had dreamt the answer to my dilemma. He explained, he had dreamt we had purchase two planks of wood from a wood yard to breach the gap between our parked camper-van in the street to the top step of the ladies house. Sighing with relief, I muttered, "How clever" He said, "Well! That's how I got in, in my dream"!

I miss those dreams terribly!

Immediately after breakfast Julian contacted the estate agent for a further viewing. After purchasing the two planks of wood we met up with the two ladies once more that same afternoon. On entering the house he sent Llewela and I up stairs to take photographs of the bed rooms and the view. As Llewela and I was ascending down the stone stair case to join everyone in the kitchen I was shocked to find Julian sealing the deal with a Gentleman's hand shake over the agreement. I'm glad he made this decision on his own I didn't want people to think I'd pressurised him into buying a millstone around our necks. I want everybody to know he bought it because he could see its potential too. Although Llewela did whisper to me upstairs, "Mum, don't let him buy it there's spiders everywhere" but luckily Julian could see beyond the spiders too. The estate agent said to Julian, "What does it feel like, to owning part of a Castle"? Perplexed about her comment I said to Julian, "She doesn't mean that, does she"? Julian pacified me by saying, "No she means it's a corner of a small Fort"

A meeting was arranged a few days later with five of us round a table, the elderly lady the seller, Julian and I the buyers, our 'Scottish' Estate Agent or 'Immobilier' who was also acting as our interpreter and the 'Notaire' who is the equivalent to our English Solicitor. He had the important job of overseeing the signing of the contract, and then the deal was done. Much easier than England, the only difference in France if one of the partners dies the property goes to the children. That's why so many run down houses can be seen in France because if there are many children involved they often can't agree to sell!

So here started our passion for renovating our dream home, although I think it became more of a 'Conservation project' rather than a 'Renovation project' in the end, trying to preserve the old building to its former glory.

Quite soon after we returned from this French trip, Julian demonstrated to me what a determined character he really was.

I call this next true story his, "Wheelie bin story."

I had gone to work on this particular Thursday morning for my usual 7am start.

We hadn't long started our fortnightly bin day collection when Julian suddenly realised after he had taken Llewela to school, that I had forgotten to put our bin out. He decided to tackle this huge task himself as we were experiencing a spell of very hot weather and the thought of having a bin full of rubbish hanging round for a month could turn out to be unpleasant.

The bin lived at the top of a very steep path, tucked away behind a gate trapped tight in to its corner by some erect paving slabs. To get the wheelie bin out even when empty by an able bodied person is very tricky; to do it when it's full is even more difficult.

When attempted by a person in a wheel chair is near impossible. It entailed trying to steady the wheel chair on the top of a slope with no brakes, then engage in dragging, pulling, shoving and rattling the bin out of its socket as it were, he then somehow managed to tip the handles on to his lap and somehow opened the gate which incidentally had a strong spring on it, then it entailed pulling it towards him down the slope, with a bin in-between him and the gate. Once he'd mastered that he then had to push the bin down a long back path with the handles still resting on his lap leaving his hands free to push the wheel chair. Baring in mind the path slabs along this path are so uneven due to the 'tree root damage', how he managed to push this heavily laden bin under these conditions is beyond me. I always pulled the bin; goodness knows how he managed to push it. I would of said it would have been a physical impossibility to pull it sat in a wheelchair.

He still had the length of the car park to master; but once he'd pushed it passed the four garages to the front of the house he must have felt a great sense of accomplishment. So, when he'd arrived at his destination with the relief of finishing the dreaded task he raised the tilted bin off his lap to its erect position. But somehow Julian's knuckles got wedge in the bin handles, and as the weight of the bin sprung itself into its erect position so did Julian, bearing in mind he had not intended to stand up that morning, something he hadn't done for thirty years neither had he engaged his brakes on the wheel chair. Our house is at the top of a slope so, down the wheel chair rolled to the bottom of the hill and parked itself between two rows of houses. In the meantime when Julian's weight was attached to the weight of the fully laden bin it over compensated and the mathematics made the bin topple over in the other direction. Julian now found himself, spread eagled over the wheelie bin. If you can imagine, one limb stretching to each corner.

He had the dilemma of either staying spread eagled on the bin or gently gliding himself on to the road and hope the tar mark didn't cause him any bodily damage.

On occasions like this, most adults hope there are no witnesses watching causing humiliation. This time however Julian was hoping a nosey neighbour had spotted his embarrassing dilemma. Once he started to take stock of who might be home that day, he realised they were all at work. There was nothing for it he would have to descend gracefully to the floor as the bin men didn't usually come until much later.

When his arms became too tired to hold on, the decision was taken out of his hands and down he went. Sitting there cross legged, he surveyed the houses once more to see who was lightly to come first to offer him assistance. The situation looked grim; it didn't look as if anyone was likely to come until late afternoon. When he started out on his journey that morning which had now turned out to be an adventure, it was then a nice sunny morning but now dark clouds were forming.

Worried it was going to rain, he started to think of strategies of where to shelter if it came to rain heavy. He didn't want to catch pneumonia for the sake of a smelly bin. His first thought was to get all the black bin sacks out of the wheelie bin then crawl inside the bin for some shelter.

Another thought occurred to him, he hoped he had enough time to crawl out if the bin before the bin men tipped him into their wagon and chewed him up into pieces. He didn't want someone blamed for his death when it was not of their doing, the secret would be to remember not to go to sleep inside the bin.

Luckily a few hours later a red parcel van called at one of the houses with a delivery. It was a wonder they didn't ask Julian to sign for it, they usually ask anything that moves to sign. Julian shouted for all his worth, "Can you help me? my wheelchair has just rolled down the hill"

The chap shouted back, "Yea, that's a likely story" and drove off. Poor Julian couldn't believe his uncharitable action. About twenty minutes later two red parcel vans appeared, the two drivers came out cautiously walking towards him asking "Are you definitely in trouble mate." Julian said pointing, "Yes if you squat down to my level you'll be able to see my wheelchair down there at the bottom of the hill"

Now convinced, one of them went to fetch the chair and then the two of them lifted him up and placed him gingerly in his chair. They explained they come across a lot of 'weirdoes' in their line of work, either on drugs but mostly drunks and are told to avoid trouble for their own safety or only attempt to help if there are two of them. When I came home from work that day Julian proudly announced he'd put the bin out, I flippantly said, "Oh, thanks" "Thanks" he said, "Is that all you can say, it took up all of my morning, I nearly got chewed up by the rubbish wagon and all you can say is thanks" My original thought was, there's no need to exaggerate. But of course he nearly was chewed up! The moral of the story is, if the job needs doing, do it at any cost.

I hope these tales doesn't make Julian sound like the local village idiot; I just admire him for not giving up at the first hurdle or giving in half way when most of us would have long thrown the towel in or in my case I wouldn't even attempt the job in the first place.

To be fair Julian was defiantly not an idiot, after obtaining his Diploma he continued his study's and was often studying into the early hours of the morning, sometimes all through the night. He was out of social circulation during these studying years, often missing out on special occasions.

The psychological example he set, must have had a long term effect on Llewela, because her studying days always took centre stage, over socialising.

The next qualification Julian obtained was in February 2002, a Certificate in Teaching Adults. Now he had a better insight into, how to better guide Llewela's learning.

Before we left to go on our first holiday to our new house, I say 'new' it was new to us, but it was actually part of an 800 year old Fort built by the Knight Templers, Julian wanted to take someone who was unemployed at the time with us, but he said the unemployed department would not let him go. Julian said, "I tell you what, I'll come with you and we will ask them together, we won't do anything illegal, if they say no, then we'll have to respect their decision" They arranged a suitable morning to go together, when Julian picked up his friend he said, "What's with the suit and tie then Julian"? Julian replied, "Watch and learn, just like money talks, suits speak volumes too" As they approached the multi-story building in the city centre, his friend warned Julian that this could take all day because the queues were always very long. As they entered the building the door attendant asked Julian, "Can I help you sir"? Julian said, "Yes I've come to see the manager about something" He said, "Come this way Sir, I'll show you where he is, he's on the top floor, have you got an appointment Sir"? Julian confessed he hadn't.

He knocked on the door, and introduced Julian as Mr Davies to the manager. Julian explained his plight, and wondered if his friend could be excused from sighing on for two weeks, he was after all saving the country two weeks money.

The manager agreed and requested his file to be brought up and explained that they only want to know what's going on. They shook hands again and they were escorted in the lift to the ground floor.

Once in the street, his friend said "How did you manage that, was it the wheelchair that got you to jump the queue"? Julian said, "Jump the queue certainly not, I told you suit and tie speak volumes, but above all being clean shaven with polished shoes says more" He was able to come with us to France, but as soon as we arrived I couldn't believe what had happened to Julian's legs, both were huge and blue. The following day they were truly awful I was sure he was going to lose both of his legs; I couldn't decide if he had elephantitis, cellulitis or lymphedema. Whatever he had, it was present in both legs and both legs were blue with black necrosis in places. I said, "I need to find a Doctor to have a look at these Julian", but Julian wasn't having any of it. He said, "No way, just dress them with a bit of iodine they will be fine" He did make me nervous on occasions with his flippant fix-me attitude. As it happened that's all I had in the house at the time, a large bottle of iodine, plenty of gauze and bandages. Rightly or wrongly I applied iodine soaks from the tip of his big toes to the top of his leg and bandaged them, then prayed for the best. My nurse's head said iodine was not the treatment in this case, but as I knew iodine suited his skin I hoped on this occasion it would not have an adverse reaction otherwise we were both in trouble. That night I thought it needed more padding, so the following morning I went to the pharmacy and with my non-existence French I bought £30 worth of wadding. At the end of our holidays Julian drove the 800 hundred miles back to England and with no dressings I might add, there was no need his legs were completely healed! How could that be? Why should iodine have healed him, was Julian listening to his body or more to the point was Julian's body screaming out for Iodine, or, was his iodine levels so low that the iodine dressings fed his iodine deficiency? I wondered if I'd ever find out. On his return home, Julian didn't visit the GP to have his legs checked out, his reckoning was, "What for, I'm completely healed" But strangely enough in the Autumn of that year Julian suffered chronic lymph oedema in both legs yet again, and on 17th October 2001 his GP prescribed Augmentin which he reacted to very badly.

The year 2002 turned out to be uneventful on the medical front for Julian, as he was blessed with good health, he took us across the English Channel once more to renovate his beloved house in France, Llewela now age 12 accompanied us on our exiting venture.

The first task beckoned all hands on deck to strip the vaulted walls of its plaster of Paris, what a dusty job that turned out to be. We lived, breathed and ate grit, but once that was accomplished Julian asked the young man we'd taken with us to start pointing the walls, realising this was not his forte he took him off that job and found him another. In the meantime Llewela started to tinker with the trowel and began pointing the walls herself.

When Julian returned and saw what had been done he asked, "Who's done this?" Llewela bless her owned up and said "I did Dad, have I done it wrong?" He said "No, now show your Mother how it's done, you're both on pointing from now on" That first year we had no ladders, so improvising was the name of the game. In order to reach the 10 foot ceiling we placed two chairs on top of the kitchen table then a plank of wood balancing from chair to chair with our out-stretched arms, we were then able to reach the tall ceiling precariously balancing on the plank. Health and safety was not our main priority that summer but we did wise up to safety later. It took six weeks to finish pointing the lounge, as every stone was unique in shape; we lovingly secured each stone back to its former place. Because of the care Llewela and I took with each stone I feel the walls are soaked in love, I adore those walls.

The following year we took two young teenagers, who were eager to learn anything Julian was willing to teach them, mainly building work. Always ready to make others feel useful he gave us all titles, not only did it make us all feel important but everybody knew every body's responsibility. He was always the pretend 'Site manager', Llewela was the 'house mother' she was responsible for all the cooking, washing every body's cloths and the general housekeeping, including washing up in the day, although we all had to join in with the washing of the dishes after the evening meal.

As Julian was constantly teaching and instructing the boys, Llewela and I tried to keeping out of his way by not interrupting his flow of teaching. Once the pointing was finished the next job he appointed to me, was to tile the unusual shaped shower that followed the contoured curve of the vaulted walls. After my poor attempt of tiling, Julian recognised something special in Llewela, she showed signs of accuracy in laying shower tiles. Julian then changed tactics and suggested from then on that I mixed the adhesive and Llewela used her precision skills to tile. After this discovery, I was only allowed to grout round her tiles and the following day wash them clean. Julian was amazed at her standard of workmanship (or should I say work-child'ship) he confessed a professional Tyler could not have done the job any better.

Llewela seemed to be collecting new titles each holiday, it had already changed from 'Chief Pointer' to 'House Mother' and now it was 'Chief Tyler' One of the young men named Anthony was given the title 'Bob the Builder' and John was usually 'Tool man Taylor' He was responsible for making sure all the tools were in the right boxes at all times, including making sure the electric tools were put on charge the night before. Unfortunately the 'Gofer' got shouted at the most, if something could not be found.

Both Julian and I realised this renovation could of taken a lot less time had we employed professionals, but this was more than building work for Julian he was teaching young men skills that they may never otherwise be taught. He wanted critics to recognise that even with handicaps you can achieve perfection. By handicaps I mean the young boys who had no experience and Julian labelled as he was 'dis-abled'. We all have handicaps; I was once told mine was my spelling!

The following summer of 2003, was a chill out year for Julian because his studying days were coming to an end, he was in his final year. I say final because he had nearly finished the final year in 2002 but sadly his lecturer died in his sleep, he was only in his 30's leaving very small children. This lecturer was so excited about Julian's project, the building of a robot that could be programmed to speak and directed visitors into the reception area at the University. All of Julian's birthday presents that year were books about robot programming.

After the lecturer's death, Julian continued to work on the project alone but when it came for the project to be marked unfortunately there was no one there qualified enough to mark his work!

Julian even suggested an outside lecturer from another university to mark his work, they declined his request. We can only assume that if the robot was successful who would take the credit, the student or the lecturer from another University?

It was concluded in the end that Julian was to abandon that year with only a month to go and re-take the final year again, choosing a simpler topic. It must have been a very mundane topic because I cannot recall what he chose.

Photograph of Julian in his cap and gown in September 2003.

On the quiet I think the degree was a double whammy, one was for his own self-esteem and the other was to know the pit falls that go with University life in preparation for what Llewela might face in the future if she chose to go to University. Unfortunately he had to keep these skills under his hat for five more years, before Llewela was old enough to draw on his university experience.

The biggest lesson he learnt at this establishment was, the lecturers weren't interested in how intelligent Julian was or impressed if he won top marks at any cost, but how well could he conduct himself in group work, exercising him team skills. In the end a lecturer took him to one side and said, "Julian to be successful in that big world out there and to retain your position in a company, you're employer doesn't want to see your individual performance he wants to see how you can jell his work force and get the best out of them.

That summer he put his new found skill to the test, when the ground level bed room floor in the house in France was in need of tiling and who better to do the job than the pretend Site manager's daughter Llewela! She set about her new task in earnest; it wasn't long before Julian came to check to see how she was getting on.

He nodded his head in an approving manner but then insulted her by passing her a very long Level to check if the floor tiles she had laid were level. To both our horror she slid the level back towards him, from one end of the room to the other wedging it under his foot plates, saying in a raised voice, "No one checks my tiles, they are absolutely level" at that she got up and went to the toilet.

Once out of sight Julian said, "Quick Olwen, check them anyway while she is out of the room".

With the aid of the level I replied "She's spot on Julian, just as she said, absolutely level"

That's what happens when you're trained by a perfectionist, you 'beget perfection' He then started calling her, 'Chief floor Tyler'

Although the work at the house was hard and the days were long, he would always find something unusual or special to do on our day off.

On our first holiday at the house, Julian came up with the idea of re-naming our 'days off' after our Christian names, that way we all had a chance to have 'our day' as it were. For example if it was Julian's day, we would all refer to it as 'Julian's day' The day was governed by Julian's wishes, what time we all got up, what and where he/she wanted to eat, where he/she wanted to go. Above all the rest of us were not allowed to spoil that person's day. In other words it was 'be nice to the chosen person's day'. Because it was only a matter of time before it was your turn to have your day.

Once home and after struggling with both Glycoside and a strict diabetic diet for two and a half years since his diagnosis, both Julian and I realised that his high glucose levels were no longer within acceptable ranges. In 2003 Julian's HbA1c confirmed our suspicion, the test results were tinkering between 7.0 and 8.7 and in September of that year Julian gave in to an additional prescription called Avandia otherwise known as Rosiglicazide, which now meant he was taking two diabetic treatments.

After taking this second treatment for six months he was plagued with irritating minor ailments, for one he developed a small sinus on his right hip and on St George's day in 2004 a large fragment of bone measuring 6.5cm in length came out of his right hip. The District nurses came in daily to pack his wound until it healed in the summer. Although he was happy to be free from wound dressing procedures, other irritating minor ailments continued to fire daggers at him, and in July 2004 he was diagnosed with Hypothyroidism and on 16th of July he was prescribed another tablet called Levothyroxine. Julian said mockingly, "Great, another tablet to take on holiday with me".

Julian was now starting to use his holidays as a distraction from ill health, and in the summer of 2004 whilst at his retreat as he called it, Julian noticed the local youngsters in the village to be much younger scooter riders than those in England. On questioning them it was true they were, the law in France allowed them to ride Scoters at the age of 14. Reminiscing about his Mod and Scooter days in his teenage life, he asked Llewela if she would like one for her birthday, bearing in mind she was only 13 at the time. And what do you think the said?

Needless to say, she said "Yes" and so on "Julian and Llewela's days" we were all dragged round Scooter shops to compare prices. The two young men including Julian made a total of three male companions to help Llewela debate which buy was best, but choosing a helmet, a padlock and a chain was another matter.

Was this a reckless father or a trusting one? He gave her such a long reign in life, but it was always attached to an unspoken rule, "Don't mess up and don't let me down" This trusting bond created confidence in her.

Llewela could not ride it until after Christmas, so the bike was parked in the kitchen in the house in France over the winter months ready for her next visit.

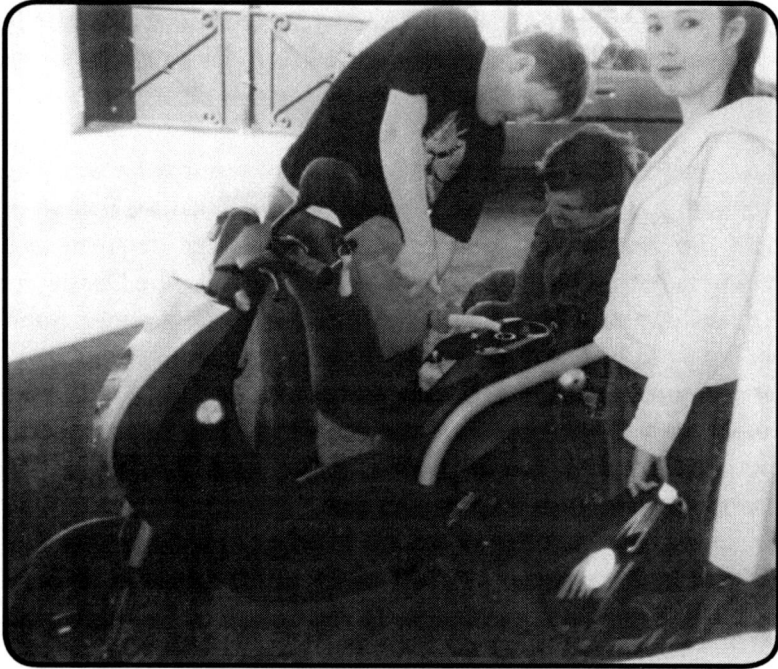

Photo of Llewela with her new toy,
"Her new Peugeot 125cc Bike"

In the year of 2005 Llewela was coming to an age where she needed to choose subjects for a career that was going to last her the rest of her life. It was a very traumatic time for both Llewela and Julian trying to choose the best subjects. This brings to mind, Saint Frances Xavier who once said in the 1500 hundreds, "Give me the boy of seven and I will give you the man". Although I grew up without electricity consequently we didn't have television, but my sister and I did go to stay with our Aunty Mew in Aberystwyth every summer holiday until we were seven. While we were there I remember watching a documentary in 1967 called 'Seven up' shown on World in Action. The documentary was produced to see if there was any truth in the fact that children of seven knew what they wanted to do when they grow up. They chose fourteen children to see if they could accurately predict what they would become as adults by the year 2000. They chose 3 Boarding boys, 1 girl from upper class background, 4 from working class, 2 from middle class, 2 from children's home and 2 wild cards from the country. The same children were re-interviewed every seven years. Surprisingly, nearly all the children achieved all their expectation except for one sweet boy who said he could not see himself as anything. Sadly he was eventually found at the age of 49 living as a hermit in the Scottish highlands in a caravan, suffering from psychiatric problems.

Point of this diversion is Llewela expressed a wish to work with animals or children. Julian was not able to see how she could fit the criteria as she did not want to work with sick animals. In his frustration he found a test on the internet to analyse what would suit her best. A test he was put through when he tried to join the army, he was advised to study engineering.

He told them in no uncertain terms that if they did not accept him as a regular then they couldn't have him at all. Years later he confessed he was an engineer through and through he should have taken their advice.

This test calculated a string of possibilities for Llewela, one of them studying Management in Tourism and Leisure. To see if it was appealing enough for her, he organised for Llewela to shadow his half-sister who was an air hostess at the time and travel on a couple of flights as work experience. She was lucky enough to fly to Johannesburg and New York, what an experience!

Even so it will still be interesting to see where her long term career will end, will it eventually be with children or with animals as she first indicated? After these two trips Llewela returned to the house in France to put the new Scooter through its paces, she must have travelled miles upon miles on that bike that holiday, and to prove her independence she would follow our car on Sunday mornings to attend church in the next village. I must say she was a great help with fetching and carrying small things from the DIY and also the odd jar of something from the supermarket.

On our return in the autumn of 2005 Julian had an appointment with a Vascular Consultant who then referred him on to a Consultant Anaesthetist to performed a Lumber Chemical Sympathectomy, which is an injection to help increase blood flow to his lower limbs.

At his follow up appointment, the Vascular Consultant recommended that Julian should start taking Horse Chestnut Extract tablets from his local herbalist to further aid his circulation. We were both surprised that a conventional doctor was recognising alternative therapy.

By the summer 2006 Llewela began to notice that other families went on holiday and stayed in posh hotels and sipped Martini by the swimming pool while toping up their tan, not grafting knee high in a building site and finding grit in their sandwiches. This particular summer Llewela was not included in the building team, she was allowed time out to do nothing but study in preparation for her GSE's

Sadly this was the last holiday she spent with Julian and I at our dream home, or as Llewela would call it half renovated house.

Looking back over the last six years, a lot of teaching went on under that 800 year old Fort roof. Things that maybe the boys would never have encountered in everyday living, Llewela and I included, we would never have discovered our potential in building work if we hadn't been introduced to it. When Llewela was 16 we brought her Scooter back to England to ride for another 12 months while she was waiting for the opportunity to get her hands on a proper steering wheel.

There were occasions where she rode the Scooter to school, not to show off but only on the occasions when Julian or I were unable to take her.

To top this year, she passed 11 GCE's 12 in all as she passed one the previous year, this was enough to gain entrance to Halesowen College. The unpredictable college bus service with their rude drivers made her even more determined to pass her driving test and on the 5th May 2007 with the help of her supporting father, Llewela Jane Davies passed her driving test. Now the world was her oyster, she was not beholden to anybody anymore. Her only problem was her speed, one day while driving in this erratic manner she looked in her rear mirror to discover what she described as a pair of eyes staring back at her, so convinced that there was someone else in the car she looked round to find she was in fact alone. This shook her up considerably, and her speed was curtailed and to her surprise she discovered her fuel gage didn't plummet like it used too. Thank goodness the 'Boy racer' in her was gone she was back on track.

That was the only worry we ever had with her. No drugs, no smocking, no heavy drinking but most of all no bad behaviour in public.

It's sad to see young girls drunk late at night staggering in the street wearing next to nothing swearing like a trooper, with their self-respect in the gutter.

Since Julian had started his diabetic treatment on Valentine's Day in 2001 he started suffering from profuse perspiration but by 2006 it had become a much bigger problem even though he was taking his Oxybutynin, there was definitely something not right. As well as the sweating he was now complaining of constant abdominal pain. As I was working full time negotiating unsociable shifts, I neglected to keep a written record of what appointments Julian was attending, what results he was getting and what pattern if any was developing as a result of their recommendation. But if Julian had a 'character of a mouse' I might have been more involved with his appointments. His favourite phrase to me was, "Stop fussing" so I learnt to be quiet, and I only got involved when he asked me to.

As time went on I was getting more and more concerned about his condition, so much so, I felt if his health continued to deteriorate at this rate I couldn't see him surviving. It seemed the more diabetic treatment he took the more poorly he was becoming, with his profuse sweating, abdominal pain and low temperature not to mention his escalated glucose levels. You didn't have to be a medical genius to detect that this was one sick man!

I mentioned my concerns at work to my ward manager; she suggested I went down stairs to a diabetic clinic to see if the nurse specialist could throw any light on my dilemma. She agreed to see me after work, I poured my heart out. Word of advice; 'never disclose everything in your heart'. She appeared to be listening intently, but then leaned forward and said, "I think your husband has accepted he's a diabetic but the problem is, you haven't." I calmly stood up and thanked her for her time, but I reminded her how ill he was becoming and if he continued to take the same treatment it will one day kill him, and when it did, would she like a personal invitation to his funeral.

She reacted by saying, "There is no need to take that attitude" I couldn't continue with this conversation anymore, I slowly turned, picked up my coat and walked out. I sobbed the whole journey home, struggling with the wickedness of it all I questioned myself, "Was I really making Julian ill?" May be it was me, but I wasn't doing anything different with Julian's care, and yet Julian was defiantly become extremely ill unable to leave his own fire place because of his state.

I could not possibly go home in this state; I pulled into a layby in an attempt to pull myself together and stop this silly crying. How could she think this of me, I didn't have a single bad thought in my head towards Julian, why would I want to either physically or psychologically harm him? I loved him.

Besides, if I was trying to harm him why would I seek help or draw attention to myself? The whole thing was quite bizarre. Surely if I had any evil thoughts and wanted to harm him I'd do it in secret.

When I eventually arrived home, Julian wanted to know where I'd been. I didn't have the courage to tell him I was too upset to come home because he was becoming more ill because someone thinks I couldn't accept he was a Diabetic.

With our Easter holiday pending, Julian was worried about the journey; well, we both were because he had become quite ill on the latest Diabetic drug. He insisted on going to France, being the strong character he was, there was no point arguing I wouldn't win. He had been looking absolutely awful for weeks but just before we went on holiday he started to look a bit better, he twisted my arm into going to France but personally I thought it was a crazy idea.

I drove down to Dover, after we'd crossed the channel he volunteered to drive for a while I wasn't happy about this but he was insistent. Driving was something he enjoyed the most in life, although you'd think he would dislike it intensely on the account it was driving that put him in a wheelchair in the first place.

It did puzzle me, the further south he drove the better Julian was becoming, he wasn't perspiring as much and he seemed to be getting more colour in his cheeks something that had been lacking in him for months. I thought maybe this holiday might be the making of him.

To my surprise Julian was well enough to drive the rest of the journey, after he'd travelled our usual 800 miles to our destination and a good night sleep he confessed over breakfast the following morning how much better he felt without his medication and how he intended to go without them for a few more days. I was shocked, he'd ventured on this long journey without taking them and more to the point without discussing it with me first. I could feel my eyes widening as he was telling me, I begged him to start taking his medication again and explained he was bound to suffer for this foolish decision.

My nursing head told me he'd defiantly made the wrong decision and it could prove to have serious consequences. But I knew I couldn't force him to take his medication, as a wife or a nurse. At the same time I could not ignore how he said he felt, neither could I deny the fact that he did look so much better visually, he definitely wasn't sweating anymore and his pasty complexion had gone, but more to the point he was starting to warm up. Since he'd been on diabetic treatment he'd been cold and clammy like a wet fish and felt these weren't physical appearances one could manifest. I decided I was going to keep a very close eye on him, I confess my first observation of his improved condition was he'd stopped shouting "Shut that door, there's a draught".

Later on that morning he said "Olwen, I can't function when I'm on those drugs, I'm all doped up after taking them, the sweat just pours out of me leaving my skin feeling so cold, but it's the terrible pain in my stomach and my kidney's I can't tolerate any more"

I agreed with him he could leave them off as long as he promised to record his blood sugar readings three times a day and if things got out of hand he would go back on the drugs, he agreed.

To my amazement he became more energetic; his blood sugar readings came down, the sores on his feet started to heel and lastly his shortness of breath disappeared. Regarding his diet whether it was good or bad diet it didn't seem to make any difference at all to his blood sugar readings, there didn't seem to be a connection except there was a marked improvement when he took analgesia. Life was wonderful again; it was lovely to see him looking so well and so active. It was as if he'd come back from the dead in more ways than one, from a physical appearance and energetically. At last we had our old Julian back, Yuppie!

He was back to his welding, grinding, cutting wood and more than that he had a clear head to give instructions once again. He even said to me take a picture of me welding and grinding Olwen, the Doctors won't believe what a recovery I've made off those tablets.

In all innocence I did as he asked, I must confess his brain didn't seem mushy at all anymore.

After returning from our holiday Julian immediately made an appointment to see his GP, he wanted him see how well he looked. Have you ever heard of such a thing, going to the Doctor to show him how well you've recovered? The phrase 'Wasting Doctors time' comes to mind, but Julian wasn't one for wasting the GP's time on this occasion he said it's only fair they should see someone who has recovered instead of being sick.

He also wanted to show off that he was well enough to drive himself to the appointment, something he hadn't felt well enough or safe enough while on treatment for months.

I stayed at home holding my breath, thinking poor Julian the Doctor is going to shred him to pieces. On entering the GP's surgery, Julian stupidly announced that he he'd been off his Diabetic medication whilst on holiday, and bosting how much better he felt. The GP was not at all amused and instructed him to recommence his diabetic treatment immediately.

No amount of excitement on Julian's behalf was going to convince the GP that Julian was better off the treatment, than on it. That day, Julian came home from his appointment not full of good humour and high spirit as he'd left, but more like a scolded cat.

With a heavy heart he did as he was told and recommenced his diabetic treatment, not surprisingly within a few days he was back to square one complaining bitterly of feeling cold, pouring with perspiration, describing his internal organs as freezing cold, low temperature, high glucose levels, unable to eat because of painful abdomen. The lounge became like central Africa, it was too hot for Llewela and I to bear. We both lived in the kitchen most of the time while he parked himself in front of the fire trying to absorb as much heat as he could, but to no avail. Eventually the bed room became too cold for him to enter at night, so he started to stay down stairs where he remained all night sleeping in his wheel chair attempting to keep warm. I was absolutely over the moon when the appointment came through the post for Julian to attend an Endocrinologist clinic. Because something had to be done to stop this ridicules situation, it was quite apparent to me Julian was now obviously suffering from some sort of drug reaction. All he needed was a medication revamp, and then our family life could return to normal function just like it did in France a few weeks previous.

But in order to get to this appointment he said "I'll have to take myself off these tablets again, otherwise I won't be able to leave the fire place" As it was, he wasn't even able to leave the lounge never mind the house. Above all he wanted his 'frozen organs' issue resolved, and secondly his abdominal pain taken care of, he was finding it difficult to sit up comfortably and bending forward became impossible. After stopping his medication it took him two days before he felt well enough to venture out into the kitchen; another four days before he was warm enough to go out into the hot sunshine in the neck of the conservatory door frame. The sun was hot enough to burn anyone, but not my Julian he returned into the lounge as cold to the touch as he went out and still complaining from of his 'Frozen organs' as he started to refer to them.

Julian's first obstacle

Julian and I turned up for this appointment full of enthusiasm that this Doctor was going to turn his life round. He listened sympathetically to his plight, of his constant sweating, freezing internal organs, absence of glucose in his urine despite high blood sugar readings in his blood, high pulse, low blood pressure, high blood sugar readings in the morning, low blood sugar readings at night after eating all day, very distended and painful abdomen, very low temperature, very low blood pressure, breathlessness and finally chest pain. What the Doctor said next was shocking to both of us; if I hadn't heard him with my own ears I would not have believed Julian. Thank God I attended the appointment with him as his witness. The Doctor said "I hear what you're saying Mr Davies, but I want you to continue with these tablets" I looked at Julian and thought he was going to cry, instead he restrained himself and pleaded, "Please Doc, No I beg you I can't take any more, if I continue to take these tablets they will kill me, can't you try me on something else?"

Doctor replied "Julian you're not listening to me, not only do I want you to continue on this treatment I want you to double up on the dosage. Look I'll show you what I mean, give me your medicine boxes and I'll write on them." Julian said "That will not be necessary I do know what you mean, I'm not stupid. But if I double up on these tablets, can I come up to your waiting area for you to just look at me, you don't have to speak to me just look at me then you can see how ill I've become on your treatment" The Doctor became frosty and replied "Certainly not, you will have to make an appointment like everybody else and visit your own GP"

Julian returned home despondent with his effort and energy he'd put into getting to this appointment. The Doctor was totally oblivious to the amount of stamina poor Julian had mustered up for this short trip to his office. Firstly he had to make the psychological decision to stop taking the tablets days before, secondly he physically had to prise himself away from the warm fire, psych himself up for the transferring from his wheelchair at the bottom of the stairs on to the Stanner chair lift, still breathless and dizzy keeping his balance as he ascended to the top of the stairs, then another transfer to another wheelchair at the top of the stairs, in an exhausted state push himself into a hot steamy bathroom to master yet another transfer and plunge himself into the bath. After bathing, his forth and biggest transfer was required to pluck himself out of the bath into the wheelchair. With hardly no breath left at all in him he slowly pushed himself to the top of the stairs, by now it had become a frightening transfer back onto the Stanner chair lift at the top of the stairs. After resting to get his breath back, he descended down on the chair lift looking like death. At the bottom of the stairs his sixth transfer on to the downstairs wheel chair. At this stage he is still not dressed, he still has to struggle into a shirt and a suit before leaving the house wearing a tie, his body still dripping with perspiration from all the effort he used to bathe himself. All this had to be done, if he wanted the doctor to take him seriously and hopefully appeal to his better nature. As he always said "Nobody takes you seriously unless you're clean shaven and wearing a suit and tie". He had to dry himself again before getting dressed. His effort is not finished yet; he still had to push himself up the back path to the car park knowing he was going to endure a cool breeze on his sweaty face, then his seventh transfer into the car. Once the journey to the Hospital was over his eighth transfer had to be done in the hospital car park this time into his outside wheel chair ready for his appointment.

Why have I repeating this long saga? It's because I want others to understand what he went through to try and retrieve back his life. The likes of you and I just have to jump into a shower get dressed and go. That day Julian had to struggle to get there with his very ill and weak body.

All this effort, only to be told to carry on and double up on the same medication that he felt was harming him. It's enough to make any able person cry.

I expected Julian to come home furious and full of rage that day, instead he returned a broken man with a whipped soul. There is no denying Julian was a very ill man that day and he was dealing with a man who <u>Could</u> have given him a sparkle of light at the end of his dark tunnel, if only he could of seen fit to change his treatment. Instead he belittled him by offering him nothing short of a "suicide concoction" in my opinion. Harsh words you may think, but if a concoction of three synthetic medications are making a person very ill, why would doubling the dose make him feel any better? But worse than that, the Doctors actions that afternoon left me feeling ashamed, that I had any connection with the medical profession at all. Because of my shame, and the hopelessness Julian felt in his heart neither one of us spoke to each other for the rest of the evening, this was the first time in my 25 years of marriage I had no comforting words to offer him. The medical profession was breaking this man's spirit, yet it was the medical profession who once labelled Julian as a 'free thinker' when he was only 19 years of age, and later the same physician marvelled at his ability to bounce from one complication to another, but still retains his <u>spirit.</u>

Now 35 years later the medical profession were trying to shackle this once free spirited young man with a barbaric bit between his teeth, to force him to go down their chosen medical road. The doctor's recommendation mounted to the same physical abuse a horse experiences in over flexing of their neck and the same mental abuse they both experienced into forced submission. Just because both are considered 'acceptable universal procedures' does not make either practice humane! Why couldn't Julian have been treated with more respect, like a Native American treats his horse, free of its mouth gaging metal bits, whip and saddle? Both could have easily been treated with kind whispering words!

Julian's first Ambulance Journey

Julian submitted to his so-called new treatment, and true to form after only two days as I heard the stair lift making its descent I rushed to the bottom of the stairs to check he was all right to come down on his own, knowing how poorly and weak he was becoming on this double strength treatment.

I looked up and saw how grey Julian looked; he was having difficulty breathing and clutching his chest and pouring with sweat once again. I realised things were much worse than ever before, now I thought he was having a heart attack. He was half way down and half way up, I couldn't think what was the best route to take to go up to be near his bed or go down to be near the front door!

I decided down was best, easer for the ambulance if they needed to be called. Knowing Julian was not one for much fuss, I asked him if he wanted me to call the District Nurse. He shook his head from side to side unable to talk meaning No. I then asked if he wanted me to call the GP, again he shook his head from side to side indicating No. I then asked, "Do you want me to call for an Ambulance" he nodded a Yes gesture this time whispering with raised eyebrows, "Quick"

The Paramedics came quickly and performed an ECG, (a tracing of the heart). To both our surprise they said his heart was as strong as an ox. There was clearly something wrong, he couldn't breathe and was experiencing terrible chest and abdomen pain. Breathing in was very painful, his face was white his lips were blue and his oxygen saturation was very low. They gave him 5mg of Morphine initially then 10mg and finally 20mg which only started to take the edge off the pain. He was taken to The Royal Worcester Hospital, where he waited for hours to be seen by a Doctor.

Eventually a nurse recorded his vital statistics, temperature, pulse, blood pressure and oxygen saturations and they also tested his urine. They discovered a large amount of Protein in his urine (yet again no glucose, I know because I asked.) It was concluded that he had a urine infection because he was excreting Protein in his urine, and he was discharged with antibiotics and instructions to carry on with the same diabetic treatment as they didn't want to interfere with what his

Physician had prescribed. I don't know how I got him home, he was so ill. He was not only weak but limp like a rag doll; he still looked in heart attack mode to me, white face, and bubbles of perspiration on his face, dark under his eyes and a blue tinge to his lips. How I got him out of the passenger side into the wheel chair I'll never know because he normally found passenger side very difficult. It was more of a dragging process really than a lift.

Once home he did as the A&E staff recommended and recommenced his diabetic medication as normal. At 6pm that evening he took his tablets, within half an hour the symptoms had returned.

Again I asked him, "Shall I call the Ambulance? Julian said "No I'd be too embarrassed to call the Ambulance out twice in 24hrs for what they think is a urine infection". We both sat up all night in the lounge, waiting for day break or at least to witness improvement in Julian's condition.

While I was waiting I couldn't help thinking, how a urine infection could cause him such severe chest pain that warranted 20mg of Morphine, it didn't make sense to me.

Julian's second Ambulance Journey

The following morning May 7th 2007 he asked me for his Diabetic medication with his breakfast, I tried to reason with him that it wasn't the wisest decision to take them. His argument was, maybe it's not the medication that's making me ill, may be its <u>Not</u> taking them that's making me ill. By now I was getting angry I could see there was a definite pattern and with a raised voice I shouted "But you are taking them, that's my point". He stupidly took them against my better judgment, and just as I predicted within twenty minutes he became extremely ill once more. It was obvious, the time span between taking the tablets and their reaction was now getting shorter, and his condition was become more critical. I thought the world had gone mad, why wasn't anyone listening to me and Julian now? At this stage I took over the situation and rang the Ambulance myself without even consulting Julian, I had too this time he couldn't even communicate with me at all. When the Ambulance arrived, the first thing I asked for was for Morphine. The two girls said they were just two drivers and they couldn't administer any drugs let alone Morphine and besides they didn't have it on board. Julian was in too much pain to be moved this time, how do I know this? Because of Julian's face of horror and his frightened wide eyes told me, his hand gesture halting us not to move him. They rang the Ambulance service to ask for another Ambulance to take a wheelchair with the patient in a sitting position. Another ambulance arrived, again just drivers, no Paramedics. Julian was pushed in his wheelchair with excruciating chest pain, with no morphine for pain relief. His wheelchair was clamped down in the back of this empty van with no escort, as far as I could ascertain, because both drivers climbed into the front cab. I was told to drive in my own car behind; this was the first horrendous journey of many I was to undertake, while in charge of a vehicle. As far as I knew Julian might have been having a heart attack in the back of this van on his own, in a sitting position with no voice to attract their attention. I refer to it as a van because it didn't look like an Ambulance. He must of felt so isolated with no pain relief, no one to comfort him verbally not even holding his hand, because when we arrived at the hospital both lady's exited the cab from the front, just as they did outside our home.

This time they bypassed casualty and took him directly to a medical ward, his biggest problem was not being able to breathe at all when he lay down. Again he tried to explain to the doctor that his organs felt so swollen and painful, it gave him the feeling his organs were pushing his lungs and heart into a confined space stopping him breathing when he lay down. He had to sit on the edge of the bed to survive really, he was prescribed oxygen and we were left to our own devices for most of the morning while I supported his balance. At one stage his oxygen levels dipped to 66% not knowing what else to do I shouted "Sats 66%" all the staff came running. Julian's eyes were bulging, his lips were blue his complexion was white and he gasped "Olwen I'm dying" A Doctor (not Julian's Consultant I might add) put his head through the gap in the curtain and said "He's got pneumonia", on the strength of this 'off the cuff remark' a junior Doctor without examining him prescribed Julian intravenous antibiotics.

I begged him to reconsider because he was allergic to Penicillin and any antibiotic made him feel unwell causing him to have diarrhoea and in some cases severe excoriation of the skin. He was not strong enough to negotiate unnecessary toilet habits. As I predicted the treatment gave him terrible diarrhoea, the nurses out of fear transferred him immediately into a side ward and Barrier Nursed him as if he had C.diff. Needless to say the tests proved to be negative.

Julian's condition became much worse and on 8th May it became apparent his Gamma GT was now elevated to 612, normal ranges should read between 0-45. What was going on?

Someone's listening

After being in hospital for seven days an Asian Doctor attended Julian, explaining he was on ward experience and was based at one of the Birmingham's Teaching Hospitals.

While the Asian Doctor took some medical history off Julian I filled in when Julian was too breathless to speak for himself. Then the Doctor asked me to step outside while he spoke to Julian alone. I didn't mind. After he finished questioning Julian he took some blood samples and beckoned me to return to Julian's bed side, but as he was leaving I felt some hostility towards me from the Doctors mannerism.

As I squatted back down at Julian's bed side, I could see he was exhausted from talking so I didn't quiz him why I was asked to leave, but when Julian regained his breath he volunteered to me the Doctors suspicion. Julian had found the Doctors line of questioning disturbing. He said, "Olwen he wanted to know who had been preparing my meals, and who gave me my tablets at home".

Julian had asked the Doctor, where his line of questioning was going.

The Doctor explained that Julian was portraying a picture of being poisoned. Julian said, "I can assure you that my wife would not do that".

That afternoon my life turned upside down, my future was pending this blood result. The consequences could be quite catastrophic for all three of us. If for some stupid reason it proved positive then Julian would never trust me again, and of course he would throw me out of our family home, Llewela would disown me because how could she befriend a mother who tried to poison her own father, I would definitely lose my job, how was I going to survive on my own? Worst still 'attempted murder' surely carries a prison sentence!

Luckily for me Roy Langford a friend of Julian's visited, I quickly ran across to the ward I normally worked on to seek refuge, comfort, support and reassurance that everything would be ok. As I unveiled my predicament to the Ward Sister she said, "Oh! My gosh Olwen, you need to hurry back to him, he sounds as if he's going into multi-organ failure" I did as she suggested and ran back to him squatting by his feet for the remainder of the afternoon neither of us speaking to each other, just praying. I don't know what was going through his mind but all I wanted to say was please believe me I've never tried to harm you. I can also remember thinking, if his organs were really packing up, shouldn't he be on an Intensive Care Unit? At quarter to five that afternoon the same Asian Doctor returned, Julian was still in the same position as he had been for the last seven days and seven nights balancing on the edge of the bed. As I squatted in front of him to maintain his balance the Doctor gently pushed me to one side and took over by gripping his upper arms shaking him saying, "Julian, Julian can you hear me? Julian's eyes were rolling, he was barely conscious his head was flopping around, dripping in sweat. He shook him again saying, Julian it's not your wife that's making you ill it's the diabetic treatment do you understand me?"

Julian's head raised a little, his lips all swollen and dribbling he managed in a low husky voice a quiet "Yes" The Doctor continued "I want you to promises me you'll never, ever take these diabetic medication ever again, do you understand me, they are destroying your organs." Julian nodded, but was unable to speak further. The Doctor explained he could not stay long as he was in a rush to catch the six o'clock train back to Birmingham, but he would be crossing off all of his diabetic treatment before he left.

I don't know how Julian felt on hearing this good news; I just hoped his good news hadn't come too late for him. As for me, it was the best news ever quickly changing into mixed emotions, what I really wanted to do was scream from the nearest mountain top because I was no longer a suspect in Julian's illness, but I was immediately brought back to earth by the fact Julian still needed me.

As Julian did not have his six o'clock diabetic tablets, neither was he offered his ten o'clock tablets and already he was starting to recover. By eleven o'clock he was able to have a bit of a conversation, he commented that he could feel the poison leaving his body and his mind was becoming clear enough to make decisions. He was taking charge of my life once more, he suggested I went home to Kidderminster to sleep safe in the knowledge that he would not be administered any more medication that night. I did as he asked after begging for some more pillows to make sure Julian remained in an upright position until the morning. Out of exhaustion I did sleep and caught up with some much needed rest. The following morning I was awakened at six o'clock by the telephone ringing, at first I could barely make out who was speaking the voice was so faint but I eventually realised it was Julian. His voice sounded so distressed, I told him to ring the nurse call bell; he said he couldn't reach it. I then told him to shout for the nurses, he said he had no volume in his voice for them to hear him. I said "I'll be there as soon as I can".

In my panic I jumped out of bed got dressed and drove straight to Worcester instead of ringing the ward first to let them know that he was in difficulties.

I arrived on the ward in twenty minutes that's including parking the car and running from the car park up to the ward. I arrived on the ward with the 'wind in my fist' as they say, I must have looked wild to the nurses huddled round the desk receiving reports from the night staff. As I approached the desk, the Ward Sister greeted me with a calm voice "Good morning, are you all right Olwen?" I said, "No Julian's in trouble he can't breathe, can someone help me sit him up. He's just rung me at home on the mobile phone"

One of the nurses got up and rushed to my aid where we found him flat on his back, without a monkey pole to aide him. He was back in his old familiar state, with a very hard distended abdomen which he could hardly bend with, clammy skin, pale complexion, blue lipped but more distressing than all, he had difficulty breathing As soon as we sat him up he started to breathe easier, but the other complaints remained. I was shocked to find him in such a state, if the medication had been stopped then my theory was wrong that the medication was making him ill. I couldn't believe I had been barking up the wrong tree. I took most of the morning to bed bath him, change the bed linen, shave him, wash, his hair and the best treatment of all he said was cleaning his teeth. He used to say, "I'm glad you force me to have a wash I can't believe how much better a bit of water can make you feel" Later in the morning a nurse accidentally left his drug chart on his bed side cabinet and to my horror I found he had been given Avandia that morning, the Doctor had not crossed this one off in the rush to catch his train back to Birmingham. When I mentioned this to the Doctor on call, he immediately crossed off the drug. The following morning, I believe it was the Professor who headed the Consultant ward round, asked his team who had stopped Julian's treatment? Another Doctor pointed out the blood result from Birmingham Poison unit. He then questioned who had requested it, the Doctors name was mentioned and unfortunately I cannot recall his name. The Doctors surrounding Julian's bed that morning seem to recognise the Doctor in question, shoulders were raised and a 'fate de complete' gesture was made no one overrode this Doctors decision by recommending the treatment or suggested alternative treatment. Julian and I then presumed that 'No treatment' was the best treatment this time.

Both Julian and I witnessed and handled this blood result; I waved the result in front of Julian saying, "This is your ticket to freedom Julian. I only hope it will be filed in the appropriate place in your notes and not get lost."

Hind sight is a wonderful thing if only Julian or I had thought of paying for a photocopying of this haematology result at the time or at least insisted that the result was selotaped into his notes, Julian's life could have been very different, but we didn't and this is where the saga begins.

Julian's condition improved so much in the next few days, it really was incredible.

The visitor

During this stay in Hospital before he turned the corner, one of the The Buffalo Brothers visited Julian called Dave Moses his title that summer was "The Grand Primo of England for 2007" Sadly Julian had no recollection of his visit, even though he stayed all afternoon and Julian joined in the conversation with only short sentences. His lack of memory of such an impressive visitor just proves how ill he must have been, because when Julian was well he had a brilliant mind and a brilliant memory but sadly not of this hospital visitor. Sorry Dave

Photo of Dave Moses the Grand Primo of England for 2007
with his supporting Lady Sue.

To emphasise how the treatment affected him, Julian went from being almost incoherent to well enough to be discharged home only two days after the mysterious Doctor stopped the treatment that he felt was poisoning Julian's organs. Although Julian still looked very ill, pale, thin and waxy I was so excited to see him on the mend; it was as if we had been given a second chance in life. If Julian was been made ill by the medication his poor body was taking a beating in the name of medicine. After 11 days of hospitalisation on the 18th May 2007 Julian was coming home, as we were leaving I asked the nurses for the name of the Doctor who had in our eyes saved Julian's life. The nurses could not help, not even with the aid of the haematology blood result slip all the nurses on duty that day including myself tried to decipher his signature on the pathology report, again proving its existence including there was such a Doctor. We wanted to thank and recognise his vidulance over Julian's case.

Once home he was too weak to do anything other than concentrate on pushing himself in the wheel chair from one room to the other. After eight weeks of this weakness on 19th July 2007 following his home coming, Julian asked me to take him to the GP practice. I asked, "Why Julian, I'm sure the Doctor will be willing to do a home visit. "You have been seriously ill Julian; you've experienced a near multi organ failure"

His reply was, "If you take me, he can then see how breathless I am on a simple excursion" At the appointment Julian insensitively asked the GP if he could be referred to a chest specialist, the GP asked "Why?" Julian with his blue lips and diminished voice whispered "Because I'm finding it difficult to breathe" The Doctor defended himself with, "I can't just do that without some sort of proof that you require a medical opinion" Julian then replied, "What do I have to do to get a medical opinion?" He was told he need an x-ray first, to which Julian agreed and I was asked if I could take him to the x-ray department on the way home. With great difficulty I managed, and then returned home to wait for the results thinking the GP would get back in touch with us some time the following week as it was now late Friday afternoon. But to our surprise the GP rang that evening at six o'clock informing Julian that his plural cavity round one of his lungs was full of fluid. A bed had been reserved for him at Worcester Hospital could he get there right away as it needed to be drained as soon as possible. Julian told the GP that after the excursion he'd endured that day, he hadn't any strength left in his body to do another transfer into the car and that he was all 'puffed out', but he was willing to have another go first thing in the morning? The GP re-negotiated with Worcester Hospital and then relayed the message back to Julian, confirming that the following morning would be fine.

To save energy he slept in his wheelchair that night to be sure he could go for this much needed treatment. After a sloppy wash and a change of clothes we left early, Julian battled with his breathing as we both struggling with his transfers in and out of the car. We arrived on the ward at the appointed hour of nine o'clock as arranged and were escorted into a side room. There the staff wanted him to sit upright in bed leaning over a table, in order for the medical Doctor to insert this "underwater drainage seal" in effect what it is, is a thick tube entering the chest wall from the lower rib cage area leading into a sterile bottle, not unlike a demy jar that's used for making homemade wine. (You may recall I mentioned Julian had one of these inserted into his right lung before, way back at the time of his big accident in 1972) Julian explained that he didn't have enough balance to sit up in bed, partly due to his paralysis but also due to previous hip surgery he'd had in 1989. He assured them he definitely could not be relied on to sit perfectly still during such a procedure. The Doctor and Julian negotiated other tactics then finally agreed to drop the back rest of the wheel chair down and he would attempt the procedure with Julian leaning over a bed side table enabling Julian to remain in the comport of his own wheelchair.

The procedure was an immediate success; Julian's lung drained 3 litres of transparent lime green fluid instantly. It happened so quickly that he started to feel faint; I called the nurse in case he did faint and dislodged the tube in his chest. But with a lot of shouting, "Julian, Julian can you hear us" he slowly came round we could see that his blood pressure had dropped considerably but once the tube was clamped for a while his blood pressure soon stabilised. A few hours later the tube was removed and a check x-ray was done to reassure the medical staff that the lung had not collapsed following the procedure. All was well and by five o'clock that evening less than seven hours later, Julian was heading for home, breathing like he normally did. So never let it be said that Julian Davies was a wimp, next time you see three litres of fluid compare it to 5 pints of beer lined up on the bar and image all that in one lung capacity. No wonder he was striving to breath.

This was a person who requested to be taken to the GP so that he could see how breathless he was on an excursion. He disliked being ill so much and took life to the extreme to avoid it. So whenever he said, he wasn't feeling very well what he actually meant was he was feeling 'very ill'.

He Conformed to the end

Once Julian was home he continued to be a very good patient still sticking to his Diabetic diet, even though he had been advised not to continue with Diabetic medication. Once home his GP referred him to a Diabetic Nurse Specialist to commence him on Insulin therapy. Julian was not keen about injecting himself for two reasons, the first being the obvious puncturing his own skin daily and the other was he was confused that if Diabetic medication was harming him he was concerned Insulin therapy might harm him too. But he wasn't a stupid man he was well aware that his glucose levels did still spike on occasions, so he decided to give the insulin a chance.

Still holding the medical profession in high esteem he thought the specialist would know best.

The first Insulin he was prescribed was Lantus, he was able to tolerate this for a few weeks then the old routine set in, cold and frozen internal organs, high pulse of 140, low blood pressure as low as 66/33, higher blood sugar readings, sores started to develop on his feet again, hard and very distended abdomen, complaining of painful internal organs, poor urine output—black urine on occasions, respirations raised to 35-40 a minutes, breathlessness, bubbling chest—bringing up clear froth but no sigh of chest infection, this low temperature of 34 degrees was of hypothermic level which meant the house had returned to its inferno state again in an effort to maintain his temperature. His profuse perspiration didn't help to keep him warm at all; its very design is to help keep you cool. It was sad to see his drug reaction was actually making him 'Disable' unable to do a thing for himself just hogging the gas fire. Physically he looked wrecked with his dripping hair and soaking wet cloths sticking to him. Amazingly throughout all of these reactions, he still didn't have glucose in his urine. We both found this very odd, strange or even mysterious; I don't know how to describe its absence.

Eventually he rang the Diabetic Nurse Specialist at Worcester Hospital for some guidance.

She initially asked him to go to visit her in person, but unlike when he insisted I took him to the GP this time he informed her he was too ill to travel. She then advised him to stop the Insulin, and she would advise the GP by phone to prescribe different Insulin, it was agreed between them to do it this way.

Consequently while Julian was waiting for the new Insulin prescription to come through the post, his condition improved once again. So much so he even venture out from the lounge into the kitchen where it was considerably cooler.

His second prescribed insulin was called Nova Rapid, Julian would be able to yet again tolerate the new Insulin for about two weeks, but then the same old routine would repeat itself and our home would become the familiar house of inferno once more. I tried not to be unkind, but I couldn't take care of him like I wanted to because the room was too hot for me to bear. As he got weaker and weaker he was too ill to wash himself and relied on me to 'chair wash' him by the fire. I'd have to draw the curtains and wear very little while he kept close proximity with the fire. If you haven't experienced this tropical exposure, I trust no one will criticise my behaviour.

There were times when I would leave the kitchen via the back door walk round the house and re-enter the house through the front door in order to gain access to the upstairs toilet, to avoid opening and shutting the lounge doors causing him unnecessary cold draughts on his cold clammy skin. Eventually the third prescription arrived by post, to try yet another Insulin. Now Julian was becoming reluctant to try any more drugs, repetition of a pattern was forming.

On drugs he became very ill, off drugs he rejuvenated.

This time the Insulin was called Noro Mix 30. And true to form this insulin produced the same side effects except he noticed the reactions were starting after a week instead of after two weeks. This time the conversation Julian had with the nurse at Worcester was very different. She said, "I have only got one other type of Insulin left Julian, if this doesn't work then I give up because although there are many other Insulin's on the market I have spent a lot of time and effort cross referencing the same carriers for the different insulin's.

You seem to have a reaction or resistance to something and I assumed you were allergic to one of the carriers in the Insulin, not so much the insulin. But if you're having the same side effects with the Diabetic oral medication, maybe I can't help you because you should feel instantly better on this treatment, not worse. Nobody should feel worse".

Julian felt awful that this lady was trying so hard to help him behind the scene as it were, that this time he was going to try very hard to make this Insulin work. Try as he might it was no good less than a week this time and he was making this dreaded phone call informing her that her last hope had failed to suit him. She told him there was no need to apologise he couldn't help the fact he was reacting to something. She suggested that as he had tried everything she had to offer, but as he always reported he felt better without treatment, maybe that's exactly what he should do. She reiterated once again that diabetic patients should always feel instantly better on treatment not worst. This time Julian told her, "Not only do I feel worse on treatment in fact I feel the treatment is killing me." When he put his feeling over this strongly she then reacted by saying, "In that case Julian, you might be on the verge of experiencing another multi-organ failure, I advise you to stop the treatment immediately as it is quite obvious to me that you CAN survive without treatment".

She wished Julian well in the future as she was leaving that after noon, and they hadn't appointed anyone in her place. With her leaving her post that day it later became a problem when other consultants were trying to contact her to see if she could verify her findings. I was sure she must have documented her telephone conversations with Julian somewhere, together with the verbal advice she was giving him periodically, but nothing could ever be found. A few weeks after he was given permission to stop all Insulin, his energy levels raised simultaneous that it caused him such a buzz, he impulsively booked Ferry tickets to cross the Channel once again. His hunger for doing physical activities was fired up again. There was so much to do and finish, illness didn't really fit in to his life style. Returning to France was one of them.

This is a photo of Julian taken not long after
his insulin reaction.

He looks so pale, thin and scraggly round the neck and his hair also became thin and balding on top he was still freezing cold to the touch even the hot sun couldn't warm him up. He was so lucky to have survived this incident and I thanked God daily for sparing him.

After stopping all treatment his glucose levels did come down, but they were still not in acceptable ranges. The mystery question was, why did they come down without treatment?

Julian remained 'treatment free' for 15 months, but that didn't stop Julian wondering why his body retained so much glucose in his blood stream and why it appeared all treatment disagreed with him so violently. He often used to say, "My gut feeling is, I'm producing enough insulin myself so why can't my body keep my sugar levels down—something isn't right there must be a missing link"! Try as he might, he couldn't think what it was. He wasn't stupid by any means, during the last eight years of his life he had obtained a Certificate in Personal Computer Repair, a Higher National Diploma in Computing, and a Certificate in Teaching Adult Learners and finally the icing on the cake was when he was awarded a Bachelor of Science in Information Technology. He worked very hard for this degree but can you believe he achieved all these qualifications while struggle with the drug reaction, organ destruction and psychological pressure to keep taking the diabetic treatment.

Recently my sister reminded me of a scene captured on camera at the end of August 2007. This was only three months after Julian had survived the near multi organ failure. We were attending my brother Glyns 'Birthday Barbeque' at our parent's home.

While we were all congregated in the orchard just finishing singing the traditional Happy Birthday song (By the way were you aware we should be paying Royalties to sing this song, but I'm sure were looking forward to the day we can sing it in 2016 with no repercussions) the ceremonial birthday cake was brought out with its candles. As Gweno went round afterwards offering everyone a piece of cake she drew back from Julian saying, "You can't have a piece can you, you're a diabetic." Julian raised his arm in the air and called out, "Excuse me everybody, I'd like a bit of attention please, I have an announcement to make. I want to inform you all that since my last Hospitalisation I am now officially NOT being treated with diabetic medication of any sort anymore" First of all I thought Julian was going to make a speech about the birthday boy, and secondly he caught us all by surprise by saying what he did. Incidentally if I had thought differently, I would have corrected him in front of everybody and voiced my opinion. But I didn't, because he was right. The Doctor at Worcester Hospital had told him to stop the treatment, the Diabetic Nurse Specialist Nurse at Worcester had told him to stop the treatment and the Physician at outpatient clinic had told him to continue with no treatment and they would adopt the wait and watch strategy, lastly one of the GPs wrote in his notes "stopped treatment" "Looks dreadful". So yes on this occasion Julian could have his cake and eat it. I say 'that day' because ironically he didn't care too much for sweet things he was more of a cheese and biscuit man really. He did eat it on that occasion because he was allowed to and besides he was making a statement.

Once the medical profession discharged him from all treatment, I set about trying to build up his frail body. I don't mean making him fat I mean correcting his damaged organs such as his liver. We knew his liver function test went higher than 600 and, at the time his half-sister had researched that milk thistle could help heal his liver. Luckily the liver is a very forgiving organ and if the offending substance is withheld it will rejuvenate itself. I continued to give him Horse chestnut Extract tablets to improve his circulation as instructed by the Vascular Consultant.

I also gave him vitamin C and Zink for his thinning hair, something else that happened following his multi-organ failure, which his GP reminded me that is what happens to men of his age. Surprisingly his hair become darker and thicker, in conjunction with that not only did the hair on his head thicken but on his legs, chest and back as well. I also gave him Dandelion Root capsule to detoxify his Spleen, Pancreas and liver. I wouldn't have believed the speed of his recovery if I hadn't witnessed it myself. Once he was fully recovered I eased off with all the herbal therapy, I thought there was no point taking something for the sake of it.

The other thing I did to help ease his discomfort was reflexology. With no training only a good book as a guide I set about massaging his head, shoulders, hands and feet.

The earliest evidence of reflexology was discovered in a tomb in Egypt dating 2500 BC with the inscription translated, 'Do not hurt me'. Native American also used it for healing, believed to be passed on to them by the Incas.

Once I learnt what part of the foot affected which organs I set about having a go nearly every evening. Why am I mentioning this, you may ask? Taking into account Julian was paralysed from the sternum down, so when I massage his liver area on the soul of his foot one would assume he couldn't feel it due to the paralysis but when he said "Oh! That's lovely, that feels as if you're actually massaging my liver, it's so soothing" I couldn't believe it, bearing in mind he had his eyes closed throughout. He had no way of knowing what I was doing as the book was out of his reach. Saying nothing, I set about conducting a little experiment of my own, after being so ill he had a lot of healing to do. I then massaged over the stomach area of the foot, this time he said it was like a tickling feeling in his stomach but pleasant, when I massage his lungs and diaphragm area he instantly withdrew a sharp and very deep intake of breath, he startled me so much I asked if he was alright. He said, "Yes, I just felt this sudden urge to take in a really deep intake of breath"

I then explained what had taken place, after that experimental every night he used to say "Don't tell me what your massaging I'll tell you" It became his guessing game, as we watched television in the evening, amusingly he was right every time. How bizarre, maybe there is something to this alternative therapy after all! But more to the point, shouldn't the physiotherapists be looking into it and conducting some research! I hope I'm not inflicting false hope to people with paralyzed limbs this book is just about Julian.

His second encounter with Insulin Crisis

While transferring from the driver's seat to the wheelchair one day, Julian scratched his bottom on a sharp piece of bad welding on the wheelchair frame. For a Paraplegic or a Tetraplegia to have any blemish at all on their bottoms was sacrilege. It's like someone having a sore on their foot and their job entailed wearing hobnail boots all day. You know both situations will get worse unless both have rest from the pressure to aid healing. Julian and I were devastated over this scratch knowing he'd have to serve a punishment for this by going on bed rest maybe even be Hospitalised for weeks on end, and Llewela and I would have to survive on our own without his wise guidance. We always did manage, but it was always nicer to have him around.

Our fears were correct, and on 11th April 2008 Julian was admitted to Oswestry Hospital, and on the 14th he was taken to theatre for surgical repair of this scratch.

Prior to going to theatre he was very anxious to speak to the Anaesthetist regarding his raised glucose levels. He expressed a wish to the Ward Consultant not to be given Insulin under any circumstances; neither did he want any Intravenous Antibiotics while he was under the anaesthetic. The consultant assured him that the discussion was between the Anaesthetist and Julian, but he could not foresee a problem as he was down to have local anaesthetic any way.

As I was working a late shift that day, I left Julian in the safe hands of the medical profession and hurriedly drove back to Kidderminster in time for my shift. The Anaesthetist did not see Julian pre-operatively as it is not customary for patients who are listed for local anaesthetic to be seen by an Anaesthetist. In other words there is nothing to assess or discuss, its only common curtsy for the Anaesthetist to introduce them self-prior to surgery.

Julian was disappointed that his request to see the Anaesthetist wasn't granted, he wanted his assurance he would not have the medication in question. On the other hand he knew it was documented on his medication notes that he was allergic to all diabetic medication including all human insulin. And after all he was wearing his red arm band stating he was allergic to Insulin and a host of antibiotics. As he was greeted in the anteroom in the theatre department, Julian immediately expressed a wish not to have these drugs. At this stage Julian was having a local Anaesthetic; I can only assume that the anaesthetist was getting irritated with Julian being insistent of refusing insulin. The Anaesthetist mockingly said to him, "How can you possibly be allergic to Insulin when it's a natural hormone in our body that we all need to survive" Julian understood that, and could not defend himself any more than he did. He eventually reassured himself with the fact he was wearing a 'Red Allergy band' which all staff were aware of its implications. The next thing Julian knew was he was waking up in recovery ward, feeling very ill and out of sorts. He was confused with time and space, thinking he was going to be fully awake throughout the procedure he couldn't understand why he was struggling to wake up and having difficulty breathing in the recovery ward instead of back on the Spinal Unit. As he was waking up he started complaining of chest tightness, shortness of breath, his Blood Pressure was 220/160, his pulse was 121 and he was perspiring profusely with face flushing and heavy-headedness. Strangely his oxygen saturation was 100%, on examination his lungs were clear with good air entry, however oxygen 3 litres was prescribed, and Diazepam and Amlodipine was given intravenously, an ECG was requested which proved his heart was normal. They also gave him GTN spray to try and reduce the tightness in his chest, which made his chest pain worst.

Julian was escorted back to the ward still feeling very ill. I contacted him by text, in my supper break from work to see how his procedure had gone. He rang me back on the ward to say, "I think they've given me Insulin Olwen" I got cross mainly because he'd rung me on the ward and secondly because of his vagueness. I asked him "What do you mean You Think you've had insulin, they either did or they didn't give you insulin. Didn't you have the operation under local anaesthetic why, can't you remember?" He confessed, "I must have had a General Anaesthetic I was out cold, I can't remember a thing" As I was working until 10pm that evening, there was nothing I could do until after my shift. When I arrived home I rang the ward to enquire about Julian's condition, after all it was only a minor procedure he was having performed, and that was to be conducted under local anaesthetic. The ward sister told me he still wasn't very well, but he had some sort of reaction to something in theatre. She said, "Unfortunately Julian is confusing matters by insisting he feels as if he's had Insulin and Antibiotics while under the influence of the anaesthetic" The Ward Sister tried to reassure me, of course he had not been given either and besides he had an allergy band on to indicate that he shouldn't have it.

Julian told me that night the Doctors mulled round his bed for hours waiting for his condition to improve. To both our surprise the Anaesthetist didn't return to his bed side that night, but gave the Doctors attending him instructions over the phone as to what to do! Later on that evening after settling the other patients down the Ward Sister was gathering up her paper work including Julian's operation notes from the printer, when to her horror she noticed Julian's theatre notes stated he was given Insulin and Antibiotics in theatre including having a General Anaesthetic. To be fair to the Sister she did return to Julian's bedside and confessed to him that his gut feeling was correct, he had indeed received Insulin, Antibiotics and the procedure had been conducted under General Anaesthetic.

Julian struggled with his high blood pressure throughout the night including his chest pain; he was given GTN spray on three more occasions that evening the second one at nine o'clock, the third at ten thirty and the forth one at one o'clock in the morning. Each time he complained it was making his chest pain worst, he later told me that he declined the GTN after the fourth time. If Julian was telling the truth, I'm asking all medical professional of all ranks, "Why" why did the GTN spray exacerbate his chest pain? It should have eased his pain, was it possible he was developing a drug reaction or allergy to abundance or all drugs including GTN spray?

Julian was eventually discharged from Hospital on 7th May 2008, which was 27 days after his admission, for a procedure that should have only taken a couple of days.

His blood pressure remained high in the regions of 193/110 following his 'Insulin and Antibiotic episode' In his discharged letter to the GP it states; 'he had episodes of chest pain and shortness of breath during his stay, he is discharged on Lisinopril Anti-hypertensive tablets' (Blood pressure medication) I felt it was a very vague note, considering how ill he'd been in their care!

His blood pressure remained high for months after he came home, but was eventually brought under control with antihypertensive. I'm glad to report that his GP stopped the hypertensive once it was with in normal range.

Following his discharge from Hospital the other lasting after effects Julian suffered from after his 'Insulin incident' was deteriation of his hand writing. To be fair it had become absolutely diabolical. On the first visit back to his Buffalo Lodge meeting, someone mocked the scriber asking "Whose craw feet scrawl is this, I can hardly read it."? Julian confessed it was his, he informed them he felt that when his Blood Pressure went so high on his recent Hospital admission, he felt he'd suffered a mild stroke. They all laughed and said "Don't be so daft", he defended himself by saying, "It's true, I choke on the simplest of things now even my own saliva, my memory is shot and I drop things constantly from my right hand. I think my blood pressure went up too high and for too long"

Who knows, he may have had one and it was never investigated. If I've said it once I've said it many times, he was nearly always right and he may have been right on this occasion too.

I can remember thinking once; the only way we will ever know is if he has a post-mortem!

Julian was automatically sent a follow up appointment for scar line inspection following the operation he had in April. I attended this appointment with him; the Doctor was pleased with the scar line but expressed a worry, "I hope it hasn't healed too quick Julian, sealing a sinus underneath"!

Life was back to normal once more, Julian taking a big interest in Llewela's education helping her sort out her apartment in Oxford, eager to give her useful University advice as he had already trod that path himself four years previously.

After obtaining BTEC at college she was accepted at Oxford Brook University and on 16th September 2008 (Julian's birthday) she began her 3 long year's stint in preparation for achieving her Degree. She moved down to Oxford a few weeks before University life started, she wanted to settle in so she could give her studying her undivided attention.

She chose not to live in the Hall of Residence, instead she moved into an Apartment a bus ride away Oxford is more of a bicycle city really. As the apartment was new, it didn't have a floor covering so Llewela asked Julian to help her put a laminating floor down. He agreed he would the following weekend. The apartment was two floors up, although Llewela had warned us there was no lift one would think with a brand new block of apartments the law would dictate there should be a lift, but we managed as usual. Llewela and Kevin at the back of the wheelchair with myself at the front lifting in tandem on Julian's instruction shouting, 'Lift' which we did one step at a time.

Once in the flat, while we were sipping coffee Julian was laying out the tools in order of the jobs on the bench. The bench saw, the electric jig saw, tape measure, set square, pencils, Stanley knife and protective goggles. He started to dish out instructions on how to best start the job. Llewela realising he was instructing her said, "Wow, I'm not laying the floor, you are Dad" He protested saying, "No, how will you learn, if I do it?" Kevin wanting to appear eager asked "What shall I do?" Llewela was getting involved in a bit of a must win over father mode here, said, "Go and make more coffee Kev" Poor Kev had been demoted to a 'tea boy' before he'd even started.

Under the supervision of Julian, Llewela as usual did a great job. Later Kevin, her boyfriend did come up to speed and regained credibility from a coffee boy by doing a few tricky cuts with the jigsaw. In fact Julian complimented him by saying, "I couldn't have done better myself Kev".

On the third weekend after the bedroom and lounge had been completed there only remained the hall to be done. As the last board required about 11 tricky cuts with the jig saw, Julian appointed Llewela to do the job. The two wills of iron clashed and they went into battle like a couple of Scottish Highland Deer's, one claiming the job could be done, the other claiming the job could definitely not be done. Kevin and I quickly retreated into the kitchen to make more coffee, we knew our place.

Llewela could be heard to start on the job, either temper or deliberate bad workmanship spoilt the first few attempts of the cut. Julian halted the operation to explain, "Llewela, when this floor is finished, will you be bringing University friends back here?" Llewela replied "Yes" What about your college friends, may be school friends and friends from work? Again she agreed they would all in turn come to visit at some stage.

He then asked, would she be boasting to them about who laid the floor. She replied, "Off course I will" Julian asked "So! Who will you say made such a shoddy job here by the door way, will you admit it was you or blame me for being a bad teacher?"

With a deep breath, and silent treatment she went ahead and did a fantastic job. After the mess was all cleared up we all sat down to a nice meal. About seven o'clock Julian and I thought we'd better head for home and make tracks up the motorway. As Llewela was pushing Julian's wheel chair past the offending corner Llewela said, "Dad I'm so glad you forced me to do a good job there, I'm rather proud of myself."

He spun the wheel chair round so fast and said in a sharp stern voice, pointing to the corner of the door frame, "That's exactly how you should feel about every job you do Llewela, PROUD".

Sadly this was Julian's last visit to her apartment, only two months later, Julian died.

What a lasting memory for a young girl to have of her father at the tender age of just 18, who was about to embark on her University life and beyond. To be proud of your workmanship always, because you never ever know who might admire it one day, is a great legacy?

You may wonder why have I mention Llewela's accomplishments so much if the book is meant to be about Julian. Well! If I had not married such a dynamic man and she had to rely on her mother for life guidance I don't think she would have achieved as much academically or practically in life. I don't mean to underestimate Llewelas intelligence but she may not have experienced the enthusiasm and the hunger for life that she can now carry with her whichever path she chooses.

He believed the other great gift you can bestow on a child besides Education is 'love for life'.

There are many many untold story's connected with Julian's past but I just wanted to highlight some of them to prove that in my eyes he had been an excellent Father.

Do you recall when he asked God for his help to teach her everything he knew, I think he achieved that, he taught her everything she needed to know in a rush so that she could survive without him.

For those who never met Julian. I hope I have painted an accurate picture of his life.

For those who did know him. I don't have to remind you he did not suffer fools gladly.

Life was very good to both of us up until Julian experienced that first blip with diabetic treatment in 2007. Then life was kind to us once again until the autumn of 2008, we pulled ourselves together after accepting Llewela was not coming home to live again as she left to go to Oxford. Although we found our lives empty we tried to chivvy ourselves along by attending social events. One of the celebrations we had to look forward to was the arrival of his half-sisters new baby girl. Julian had been asked to be the Godfather, for weeks he refused because he felt he was too old for the post but I reassured him by reminding him that although the Spinal Injury Physician could only promise him ten years survival in 1972, he had in fact out witted him by 28 years extra survival. And who was to say he could live as long as the next man especially now the diabetic treatment had been stopped. And, hadn't God promised us all three score and ten years life on earth, in my reckoning that's seventy years. After much persuasion he agreed to become the Godfather to his niece, a responsibility he would have taken very seriously had time been kinder to him.

The beauty of <u>our</u> lives is that we don't know the length of our string, poor Julian had to live every minute of his life on the edge. How dare any human being put a time scale on any body's life, even those with cancer? He must have felt on occasions that he had a time bomb attached to his side, or worst still living on death row for the last 38 years. What a way to live, he never showed any fear of this, but he must have thought of it from time to time. We on the other hand don't even give our last breath a second thought. Aren't we lucky to be living unpredictable life lengths? Maybe that's why he lived each day in the fast lane and to the full. May be we should reconsider and do the same.

The only thing he had between the photograph taken on the Baptism day' seen on the front cover of the book and his 'Death day' was Insulin, Antibiotics and Diuretics which he begged not to have.

Does he look like a dying man, Julian died just over nine weeks later.

Incidentally two days before the Baptism Julian advised me to re mortgage the house, he was very careful about taking care of me and the thought of giving me reckless advice was unconceivable.

Thirteen days after the Baptism Julian and I attended a Social Ball; it was an evening gown and tuxedo event. As it was more practical for me to go to the bar for the drinks than it was for Julian, struggling pushing the wheelchair and perform acrobatic acts with a tray of drinks I offered as I usually did to do the drinks patrol. Although I do acknowledge it's not etiquette for a lady to buy drinks from the bar, I'm sure onlookers understood why I undertook this role. As I was walking back from the bar with the tray of drinks, there were many comments made regarding one particular pint of beer, mainly what's in that pint glass? I just replied to everybody with the same girly answer "Beer" I distributed all the drinks to the appropriate guests at the table, when all of a sudden Julian said, "What's this Olwen, it tastes disgusting, in fact it tastes of vomit." As most men who are given a pint of beer take a large swig, if not half a glass down in one gulp before they say that's a good pint or a bad pint. To re-check his senses he smelt the pint again, he said, "It still smells like vomit". Needless to say he did not drink the remainder of the beer. I went to fetch him an alternative drink, this time out of a bottle. He said, "Those pipes couldn't have been cleaned, to pump something as disgusting as that out" I confessed I wouldn't be surprised if the beer pumps hadn't been pumped as I had to wait at the bar for ages for the bar staff to arrive and then wait for them to remove their coats. I didn't see anyone draining the dregs or testing the beer before pulling the first pint. The function was not held at a place where the bar was in regular use. So Julian may well have had stagnant gunk that was left in the pipes since the last time the bar was open. The reason I've mentioned this small incident was by the time we were leaving that night Julian was soaking in perspiration, people were coming up to him greeting him like they normally did, with a hand shake and a sincere slap on the back. Except this time they said, "What's the matter with you Julian, I can see steam coming from your jacket, you're soaking wet" He told me after, if we hadn't taken guests with us that night, he would of come home as soon as he'd tasted the bad pint.

The beginning of the end

Ten days after that social event, on the morning of 30th of September 2008 at 3am Julian woke me to say, "There's something not right here, the bed is wet" On went the lights, I then pulled back the bed quilt and to my horror I found a fountain of puss cascading up about five inches in the air, coming from his hip. I had to think quickly, there was so much of it; I needed a vessel to catch it. I dashed into the bath room and snatched a measuring jug; I placed it just under the fountain. (Sorry about the grafics this it's not for the faint hearted.) When it appeared to have finished there was 3 pints collected in the jug, goodness knows how much was in the bed.

(By the way I've thrown the jug away, in case you decide to come, visiting)

For the first time in my life I felt I was saying my final 'Good Bye' to Julian, this was so serious. I'd never had this feeling before, a panic set in me that we were becoming trapped, what if no one believed us about the Insulin. I might have to watch him die this time, unlike the last time when he was spared at the eleventh hour. I suddenly felt like Bonnie and Clyde with no way out for either of us. I felt something griping my heart and squeezing the living day light out of it.

I tried to convince him it was serious while he tried to make light of the situation by saying, "No, it's ok now it's better out than in, isn't it?" I reminded him that if this needed surgery, then he needed to think again because the Insulin issue had not been resolved on paper, I asked him to remember the bridge, and we need to cross it. After a major clean-up of changing the bed cloths, followed by a bed bath and a secure bulky dressing in case it started to ooze again, we both stayed awake waiting for day break. When morning came, Julian wanted me to call the District Nurse to assess the situation. She visited mid-morning after inspecting the sinus she contacted the GP who later visited himself mid-afternoon, later about tea time his colleague called. They were of the same opinion that he needed to go to Worcester Hospital, but Julian was keen to be treated by his "Spinal Nurses" as he called them. Julian haggled and begged the three of them if he could attend Spinal injury outpatient clinic, designed as more of a drop in clinic originally but over the years it became so busy due to lots of follow up clinics that it became necessary to make an appointment. The GPs agreed Julian could arrange his own appointment and after some phone calls, the staff nurse managed to fit him in on the 9th of October 2008. Which meant, Julian had to wait another nine days before he was seen at Oswestry? During these nine days Julian and I spoke often about the bad pint of beer he had on the Saturday night previously. The question we were asking ourselves was, did Julian feel ill that night because he was brewing an abscess anyway, causing him to feel rough or did the bacteria in the bad pint of brew float around and settle in his weak spot which was his right hip the very place he had had a Gerdal Stone operation 18 years previously, or was it the result of the minor surgery he'd had in April, where the consultant had raised concerns about developing an abscess at a later date. Either way his immune system must have been down to allow this abscess to get hold of him like it did. But which came first the chicken or the egg?

I don't suppose I'll ever know unless I ask a microbiologist the question, "What are the chances of connecting bad fungal growths in beer pipes and the formation of an abscess". Although I have since asked trained barmen, what's the possibility of contamination? Their answers were the same, they were not medically trained but confessed that "Dirty beer pipes can cause untold health issues" I recalled that particular night the Bar staff consisted of one lady, rushed off her feet and one very young boy who obviously had never worked behind a bar in his life before because he had no idea what drinks went in what glass never mind checking if the pumps were drawing good beer or the temperature of the beer in the kegs were correct before the doors were open to the guests that evening. I don't know why Julian did this, but he wrote a note and stood it by the pint for the Barman to collect later. The message was, "This is the worst pint of bitter I have ever tasted in my life" The message fell on deaf ears, because it was the same young man collecting the glasses who picked up the note. So strong did Julian feel about this bad pint, he asked me to take a photo of the half-drunk pint, with the attached massage. Why! I don't know, because he always asked me to put my camera away. The question remains, which brew caused the abscess? Was he brewing for an abscess or did the brew cause the abscess.

Julian's Third Ambulance trip

On the morning of the 9th of October 2008, I got up at 3am to bed-bath Julian; change his bedding and his wound dressing. I then helped him get dressed into a track suit he'd had for his birthday 24 days earlier, I wanted him to be warm for his journey. An electric hospital bed had been delivered from the Social Services for Julian's use during the last nine days of his life at home.

I made us both his favourite breakfast, poached egg on toast. As he took his last mouthful he was startled by the loud door bell, the Ambulance men were punctual they arrived as promised prompt at five thirty in the morning. In the rush to finish his tea he dropped his half-drunk cup down the side of the Welsh dresser.

While Julian was fussing about cleaning it up, I was getting stressed because Julian might be seeing his family home for the last time and all he could think about was spilt tea. The realisation must have dawned on him eventually, because when the Ambulance men were making small talk about what's the best way to get the stretcher out of the house. I noticed Julian had stopped talking; his mind seemed preoccupied with something else. Then maybe silently, Julian was saying his good byes to his familiar surroundings.

Luckily for the ambulance men that morning, because of Julian's forward thinking eighteen years previously when he asked his brother to hinge the garden panel the convenient opening into the garden once again served its purpose.

The ambulance men commented, "It's a shame more houses don't have access like this, it makes our lives so much easier. It has been known for us to take window frames out to get patients out" Julian still wasn't joining in with this conversation, not even with its interesting facts.

Julian's last short journey from the house to the ambulance seemed effortless and unreal, I felt numb as they glided him on the stretcher out of the lounge through the kitchen and the conservatory, up the back path and then through Wayne's adapted fence straight into the ambulance. I followed in the car neither of us knowing what lay ahead of us, but I was right to worry. Its funny how the little man inside your heart tells you "Be on your guard, something is not right."

Julian was greeted by his extended family as he considered them, because most of them had known Julian on and off for the past 37 years. To other patients they were just staff, to him they were his friends. Julian knew about the staff's children, their hobbies, where they went on holidays, what their ambitions were. So you can understand when he used to say, "When I'm ill, and get wheeled through those doors I feel a sense of relief, I know I'm safe and my friends will make me better."

I was glad he had this confidence in them, because when I couldn't make him better it was a safe haven for me too knowing they could heal him.

After Julian had been clerked in, he was then transferred on to an examination bed to assess the extent of the abscess, the nurse attending said, "Oh! My gosh Julian, I didn't realise what I was dealing with when I was on the other end of the phone, you should have been seen sooner"

A little while later the Doctor who was clerking him noticed it stated in his notes that he was a diabetic, and it was Hospital policy to commence diabetic inpatients on a sliding scale Insulin the night before prior to surgery. (This is a steady flow of insulin dripping into the veins via a pump). Julian said he understood their Hospital policy, but he reserved the right to refuse the Insulin as he was allergic to it. The Doctor insisted he'd have to have it, it was Hospital policy. Julian tried to explain his previous reaction to all diabetic treatment. At that a Staff Nurse entered the examination room to borrow something, when she overheard the conversation regarding the Insulin, she stopped in her tracks half way across the room, and said to the Doctor "Don't b . . . . give him Insulin, I was on duty when he was given Insulin last time he requested then not to have it and we thought we were going to lose him that night.

Julian felt a relief in her support but I started to feel frightened, for the first time ever I didn't have the same confidence Julian had. Because I knew dealing with Insulin was out of Oswestry league, and I was sure if he continued to refuse treatment they would wash their hands of him and transfer him straight to Shrewsbury, where Julian's choice of treatment would be taken from him. The Doctor could not be convinced, even though he had suffered the 'insulin incident' at this very hospital only four months previous in April 2008. Question was if they were to transfer him, would they send Julian's medical notes with him including the incident that happened in April 2008 to Shrewsbury.

The following morning on the 10th October 2008 Julian Paul Davies was taken to theatre, for debridement and washout of his abscess cavity. He went to theatre that morning hoping the staff would be more vigilant of his 'red allergy band' on his wrist than they were in April that year.

On his return they had honoured his wishes regarding refusal of insulin but they felt differently about the antibiotics. When the surgeon visited him later that evening, he explained that he was pleased with the surgery after debriding the cavity and giving it a good irrigation and the tissue in the cavity looked healthy. The wound was packed, with instructions to leave well alone for 48 hours, with recommendations to commence Vacuum Assisted Closure therapy in a few days' time. It was not my imagination or Julian's that he could not tolerate antibiotics, by the fourth day Julian's body was reacting to the point of pain. He experienced chest pain, low temperature of 34 degrees, bubbly chest, breathlessness; his respirations went up to 35 a minute, his urine output decreased, his pulse increased to 128, the diastolic dropping into the 30's.

Julian struggled with the Antibiotics until the 14th of October, and was constantly badgered every day to take insulin. Julian tried to reason with them saying that the insulin had similar reactions as the antibiotic on his body. If he was to accept the insulin he wouldn't know which drug caused him the most discomfort. The reaction of the antibiotics was now raising his blood sugar levels, his condition was deteriorated so much now the Doctors wanted to discuss his Rhesus status with me. How could this be, this was only four days following a simple surgery and we were already discussing Rhesus status! They also wanted to clarify in the event of a cardiac arrest could they administer insulin and antibiotics?

Julian said, "Yes I want to be resuscitate, but defiantly NO, NO, NO to the insulin and the antibiotics in fact I don't even want the antibiotics you're giving me right now, can't any of you see how ill I've become on them"?

That night I was at my wits end, mainly trying not to cry out of hopelessness in front of Julian. This was like disavow with Julian sitting on the edge of the bed yet again with me squatting in front of him in case he over balanced and feel to the floor.

As I was squatting on the floor supporting him, I slumped my forehead on his knee and begged him, "Please Julian let me ring Gweno". He replied flippantly, "What for, she can't do anything". I said, "May be not for you, but she can be strong for me." Still gasping for breath he said, "Quick, tell her to come quickly, tell her I need her right now" I couldn't believe his change of heart. With my mobile phone in one hand and trying to keep his balance with the other hand I texted Gweno, 'Come quickly, Julian's asking for you. In a lot of pain-breathing very difficult' This was a huge step for Julian as Gweno had recently become a healer, but Julian wouldn't have the subject mentioned in the house at all, he would say, "I'm a Christian and don't believe in things like that." I don't know what he thought Jesus did, not that I'm comparing Gweno to Jesus.

Luckily Gweno had her mobile switched on, and bearing in mind it was one o'clock in the morning when I text her. Gweno arrived very soon afterwards; as she tip toed into the side room she quietly took off her coat and mimed with her index finger to her puckered lips, the silence gesture. Julian said, "Oh! Gwen, where have you been?" I was puzzled, how did he know she was in the room he had his back to the door and the blinds drawn. So I asked him, "How did you know she'd arrived?" He said, "I sensed her entering, and I also know she's been sending me healing for the last twenty minutes, I can still feel the imprints of her cold hands on my kidneys." I was shocked but she did acknowledge that she had been sending healing throughout the journey over his kidney area. Surprisingly quite soon after Gweno started the healing, Julian appeared to breathe much better the pain he'd experienced for the last few days started to subside.

Whether you believer it or not, there was definitely a dramatic change in Julian's conditions by four thirty that morning. I couldn't believe the transformation that had taken place in very ill man a total non-believer in the art of healing. Julian was concerned that Gwen was working a long shift the following day at a Nursing Home 20 miles away, her hours were 8am until 8pm. Not only was the day's long but the work load he knew was very physically and very demanding too. He begged her, "Please go home and get some sleep before you go to work." She agreed she would.

The following morning the 15th October Julian was assessed by a visiting medical doctor who documented in his medical notes that he <u>did not</u> need any further diuretics due to his Creatinine levels being acceptable. Julian was prescribed and given diuretics against this recommendation eighteen times more. After watching Julian suffer yet another harrowing night I rang my mother asking if she could contact Gweno, telling her Julian is very ill again could she come quickly. Julian was really sorry to ask, he knew it might risk losing her job, but he said he will make it up to her when he got better. Unfortunately he never got that opportunity, but may be one day I can on his behalf. Mum said she would try, but poor Gweno had only been at work at the Nursing Home for about two minutes when Mum's phone call came through. Nick her boss was excellent; I think he had a soft spot for the situation as he is a twin himself.

Gweno came like a faithful dog, and stayed with Julian giving him healing until 7oclock that evening. She then took some time out and went to our parents' house for a bite to eat, she intended to go home from there but was still worried about Julian so she returned to his bedside to offer him more comfort this time she massaged the back of his neck and his feet. It was ten o'clock when she finally left, and this time she did go home to Welshpool but she promised to return the following morning.

As soon as she went Julian became very ill again, following another dose of Antibiotics; all through the night he kept asking for Gweno and wondering when she would be coming. Saying things like, "If I can just hold on until the morning, she will make me better." By now he had such faith in her. Gweno was aware of Julian's strong feelings about any additional visitors, he didn't wish to see any one while he felt and looked so ill, "I'll let them see me when I'm better", he assure us.

The following morning Gweno decided to take the bull by the horns, and go against his wishes and bring a friend. Contacting her friend made Gwenos late, and poor Julian thought Gweno was never going to come. He kept repeating, "Where is she, she's never this late normally". She didn't arrive until ten thirty but as she walked in with her head down and both her palms raised in a surrender position she said, "Julian, I know how you feel about visitors, but you're far too ill for me to deal on my own, so I've brought a friend who is also a healer" Before he had time to object, Gill had waltzed in and while she was taking off her coat she introduced herself.

Julian glanced backwards over his shoulder and said, "Thank God, if you can help Gwen then welcome aboard" and after this first encounter he always introduced Gweno as his sister-in-law, me as his wife and Gill as his new 'best friend'.

Both Gweno and I were shocked at his quick acceptance of Gill, the first thing they both did was put on some quiet Angelic music in the background. I couldn't believe what a difference lovely music could do to a tense atmosphere. They both stayed until two in the afternoon and as they were leaving, Julian thanked them and said, "I can't believe how much better I feel, I feel well enough to doze off and have a little sleep" One could think this was all psychological brain wash stuff, but don't forget I wasn't totally converted either. What semi-convinced me was the fact his recovery had physical aspects to it. He wasn't sweating any more, his abdomen was defiantly not hard and distended any more in fact it was softer, his breathing was normal, his observations were normal, the only thing I couldn't see was the fact he said he was pain free. Just to be able to recline a little on a big pile of pillows was a great step forward, instead of balancing on the edge of the bed. I couldn't believe he'd drifted off to sleep before they'd even left. But this tranquillity was short lived, as soon as they'd left he was woken by two nurses to give him more antibiotics, his hard painful and distended abdomen had returned within ten minutes along with all the other side effects.

Both Julian and I were constantly asking the Consultant, the junior Doctors and the Registrars to contact Worcester Hospital or Kidderminster Hospital to try and obtain copies of the medical notes to clarify that Julian did have problems with Insulin.

I was sure that the medical professionals were duty bound to obtain notes from other Hospitals if the Patients safety was at risk.

When Gwenno visited the following day I asked her if she could stay with Julian while I went up the corridor to find a pay phone. I wonder why all Hospital pay-phones never work when you need them the most, the very place where you need to make contact with the outside world. Then there's the issue of the mobile phones, that's another stumbling block when you discover they are forbidden in some Hospitals and not in others. I don't know why they can't have a universal rule, either they interfere with Hospital equipment or they don't. In some Hospital some Surgeons use them outside Theatre corridors! I eventually found a pay phone that worked, I was anxious to speak to the secretary of a Medical

Doctor Julian had been under his care as an inpatient some years previously.

The secretary explained she could not disclose any information about Julian's medical care to me over the phone or any allergies he may have had. But she could send it direct to a Doctor who was taking care of him at the time. She said if I could give her an appropriate fax number she could fax them that minute. I returned to the ward to quietly ask one of the junior Doctors for the necessary fax number, but the Consultant overheard our conversation. With an almighty voice, the Consultant shouted down the corridor, "NO MOORE REQUESTS, the endocrinologist has no recollection of Julian Davies or the unusual case surrounding him, I don't want to hear another word about these notes EVER again, is that clear?" He was so loud, and so stern that I jumped and even the ward staff stopped in their tracks too including the visitors. I turned to the Doctor and said, "Something will only be done about cases like Julian when the same thing happens to a member of the medical family" He said, "I am so sorry, my hands are tied I cannot help you. I've been asked not to get involved. This would never happen in my country; at home we would try and obtain as much medical information as possible to see a bigger picture"

I thanked him for trying, but I assured him I was not giving up.

His big plan

On hearing the fiasco outside his side-room with the Consultant, Julian said, "I've been thinking about ringing the Police to get the Doctors to stop all these treatments, but I might run the risk of them banning you from visiting. I can't afford that, I need you to help me balance on the edge of this bed when the side effects get really bad. I accept now that my notes are not going to materialise from either Kidderminster or Worcester so I'm going to conduct an experiment"

At that exact moment I felt like screaming on his behalf at the top of my voice. The two of us felt the same panic one experiences in a nightmare, when your screaming for all your worth and not a single sound coming out. At the same time both of us struggling to behave with dignity knowing the shadow of death was hanging over him. It was just like being on death row, except people on death row at least have years to appeal while Julian was constantly negotiating over the next few hours of his life. It felt as if all the doctors were shooting arrows at his immune system with their constant psychological persistence badgering him to take these drugs.

The very mention of the word 'experiment' un-nerved me I hoped it didn't involve me doing anything illegal but I agreed to hear him out. He said "As they obviously don't believe that I have an issue with Insulin or Antibiotics, I'm going to do something really brave I'm going to take all the Insulin and antibiotics they offer me, then they will see how ill I will become then someone hopefully will shout, 'Stop this! these drugs are killing him' Then BINGO they will write in my medical notes; I will ask for a copy of it then translate it into French and then we'll simply stick the French/English translation together back to back and laminate it together. So when we go to France, we can just produce the translation. What could be simpler?"

Julian always made things sound so simple. With Julian's mind everything was always simple, it was others who made things complicated.

I was very, very worried. I queried him, "Yes, but what if things go too far and nobody stops the treatment?" He said, "It's a chance I have to take, because at this moment in time no one is taking a blind bit of notice of my requests anyway".

So I'll do exactly what they want, there's bound to be <u>one</u> doctor amongst all of them who will be able to recognise a sick man when they see one"

I was prepared to be his advocate, but I wasn't prepared to do nothing that would jeopardise his life. This was not exactly illegal I admit, but there was something morally not correct about his request. His mind and body was definitely struggling with his 'human rights'.

It was as if I was living a negative existence in the real world, it's illegal to assist in euthanasia. In this crazy existence Julian and I were conforming to a type of euthanasia by allowing him to accept drugs we both knew he was reacting to and allergic too? (But I had no proof) I didn't know which one was the best out of the two evils! I couldn't do right from doing wrong either way.

He reassured me by reminding me that his liver function tests would soon escalate, and someone was bound to notice those results. That was true, that's not something anyone could conger up.

He was hoping he would be allowed a much needed sleep before this 'experiment' started, but that was not to be. He was soon baited in to starting a different type of antibiotic, this time an antibiotic he knew disagreed with him. But he agreed to conform, this time for completely different reasons he felt it was a means to an end to all this misery and painful reactions.

To me it was like agreeing to have all your teeth pulled out at once without a local anaesthetic. How could he go through with this, this was stupid and dangerous and irresponsible, to take something you know you're allergic to. Sensible people just wouldn't risk it, but I realised he was cornered and had to try different tactic.

He did how ever make this doctor promise if this Antibiotic inflicted pain on his body the Doctor would stop the treatment immediately. The Doctor agreed, and in order to strike while the iron was hot before Julian changed his mind the Antibiotic was given within minutes of Julian agreeing. But he was tricked, they administered two antibiotics at the same time whereas Julian only agreed to have one at a time. That afternoon on the 15th October 2008 which happened to be a Sunday afternoon Julian had his first dose, with in ten minutes he was back to square one with all the signs and symptoms except this time the reaction seemed much more severe having breathing difficulties, chest pain and now physically doubled up with abdominal pain.

It was at this point I was truly convinced 'Julian Paul Davies' could no longer tolerate any medication at all, not any anymore!

What was going on?

As his pain started to erupt he said, "Olwen, quick get the Doctor back" I rang Julian's call bell and I asked the nurse to summon the Doctor quickly. She must of emergency bleep him because he was at his bed side with in seconds.

What Julian asked the Doctor next, shocked both the Doctor and myself. He said, "I need you to reverse this antibiotic right now, I need an antidote quickly I can't stand this pain anymore" The Doctor looked at me as if I'd put him up to it, I defended myself by shrugging my shoulders saying, "I had no idea what he was going to ask you, except as you can see he's in agony, quickly do something to help him" All the Doctor was able to offer him was a shrugged shoulder gesture to match mine and say "I'm sorry Julian I'm afraid you'll just have to ride the waves out on this one" No attempt was made to ease his suffering by contacting the hospital pharmacy for advice, or contact the central poison unit for advice not even offering additional pain relief, nothing but a hard hearted remark. Not even when Julian begged the Doctor, "Please Doc, I can't, I can't go through with this pain for the next four to six hours, I've only just had the injection, please I beg you help me, I feel as if I'm dying" Julian had his one arm out stretched in a begging gesture while the other was hugging his abdomen. At that the Doctor turned on his heels and with a swish of his white coat hurridly walked out of the room. I was finding it increasing difficult to believe I was in a Hospital in England, it just felt as if I was somewhere foreign dealing with a language barrier with no money to pay for a decent Doctors. They could not grasp Julian's request "No more drugs, please I beg you" it seemed a simple statement to me. What part of this simple English request couldn't they understand?

Poor Julian had to endure the next eight hours exactly as the Doctor predicted by riding the waves and hope his heart didn't give up before the drug wore off!

Julian's Forth Ambulance trip

The following morning Julian's condition hadn't fully recovered from the two antibiotics he'd been given the afternoon before. An emergency doctor was called yet again as Julian was still complaining of terrible chest pain, several ECGs were performed but they said his heart remained strong as an ox, although all his other usual signs and symptoms were present with raised blood sugar. The congregating Doctors were trying to get Julian to take more Insulin, Julian insisting he wasn't well enough to take it on top of the antibiotic reaction.

Because of his refusal of the insulin the doctors wanted to transfer him to Shrewsbury where they could monitor him better, with access to an Intensive Care Unit. Julian was too ill to fight but at the same time he was worried if he refused their drugs the transfer to Shrewsbury would be imminent and Oswestry might Black List him from the unit, his arm was twisted he simply had to go.

They were preparing to 'Blue light' him to Shrewsbury and while the kafuffle was going on I managed to contact Gweno informing her that Julian was just about to be Blue-lighted to Shrewsbury Hospital. She once again left work and arrived in time to wish Julian well before he left, he boarded the ambulance on that beautiful crisp-sky-blue morning of 16th October 2008. I was asked to travel separately yet again, how anyone can think this is safe is beyond me. Another terrifying journey, this time travelling down a dual carriage way following the Ambulance not knowing if Julian was breathing or not. Gweno and I followed in separate cars behind so she could return to work if needed. As Gweno and I entered the Casualty department poor Julian's voice could be heard trying to fight his corner regarding the insulin issue. It was as if someone had sent an errand-boy ahead of us with a message to warn the Doctors, 'beware of this patient he will try to refuse all treatment'.

It felt the Doctors had taken the attitude they weren't negotiating with this one, because I overheard someone saying, "Ok, let's ship him out" and he was soon transferred to the Medical Emergency Centre. There Julian came across the most obnoxious human being who carried the title of Senior Medical Doctor. This Doctor did not possess a streak of kindness, he had no compassion, no sympathy definitely no listening skills and no bedside manner. Julian begged him not to prescribe Insulin, "I'm too ill to take it, please let my organs recover before you start again" The Doctor kept denying his request. Then Julian begged him again, "Then please let him go home" again he denied Julian's request, Julian asked "Why" his reply was "Because your too ill to be discharged" Julian then begged him, "In that case will you let me go home to die."

This man was heartless because this man denied a begging man the right to die in his own bed, except this time he mocked him by tossing his head back asking, "And how would you get home?"

Julian said, "By Ambulance, the same way I came". The Doctor laughed out loud and shook his head from side to side, "If you're taking your own discharge then the Hospital will not supply you with transport." He then encouraged the medical students to laugh too, there were plenty of them they seemed uncomfortable but grudgingly joined in anyway.

There is a verse in the Bible that says, "Don't laugh at someone who has been humbled, it's the Lord who humbles a person, but the Lord also raises him" (Sirach 7, v11.)

Julian then said something heart breaking. He said aloud, "I wish I had cancer, then you'd arrange for me to go home wouldn't you, I just want to say good bye to all my friends in my own home" Julian pleaded one last time, "Please I beg you, how else can I get out of this building."

The Doctor said in a sarcastic, low tone and slow manner, "Only if you take the Insulin!"

Julian's reply was, "If that's the only way I can escape, then I'll have to take it" and then threw his head back in a defeatism gesture. To me it was like saying, take the poison then you can have your freedom, it was an absolutely diabolic situation. Seeing Julian so defeated, I got very angry and turned to Julian and said, "Julian if you really, really feel and believe that the Insulin and the antibiotics are slowly killing you and you continue to take it" then I turned to the Doctors and pointed at al of them standing in a semi-circle round his bed, ". . . and all of YOU continue to force him to take these drugs, then I tell you what, YOU can take care of him, because I'm off, I can't take any more of this physiological torture, he has become more and more ill in your care to the point of been critically ill". I turned away from the Doctors to face Julian and said, "Don't you bother about concentrating about getting better Julian Davies, concentrate on how to cope with going through a divorce. I've had enough of fighting your corner I'm exhausted of constantly being on your guard day and night I feel physically sick all the time. I just can't take any more, I feel weak, I'm hungry and I don't know when I had my last drink and look at me I'm like skin and bone my clothes are hanging on me."

I stormed off the ward, as I did so I could hear Julian crying loud "Please don't leave me", then I could hear him sobbing as he repeated "Please Olwen, I've got no one on my side, NO ONE BELIVES ME LIKE YOU" he shouted. I collapsed in the corner of the day room, and sobbed. I felt so weak, I was shaking I did not know if it was from rage, mal-nutrition or dehydration or if it was my immune system crumbling. How could they allow two people to become so distressed? It felt like we were both in Prison, but out of Prison.

I realised as I was squatting in the corner of the dayroom that I too was becoming ill now, I was worried of how much fight and strength I had left inside of me. I started to feel even more nauseas when I realised what a cruel thing I'd just done to poor Julian by abandoning like I did in his hour of need!

I must have been sobbing on the floor for about 20 minutes before any one came to find me. When this young male Doctor eventually did find me he said, "Don't abandon your husband; he needs you more than ever right now." I thought to myself, you silly man you're missing the point, what Julian needs is the right diagnosis and then the right treatment. I loved him too much to leave him. There were a lot of young female Doctors witnessing our anguish, didn't any of them have <u>1oz</u> of female motherly compassion in their body to try and comfort or even listen to our plea. God help their children when they come along because their children will be raised by heartless empty shells, because I couldn't honour them with the caring title of a 'Mother' or a caring female 'Doctor'

He escorted me in a clumsy elbow hold back to Julian's bed side, I felt like a starved whipped dog. The situation was hopeless I had never been down such a dark pit as this before in my life.

We were left alone, to make it up I suppose. I apologised to Julian, sheepishly and explained I was desperate that not one of those Doctors that was gathering round his bed could find pity in there heart towards our plight. We hardly spoke for the remainder of that day, my silence represented shame for my behaviour, and Julian's silence represented defeat because for the first time in his life he was unable to find a solution to this desperate predicament. Who knows, his silence might have been spent questioning my loyalties after that little outburst. All this rubbish was now starting to affect our relationship we'd had such struggles throughout our marriage, but no matter how bad things got we always laughed before, during and after our struggles. The trouble this time there was nothing funny about this situation. Family and friends would send massages "Make sure you have time out, to sleep, eat and drink". But I didn't want to leave Julian in his vulnerable state in such a threatening environment to defend for him-self. If I felt comfortable that the nurses and the Doctors had his best interest at heart I would leave him and even go back to work and visit him on my days off but the trust wasn't there. That night at eleven o'clock I was desperate to go to the toilet so I pushed his bed by the wall and I placed his feet on a chair then wedged him tight with pillows and raised the cot-side up while I was away. As I was leaving he said "Please don't be long, please I beg you don't belong, they might give me something when you're away" I rushed to and from the toilet and when I got back, there was an elderly lady who was obviously confused, at Julian's bed side. Julian said, "Quick Olwen, have a look to see what she's doing". After placing my hand bag down, I went to investigate only to find she had removed Julian's dressing, and had her hands inside the wound.

Some might think there was no need to repeat this incident but it had become impossible for me to trust anybody, twelve hours later again I needed to go to the toilet on my return this time the same old lady had put Julian's toilet bag in her locker and was wearing my jumper. Needless to say, this was a mixed sex bay. The nurses usually gave Julian his Insulin in his abdomen, but that particular evening while Gill and Gweno were visiting, a ward Sister approached Julian from behind and gave Julian his insulin in his arm. There was no warning that she was going to do it, there was no verbal consent obtained, no unit number checked or questioned if he was allergic to anything. At this action Julian turned round with such thundering eyes and said, "What are you doing", and then a long loud ahhhhhhh. "You have just injected me with that insulin haven't you, that was the most painful injection I've ever had" Incidentally, that injection site remained both painful and solid up to his death. Gill who has no medical background at all had the courage to ask the ward Sister, "Why are you still giving Julian Insulin when he is wearing a red arm band indicating he is allergic to Insulin." The Sister then turned to Julian with raised eye brows and said, "You're not, are you?" He replied, "Yes." There were no repercussions from this conversation as far as I know. No investigations or questions asked, no apologies, in fact there is nothing written in the notes by this Ward Sister to say she had given the insulin without first checking with Julian verbally or checking his arms for an allergy band, or that a visitor (Gill) had questioned her administration of the Insulin. In fact, staff continued to give Insulin three to four time a day, even though Julian verbally requested it not to be given, each time.

I hastened to add, neither of his armbands were checked prior to administering any medication.

Looking back, staff would often ask Julian why he didn't administer his own Insulin, other patients do and their a lot older than you? He used to answer them all by saying, "I use to, until I started having reactions to it!"

On reflection, he always displayed a body image of refusal when the staff would give him the injection; he had started to look away. As if to say, you won't let me refuse it, but you can't force me to look at something I believe is harming me.

Julian stayed on this ward until the 20th of October 2008 having four bed space moves before eventually been transferred to another ward upstairs.

The worst night ever

Here he said he felt claustrophobic as soon as he was wheeled on to the ward, to be honest the beds were confined together with six beds in a bay and the ward was stiflingly hot, and the windows would only open a few inches. Still suffering from hard distended abdomen he felt his stomach had been crushed into a small space and because of that, all he'd had to eat that day was two table spoons full of unsweetened semolina. Beyond understanding that evening his glucose levels were high, consequently he was then given his six o'clock Insulin. He immediately became agitated then he progressively became restless with his arms eventually becoming nasty, he started to perspire profusely this continued throughout the night, he was extremely pale, by eleven o'clock he demanded that I sat on the edge of the bed next to him, he was almost animal like. I didn't mind his attitude; I knew it was the Insulin making him behave like this; it had to be he'd only had insulin when he started to feel out of sorts. I'd never nursed such a sick person in the whole of my nursing career ever. I would expect to see someone like this in a drug rehabilitation unit, struggling to come off drugs. By midnight he was gasping for breath, he took the oxygen mask off and threw it at the nurses stationery (the nurses never flinched an eye lid not even to ask if I needed assistance) he then rammed the tube down his throat where it remained most of the night biting on the tube as if he was chewing tobacco to keep it in place. I can only half imagine what it was like for him inside his head, but it was a total nightmare for me just watching him. The whole scenario was so difficult, he wanted me to sit next to him at the same time massage his abdomen which was so swollen and rock solid and massage his kidney area at the same time. I didn't know what to do first, but at three o'clock his psychological behaviour worsened not only was he very confused but he'd become viciously aggressive, his respirations became much faster, he was trying to stand out of bed and sit in an arm chair in the other corner of the ward. Something he hadn't done for thirty four years, adding to this struggle he was hallucinating that ferocious dogs were chasing him and barking and he was trying to get away by climbing to the bottom of the bed. His behaviour was so realistic, that I could almost imagine the dogs chasing me as well. Silly I know, but this was in the middle of the night pitch black outside with no moon light for comfort. He was describing these Doberman's with their white teeth, their dribbling saliva and their bad breath.

His organs generally resumed back to almost normal after about six hours, but on this occasion his organs remained swollen and hard all through the night and at half past four he started complaining bitterly of liver pain then the agony in both of his kidneys. By five o'clock the aggression and the hallucination had subsided it was now replaced by constantly calling my name I kept saying "I'm here" Then he'd remember and say, "Oh! Yes I forgot your there" By five thirty he said "Its ok, Ol, the Poison is leaving my body now, don't worry it will soon be light". He was referring to the Insulin as the poison. By twenty five to six he pushed me away really cross and rough saying, "No more massage, I can't bear it any more, my skin is crawling with spiders, inside and out."

By five forty he complained of excruciating abdominal pain then at six o'clock he said "That was the worst experience I've ever had Olwen, but don't worry my brain is coming back to normal now, it's been swollen tight inside my skull all night. I don't know what Insulin they gave me last night, but I can't take much more rubbish like that". We tried to make sense out of the horrendous night. We questioned each other could it have been a different insulin or was it the same insulin with a build-up of the insulin, or maybe his body had reached some sort of saturation point. Whatever it was we both agreed he'd never reacted or behaved like that before. At six twenty I noticed large purple rings on Julian lower back, both cheeks on his bottom and back of his upper thigh. I could not disclose to him what they looked like to me, they resembled the purple mottling rings that appear after someone's died. Whatever happened that night was down to some sort of awful reaction, but what? All I knew was they were not there the night before and they were there the following morning and they did not disappear, but eventually became black necrotic hard crusty areas, that would obviously need to be debriding at some stage. It frightened me to think how deep these hard crusty necrotic area went. This was awful; my life was out of control I spent all my nursing career healing people not mutilating them. I was so upset about these black rings, that I didn't want to go back to Oswestry now in case they blamed me for his skin condition. The carers or relatives were always held responsible for the condition of

175

the spinal injured person's skin. I prided myself on the fact that Julian had never, ever had a pressure sore in my care of 29 years. He had had cuts, abrasions, burns and abscesses but never a pressure sore, even osteomyelitis but never a pressure sore. Even though the Consultant who put this fear of God into us the carers, about their skin care had now retired and passed away. I know because I attended his funeral, but I still lived in fear of his criticism.

About six o'clock that morning the night duty doctor was bleeped to see to Julian I don't know why they called him then it was in the dead of the night when we needed him most. When he came he took blood samples for liver function tests and full blood count.

At seven o'clock Julian appeared perkier, and said "I feel so hungry, I need to soak up the remainder of this poison now." he kept looking wildly round for the breakfast trolley. When it arrived he asked to be served first, but it wasn't like him to be so forthright. At the same time it made me smile, he sounded like Oliver Twist asking for more. His big bowl of porridge arrived, but sadly he was only able to eat two tablespoon full and then he pushed it away saying, "Take it away, I can't eat any more my other organs are too swollen they're crushing my stomach."

At eight o'clock the morning staff came to record his observations, his blood pressure was 223/87, goodness knows what is observation were during the night no one came near us.

The top reading called the systolic reading, suggested his body was under considerable stress and the bottom reading suggested there was still signs of some activities going on, but what?

When I started my training I was told to use this as my guide line, the top reading should be 100 plus your age and the bottom reading should never be above 80. They also told me the top reading can be brought down if you force yourself to chill out by resting or de-stressing, but if the bottom reading was elevated only medication could bring this one down. It's the bottom reading that indicates if you are hypertensive or not the top reading only indicates white coat syndrome, or how worried or stressed you are at the time. The 'S' in Systolic readings rhymed with sky, and the 'D' in Diastolic readings rhymed with die or someone else told me once associate Systolic with stress, Diastolic with death. In other words it's the bottom reading we need to concern ourselves with.

It seems to me modern day medicine moves the goal post daily, I don't understand why some GPs prescribe hypertensive drugs to people with diastolic below 80 just because their systolic is above 120? Any way I digress, his oxygen saturation was 88% even though he'd been on oxygen therapy all night, his pulse was112 and not budging.

At nine o'clock the Consultant did his ward round, and insisted that the Insulin had nothing to do with the horrendous night he'd just had.

Julian kept interrupting the doctors round by begging them, "Please read the nursing kardex, your nurse said I've been a nuisance all night, saying that they have spent more time writing about me instead of caring for the other patients". The Consultant replied, "The nurses notes are nothing to do with us." Julian froze for a moment, and appeared perplexed by his comment and said slowly, "Well! What's the point of nurses documenting everything if no one is going to read them?"

Julian was really puzzled and unable to move on from this topic, he continued the conversation but kept repeating the same question in different ways. Still in dismay, he eventually turned to me and said "Don't you have to document everything at your Hospital, Olwen?" I replied "Yes, Ju it's a legal requirement".

In the end Julian shrugged his shoulders and said "You needn't bother; the Doctor says it's nothing to do with them, no one looks at them by the sound of things"

I smiled, Julian still insistent said, "No! I'm serious, Olwen, something big went on last night, and the Doctors won't take any notice of what the nurses have documented, that not right that's defiantly not right and the nurses aren't telling the doctors what went on, so how will they get to know"? Julian of course was right, this was very serious.

The Doctor turned his back on Julian ignoring his chuntering about the nursing kardex, and said to the young medical students, "He seems reasonable now, except for his blood pressure." Julian tried to join in the conversation again even though the Doctors turned their back towards him.

Julian tried to protest by saying, "It's only because I haven't had my early morning Insulin yet, otherwise I wouldn't be in a fit enough state to speak to you" Still ignoring Julian's comments, the Physician instructed the medical students to carry on with the Insulin, on hearing this Julian raised his voice, "Please Doctor I beg you don't force me to take the insulin not just yet, my blood pressure is still far from normal and my stomach is still so painful. Look at it Doc it's huge I look like a Biafrian child, what's the matter with me"? They were so rude; they never even glanced at his extremely distended abdomen never mind answer him, much less attempted to palpate his abdomen. The entourage of Doctors swiftly walked away with out as much as a bye-your-leave.

By now Julian was petrified of any repercussions of what happened in April, he didn't want history to repeat itself when his blood pressure was allowed to escalate to 288/188 which is when he felt he suffered a mild stroke. But if he was to accept Insulin on top of an already high blood pressure, that might tip the scales enough to cause him to have a massive stroke added to the fact that his frail body was becoming too weak to fight these drugs.

All the Doctors must have left their common sense at home that day!

On the 21st of October 2008, I found myself ringing Gweno yet again in distress saying he's very ill again. Her reply was, "Olwen, this has got to stop Julian cannot carry on like this, his body cannot take any more rubbish, let's get some legal opinion."

I said, "I can't afford solicitor fees and I knew Julian wouldn't agree to it either."

She reminded me that our cousin was a solicitor in Oswestry, she was sure he would help. She said I'll ring Mum to arrange an appointment. I said I'd have a word with Julian first, she agreed to hold fire. I mentioned it to Julian and of course he refused and said, "If this treatment kills me, then I don't want you burdened with a debt of a solicitor" Eventually after I brought the subject up a couple of times, he agreed that he could come but warned me, "Let him come then, but I'm telling you right now cousin or no cousin he'll want paying and we haven't got that sort of money." I text Gweno with the simple message, "He's agreed" Unbeknown to me, Gweno had rung Mum up to ask her to contact Richard to pre arrange a visit. When I gave Gweno the nod, Mum contacted Richard immediately. Bless him he said, "I am very busy right now Aunty Ei, when did you want me to come?" She replied "NOW".

The day the Solicitor came to visit

They say blood is thicker than water, I don't think I'd seen Richard since I was a child. But when your chips are down, its then you get to know who you can count on. True to form this cousin of mine turned up that very day in his lunch break, making the 40 miles round trip. When he arrived he asked, "Can we talk somewhere"? At this the tissue viability nurse had just arrived from Wolverhampton to redress Julian's wound and do a check on her vacuum pump, I felt safe leaving Julian alone with her.

I brought Richard up to date with what had happened so far, Richard asked if he could have a word with Julian to see how he felt. Richard advised him that while he had his 'full faculties' he could refuse any treatment, especially if he thought the treatment was harming him. But the minute he could not make his own decision, they would get a psychotherapist involved to assess his mental state and they would then by law empower the trust back to the medical profession.

He also pointed out that I didn't possess any power over Julian's care at all while he was an inpatient. There was no point Julian asking me to request anything on his behalf. Julian was the only person who could demand what he wanted the medical profession to do.

Julian's reply was, "You don't know what they are like Richard, you just don't know what they are like, they agree verbally to one thing then half an hour later the nurses do the exact opposite and claim the Doctor forgot to inform them of the change of treatment".

At that point I saw the same hopelessness in Richards's eyes, it just mirrored the hopelessness Julian and I felt about the whole situation.

There was no more Richard could do, he had done what he set out to do and that was to advise us.

I can honestly say I'd never witnessed such 'persistence' in insisting that treatment should be administered at all cost to anyone, in the whole of my nursing career. So to any outsider who thinks, why didn't Julian stop the treatment himself? I don't know of another man alive who could have fought verbally any better than Julian, or struggled to survive as much as he did. All I can say is I think they were right when they jokingly said he had a heart as strong as an ox, he must of to have survived this long.

Julian's days of dehydration

The following day, Gwen came to visit thankfully it was her day off this time. As soon as she arrived Julian asked her to ask the staff for a cup of tea, so off Gweno went to the nurse's stationary; she was told the staff will be round shortly with the tea round. Half an hour later Julian was still gasping for a drink said, "Can you ask them again Gwen", poor Gweno went to the kitchen this time and trying to be helpful she asked the domestic if she could make Julian a cup of tea, if the staff were too busy. The domestic with her hands on her hips and a frosty reply pointing to a sign on the door "No unauthorised persons are allowed in this kitchen". So Gweno went down to the vending machine in the basement to purchase a cup of tea, following this refusal she did this every time she visited. Surely getting a cup of tea from a kitchen which was only a few yards away from his bedside, was far safer than walking the length and breadth of those long corridors with hot steaming drinks in cardboard cups up and down stairs. The point of mentioning this incident was, the obstacles Julian faced on a daily bases were both big and small. Life was just one big uphill struggle you could tell he was thirsty his lips were all crisp and dry he was totally dehydrated it wasn't rocket scientist. At home Julian's constant companion was his mug of tea, when I say mug I refer to those mugs that hold 500mls of fluid or just under a pint. Since his accident in 1972 Julian had been drinking large volumes of tea at that rate ever since, this was the advice he was given all those years ago. It was imperative he drank plenty in order to keep his kidneys flushed; he was told it would prolong his life, if he abused this advice he would risk dyeing young with kidney failure. This fear travelled with him everywhere he went, it used to be embarrassing for Llewela and I when we went visiting, he would always ask for a cup of tea, if we got to know them a bit better he would say "It's alright for Olwen to make me a cup of tea isn't it I've brought my own mug?" Julian used to pride himself on the fact that he had two plump kidneys, not two dried up prunes for a pair of kidneys. The Doctors even used to say to newly paralysed patient "If you have kidneys in the same condition as Julian when you're his age I'll be proud of you" You may wonder how he knew this; well he knew this because he went for regular IVP. We both tried to be reasonable with all the staff during the last five weeks of his life even though we were so frustrated with the whole situation. We were worried that staff would brand us the difficult couple or the contrary couple or worst still the mad pair or the couple with crazy ideas.

No one, it seems could see life through Julian's eyes because no one was listening. After all everybody knows your cells receive nutrients for energy much more efficiently when you're hydrated.

Then one afternoon an Indian Doctor came to take some blood samples off Julian. Julian asked "What's it for? The Doctor ignored him, after a long uncomfortable pause Julian repeated the question this time asking why he was taking the blood, thinking he hadn't heard or understood him the first time, after another long pause the doctor abruptly said; "Because I have to" I don't know where his introduction or verbal consent was or his explanation about what he was about to do was I'm sure? But Julian was very polite towards him, suggesting he tried his feet informing him he wouldn't get it any anywhere else as his veins had all but collapsed by now because he was too dehydrated" To me he seemed ruthless digging at his hands and arms, but when he admitted defeat and took Julian's offer to attempted his shins and feet he kept apologising saying, "Are you sure I'm not hurting you". Julian must have repeated about half a dozen times "I'm paralysed; I can't feel my legs so don't worry".

As Gweno arrived to visit, I was summoned by the Senior Doctor into the office as I walked towards him I was thinking of all the questions I wanted to ask and all the answers I was hoping to get, answers such as, why was his diastolic often allowed to go as low as 30 at the same time his pulse allowed to stay as high as 140 for so long without any treatment or concern.

Why did his temperature always dip to 34 degrees when he was on medication?

On entering the office the Doctor greeted me with, "I see that Jack Russell is here again" He was referring to my sister, but the comment was not said in a humorous manner and as I always felt uncomfortable in his company it seemed like an unprofessional comment to make. I replied, "If you are referring to my sister, then yes"

He then shut the office door which made me wonder if he had some bad news to tell me. The comment he made next has haunted me ever since, he said "Mrs Davies, I have a question I want to ask you, are you sure you are a real nurse!" As the comment was made one to one behind closed doors I cannot prove what was said, but as I took in what he said I felt as if all the air had been sucked out of my lungs. My soul felt ripped, when people use the phrase! 'They hurt my feelings' This was it, this was the hurt that I'd obviously never experienced before. Seconds later I became so numb and unable to speak or defend myself and felt my eyes well up.

Inside my head I could hear myself thinking; yes I am a real nurse a qualified one at that, but Julian's too poorly for me to travel to Kidderminster to fetch my certificates to prove my worth.

I didn't react; instead I stood up like a zombie and left the office with my unanswered questions. He didn't call me back to apologise, he just let me go. You hear of people walking under a bus when they've had bad news, lucky for me there wasn't a bus. As I was walking out of the office I was thinking he should be questioning his own junior Doctor not me. The Doctor who is attending Julian right now doesn't understand the meaning of the word <u>Paralysed</u>?

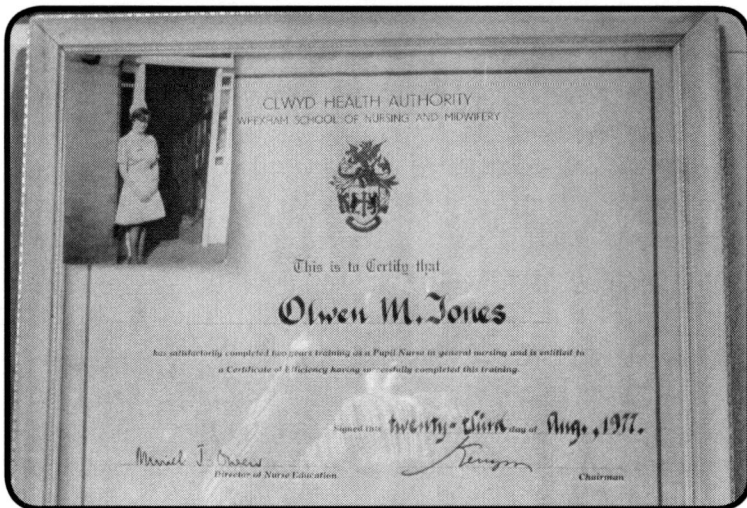

This is my proof that I was a real nurse in my nurse's uniform and my certificate for completing my nurse training as a State Enrolled Nurse in August 1977.

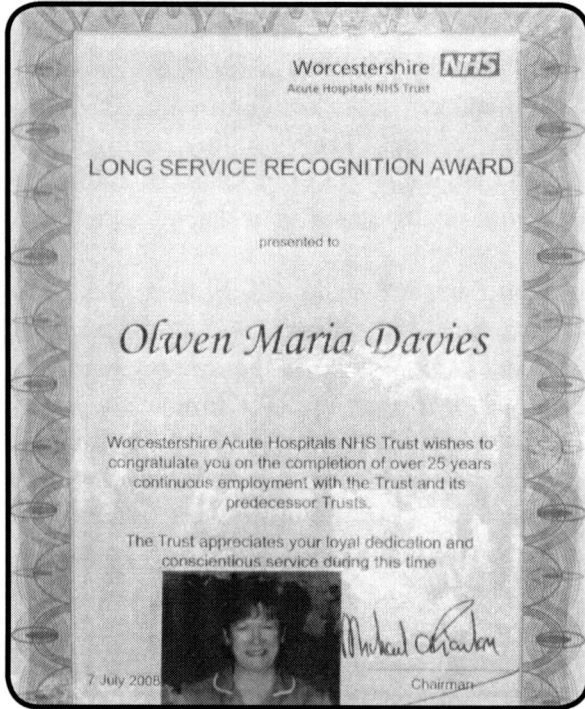

This is a photograph of my certificate of 25 years' long service presented to me in 2002.

As I approached Julian's bed I heard Julian saying to the Doctor, "Why are you bothering, I'm dying" another doctor was now attempting to get a sample of blood. They both locked eyes for several seconds, there was an understanding in the statement but nothing was said.

I've wondered since, did the Doctor think I know your dyeing but I'm trying to find out what's making you so ill. Poor Julian's body wasn't helping at all by not supplying a blood sample.

Eventually he said, "I'll be back in the morning". Julian got hold of his wrist and said, "If they don't stop this Insulin Doc, the morning might be too late" They starred at each other and again nothing was said, he just picked up his syringe and went.

He did survive the night but only because the Insulin was withheld on one of those rare occasions.

Two days later the Consultant called to see Julian I wasn't present at this consultation as Gwen had suggested I drive back to Oswestry to our parent's home for a bath. This was a 36 mile round trip. She promised she would stay at Julian's bed side the whole time I was away. Julian had become insecure during this particular Hospitalisation, no doubt through lack of trust.

That afternoon his mother visited, evidently Julian had not been able to stop her from coming to visit; he always tried to stop her visiting if he felt unwell from the Insulin. This was the first time she had seen him so ill. With hind sight this was probably a good thing, it may have been a bigger shock if she hadn't seen him like this, but I think Julian was constantly trying to protect her from any worries and of course trying to sort the Insulin situation out himself, after all he was a grown man and could normally sort his and everybody else's problems out.

Gweno told me later that his mother looked shocked at how ill he looked.

He said to his mother "Mum I've been close to death 5 times since I've been in here, just let me get this Insulin out of my system and I will start to feel better.

The Consultant heard Julian saying this to his mother from the nurse's stationery, he walked over to Julian's bed and proceeded to tell Julian "I can't help you any more, I'll discharge you to Oswestry on Monday" and turned on his heels to walk off.

His mother then went to question the nurses at the nurses stationary asking, "Do you think the Doctor has thrown in the towel?" the nurses replied "Most definitely"

Julian's fifth Ambulance transfer

On the 27th of October 2008 Julian was transferred from Shrewsbury Hospital at eight o'clock in the evening on a very, very cold night to The Robert Jones and Agnes Hunt Orthopaedic Hospital, he was sweating profusely, my heart was breaking for him. He was exposed to a very cold winter night and there was a flurry of snow falling on his sweat pouring face. I know the last thing on earth that he would have liked while he was sweating, was freezing cold air and snow on his skin. What he really wanted was the heat of Africa in his own living room, but I knew he was happy to go back to his sanctuary his beloved hospital to be looked after by his spinal nurses as he so fondly called them. I followed in my car, after he was settled in to his bed space; a Doctor did a courtesy call to greet him back. I begged again, "Can't you look into Julian's case, please, there's something wrong, he should be able to take Insulin and all the other tablets including antibiotics. What's the matter with him, the whole thing is making me look and feel stupid. We must be missing something, can't you help us." He replied in an aloof manner, "I have no interest in Diabetes, and don't profess to know anything about the condition. It's too complicated for me I'm an Orthopaedic specialist not a medical one."

To this Doctor I say, "May you and your family live long and healthy lives, free from Diabetes and its complications, because if they are ever afflicted with the same suffering Julian was going through, then I could assure him, he like me, would find a huge and sudden interest in Diabetes in order to save their lives."

This Doctor incidentally has now been promoted to Consultant status!

God help us all who comes under his care with that dreaded complaint called 'Diabetes'.

Teaching Tibetan Chant

On the 28th of October 2008 Gill came to give Julian some more healing, but this time it was different. She said, "Julian today I feel guided to teach you how to do sound healing."

I thought Oh! Oh! She's gone too far this time, Julian won't wear that.

It could all fall apart now, I thought but to Gweno's and my surprise, he said to Gill, "Ok, bring it on I'll try anything, anything at all to make me feel better, I'm feeling so very ill right now."

Gill started to hum and it wasn't long before Julian joined in. He was sat up in bed crossed legged, with his head bowed forward sometimes with a sheet over his head like a tepee but always with his eyes closed both humming away, they sounded like a couple of Tibetans chanting away.

This chanting made me reminisce of our ancestors from my Father's side of the family, who had emigrated to Canada from Welshpool district in Mid Wales . . . . of them went together around 1912 about the same time as The Titanic went down. They had purchased the land, but of course on arrival they had nowhere to live, only the shelter of their horse drawn carts. The local Native Americans Indian tribe called Cree Nations took pity on them, and as far as I know the male of the tribe took our men folk out teaching them how to survive in the wild by hunting and fishing, they mainly hunted Buffalos. The females of the tribe taught the women folk how to cook, pick wild berries and forage in the woods, teaching them what was safe and what was not. They also taught the men how to build their own Tepees. There they lived side by side with the local natives by the river for twelve months while they built their own cabins. Learning only to take from the land what was needed. Aunty Kay told me this when she came over to visit us.

I was brought back to reality when Gill finished her chanting and told Julian she wasn't able to come the following day. Julian looked frightened, he had started to rely on her and Gweno it was sad and pitiful to see such a strong, intelligent, independent character reduced to such a pitiful voice saying "Gill, I don't think I can manage without you, I'm so much better when you and Gwen are here" Gill assured him, "You will be absolutely fine, but I don't know why I was guided to teach you sound healing but there will be a reason".

After Gill left, Julian slipped into a tranquil sleep, but not for long because soon afterwards he was awoken for his five o'clock Insulin. Ten minutes later it all began again, shortness of breath, high pulse, low blood pressure, very low temperature, abdominal pain, terrible pain in his head not like a headache but pressure in the skull he used to say, sweating, gasping for breath repeating the same thing "Olwen, I'm dying, can't you stop them giving me this Insulin ?

I said, "No, Julian you know the score Richard told you, you have to refuse the treatment yourself, otherwise they will think I'm trying to stop you receiving treatment. I can see for myself that you're suffering from some sort of nasty drug reaction, but the fact remains Ju, only you have the authority to stop their practices" I was genuinely worried that if I was accused of trying to stop Julian's treatment, the Hospital could bring an injunction against me preventing me visiting. The following day Julian seemed more positive and forthright with his attitude in trying to gain control over his own life. Julian asked the Doctor if he had any bacterial growth in his wound swab or in his blood, to which the Doctor replied there was no growths. He said, "Good, at least my system can now have a rest from the Antibiotics, which will help relieve this terrible pain I have in my abdomen not to mention the risk I'm taking in contaminating and infecting my wound with diarrhoea" but the doctors answer was still "No, the antibiotics must defiantly continue" Contradicting this statement other doctors were confusing him by spending hours trying to convince him he had osteomyelitis in his wound, angered about their conflicting statements Julian challenged them by asking them to prove to him he actually did have osteomyelitis. Julian had fired up in them a battle of wills, the war was on and they needed to win at all cost. The most accurate confirmation would be to undergo an MRI scan, and amazingly one was conjured up just like magic for that very evening. Talk about jumping out of the 'pan into the fire' Julian was now faced with an additional pressure, but could hardly be seen to be backing out after he demanded proof. His body might have been weak, but he still possessed a warrior's heart because he then said "Olwen, I'll have to try and conquer this phobia, but I can't do it while I'm all drugged up like this. I need all my faculties about me, I'll see if they will give me a fighting chance by letting me off the six o'clock drugs" You see, Julian had developed a condition called CHLOSTRAPHOBIC since he'd started on diabetic treatment! The three main character changes I'd noticed in Julian since he'd been taking diabetic treatment was the physical reaction immediately after, his argumentativeness and lastly uncharacteristically his most embarrassing condition of all claustrophobia.

Julian's Claustrophobia

When Julian was first prescribed Diabetic treatment in 2001, he found it increasingly difficult to be in a confined space, such as lifts. One could start to understand how much will power Julian Davies had, when one considers these facts. The only way he could manoeuvre from one room to another was in a wheelchair and to ascend or descend from one floor level to another was via a lift. So he had <u>no</u> alternative but to travel in an escalator, I often over heard people jokingly say, "You lazy thing, using the lift" not realising he was fighting a private war inside his head, against a condition called 'claustrophobia' never admitting it of course as he considered it as a sign of weakness. The very thought of entering this scanning machine head first, terrified the living day light out of him. And if I could have jumped inside that tunnel in his place I would of, anything to avoid his dreadful anguish he was harbouring inside his chest. This of course was a 'do or die' situation that evening either he refused to undergo the scan procedure and continue to take the antibiotic or accept their investigation and force himself to endure a horrendous time in a restricted tunnel they called a scanner. He was hoping the scan result would prove he didn't have osteomyelitis consequently he would have a stronger case to protest against the doctors who insisted on prescribing Intravenous Antibiotics, which he knew would prevent him suffering further physical and extremely painful side effects. Still at loggerheads with the medical profession Julian spent the entire afternoon haggling with the Doctors to let him off his six o'clock drugs, he wanted to be 'allergy free' to gain ground in regaining his strength before he went through what he called a 'pot-holing' like procedure.

Eventually the doctors gave in, and his request was honoured but he was sure there was a price to pay later. At seven o'clock the porter arrived to escort him up the famous quarter mile long corridor to the x-ray department. I couldn't imagine people who are escorted to the electric chair suffering much more anguish than what Julian was experiencing on that journey. I can remember thinking how eerily quiet the radiography department seemed as we entered through the doors. There was of course only Julian as a patient in the department that evening; it felt as if we were like 'thieves in the night'! I helped the radiographer transfer Julian from his bed on to the Radiographer's scanning machine, and then I was asked to take a seat outside. I didn't mind, but I did inform them about Julian's claustrophobia. They assured me he would be absolutely fine, they had come across lots of people like this and they always manage. I was soon summoned back into the department, as I walked in and looked at Julian's face I took a sharp intake of breath as I saw how poorly Julian had become in just a few minutes his lips were blue, his eye balls appear to be bulging and he was as white as a sheet. Julian was half in and half out of the scanner, he tilted his head backwards and looking at me he said, "Olwen, I can't do it, I think I'm going to be sick and I've got this terrible pain in my chest"

The radiographer suggested we took Julian back out of the scanner and re-entered him feet first, he might manage that better. Julian said, "I'll try anything, I know I've got to do it but my chest is so painful I can't image a heart attack being this painful" So that's exactly what we did, I helped them transferred him back onto his hospital bed then turned the bed round, so his feet would be facing the opposite direction and lastly we transferred him back onto the scanner trolley. Yet again I was asked to step outside, as I passed the staff I quietly asked them if they had cardiac arrest facilities at hand because he's complaining his chest pain is getting worse. Just as before I wasn't left to stand in the corridor for long, I was soon called back this time invited me to stay. I was asked to put on a lead apron and lie on another trolley so I would be close enough to be able to speak to Julian throughout his ordeal. As the scanner steadily took Julian in, I too seemed to be drawn in after him, then Julian said, "Olwen I'm ever so sorry but I need to get out again, I can't breathe and my chest pain defiantly getting worst" I signalled to the girls, "Get him out, this isn't working" This time they recommended he had some oxygen, although normally in ward situations only doctors can prescribed oxygen!

He agreed to try again, but there was hardly enough space for his head let alone for a mask on his face, but in addition to the lack of space they asked me to hold the mask tight over his face. This was awful, my hand was crushing the mask over his face no wonder he felt as if he was suffocating. It was making me feel sick watching him struggling to breathe, and his poor little eyes were making sudden movements like a trapped rabbit. He muffled through the mask, "It's like being in a coffin

Olwen" I tried to put myself in his situation, paralysed from high chest down, with the machine taking him in a jagged movement because his shoulders were wedged tight at the sides, suffering this tight chest pain with no space to take a deep breath and someone holding a plastic smelling mask over my face, pressing hard on my face because there wasn't enough room for the hand.

He looked at me and said, "Olwen, I can't do this, my heart feels as if it's going to explode. I think I'm going to have a heart attack" At this stage I wanted to shout stop everybody, this is too dangerous and totally inhumane but instead of been hysterical I tried to calm the situation down and asked him, "Wait a minute, what would Gill tell you to do?" I was thinking more of deep breathing technique, not that he could take a deep breath there was no room. But to my surprise he said "She would tell me to sing". "Sing!" I said, "Sing what?"

That chanting she taught me yesterday" I asked him, "Have you got the courage to hum it loud, Ju?" thinking if he could sing then it might expand his lungs to take deeper breaths! He said, "I'll have a go" Then I thought if he's got the courage, then I can't be seen to be doing any less.

So for 40minutes we both hummed, and I didn't care if the world and its mother were laughing at us. If this could bring a means to an end to his 'drug for-bidding lunacy', it was worth all the humiliation in the world. As he was coming out of the tunnel, he tilted his head back and looked at me with large protruding eyes and gave a weak smile he said, "You've got nice perfume on." I wanted to sob, this was so like Julian. He looked and sounded as if he was taking his last breath, but still found a microscopic streak of goodness amongst this terrible turmoil to pass a compliment. As I looked down at him I noticed how much weight he had lost, I noticed his long scraggy neck, his protruding clavicle bones, the blackness under his eye sockets, his bulging eyes, his white pasty face and his dripping hair sticking to his scalp as if he'd just come out of the shower.

I couldn't help thinking, what have I allowed these doctors to do to him? I brought him here for them to make him better but day by day minute by minute I could see him getting worse. He even looked worse after 40 minutes ordeal in this awful chamber.

As we returned to the ward it was then approaching nine o'clock, he was greeted by three Doctors who approached him like a pack of wolves to remind him he had been given a reprieve before he left the ward to temporary omit his six o'clock drugs. I couldn't believe my ears, what was the matter with these men, why were they behaving like bullies towards Julian?

Julian pleaded with them once again, "Please, please I beg you I'm exhausted from the ordeal of the scanner; I'm not strong enough to take any more Insulin it's still too soon I've still got chest pain from the claustrophobia. Please let me have a good night sleep and then I'll be stronger in the morning to take your drugs"

They threatened him with these words, "If you don't take the Insulin and the antibiotics right now, then we will have to arrange transport for you to be transferred to Shrewsbury tonight"

With those words, he admitted defeat and submitted to their enforcement of drugs. That night I agreed with Julian, that this was now definitely plain and simple BLACK MAIL. It didn't make sense to me, forcing someone to taking insulin at nine o'clock at night when they knew he <u>hadn't</u> had his evening meal before the scan and of course there was no kitchen facility's available at this unearthly hour to get another meal for him to compensate the insulin. In addition to this the doctors were constantly failing to gain access to his veins; consequently he didn't have an Intravenous drip to help regulate the insulin either!

Why were the three of them acting so irresponsible, it was as if they had to have the last word no matter what? All Julian wanted was to feel well again, but they played their trump card when they mentioned Shrewsbury, they knew how frightened he was about been transferred there. It goes without saying as soon as he had his Insulin his condition worsened, just as he'd predicted he obviously hadn't had time to recover from his traumatic experience of his claustrophobia. It's a wonder his Adrenal Glands didn't give up on his fight, fear and flight that night as his stress factor was put to the test?

Rejection

Julian's condition progressively got worse that evening, and he struggled through the next day on the account he was given the Insulin regularly having to listening to such comments as "The Doctors must know what they are doing" from qualified nurses.

But when something does not sit comfortable with nurses conscious it's their duty to become the patients advocate. Believe it or believe it not that's all I was trying to do, but evidently the nurses had now joined forces with the doctors and become bullies, in a gentler way granted but bullies never the less.

While Gweno was visiting that evening she relived me for a few minutes, so I could pop to the toilet, as I was returning to his bed side I thought, I can't take much more of this. Feeling nothing but despair I collapsed into an arm chair in the waiting area. As I sat there thinking how could Julian and I get out of this place, this situation, this dilemma, this crisis. I felt as if I was suffocating, it was as if we were both been swallowed up in quick sand and no one was offering a helping hand.

I don't know how many minutes I'd been sat in the pitch darkness, but someone noticed my silhouette in the moon light, and asked, "Are you all right." I don't think he realised who he was speaking too otherwise I don't think he would not of engaged in conversation with me.

I replied, "I hardly think so, I can't get anyone to listen to my husband's wishes." He suddenly realised who he was speaking to, it was Julian's consultant.

Still in darkness I asked him if he was married, he said he was. I asked him if he took marital vows in his faith. He said of course he had.

Did he also say he would take care of his wife in sickness and in health in his vows?

He again replied "Yes".

"Well that's exactly what I'm doing I've taken care of Julian while he's been healthy, and now I'm trying to watch out for him while he's sick. Please can't you listen to his plea, I'm only trying to do what he requests of me? His requests not mine. I know he's got a high blood glucose reading, but he's allergic to your treatment. I know he's allergic to

Diabetic treatment his diabetic specialist in Worcester told him he was, so why do you insist on giving him a drug he knows he's allergic too can't you take his word for it. Please can't you help us?"

He then tilted his head back and looked down his nose at me and said, "I don't wish to carry on with this conversation anymore; you better return to your husband's bed side I think that's where your place should be right now."

Yet again, Julian was right, <u>they don't listen</u>. Out of frustration I called out of the darkness down the corridor as he so rudely walked away. "One day I will find out why he has such a reaction to your treatment, dead or alive, mark my words, I will, and when I do I will come back and let you know why. Do you hear me?"

I couldn't believe I was dealing with so many Doctors and Consultants who had such closed minds, to the point of been sealed. (Neither could I believe I was shouting at a Consultant, a title Id bowed and scraped too my entire nursing career)

After Gweno left I was squatting as usual supporting Julian on the edge of the bed, when a Doctor just stood in the door way saying nothing just staring at us. I might of misunderstood the next few seconds but he appeared to be smirking, in my frustrations I did something unforgettable rather than unforgivable, from deep within my soul I wanted to shake him by the throat but as both my hands were tied up at that time holding poor Julian up, I wanted to do the next best thing and throw something at him. I couldn't reach anything, so I grabbed my glasses off the top of my head and through them at him, screaming "What are you doing to my husband, why won't you stop all this?

Julian barley able to talk, whispered in my ear as his head was slumped on my shoulder leaning very heavy on me, he now obviously couldn't take his own body weight any more. Julian tilted his face towards me and said with a **little boy look** who was sharing a secret with his best friend

"The Doctor knows what he's doing, don't shout at him he might throw you out and I need you to hold me up I can't breathe without you." It was so pitiful to here Julian reduced to this, I fought the sadness out of my heart so I didn't cry in front of him. He made it sound as if I had become his lungs, when he said "I can't breathe without you" I felt as if I was his donor sharing our lungs so he could survive. Because of what he said, I got a second wind and I picked up an empty tissue box and threw it at his feet, he jumped like a little Leprechaun. A nurse came running to his defence, asking if the Doctor was all right, which made me even more furious; the nurse was more concerned about the Doctor having an empty box of tissues attacking his feet, whereas poor Julian was gasping for breath and struggling for survival from their forced toxic drugs. I didn't hear any one asking if Julian was all right. The Doctor smiled and calmly said, "Yes, I'm fine" then referring to me, "She's just a bit upset" (A bit!)

No time to say Goodbye

Both of us had a terrible night, neither of us slept again Julian in pain and I on guard.

That morning the Doctors were on his case yet again, wanting to transfer him to Shrewsbury, Julian could only whisper now to the doctors "Please don't send me to Shrewsbury, I shall die if you send me there, it will be my death sentence." But it was the black list issue that made him agree to go in the end at the same time he was beginning to have his doubts about his lovely sanctuary. Julian couldn't get them to understand, the only reason his condition was deteriorating was because he was being administered drugs that were reacting badly with his body. Have you ever been involved in an argument when your opponent has been so obnoxious that the only way to win the argument was to either knock them out or give in? This was one of those moments in Julian's life, as he didn't have the strength to blow never mind knock someone out so he was forced to take the latter option and give in. On 2nd November 2008 it is documented in his notes, "Patient not happy to go to Shrewsbury, would rather die here at Oswestry, because he thinks he was not treated well there. I persuaded him again, and he agreed" Julian was agreeing to something against his will, this surely was bullying of the highest degree but having the audacity to document and admit bullying, its beggars belief. Later in the paragraph the Doctor wrote "?? Panic attack" What was he saying, couldn't the Doctor differentiate between a critically ill patient and a fake panic attack? Can you see what Julian was up against; he was first denied the chance to die at home then for the second time he was denied the opportunity to die in what he considered to be his sanctuary.

How could they be so callus? For his journey they injected him with 60mg of Diuretics a drug he consistently told them he reacted to. With the instructions documented **inside** his medical notes 'observe Blood pressure', but the notes were sealed inside an envelope and I didn't hear any nurses verbally pointing out to observe blood pressure to the Ambulance crew! Accompanied by the fact Julian did not have an escort nurse, so who was looking out for his lowering blood pressure? Diuretics are notorious for dropping blood pressure, interestingly his blood pressure recording just before he was administered the Diuretics was 104/82, so to this day I don't understand why it was given minutes before he entered the Ambulance. There was a sense of rush about the place, the staff were packing his belongings, notes and paperwork being gathered up, furniture being moved to make space for the ambulance stretcher and I was in limbo thinking 'slow down, things don't need to be like this, everything is out of control' Julian's not getting the best deal here! But all I could do was help to balance him. The Blue light transport was awaiting us, we had to go.

Julian's sixth Ambulance journey

On the morning of 2nd November 2008 little did Julian know he had just spent his last night at his beloved sanctuary? Not realising he had greater battles ahead of him, barley coherent enough to be able to say good bye to his 'safe corner to hide', the one place in the whole wide world in the last thirty four years he felt safe when he became ill. The fun and games he'd had over the years with the female nurses, the male orderlies the occupational therapist staff the physiotherapists last but not least the other patients. The pranks they got up to, incidentally which would not be allowed today because of health and safety in the work place. Agnes Hunt would disapprove of the modern ways I'm sure, the lack of humour found in all Hospital these days, including her own hospital.

They have now scientifically proven that laughter produces endorphins, which helps with pain control, Agnes Hunt with the help of her "old wives tales" had worked that out years ago.

What better way of dealing with pain than through laughter, as the old saying goes 'Laughter is the best medicine' not to mention how cost effective it is.

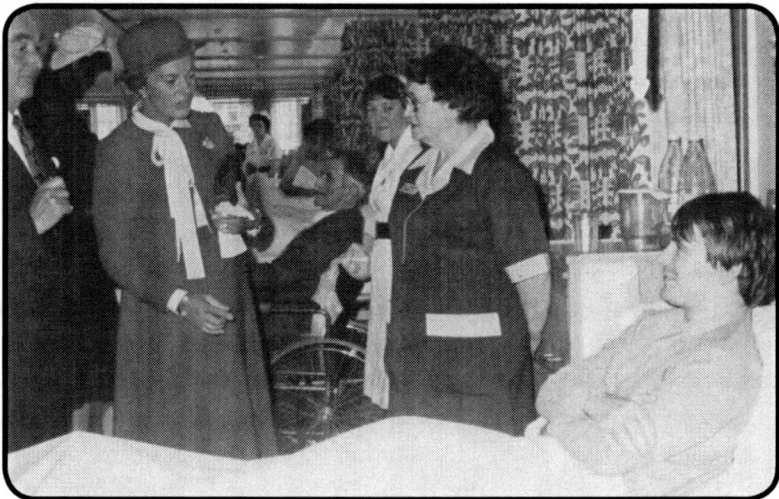

Photograph of Julian sharing a joke with the Hospital Patron
H.R.H the Duchess of Kent.

Fondly known as the 'White Rose of York' who in later years struggled to face gruelling battles against her own health. And while in exile away from the glamour circles, she fetched and carried for patients in Hospitals and Hospices even emptied bed pans.

Still reminiscing, I recalled the large portraits of Agnes Hunt in the corridor depicting her adult life here at her own Hospital.

You see it was not just Julian who had an affinity with this Hospital; I too had developed a love for the old sheds. To give you a brief out line of how I had developed such affection for this couple, Robert and Agnes.

At the age of twenty I attended an interview at The Robert Jones and Agnes Hunt Orthopaedic Hospital where they offered my twin sister and myself a position on the Spinal Injury Unit as long as we agreed to embark on their Orthopaedic training the following autumn, to which we both agreed. During my training I came across a biography of Agnes Hunt in the hospital library. I found this woman fascinating, so much so that she became my heroin; my whole career from then on was based on her belief that all sick people need good food, fresh air and above all plenty of laughter. She believed no one would get better without these three tonics.

She was born into an aristocratic society, so nursing did not usually go hand in hand with these high society ladies, but she had suffered much pain from osteomyelitis in her hip from the age of ten. And when she was once confined to bed as a child, she was caught crying by her clergy who wrote in her birthday book, "Reared in suffering thou shalt know, how to solace others woe. The reward of pain doth lie in the gift of sympathy"

This 'scribe' must have made such an impression on her young life and because of her own suffering she once wrote, she believed she was 'sent to earth to help other cripples'.

After completing her nurse training she 'sent word' to her mother asking if she could convert one of the family homes into a care home for children with TB of the bone, which was so prevalent in those days. The children who were afflicted by this skeletal disease were referred to as cripples in those days. Her mother agreed to bequeath one of the houses, Agnes chose the family home in Baschurch Shropshire and she started accepting 'crippled children' Children arrived in droves by word of mouth and by 1921 she was full to capacity and had to house some of them in the garden sheds. She eventually had to move to a bigger premise which later became known as The Robert Jones and Agnes Hunt Orthopaedic Hospital. She opened this hospital with only 320 beds, the 'quaint' aspect of this establishment was the beds had wheels, and patients could be pushed down the lanes and sometimes into Oswestry town itself to do their shopping. In 1926 Agnes was honoured with the title 'Dame Commander of the Order of the British Empire' Apart from her three ethos, she also expected her nurses to abide by the practice of good common sense, gentleness and kindness empowering hope and joy to those who were suffering. Hospitals to Agnes were for the good of the patients, and neither medical nor hospital etiquette should stand in the way of that aim. Wow! What went wrong?

If only Agnes had been in charge when Julian needed her most, sadly he was 60 years too late. Dame Agnes Hunt sadly died in 1948.

Then there was Robert Jones, a man who I had a lot of admiration for. He, like Agnes had the same ethos about nursing and doctoring. They both seemed to have listening ears and caring hearts but above all were forward thinkers. They would have found Julian's case unusual and exiting, not annoying, like the Doctors that were taking care of him did. They would have thrived on solving his mysterious complaint. Robert Jones was born on 28th of June 1857 exactly 100 years to the day of the birth of my twin sister and I. So we had more in common than most, we shared his birthday. He was knighted in 1917, and from then on was called Sir Robert. He died sixteen years before Agnes in 1932 age 75years.

In desperation I would walk the long ¼ mile long corridor begging Agnes and Robert to intervene in Julian's case, but in the end, not even their Pioneering Hospital could save Julian's life and all the Doctors had to do was just 'Listen' Why had my two heroes' let me down in my hour of need.

Photograph of my Heroin, Dame Agnes Hunt, 'Commander of the Order of the British Empire'
(The title Dame carries the same weight as been knighted a Sir.)

Sir Robert Jones 1ˢᵗ Baronet, Knight Commander of the Order of the British Empire, CB.

Sir Robert Jones was knighted in 1945, but I have no idea what date when either of them felt the touch of a sward on their shoulder by a sovereign. The original Knight had to prove he would 'Protect the weak, the defenceless, the helpless and to fight for the good of all'

Suddenly I felt as if I'd been in a time warp, reality struck me, Julian was boarding the Ambulance. As he boarded, the Ward Sister called out "Julian, take everything they offer you" these words have stayed with me ever since.

It's a short sentence, but why should these few words haunt me when I recall Julian's last few minutes at this hospital. One day maybe, it might be revealed to me but until then I fail to understand why would she want Julian to take something that he believed his body was reacting to so badly, couldn't she see how the treatment was making him suffer?

Yet again I rang Gweno at work, "Please come, they're taking him again by blue light, and I don't think he's ever coming back" Bless her, my faithful companion managed to get there just before the Ambulance pulled away. This time they allowed me to ride in the Ambulance while Gweno drove once more alone in her car behind.

They insisted I sat in the cab with the driver, but I wanted to comfort him so much and hold his hand tell him comforting and positive things. Although I was only a few feet away, I felt I might as well be miles away. On the journey the Paramedic took it upon himself to lower the back rest down, and then there was a big kafuffle a lot of moving around in the back. He said he's gone off, he's not breathing. I quickly turned round to find Julian lying completely flat. I said, "Please sit him up, quick, he does this if he lies down.

This is one of the reasons he's been transferred because he can't breathe when he is lying down." He wasn't keen at first, at the same time I felt as if I was interfering. To be fair it's a natural instinct of any first aider or any medical person, if a patient stops breathing they lye them flat and administers CPR, but in this case Julian needed the opposite.

It must have been difficult for the paramedic to go against his instincts and training, but he did eventually do what I suggested and raised the backrest to its original position. As he did so Julian drew in a deep breath, and to the Paramedic's surprise informed the driver, "He's breathing again, but his oxygen levels remained very low" even though I could see he had increased his piped oxygen.

On arrival Julian was taken straight to the Medical Admissions Ward where he was recommenced on antibiotics once more and of course eventually more insulin. The battle was on going and still true to form his very predictable reaction flair up ten minutes after been administered any drugs.

The following night at about eleven o'clock it was necessary to emergency bleep an on call doctor, this particular doctor however was more concerned about saving Julian's life rather than getting into a confrontation over whether he should or should not have Insulin. He was concerned that his blood pressure was too high, he explained he must have terrible pain somewhere for it to be this high, let's treat the pain first he said. This young Doctor was like a breath of fresh air at last we'd found someone who was treating Julian holistically instead of wearing blinkers and homing in on this, one dare I say it stupid diagnose 'so called diabetes'. I really wanted everybody who was treating Julian to think outside the box. This Doctor gave us fresh hope, I recalled watching a Japanese concentration camp film once and one of the prisoners who was a lay-preacher said, "A man can tolerate a huge amount of pain and punishment as long as he has hope, once he has lost hope that's when he dies"

Julian used to say, "I'm not dead until I'm dead" he didn't consider dying as dead, one can recover.

At this stage we both had hope that this compassionate Doctor was going to listen, and then turn Julian's life round. I can remember saying to him, "Thank God, thank God some ones listening at last, if you give him strong analgesia I know his high glucose levels will come down then his insulin won't have to be administered" He said, "Never mind about the insulin, stops talking about the insulin I don't want to know about the insulin I will discuss that later, in the mean time I want to discuss his resuscitation status before we go any further"

I told him there was no question both Julian and I had discussed before, that if there was a chance of surviving cardiac massage was to be carried out in both our cases, unless our minds had gone in which case neither of us wanted to survive. True to my word as soon as he was given morphine injection his blood glucose plummeted from 25 to 7 in only ten minutes.

This should have raised alarm bells with the medical sector let alone me, why should blood sugar come down with analgesia. It was obviously due to some fact I had not yet worked out, unless it was something to do with his Adrenal Tumour.

That night Julian felt as if he was having a hypoglycaemic attack, by morning I couldn't believe what a good recovery Julian had made over night. As his blood sugar reading had come down to 7 it wasn't necessary for him to have the insulin throughout that day including the following morning. Because of this sudden recovery he was transferred mid-morning to another ward where it was dark and bleak with no window to give anyone hope of ever getting into the outside world ever again. I'm sure people in prison see more sky light than these poor patients did in this occupancy, absolutely totally soul destroying, just artificial light and extremely hot atmosphere. Agnes and Robert would have turned in their grave for lack of fresh air.

As soon as he arrived on this ward, the old insulin battle began again and once again insulin treatment was recommenced. Within a short time he was breathing like someone with emphysema, he was now reacting to the drugs sooner than the usual ten minutes. That afternoon his brother and his frail Father came to visit. Julian found talking very difficult while he was breathing like this, he suggested in a gasping and husky voice "Why don't you go for a cup of tea Olwen and a bit of fresh air while Dads here, but leave Gweno here to help me sit up I trust her with my life"

Good bye Papa

While I was away, Julian said to his brother, "If anything should happen to me, I want you to promise me that you will look after Olwen for me." His brother got all emotional naturally and said, "Don't talk like that." Julian then got cross and said, "Stop crying and listen to me, while they keep giving me these drugs I will die, promise me you will look after Olwen when I'm gone". In the end he promised. Then Julian turned his attention to his Father and asked forgiveness for being such a difficult son, and said he was sorry. His father agreed that he had been a difficult son but did not offer a pardon for his son's behaviour, not even on his death bed. I don't know what it did to Julian's feeling, but Gwen's heart was breaking just listening. Feeling embarrassed that she was intruding on such sensitive matters, she asked Julian, "Would you like me to leave, so that the three of you can talk freely." Julian said, "No I have nothing I want to say to them that I don't want you to hear Gwen" His Father not forgiving him might have been an over sight, but Julian used to say he had spent all his life from the age of five trying to gain favour with him.

After the two of them had left and Julian repeated what took place that afternoon, a song from the 70`s came to mind called, "Seasons in the sun" by Terry Jacks. Some of the lyrics in the song are so heart breaking, but poignant,

"Seasons in the sun".

"Good bye Papa its hard to die.
When all the birds are in the sky.
Little children every where.
When you see them I'll be there"

The song goes on, but ironically since Julian's death, it has been on the radio constantly. Like so many other songs that pull at your heart strings, if the lyrics fit the moment it can rip your heart apart.

That same afternoon his mother also visited with her husband and Julian's half-sister. Soon after his Father left his mother begged him to take all the Insulin that was offered. Julian looked at her with drugged up eyes and said "Mum! I'm trying, but when it makes me so very ill I sometimes have to refuse"

He looked like Buddha with one towel wrapped round his head and another round his neck and a bath towel over his tummy which was so swollen. When I say he perspired, I mean he soaked a bath towel every 90 minutes.

After the psychological build-up of begging forgiveness off his father, the topic had left him exhausted and trying to defend his refusal of insulin at times to his mother it sapping his energy further, he could barely stay awake so he asked the three of them to leave.

The following morning he was moved to yet another ward, he was now getting distressed with all the moves. As his bed was being pushed on to this ward he said, "Olwen, this is not a good place to die" As the porter parked his bed into his bed space I asked, "Where do you consider a good place to be then Ju". He said, "On a mountain top, sitting with your legs crossed and a Buffalo skin wrapped over my shoulders, with no one for company no food or drink, just waiting for death."

"Where do you imagine this place to be?" he replied "With the Native American Indians of course, they knew how to live and how to die with dignity". He didn't appear disoriented at this stage, just very ill.

Hungry for this mountain top he felt he couldn't breathe on that ward, to be fair the heat on the ward was stifling. The large windows only opened about 2 inches; we felt as if we were breathing everybody's yesterday's germs not to mention the day before that stretching back year.

No wonder they say germs grow in Hospital, this was the perfect breeding ground for them. This ward should have been renamed 'Germ Incubation ward'. The smell of the last 20 years of hot dinners, the smell of lingering used bed pans and commodes, talcum powder and deodorant spray, body spray, lady's perfumes and aftershave behaving like visitors lingering and refusing to go, day in day out. Julian was right this was not a healthy place to be, never mind die. The air was so thick it got stuck at the back of your throat and up your nose. Julian was obviously having difficulty like me breathing in this thick atmosphere. He did what he'd done so many times before, he pulled off the oxygen mask and pushed the oxygen tube to the back of his throat, in order to get maximum effect from the flow of oxygen directly in to his lungs.

That afternoon he asked if he could be moved next to the window, the nurses asked why he explained that he found it difficult to breathe in the hot atmosphere and the beds were so close together he was beginning to feel claustrophobic. To be fair the beds were so close together one could touch the neighbouring bed.

At 8 o'clock the following morning Julian took another turn for the worst, there was no one around. So I shouted for help, a nursing Sister popped her head round the corner to see what was going on. I called out, "He's going off quick, get the blood pressure machine and bleep the Doctor". She did as I asked, but kept informing me "I'm not supposed to be here, it's not my bay."

All I kept thinking was, "Does it matter whose bay it is, if you're saving someone's life and besides where was the person that was supposed to be in this bay, anyway?"

She soon came up to speed to what had happened, and tried to reassure Julian by saying, "Hang on in there Julian, the Insulin will soon be out of your system, then you'll feel better."

At that a Catholic Deacon came to the bottom of the bed and stared at Julian for some time, he then came close to my side; bearing in mind an emergency situation had got hold of Julian's bed space by now. There were leads everywhere, but he managed to climb over them somehow, it was as if he was invisible. No one asked him who he was or could he leave, no one seemed to notice him amongst the chaos. He whispered in my ear, "This young man is very ill, would you like me to arrange for him to have Sacrament of the Anointment of the sick"?

Julian heard and opened his eyes wide, and he mustered a loud "NO", I then said to the Deacon, "Can someone receive the sacrament more than once in their life"? I didn't want Julian to think I was giving up on him. He said nodding his head saying, "It can sometimes strengthen one." Julian slumped back onto a pile of pillows and said, "Ok if it will strengthen me then I'll agree". At that the Deacon made the sign of the cross on Julian's forehead and then swiftly left.

Julian spontaneously opened his eyes wide again and said something unlike him, "Quick call the Deacon back, I need him, he's got healing hands."

As Julian was being taken care of, I ran as fast as I could down the corridor to try and catch him up, maybe he was just as good as having the Priest if Julian felt he had healing hands but it seemed as if he'd vanished into thin air. About 20 minutes later the Priest arrived, the commotion had settled but the after math of the emergency was still evident with leads and tubes still present but the staff had all merged into the walls so it seemed. A Doctor still hadn't materialised when the Priest left, evidently the Deacon had had time to drive in to Shrewsbury city centre to fetch the Priest from the Cathedral and conducted Julian's last rites, before a Doctor could be summoned. In other words it was quicker to get a Priest to help you on your journey to the next world than it was to get a Doctor at Shrewsbury Hospital to help you stay in this world. I know they are busy in big Hospitals, but bigger isn't always better. The bleeped Doctor eventually arrived four hours later just before lunch time, by which time Julian's condition had started to improve. Needless to say, his instructions were the same as all the other doctors; continue with the insulin as normal. The following morning I was desperate to go to the toilet, I begged Julian to let me go. His insecurity was worsening me; I tried to reassure him I'd be quick. He said, "I'm so frightened, and I didn't know what they might give me next" I pushed the bed against the wall and wedged him with pillows to support him before I left. As I was ran back to his bed side, porters were pushing Julian's bed off the ward. I couldn't understand why no one had mentioned that he was on the move again before I went to the toilet. I called up the corridor after Julian, "Where are they taking you Julian?" he shouted "A ward upstairs" I grabbed my cardigan and handbag and rushed behind him asking, "What about packing your clothes? He shouted, "They've packed them" What about the Intravenous antibiotic they wanted to give you? He said "They've given me that" What about the Diuretics they wanted to give you? "They've given me that too." What about the Insulin? "That too" I said, "I don't understand how they had time, I was so quick."

The blindness

By the time we arrived on the ward, it was evident that Julian had gone completely blind, and his hearing was also affected he'd become partially deaf.

Was it my presence that made the staff behave in this manner, to administer intravenous medication in such a rush fashion, in my opinion this was both foolish and dangerous.

I'm sorry if my presence caused Julian any harm, but I was only at Julian's bed side not because he asked me to be there but because he begged me to be there. So the wife in me wanted to comfort and protect him, but also the nurse in me could see he was not receiving fair play.

All through that night he kept asking, "Why have the nurses turned off all the lights?"

I kept repeating the same answer, "They haven't, the night light is still on Julian."

He would repeat, "It's so dark, I can't even see the street light, what's going on?"

Later on he said "Is it a starry night Olwen? I'd answer "Yes". He would then question again and again, "Why can't I see the stars?" then he'd ask, "What about the moon, is that out?" I would reply, "Yes, full moon". Well why can't I see the moon either?" He even behaved like a blind man, turning his head in sudden sharp movement when a tiny sound was made, and say, "What's that, what was that noise?" During this time of blindness he had only passed 70mls of urine in 10 hours. They continued to give him the diuretic at the same time restricted his oral fluid intake. By the following morning he had only passed 4mls of urine in 4hrs. The general rule of thumb in Intensive Care Units is; we should all produce at least 30mls every hour. Where did that leave Julian then, only 1ml an hour and not even nursed by high dependency nurses!

It appears to me; he was more poorly than ITU standard then!

The Doctor had agreed that if his blood glucose came down to 12, the Insulin could be withheld. His blood sugar reading that morning was down to 6.6, the nurses were still insisting that he should have the insulin their reasoning was 'That's what diabetics do, they take insulin'.

Julian pleaded with them saying he felt as if he was slipping in to a hypoglycaemic attack, his organs were too swollen to eat to raise his sugar levels, he didn't have an intravenous access to give him a glucose drip but they still wanted to lower his glucose levels even further.

Eventually one of the nurses did show him some compassion, but this was the only time a nurse showed any empathy. Some days previously Gweno and Gill had arranged for a Chronologist to visit Julian. Julian was in agreement with his visit, anything to try and solve the mystery of why he couldn't tolerate any treatment; a verbal consent was obtained from the Ward Sister and the Consultant. He arrived at 10am to conduct his allergy testing and by 12 mid-day he had completed his session. His findings were, Julian should avoid white re-fined food, and his oxygen issues were due to a reaction to some medication and the current medication was also affecting his liver function. He suggested Julian would benefit from eating a banana each day to increase his potassium, and try to increase his magnesium levels somehow. He recommended 'True Food Magnesium' and 'True Food GTF Chromium'

Julian thanked Ben in a strange way, by turning his head away from him and tilting it up like a blind man with his ear to the speaker. This was the first tell-tale signs that he had indeed gone blind, but there were others later. Another was just after Ben left when a nurse handed Julian his medication. I could not believe what he did next he puckered up his lips when she placed the antibiotic capsule in-between his lips and he started to suck on it, making kissing noises. He kept saying, "This is blocked, there's something the matter with this, it's really blocked"

Thinking he wanted a straw I placed a straw in his drink so that he could take his antibiotic capsule, I took the capsule from his lips and replaced it with the straw. He then franticly blew bubbles all over the place, there was such a mess and proceeded to say, "That's better, it's not blocked any more" Evidently he mistook the capsule for a straw.

When I gave him the straw he naturally blew down it to unblock the blockage. This was further proof that his sight was still absent.

—Still asking who's turned out the lights, I repeatedly told him no one had, it was now day light.

—As well as not been able to see, he also spoke very loudly due to his deafness. He was fast becoming a stranger, not the Julian I knew. Throughout all of this, he looked like a frightened rabbit, a very sick rabbit at that. He had become so pale, grey looking, he had black rings under the eyes, constantly pouring with sweat his hair still sticking to his scalp, I noticed that day how much further weight he'd lost since that awful night in the scanner, especially around his neck.

Then at exactly three o'clock that afternoon Julian's vision returned, just as if someone had turned on the lights. I can remember glancing up at the clock as I commented to Julian what a nice young man Ben was, and that he was a lot younger than what I expected. Julian replied, "Was he, I don't know I didn't see him, I kept telling you I couldn't see anything?" Every nurse and Doctor who attended Julian from then on were asked by either Julian or myself, why had he suffered total blindness and partial deafness immediately after been given the combination of drugs in such a hurry on the other ward? No one offered any explanation why the blindness should occur, or why it should have lasted for 27 hours. I also asked, was it normal practice to give so many drugs together and so quickly? There was never any explanation offered for their colluges behaviour. Incidentally his partial deafness never recovered. Gweno trying to do her best for Julian went into Shrewsbury city centre and bought the two bottles of supplement Ben recommended, but the situation as it was I was too frightened to ask the doctors if he could stop the traditional drugs in exchange for these alternative therapy. Desperate as I was, I would not meddle in Julian's medical care behind the doctors back and jeopardise his life.

After this incident Gweno bought me a little red note book from the WRVS shop, for me to start jotting down any questions Julian had for the doctor. Although I was writing about the daily goings on in my diary, this book was to be kept specifically for questions Julian wanted answered. Because there was so much going on with Julian in a day, by the time the ward Physician did his flying visit at 5pm both Julian and I would forget what we needed to ask. The window of opportunity was so small. The little red book came in quite handy, not only to remind us of the questions to ask but also to reflect on the answers later. Julian dictating his questions and I became his little secretary, I decided to write his questions in blue and their answers in red. One of the questions I wrote down was, "Did Julian, suffer heart failure?" the Doctors answer was "No". I also wrote "Did Julian have fluid on the lungs? The answer was "No" again.

Once they had answered no to both questions he asked, "If my heart and lungs are fine, could the diuretic be stopped? Their answer was "No"

It didn't make sense to either of us, why did he need to continue with the Diuretics when it's obvious he was becoming so dehydrated.

Another question I wrote was, "Could the Doctor explain why the liver function tests became so elevated when on diabetic treatment?" His answer was, "I don't know."

I wrote, "Could he explain why did the nurse say, after he he'd received Insulin and realised he didn't have Intravenous fluid to compensate the reaction he was suffering, why did she advise him to 'drink plenty of water to get rid of the toxins' why did she use the word toxins unless she felt he was allergic to the substance?

The Doctor had no explanation and consequently did not reply.

I wrote the nurses comment "I can't believe you haven't got Intravenous fluid infusion in progress, in case something like this happens" Another blank space in my little the red book.

Another question I wrote, "Can a test for Insulin resistant or insulin allergy be conducted under NHS control"? (To back up the Chronologists findings) The Doctor said, "There was no such tests available"

I wrote, "Could he obtain the old Worcester X-Rays to compare with when he had 3 litters of fluid drained from his plural effusion, the Doctors should have documented that there was some residual left in the base of the lung, but were happy for this to remain. They verbally said at the time, they would adopt the 'watch and see policy' couldn't they do the same, instead of insisting on continuing with the diuretics drying him out further. The answer was still "No".

I wrote, "Julian had Hepatitis C when he was in his mid-20s could that have impaired his liver, affecting his liver function tests? The Doctor showed no interest in this piece of information at all, except to shrug his shoulders and pull a face.

I wrote, "Why every time he received Insulin did his temperature plummet to below 34 degrees and would only return to normal when the insulin was stopped."

"I don't know why that should happen" was the reply.

I wrote, "Why did Julian never have glucose in his urine, didn't he find that strange when his glucose levels were so high?" This answer was longer than one syllabus, "We don't test urine any more as standard practice it's not considered a valid test"

213

This time I replied saying, "If that's the case, I suggest someone should be informing 'Aldi Food Stores' if doctors don't consider urine lab stick testing for Glucose as a valid test anymore and what's more someone should also inform all the Banks, because prior to signing for my second mortgage two days before Julian became ill I had to sign a medical declaration stating I did not have glucose in my urine. I wrote, "Will we need to make arrangements to get oxygen bottles delivered once he's discharged?

His reply was, "No, he will learn to manage to go without oxygen before going home" Julian replied, "But I've been on it now for four weeks, and our friend's mother was also on insulin and she had oxygen cylinders delivered to her home, didn't he think there was some similarities in both cases? Another shrug of the shoulders, "No, Diabetics don't need oxygen".

I wrote, that the Tissue viability rep had said, "Patients on silver nitrate treatment didn't need oral or intravenous antibiotics." He said that she was entitled to her opinion but he still wanted the antibiotics to continue.

I haven't quoted everything I wrote, I've just plucked out a few examples of the type of questions Julian wanted answered. They seemed like reasonable requests to me just substandard answers.

Off course Julian didn't ask all these questions in one go, they were asked at different intervals.

I must confess it had been some years since I'd seen so much antibiotics used. Not just on Julian, but what I witnessed with other patients too. I didn't deliberately listen to other patient's complaints but one couldn't help noticing trays upon trays of antibiotics going to most patients.

One weekend a young man in his early 20's was admitted into the bed opposite Julian on a Friday night with what he claimed was mouth ulcers, he had suffered with them for years but they were particularly bad that weekend. I recognised them, as our daughter suffered dreadfully from the same complaint. To suggest to these sort of suffers to apply baby teething gel on, was like insulting their pain threshold.

When I saw this young man having intravenous antibiotic, for what he said was mouth ulcers.

I commented, "They must be very bad to warrant that sort of treatment." He said, "Your right, they're extremely painful but antibiotics won't do them any good, this Hospital is Antibiotic mad." On the Sunday morning he took his own discharge, unlike Julian he was able to walk out.

Later that evening a Doctor came to Julian's bed side and randomly blurted out in a rather harsh manner that he had a mass in his heart and a clot in his lung. We were both shocked neither of us had requested to see a doctor, so why were we graced with his company at such a late hour? Julian went into shock and couldn't talk, so I asked on his behalf how he'd discovered this thinking I hadn't left his bed side long enough for anyone to conduct such investigations. He didn't give us an answer. I broke the silence by asking how long had they known?

He boldly announced, "Two weeks" then turned and walked away with his white coat swishing behind. We were both left numb; thinking may be there wasn't much point fighting his allergy issue any more. We both sat up all night as usual, but silently this time just staring at the floor.

The following morning I asked all the Doctors surrounding Julian's bed, why Julian had not been treated during the last two weeks for this clot on his lung.

To which they all looked perplexed and all joined in, "We don't know where you got that from."

Julian then questioned them, "So you don't know anything about a mass I've got in my heart either then" They all agreed they didn't, Julian then looked at me then said to the Doctors, "We couldn't both have imagined it, a Doctor definitely came to my bed side last night around mid-night to inform both of us of these two conditions"

Julian and I could only assume at the time that the Doctor was talking to the wrong patient and the wrong relative. While the Doctor was still there Julian asked, why do I need to continue on hypertensive drugs when my blood pressure on occasions is as low as 66/33?

No reason was given, neither was the treatment stopped. While on this ward Julian asked the Ward Sister why no one was sharing information, she asked "What do you want me to do Julian". He said, "You know I'm a complicated case, and I know I'm like a thorn in your side, can't you hold a meeting with everybody to try to get me sent home?" The Ward Sister agreed, she set about arranging a multidisciplinary meeting involving the Physician, the Dietician, Social Worker herself the Ward Sister and of course Julian. This was to take place at 5pm the following evening. At a quarter to five the Ward Sister informed Julian that the meeting had been cancelled, but she would try to rearrange it for the following evening for the same time. At lunch time the next day the Ward Sister confirmed that the meeting was still on schedule but this time Julian was not welcome, but I could attend in his place. We both wanted to know why the change of plans was necessary. I was furious with this underhandedness; I would no longer be the silent party at this meeting but Julian's spokesperson. And as Richard my cousin the solicitor had already advised Julian I had no voice in his care legally, then anything I had to say on Julian's behalf was worthless. We both knew they'd all over ride Julian's wishes. I felt like cancelling this futile meeting but Julian insisted I should try to defend him, because of his stamina I then had to find someone to sit with Julian while I was attending this meeting. Gweno like a true trooper turned up like a loyal buddy, Julian appeared unsettled and kept repeating, "It's hopeless, it's hopeless Olwen I'll never get my say, this meeting will never take place, mark, my words" I also felt now while the medical staff were dealing with me on a one to one behind closed doors they could get away with saying anything to me, but once there was a gathering of people in an official manner and notes would be taken they could not afford for anyone to quote them saying anything that might incriminate them later, especially if it was one of their own people doing the quoting.

I was beginning to think like Julian, they were too much like cowards to go through with this.

By six forty that evening Julian's predictions was fast becoming a reality, when I enquired at the nurses stationery what was going on, the Staff Nurse seemed surprised, "I thought you'd of guessed by now, the Consultant, Dietician and the Ward Sister have all long gone home" Not one of them had the courage to let Julian know, what his future plans were. Needless to say the meeting never took place and consequently the issue of the insulin was never discussed at the multidisciplinary level. I have often wondered since, why a pharmacist wasn't invited to attend this meeting to throw any light on this unusual and difficult medical case?

That evening Julian said to me, "Olwen, I've got to get out of here somehow, the Doctors have even turned my own mother against me" I said, "I don't think so Ju"

His reply was, "Yes they have, she doesn't even believe me any more when I tell her the treatment is harming me, they've even convinced her that you're trying to stop my treatment. Oh! Olwen, there's only you who believes me now"

Julian's final negotiation
with the Doctors

The following morning on the 6th of November 2008 on the strength that he believed his mother no longer believed him, he begged me to ring Worcester Hospital to speak to any nursing staff I used to work with. Again I had to ring Gweno to ask her to trek the 40 mile round trip from Welshpool to sit with Julian while I went outside to use my mobile phone as the kiosk phone was out of action as usual.

I managed to contact my previous Matron at Worcester who was shocked that the Staff was administering insulin to Julian knowing how he suffered the reactions in 2007. She said leave it with me I'll ring you back. She was going to discuss the issue with one of her ward managers.

I was concerned the reply might take a long time to sort out; I felt my place at this point was at Julian's bed side, mainly in case he took a turn for the worst. Luckily I only had to wait a few minutes she returned my call immediately.

She said, "Ok it's all sorted Olwen, I've spoken to the other two Ward Sisters and the Consultant has accepted Julian on the Orthopaedic ward, there's a side room all set up for him. All they have to do is get the Consultant at Shrewsbury to ring the RMO on call at Worcester and they will confirm the transfer" I asked if we had to pay for a Private Ambulance, she said no once they have agreed she would arrange their hospital transport to come for him. She emphasised that the RMO was waiting at the desk for the call right now. I assured her I would get them to call her as soon as possible, this was mid-morning. By mid-afternoon nothing had happened, and by four o'clock Worcester Hospital was on the phone asking Shrewsbury nursing staff, "Where is he, we have been waiting all day for the transfer, it might be difficult to arrange transport now as its Friday night" When the Physician eventually visited Julian at 5pm, he was aware that several messages had been left for him to negotiate Julian's release. As Julian had been given insulin all day but had not been able to eat, it had affected his blood pressure the physician used his low blood pressure of 76/55 as reason to refuse his realise to another Trust. Julian tried to defend himself by saying, "Please I beg you take

218

me off this Insulin then I'll prove to you how quick my blood pressure will return back to normal, but not just my blood pressure, I will start to feel better, I will eat better, I will heal better, I will breath better, I will drink better, I will pass urine better, I will simply get better then you can send me home. Please I beg you; I know I'm a thorn in your side I know I'm not one of your straight forward cases, please let me take my own discharge"

I did intervene at this stage and plead on Julian's behalf, "Please I beg you, if you won't permit the transfer then let me take him home, I realize his case is very complicated. Without this Insulin I know I can make him better, please let him have a second chance" Julian butted in, directing his disbelief towards me saying, "What do you mean second chance, I haven't had my first chance with these doctors yet" This last comment Julian made, made the doctors dig their heals in even deeper and Julian had no say after this debate.

That afternoon I reluctantly contacted Llewela asking her to do the long journey from Oxford to see her Dad again; I just felt there was a big change in him since she last saw him. At the same time I wanted to protect her, I didn't really want her to see him like this.

But luckily that evening Julian's cognitive improved enough for him to have a bit of a conversation with Kevin and Llewela. Unfortunately when she arrived she witnessed her father asking another Doctor, "Why are you forcing me to take the Insulin and the antibiotics." The Doctor replied slowly, "We are not forcing you; we're just going to keep asking you until you agree to take it." Our daughter then stepped in in his defence by saying, "That's forcing him."

Up to this point I don't believe Llewela had a specific opinion of any of the medical staff that were administering care to her Father, she just wanted to see him better and thought he was in the best place. But even this scène made Llewela express an opinion in her father's favour.

Julian asked again, "Please let me go back to Worcester Hospital they're expecting me, the bed, the doctors and nurses are just waiting for your phone call.

I feel the Doctor was playing for time, Julian now looked awful he looked under nourished, waxy, black rings under his eyes, the perspiration would not stop, they knew how bad his abscess cavity had become, in his defence he then turned the situation on to Julian by asking, "Do you think it's fair on the Ambulance men to take you all the way to Worcester with such a low blood pressure?"

I could see what he was doing; he was putting the onus back on to Julian's shoulders, by trying to make him feel guilty, if his blood pressure dropped any further the poor Ambulance crew would be held responsible for his survival. He even graphically described that if he took a turn for the worst they might have to pull over into a layby to resuscitate him. Julian said, "Ok, I'll sign anything relieving them of that responsibility, I am prepared to accept any consequences, just please, please release me"

The Doctor said, "No, we will assess you again on Monday morning after the weekend."

Julian replied, "If you intend for me to continue on this Insulin until Monday morning, then Monday will be too late for me!" But that was the Doctors final word on the matter, as he patted the bedding and repeated, "Monday, we will see on Monday" Julian then slumped, his head forward, and closed his eyes in a defeated gesture then shook it from side to side. After the Doctor had gone Julian then tackled Kevin by pointing out to him that he was dying. Both Llewela and Kevin was trying to make light of the situation, but Julian was insistent "No, I'm serious, I'm dying this Insulin is killing me" For some reason he appeared to be surveying the ward by making sweeping glances up and down the ward, as if he was checking to see if anyone was listening. If the situation wasn't so serious, it could have been interpreted as comical. He then paused and directed his instructions towards Kevin. "Right Kev, I'm going to give you permission, but only if Llewela wants to, to marry Llewela, but only if Llewela wants too. Do you understand me? You can marry Llewela with my blessing. But-if you mess her around once, just once, I'll come back and I'll haunt you like you've never been haunted before. Do you understand me?" (I confess he did use the odd swear word, during this warning to his future son-in-law)

Kevin said, "I understand Julian, I won't mess up I promise I'll take good care of her."

The reason I have mentioned this very personal and private part of our family life, is because I want people to know how particular Julian was about "dotting the I's and crossing off the T's" up to the point of death. He'd already predicted to the Doctor only one hour before if the treatment was allowed to continue, come Monday he would be as good as dead.

After Llewela and Kevin left to go back to Oxford that night, Julian had his usual bad night. The following morning on Friday the 7th of November 2008 it felt as if all the plugs were being pulled in preparation to get Julian fit for his transfer to Worcester Hospital on Monday morning. Arrangements were been made for Julian to have a Central Venous Pressure line inserted in to his neck leading very near to his heart in the x-ray department and a Neso-gastric tube into his nasal passage passing into his stomach for liquid diet. He returned to the ward about six o'clock that evening in time to start his liquid feed. It was to continue for 20 hours leaving 4 hours rest before starting the next regime. The Consultant came round that evening and said if you improve over the weekend, we still consider transferring you on Monday. Julian still frightened about his mortality, if the insulin was to continue asked one last time for it to be stopped. The Doctor insisted it had to continue, Julian gave out his last and final distress call, "NO, NO, NO that's too late I can't take any more Insulin, I'll die here if I have to take it over the weekend, it will make me too ill I will <u>have no</u> fight left in me by Monday if this treatment is allowed to carry on. This comment was just too much for me to bear, I left Gweno holding Julian as I ran out of the ward sobbing uncontrollably. I quickly rinsed my face in that microscopic dirty sink in the toilet, the water was freezing as usual, and then I rushed back to his bed side. That evening Gweno text me these words, 'When the two of you get out of there, Julian needs to complain to the Courts of Human rights on the grounds of **malnutrition, dehydration, and sleep deprivation'**

This text just amplified what Glyn my brother had already said to Julian at his bed side a few nights previously, but Gweno was not aware of Glyn's feelings or the comments he had made to Julian already. It wasn't just me others could see the injustice he was suffering too.

I pondered on these three words Gweno had mentioned in her text.

Malnutrition - I confess he hadn't been able to eat since he'd been on drugs, as he felt his painful swollen organs were pressing on his stomach.

Dehydration - I confess he was suffering from this too, with the fluid restriction which is a basic human right, and the additional

Diuretics, (water tablets) they insisted he had which exacerbated his already crisp body, with the added problem of constant perspirations brought on by allergy.

Sleep deprivation - I confess he suffered with this for 35 nights no wonder he was look as ill as he did. He was unable to sleep because of the severe pain in his abdomen, and the breathing difficulties he was experiencing when he lay down following treatment.

Putting things in order

Things seemed pretty grim for Julian now; there was no escape out of this building or from this toxic Insulin. So that night at ten o'clock after the night staff had taken over from the late shift, he asked one of the nurse's for a couple of sheets of paper from the office.

I didn't know what lay ahead of me that night but it seemed Julian wanted to put his life in order before the Insulin took over his mind for ever. He said, "Get comfortable it's going to be a long-long night, because I don't think they're going to give up on these drugs, until I'm dead"

If the situation hadn't been so serious, it would have been a beautifully romantic night. First we waited for the moon to appear then the stars popping and twinkling, the song 'Starry, Starry night' by Don McLain came to mind, many times during that night and we both hummed or sang it quietly. The chorus goes like this-

"Starry, starry night"

Now I understand what you tried to say to me,
How you suffered for your sanity,
They would not listen, they did not know how.
Perhaps they'll listen now.

Neither of us could remember the next line so we just repeated what we knew.

As you may have guessed, it was on the strength of these lyrics the title of this book came about. "They wouldn't listen, they didn't know how."

Once I made Julian comfortable and secured him in a sitting position with pillows, I then dragged a chair in front of him to prevent him over-balancing forward and head butting the floor. Then the long night started, I felt like a one armed secretary taking notes. He started to instruct me in what order things should be done in the event of his death. My first important instruction was to make sure I did not accidently cancel Llewela's car insurance, before she finishes University. He then systematically went through all our financial issues starting with our standing orders. Then onto practical issues, like "Don't forget the very next day after my death, ring the Mobility Car Company and ask them to pick the car up immediately, you don't want nasty letters demanding money after my death day" I sobbed and said, "Please Ju don't make me do this anymore, it's too sad". He urged me on by saying, "Come on it's something we've both got to do, I need to know you understand what to do if I die" We bravely knuckled down again, he then said "Get one of the Buff members to help you sell the quad bike, and ask someone who knows a bit about cars to help you sell the half renovated Porsche, neither of them will fetch much money there both unfinished projects" He also said, "Don't forget you've got my blessing to sell the house in France, but check first I think French laws says property gets handed down to the children not the wives because of second marriages" About my funeral, Cremate me Olwen, and scatter my dust where ever you think best, and don't get all screwed up about where. Don't go to a lot of expense of burying me, I don't want you feeling guilty about looking after a head stone.

Anyway I don't want you to be chained to Kidderminster because you feel you're the caretaker of my head stones. One last thing, I should like a Buffalo funeral if they think I'm worthy of it. Can you see to that?"

Throughout the night I wrote, we sang quietly, we talked, and even laughed at times but most of all we both cried gently with my head resting on his chest, sobbing quietly so not to disturb the other patients who were all sleeping.

When he'd finished instructing me, he made me read it back just to check I understood exactly what I had to do. Then we just reminisced about our life together but there was one haunting request he begged of me, "Olwen, whatever happens don't let others suffer like I have" I did agree but he didn't tell me how I could for fill his wishes on this one! Then at day break he startled me by suddenly asking me, "What have you called this list?"

I whispered, "Nothing, there's no title, what do you want me to call it?"

He thought for a moment then said, "Call it, 'In case Julian dies', list" I said, "No Ju, I don't like that title" He insisted, "Write it down, go on and then put it on the fridge door when you get home, that way you'll know exactly what to do in what order, and don't deviate from it, that's exactly how it should be done." Oh! Ju, then there was more sobbing from the both of us. Then he cupped my face in his hands and said, "I **will** die here, if they don't stop this treatment you do know that don't you"?

I said, "Yes, I know Ju"

I could not understand why Julian and I were treated so badly when we both tried to be so kind to everyone we'd ever met.

To much for to long

The following morning, which was the Saturday 8th November 2008
I recall was very sad after he had been given his usual 8am insulin his
mind had been affected so badly he kept repeating the same things over
and over again such things as "Who's the Queen of England?" I would
answer him, and then he would ask, "Who's the Prime Minister?" again
I would answer him. There were several questions similar to this, which
he would repeat over and over again. Until in the end it drove one of
patients in the opposite bed to intervene by asking, "Why is he repeating
the same question over and over again?"

I explained, "Keeping his sanity is important to him, especially Julian
because he has such a brilliant mind" That afternoon a patient in the
next bed had noticed Julian perspiring and how he'd complained of the
cold a few days previously. He called over to me and said "You know
what's the matter with your husband don't you, he's got Frozen Organ
Diabetes" I hadn't discussed Julian's condition with any of the patients
in his bay, so what made him make such a statement. I asked him "What
made you say that?" He said, "I read about it in my Diabetic magazine
this spring, when I get home I'll see if I can find the article and I'll send
it to you.

That afternoon I started to smell decay around Julian's bed, it smelt
like dead flesh and offensive smelling puss, it became progressively worse
each hour. So much so, the domestics started to go up and down the
ward spraying air freshener. This man was desperate to be nursed in a
side ward now, for the sake of others as well as himself. The next day
being Sunday 9th November 2008, Remembrances Sunday. As tradition
has it, the two minute silence was expected and respected by all. There
was nursing staff, patients, Doctors and Domestic staff all stood to
attention, those who could and faced the television.

After the silence was broken by the Chita-chatter there was an
almighty guttural noise from my right side. To my surprise that noise
was made by Julian, taking a very noisy deep breath. He said in a slurred
speech, "I tried to hold my breath for the silence"

This was so like Julian, still wanting to do the correct and etiquette thing right up to the very end. Julian's breathing had become so very noisy over this last weekend.

As lunch time approached Julian was given yet another dose of insulin, this time his body reacting within minutes of receiving it, because Julian said something I never wanted to hear him say,

"Oh! Olwen something has just gone horribly wrong, I've just been given my last lethal dose of Insulin it's all gone terribly wrong. I wanted the Doctors to stop the Insulin not me. It's all been a complete waste of time, a waste of exercise, it's all ruined I'm ruined. I can feel my self-losing my mind, Oh! Olwen my brain, my brain is hurting so much; I can start to feel it swelling up inside my skull I don't think I can recover from it this time. Oh! Olwen it's so painful."

About ten minutes later, it became very apparent to me what he meant, his body was shutting down as I watched him. It broke my heart that he knew he was forced to commit suicide, this was an absolutely and totally unnecessary death. Immediately I started to notice physical changes taking place on his body, his lips became swollen and he was dribbling from the corner of his mouth, his arms became so swollen they looked as if they'd been injected with gallons of water, in fact his outer skin was becoming transparent with fluid even his eye lids were filling up with fluid including sacks had started to develop under his eyes. My husband wasn't the thin undernourished man any more he had suddenly become water logged.

The last two nights had been very long and lonely nights, whereas the previous nights I had spent with Julian I had been lucky enough to talk to him, asked his advice and discuss things. These two nights were preparing me for a life time without Julian, a life of no communication. I could only look on as his condition worsened and wait for the morning alone. He used to say each night as it got dark, "Let's settle down and wait for the morning it will be much better when day light breaks."

As day break broke on Monday the 10th November, I was kneeling on a pillow in a squatting position in front of Julian who was sitting on the edge of the bed still. My initial reaction was he'd made it through another night and that was a blessing, I acting up as a watchman making sure he didn't over balance and fall to the floor.

I had my head on his lap, when I thought I heard Julian say something I looked up and he whispered, "Olwen, why aren't you stopping these people giving me Insulin" I looked up thinking that was a proper sentence. I half stuttered, "Julian I'm trying." He said, "But you're not actually stopping them are you, so you're no better than them are you"? His head was bowed down towards the floor as he spoke to me, his lips were still very swollen and he was dribbling.

I howled and sobbed in his lap, he then with a heavy hand banged me on the head, as I glanced up again to see why he'd done such a thing I realised he was trying to be affectionate by stroking my hair, but instead of stroking my hair he was dragging it with a heavy fist. It was his way of saying sorry, he didn't mean to make me cry. His hands and arms were so full of fluid by now they looked like the Michelin man arms his skin looked ready to burst.

This kind and gentle soul was now **out of control,** with the only two limbs that he'd been able to use since his accident in 1972.

Those were the last words he ever uttered to me. "You're no better than them."

I have to live with these words. I a nurse who had nursed and served many strangers over the years, but try as I might I could not save the only man I had ever loved.

With afterthought I'm glad he blamed me and not God, after all God hadn't done anything wrong but I had. This man was now fast becoming someone else; he didn't look like my Julian any more.

At ten o'clock the Physician appeared on the ward, as he approached Julian's bed he realised how ill he'd become over the weekend and in an alarming tone said, "This man is very ill"

I then said, "I know, he has been like this since Friday night when you insisted he was to continue with the Insulin. I've been asking for a Doctor to see him but no one's been near him over the weekend". He said, "Your husband has been seen over the weekend Mrs Davies." I replied "Well I haven't seen anyone, and I haven't left his side." He then said, "They have documented they have seen him in the notes, are you calling my Doctors liars Mrs Davies."

I deliberately left a painful silence to fall between us and raised my eye brows, hoping he would get the impression that I meant, if the cap fits, wear it. (Nobody came)

Suddenly there was a lot of kafuffle, phone calls made, ECG done, blood pressure taken, blood samples attempted.

And then a gentleman with a very long pony tail approached the bed. As far as I can remember he did not introduce himself, I assumed he was from the psychiatric department, who else would be allowed to wear a long pony tail hair style half way down his back for work. It would not be deemed professional in any other sector in the National Health Service to have such a hair style. I assumed he had been summoned to assess Julian's mental state and consequently section him just like my cousin the solicitor had warned us. When this 'long haired' gentleman asked me to help him lie Julian down so he could examine him, I pleaded with him, "No, please don't lie him down he will stop breathing if you lie him down" He was irritated by my refusal and instantly snatched back the curtains, saying to me "Excuse me can you leave right now" he summoned a nurse and with a gesture of his hand he asked a nurse to escort me to the rest room. I realised as I was leaving, I would never see Julian again as I fondly remembered him. As the curtains were being dawn round Julian's bed for the last time I also realised Julian's curtain of life was also being drawn to a close. There was a certain heaviness cocooning me as I left his bed space. As I was walking slowly away, I felt as if I was heading for the Gallows to be severed from Julian's side, it sounds a bit mellow dramatic but we had been joined at the hip for the last 29 years. Someone must have aided this 'pony tail' man's instructions and lowered poor Julian down because the next thing I heard was the same 'ponytail man' calling out "He's stopped breathing quick I need some help hear". This was 12mid day; I remember glancing at the ward clock as I tried to get past this jungle of whit-what of disorderly trolleys. There was a dinner trolley, a domestic trolley, a drinks trolley and a linen trolley, and a couple of skips fully laden with dirty linen all congregating by the nurses stationary. I can remember thinking there will be a cardiac arrest trolley joining this little lot in a minute, and I wondered how it was going to find its way through this obstacle course of trolleys. The smell coming from the food trolley sickened me, as I realised Julian would not be sharing a meal with us again. Life was carrying on as normal while Julian was struggling to survive without me at his side. There was a lot of shuffling and scrambling going on, staff rushing in and out of Julian's bed space.

I knew in my heart of heart that this was the end; the insulin issue had gone too far. Just as I feared all those weeks ago when Julian was at home and I reminded him that the insulin issue had not been properly addressed, how right I was to worry. I suddenly slipped into one of those strange modes when my body was traveling at a different pace to my environment. It seemed to me as if I was walking in slow motion, while the nursing staff were running past me fast. But on this occasion I also felt invisible, no eye contact, no excuse me, not even are you alright.

As I wondered up the corridor I glanced up to see my parents approaching, with Tracy my sister-in-law and Gill, Julian's 'new-best-friend' as he referred to her.

Funny how people turn up when you need them the most, that's why we should never under estimate the power of prayer. I don't know how Julian and I would have managed without our faith in this trapped, suppressed and imprisoned building we were living in during the last five weeks.

The five of us sat in that small minimalistic room for what seemed like ages, I recalled in my private thoughts how our friend in France had suffered the same complaint as Julian only six months previously, except her abscess was in her abdomen. She could not be operated on consequently the poison was not released, so in theory Julian should have had a better chance at least the poison in his abscess had evacuated itself. She was nursed in an Intensive Care Unit on constant morphine while Julian had no opiates' and no High Dependency Care.

The end result was, our friend was discharged home, and Julian died.

I know the medical profession feelings on the topic are, no two patients or conditions are ever the same. I agree, but this was the 21st century, and when was the last time you heard of someone dying of an abscess?

After two hours had passed I ventured out onto the main ward to see what was going on. I went like a little girl with no Julian to encourage me to do the right thing. One of the nurses said she would get a Doctor to come to have a word with us. When he eventually came I have no recollection of what he said, I don't know why, maybe I didn't like what he was saying and I blocked it off.

After the Doctor finished talking he or they got up to leave and we were asked to wait yet again.

Sometime later I ventured out onto the corridor once more to see if there was any more news of Julian, and to enquire when we were allowed to go back to sit with him. I was informed abruptly by a nurse rushing past with a bowl of water that Julian had already been taken to Intensive Care Unit at three o'clock and that I needed to pack his belongings and go down to the basement. It was now four o'clock I rushed back in to the waiting room to let my family and Gill know, "He's gone, they've taken him already". We all hurried back to his bed space, the emptiness suddenly hit me there was no bed and no Julian. Everybody hurriedly helped each other pack his cloths and belongings, it all seemed to be scattered everywhere somehow. They were all trying to find old carrier bags in his locker and were ramming everything and anything in any which way so we could hurriedly catch him up. For no reason at all I stood still for a moment, they all looked like tramps rummaging in bins. Nothing felt real, I have no recollection of a nurse escorting us to the Intensive Care Unit; in my head I felt we had to find the department our self. I could be wrong on this point but I remember sitting in a room for another two hours with no word of what was going on; thank God my family were there and Gill. Eventually at six o'clock two Doctors came to inform us that Julian needed an Intensive Care bed but they didn't have one at Shrewsbury, so he would have to be transferred to Telford that night by Ambulance. We were told he had been ventilated and they had inserted another Central Venous Pressure line into his neck, an Arterial line in his arm, so they could have a good access to his circulation. And yet another Naso-gastric tube was introduced into his stomach, this time it was to aspirate not to feed.

I sat there feeling numb, the whole situation felt quite bizarre, as I recalled only two nights before on the Friday night Julian was told in no certain terms that he was too ill to be transferred by Ambulance to Worcester Hospital because it was unfair on the Ambulance men to deal with a patient who had such a low blood pressure. After taking insulin all day Saturday, Sunday and Monday morning a drug he felt was harming him, he was now intubated and in a critical condition. At least on Friday night he had his full faculties to negotiate his wishes, whereas now after following their instructions and treatment he was unconscious.

And here we were only 72 hours later expecting the poor Ambulance crew to travel with the same patient at nine o'clock at night on a cold dark winters night with an unconscious patient who needed a Doctor and a Nurse as an escort so they could be in attendance of a Central Venous Peripheral line, a Naso Gastric tube, an Arterial-line, a Morphine pump, an Insulin Sliding Scale Pump, Intravenous fluids, oxygen therapy and Intubated. As I sat there with my family who were talking amongst themselves, I remember drifting off in my thoughts wondering what Julian would of thought of all of this. For a start he would have been cross about wasting tax payer's money on unnecessary Ambulances being carted across country all because of a drug allergy. If only they had listened to him in the first place; he could have been home and healed by now.

I could almost hear him shouting; "I told you this would happen if I continued on those drugs"

Unfortunately this is a sentence they will never hear from his lips. Only I can hear the echoes of that sentence in my head, and only I can verbalise the fears he endured.

Julian's 8th and final journey by Ambulance

My family left to go home after the Doctor had updated us on his transfer, Gill bless her offered to take me to Telford in her car, but we were warned not to travel at the same speed as the ambulance. Without her kindness and no Ambulance to follow, I know I would not have found the hospital in the pitch dark on my own, mainly due to lack of sign posts and secondly my state of mind. It left me wondering how do people with no family or friends to call upon manage. And what were the bus services like at ten o'clock at night from one hospital to another. How sad to think the elderly could be so cruelly parted from their loved ones at the end of their partnership all because of transport issues, more fighting it could of quite easily of have been me!

Gill and I sat and waited for Julian outside the Intensive Care Unit at Telford, we arrived at eight o'clock but Julian didn't arrive until nine o'clock, so much for a fast Ambulance! It was after ten o'clock before I was allowed in to see him again, it had been 10 hours since I last saw, touched or spoke to him. Gutted that I was not able to communicate with him anymore, I held his hand with both our thumbs clasped, like blood brothers do and I said quietly inside my head 'Julian you will have to find a way to communicate with me, I still have so many unanswered questions. I need to know things like, are you ready to die. Julian please squeeze my hand if you're not a Diabetic'. At that I felt a large spasm radiating from his thumb into mine. I was so shocked I immediately looked up to Gill and said, "Did you just do something then?" She shrugged her shoulders and said "No" I explained what had happened.

She stepped back away from the bed with her hands behind her back, and suggested I asked some random questions, some that requiring positive answers and some that required negative answers.

I was amazed with the result, if the answer were a defiant 'no', there was no response but if the answer was a defiant 'yes' not only did I feel a physical spasm I could also visibly see Julian's muscle jump. The accurate answers were uncanny, spot on and correct each time. Now I had discovered a way of communicating with him, I didn't feel so completely cut off from him.

At about 12 midnight I said to Gill "I think he's as safe as he's going to be now, these girls are recording and monitoring his every move, they're documenting things all the time' and I realised he wasn't going to wake up and ask for me while he was in this condition. Not like he did during the last 5 weeks, although I would have preferred him in a wake-up state than this.

So Gill and I went in search of the dining room for something to eat. From my recollection it was my first hot meal in five weeks, if you can call baked potato and baked beans a meal. We returned to Julian's bed side to say good night to him. Gill drove me back to Shrewsbury some 20 miles away to pick up my car, then we both parted company at one of the roundabouts we flashed head lights as she headed for Llanfercaerinion another 40mils away, and I drove in the opposite direction to Oswestry some 20 miles away to sleep at my parents. Poor Mum and Dad they too had had five weeks of turmoil, then to hear a loud knock on the front door at one o'clock in the morning must of frightened them out of their wits. I slept for England that night, having a bath next morning was like receiving a million dollar bill; during the last five weeks I think I only had one bath.

My daily wash consisted of a freezing cold wash in a sink that could barely accommodate enough room for a pair of hands. The hot tap looked as if it hadn't worked for years. It was like camping with no facilities, not even a bed. My nights consisted of sitting in an arm chair on good nights, on bad nights it entailed sitting on a plastic chair but most of the time I spent squatting on my knees on the floor. Although I was offered a bed at Oswestry for the last two nights Julian spent at Oswestry, unfortunately he was too poorly for me to leave him.

After I bathed and had breakfast at my parents, Telford Hospital rang asking if I could return the Doctor wanted to speak to me.

With a heavy heart I returned, not knowing how to get to the Hospital on my own. I lived in the days of no 'Tom-Tom'. Julian used to humorously say, "Why would you want a Tom-Tom, when you have a Ju-Ju?" Well at this precise moment I wished I had a Tom-Tom or better still my Ju-Ju. So with the help of my father's direction scribbled down on a piece of paper I started my journey, as I approached Shrewsbury the sky was ablaze with an orange hue, for as far as the eye could see over the Shropshire planes, it looked as if the world was on fire or just been formed. It was so moving I felt compelled to stop the car and take a photograph. It does sound like a bizarre thing to do after the hospital had contacted me return to speak to the doctor. But the sky was so overwhelmingly bright, bearing in mind this was early morning. One would expect this sort of orange sky line on a late summer evening, not a cold November morning. Nothing seemed real any more, once I'd snapped the shot through the driver's window I was then drawn to get out of the car and gaze at the sky, in my terrible dilemma I stretched out my arms and screamed to this churned up orange sky shouting "God what more do you want of me?" I felt my faith was being tested. I then went back in to the car and slumped over the steering wheel and sobbed repeatedly saying "Please God help me, please God, please God help me!"

Photo of the sky, on the morning of 11th November 2008 on the road to Telford.

I managed to pull myself together so I could continue my journey; I had to Julian needed me. Feeling this deep hopelessness, I remember thinking, 'Julian; what's going to become of us' and to try and distract me from my dilemma I inserted a CD in to the player, it was a free CD that came with one of the Sunday newspapers I bought on remembrance Sunday. The volume switch must have been accidently touched, because out blared Russell Watson singing, "You raise me up". The lyrics were so poignant I could not fail but to sobbing uncontrollably,

"You raise me up".

"Then I am still and wait here in the silence.
Until you come and sit a while with me.
I am strong, when I am on your shoulders.
You raise me up to more than I can be."

Listening to the first verse made me aware that Julian and I were so far apart at that moment, I was so lost and alone and what I really wanted him to do was to sit a while with me and direct me to his side. The second verse reminded me, of when I first met Julian, I had no confidence I was a timid country girl, unlike him street wise and a know it all. However, he coaxed me to do things I would never thought capable. He would often ask "Why can't you do things?" "Why can't you pass your driving test? "Why can't you change a spare wheel?" "Why can't you do your nursing conversion?" "Why can't you use power tools?" "Why can't you build a stair case?" "Why can't you drive a camper van?" "Why can't you drive on the right?" Of course with his help, I could do anything; anyone could with his help. As I look back on our life together, and listened to the words of this second verse. He did make me strong, and he did raise me up to more than I could ever be.

I realised the song had given me hidden strength to complete my journey. I can remember thinking whatever happens in the next few days, I had definitely become over the years a better and a stronger person for meeting Julian. Was this a coincidence that I heard this song at this precise time or was there some one pulling the strings somewhere? I will never know. But to my surprise I did manage to find Telford Hospital, it must have been a combination of my Fathers map, along with the power of prayer. On arrival the Consultant took me to a sitting room to explain the seriousness of Julian's condition. Firstly he took history of his medical background, and explained he needed to be taken for some surgery to de-slough some necrotic tissue from his hip area. Secondly he was asking about the Insulin issue, and what type of Diabetic treatment he had been on during the last few months. I told him nothing for the last 15 months, his reply was, "He can't possibly be a Diabetic if he hasn't had any treatment, he would of died" The Doctor got up to go, when I said "By the way he's never had glucose in his urine" he then said "Well that clenches it then, he definitely can't be a diabetic" As the Doctor was leaving with the escorting nurse, the nurse pointed out to the Doctor that Julian had been transferred from Shrewsbury Hospital with a sliding scale Insulin which was still in progress. He paused a little then said, "Stop it immediately, actually how much is he having? She quoted the amount. "Eerrr, well maybe we will turn it down to 0.5ml an hour, just while he's having surgery, then we will stop it when he returns to the unit. Is that ok with you Mrs Davies?" I said "Thank God, thank God some one's listening to Julian at last." He warned me, "We're not out of the woods yet you know Mrs Davies. He still needs to get through this big operation" It was also at this meeting the Doctor discussed his rhesus status. I said "No, he'll want to live at all cost, I too would like you to performer cardiac massage on him if the need arises. I stayed with Julian until about 3am, the night staff said they had made a bed for me in the rest room; it consisted of a pillow and a few blankets on a sofa. I was glad of anything, but most of all I wanted to be near Julian, but now I realised I too was getting weak.

Tuesday 11th of November

This was the morning of Remembrance Day I wondered what lay ahead of me today. I got out of my make shift bed at about five thirty. Two and a half hours sleep; it was certainly a good top up. I got dressed no breakfast as normal and walked over to Julian's bed side, not knowing what to expect. The night staff informed me that during the last two and a half hours I was away they had given him 6 units of blood, and had struggled to maintain his blood pressure at 88/44 and his pulse was racing like mad at 164 beats per minute. His poor heart must have been so exhausted, although it had been higher than that on several occasions over the last five weeks.

Julian went to theatre on Tuesday the 11th of November 2008 at 1pm on Remembrance Day, a day which I'm not lightly to ever forget!

I spent all afternoon waiting for Julian's return in a small but comfortable day room, on my own. Before anyone has any hang ups about my solitude, at this point in my life that's exactly what I wanted and needed, to be left on my own with my own thoughts and prayers. It gave me time to put things in to perspective, the life I had before Julian, the life I had with Julian, but left me wondering what type of life I had before me now. I remembered at one stage thinking of one of Winston Churchill quotes, when he famously said "Never, never, never give up"

I thought that's what we would do, soldier on as always.

As they pushed Julian's bed passed the door way of the rest room at 4 o'clock, I quickly trailed behind the entourage of theatre staff escorting Julian back to his bed space, attached to so many tubes and pumps. I can remember thinking as I trailed behind, "Thank God, he has at least survived yet another vast hurdle in his life, which meant he was still in with a chance"

If the Doctor stops the Insulin as he promised, then Julian could start his long journey to recovery finish the house in France and see Llewela through University, watch her get married and enjoy his grandchildren grow up. He had so much to live for.

But unbeknown to me they had found such horrors in theatre; I could not begin to imagine. As soon as I pulled up alongside Julian's bed, the Staff Nurse asked me to return to the rest room, there would be a Doctor along shortly to speak to me about Julian's operation.

This meeting I thought could go either way, good news verses bad news.

I was surprised it was the Consultant Anaesthetist who came to speak to me not his surgeon, it was the same room that I had sort rest the night before on the make shift bed now converted back to a settee to help me absorb the news he was about to give me about both our future. The atmosphere was very much different now, instead of tranquil rest I had the night before it was now tenser with anxiety. We both sat down, he introduced himself, and he explained that the Surgeon had asked him to speak to me on his behalf. He proceeded to inform me that the Surgeon had not seen anything like it in 30 years. He said it was too horrible for words he described it as excavating; the more he removed the more that had to be removed. He said a large part of his lower spine had disintegrated into powder; you could almost blow it away. He had no idea how far into his body the decay went before reaching healthy tissue. It came to a point when they asked themselves how much more could they remove? Both cheeks on his buttock had been removed; the flesh behind his upper leg had been removed. Part of the bowel was affected and needed a colostomy, but felt that had to be done at a later stage.

I wondered why this man was not sparing me anything, he wasn't holding back on any information. All I kept thinking was why are you being so graphic; I don't need this all on my own.

I was sure if I hadn't been a nurse they wouldn't tell other relatives as much.

Unless he thought I would insist that he was to be saved at all cost, as I had expressed before he went to theatre.

He continued to say that it was agreed amongst the staff there present, that it was absolutely too inhumane to keep a human being alive in this condition.

Instructions were given that Julian was to be taken back to the Intensive Care unit and his relatives informed immediately so they could say their Goodbyes before switching off the ventilator.

He was also seeking permission to carry on with the Insulin and the Antibiotics therapy, for the first time I agreed on Julian's behalf. I don't know why he bothered asking, everybody kept reminding me that

I didn't have a say in his care anyway. Julian's fight was over now, so was mine, they could do what they liked.

Just as Julian said to me before he lost his mind, things have gone horrible wrong funny how they both used the same word 'horrible' to describe Julian's condition! They'd won; I hope they were really proud of themselves because I certainly was not. I had failed Julian miserably; I just hoped that by carrying on with the insulin his organs would not be in excessive pain, as they had been when he was conscious. The only comfort I had was; he had returned from theatre on a Morphine pump and I was hopeful the pain that was caused by the insulin was then cancelled out by the morphine. I told him I was not surprised about the state of his flesh, this necrosis had started that one awful night Julian had at Shrewsbury when he was hallucinating, when I witnessed those large purple rings on his buttocks and on the back and legs the following morning. I knew something serious had happened to his skin that night. Julian had predicted that something 'horrible' like this would happen to his skin if they continued with the insulin and antibiotics, but neither he nor I had visualised that it would be as horrific as this.

He then of course went onto the subject of continuing with Julian's life. I realized things seemed hopeless but at the same time I was a wife first, who did not want to play god (with a very small g) determining Julian's life or death. Secondly I was a nurse who had to save and preserve life at all cost weather it was a relative, friend, stranger or even someone I disliked. So I thought; when he had his accident all those years ago he survived against all odds, surly he could survive again. After all, this abscess was small fry compared to his big accident. My heart still wanted to pull out all the stops to prolong his life; he loved life with such passion. He never gave up on anything, anyone not even himself, and especially not on any problem; in fact he seemed to thrive on solving people's problems I'd go as far as to say he even went out looking for them. Who was I to give up on him; he had never given up on anyone especially Llewela and I.

The Doctor then said, "I understand how you feel but he has years of surgery ahead of him, the most urgent procedure he has to undergo is a colostomy, the second procedure is muscle transfer and later extensive skin grafting and for this he'd have to be nurse prone, may be for years" In my head I was trying to grasp how he'd mange his colostomy bag if he was lying prone! Then he will have to spend years lying on his abdomen while he has extensive muscle transplant before even thinking of skin graft." Positive as I was, not even I could put him through this. Looking after him was not the problem; I would give up work and live a life of poverty if it meant Julian was having a quality life style. Not forgiving myself, for putting him through this stage of his life, was my problem. This man's life had been an uphill struggle since his accident, but up until now nothing perturbed him. Who was I to punish him even further? I half-heartedly agreed, and promised I would contact the immediate family to say their farewell's.

I just hope wherever he is, he has forgiven me for my decision and I did it for the right reason at the time. We can all live in regret, please forgive me if I made the wrong choice on your behalf Ju.

He was a kind soul, so I'm sure he will have forgiven me.

Final Goodbye's

I now had the big task of rounding up everybody who loved him, to give them an opportunity to say their Goodbyes. Where did this massive circle stop?

I once mentioned to Julian's Mother when she visited Julian at Oswestry that I felt a huge responsibility keeping Julian alive. I don't think she understood what I meant at the time. What I meant was, I didn't have to keep him alive just for my selfish reasons but for our daughter, his brother and sisters, of course for her his Mother, my family loved and respected him, especially my twin sister who loved him like a blood brother, he helped her with her conversion when she returned to nursing against her will, he had faith in her when she felt no one else did, and she never forgot his steadfast belief that she could do it. Unbeknown to me they were in constant touch with each other, him with his computer skills her with none. He would talk her through each screen on her lap top sixty miles away while she sobbed over the phone saying her lap top screen was blank, but he took no notice of her crying just calmly told her what buttons to press; he took no praise for this. My own blood brother had a great comradeship with him communicating many nights until the early hours of the morning, my other brother who he had great admiration for who like him would not boast about his skills. Julian would often say I'll ring Ali he'll know the answer, and sure enough he would. My parents who were very fond of him and respected his achievements, they were aware he was sometimes sharp but only when he was right.

Who else did I need to save him for? Over the last 30 years because of his disability he has taken young boys who are now young men under his wing, to teach them skills that they would not normally be taught. He would undertake this challenge of educating these youngsters seriously by going as far as taking them to France to teach them how to do building work. It was work that he would have found physically difficult but had satisfaction passing on his skills to the future generation.

The Buffalos, which he regretted not joining earlier once he did join he just plunged his whole heart and soul into it. Although he had only been in the organisation for 3 years, he had gained great respect amongst the brothers as they referred to each other. The first time he came home from the first meeting he said, "It's a fantastic organisation Olwen, they even look after the widows if something happens to one of the members." "Really" I said, "And why would I need to know about that?" Well! He said, "You never know, it's a peace of mind knowing someone would keep an eye on you." On other occasions I would split on him by telling someone, Julian did that, it might have been making a load of unexpected pamphlets for a social event. He would go mad with me for informing on him. Why did you tell them? it's all ruined now, as if he was secretly collecting Brownie points for all his good deeds. Well I certainly think he collected enough to get through those pearly gates. There were many more people I had to save him for, too numerous to mention. Patients from The Spinal Injury Unit, who he had vetted, supported and encouraged over the years a young man by the name of Dave Weaver for one. People from all walks of life admired this man, it's a wonder he hasn't dropped something from a great height onto my head to stop me writing these admiring words.

The pressure was huge to preserve this man's life, when the entire world would be falling apart Julian always knew what to do. My next task was to select a small number of people to say their goodbye; the room was too small for all his friends.

I apologise to anyone who is reading this book if you felt I have left you out by not asking you to his bed side, but if you were visited by a robin between November and December 2008 then rest assured Julian came to visit you instead to say his personal goodbyes, so don't worry about it.

My first phone call was to our daughter, who had only started University that September in 2008, she had been in her new abode only 8 weeks when I made this sad phone call. In my telephone conversation I asked her, "Please don't drive up on your own Llewela, can you ask Kevin to bring you to Telford." She agreed she would, my second phone call was to Julian's brother, who I asked if he could inform his Mother, but not by phone could he let her know in person and also, could he drive her and his step father up. He too agreed he would do so.

His sister was abroad on holiday at the time in a country I can't remember, and as I want the book to be word perfect I will not risk mentioning the wrong country.

My third phone call was to my parents, but I didn't want them to drive cross country with something as heavy as this on their mind either. Luckily they rang Tracy my sister-in-law to see if she would take them. My parents arrived first with my sister in law, we sat for some time talking to Julian and holding his hand reminiscing about the good times in-between watching the staff mulling round him like ants, none of the staff appeared to speak to each other, all knowing what the other was doing. Then Julian's Mother came with her husband and off course Julian's brother as he'd chauffeur them as he'd promised. His mother commented about the tranquil music in the back ground. It was very sad and moving to see how very upset his brother was, he was visibly breaking up. To try and console him, I said hold Ju`s hand like this, in a clasped fashion like blood brothers do. Then ask him a question, if the answer is yes he'll give a small spasm in the crook of your thumb. He said, "I can't Olwen, I can't."

So I stepped forward and said, "I'll hold his hand, you ask the questions". The staff asked if all the family were present, I quickly said, "No Llewela his daughter hadn't arrived yet" The staff nurse continued "The Doctors are concerned that the machines must be switched off as soon as possible"

I then went to phone Llewela again, this time when she answered she was whispering, I asked, "Why are you whispering Llewela? She said she was answering her mobile in a lecture.

Why are you still in Oxford Llewela.? She said, "Dad will be upset and cross with me if I miss out on too many lectures." That was true he would have been, he put education before everything.

My intention was to explain to her how poorly he was when she arrived at Telford, but I was forced to tell her there and then that they wanted to switch everything off today, but the Doctor was holding back until she had seen him.

(As I'm writing this, there is a black bird banging on the window with its beak and flapping its out span wings, a bee is buzzing inside the window and the mobile phones making funny noises)

She said, "Ok in that case I'll come"

While waiting for Llewela to arrive, I was conscious that everybody in the immediate family was not going to be able to say their Goodbyes. My sister for one and Gill his best friend was another and of course his half-sister who was abroad on holiday with her husband with Julian's God child.

My mind wondered what if Llewela was not able to get there in time, how could Llewela put an "Amen" to this chapter. An idea came to me, or was it Julian putting the idea in my head if I could get Llewela to speak to Julian on the mobile, that way she would get a chance to say her goodbye, and only she would know what had been said. This idea was so much like Julian, I realised I had to think like Julian otherwise nothing would get done.

I was worried that his mother might think this was a sick idea, before I made the phone call I held his hand and asked Julian do you want to hear Llewela's voice on the phone in case she can't make it in time. The spasm in his hand went wild; I spoke out loud, "He said yes".

I took a chance, and dialled her number explained to her what I intended to do, but if she wasn't up to it Dad would understand. She said she wanted to, my brave little girl had to say goodbye to her Father for the last time over the phone. I don't know what was said and it's not for the world and its mother to know, not even her mother.

The idea got hold of me then, what about Gweno who was in Scotland; she could also say Goodbye to him. So I did the same again held his hand and asked the same question, again a strong response spasm between the thumb and index finger. I dialled her numbers and explained to her what she could do, she agreed to speak. I still don't know to this day what she said to him, except she was glad that she had the opportunity to say those parting words. Then I thought of his best friend Gill, again I asked Julian if he wanted to speak to her, same response. I placed the phone next to his ear.

My last request for an answer off Julian was, did he want to hear his half-sister voice? This was the biggest response of all. Before dialled her number I asked his mother do you think she'll want to speak to him. She turned to her husband and discussed it, they decided no.

At that Julian's hand was going mad, I said "But Julian wants to hear her voice, please please ring, it's what Julian wants, it's not me it's him look".

She said she would try, once again they were engaged in conversation, the spasm in Julian's hand was jumping all over the place I intervened, "Please, he's begging to hear her voice".

I had such little communication with this man who was about to stop communicating completely in an hour or so and still people weren't listening, not even his mother now. Julian and his half-sister were so close when she was growing up, he was her father figure, what was I to do?

Against my better judgement or my very worst judgment ever I insensitively grabbed the phone off his mother and placed it to Julian's ear and said Ju, it's your little sister.

May be this was one of the worst moves I ever made in my life, because when I took the phone away from Julian's ear and spoke to who I thought was going to be his half-sister her husband said, "What's going on." I did it for the right reasons, but on reflection and with hind sight I believe now it may have ruined our relationship for ever. We all have to live with regrets; this will be mine for a very long time and I do seek forgiveness on this one. On the other hand the others were glad they had that opportunity to say their farewell.

Llewela then made a pleading phone call to me about twenty minutes later, saying, "Mum if Dad is in pain please don't wait for me, I don't want him to be in pain for one single minute longer than he has to, just because you're waiting for me to say goodbye, promise me Mum please promise me."

I said, "I promise." Julian was so pumped up with morphine I'm sure he wasn't in any pain, which then makes you think if he had so much morphine on board, how could he communicate with me? Well I don't know the answer to that one, but maybe it's a study all ITU staff throughout the land can research with future unconscious patients.

All I know is when I asked him negative questions that required the answer NO I had no response, but when I asked positive questions that required the answerer YES I had a reaction.

About an hour later, I heard Llewela's voice at the entrance of the ward I wanted to run out to greet her and warn her not to look at all the tubes; just see your Father there. But I was too late she had already arrived at the foot of his bed. I turned to Julian and leaned over his chest saying Llewela's come to visit you Ju, Kevs brought her. When all of a sudden I heard an almighty noise come from the bottom of the bed I couldn't make it out. I'd never heard such a noise, it sounded like a wolf trapped; the noise was so deep it didn't sound like a young girl's voice at all. As I turned my head I could see it was Llewela, she sounded like she was feeling the pain of the world, and she probably was. I turned to Ju again and said, "Listen to her she's crying like a branchy or is it a mouse". Which may have sounded harsh to any one listening, but to the three of us we understood what it meant. Once, when Llewela was a child, she trapped her fingers in a door and howled but Julian pulled her to one side and said, "Llewela are you a mouse or a Davies", she knew she wasn't a mouse so she must have been a Davies. She sobbed, "I'm a Davies", in that case "Davies's don't cry". She immediately stopped, and as far as I knew she'd never cried again in front of him. But this time, it was alright to cry.

The Doctor was informed that Llewela had arrived, so we were urgently ushered into the rest room except I noticed Llewela was missing. I went back to look for her and found her next to Julian, I said "Llewela you need to come quickly, the doctor is waiting to talk to all of us". She said, "I don't need to listen to what he wants to do to my Dad what I need to do is to talk to Dad." Kevin said, "I'll stay with her" Llewela said "NO, I need to speak to him alone, what I've got to say to him is between me and him."

Kevin and I reluctantly left her to have some private time together with her father.

What I didn't want to do, was to make the sole decision that Julian's life should end that day, my heart was thumping away as Kevin and I joined the others in the rest room. The Doctor introduced himself and emphasised how grave the situation was. I was worried I would have to say in front of everyone, that I was making the decision that the machines should be turned off. But in actual fact I never uttered a word; the final decision in the end came from his Mother. It was only right she was allowed to raise the flag of surrender on his suffering body, who better to make this hard decision than his own mother; she gave life why should someone else make the decision to end it? Her final words on the matter was, "I don't want him to suffer any more" and I couldn't have agreed more.

My mind drifted off at this point, I was still thinking shall I stand up for Julian even at this late stage and shout, "No, no I want him to live" but then I thought of our agreement that both of us wanted to be resuscitated at all cost unless our minds had gone. There was my answer; his mind had gone, in my opinion it had been stolen and destroyed by the medical sector. Burglary had taken place and they had left his head empty. The hopelessness of it all was now over, no more pain, no more fighting, no more anguish over taking something his body revolted. Just no more, no more! Exactly what he'd been begging for, for five long weeks, please no more!

I drifted back into reality, not that any of it felt real. I don't know what I'd miss but I heard the Doctor explaining that he would be turning one syringe pump off at a time, bearing in mind he had about 8 syringe drives, about 4 bags of Intravenous drips, blood and insulin drive.

Other tubes consisted of a urinary catheter, drains from the wounds, an E.T tube to maintain his air way, a nasogastric tube, also he had an oxygen mask, blood pressure cuff, pulse ox meter on his finger to measure oxygen level and this was one mental picture I had buried deep within my soul not to revisit again.

We all then returned to join Llewela and Julian, in that tiny side room. Everybody in their turn came to say their Goodbyes, his Mother was intent on not saying the phrase 'Goodbye', but in her farewell she accidentally said Goodbye. To try and pacify her I told her; if I remembered correctly the phrase Goodbye derived from "God bless or God be with you, and both were a nice thing to wish someone. With no acknowledgment I'd spoken, she left, being more distressed about where she had left her mobile phone. I know shock can affect different people in different ways but at this sad time we should have been comforting each other not fighting from different corners.

My family went to wait in the rest room, to allow Llewela and I quality time with Julian.

One of the Staff Nurses commented how lovely the angelic music was, and was it Julian's favourite type of music? Llewela and I looked at each other and replied in unison, "No".

But we explained since he had been so poorly my sister and her friend had introduced him to this type of Angelic music, and when the CD came to the end he would often ask for it to be switched back on. He used to say it's so soothing and it helped his pain.

Looking back I think it must have helped all of us on that last day, especially regarding the atmosphere between his Mother towards myself.

While there was only Llewela, Kevin and I at Julian's bed side, we made small talk with the two nurses. I mentioned that the night before, with the aid of the hand spasm communication that I had said to him, if he was to be faced with two doors at the end of his journey, through one door he would be able to slip easily in to the next world but through the other door it will lead him back to Llewela and I. This door however will lead him back to pain and suffering and above all the biggest struggle he'd ever endured, but if he wanted to choose the other door, Llewela and I would understand. Although at first we'd feel he had chosen the wrong door for us, but whatever he did, he would do it with our blessing. The nurse said that was so lovely, a short while later when the last pump was about to be turned off the staff nurse said, "Quick look at the screen" I couldn't see what she was showing me, except his observation were threading." She walked over to me put her arms around my shoulders and pointed to the screen and said, "Look he is choosing his path, he's going through his chosen door". At that we sobbed, the nurse with swimming eyes soon pulled herself together. I walked over to Llewela to hug her, and over her shoulder I could see the clock it was exactly 3 o'clock. I then turned to Julian, who still looked so alive and said to Llewela, "How can he be dead, he's still so warm."? I then collapsed on his chest and sobbed, whispering "Oh! Julian I'm so sorry, what have they done to you Ju, what have they done"?

Still sobbing I said, "Julian how will we ever manage without you, there will be no more stories."

Nobody cared for me like he did, nobody understood me like he did, who was going to squeeze my hand when no words would do, who was going to wink at me across the room when I did well, who was going to complement me when I'd done a good job, who was going to hug me when I felt despair, who was going to say it will be all right when I couldn't stop crying, who was going to encourage me when I felt like giving up, but most of all who was going to say 'I love you' many times a day especially when I least expected it.

Then the hymn "Breath on me breath of God" came in to my head very quietly at first, I could almost hear the congregation in our church singing it. Then it became louder and louder in my head until I thought the roof was going to blow off.

Then my thoughts drifted to when Llewela was first born and how Julian raised this tiny baby above his face while he was lying in a Hospital bed saying, "Please God let me live long enough to see her come of age". We both took that coming of age to be 21, I realise now Julian was dealing with a modern God and coming of age is actually 18 in this country! In that case we should be careful what we ask for, but more importantly we must be careful what deals we make with our maker. Maybe we do always get what we ask for in life. It says in the Bible, "Knock and it shall be opened, ask and it shall be given" Maybe in future we need to think bigger, and then we won't be disappointed. I don't know how long I was wrapped in my private thoughts when Llewela suddenly said, "Ok, let's go, Dads not here anymore he's gone" She sounded so strong, as if the strength Julian used to have had now suddenly passed onto her.

Of course she was right; spiritually Julian was not there anymore, only bodily.

How glad I was that we had introduced her to 'faith' all those years ago for such moments as these. She had understood from his teachings, that his soul had left his empty shell on earth and was now traveling on another journey heavenward.

I realised he was not going to speak to us in his old familiar way again. I kissed him one more time on his forehead before we left, and whispered "God bless you Julian, I love you".

The three of us then went to join my parents, Tracy my sister-in-law and from nowhere my other sister-in-law Sue had arrived.

I then thought I must ring Gweno and tell her. I rang her on her mobile, and said "It's all over" She said, "I know it, what time did he die?" I said "3 o'clock". She said "I knew that too, we're half way back from Scotland I'll speak to you later".

Once Id finished on the phone to Gweno, we all meandered outside into the fresh air. I hadn't felt the elements on my face much for 35 days; I can now understand how people trapped in Nursing Homes must feel when they are cooped up inside a central heated building year after year.

To be honest I felt more like a Welsh pit pony emerging out of a dark mine, a place I had no wish being but worst of all I was surfacing alone with no Julian at my side. It felt as if my journey had run out of road and I had also lost my navigator of life.

It was about four thirty in the afternoon by now, the sky looked grey and fit to snow. As we were negotiating who was going home with whom; I turned to Llewela and asked her was she going to Nana Nooks house or Aunty Gweno's.? She said, "Neither. I'm going home to Oxford, I've got an exam in the morning and Dad would be cross with me if I failed it".

I said, "Llewela you don't have to put yourself through this, the lecturers will understand."

She said, "I don't want anybody to know about this, people say the most stupid and inappropriate things, when they think they are being helpful. I know they have already" She did as she thought best, and returned to Oxford.

Tracy my sister-in-law insisted on becoming my passenger saying, "I don't think you're in a fit state to dive alone" It was true I think I felt capable mentally but not confident enough to negotiate Telford roundabouts with its lack of sign posts. Tracy made a better passenger than a navigator we landed up traveling up the motorway in the opposite direction to Wolverhampton, never mind Tracy, it was a kind offer.

That evening Gweno filled me in with the details about her early return from her holiday.

On the morning of the 12th of November she went for a walk round Edinburgh Castle with her partner Elwyn, when a robin red breast flew into their path her partner said "Look at that cheeky robin he's so close I could kick him", he kept flying a short distance then into their path again. They decided to sit on a bench to admire the view; this time the robin flew between their heads, then he landed on a wall level with their eyes. Elwyn her partner said, "This is silly now; why is he behaving like this? Gweno said, "I think its Julian telling us he's leaving".

At that Llewela rang Gweno and said, "I don't understand Aunty Gweno, Mum says Dad can't speak." Gweno said, "No but the two of them have found a way of communicating, you need to go to Telford your Mum needs you"

As they got up to go the Robin was hopping behind them both as if it was ushering them back to the Hotel. As they approached the Hotel Elwyn said, "You go and pack the bags and I'll pay the bill. She said, "I don't understand, why are we leaving"? He said, "Your sister needs you, and you're not going to settle until you see her." But she's 600mils away, and you've looked forward to this Holiday so much. He said, "I know, but bloods thicker than water, let's get going."

He paid, she packed and they both jumped in the car. As they settled in for this long journey they both noticed the robin was on a post just level with the wing mirror. She said, "There's that robin again, I'm sure he's brought a message."

At that she had terrific pain in her kidney area, her partner said, "Sit back and relax we've got 600 mile journey ahead of us." She said, "I can't, the pain in my kidneys is too bad". She endured this pain for most of the journey then suddenly the pain suddenly went, Gweno slumped back into the seat and said "My pain has gone, I think he's just died" and she asked what time it was. Elwyn said, "Its exactly 3o'clock" she looked headword and saw an unusual formation in the sky she spontaneously grabbed her camera and took a photograph of it through the passenger's window.

Could it of been Julian's spirit leaving earth in the form of an aura. Nurses dealing with the dead, believers and non-believers leave the dead for one hour making sure the window is slightly opened giving access for the spirit to leave, why would we do that if it wasn't necessary?

Scientists would argue when a person dies the soul dies too, due to electric impulses ceasing to pulsate. Whereas the Bible tells Christians the humans consists of a body a soul and a spirit. The body is the physical form; the Soul is our intellect and our emotions, whereas the Spirit lies dormant until we ask the Devine to come into our lives, then the spirit becomes active in other words when we are blessed with the presence of the Holy Spirit at our Baptism.

Was it possible that Julian was visiting Gweno all those miles away, to let her know he was leaving. I don't know but they were very close, will any of us ever know for sure? But one does hear of such coincidences when people die.

This is the photo she took at the exact moment of his death, at 3pm just as her pain subsided.

It's not unheard of to see unusual sky light in the middle of the day; it was once reported of an 'unknown light' in the sky on 26th January 1938 when three children saw a vision at 'Cova' in Portugal which was also seen across Europe at the same time.

That night I slept in my old teenage bed, at my parents. I slept mainly through exhaustion that night but woke up feeling sick, angry and frustrated wondering why no one listened to Julian. Still feeling gagged with a terrible sense of hopelessness but at the same time feeling relived that Julian's days of worrying about being black listed from Oswestry were now over, as well as his blackmailing days of take drugs that he felt was harming his body were now also over. And I didn't have to hear him say any more that he felt he was imprisoned against his will in any more, those begging pleas were finished, and I didn't have to hear him say, I feel as if I'm committing suicide when they force me to take their drugs.

Sadly his freedom of choice to die wherever he wanted to had long been taken away from him. It felt like experiencing turmoil and peace at the same time, an awful mixed up feeling.

What next

The last 28 years of my life was about Julian and I, what was the next phase of my life going to be about? I woke up early that morning it was Thursday the 13th November 2008, I said my prayers as normal, asking God to keep Llewela, Julian and Kevin free from harm. I realised everything had to change now, but did this prayer have to change too?

No, I decided that this was one part of my ritual that would not change, and it hasn't. I've added others to my daily prayers, but Julian's name has remained sacred in my daily prayers.

As I got up that morning my Mum said, "Why don't you have a nice bath." I thought that was just the therapy I needed, as I emerged into the lovely warm water I cried knowing how much Julian loved and adored his daily baths. Sadly this ritual had became more difficult for him in the later years. After my long soak, my first task then was to check that Llewela was alright after her ordeal the day before, and to wish her well with her exam. When I rang, using the mobile not something I was familiar with but she eventually answered the phone. My first question was, "Why did you take so long to answer, Llewela?" She said "Mu-u-um I can't believe you used that phone!" I said why? She replied, "You used Dads mobile; it came up as DAD CALLING".

I learnt a lesson that day; that every action we make in life can have a lasting effect on others whether it's a negative or a positive one.

The foremost thing on my mind that morning was to contact Telford Hospital to see if the Doctor had written in the notes, that he felt Julian was not a Diabetic. It was proving near on impossible to speak to this Doctor, but I had no intention of giving up until I had spoken to him. I left several messages asking him to return my call.

That afternoon Telford Police Station rang asking if they could arrange a time and place to make a witness statement about Julian's last few days of his life. I had nothing to hide so sooner the better in my opinion, we arranged to meet the following Monday on the 16th November at 3 o'clock at my parents' home.

The next few days appeared to meander into one except I do recall getting ready to go to chapel on the Sunday evening. When my Mother asked me, "Where are you going Olwen?" I said to your chapel. She replied, "You're Father and I weren't thinking of going tonight, we were going to keep you company" I said, "No, I've got a lot to pray for, a lot to ask for and a lot to be thankful for." The Sermon that night was about the 7 foolish virgins and the 7 wise virgins.

Mum apologised, thinking the Sermon might have been insensitive as Julian had only died three days before. I said, "Mum before I go to listen to God's word I always ask him to choose an appropriate Sermon or Homely to help me through that week." Puzzled, she asked, "How did you think this one helped you then". I enlightened her by saying, "Just before going into chapel, I was worried about what sort of buffet should I prepare for Julian's funeral." The answer was in the sermon, don't be caught out with curled up cucumber sandwiches, but be prepared like the 7 wise virgins and put on a good spread".

Not only was God giving me a message, but Julian was too you'd never find Julian doing a shoddy job, and he would not have expected me to do one either.

The following day was Monday 16th November, it had taken me three days to track down the Doctor who appeared to side with me regarding Julian not being a Diabetic, when I did manage to speak to him he said "Of course I have written in your husband's notes, this is an Intensive Care Unit I have to document everything that happens."

Relieved that he had given me verbal confirmation that he had documented his belief that <u>Julian could not possibly of been a Diabetic, as he could not have survived the last 15 months without treatment,</u> made me feel uplifted.

Only time will tell now if he is true to his word, will he or won't he have documented this or if he has, but it appears to be missing at a later date will it mean that the notes have been tampered with!

I was apprehensive about this 'witness statement' appointment I had at three o'clock, I wondered if this was normal procedure? Worried I might get the order of how things actually happened wrong I spent the next few hours trying to piece together the last few days of his life. The policeman arrived prompt at three and did not leave until gone five o'clock that evening. I asked him if it was normal practice to make a statement after a hospital death, he confessed 'No' it wasn't normal practice it was because someone had made an accusations against me, that's why it was necessary to get a statement and as he was leaving he said, "I don't think she's got much grounds" I took the phrase 'she' to mean his mother. He said he was going to get the statement typed as soon as possible and get a copy sent to me by post.

As soon as he left we all sat down for our evening meal, but just as we finished the doorbell rang. Mum invited the caller in and introduced me to their friend, she explained to him that we'd only just said goodbye to another caller jokingly saying it was one of your people actually. She proceeded to tell him that I had recently become a widow and encouraged me to tell him of my plight. I was hesitant to divulge my private life to a stranger, he might be Mum and Dads friend but he was still a stranger to me. Mum said, "Its ok, he used to be a Chief Inspector Olwen".

I hadn't got out of the practice of asking Julian's advice yet, so silently in my head I asked him, was this man to be trusted, and could Julian give me a sign. To break the silence I asked my Mums friend where he was policing before he retired.

Well, I don't know if you have ever heard of it, it's a place called Stourport-on Seven and I covered Bewdley, Kidderminster and surrounding areas.

Suddenly I trusted him, and after listening to Julian's fraught medical experience his comments were; "Clearly something is not right, and if you're thinking of cremating him, I strongly suggest that you reconsider and have him buried."

That night after he had gone, I rang Llewela to ask her what she thought; she said "Mum you do what you think best, whatever you do it won't bring Dad back"

As I lay in bed that night I thought, what a day, and were all my days going to be like this until I found out for sure how he died?

The next few days were spent studying some suitable hymns, and ringing the funeral directors regarding cost of bringing Julian home. I started to ring friends to let them know that Julian had passed away. I needed to ring one friend in particular, Maureen Brewer to ask her if she was still very particular about cutting triangular sandwiches. After I rang and asked her about her skills she asked, "Do I need to sit down, Olwen?" I said, "Yes." She understood straight away that I was ringing with bad news. Julian was right to choose Maureen, straight away she said we need to form a committee, and this needs to take place in Kidderminster.

This was so much like Julian, there was always a committee involved in everything he did. He used to say, it's the only way to get the job done right.

A committee was formed and a date sorted for this meeting, I returned to Kidderminster and strangely enough while I sat round this table I glanced round and realised I had chosen either Brownie leaders or ladies who had some connection with taking Brownies on camp, either way they could all be relied on to turn up trumps on the day. Subconsciously I had chosen 'doers' to do the job on my behalf. I was sure after the event the mourners would not even notice how much food had been prepared for them and definitely not recall what sort of food was there. What I didn't want was Julian's farewell to be associated with an inadequate amount of curled up cucumber sandwiches. No, this committee forming was part and parcel of Julian's make up, it had to be a banquet. Even if it meant I had to go out and get a second job to pay for it, this was after all in effect Julian's last party. I use the phrase loosely but I'm sure Julian was there looking down with approval of the effort his friends had put into his send off.

Julian lived by this personal principle; everything he took part in had to be of the highest standard with the maximum of effort, to achieve maximum result with no room for sloppiness or second best. He used to say, if you do the job right first time round you don't have to keep going back to correct or mend it. Sometimes you only get one shot at some things in life and going back to correct them is not an option; this was one of those times.

Friday 21st November 2008

A few days later I had another phone call this time asking me to attend the mortuary in Telford to identify Julian's body, folks who spoke to my mother kept asking, "Why!, don't they know who he was by now, he was an inpatient of theirs for five weeks"

Luckily Gweno happened to have a day off that day. She offered to come with me, thank goodness for twin sisters everybody should have one it's like having a second opinion off your own shadow.

It was going to be a 'heavy duty' day, doing things I'd never done before.

My first port of call was the mortuary; I was really worried about this visit. I thought it was going to be very clinical with white sheets, and metal surroundings. I was worried people attending would have no feelings; if this was their every day job they might have become flippant with their attitude. But to be fair the two ladies were very pleasant and kind.

After some form filling they asked if we were ready to go in to identify Ju. I braced myself in case I fainted or did something out of character or reacted badly.

As the door opened, I couldn't help my reaction the words just came out of my mouth.

"Oh! Julian they have dressed you up like a king".

Whatever he was laying on was camouflage with a drape to the floor, the crown of his head was facing an outside window, and streaming in over his whole body was a beam of sun shine.

Draping over his body was a majestic scarlet colour velvet type material, and round the edge on the floor was a single row of gold fringe tassels.

The reflection of this majestic coloured cloth seemed to reflect onto his face giving him somewhat high colour to his cheeks. It may not have been the combination of the sun and the cloth; it may have been makeup that they might have used. I didn't ask, and it didn't matter what mattered was my lasting impression of him dressed all regal, and royal like. Almost King Arthur like.

Gweno and I kissed his cold face as we would normally greet him; Gweno asked if she could see his red arm band that stated he was allergic to Insulin and most antibiotics. We were worried that it had been removed, but it was still there. We toyed with the idea of asking for it to be removed, but thought better of it reminding ourselves that he was going to be buried not cremated.

When we were escorted back into the small office, I was asked to sign a form to confirm that I was identifying Julian Paul Davies.

Then I was asked to sign an additional form, this time it was a Consent Form giving them permission to replace 5mls of blood which had been taken at his time of death.

I couldn't understand why I had to give anyone permission to replace a blood sample to a dead body. I said, "Throw it away, Julian has no use of it any more" They said, "We can't, it's not our property to throw away, we have to return it back into its rightful owner."

As I sighed I said, "I wish someone had paid half as much attention to detail when he was begging for mercy and not to have any injections when he was alive. No one asked for my permission or consent then" Contradicting matters I recalled my cousin the Solicitor had informed me when he was alive I had no voice to defend him, but now in death I see I have a voice, bizarre don't you think" The Coroners clerk said, "Well! You will have to take that up with the staff concerned."

I said, "Rest assured; these sorts of practices cannot carry on, remember these 3 names, JULIAN-PAUL-DAVIES you will hear them again, and when you do you can say to yourself, I had some dealings with his family.

As I walked down the corridor I suddenly stood still, and turned to Gweno saying, "Taking into account that Julian had at least 6 units of blood in the last 24hrs of his life I don't rightly know who that sample belonged to"

She agreed and shrugged her shoulders, leaving me bewildered had I done wrong by giving them permission for the sample to be returned into Julian's body.

My second port of call that day was to pick up the Interim certificate from another part of Telford, then go to Wellington to register the death, along with his birth certificate and our marriage certificate. Don't they ask for strange things, a 'marriage certificate' I ask you? Was this to register the death of our marriage? As it turned out the Interim certificate wasn't ready, so the second worrying journey didn't have to take place that day. Good job too, we were only two girls from the mountains; we were not street wise to the fast moving city driving.

Our trek out was not yet over, I still had a third place to visit. I had an appointment at Telford Police station to see a Detective Inspector regarding a revised witness statement I had compiled because if the Inquest was going to rely on the typed statement, the Police statement they had sent me was written in the third tense, which I felt had lost what I was trying to express.

Gweno and I were both kept waiting in the small foyer for about an hour, at some point I whispered to her, "How did I land up here?"

Eventually we were both escorted into a small room with a table and three chairs. I handed over my personal statement which he read. I replaced his four pages with my fourteen pages.

On being questioned about some of the points I'd written, the Detective Inspector said, "You seem to be nervous Olwen, why's that?"

"Your right, I'm nervous, it might be something to do with the fact I'm in a Police station being questioned about possibly harming my husband before his death, and when I was young my mother told me never to get involved with the Police." He leaned over the table and surged his head towards me saying, "I can assure you, you are not involved with the Police because if you were, you would be questioned in a cell and you would not be allowed to go free. You are making a statement to help the Police with their enquiries."

The interview was more relaxed after his outburst. At the end he balanced back in his chair, and raised his arms above his shoulders and clasped his hands behind his head and said, "Where exactly is this going Olwen?" "Are you going to sue the NHS for neglect?"

I stopped for a minute took a deep breath and said "And what good do you think that will do me, it's just a dead man's money, how can I enjoy dead man's money how will I spend it with a clear conscious?" No, firstly I want Doctors to look into why people like Julian have such a reaction to diabetic treatment, and secondly why there is such an explosion in diabetes type two in the world. Maybe there is some other type of Diabetes out there and they need different treatment, but something is definitely WRONG. You too can remember these three names, JULIAN—PAUL—DAVIES. I've asked someone else to remember these three names at the Coroner's office this morning. Then one day you too can say, I had some dealings regarding that man too"

I walked out of the police station saying to Gweno, "I can't believe I spoke to him like that, I just had a surge of power from somewhere inside me to voice my opinion"

Gweno drove me back to my parents then I drove back to Kidderminster to meet up with my friends to discuss the buffet for the funeral.

That evening as I stood at my kitchen sink filling the kettle, in the silence of my home I said quietly as I sighed, "Oh! Ju, how can I best defend you at this Inquest without your help" as I turned to face the cooker I flicked on the radio in passing and suddenly a loud noise filled the room which made me jump initially then trembled at the knees. I managed to stagger to the chair before sitting down, still shaking these were the words that blasted out at me,

> I feel it coming together.
> People will see me and cry, Fame.
> Light up the sky like a flame.
> Baby, remember my name.

By now I was in floods of tears and unable to move from the chair to turn the radio down.

The whole incident was just too over powering.

The words were only poignant to me that night because I had asked two people that very morning to remember his name. Was it a coincidence or was Julian connecting with me through music? The lyrics in the line that said, 'Light up the sky like a flame' reminded me of the morning on the road to Telford, when the sky was lit up like a flame!!!!!

The following day after my meeting with the girls, I returned once again to Oswesrty.

My Coming home

On Saturday night Llewela rang me at my parents saying she felt it was now time for me to come home for good. I said, "No Llewela, I don't like leaving your Dad; on his own in Telford". She said, "I can understand how you feel Mum, you need to start sorting out the post there might be some nasty bills there" what she probably meant was stop running away mum and on the pretence of the bills I agreed to come home.

On Sunday 23rd November 2008 I drove home alone, realising my flying visits to Shropshire were now coming to an end. Llewela and Kevin drove from Oxford to meet me in the car park outside our family home; this was arranged so I didn't have to deal with sorting out familiar things that might be painful. As soon as we entered the back door the front doorbell rang, it was Michael and Joanna, Llewela`s God parents they had come to offer a helping hand too. A few minutes later Julian's brother and family turned up, things were becoming a bit unreal now; it was beginning to feel like a party. Then Jo, bless her demolished the party atmosphere by saying, "Come on let's take advantage of all these men, and shift some of these things what about this bed Olwen? Do you want them to take it up stairs or do you want them to take it into the garage?

I said "No, it belongs to the DHSS, it can go in the garage and I'll ring them in the morning to pick it up." The four men dismantled it and relayed the frame into the garage.

When all the furniture was set back into its original space, and the cups of tea and coffee drunk Joanna and Michael kindly invited Llewela, Kevin and I for an evening meal. I thanked Julian's brother and family for coming, but before going to Joannas house Llewela said, "We're going on a small detour first shopping, and we're going to buy you an electric blanket". What a thoughtful thing to do, she thought a cold bed would make me miss Julian even more.

There is always an old fashion Italian welcome to be had at Joanna's, and on this particular night I appreciated the fuss. After a pleasant evening at Jo's I said my goodbyes to Llewela and Kevin as they returned to Oxford and I returned home alone.

As I was tidying up that night I quickly pulled back a curtain and there in front of me was Julian's one and only empty pair of shoes. It took my breath away; who could ever fill these shoes like he did. This was the only thing Julian never wore out; he just kept polishing the same old pair.

Still feeling sad in the quiet of the evening, I collapsed on the settee closed my eyes and gently said, "Oh, Ju how will I manage without you?" With my eyes still closed, I felt as if someone big was hugging me, like the Michelin man in the tyre advert. I was engulfed in something squeegee, all around me it was like how you would imagine a cloud hugging you. "I said silently, Julian is that you?" I didn't want to open my eyes in case the feeling went away. When the hugging feeling slipped away and I finally opened my eyes, I smiled and felt privileged that I'd been hugged by someone or something not of this world. This was the one thing I was going to miss the most in life, his hugs they were always long and meaningful, just like that experience was. A good hug solved every problem, it's hard to continue a row if your hugged in the middle of one. That was the other trick he had up his sleeve, an abundance store of hugs. The electric blanket gift turned out to be a big success, how right they both were I slept like a log that night.

As my main purpose for returning home was to deal with all the brown envelops, I thought I'd better start but where? Julian had taken over all the bills and paper work years ago.

The big pile of post was humongous, I wish now I'd taken a photo of how high the paper bumph had become after only 50 days of unopened correspondence. I was worried I was out of control, so I went into both bedrooms the lounge, kitchen, Welsh dresser, draws, cupboard, desk, bill box, even tins and boxes, including the attic looking for any correspondence, then piled them all together with the most resent post on the lounge table. Armed with a telephone, a bin and a shredder with lots of tea I systematically went through each item. The reason it took so long was because nearly every scrap of paper I dealt with I had to ring them up to confirm the amount I owed, pay by card or send a cheque at the same time inform them of his death. Those were the toughest conversations to make, when they insisted on speaking to Mr Davies. It was hard to keep repeating the same old thing, "I'm sorry it's not possible for you to speak to him he's died"

This mountain of paper work took weeks and weeks to sort out, often on my days off I would sit down at eight in the morning and not leaving the table until ten at night. As soon as I made a dent in the pile the post lady would drop more off, lots of it was bumph granted but it still had to be dealt with. While dealing with all this paper work I had a phone call from 'Adult Protection Allegation Department' asking if they could speak to Mrs Davies. I asked him to repeat who he was representing; he said it again and then went straight into a spiel. I said, "Excuse me I'll have to stop you there; you mentioned the word protection, who needs protecting?" He continued, "It's regarding your husband death, someone has been in touch with us asking us to investigate" I asked, "Am I allowed, to ask who's brought these allegations against me"? He replied, "I'm afraid that's confidential information Mrs Davies"

In that case, I have nothing to hide so fire-away I've got all day, ask me anything you like. We were on the phone for about an hour, he concluded the conversation by saying. "It sounds as if everything is straight forward I don't think you have anything to worry about; she doesn't seem to have a case" We said our goodbyes and as I put the phone down I thought to myself, he said 'SHE'

I assumed the phrase 'She' meant his mother had contacted the Adult Protection Allegation Department. All this concentration started to drain me so I decided to go back to Welshpool one more time for some 'twin-time' before detaching myself from Telford district completely. My sister and I talked into the night about all sorts, then the following morning on the 27th November I drove back calling at my parents on the way, good job I did there was another message awaiting me. I had been summoned once more back to Telford Police station to make a further statement regarding additional accusation against me made by my mother-in-law. Yet again I found myself heading into the heart of this busy town full of roundabouts, dual carriageways with no signs to guide me to the Police Station. I found it by accident more than knowing, as I sat in the same corridor alone this time I cried gently mentally saying, "I'm here again Ju, how could I land up in this Police station so many times when I haven't done anything wrong?" I pacified myself with the thought that I had to be there so it could be documented that I was not a danger to others, and to prove my innocence.

Funny how things happen, instead of driving home afterwards I drove in the opposite direction to my parents' home and as I entered their front door the phone rang. I answered only to realise the call was for me, it was the Coroner's Clerk from Telford informing me they had opened the Inquest into Julian's death that afternoon, this was 15 days after he died.

It was turning out to be a bit of a drain on the psychology side, and because of that my parents persuaded me to stay the night and return home early the next morning.

Julian's coming home

Just before I left the following morning on 28th November, the Funeral Directors rang me at my parent's home to say they were taking Julian's body home to Kidderminster later that afternoon and the burial certificate was going to be with him so I didn't have to worry about going to Wellington to register the death, it had already been done. It was one less nightmare journey for me to worry about.

I informed the immediate family that Julian was coming home. This was not the plan Julian and I had in mind, Julian was convinced he would be coming home a well man! I on the other hand had not been so convinced that things would pan out for the best, but at the same time I did not envisage this separate journey.

The rush was now on; I wanted to be in Kidderminster for when he arrived. That particular morning the sky was a very dark grey, with heavy rain. Coupled with this heavy weather and the thought I was traveling ahead of Julian in very sad circumstances made my journey almost depressing. I say 'almost' because when we first met he said, "I don't do depression" so there was never any time allocated to depression in our relationship. Luckily for both of us we were both blessed with happy hearts. To try and raise my spirits I slotted in the freebie CD which I hadn't finished listening to yet. Looking back I don't think it was such a good idea, the lyrics just pulled at my heart strings even more. Originally it was a hymn but it was recently made popular by Will Martin the song was called "Going home" I was more familiar with the 'Hovis' tune in the bread advert,

> I'm just going home.
> Work all done, laid aside.
> Fear and grief no more.
> Life has just begun, life has just begun.

From what I could remember I cried almost all the way, I cried with the rain and the sky cried with me. What moved me the most was, I could almost imagine the Virgin Mary leading Julian through to the other side, to where his new life was just beginning.

The following Saturday 29th November I went to the church Julian, Llewela and I used to attend. Mass was being said for Julian, I sobbed gently realising if Julian had already arrived in heaven; he had already seen the face of Jesus. Shaken by this sobering thought I left the church crying and headed straight back once more to Oswestry, this time to see my youngest brother Alwyn who was going to remove the hand controls from Julian's car and of course the tow hook so that the Motor Mobility company could have their car back first thing Monday morning. Looking back I'm sure I could have managed, I had on several other occasions under Julian's supervision, but he wasn't supervising this time. As they say horses for courses, this was something Alwyn could do to help.

While Alwyn was doing this favour for me, my parents took me into town to look for an outfit for the funeral, I could not believe I'd gone from size 16/18 to a size 8. The same size I was on our wedding day!

I returned to Kidderminster the following morning with my size 8 black Dress, this time to stay.

While I was off sick I had to periodically keep my work manager up to date with what was happening. And on one of those visits I met the Diabetic Specialist Nurse in the corridor the very one I had sought advice from when Julian was originally critically ill on diabetic treatment. As she approached me, in my frustration I thought this is my opportunity to give her my special invitation as promised, to attend Julian's funeral. I engaged in conversation first by informing her, "Julian did die you know, just as I predicted he would if he continued to take the treatment" that's as far as I got. She retaliated by saying "I don't want to continue with this conversation" she turned on her heels and went back up the corridor the other way. I have not seen her from that day to this; evidently I was still dealing with people with blinkers, cloth ears and closed minds. The three little monkeys came to mind, see no evil, hear no evil and speak no evil. Again I felt gagged and abandoned this time left alone in a corridor.

I returned home to start my funeral arrangement in earnest, I have no idea how the elderly manage in these situations. My list seemed endless and everything had to happen in chronicle order. My first job was to choose a photograph for the local newspaper to announce his death, and then make arrangements to see the Priest to negotiate a date and time of the funeral, and finally place it in the local paper. I had to make a Bank appointment to remove his name off the bank account, contact the Buffalo's to see what needed to be done for a Buff funeral, return the wheel chairs, cushions and bed to the DHSS, complete bereavement forms, phone up the ladies who kindly volunteered to help with the food, to make final arrangements of what food to order or prepare, order the wreath, decide how many funeral cars, finalise what hymns to sing and in what order, then with Llewela ask the Priest to proof read the service sheet before printing. Incidentally, the Priest was more concerned that he was not committing himself to a Masonic funeral, why I don't know.

I had to organise who would be the ushers, who would do the readings, who will carry the coffin, book bed and breakfast for relatives living away. I wanted it to be perfect for Julian, with no regrets. There were no regrets with our life together and I didn't want to let him down at the last hurdle. The last funeral we both attended was Rose's funeral and as she was taken by a horse drawn carriage, Julian was very taken by these two beautiful horses, he tuned to me and whispered, "Olwen, that's so beautiful" and because of that comment I thought he deserves one last beautiful gift, after all there wasn't going to be many other occasions where I could spoil him. So the two beautiful horses were asked to draw the glass carriage, escorting Julian on his last journey to his place of rest.

But I had one last job to do, Glyn had rung to say his mind was troubled regarding the last conversation he had with Julian. Glyn had mentioned he was reading a book about Peter Collins the Gran Prix racing driver from Stone, just outside Kidderminster. Julian asked if he could borrow it. Glyn jokingly said, "Get lost, it cost me a lot of money and I haven't finished reading it yet" Because of these last few words they exchanged, Glyn wanted the book to be placed in the coffin with him. Timing was imperative I had to travel to Oswestry to pick up the book and return back to Kidderminster in time for the Funeral Directors to seal the casket at four o'clock before being taken to the church that evening. I managed to fulfil Glyns request, and that night at five thirty Julian's body was taken to the Church, before entering one of the bearers quietly asked me if there was a fourth man I could appoint to help carry Julian into the church. I looked up and saw Masimo De`Angelo approaching the church a young man Julian had long admired. It choked me to ask him, but as I asked him it reminded me of a film called the 'Gladiator' who called out in the arena, "This man was a soldier of Rome, who will help me carry his body" Masimo agreed without hesitation, willingly took his weight. Thank you, Masimo.

Photograph of Masimo De`Angelo

Then a short Mass was said to welcome Julian into the church, the Winchester coffin was draped in a shiny black and maroon pall to the floor. After Mass I placed a gold framed photograph of Julian dressed in his cap and gown on his coffin, to remind us all what a learned man we were laying to rest the following morning.

The day of the funeral

On the morning of the funeral I rose before six, and as I stood at the sink waiting for the kettle to boil looking through the kitchen window I started to day-dream wondering what the day ahead held for me.

Was I going to protect my feelings by behaving as hard as nails and not show any emotions, was I going to collapse and let myself down by sobbing all over the place, or was I going to do something even worse by collapsing into the grave, begging him to take me with him.

I just didn't know; emotions can be so unpredictable when you're under stress you never know which way they will react, but most of all I didn't want to let Julian down.

Then something frightening happened, I started to shake all over I was behaving like a person suffering from Parkinson's. My arms and legs became freezing cold, I started to perspire but worst of all I couldn't move, my feet appeared to be fixed to the kitchen floor.

This lasted for some time; I thought if I don't move from this spot soon my relatives would be knocking on the door and I needed to let them in. I needed to pull myself together and quickly because Julian was being buried at ten o'clock. I also needed to make some last minute phone calls. Slowly I made my way through the lounge but only able to shuffle like a penguin as my hips were still fixed, then on all fours I crawled up the stairs. Still shaking I began to realised I was suffering from shock. For the first time in 29 years Julian wasn't going to be there for me, the one day I needed him the most—his funeral day.

I slowly made my way to the bathroom and there immersed myself in a deep tub full of warm water. Since that day, a tub full of warm water has become my haven and sanctuary.

I've come to believe that a bath can be cleansing as well as having therapeutic values. Therapeutic because it helps you relax and also gives you time out to plan the day ahead or it can be a place of sanctuary where no one can disturb you. Then when I get out of the bath and ceremonially pull that plug and listen to the gurgle, gurgle of the water disappearing down the plug hole taking with it all my sadness leaving my soul as well as my body that much lighter. They say water can be a great healer; using water to baptise is a sign of cleansing and healing the soul.

Old wives tale used to say, babies appeared much healthier after they have been baptised. I prayed that morning for strength to appear strong even at my weakest moments, that I would say the right thing at the right place but most of all that I would conduct myself appropriately and not bring shame on Julian's name or his memory. Llewela and I chose the hymns because they meant something to all three of us; the entrance hymn I chose "I hear you calling me in the night" Well! Every night after his death at 3am I would hear the bedroom door handle rattling. Of course the original words in the hymn refer to God calling us to him, but on this occasion the hymn had a double meaning. The other reason I chose it was because every time we used to sing it in church I would have this over whelming feeling to cry. I would cry all the way through the hymn. Julian at the beginning would nudge Llewela and say, "What's the matter with your Mother?" in the end they would say to each other, with their head tossed in the air "It's that hymn again" I cannot explain why I felt this over whelming feeling to cry each time I heard the hymn, because I never sang it all the way through I couldn't I was always to upset.

The second hymn was "Jesus remember me as I come into your kingdom" I hoped God would remember Julian, he had worked so hard during his life time on earth to get everything right, to enable him to get through those pearly gates.

The third hymn was "Lay your hands gently upon us". Gweno and Gill did that every day in the name of God until the last few days of his life and I wanted them to know that he got a lot of comfort and relief from what they did, on occasions he would say he couldn't have managed without them.

The recessional hymn was chosen in memory of all the Pilgrims who went to Lourdes, in the South of France joining in with thousands of other pilgrims singing in unison "Ave Maria"

It's a very moving experience to be part of this service in the Pyrenees; you don't have to be Catholic to join in. In fact I think it's more powerful if you're not a Catholic, if you ever get the opportunity to go there, it's wonderful to witness young people helping the very sick and disabled. We often run the younger generation down, but remember the millions of good teenagers who are willing to help less fortunate souls than themselves as they comfort and serve the dying in Lourdes. There appears to be an aura there that cannot be described, you have to experience it to know what I mean. There would have been lots of people at Julian's funeral who would have escape to that small town in France while this hymn was being sung; in fact they would have found it difficult not to raise their hands in the air as if they had a lit candle in their hand. If I'm lucky enough to have anybody attend my funeral I would like candles lit when they sing "Ave Maria" so the lit candles can guide me on my way. I'm just sorry I didn't think of it for Julian.

I had a book called 'Celebration of life' placed in the hall where the food was served for anyone to simply sign or enter a small comment of remembrance about Julian. (Incidentally if any of you haven't signed it yet, do pop round. You're sure of a Welsh welcome, and a cup of tea.) In this book you will find a small verse about music, and it reads like this-:

Music.

How many of us stop and think
Of music as a wondrous magic link with God,
taking sometimes the place of prayer,
When words have failed us 'neath the weight of care?
Music, that knows no country, race or creed;
But gives to each according to his need.

It sounds a bit heavy and doesn't flow easily like a poem, but the gist is there. I think it's true that sometimes music can take the place of prayer. The words in a song can also possess a powerful message if it happens to be appropriate at the time. It can stir up some very powerful emotions, which can crumble the strongest of men or send a baby to sleep. It can also affect a large number of people to a standing ovation. After all didn't David in the Bible put all the Psalms to music so he could remember them better after tending to his sheep?

I chose Gill to walk me down the Aisle, who better than Julian's latest "best friend" to accompany me to be my strength and prop on this sad day. What a rock she was too, nothing perturbed her.

I felt like a little girl who needed to be looked after in case I got lost.

I chose Ben Kelly to do the first reading. I think secretly Ben and Julian admired each other from afar. The two of them were on a different Plato of intelligence, although Julian could not read Ancient languages like Hebrew, Greek and Latin but they spoke the same language when it came to complicated maths or discussing the innards of a computer.

I chose Melissa Goodwin to do the second reading because she was amongst the first in the family and circle of friends to obtain a cap and gown. To him she symbolised sticking power.

In days gone by young people who obtained a degree were children from learned parents like teachers and other professionals. So to get a degree off your own back struggling against all odds was something he admired. After the second reading the Deacon did the Gospel reading and the Priest followed with the Homely. Following the Holy Communion as a normal part of the Mass, the Priest asked the congregation to exchange a hand shake as a sign of peace, greeting everyone in arms reach saying, "Peace be with you" I drew a deep breath and with as much courage as I could muster I walked across the empty and lonely Isle to Julian's family to offer them the "the sign of peace". I was sure that this gesture would mend the rift between us in front of all that was gathered there that day. Sadly his mother could not find it in her heart to offer me peace, but instead offered a barrier by turning her back on me. It must have taken a lot of courage for her to display this action in front of everyone that day. But I have comforted myself in the knowledge that I have never harmed her son in any way shape or form, the only crime I ever committed was to love and care for him and one day if we both wait long enough she will discover how much I loved him.

It became apparent to me that day that she and I will never make peace with each other in this world as she has vowed that she will blame me for her son's death right up to her dying breath. That does not leave me any time to make amends.

Clive Williams then read Julian's eulogy before John Marks the Buffalos Funeral Marshal conducted their Funeral Ceremony, the brothers were asked to step forward to the front of the church to form a circle round the coffin leaving a space where Julian would have once been, they deliberately left that space near to where I stood. The circle as far as I can remember went up the centre Aisle round the coffin and extended up the two side Aisles. The Funeral Marshal first explained what the Buffalos were about, then instructed the "Brethren, form the link." once this was done, he repeated off pat "One Brother is absent from our circle. We therefore leave him in Gods keeping until that glorious Day when Death shall be swallowed up in victory and our broken link is complete again. May he rest in peace. Amen"

273

With hands still clasped the members sang their hymn "Absent Brethren" Afterwards the Funeral Marshal waited for each member attending to place a sprig of ivy upon Julian's coffin.

As a word of prays, I had many friends and family say to me afterwards "What lovely voices the men had" considering they sung the hymn unaccompanied.

So, well done and thank you for turning up so early on such a cold and drizzly morning.

I was familiar with this ceremony the Buffalos do at funerals; only because about two months previously Julian had insisted I attended one of the Brothers funerals. He wanted me to witness what took place at a Buffs funeral just in case the occasion arose that he went before me and I would not feel uncomfortable with the ceremony. You see Julian always thought of everything.

After the service the members then dispersed quietly.

Just as you thought the Mass was over, Gill let go of my hand and stood up and walked to the front of the alter, then turned by the coffin and proceeded to explain that when Julian was so very ill in Hospital; one day when she was visiting him an over whelming feeling came over her to sing. Julian said, "If you want to sing Gill, you sing." She explained to him that the song was in Welsh. He said, "That's ok, sing" The song was called 'Ar lan-y-mor.' Julian was familiar with this song and joined in with her. When he used to go to his lovely Pendine Beach all those years ago he used to join in with the locals in pubs and sing along with them. Gill had explained to him when he was in hospital that she could only remember the first verse and the chorus. He said never mind, "Just sing" The title of the song transited means, 'By the sea edge' while we joined in with the signing at his bed side our minds drifted across the miles to Pendine Beach.

Gill must have struggled with this unfinished business of not knowing the rest of the verses. So when I asked if she would sing at Julian's funeral, she said it would be an honour and she knew the very song to sing and set about learning the remainder of the lyrics.

Some of you might think it would not have mattered about the correct words, because the congregation would not have understood them anyway, but you forget half of the congregation were Welsh speakers, so they would have known and anyway it mattered to Gill.

I don't know how she had the courage to say, "This is for you Julian" then touched the coffin, and looked directly at the coffin throughout her performance by singing unaccompanied with such a beautiful Angelic voice. Julian would have been so proud of her. Thank you Gill, I think we were all left emotional after your performance.

Llewela would of liked to have read a poem, but it was suggested it might be too upsetting for her if she faltered by crying half way through. She later confessed "Dad wouldn't of been upset with me if I'd broken down half way through the poem, he would have been proud of me he was always proud of everything I did" Anyway it was not to be, the congregation then stood for the Recessional hymn which was "Immaculate Mary" the six bearers stepped forward and took charge of one handle each. We all remained in our pews for the first few verses then steadily the bearers started their journey down the Aisle. When Gill took charge of me by guiding me to follow the coffin I was so grateful. Up until then I felt I was still holding my own, but if I had to have waited for the sixth verse trying to sing the words, "In death's Solemn Moment our mother, be nigh; as children of Mary, O teach us to die" I don't know how strong I would have been to actually sing those words because Julian was so brave at the end, I felt he had taught me how to die but the very words would have choked me.

Still strong, I held my head high and walked behind the entourage of bearers. Then a sneaky thought entered my head that weakened my defence as I allowed my mind to reminisce and wonder. I recalled the last time I had walked down this Aisle was on our wedding day 28 years previously. Although we were married in this church we actually attended another on a regular basis. When he proposed to me all those years ago, the one thing that bothered him the most was being pushed down the Aisle by someone else. He confessed to me once the act of being pushed down the Aisle symbolised him being pushed in to marriage. But as he knew this was not true in our case he was able to overcome this fear. He knew his other option was to get married at a Registry Office, he didn't feel comfortable with this alternative either because he said he would not feel truly married if he took his vows anywhere other than in a church.

(I want to point out, this was his personal opinion, I hope it's not offended anyone who's been married in a Registry Office, after all life is about making personal choice and this was his.)

On our wedding day we both held hands as his brother pushed the wheelchair down the central Aisle. I felt I was once again going down the same Aisle but not arm in arm like we were on that special day, this time separated by a box as I lagged behind. That's when I felt this sudden urge to lurch forward to touch the coffin. If it wasn't possible to hold hands on this our last journey together in public at least I wanted a small contact with him.

I had another attack of weeping half way down the Aisle, remembering he did not want to be pushed down the Aisle on our wedding day so I had requested an extra pair of handles to be fixed onto the coffin so he could be carried more effortlessly. But health and safety prevailed on the day, and the coffin was pushed down the Aisle on a trolley with wheels yet again. I didn't mind, and I'm sure Julian didn't mind either. I was just struggling with the fact that on both occasion the options had been removed out of both of our control. As our journey down the Aisle came to an end, I was still thinking about our wedding day when I recalled that our married life had started at 3oclock in the afternoon and Julian died at precisely 3 o'clock in the afternoon; in effect our married life began and ended at 3 o'clock and how strange we were married on the 3rd.

As the coffin was leaving the church a mourner stepped forward and touched one of the bearers' arms asking, "What do you have to do to join this organisation called the Buffalos?"

I overheard him saying, "See me after wards"

This mourner had been my Night Superintendent for years and curiously enough Julian had been pestering me for three years to ask him if he would like to join the Buffs. I would reply the same answer every time, "I don't think it would be his cup of tea" how wrong I was.

That person that begged entry to join the lodge on the morning of Julian's funeral was Gaj Narsingh. I feel that Julian had asked me to intervene in life so many times, but in the end Julian had to do the job himself by asking Gaj on his own funeral day.

I could almost hear him say, if you want anything done round hear you have to do it yourself.

As I stood outside the church looking at them gliding Ju's coffin into the beautiful glass carriage, I hoped Julian was proud of his send-off but not just the send-off but our married life together too from beginning to end, no regrets I hope only the fact that it had been shortened by miles.

Photograph of Daisy and Poppy drawing Julian's glass carriage
which took him on his last earthly journey to his place of rest.

As the Horse Drawn Hearse pulled away and the two Mourning
cars slowly followed, I was amazed how much respect every one gave to
the procession of mourners, even a gentleman of the road who was busy
attending to his bottle of spirit slouching on a bench suddenly realised
a funeral party was passing stood up to attention and quickly hid his
bottle behind his back with one hand and with the other slipped off his
peaked cap, then bowed his head. Julian would have probably smiled
at this because Julian could mix with anybody. Folk were just people to
him, all dressed in different cloths and all possessing different skills and
accents. Standing at the graveside there appeared to be a great heaviness;
the sky was dark grey and a dismal drizzle started to fall. Joanna bought
some single roses for the immediate family to toss onto the coffin as a
last gesture of love. After the burial we all returned to congregate back at
the Hall for something to eat.

At this stage I would like to say a public thank you to all the ladies
who helped with the food and made everything go like clockwork,
but most of all to the lady who came up with the idea of welcoming
everybody with trays of hot tea at the entrance. What a lovely touch,
it made us feel really greeted as it enticed us out of the cold. So thank
you Amanda, Jenny, Sue, Kay, Joana and of course Maureen. I couldn't
believe how far and wide these people had travelled to pay their respect.

Canada, Preston, Barmouth, Cornwall, Devon, London, Yorkshire, Summerset and Lake Vernwy

To add a nice touch to a sad day Julian's Buff Lodge gave me a list of condolences they had received from around the world. One from Victoria Australia, one from Queensland Australia, one from New South Wales Australia, two from Canada, one from Spain and another from Gibraltar. There were many others from the British Provinces. Julian was a Certified Primo just about to be raised to the Third Degree (Knight of the Order of Merit) as well as being the Web Master for the Worcestershire Province.

I have very little recollection of what I did that evening except I remember dwelling on a sympathy card I'd received the words reaffirmed what the Buffs had said in their service that morning, how our family chain was broken and when God calls us back one by one, the chain will link again. I wondered how long it would be before we saw each other again!

The following morning I visited his graveside alone, I wanted to spend some time with him and read other peoples thoughts on the cards attached to the wreaths and flowers, but as I approach I thought there was someone already there and sure enough there was, it was Julian's Uncle from Canada. After we both said a few words at his grave I accompanied him up the hill to visit his parent's grave. It was this gentleman's mother that Julian brought back from Cornwall in the campervan. I informed him that it was Julian who put his parent's head stone in place, explaining he'd over engineered the job as usual, but years later the council attached a vibrating machine to the headstone testing it for movability due to recent vandalism in other parts of the cemetery, Julian rang up the council to complain and said that an earth quake would not shake that much. The explanation he got was, "It was health and safety issues regarding vandals" It made Julian angry that the deceased relatives were held responsible for the vandals health and safety. As we strolled up the hill he reminisced about the last conversation he had with Julian, a comment he felt was strange at the time. He said Julian could foresee that the price of fuel was going to escalate so high one day, that it would affect the cost of living so much that cargos would have to be transported by hot air balloons.

I must confess he did say some wayward things sometimes, but they always came true in the end.

I often used to say to him about other topics, "Yea, that sounds a likely story" Then landing up having to apologise. I wonder if his Uncle ever gave this hot air balloon idea any more thought on his return to Canada. Indecently he was a Professor at Fredericton, New Brunswick University. I think we will have to use the 'watch and wait' policy on this one to see if this is yet another prediction that Julian got right. There might be something in it, if the price of petrol becomes too high we might be forced to buy local, eat seasonal or even grow our own food.

That evening by the fire and behind closed curtains I remember smiling to myself about some of the fond comments I'd seen written on the wreaths and flowers that morning. His niece and nephew had written "The Stilton's safe and the kettles always on Uncle Jue" Everyone knew he loved his Stilton and as he'd enter his brother's house he always call out, "Put the kettle on AJ"

His Uncle Sid, bless him slipped me a cheque on the day of the funeral to buy a new frock, he winked at me and said, "I know how tough it can be financially at times like this" I rang him that night to tell him I'd put his money towards Julian Horse Drawn Carriage his last journey on earth. Bless him he cried but I promised I'd send him a photo of the glass carriage in his Christmas card.

Since the Funeral, Julian's mother has been quoted by others saying, "I don't know why Olwen asked those Buffalos to Julian's funeral" I hope by including this part of Julian's life I don't portray myself as telling tails out of school, but I feel it necessary to explain my actions in defending my decision.

This book came about as part of my healing to de-clutter my mind; I've decided to include this part so it won't come back to haunt me at a later date. If I "say it as it is" and write the truth then I'm sure I won't have to reproach myself.

The conversation went like this, while Julian was on his death bed, but still with his faculties, Julian's mobile phone rang and his Mother answered it saying he wasn't well enough to receive the call. On hearing this, Julian asked "Who is it?" His mother said, "It's one of the Buffs". Realising who it was, he said, "Yes, I do want to speak to him", and took the mobile off her. He continued to speak informing the caller (The caller that day will know who he was if he's reading this.) that he was dying, and that if it was possible he would like a Buffalo Funeral, at this stage his mother tried to take the phone off him, saying "Don't talk like that, Julian". This is the very reason why Julian had a Buffalo funeral; I need to explain it was HIS WISH; not mine.

So to any Buffs out there who are reading this book and attended his funeral, I say to you all "Thank you for your attendance, and for making his farewell so respectful."

I am reminded not to mention how many of you came, but I'm sure he'd like me to thank the six Bearers who honoured him by carrying his coffin that day, they were Brother Mark Harris R.O.H PGP 2008, Brother Gerry Criddle, Brother Mark Bell R.O.H, Brother Colin Vaughan R.O.H Deputy PGP 2008, Brother Alf Wilkes K.O.M. and Brother Clive Williams R.O.H PGP 1997

I read of a Native American Indians third law which states, "Show great respect for your fellow beings" and I consider being a bearer is the last respectful act one can perform for a fellow human-being.

16th December 2008

Three days after Julian's funeral, was the eve of Llewela's birthday. Do you remember I recalled Julian making a divine deal when she was born to see Llewela come of age? It appears God kept his word and had prolonged his deal for as long as he could because Llewela became 19 years of age three days after Julian's funeral.

How ironic that Julian had his big accident just before his 19th birthday and Llewela became an orphan in effect just before her 19th birthday. Not the same I know, but both were a life changing event. I wanted a sense of normality to creep in to Llewela's birthday that day. So we ventured to Merry Hill, I must say Llewela had been a brick throughout this entire ordeal and her boyfriend Kevin was a big support for both of us.

The first Sunday after Julian's funeral, I went to my regular church as usual and after mass one of the parishioners asked me "What's happening now then, Olwen", I said, "I don't know, but I feel like Queen Boudicca we both witnessed our loved ones suffer injustice.

I told him that I felt as if I was travelling from the North gathering momentum heading South in my chariot single handed fighting for justice, anyone was welcome to accompany me, but low behold if any one tried to block my path. He said "Good for you Olwen, keep it up"

It was true, I did feel Julian had been violated like Boudicca's daughters, and all Boudicca and I could do was stand back and watch the humiliation. I did struggle at first, whether to do 'something or nothing' about this diabetic dilemma or to take up arms and fight the injustice that he had endured, in the process protecting others might follow in his footsteps.

History states that Queen Boudicca once said, "I am fighting for my lost freedom, my bruised body and my outraged daughters. Consider how many of you are fighting, and why?

Then you will win or perish. That is what I, a woman plan to do. Let the men live in slavery if he wants to." Like Boudicca, I wanted to fight for Julian's lost freedom, his broken body and the outrage I felt towards everybody who would not listen to his agonising plea, or did **I** want to live the rest of my life in slavery thinking I could of done something to stop others suffering like he did. While there was a small chance someone might take notice of me, I have to try. Otherwise I will not free myself of the memory of seeing him dyeing, fighting at the same time and with his last breath begging me not to let others suffer like he did.

That same Sunday I took Julian's unfinished chain mail-armour for one of the Altar boys to finish. He was only 12 at the time but had taken Julian's death to heart; he considered Julian to be his friend and seemed pleased Id asked him to finish this task. Their ages were miles apart but they seemed to have an affinity with each other! His name is Aiden Pinder, he's a good scholar and I know one day he will make Julian very proud.

Our first Christmas without Julian

The next few days were a bit of a blur, which quickly brought us up to Christmas. The question was; where was I going to spend it without offending some anyone? I was very lucky I had five invitations to spend Christmas with them. So not to offend anyone I decided to spend it distributing soup to the homeless. When I told a very learned man in our church of my decision, he burst my Christian bubble by reminding me I was very lucky to have so many homes to choose from. Why did I want to insult any of them by not taking up on their kind invitation and especially this Christmas more than any, because I would need their support? If I was to go amongst strangers on this special day no one would offer me a shoulder to cry on because they would be so wrapped up in their own problems to spare a thought for me! He suggested I did it in a few years' time when I was feeling stronger. I took heed and but then had the problem of who to spend it with, I discussed it with my work colluge Gaj do you remember Gaj the one who requested to join the Buffs at Julian's funeral, who said, "Who would Julian be spending Christmas with, if he was here?"

I said, "With Llewela and myself, of course".

There lay my answer; my destiny was going to take me to Halesowen that first Christmas. I woke early that morning and while lying in bed trying to put things into perspective I noticed the excitement and cheer of Christmas past was missing in the house, my mind wondered to what the original Christmas day was all about. How Joseph had walked the eighty mile journey from Nazareth to Bethlehem with his heavily pregnant wife Mary on a donkey.

Not only did she give birth to her baby son amongst the hay and animals, she had no female companion like a mother or midwife to reassure her or any pain relief to ease her discomfort.

I remember sobbing uncontrollably as I tried to imagine the two of them all alone in this stable struggling with this little miracle. How different it was when Llewela was born nineteen years previously, born in a clinically clean environment with Doctors at hand if I needed them.

I then thought of all the gifts that would be exchanged later that day and what the original gifts were offered all those years ago. Gold,

Frankincense and Myrrh, gold recognising his royalty, frankincense when used as incense was considered as moving into a new spirit and myrrh when mixed with oil was used to embalm a corpse. The shadow of the Roman cross had already fallen over his little face. The three gifts represented a beginning a middle and the end of this baby's life.

I pulled myself together thinking how glad I was knowing there was life after death, otherwise the word 'corpse' might have dwelled too much on my mind and ruined the celebration. I quickly bathed and dressed before driving over to the 'Smith household' to join Llewela and her boyfriend.

I was very apprehensive about the day, it was the first Christmas day I'd spent away from Julian for nearly thirty years. In fact, I did have a very interesting day keeping company with the Granddad in the family. He too was a widow, he told me of lots of stories from the past that his grandsons didn't even know. They said a few times in the course of the day, "I didn't know that Granddad" he'd reply "You never asked" Word of advice, question the older generation to near exhaustion they love telling us about the good old days and we often learn so much and realise what dull lives we actually lead compared to theirs! I watched a film once, when an old lady was looking at a photograph of herself in a swimming costume and she said, "You see my dear, I haven't always been old"

One of the tales he told me was when he ran the Boys Brigade; he had a funny feeling about this one boy but could not put his finger on it. It was little things like he had the smallest of feet and hands for a boy. It was some twelve months later the boy was discovered to be a girl, needless to say there followed a long investigation in to how she managed to hide her identity for so long.

We wrote to each other on and off for two and a half years. He had the most beautiful handwriting for any age, but to have it at 90 years of age was absolutely marvellous.

They tell me now education is trying to discontinue teaching hand writing in schools and only use computer writing to correspond. I believe there is a state in America conducting a trial study to see if it will work! Can anyone explain to me how will these children when they become adult, quickly scribble down a quick note if they have never been taught how to write? Long handwriting is nearly extinct already. Handwriting could be fast becoming a thing of the past. Well that's progress for you! Thank you the 'Smith family' for your kindness extended to me that day especially Chris and Dave, Kevin's parents for their hospitality and Steve his brother for his efforts in the hot Kitchen.

Sadly Bob Jennaway passed away on the 16th May 2011. How strange Kevin's grandfather died on Llewelas grandfather's birthday.

The next family gathering was also going to prove to be a bit difficult. It was our annual Christmas get together that Julian instigated all those years ago, at my parents' home. We used to call it our pretend Christmas day which was always held on New Year's Day. May be New Year's Day was more fitting if our calendar year if the years are calculated according to Jesus's birth.

The question was, was it going to continue in its old familiar way the answer of course was why stop a good thing? We just had to have the courage to carry it through.

It did take place, but I asked if it could be held on another day other than New Year's Day so I could be left alone with my thoughts and not be bombarded with chitter chatter on the usual chosen day. To my amazement I quite enjoyed this other day they chose. An elderly lady did say to me once; when you become a widow and you attend these function alone that's when you realise, you truly are on your own.

When Julian instigated these gatherings, Gweno and I decided to stay focused on the origin of Christmas by theming the day each year. The theme would always be chosen the Christmas before allowing us time to collect the appropriate gifts, wrapping paper, tree decoration, Christmas cards and table decoration to match. We tried to connect with the crib, choosing such topics as angels, stars, royalty, shepherd, cherubs and doves and so on. The last few years were proving to be more difficult to find something different, but at the 2007 gathering Julian suggested a Robin as a theme. Gweno and I looked at each other and agreed 'as legend has it' the little red Robin had dipped his chest in Christ's blood at the cross and that was enough reason for our theme for 2008 Christmas. Throughout the year Julian would have seen Robin Christmas paper coming into the house along with Robin Christmas cards, Robin serviettes, presents associated with Robins, Robins for the tree and Robin table decorations, he even design and printed the Robin place names, so when people outside our family who didn't know about our annual themes started telling us they had a Robin nesting in their garden for the first time ever, especially when these sightings were made by people who were unable to attend the funeral this left Gweno and I wondering; what was going on? When I told one of his friends who had inherited a Robin in his garden; that Julian had chosen the robin as a theme for Christmas 2008, his children fondly started to call their Robin 'Julian'.

That first Christmas at my parents we had an additional guest at the table it was Gill and her husband, Julian new friend who had now become my new close friend too. Many photographs were taken that day and this is when I first encountered Orbs. These Orbs were only present on photographs when I was caught on camera laughing.

One of the gifts I received that day was a CD off Gweno, by the artist Enya. While I was driving home to Kidderminster that night I decided to listen to my new CD the album was called "And Winter came" the song that affected me the most was The Spirit of Christmas Past. The lyrics go like this—

> When tears are in your eyes, it's time to look inside;
> Your heart can find another way,
> Believe in what I say, don't throw this time away.
> Tomorrow will be Christmas day.

I couldn't think why I was so affected by these four lines, was there a message for me here from Julian or was I trying to read too much into these lyrics. This is what I made of the supposed message.

The first line, while I'm crying; I need to look deeper into why Julian died like he did.

The second line; I'll find a way somehow to the truth, I just need to listen to my heart more.

The third line, indicated to what Julian said, "Don't let others suffer like I did"

I need to believe in what he said and not to waste time doing trivial things like house work, until I find the cause of his death. The forth line; there will be plenty of time to celebrate lots of Christmas's once the jobs done. I am well aware there will be plenty of readers out there who will disagree with my explanation of these lyrics but for the time being I ask you to just humour me for now.

It felt odd returning home that night with only presents for me, how sad Julian didn't have any at all. I just hope that where he was, he'd have an abundance of everything.

The only gift I had for Julian that Christmas was a laminated Christmas card that I left on his grave tucked into a Holly Wreath. It read like this—

> **I'll miss you this Christmas.**
> It's hard to understand why some things happen as they do.
> No other husband in the world was loved as much as you.
> But sadly, you were taken to a very special place
> No longer shall I hear your voice or feel your warm embrace.
> And yet, I know for certain, we shall one day meet again and
> That's the thought that helps me through the sorrow and the pain.
> So even though this Christmas will be lonely, it is true.
> I'll keep you in my heart until I'm back once more with you.

The words were true about missing his voice and his embrace. Thoughts that crept into my mind often and still do, are "I can't wait to get home to tell Julian" then a second later the realisation I can't. Other things like people I've met in the street or not seen for ages, the news they had, I wanted to rush home to tell Julian. Food I might of bought, then on the way home I'd think, I hope Julian will enjoy this, or worst still if I didn't know how to do something I'd think, never mind I'll ask Julian when I get home he will know how what to do!

Strangely that first Christmas I only received one Christmas card, but 99 sympathy cards mostly from people who couldn't attend the funeral which made me think there could have been even more on his funeral day. I wasn't upset about the lack of Christmas cards; it would have been difficult to appreciate the sentiment behind the two different sets of cards. One of joy, the other with sadness but the reason I'm mentioning this solitary Christmas card is because it was sent by our friend in France. Was this card yet another coincidence or was it intended to stand out of the crowd as a reminder that dyeing from an abscess in the 21st century was not normal in this day and age. Shouldn't he of survived like her. Was it another sign to continue with the diabetic issue?

Just as some poignant lyrics appeared to direct me to continue with Julian's cause, there were others that just played on my emotions. One such song which did just that was—

"All I want for Christmas"

I don't want a lot for Christmas.
I just want you for my own.
More than you can ever know.
Make my wish come true.

I felt like screaming, "Stop teasing me, I know I can't have what I want this Christmas"

New Year's Eve was approaching fast, yet another emotional function to attend. As a family we usually went to our friends Jo and Michaels for this celebration. That first New Year's Eve they invited Llewela, Kevin and I they pointed out it would be low key affair on the account that Julian was missing. I said "No, I beg you do everything just as if Julian was there." As usual, there was a houseful of Italian people, an abundance of Italian food, Italian music and a lot of happy chatting. At the stroke of midnight they all went outside into the garden to watch the fireworks to welcome the New Year in. Afterwards everyone was offered a hand held sparklers; I didn't join in with this tradition instead I ran into the house for my camera. As I was taking the photographs, I said quietly "Julian can you hear the laughter, they're having such fun wouldn't you just love all of this".

And I continued to take more photographs. When I had them developed, I couldn't believe my eyes the photographs taken of when I said, "Wouldn't you just love all of this" they were covered with Orbs. If it was true that Orbs that appear on photographs represented spirits or visiting angels and loved ones then Julian had brought a ruck of friends with him that night. He appeared to be having a party of his own. Trust Julian to do something big like that, he always liked to involve everybody.

Once New Year celebrations were over I decided to tackle the conservatory, it was full of what other people would consider rubbish, but to me they were things I'd put off shifting because of the emotion they had attached to the task. The task was to move all the tools that were stacked in the order of the jobs, intended to be taken two days after Julian became ill to the house in France.

The Ferry was booked, Formula 1 Hotel room was booked to break our journey, and our passports were in date, including the euros exchanged. Nothing to do except go, with hind sight maybe that's what we should have done just gone 'burst abscess and all'. The French might have taken more heed of his reactions and withheld the Insulin. Even with the language barrier it might have been easier to deal with than the cloth ears doctors he was dealing with. I know I mustn't dwell on that, and I know 'maybe's' don't mend situations.

Getting back to the painful task in hand; I made the many journeys backwards and forwards from the conservatory to the shed. I sobbed with every load, thinking how could it of gone so horribly wrong! The damp drizzling weather didn't help my low mood either as I sobbed with every arm full.

Although I felt very comfortable living in the house on my own, I didn't feel totally alone. It still felt as if Julian was still living here, just didn't happen to be in the same room as him, as if we kept missing each other in the physical sense. Because his things were still about, his shoes his cloths his wheelchairs, his quad bike, his disabled truck the stair lift and his bath seat.

While Llewela was on her Christmas break from University her laptop failed to function so she asked if she could borrow her Dads laptop. I said of course, anything to make sure her studying continued. A few days later after she returned to Oxford she rang me asking, did I know that Dad had written a letter to the Consultant at Oswestry?

I said, "No" She said, "I'll print it off and send you a copy in the post?" Two days later a copy of the letter landed on the door mat.

The letter was dated 2006 and as the letter was never finished consequently it was never sent.

I am sure Julian won't mind if I re-type it out in this book for the good of others, I hope no one try's to do me for copyright. When he was alive we shared everything, I'm just doing the same now—sharing.

Julian Davies BSc (Inf. Tech), HND (Comp. Science)
Kidderminster,
Worcestershire.
DY10 4JW.

Mr ////////// M.B.Ch.BM.Med.Sci(Trauma)FRCS
Midlands Spinal Injuries Centre.
R.J & A.H Orthopaedic & District Hospital NHS Trust.
Oswestry.
Shropshire.
SY10 7AG.

13TH May 2006

Dear Mr //////////////////

First, may I take this opportunity to thank you for my recent operation which, touch wood, is healing nicely and I am still hopeful for a successful conclusion.

Whilst I was in hospital you referred me to a Registrar regarding my diabetes on which we couldn't agree and I didn't see again. Now, on reflection, bed rest is a wonderful opportunity for perusal on one's problems, I wondered if I could apologise to him and take up the matter with him.

The problem we had was that doctor assumed that I would not accept the fact that I was a type 2 diabetic. But I know I have diabetes but not type 2 the Doctor in question would not listen to my reasoning which was not helped at the time by me not remembering the name of the diabetes I think I have, added to his refusal to accept that there is this other type of diabetes. Once at home again and on my computer (still on my bed rest I would like to add) I think I have Hepatogenous Diabetes. I know I have a liver problem, I know it's enlarged; I know I have a spleen problem with 4.5cm infarction. What I want to know is what is meant by statement such as "patients with cirrhosis have insulin resistance" and "impaired glucose tolerance" and there is no definitive test to distinguish type 2 diabetes from diabetes caused by liver cirrhosis. Is an LFT`s of 643 high? Should I have been put on Metformin when I have a liver problem and why did I collapse with `Metformin-associated lactic acidosis?` Why do my O2 levels reduce and my lungs collect water when I use Insulin (3 litres drained Sept. `07)? Without treatment my sugar levels are 11-13 and whatever medication I took, some at the minimums and maximum, my sugar levels never changed. Lastly, why am I so fit and healthy without diabetes medication and so so, sick when I am on it?

(The letter ended abruptly here)

As the letter was never signed or sent; maybe he felt the questions were there but not the answers, he was obviously not happy with the way the letter lent itself with too many questions and not enough satisfactory answers. On the other hand with hindsight, if he had sent the above letter unfinished as it was, and some Doctors had found it and read it, it may have thrown some question into his treatment and furthermore, additional investigations may have been instigated to see why he was suffering so badly at the hands of the treatment forced upon him. What I need to know is, are there any more cases like this out there? If there is, voice your concerns and let Doctors know your suffering too like poor Julian did. Don't become a statistic like Julian, if you're suffering at the hands of diabetic treatment have the courage to say "I too would like to share my experience"

Winter of 2008

Winter came and went taking with it its snow. The first thing I intended to do was to see how difficult or how easy it was to obtain copies of medical notes. I started by applying for Julian's medical case notes in January 2009 six weeks after his death, I didn't even know how to set about this task. I didn't even know if I was allowed to.

So I started with Worcester Hospital, with a simple telephone conversation. They were very helpful and advised me to apply in writing, not forgetting to enclose the appropriate fee, on receiving this request and payment they would copy and forward the notes.

That was simple enough; I then went through the same procedure with Oswestry Hospital, same answer, same request in writing enclosing a fee.

The next Hospital was Shrewsbury, same procedure.

The next Hospital, Telford, again the same procedure.

Last but not least, his GP medical notes?

Not only did I want the medical notes, I wanted the nursing notes, the results of any tests, copies of any x-ray's, MRI scans, ultrasound scans, CT scans, as well as written reports of these scans.

Including records of such things as the medication charts, the observation charts the diabetic charts and any fluid balance charts.

I am specific in quoting what I requested, because lots of these copies were missing, which meant a true bigger picture could not be seen. I had to apply, and reapply for the same paper work and in most cases, I had to pay again as it was a separate request.

Things I was looking for when the notes arrived were, did the Doctor in Telford actually write in the notes that he felt "Julian was obviously not a Diabetic!"

As I feared he had not, was it an oversight, or did he scribe this and was later deleted, or was it not filed in the notes, maybe filed in the wrong notes or was it removed, I will never know. The other documentation that was missing from the medical notes was the comments from the doctor describing the condition of Julian's skeletal frame. What puzzled me was why did the Doctors at Telford tell me the gory details of Julian's bones and how it had disintegrated into fine powder in theatre, then not documented in the notes ?

Yet again I'm left feeling as if I've got a vivid imaginative mind.

I also wanted to see if the Doctors had documented what had taken place on the 14th April 2008 the night Julian had a reaction to Insulin following his minor surgery. He had requested not to have Insulin from the nursing staff the Doctors the Surgeon and the Anaesthetist. The Anaesthetist claimed he'd never heard such rubbish and besides how anyone can be allergic to insulin, every human needs insulin to survive it's a natural hormone. I couldn't find any documentation about this incident. Why not! The drug chart indicated he was given the Insulin, even though he was wearing a red allergy band. In addition to disregarding his request he was administered an unprepared General Anaesthetic and while in this disadvantaged state of unconsciousness he was given the very drug he requested not to have. I know he wasn't starved for this procedure, because I prepared his breakfast at home before I drove him to the hospital. Why should he be starved he was expecting a local anaesthetic. Documentation of this hospital episode is very sparse; reading the notes you would not conclude he was very ill. The only thing that was mentioned in the copy of his discharge letter to the GP was, discharged on hypertensive drugs.

Could this be classified as physical abuse?

More unanswered questions! The water is not getting clearer but murkier.

As I watched the post daily for news of the medical notes my sick leave came to an end, and I had to return back to work. I discovered later that I had been thoroughly investigated after the accusations from his family. Not only were my in-laws gunning for my job, they were also after my pension and worst of all to tarnish my reputation as a nurse, and lastly to lock me up and throw away the key. I know this people kept ringing me up warning me of her intention and to be careful.

I don't rightly know who was involved in my return to work plan, but I believe there were some top Hospital Authorities, the CID from Telford Police and my managers. Rightly so, if I was a danger to the public the last place I should be let lose is amongst patients who were sick and vulnerable.

Once everything had been investigated my place of work allowed me back to work after I signed a witness statement regarding my mother-in-laws unfound accusations of contributing towards Julian death. I returned back to work first week in January 2009, a fresh start to a new year, a new beginning to a life without Julian.

I think one of the hardest things I had to do each day from here on was to travel in my car past the cemetery, at the beginning of each shift and then again at the end of each shift knowing he'd been laid to rest at the back of my work place. As I passed the entrance of the cemetery each day, I would do the sign of the cross then blow him a kiss.

Spring 2009

Now winter was over I started to evaluate my life, knowing Julian loved his so much I realised I was lucky to still have mine, so I should appreciate it and live it as he would have if he was in my shoes. Strange, when we're searching for guidance we find it in the most unexpected places.

I found mine in small print on the previous year's calendar, it read, Psalm 116 "I will walk in the presence of the Lord, in the land of the living" to make sure I didn't lose sight of that I decided to frame the beautiful scenic sun set picture.

Spring bought with it new life, not just this single life that I was trying to adjust to but other small things were that I hadn't even notice were taking place too.

I didn't watch television any more, whereas before we were both telly addicts. After his death I felt if he couldn't watch television then I wouldn't either.

I always slept on my left side; I started to notice I was sleeping on my right.

I use to dream of Julian in the wheelchair; I started to dream of him walking. He used to be in dark cloths, I was now dream of him in white cloths.

I used to do big weekly shopping; I was now only buying what I needed. In fact I dined out more with friends than in.

I never use to touch the bills, I was now dealing with them on a daily bases.

I never used the front door because the front door was not wheel chair friendly, in fact I didn't possess a front door key I had to ask Llewela to have a copy of hers.

I never used to keep a diary, I now realise the importance of keeping one. You never know when a Police man might come calling asking about my where about. With my poor memory it could keep me out of trouble.

I never use to eat red apples, now I love them. (Julian's favourite)

I disliked olives intensely but now I adore them. (Llewela and Julian always loved them)

Our focal point was always the lounge; my favourite room in the house then became the kitchen.

As time went by I did started to use the back door, at about the same time I bought a small statue for the garden. It was a statue of a lady with her head bowed on her bent knees, crying. Every time I passed this weeping statue I used to leave my sorrow with her. So when I entered the house I'd leave my sorrow outside, and then when I left the house to visit someone, again I would not take my sorrow with me as an unwanted guest but leave them with my guardian of sorrow. I did realise that one day I would have to experience the sorrow, maybe soon maybe in 30 years never the less one day, but not right now.

Photograph of my 'Guardian of sorrow' statue.

Although I was struggling trying to accept that Julian was never coming home again.

Repetitive songs on the radio didn't help my healing, one such song that I managed to tune into constantly was Abba, "Knowing you"

No more care free laughter's, silence ever after.
Walking through an empty house, tears in my eyes.
Breaking up is never easy I know.
But I have to go this time, it's the best I can do.

Poor Ju, he always did do his very best.

Summer of 2009

Summer was soon upon me, and what a lovely summer it was too with its long beautiful hot summer days. I spent all my spare time working on the patio under the shade of the parasol filing his medical notes into folders, and reading and re-reading the notes in preparation for the inquest. Researching what the medical profession missed, more importantly what I had missed!

It was so difficult for Julian and I when we didn't have accesses to information, at his bed side.

As I was looking through his notes, the one thing he complained about the most was pain.

Julian was normally blessed with a high threshold of pain; that included his childhood mischievousness which often resulting in painful accidents. I'm sure he would have curtailed his adventure if he could not have tolerated pain. Even when he did experience pain he had this ability to push himself beyond and endure considerably even more pain before submitting to it. What I'm saying is; when Julian said he had pain that to me meant he was in agony. I recalled I had saved a cutting from a newspaper before he became ill. On my return home I found the cutting which I'd saved from the Mail on Sunday dated 28th September 2008, which was two days before Julian's abscess burst. I remember showing this article to Julian because the topic was so interesting. It was about a bizarre experiment done ironically at Oxford University.

The academics at 'Oxford Centre for Science of the mind' studied 12 Catholics and 12 Atheists to see who could endure the most pain, the study was to see if Faith helped with pain relief. They used the latest brain scanning techniques and sessions in an MRI scanning machine. They discovered that while Catholics studied the image of the Virgin Mary they discovered they could activate parts of the brain that controlled pain. The result was Catholics experienced 12% less pain than atheists did. I couldn't tell you why they chose Catholics and not any other Christian faiths, I can only imagine that Julian's faith helped him over the years but at the end, the pain was too great even for poor Julian to bear, which would explain why others who have suffered like Julian, taking diabetic treatment, were prescribed Morphine for their pain.

It was his pain that was his main cause for refusing his treatment, the most profound rule of nursing is, "Pain is what the patient says it is."

My Longed for Letters

I call this chapter 'My Longed for Letters' because it was what we both longed to see during his last five weeks of life. They were conformation that he did have difficulties with certain drugs.

Finding proof in Julian's medical notes confirmed it wasn't the figment of my imagination that Julian was truly suffering at the hands of his treatment.

There were 15 documentations in his notes stating he had difficulties with insulin, antibiotics and diuretics.

The first letter I found was dated 12th May 2007 in his GP notes; **"Looks dreadful, stop new insulin, sweaty and a degree of breathlessness"**

The second letter I found was dated 20th May 2008 dictated after his follow up appointment at Oswestry informing Julian's GP that his "Sore was completely healed. **Presently refusing medication, his condition improves"**

This letter confused me; it said Julian's condition was improving without the compulsory treatment of insulin which they insisted he had to take while he was in their care, less than one month previously. Mmm.

The third letter I found was dated 8th June 2007 **"Diabetic nurse feels illness is related to insulin—stop insulin."**

The fourth letter I found was dated 19th July 2007 in his GP notes following his near multi-organ-failure stating, "Patient wishes a referral to a liver specialist as advised by Diabetic Nurse at Worcester. He also requested to be referred to a Respiratory Consultant as advised by an Anaesthetist at Oswestry. Patient Feels lungs are shot since near-multi-organ-failure earlier in the year.

The fifth letter I found was dated 15th August 2007 from the Chest Clinic to his GP stating,

"He is feeling a great deal better in himself following lung drainage and has not been recommended on insulin treatment. As you know, he has **felt very unwell whenever he has been on oral hypoglycaemic and more resent insulin**. For our part we have decided to adopt a watch and see policy"

The sixth letter I found was dated 2nd September 2008 sent by a Diabetic clinic to his GP stating, **"Patient became unwell on Metformin resulting in extreme chest pain, he was found to have splenomegaly with splenic infarct.** Diabetic medication has been stopped and the insulin's have made him very ill. He has not been on any diabetic treatment for a considerable time. In clinic he told me today that he **felt well and optimistic for the future** and is looking for employment"

The seventh letter I found was dated 8th September 2008 sent to his GP from a Consultant Physician stating, "Julian showed no evidence of diabetic retinopathy. He has had bad reaction to quite a lot of medication especially diabetics". He carries on to say that **Julian felt well and optimistic for the future,** and would like to see him again in 5 weeks. Julian was rushed into Hospital exactly 5 weeks to the day following this appointment; needless to say he did not attend this appointment.

The eighth letter I found was dated 10th September 2008 sent by the Specialists Registrar in Respiratory Medicine to the GP. I quote, "Julian's chest x-ray showed no re-accumulation of fluid in the lungs. There are chronic changes at the base of the left lung he has no respiratory symptoms or weight loss. Mr Davies is very wary about taking any oral hyperglycaemic agents; he is well in himself and **I discharge him from the clinic."**

This was four weeks before he was admitted with the abscess. Once he re-commenced on the diabetic treatment his symptoms of plural effusion returned immediately, his lungs always recovered once he was off the treatment. Doctors would diagnose him on a regular basis that he had pneumonia, only to recover 4hrs later. Physiotherapists would document chest clear diuretics not necessary. He died exactly nine weeks and four days following this appointment.

The ninth document I found was dated 9th October 2008 on his admission day to the hospital and I quote, "I called his Diabetic Consultant who was not convinced that he is allergic to insulin and wanted him to be on sliding scale of insulin per-operatively."

How could this Consultant possibly recommend treatment to Julian, from the heart of Worcestershire when Julian was being treated in Shropshire a good 70 miles away? The distance was not my problem; my problem was Julian had never clapped eyes on this Doctor and vice-versa. This lack of contact between them certainly disturbed me, because on the basis of this telephone conversation that **he couldn't remember Julian Davies and his unusual case** was correct. What made his vague non-committal statement so dangerous was on the strength of his opinion; Julian had to endure a continual admission of insulin up to the moment of his death. The doctor Julian actually saw at this Consultants clinic could barely speak English. Julian died four week and six days following his admission, after struggling with the excruciating side effects of their drugs.

The tenth document I found dated 15th October 2008 the day Julian agreed to have Erythromycin Antibiotics under duress, as long as it was stopped if his body could no longer tolerate the treatment or its side effects. On the same date the Doctor wrote in his notes ten minutes after receiving the Antibiotic, "Arrived on ward patient feeling unwell, conscious, able to complete sentences but was burping. Blood sugar 24.5 sweating, abdomen looks distended. Girth measurement 139.5 cms (that's 56inch waist, he normally wore 48inch waist trousers that's an increase of 8inches or 20cms) explained to patient Haematology and Biochemistry results are well with in normal limits. **Julian enquired about an "antidote" for Erythromycin.** He feels it is the Intravenous Antibiotic that is making him feel this way. Have told him that to my knowledge, I don't know of antidote for Erythromycin—Plan is ECG, Monitor something . . . (illegible), Stop antibiotic, Discuss with consultant"!

The eleventh proof rather than letter was the MRI report dated 29th October 2008. On many occasions Julian begged the Doctors to omit his Antibiotics unless it was absolutely necessary, due to the reaction he had to endure. They told him that he defiantly had osteomyelitis and had no <u>alternative</u> but to continue with the Antibiotics.

When I finally obtained the MRI scan result, following his death. The report stated, SUGGESTS osteomyelitis three times and the word POSSIBLE osteomyelitis once in the report. It also states—"although the signal changes seen here may be reactive in nature." (What does that mean? Is the word signal a misprint and should it read—single? And I don't know what reactive in nature signifies.)

But there was **nothing in the report to say Julian definitely had osteomyelitis** and it was not documented in the report that it was imperative that he was given Intravenous Antibiotics otherwise it would become life threatening.

This is what they were threatening Julian with, before and after the MRI scan that the consequences of not having the antibiotics would be life threatening. He took their heavy doses of antibiotic for another 13 days on their recommendation that they said he defiantly did have osteomyelitis.

The twelfth letter I found was dated October 2008 was from a Consultant Haematologist to Julian's GP, confirming he did not have cancer. The investigation that had been conducted was called 'Bence Jones Protein Test', it was requested on the strength Julian had Protein in his urine. It's a useful test to detecting or excludes the presence of cancer cells being present somewhere in the body, the cells are small enough to filter though the kidneys and make their escape through urination. Incidentally Aspirin and **Penicillin can cause a false positive Bence Jones Protein test.** This is further proof that Protein should not be present in the urine? And if it is they usually investigate something as serious as cancer! This letter was not available to the hospital doctors because it was filed in the notes they didn't feel was necessary to obtain from Worcester.

The thirteenth documentation I found was dated 2nd November 2008, it revealed that he had an enlarged heart even though earlier that day an ECG Report stated no change. What had happened in a couple of hours to change this, what strain had he endured to have an enlarged heart later that day? His hospital records state, he was given Metronidazole 400 mg twice that day, something he found difficult to tolerate, he was also given Flucloxacillin 1.5 gm. 4 times that day something else he kept telling them he was hypersensitive too, this being his third day of treatment a drug that contains penicillin. He was also given Furosemide 40mg to an already dehydrated body, and lastly he was given Actrapid insulin12 units which he knew he was allergic to—quite a mixture don't you think. Was this concoction too much for Julian's strong healthy heart to endure?

Ten days later Julian was dead.

The fourteenth letter I found dated 3rd November 2008 was written by a Clinical Psychologist recommending I quote, "The couple would like further investigations regarding Julian's insulin to see if it is considered to be the appropriate treatment and is it safe for him. Perhaps, **they feel if this had been properly addressed they can then understand why it is necessary to continue with the treatment.**" No investigations into his allergy were ever carried out; consequently this Clinical Psychologists advice was not heeded or acted upon. Not much point asking for her opinion, she was obviously picking up a wage packet for not accomplishing any life changing treatments on a monthly basis! Mmm. Sounds like easy money to me! Julian died nine days later. The fifteenth documentation I found dated 4th November 2008 by the Tissue Viability Rep from Wolverhampton, "Wound bed clean, change dressing in three days" Verbally she told both of us the properties in the dressings she supplied **did not warrant additional oral or Intravenous Antibiotics**. Julian and I asked her to relay this to the Doctors as he found it difficult to tolerate any drugs any more. Julian also stressed to her that his wound would break down beyond belief if he was to continue with these drugs.

Her reply was, "I cannot get them to listen Julian; they are from the old school."

During the first week of the five he spent in hospital during his last stint, before Julian was recommenced on insulin, she said she hadn't seen a wound react as quickly as this to the treatment. It was true you could see granulation taking place each day, it was like clean bunches of grapes growing inside the cavity. The treatment obviously suited him I thought nature was wonderful, if I hadn't seen this with my own eyes I would not have believed it second hand. Julian lived in dreadful dread that the insulin would destroy all her good work beyond all recognition.

How right he was to fear this tissue destruction, in my opinion his body suffered decomposition and decay while he was still living! Eight days later he was dead!

Was I over reacting when I was constantly quoted in Julian's notes, "Wife seeks further tests regarding drug issues".

To clarify what Julian endured and what Julian refused during his last five weeks in these three Hospitals. He was prescribed Insulin 76 times, contrary to popular belief he was only successful in refusing insulin 6 times at Oswestry, on those occasions for good reason because his blood sugars were too low, if he had taken the insulin on those occasions he would of suffered a hypoglycaemic attack. The Doctors were emergency bleeped to attend Julian 6 times at Oswestry after having reaction to the insulin. There were many occasions when a doctor was contacted I'm only quoting the emergency call outs.

He refused the insulin 9 times at Shrewsbury Hospital, granted the sugar levels were still high on those occasions, but he felt too ill to continue. At this point I should point out that it was documented on his medication chart in the "Additional information section" that the patient is sensitive to insulin and was wearing a red allergy band, warning staff of the same. Why was he administered this drug?

Doctors were emergency called out to Julian 20 times to investigate his reaction to the insulin at Shrewsbury Hospital, but each time they would say, "Continue with the insulin". These emergency call outs are recorded in his notes and are not my say so. And of course there were many other call outs, I'm again only quoting the emergency call outs.

On the 2nd November 2008 it was documented in Oswestry notes that Julian had said, "I would prefer to die than take Insulin or go back to Shrewsbury" Can you see how desperate this man was, not only did Julian say it but a doctor actually recorded his comments and wishes in his medical notes. Don't forget Hospital Medical notes are a legal documentation.

After reading these letters I sought professional help and approached a Medical Solicitor for guidance regarding my next move, her reply was "Unfortunately your husband is dead and it would now be very difficult for us to prove a case"

So, at what stage would it be best for the law to help and defend its subjects, if it's not possible when they are alive, sick or dead? Can someone enlighten me? Where is our window of opportunity?

On the rebound of this reply I then approached "The Action Against Medical Accidents" (A.A.M.A) and on 7th December 2009 I received a reply apologising that their findings were disappointing. Then it went on to say that, they knew of an attempt some years ago to bring legal action in relation to human insulin, when the Insulin became more widely used, such claims and allegations that there were reactions to such drugs could not be substantiated legally. That's not to say there was not a problem. (Another dead end alley)

If these two professional bodies could not find a case maybe I had misled the Doctors regarding these three little words, Reaction, Side effect, and Allergies.

Maybe I wasn't clear on those words either?

This is the definition I found—:

Side effect - often mild but can be life threatening. (The drug threatened his life first then he died)

Allergies - abnormal sensitivity to substance innocuous to most people involving the immune system but sometimes deadly. (His immunity was affected by the Adrenal Tumour, and the drugs proved to be deadly in his case)

Reaction - action resisting another chemical change causing decomposition. (The drug reaction caused his flesh to die first and his body to die later)

Not much difference with any of them really, they all carry the same sentence; either 'cause for concern label' and more worryingly the 'death sentence'

But I had to do something, the echo what he said at his bed side haunted me, "I feel as if I'm forced to commit suicide, every time they make me take these drugs"

All Julian was begging for was investigation into his reaction, then the appropriate treatment. Nothing more than what everybody else in this country is entitled to.

Desperately not knowing who else to seek help from, I was bothered by something both my brother and sister had said at his bed side, which was "If you get out of here Julian you need to contact the Courts of Human Rights regarding your forced treatment". I can remember thinking at the time, "What did they mean, **if** he gets out!"

How true their words had become.

I did what Glyn and Gweno recommended, a task they'd given Julian to do but now I found myself doing on his behalf. But before I contact The Court of Human Rights, I thought I'd better check first to see if Julian's human rights had been affected.

Human Rights Act 1998 in UK.

They are—: Right to life.
The right not to be subjected to torture, inhuman treatment,
degrading treatment, or punishment.
The right to liberty and security.
The right to respect for privacy and family life.

They should—: Have access to services, treatment and support.
Communication.
Being treated with respect.
What health and social care service providers are expected to do?
Give feedback and making complaints.
Freedom of movement in your own country.
Freedom to do what you wish. (as long as it does not harm others)
What the law says.

The Law on Consent

One of the acts of human rights is, 'what the law says', well what does the law say about consent?

How many types of consent are there? There are two, one is written and the other is verbal consent.

Both should respect all the ruling laid down by . . . , they are-:

- Consent before all examination.
- Consent must be voluntary and not **under duress or undue influence from health professionals,** family or friends.
- Consent should be informed, patient receiving sufficient information before consenting.
  (Barks (1979) defines "informed consent" as the right of every human being to determine what shall be done to his/her own body.")
- Consent can be withdrawn when Patient changes their minds.
- Capacity consent, one must be capable of giving it.
- Consent does not have to be given, under entitled to **refuse treatment, and their choice must be respected.**

A more elaborate explanation of the right to refuse treatment,—:

> It is a basic principle of law in this country that an adult, mentally competent person **has the right to refuse treatment and take his/her own discharge contrary to medical advice for a good, bad or no reason at all.**

Also King's (1981) views states, "Individuals have a right to knowledge about themselves, **a right to participate in decisions that influence their life, their health,** and community service and **a right to accept or reject health care.**

I feel none of these were adhered to; medical staff failed in their care of duty when they excluded Julian from taking part in his own Multidisciplinary meeting, then cancelling it with no further date arranged. The other was the right to refuse medical treatment.

During those five weeks he lived in fear of many things, fear is a terrible condition to suffer from. This was not something Julian was familiar with; he had no place for it in his life.

There is, an old wives tale that claims 'People who live in fear cannot heal' I assume it's because it affects their immune system!

These were the type of things he lived in fear of—:

Fear of being black listed from Oswestry, if he didn't take the medication at Shrewsbury

Fear of having the next insulin, knowing what pain and suffering it brought with it.

Fear of dying in Shrewsbury amongst the Doctors and nurses who blackmailed him into taking the insulin, and not amongst his family and friends in his own home.

Fear of not been able to stop the insulin in time before he died prematurely.

Fear in the end of seeing the Doctors who mocked and humiliated him approach him.

Fear of not being allowed to be transferred to Worcester Royal Hospital where he knew staff believed he had a problem with insulin.

Fear of never having access to the Worcester or Kidderminster notes before something serious happened.

Fear of never seeing the pathology report that indicated he could not tolerate diabetic treatment.

Fear that we would not find the Doctor who did the blood test in time. (He was never found)

Fear of being left on his own in case the staff gave him medication he felt was harming him.

Fear of never coming home again.

Fear of leaving me a widow.

Fear of leaving Llewela without a Dad when she needed him most.

Finally fear of his mortality

Julian was subjected to all of the above.

I did contact the Courts of Human Rights in Strasbourg but in their correspondence they emphasised so much on time scale, I lost momentum while I was concentrating so much on gathering information for the Inquest, in doing so I missed my window of opportunity. At the time I was trying to prioritise the paperwork, it now leaves me wondering if they are all 'much of a much-ness' as they say leaving us relatives and patients out in the cold! Why should time matter?

The Nursing and Midwifery Council states Nurses must respect patient's refusal to treatment just as much as they would if they consented. A record of refusal to consent must be documented.

I did not find any documentation in Julian's notes that he repeatedly refused treatment, only on his drug chart. With hindsight, what might have helped Julian's case is if he had in his possession a living will. This is a binding form one signs for 'Refusal of Medical Treatment or Procedure' it is not a binding to request specific treatment you would like to be undertaken but a refusal. For the form to be legally binding, it must be written signed and witnessed and not necessarily by a Solicitor. Your GP must be made aware of this 'Living Will' including all other medical teams, carers and family members. If you're travelling you need to take a copy with you.

Oh! Hindsight what a wonderful thing!

Post Mortem Report

In the spring of 2009, I requested a copy of Julian's Post mortem report; it arrived on the 16th May 2009 which also happened to be his father's birthday. It was sealed in a double envelope with the words, 'WARNING, MAY CAUSE DISTRESS' on the second inserted envelop.

The front page had simple information on such as Julian's name, date of birth and so on.

The document stated his date of death was 13th November 2008, this was incorrect Julian died on the 12th November 2008.

It stated he was admitted to Oswestry Hospital on the 10th October 2008, this was incorrect, he was admitted on the 9th October 2008.

It stated he was admitted with a pressure sore, incorrect he was admitted following a burst abscess.

At this stage, I was still on the front page and I was beginning to wonder if the content of this Post Mortem Report was going to prove credible, if they couldn't even get the basic information correct? As the outer envelope stated it may cause distress, I decided to replace the bulk of the content back inside the envelope and went directly to work for a late shift.

When I returned home from work that evening I continued to deal with some more post. As I was about to retire to my bed, bearing in mind the time was approaching two in the morning I foolishly decided to open the Post Mortem report. I had originally intended to read it when there was someone else in the house, I don't know if tiredness or inquisitiveness got the better of me but I think I was intrigued to see how much information was correct or incorrect in the report.

Looking back I don't think I was adequately prepared to read the content especially about the state of his flesh, but to read that his blood glucose levels were only 1.4 when he died saddened me. Was it the Morphine that contributed to his hypoglycaemia?

I feel, to appreciate the remainder of this Post Mortem report you will need to find a tape measure, and all will be reviled as the chapter unfolds. The Pathologist has categorised his findings under nine systems and then his final conclusion.

<u>External Examination</u> he starts by describing Julian as 5ft 9in obese white male weighing 12 stone. The National Body Mass Index categorises 12 stone male to be of normal weight, not over weight and certainty not obese. He was overweight when he was admitted five weeks previously I admit, but it did at least confirm what I suspected that he had lost four and a half stone in weight during the last five weeks of his hospitalisation.

The report went on to describe his abdomen as distended, which was exactly what Julian complained of accompanied by excruciating pain every time he took the medication. Nurses recorded his girth measurements on a regular basis which fluctuated from 134cm to 150cm in hours. Before his admission he was wearing trousers measuring 48inch waist, which is 122cm. Have you got that tape measure handy? When they started the girth measurements his abdomen had already increased by 5 inches (12 cm) since admission. This increase could <u>not</u> have been due to diet intake, because he complained his organs were too painful and swollen to eat. This was 16cm difference, for us oldies that is over 6 inches, how would you like your waist line to go up and down every 4 to 6 hours daily accompanied with excruciating pain?

The report moves to his sacral area, where he states he had complete skin loss extending 25cm by 23 cm extending down to the bone. (That's 10inch x 9inches) I find this too disturbing to discuss, except Julian predicted this would happen.

<u>Respiratory system</u> he concluded the left lung weighed 980g while the right lung weighed 1100g

Two normal healthy lungs should weigh 2.3 kg. He had 500mls of plural effusion on right side.

<u>Cardio Vascular system;</u> he concluded his heart weighed 600mg. Double the weight of a normal male heart, which should weigh 300mg. He could tell he'd suffered a myocardial infarction (heart attack) in the past, which was true he did suffer this at the age of 18 when he originally became paralysed. Julian's heart was normal on 12th October 2008; 30 days later it is recorded he had an enlarged heart. He also stated he had 70% atheroma of the heart, otherwise known as Kounise Syndrome, which is thickening of the heart vessels caused by Allergy Angina which could progress to acute Allergic Myocardial Infarction. This type of Infarction

is brought on by **Medication Allergy** which damages any smooth muscle of the heart vessels. Medication such as Penicillin, Cefuroxime, Vancomycin and Insulin are amongst the long list of possible allergies. There are three types of Kounise Syndrome that cause atheroma, Type 1 affects a healthy heart, Type 2 affects Angina sufferers and Type 3 affects patients who have a history of Coronary Thrombosis prior to the allergy. In most cases when one discovers an allergy one discontinues the treatment, but in Julian's case there was no alternative he had to continue to take them, causing further damage to his heart.

Was his heart enlarged because his pulse rate was allowed to beat at about 145 times a minute constantly day and night for nearly 35 days, only dipping occasionally to 115 when treatment was stopped? His blood pressure most of the time was 80/50 while his respirations were up to 30 and above on many occasions, his system was obviously struggling.

His ECG prior to his surgery on the 10th October 2008 indicated Julian's heart was normal. A healthy heart depends on a flow of sodium, potassium, calcium and magnesium through the cardiac cells. Imbalance in the levels of these minerals as well as increase of toxins can prevent the impulse forming normal arrhythmias. In Julian's case he was struggling with the toxins from his allergy's causing shortness of breath leading to lung insufficiency producing pulmonary oedema. This excess work that was curtailed by the heart to shift the fluid from the lungs turned the heart into a work horse, trying to catch up with itself. In doing so the heart became more muscular hence the term 'enlarged heart'.

I applaud the nurses for conducting and recording these clinical observations, but what was the point of collecting this data if abnormalities weren't acted on. No one ever discussed the possibility of commencing Julian on Digoxin to control his fast and irregular heartbeat beat.

The sad thing is, an enlarged heart can be a temporary complaint if the underlying cause is treated, in Julian's case if the allergic medication had been stopped.

These findings are screaming out at me, "He needed Intensive Care input in order to correct his heart impulses."

Gastrointestinal system. He stated his Intestinal to be unremarkable; I don't know what he means by this remark?

He stated his liver was enlarged weighing in at 2500g where as a healthy male liver should only weigh 1400g. Could this be because his

Gamma GT liver function test result was always elevated when he was given Insulin and antibiotics?

His Pancreas was also reported as unremarkable, why would he say that? Did he expect it to be in poor condition because of his long term high glucose levels which would normally display Pancreas damage?

The Pathologist states that the right kidney was somewhat enlarged weighing 180g, whilst the left kidney was rather small weighing only 100g, why would there be such a difference in size so suddenly after all these years. A healthy kidney should weigh 130g. For years Julian took care of both his kidneys and prided himself that they were always in mint condition? Could this be, when he was given medication that he claimed he was allergic to, he always complained bitterly of pain in both of his kidney region? Either my sister or I would have to constantly massage his back as he swayed backwards and forwards repeating, "The pain in my kidneys is excruciating"

We knew that his kidneys were in fine fickle before this last Hospitalisation. Could it be because he drank so much fluid since his accident in 1972, that he was able to maintain their plumpness? However his kidneys may have taken their toll when his oral fluids were restricted and then enduring the constant impoundment of diuretics during the last five weeks of his life forcing his body to become dehydrated.

Reticuloendothelial System.

His spleen was described as grossly enlarged but soft, it weighed in at 800g, where as a healthy male spleen should weigh 150g. What made his so BIG? Spleens are normally our filters, cleansing our bodies of its bacteria and viruses. The white cells attack and remove any foreign bodies, this keeps us free from infection. So what was Julian fighting so hard to make his bulk up five fold in weight and double up in size like it did?

Also the average length of Spleens is 11cm, so when he suffered two splenic infarct, (holes) one of the holes measuring 4.5 cm in length, that is quite a gash in a relatively small organ!

Even a Haematologist could not offer Julian an explanation for these infarcts, when it was discovered in May 2007 the infarct had increased to 6.7 cm long and 4.7 cm wide. That's another big hole! An enlarged spleen is called Splenomegaly, when its enlarged it can cause pain in the abdominal region and in the chest, this sounded familiar. Common cause of enlarged spleen is liver disease we know his liver function tests were very raised at times. Direct trauma, infection or abscess could also enlarge it. Oxygen starvation can also cause the tissue to die resulting in splenic infarct. That would explain when his oxygen levels depleted to as low as 66% on occasions it may have caused death to some of the splenic cells.

Endocrine system.

The Pathologist report goes on to say that the Pituitary gland was normal; however the cranial cavity was not examined. How then, could he say the Pituitary glands were normal if it was not examined? I was not the only one who raised this concern; a retired Consultant also asked me the same question in church.

But more perplexing was why didn't the Pathologist examine the brain at all, he must of read my Police statement that I had said Julian use to be beside himself with pain in his brain 10minutes after receiving medication. The Pathologist had access to all the notes including my Police statement. Wasn't he the slightest bit interested to see the state of the brain? or at least curios as to why he complained like he did, especially when he had lost his faculties for two days before they intubated him, then transferring him to Telford, coupled with the fact that this decided patient wife and mother-in-law were at odds regarding his death.

He stated he found the Adrenal glands to be Atrophic. Atrophic is a medical word meaning shrivelled up.

Musculoskeletal system this was the last system he examined; here he found numerous bony protrusions down the length of the thoracic and lumber spine, with one vertebra measuring 7cm. That didn't mean too much to me until I got the tape measure out again to remind myself how long 7cm is. Wow! Don't you think that's an almighty vertebra body!

Why was it so big? Guess what, I Googled it, to my surprise I found I quote; "In some cases of Adrenal Tumours patients can have bone that becomes over grown."

The plot thickens, although Julian sustained fractures of his cervical region in 1972, the Pathologist declined to examine this part of his spine, if I had been in his shoes I would have been at least interested to see what had happened to these fractured sites as a result of sitting down for 34 years. Neither did he mention the Gerdal Stone operation he underwent 19 years previously, when Julian had the head of his femur and upper shaft removed, totalling four inches in all. Supprisingly ten years after this surgery it was noted on x-ray that nature had taken over and 're-formed another miniature head' on the shaft of his femur. When we first saw this on x-ray Julian humorously commented, "I told you I was clever, I've grown another head"

These fracture cervical which caused him his paralysis 34 years ago and the Gerdalstone operation that took place 19 years previously may or may not have affected the outcome of his findings, but it was his job to 'recognise and report' what he found.

It was after all Julian's constant reminder to donate his spinal vertebras to Scientific Research although it wasn't Julian's original gruesome idea or wish to give away his backbone. When Julian first had his big accident the Spinal Injury unit discovered he had an extra vertebra in his back, this was discovered when a junior Doctor was counting his injury from below up while the other doctor was counting from above down consequently they came to a different diagnosis, this is when he was approached to donate his unusual spine to research. Julian was asked to sign a consent giving them legal possession of his vertebras. For this reason I was trying to carry out Julian's wishes. Even if I had decided to keep a low key on this topic; I couldn't have because I had many friends contacting me to remind me of his wishes.

This might sound harsh and callus, but believe you me before Julian's death I had nothing but love in my heart for this man, but since his death I have had to toughen up.

The Pathologist knew of this request because I contacted him to warn him that someone might be in touch about his backbone. So I'm perplexed as to why he didn't explore the rest of his vertebras.

As it happened when I did approach The Charles Salt Research Centre, at his beloved Hospital, they were rather uninterested but would accept a slither of the bone just for analysis.

I felt like saying, "Woopydoo, don't force yourself", I didn't particularly want to put him to rest without his backbone anyway; I was just trying to carry out his wishes.

As the Pathologist was aware of the difficulties Julian's mother and I were having over his death, one would think he would have covered every avenue regarding attention to detail in preparation for the Inquest.

Why would he leave himself open to questioning like this? I felt a lot was left undone, and to add insult to injury, a separate letter accompanied the Post Mortem reminding me that Julian's body belonged to me up to the very second he started to performed the Post mortem, during that time Julian's body belonged to him and the crown, when he was finished then his body became my property once more.

Poor Julian, he was never anybody's property he was always his own man.

Pathologist Conclusion

The final conclusion on the Post Mortem report regarding the cause of death prior to the Inquest was,

- Firstly due to his Tetraplegia and the longstanding pressure on his sacral area. (Referring to Julian sitting down for 34 years)
- Secondly was his poorly controlled Diabetes (not through lack of trying on Julian's behalf.)
- Thirdly because he had suffered a myocardial infarction (heart attack) when he first had his accident in 1972, it stated <u>it may have</u> been the cause of him having recurrent pleural effusions.

Now this is my personal opinion.

The above is the Pathologists professional opinion this is my personal opinion and as he is allowed to use the phrase '<u>it may have been</u>' on a legal document in a Pathology report I too will use it here in my book.

The plural effusion <u>may have</u> been the reaction of the Insulin allergy, or <u>it may have</u> been as a result of the adrenal tumour or <u>it may have</u> been the result of a reaction to the antibiotics. In fact <u>it may have</u> been because he had right lung collapse twice in 1972!

I feel, blaming Julian meant he couldn't defend himself; he definitely couldn't defend himself in life and most certainty not in death. Don't worry Julian while there's breath in my body I will try to defend you in your absence, and prevent others suffering the same fate.

I thought in this country we were allowed to practice our freedom of speech.

I think you'll find that Selman Rushdie was allowed his freedom of speech, regardless of whether he upset other parties or not, but unlike him I don't intend to upset anyone I just intend to tell it as it is. Unfortunately for poor Julian, who incidentally was a British citizen, was not allowed his freedom of speech to be expressed, not even in his own country. Neither were any of his other requests honoured mainly choosing where to die. With hindsight maybe we should have gone abroad, if nothing else we could have herald a bit of respect and attention by saying, "Were British citizens you know" and seek refuge in a British Embassy. Questions still remain, "What ever happened to Julian's fit body to became such a mess in such a short time"

Preparing for the Inquest

I had never attended an inquest in my life before, so I didn't know what it entailed or what to expect. Was it like a court case? Was it informal? Was it formal? Was it held in a Town Hall? Was it held in an office? Was it held in a Police station? Was it held in a Court room? Someone even suggested in some cases it can be held in a Public House!

No one knew.

Then I wanted to know; was it conducted in a manner of Police verses relative, or was I just going to listen to what was going to be said and have no input, or was I going to be able to ask questions and did I need to defend myself, or was there no question of defending myself, more to the point did I need to defend Julian?

No one knew the answers to any of these questions either. There were plenty of stories to frighten me, but nothing of any use. Again I decided to be like one of the 'Seven wise virgins' and go prepared. I would get as much information as I possibly could to defend myself and Julian giving him as much of a fighting chance as possible and hopefully get as much justice as I could. It would have to be in death I'm afraid, because he certainly didn't achieve it in life.

Having read the Pathology report, I decided to dedicate the next four months totally to Julian's case. It lead me to be in contact with professionals that I didn't normally mix with such as the Coroners Clerk, the Independent Pathologist, Police Detective Inspector at Telford Police Station, Registrars at Wellington Coroner's Office, Adult Protection Allegation Department, Solicitors, Retired Detective Inspector, Retired Paediatric Consultant, Local MP, Retired Orthopaedic Consultant, Medical Solicitor, Independent Complaints Advocacy Service, Human Resources, University Queen Elizabeth Birmingham Hospital, Poison Unit Researching, Retired Police Constable, and numerous Pharmacists.

My biggest task now was double check that all the medical notes from all five hospitals were filed in their correct folders including the GP notes. I purchased six folders for the task, but I didn't just want them filed, I wanted them in chronological order. If I needed them on the day of the inquest, I needed to be able to put my hands on the smallest of detail quickly at a moment's notice.

There was no time to cry or fall apart, I had to keep focused. Looking at the list above, I can't believe I was involved with so many learned people, trying to break new ground on behalf of Julian. If only he was here, he'd know how to help me.

Needless to say all this was all done in between working full-time; I can't confess I was running a home as well, because during that time I became a bit of a 'Miss Havisham' in the Charles Dickens novel called 'The Great Expectation 'with my cobweb filled home.

One day while I was at work I was discussing allergies with a colleague in the kitchen, when a Consultant Anaesthetist walked in, to reassure him we were not talking about him I decided to involve him in the conversation by saying, "We were just talking about allergies in general and the different degrees of them". He said, "What do you mean" my friend directed the conversation on to herself, by saying "Well I have a slight allergy, when I eat bananas my tongue tingles but the last time it happened it swelled up and I was rushed to the nearest A&E."

He became very cross saying, "Don't you realised how very lucky you've been up until now. Do you carry an anti-histamine pen with you everywhere wherever you go?"

She replied, "No" He said, "Have you stopped eating bananas? She confessed she hadn't made a deliberate effort but she hadn't had one since the last episode of tongue swelling, but if it was as dangerous as he made out, she would stop eating them.

I stood there speechless, thinking this man has never seen this person having a reaction, yet he instructed her, never to eat bananas again if she valued her life.

Why wasn't someone like him on my side when Julian was clearly having so many reactions when he was administered either insulin or antibiotics? Thank you Doctor Gaja, you restored my faith in the medical profession that day. He has since retired, but I do hope there will be plenty of others just as wise as him following in his footsteps.

The weekend before the Inquest I received a message from a friend who had been to a psychic supper, she claimed she had a message for me off Julian, "Tell her to listen to 'Pie Jesu' by Andrew Lloyd Webber from a CD called "Requiem." She said I needed to listen to it before the Inquest.

Curious as to why I needed to do this, Gweno seemed more curious than I so she purchased and sent me the CD in the post, but when I heard it I sobbed, it was a Latin text from the Bible sung at Latin Mass specifically for the dead. When translated it means "Merciful Jesus, who takes away the sins of the world, grant them eternal rest"

Worried that this message meant, Olwen let me rest in peace. I then went on the internet and looked up Sarah Brightman singing 'Pie Jesu' in case I was barking at the wrong tree.

It stated that Andrew Lloyd Webber had composed the music in sorrow over the loss of his Father, it went on to say that in September 1997 at a concert in Edinburgh Sarah dedicated the song to all those who lost loved ones, then at another concert of the Luna tour in the year 2000, she dedicated the song to those who lost their lives due to political conflicts.

Oh! My, what was Julian trying to tell me? I certainly felt he'd died amidst a political conflict, and I was still fighting his medical political campaign.

Was this a Devine message or just another coincidence that the words just happened to be appropriate to me, but how was this person who sent me the message to know what 'Pie Jesu' meant to me!

Frantically trying to get everything in order I realised I didn't have any proof that Julian had a tumour on his adrenal gland, and although I had sent a letter to Oswestry requesting confirmation for this diagnosis on 30th May 2009, I received a disappointing answer on 26th June stating

"I cannot see that Mr Davies had any growth on either of his kidneys" I say disappointing because that meant Julian was telling me 'porky-pies' about his tumour! Why!

Not satisfied with this answer I requested in writing a copy of all his investigations, maybe someone had over looked a small detail. What I was looking for was copies of his Ultra Sound Scan results, the MRI scan results, and his CT scan results. By the 21st September 2009 I still hadn't received any scan results, in the afternoon I contacted Oswestry by telephnoe to see what the holdup was. They said they'd received my request for the results but they needed a cheque to release them, I protested informing her I'd already paid for them once but they weren't included with the photocopied reports. She explained that this was now a new application, I thought blow the cost I need these results for the Inquest in three days' time which was going to take place on the 25th

September. Realising my emergency she recommended if I wanted to be sure of their safe delivery in time for the Inquest, I should travel up in person to pick them up from her the following morning. I agreed it sounded a safer option, I arranged with her I would be at her office at ten o'clock the following morning 22nd September 2008 to pick up the results. I arrived prompt at ten o'clock, but was very nervous about knocking on the Consultant office door in case I came face to face with some of the Doctors who denied Julian's constant request not to have treatment. I had no choice but to 'Just Knock' thinking all I had to do was to grab and run with the report. On entering the office I was relieved to find no Doctors present, unfortunately she didn't have the report to hand over to me, what she did have was a request slip for the Radiographer to issue me with a written report and a copy of the DVD of Julian's MRI scan. What she asked of me next nearly rooted me to the floor, before she could hand over my permission slip she asked me first to sign a declaration form, confirming I would not sue the hospital on the strength of these results. Shocked at her request which, incidentally was not even mentioned the afternoon before, I signed under duress. I kept my cool and my personal opinion to myself; on the grounds that in two days' time I would have to face these doctors in a court room, why make waves?

But how many more times did I have to be gagged!

After I handed over another cheque I sat in the waiting area thinking about the declaration I'd just signed, what a cheek after all they'd put Julian through. Without confrontation I'd managed to drive off the hospital premises with a DVD copy of Julian's investigations and their report, which I kissed before I placed on the passenger's seat thanking God for letting me have them. I side glanced periodically at them on my journey home not believing I was in possession of them.

On the 24th September 2009 the morning before the Inquest I had the courage to ring the Nursing Midwifery Council (NMC) and asked them how serious was it, if nurses continually give a patient a drug that's written on their allergy band, and on the front of their medication chart under allergy even if the Doctors insists the patient needed it.

The reply was, "This is very serious and needs reporting to the Nursing Midwifery Council, and had any one reported it to the General Medical Council yet?

323

I said no, but I can't afford to make waves just yet, as the Inquest was the very next day.

She advised me to contact her the day after the Inquest, and also I needed to contact GMC immediately.

The night before the inquest I was searching my soul for guidance or a <u>sign</u> that everything would be alright the following day. Exhausted from spending every waking minute studying Julian's medical notes I felt the need to chill out and stop even thinking about the notes and do something relaxing.

As I was still not watching television I retrieved into the kitchen, it had become my place of solace. With no electric lights only the flickering light of a candle for company and the sound of Enya CD in the background, my guidance seemed to come from the lyrics in one of her songs—

> If you really want to, you can hear me say.
> Only if you really want to, you will find a way.
> If you really want to you will seize the day,
> Only if you really want to, will you seize the day.

With these words, I decided to go to the Inquest with confidence that everything would be alright and that even if I didn't find a way, I would one day surely seize the day. Either way I had to turn up, it was a hoop of fire I had to go through. I decided to do the job like Julian would expect me to, and that was to do the job well. I just hoped he was going to be proud of me! With this positivity in my heart the kitchen seemed to light up like a pink and orange hew, bewildered by this glow I looked through the kitchen window and it reminded me of those lyrics again, "Light up the sky like a flame" just like it did on the morning I was traveling to Telford to discuss the termination of Julian's life. The sky was so impressive I felt the same urge to reach for my camera once again. I know Id asked for a sign, was this it? It then left me wondering; what these signs of nature meant to our faith and spiritual life. God has chosen the sky to communicate with us many times before, a rainbow for Noah, a star for baby Jesus, thunder and lightning when Jesus died on the cross, the sun for the Portuguese children at Fatima so was this my private sign or just another coincidence, what do you think?

Photograph of the evening sky on the eve of the Inquest.

Poor Ju, I'm sure he hadn't intended for me to go through this Inquest on my own, in the past he'd always protected me from life's unpleasantness unless I had a lesson to learn.

The morning of the Inquest

On the morning of the 25th September 2009 I got up early, bathed and dressed in a black dress. I had been wearing black for the last ten months even though lots of people tried to entice me to wear brighter colours. I felt I couldn't, not until I was in possession of his death certificate. It was hard to believe, it had been 10 months since I last saw, touched or spoke to him.

That morning I planned to drive to my sister in Welshpool, and then her partner was going to drive us both the remainder of the journey to Telford Magistrate Court. Unfortunately at the last minutes he wasn't able to take us. Feeling stress coming on, I said to myself "Please Julian, send me someone" I didn't want Gweno or I, to be all wrapped up in maps and Sat Nav's which may of sent us in the wrong direction, making us late for the Inquest. At that there was a phone call a well-wisher Clive. I mentioned the change of plans and he said, "You're not thinking of driving all that way to Welshpool to pick up your sister then back tracking across country to Telford to face the music of an Inquest.?" I said, "Yes, there's no other alternative" He said, "I'll drive you both there before that happens". So that's what he did, and what a good job he did, if Gweno and I had known what lay ahead of us we might not have turned up at all.

Actually that's not strictly true I had to attend, the courts letter stated if I failed to turn up a £4,000 fine would be incurred. We made arrangements to meet Steve the ex-policeman outside Telford Magistrate Court at twelve mid-day. Synchronisation was perfect, surprisingly traffic allowed both parties to drive into the car park at exactly the same time. After the four of us exchanged greetings and introductions, Steve suggested that we should go for a coffee. As we headed towards the Magistrate Court Julian's Mother was sat outside on a bench with her husband and his half-sister. I nodded to acknowledge them as I passed, but she continued to be hostile towards me. I sympathised she had lost her son but I was not the cause of his death I hoped the truth would be revealed that afternoon.

The four of us entered the building, double-checking at the reception what time Julian's Inquest was due to start. Once in possession of our coffee Steve said, "In case you are given the opportunity to ask any questions at the end, have you thought of any?"

I said, "Yes 20" "Twenty," he said laughing. "I think the Coroner will only allow you to ask a couple questions, let's have a look to see if their valid ones. We'll cross off the ones that are not."

I was quick to remind him, "Never mind the questions, I still wanted 20 answers in any case."

He laughed again, but to his surprise he found all of them to be sensible questions. When we were discussing the 14th question, the door to this microscopic cafe opened. My heart sank and my bottom jaw must have dropped too because in walked my mother-in-law, Julian's step father and his half-sister. I thought my heart was going to stop.

If the roles had been reversed I think I would of walked out again, due to the confined space but it was a free country and they had just as much right as us to be there.

Steve turned to me and asked "Do you want to continue this somewhere else"

I looked at the clock, the minutes were ticking away I said, "No lets finish I need you to revise my questions quick" There was no verbal exchange between my mother-in-law and myself, not even head nods this time as she had already made her feelings known to me outside. Maybe both parties were at fault, both thinking they had done no wrong.

We finished discussing the remainder of the questions quietly. I remember praying quietly, please God help me keep focus and get through this with dignity.

He then got up and said, "Ok, let's get out of here". We all rushed out like little chicks following a mother hen. "Where are we going now Steve", I asked in the corridor.

He said, "We need to find which court room it's held at"

He established it was court room number six, and coaxed us in with a hand gesture. I couldn't understand why so early. He approached a young lady and said, "Excuse me, are you the Courts Clerk"? She replied she was. "Then you must have the itinerary of the afternoon then?"

She said she had, and continued to inform us who were going to be on the stand first and that we would all be expected to swear in an affidavit on the Bible.

Steve then asked "Could you tell Olwen the seating arrangement in this court room this afternoon".

"No problem," she said, "Olwen you will sit here, with whoever you choose to sit with, then there will be the two Solicitors representing The Orthopaedic Hospital sitting next to you, then on the end will be Mr Davies's Mother and Stepfather.

Facing you on the left will be my colleague and myself, on the top bench will be the Coroner.

We will all enter and sit in our places, when the Coroner is ready to enter I shall ask the Court Room to stand while he enters and once he is seated everyone will be asked to sit".

He thanked her for her time, then turned to us and said "Ok, outside now" again we followed him hurriedly. Once out side he asked me if I'd brought the files with me, I told him they were in the car, shall I fetch them? He pointed out, "There's no point having them if it's going to take you absolutely ages to find out one small fact"

I said, "Steve, I have been studying these notes for four months solid, I know exactly where every single detail is, I can find anything at a moment's notice"

"In that case you stay here with me and let the other two fetch the folders, we'll carry on discussing the case" Unbeknown to me Steve had jotted down the order of appearance of all the Consultants on the stand in his note book.

With my 20 questions he systematically went through all the questions jotting the name of the doctors against each question. For example, the first Doctor on the stand I was to ask question 5, 8, and 10. So not to ask the same Doctor to return to the stand 3 times, I could ask him all 3 questions at the same time. Clever Steve!

Clive and Gweno had joined us by now, after struggling with twelve heavy folders between them but they still had to negotiate two flights of stairs before reaching Court room number six.

So my worst fears were coming true after all, it was going to be held in a 'Magistrate Court', the name of the room itself 'court room number 6' suggested the afternoon was going to be formal unlike what so many other people tried to convince me.

I would like to say a 'a big thank you' to my family for showing me support that day none of you had to attend, after all this was my battle but you all looked so smart in your suits, and I'm sure Julian would have been proud of you too. We all knew his feelings about wearing a suit, how others take you seriously if you've taken pride in your appearance.

Poor Julian must have felt at a disadvantage when he was in those Hospital beds, trying to get his point of view over. He said once "They won't take me seriously in here Olwen, because I'm not wearing a suit" Poor chap he was as naked as a jay bird under that bed linen, which must have made him feel so vulnerable.

At one o'clock the four of us approached the Court room with my family in tow. I was really glad Llewela was not there to witness this tug of war surrounding her father.

I think I would have fallen apart if she was there. As we were walking down the corridor Steve asked me, "Who are you going to have sitting next to you on the front panel Olwen?" I half turned my body towards Gweno and said, "Gwen do you mind if Steve sits next to me?"

Gweno said, "Anyone Olwen, anyone I don't think I'll be much use to you".

We all took our appropriate seats I can remember thinking; I can't feel the presence of Julian's mother in this court room or his sister. They both had an 'air' about them; you knew when they were around without seeing them. I did not look round I decided to stay focused on my tasks, I arranged my folders on a large side table in order of Julian's Hospitalisation's I couldn't believe I had accumulated 12 thick folders.

Then I arranged my questions in order of the itinerary. Then prayed "Please God, help me do justice to Julian's case" this was my very last chance, no more chances after this".

Steve was just giving me last minute whispering advice when the Coroners Clerk walked into the court room and announced, "The court will now rise."

Hearing those words made me realise how formal the next couple hours was going to be. The Coroner made his entrance and then he invited us all to sit. He introduced himself, and then turning to me went on to say. "I have this afternoon to resume the inquest into the death of your husband, Julian Paul Davies. He also mentioned that inquests are always traumatic. We are revisiting the last few months, days and hours of your husband life.

He asked the Solicitors representing the Oswestry Hospital to introduce themselves.

He said, "In view of the circumstances surrounding his death and the concerns which you yourself have raised, I determined that it was appropriate that a post-mortem investigation should be carried out. I must remind you that this is an inquest into the death of your husband and not a trial.

He gave a brief account of Julian life, his medical history his last Hospitalisation which he referred to as a "Rocky Road".

He then said, "Now in view of the allegations which you made I decided that this was nearly what we call an "Article 2 Inquest" under the Human Rights Act, because you alleged that your husband was given insulin against his will.

I was asked to take the stand first, and swear an Affidavit.

He started to question me about our past history, where we met, how long we'd been married was it a happy marriage, he mentioned the off licence and so on.

He asked how long had Julian been a diabetic?

He said "In fact I have a letter from Mr Jenkins. You know Mr Jenkins, do you?

I replied "No, Julian never met him"

"You never met him, but your husband did?"

I said "No, we saw a Spanish gentleman".

"Okay, Mr Davies was seen by his colleague, and this was on 19th August 2008?"

I then went through the lengthy history of what happened to him from the year 2000 to his Hospitalisation at Worcester Hospital, where the blood was taken and sent to the Birmingham Poison centre. I pointed out that I had seen the blood test result but could not decipher the signature.

I think it was about this time when Julian's mother, half-sister and stepfather entered the court room. Now I could defiantly feel their presence, I could hear the ruffling of her garments, the clunk, clunk of her crutches and the metal noise of her husband's walking stick. She was apologising to the Coroner for her late entrance but said she had been told the wrong time, we were told it was one thirty start.

While the Coroners Clark got up and directed them to their seats, the Coroner himself said, "I can't see how you thought otherwise Mrs Atwel everyone concerned was informed by letter of the same time". The Inquest came to a standstill while they settled the two of them down and fetched a chair for his half-sister to sit next to them. The Coroner welcomed them and in fact he was kind with his words for this late entrance to the afternoon hearing.

He then turned to me on the stand to resume my questioning by saying, "I think we are at one that everyone agreed that he had got diabetes?"

I replied, "He had high glucose level in his blood, yes. But when you're looking after someone, you have to take care of them as a whole in a holistic manner"

"What sort of holistic approach do you think the Doctors ought to have taken?"

"They might have been able to investigate his diabetes, because there's more than one reason why you have raised glucose levels in your blood. For example if you have something the matter with your Adrenal Gland or you're suffering from pancreatitis there's a huge long list of things."

The Coroner asked, "Your original concerns were that giving your husband insulin, killed him?"

I said, "That's what he believed" "Sorry" said the Coroner. I repeated, "That's what he believed" "He believed" I continued, "That's what he kept saying to me all the time. In fact, I'll tell you what he told me at the very end. He said, "Olwen, you are no better than all the Doctors and nurses. You are not stopping them" and I said, "Julian, I am trying" Then he said, "But you're not, are you?" "You can see it's making me so ill. It's killing me and you're not stopping them. <u>I have to live with those words"</u> He responded by saying "But insulin was the only way forward for him? I replied

"Julian did have high glucose levels, but he never had any glucose in his urine. Nobody investigated that" The Coroner asked "Is this the reason why you wrote to the Trust to allege that he was given insulin against his will?" I said, "He kept begging not to have it" "Sorry" the Coroner said. I repeated, "He kept begging not to have it. So whether it was good for him or not, if he said he did not want it, he should have been allowed to make that choice."

"Would you have preferred for him to have died without having insulin treatment?"

I said, "He wouldn't have died such a terrible painful death, because his organs were in absolute agony. He didn't have morphine until the last two days at Telford."

"So, you are only following his wishes. Thank you very much."

(I was really angry at this point)

I said," Excuse me, what are you suggesting?" "Sorry" again, said the Coroner

I recapped in a raised voice, "Are you suggesting that I was helping him with his death?"

His answer was, "No, I just said, you were only following his own wishes that he didn't want to have the treatment, and that is what you were saying to the doctors?

The coroner then asked his mother if she had any questions. She started to say about one day when she and her daughter was visiting, but the coroner intervened by saying is this a question? She carried on, the coroner intervened again and said, "Is this a question or a statement on your part?"

She stopped. I was asked to stand down and the consultant from Oswestry was then put on the stand. He unlike the rest of us put his hand on the Koran to take his oath.

After the history was given the coroner asked, "Was he grudgingly taking it or did he agree willingly. "We had (words not clearly audible) because we discussed with him all the time and on a daily basis, actually. The coroner then asked me if I had any questions.

I replied, "Yes three"

"Julian did take his insulin at Oswestry and I noted from his notes, he refused insulin 6 times and on those occasions his blood sugar reading were below 6. So you knew he was frightened of taking insulin when his reading were that low. Was that a valid reason not to take his insulin?"

"The other point I would like to make is when he was at Oswestry his pulse after taking insulin went up to 125 and stayed there for five days and then went up to 140 and remained there for a further seven days. This is the sort of reaction he was getting from the insulin"

"The third question is I'd like to ask, while he was wearing a red armband; both doctors and nurses still gave insulin even though he was wearing the red armband" "I just wondered what the Hospital policy was on the wearing of a red Armband?"

The Consultants words were, "I think, a red armband indicated some allergy to a specific drug, but I can't remember what the red armband is."

The coroner intervened by saying to the Doctor, "But you do accept, don't you, that it is quite apparent from all the statements that he did have some sort of allergic reaction to the insulin treatment?"

He defended himself by saying that he asked his medical colleagues opinion who had contacted Julian's Doctors at Worcester and that he was not aware about any reaction to insulin.

The coroner then enquired; was he the consultant Mr Davies never saw?

The Coroner then went on to say, "I think it is fair to say that Mr Davies was saying he had an allergy, even if the medical personal who were looking after him could not find any evidence of that allergy, I think it is absolutely correct that one should make that quite clear."

The coroner then asked Julian's mother if she had any questions. She said "Yes, My son had a horror of catching MRSA, or C. diff. Did you tell him at one stage if he didn't have the insulin his body would turn gangrenous and rot and he would die? Did you ever tell him that?" (She was very angry at this stage and was shaking a pointing her finger at him.)

The consultant replied, "Yes, I told him immediately, the first day when he had been admitted."

His mother then said, "I know! You give birth to them, but it seems once they get married you have no control. Okay".

The next person that was called to the stand was the Consultant Physician with a special interest in Diabetes and Endocrinology at Shrewsbury Hospital.

Before the questioning started, the coroner turned to me and said, "I think it appropriate, Mrs Davies to say that I did write to him to ask for his advice on different forms of diabetes so that I could get myself up to speed in view of some of the comments you made in your statement."

(These are my words now, my after thoughts as it were. I was dismayed as I think most right minded people would be, to find that he had particularly selected this doctor to seek advice on the treatment of diabetes. This selection invites criticism of him and throws doubt on the impartiality of the inquest. Do you the reader consider that this decision was professionally ethical? I feel I needed to put my personal opinion in at this early stage, as I think it would lose its impact if I was to mention it at a later stage.)

333

Once on the stand, this Physician was very vague in his answering throughout. Baring in mind he had the most to do with Julian, and he claims on oath that he had a special interest in diabetes and endocrinology. "The coroner asked; were the antibiotics and insulin given to him against his will?"

The physician said, "I was never aware of him getting any treatment against his will"

"Although you might have been aware that he had previously refused both?"

"Yes, myself and other members of the medical staff had frequent and sometimes lengthy conversations with him and obviously when he was given a treatment we believed that he had accepted that and had given consent. It is a while ago, I can't remember all the details. But certainly I remember him being very concerned that the treatment he was being given was upsetting him.

Coroner asked, "Was this the first person you have come across who has refused insulin and antibiotics?" "Not the first, we have many people who are concerned about starting insulin treatment" "How did he accept your advice?"

"He was a very logical person, he said Okay, I understand if I have to take it, go ahead"

He then asked the physician to read the last paragraph of his own statement which reads like this.

"Clearly Mr. Davies was reluctant at times to have anti-diabetic treatment or antibiotics"

The Coroner followed with, "Yes, it is the case isn't it, and you correctly say, that he was reluctant at times to have his anti-diabetic treatment and antibiotics and that reluctance was obviously built upon his own feelings, his own body feelings, whether or not you and your colleagues could actually particularly put your finger on the allergic effect that he suffered.

The coroner turned to me to ask if I had any questions. I replied, "Yes, I just wanted someone to explain to me why our daughter had to witness her father begging the doctor "Why are you forcing me to take this insulin" The doctor replied, "I'm not forcing you I'm just going to keep asking you until you agree to take it" and our daughter then said, "That's forcing him"

My second question is, "When I read through the notes there was 20 episodes when a doctor was emergency bleeped 10 minutes after Julian had had the insulin

He said, "I cannot answer that."

I replied "But there was a pattern, 10 minutes after he . . . .

He cut me short by saying, "I don't believe there was a pattern" he was then asked to stand down and the Consultant in Anaesthetics and Intensive Care medicine at Telford Hospital was asked to take the stand. (What this consultant said confused me on the day. Now that I'm in possession of the transcript of the inquest, I'm even more confused).

I quote word for word; he said "Mr Davies was an insulin dependent diabetic and there for long period without insulin, I wouldn't have thought he would have tolerated long period without insulin. Just occasionally some patients have what we call a very high threshold, so they can run a high blood sugar, but you don't see it in the urine." End of quote, please read what he said again because I can't make head or tail out it, can you?

(These are my comments again. While Julian was under this Consultants care, this is the very Consultant who told me that Julian couldn't possibly be a diabetic if he had survived 15 months without treatment and be well. The other thing he mentioned to me after his last operation was how the lower half of his spines process and sacral bone had disintegrated into powder.

None of this was mentioned in the operation notes or by the pathology report and again was not raised at the inquest. Three places I expected it to be mentioned. Was this fact or fiction? I will never know, as everyone is <u>keeping stump</u> about this one. I mentioned before Julian and I were avid television viewers. Amongst other programs, we mainly watched documentaries and were always fascinated by archaeologists digging skeletons from hundreds of years ago sometimes thousands of years ago and still be able to tell what they died of. So put yourself in my shoes, what do you think happened to Julian's bones to disintegrate into powder like this while he was still alive, while other skeletons survive for thousands of years? One could only imagine it was some sort of very powerful reaction. Right or Wrong?)

The coroner then called me back to the stand for further questioning.

After a brief out line of Julian's case, he said "There were times when he refused treatment and there were times when he took the treatment, Mrs Davies.

I said, "Yes under duress"

The Coroner answered "I had the investigation officer from West Mercian Police to investigate all the allegations that have been made in every respect."

I butted in, "But Julian knew he would be safe at Oswestry, but he also knew if he refused treatment at Shrewsbury, Oswestry would black list him and he was absolutely terrified of being black listed from the Spinal injury unit, so he had to take the treatment.

The coroner sympathised with me by saying, "You were torn between the obvious effects that these treatments had so far as your husband was concerned, maybe not generally and also trying to keep him alive?

Lastly the Honorary Consultant Pathologist was asked to the stand, he asked the family if they were content to stay during this evidence. Then turned to me, are you Mrs Davies.

I nodded a yes gesture. No one left the room, so I assumed there was no one with a fickle stomach present.

He read the same pathology report I had in my possession.

The coroner asked me, had I any questions for the pathologist, I replied "Yes".

I said, Julian used to go to the Orthopaedic Hospital for regular tests on a one to two year period interval, he'd come home one day and told me that he had a tumour on one of his kidney on the Adrenal Gland.

After Julian's death I wrote to Owestry asking for more details of this, they said there was no record of this. So I could not understand why would he tell me that, if it wasn't true. He even used to say it's nothing to worry about but could this have disturbed his glucose levels?"

The Pathologist appeared to look over my head towards the Consultant Physician from Shrewsbury Hospital and mimed to him saying, "I wasn't aware that he had a tumour." As I looked round to see who the Pathologist was corresponding to behind me, I witnessed the Physician closing his eyes, shaking his head from side to side, sighing deeply, crossing his arms but raising one hand to his worried forehead.

As I turned round to look at the Pathologist he shrugged his shoulders and shaking his head from side to side saying "I am not sure where that story came from"

He was the only person in the land who had access to examine his Adrenal Glands and yet he was the one looking perplexed at me! He was holding Julian's Pathology report in his hand as he spoke on oath. The Coroner then asked Julian's mother if she had any questions, she said yes, she would like it stated on the death certificate he died of diabetes mellitus first and tetraplegia second.

The Coroner then brought the Inquest to an end by saying, "I am going to close the inquest, the day has been long and it's been emotional for everyone. I think this has got to be the opportunity to say that Julian Paul Davies's death has affected a great number of people.

(I felt like saying that his **life** had touched many, many more.)

The Coroner continued, "And it is sad that there should have been a breakdown between the family, and I just hope that can be repaired."

In reference to the above remark about family breakdown, I had requested police protection in the court room for that day, so that I could feel safe to deal with any questioning I was to undergo that afternoon. Luckily the day was uneventful in that no verbal confrontation took place between Julian's family and mine on that day or since.

The Coroner concluded the inquest by saying, "On behalf of Her Majesty the Queen may I thank you for your attendance today" The court was asked to rise while the Coroner left the court room.

My family said their goodbyes outside the Magistrates Forecourt on that hot sunny afternoon.

A bit dazed after the day's event, my sister was taken to Welshpool and I was driven back to the Midlands.

If there was any one present who felt there was more said in that court room that day, you are correct because the Coroners Sectary has condensed the above script to what SHE thought I needed.

The traumatic afternoon lasted three hours it started at one o'clock and ended at four o'clock.

It took eight months for me to obtain the transcript of the afternoon events in that courtroom.

Looking back and re-visiting that court room through the eyes of this transcript report, I don't think I could repeat that performance ever again. I don't know where I got the hidden strength from, unless it was a divine intervention answering my prayers to help me give Julian his last chance at justice?

I felt on that day it was me verses all the intellectuals in that room, without a Julian at my side.

I must point out that this is an unusual case, so don't think in the future if you are ever called upon to give witness, your time would be as traumatic as mine. My sister had to give evidence at an Inquest some years ago and she recalled the two cases didn't compare.

I was surprised there were no nurses there available for me to ask questions, after all it was the Doctors who prescribed the Medication but it was the nurses who repeatedly administered the drugs. Only one nurse declined to give the insulin at Shrewsbury hospital, and that was only when I said, "You do know Julian's wearing an allergy band, don't you?" He was not aware, he went away and on his return he said, "I'll put you down as refused Julian, is that ok?"

When I asked him why he'd shown such pity towards Julian he said, "I need my PIN number to practice in other Hospitals, you see I'm a Bank Nurse and I move from Hospital to Hospital." That's how serious it is to give someone drugs that they are either allergic to or who refuse treatment!

The following day after the Inquest I couldn't bring myself to contact the Nursing and Midwifery Council or the General Medical Council as I promised, purely because I wasn't the nurse administering the drugs, and what I witnessed was in a wife capacity and thirdly there was no point making waves with the GMC they have Barristers pouring out of the wood work in Harley Street to defend them. More importantly I still had to consider my employment I was still working for the NHS, how would I survive without an income?

Besides poor Julian was dead, no amount of action taken now would ever resurrect him it was all about self-preservation for the time being.

On the 3rd of October 2009 what would have been our wedding anniversary, I received through the post not an anniversary card as we usually did but Julian's death certificate stating his cause of death. Not quite the same was it, at the Inquest his mother had requested the order of cause of death to be changed. She wanted Tetraplegia to be listed last, I see her request was nearly honoured.

Cause of death read like this, firstly bilateral Bronchopneumonia, secondly extensive debridement for necrotising fasciitis and thirdly Tetraplegia and lastly Diabetes Mellitus.

None of it sat well with me, but I don't suppose I will ever have the power to change what was written on his final certificate. I wondered if I have got the stamina to find out what he really died from.

My only regret after the inquest is; I failed to ask who instigated the urine analysis to be conducted to confirm drug abuse. Was it the social services on the strength of his Mothers accusations or was it the Staff Nurse who wrote in Julian's notes "wife not to be left alone with the patient" Reading those words made my blood run cold. How dare anyone write such a thing, without following this through with the Police? I was never approached by the Police while he was an in-patient about this damming documentation neither was I questioned about it after his death. So was I considered safe by the police or did they neglect to interrogate me on this subject? What the nurse wrote was derogatory to a person in my position as a Staff Nurse without proof that I was a danger to his welfare.

As it happens, I was investigated separately by my place of work before returning back to work and I was declared safe to practice.

It's true that his Creatinine levels were 7.610 on the 10th November 2008, which I presume that's why they instigated the investigations into Amphetamines such as Benzodiazepines, Cocaine, Methadone and Opiates level in his urine. But Julian's Creatine levels could have been elevated due to drug allergy such as antibiotics, insulin and diuretics; not illegal drugs that they suspected I might have been giving him. Where in goodness name did they think I was getting them from, I was at his bed side day and night!

The Crossroads in my life

With the Inquest over and after receiving the Final Death Certificate, I wondered what I should do next. Should I look forward to the future and shut the door on the past and try to forget what had happened or should I choose the same rough and rugged road Julian was forced to take when he was cornered into saying, "Don't let anyone suffer like I have" The first option sound safe and almost exciting, fresh start new beginning! But my conscience wouldn't let me ignore what he'd gone through, besides I would have to struggle with my guilt daily if I'd opted for the 'easy life'.

Friends and acquaintances became my 'devil's advocate' by saying, "Forget it now, it's done, it's finished, it's all over", but when I used to turned the conversation on its head asking, "What if one of your children suffered the same fate as Julian, in say in 5 or 6 years from now, wouldn't you wish then that I had done something NOW to prevent your child from suffering"?

Their cajoling me into giving up on the Diabetes dilemma would stop; life feels very different when loved ones are at risk.

Of course no one knew Julian's whole story they only knew snippets of it, so how could they advise me. They hadn't experienced the pain of watching someone they loved ebbing away at life as I fought this psychological warfare to try and save him.

Gweno helped me put things into perspective when she said, "We sometimes have to experience hardship in order to be shocked into becoming better people, and just like the spring flowers there is always a better display of bloom from the bulbs after they have experienced a harsh frost the previous winter" Did she mean, Julian had to experience a terrible end so that others would have a better outcome?

Although I was full of determination I was hindered by the negative-ness of what others had to say, mainly reminding me that I couldn't change anything on my own. May be I couldn't, but was I on my own here? There must be a few people out there who I could rely on for help?

I decided to make a list of whom I could count on and who believed in me.

- To start with there was my faithful Sister, who was at his bed side more days than she was not, she believed me.
- Then there was my parents, who sat and watched him struggle for breath all through the night, it's not something people in their late 70`s should witness. They believed me.
- Then there was my parents friend, the retired Chief Detective Inspector, who said "Clearly there was something not right, I certainly hope you're not thinking of cremating him?" he believed me.
- Then there was yet another family friend who was a retired Paediatric Consultant, who intervened one night and rang the Hospital, and was advised to comfort me and get me to see sense. I know this because the conversation was documented in Julian's notes. He incidentally said after Julian's death, "I didn't think it would come to this." Thank you for trying though. He believed me.
- There was my cousin who was a Solicitor, luckily he came to visit Julian at Shrewsbury Hospital and saw how ill he had become. He had a saddened face as he looked at Julian struggling to breathe? His advice was "If you feel that this treatment is harming you, while you are in your right mind you have the power to refuse it". Julian replied "You don't know what their like" He believed me.
- There was the retired Police Constable who gave me support and sat by me throughout the Inquest, he believed me.
- There was my other cousin a Retired Ward Sister who was horrified that Julian's refusal to accept treatment was denied. She believed me.
- Another nursing Sister Helen Frogget who felt strongly that Julian's suffering stemmed from his Adrenal Tumour. Her father had also been treated with Insulin for 12months, it was stopped when they realised it was the chemotherapy that was causing him to have altered glucose levels in his blood. She believed me.
- A retired Orthopaedic Consultant, who happened to be Julian's friend, was constantly chasing me for updates on Julian's case offering help and advice. He believed me.

- There was the Matron I worked with at Worcester Royal Hospital who reserved a bed for his transfer from Shrewsbury up to the eleventh hour, she believed me.
- There were lots of nursing friends who were of the same opinion, but how could all of these professionals be wrong?

Their support and encouragement helped me to decide which path to take; besides I know for a fact Julian would have done exactly the same for me.

Living with regrets

We all have them, this is one of mine.

After the inquest I re-read an A4 page a colleague from work had put together for me to ask at the Coroner's Inquest. I regretted not paying more attention to his line of questioning, after the event his list makes perfect sense now. As I didn't know the tone and depth of the Inquest I went in blind. If I was ever involved again I'd go in with both barrels loaded as it were and not leave one stone unturned. My colleague's questions went like this—:

1. Did Julian have diabetic mellitus?
   a) Any record to show controlled and stable readings during active treatment with insulin?
   b) Any fasting and random glucose levels records available.
   c) What diagnosis, influenced treatment and changes in treatment while he was receiving treatment in your care.
   d) What steps were taken to rule out any allergies and any evidence to show the elimination of any allergies?
2. Why were Julian's expressed wishes concerning his treatment refused?
   a.) Any evidence of team meetings concerning his enforced treatment.
   b.) Any documentation of trial periods that demonstrated that insulin improved his condition.
3. What was the main cause of his death and any contributory factor that exacerbated his signs and symptoms?
4. What reassurance can you offer me that my husband had the best medical and humanitarian care that the trust provided for my husband while he was receiving treatment in your care.

Gaj, I am so sorry I should have drawn on your years of nursing experience, I realise now. These are powerful questions and all of them still remain unanswered. With hindsight I should have taken you as well as Steve in to the court room. Steve with his policing skills and you Gaj with your over thirty years nursing supervision. I noticed some one wrote in your retirement book, "Thank you for your friendship, wit and humour but most of all your wisdom"

343

All those learned people!

Looking back on Julian's medical history I feel I have to commend his GPs for pulling out all the stops and disregarding any cost when requesting the necessary investigations that Julian needed, but then I equally admire Julian for continuing to attend his follow up appointments even when Julian no longer took any medication for his high glucose levels. He tried to attended every clinic appointment even during those fifteen months he was drug free from diabetic treatment in fear of being 'Black listed' and denied access to his 'safe house'.

These are the eight follow ups he remained faithful to—:

1. He never missed his Endocrinology appointment with his Endocrinologist, even though it was the hardest one of all to attend because this was the very Physician who requested Julian to double up on his medication, even when Julian tried to reason with him explaining he felt it was the prescription that was harming him. Apart from the 'Black list' issue he also went in the hope he could one day make peace with him, but this was not to be. Each time he attended he was always ushered in to see his clinical Assistant and was told he was away even though he could hear his voice in the next room.

(2) He never missed his Haematology appointment with his Haematologist, who unfortunately could not shed any light on why his Spleen had become so enlarged eventually measuring 19.5 cm in length; whereas a normal Spleen should measure 11.5 cm. He could not explain how Julian obtained two infarcts within his spleen; the first one measuring 4.5 cm in length and the first was diagnosed before he experienced the near multi organ failure, the second infarct measuring 6.7 x 4.7 cm developed during his stint in hospital while he was suffering the near multi-organ failure. What neither Julian or I were aware of at this stage was he'd also suffered another lesion this time to his right Adrenal gland measuring 5.6 x 3.1 cm this was some

gash but in keeping with the Adrenal Myelolipoma diagnosis. All this was documented on 14th May 2007. But what the Doctor could assure us that day was Julian did not have cancer of the spleen or anywhere else for that matter. This was a huge relief to Julian but a total shock to me I wasn't even aware that Julian was being investigated for the big 'C' apparently it was Julian who originally queried if he had cancer because of how ill he had become. Unbeknown to me a cancer test called 'Bence Jones Protein test' had been requested due to the fact he'd lost three and a half stone in weight in a short time. No further explanation was given for his sudden weight loss, at this stage or later.

(3) He never missed his Chest clinic appointments either with the Respiratory physician, although it was his Clinical Assistant who always saw Julian at the follow up appointments. At his last appointment the Doctor could see how much better Julian looked and felt, after listening to Julian's recovery story he ventured to say continue as you are without treatment and we will adopt the 'watch and wait strategy' Julian was concerned that his glucose levels were still too high, and asked what should he do if he was ever Hospitalized again, could he possibly document in his notes that he was not to have diabetic treatment. The Doctor said "Don't worry we'll cross that bridge when we come to it." But that left Julian worried who was going to speak up in his defence not to have the treatment should the occasion arise! Unfortunately Julian did find himself at that bridge, and just as he feared there was no one there to speak up for him. As regards to his lungs, Julian was pleased to hear that the drainage of his left plural effusion had not re-accumulated. But they had detected a nodule at the base of his left lung but no Pulmonary Embolism, thank goodness. One last question was asked of Julian at this last appointment, had he been exposed to asbestos?

(4) He never missed his Vascular appointment with the Vascular Surgeon either, who had referred him to a Consultant Anaesthetist for a Chemical Sympathectomy. It was so nice to see a bit of humour and banter creeping in to the medical

correspondence. In one of the letters following his first injection he wrote, "Mr Davies is absolutely delighted. You know what's coming next! You are a victim of your own success once again and Mr Davies and I would be very grateful if you would consider a second chemical lumber sympathectomy on the left side"

Following the second injection, he was advised to start taking Horse chestnut tablets to further improve his circulation. He advised Julian to get them from any high street herbalist. Here was a surgeon combining the old and the new way of healing. Comforting to see!

(5) He never missed his annual Diabetic Retinopathy Screening follow up either with the Screening Manager. He used to attend this clinic alone; he came home once saying the specialist had asked him if he was sure he was a Diabetic, only he didn't appear to have any determination to indicating he was a Diabetic. Julian informed him that his glucose levels are definitely raised. The reply from the specialist was "Well, if your GP says you are, you must be." These comments didn't make sense to me at the time, but rest assure they have haunted me since. On the other hand if the specialist didn't make these comments to Julian, then why did Julian lie to me? Comment sent to GP was, 'For annual recall'; as he scored better than average considering he'd suffered with high glucose readings for more than eight years. Julian of course was unable to attend this next appointment in September 2009, because he died 67 days later.

(6) He never missed his Diabetology appointment, although he never met the Consultant Physician himself he was seen by his colleague. This is the Consultant who informed the Hospital Doctors who was taking care of Julian at both hospitals, as well as the Coroner at Julian's Inquest after his death that he did not recall this unusual Diabetic case' Of course not they never met why should he remember. But on the strength of his verbal sayings, Julian had to endure four long weeks of medication he was allergic to. At this particular appointment Julian was put

under pressure to re-commence the diabetic therapy again. It didn't help the fact the Doctor spoke very poor English; to try and explain he had just survived a near multi-organ failure was proving difficult. When Julian was getting the upper-hand of the debate the Doctor stepped outside to discuss Julian's case. On his return he explained he'd had a word with the Consultant, to which Julian suddenly realised he wasn't being seen by the Consultant as arranged by his GP, "Excuse me but who are you, my GP sent me to see a Consultant in Diabetology because my case is so complex is it possible that I can see him"? He said, "No" and gave a nervous laugh. Julian continued, "I don't mind discussing my case in the corridor if he hasn't got a spare office" He still refused and continued to explain he should start on a new drug called Sit-a-glip-tin. Julian said, "Please no more drugs I don't trust drugs any more". He assured us that it had been passed as safe in 2006. I don't know what happened about the prescription of this wonder drug, but Julian was never started on it. Seventy days later Julian was dead. Since his death I've had a chance to look up this new drug, worrying that may be if he had taken it he might still be alive today. Well I don't think so, because it carries some serious warnings.

The first warning; one should not take Sitagliptin if one is allergic to Metformin!!!

The second warning it can cause Lactic Acidosis which is a medical name for Multi-organ-failure, and as he'd already experienced one near multi-organ-failure why would he take a drug to induce another?

The third warning is its make up, it contains Metformin!!

Fourthly Metformin should be stopped before a CT scan is done, because of the reaction it may have with the dye in the injection.

What else can it do? It can interfere with other drugs such as Diuretics and thyroid replacement; it can raise your blood sugar!

Equally there are other drugs that can lower the glucose levels such as anti-inflammatory, Aspirin, Warfarin and Blood pressure tablets. Julian was right to be cautious, he saved himself additional suffering by not going back to the GP begging for this new drug. No wonder he found it hard to control his glucose levels I appreciate he hadn't yet take the new drug but he had taken Metformin.

Even more interesting; when drinking alcohol and taking Metformin and Sitagliptin it can lower blood sugar readings. "That sounds good I thought" No that's bad, because over a time it can increase the risk of developing Lactic Acidosis. The trouble is; it doesn't happen instantaneously it starts slow and builds up.

So when Julian used to come home from the Buffalo meeting and tested his blood sugar to find it had gone down, he claimed it was the Beer; guess what Ju you were right again it was the combination of the beer and Metformin!

(7) He never missed his annual MOT as he called them, at his beloved sanctuary on the Spinal Injury Unit. Failing to attend these carried the same penalty as Baseball, three strokes and you are out.

He came home from Worcester Hospital following one of these appointments, and told me they had found a TUMOR on the outside of one of his kidneys, I asked do you mean the adrenal gland. He said, "That is it". I enquired, "When are they going to remove it?" He said, "Never, I think" they say it's benign, but could change cancerous. But they are going to keep a close eye on me and scan it every year."

I offered to go with him next time he went. He said, "No thanks, I'll be fine." He never did let me attend those appointments with him. This insignificant mention of a tumour was hardly mentioned again, possibly because he didn't want to worry me. Unbeknown to me he had confided in Gweno, so evidently he was unloading his worries somewhere else.

(8) He never missed his Diabetic clinic appointment with the Physician, the last time he attended this appointment on 21st September 2008 Julian explained how well he felt, now the treatment had been stopped in fact he was well enough to seek employment.

When the Green paper was launched on 24th January 2006 by the Labour Government empowering people back to work, we were inundated with pamphlets urging disabled people back to work. Julian's health in 2006 would not have held up to a full time employment at that point.

To be fair to Julian, he had been working self-employed full time until 1988 and when Llewela came along he became a 'house father' but as the turn of the century approached he was struck down with one ailment after another.

After eight years of drifting from one minor sickness to another he was able to say at last, that he was blessed once more with a 'feel good factor', the Doctor wrote this in his transfer letter, "He's optimistic for the future and is looking for employment at present" Julian had in mind to teach at the local college, but 59 days later Julian was dead!

Unbeknown to me, Julian had taken this next stage of his life very seriously because Llewela had already escorted Julian to two interviews while I was at work, neither of them told me of their activities. When she divulged this to me three years after he died I asked why she hadn't told me before. She said, "I think Dad declined both posts, because access into the building for the interview alone was too difficult, let alone working there full time".

As a result of Julian's unexpected sad end, my sister sent me a cutting from the Daily Mail dated the 29th November 2010. It had a full page dedicated to the topic of statistics of deaths in Hospitals. It was based on 147 Trust Hospitals. To my horror Shrewsbury and Telford Hospital NHS Trust scored top marks, they had the highest incidence of death occurring in their care. They will probably argue they have the most poorly patients in the land admitted to their Hospitals, but then I hear the haunting voice of Julian calling out to a patient in the opposite bed to him, "Have you noticed no one leaves this ward alive?" Out of embarrassment I said, "Hush Julian, the Doctors and nurses will hear you" he said, "Good, I want them to" then proceeded to repeat it even louder for the elderly deaf gentleman and the staff to hear.

I'll say no more on the matter except we all have to speak as we find, and I'm only retelling Julian's experience. These figures were disclosed by Dr. Foster-Hospital Guide 2010. The frightening thing is the authorities are now talking of closing Telford Hospital and joining forces with Shrewsbury Hospital, in this medi-Evil town of Shrewsbury. I sincerely hope that all the staff who will be employed in the future running of this humungousley huge Hospital (when it is built) will have a breath of fresh air injected into their nursing care and that they will become the patients advocate and protectors, and the cloth eared Doctors exchange theirs for a pair of listening ones with sympathy and empathy in their hearts. On the strength of the newspaper clipping my Mother has made her four children promise; whatever happens if there is ever a reason she has to attend Shrewsbury Hospital, we will do our utmost to prevent her attending that hospital because it will be against her will. She has also expressed the same wish to her friends who have been dismayed at her strong feeling towards this matter. But now some of those friends have had cause to be treated at this very Hospital. They are now ringing her saying they now know why she feels so strongly. So strongly did one friend feel; after one episode in this hospital she said she would never ever go back there again? She kept her suffering a secret and died at home. How sad is that, if only Julian could have done the same? It's not right; every Hospital should be everybody's sanctuary. It's not just my Mother who is worried, I read in the Universe Sunday newspaper on 23rd October 2011 for UK and Ireland that Bishops are speaking out for patients dignity to be restored. How ironically I read this article in Kidderminster but the Bishop was from Shrewsbury, he said, "Could it be that we have begun to dismiss the cries of the weakest in the place where they expected to receive the greatest care because their impaired lives no longer seem to have any great value?"

Did Julian also have a will of iron, enough to speak out like he did about his own survival, he was obviously willing to risk being accused of unfounded accusations of malpractice.

Julian was always concerned when he was dealing with Doctors that his nakedness put him at a disadvantage but it was not just his nakedness of cloths but nakedness of human dignity and respect. Sadly since Julian's death, Gill that is Julian's new friend has also now suffered at the hands of the medical profession who yet again refused to listen. Their lack of listening technique led her family to heartless social services, blinkered Doctors with their unkind words who psychologically supressed and cornered the parents and the carers into total submission of 'silence' and eventually after the horrendous event had to defend themselves in a court of law. Listening to their harrowing experience echoed 'Disavow' tipped me over the edge into publishing this book, because Julian's words rang out even louder and clearer this time, "Don't let others suffer like I have" I don't think he totally meant at the hands of just the Diabetes issues now, but at the hands of everything that was wrong, such as our chemical soaked world, the nurses who think Doctor knows best, to the non-listeners with their cloth eared professionals wearing blinkers!

What happened to good old fashioned caring, and listening skills. May be our society has lost the art of listening to the little voice inside called conscience but most of all to our bodies. If only the Doctors had listened to Julian when he tried to explain that he felt the treatment was harming him I fear his life would not have ended when it did. When Julian said it's gone horribly wrong I see what he meant now, when I read some scribe written on papyri of ancient Egyptian medicine scrolls. The wise Amenemope wrote, "Don't mock at the blind, do not scoff at the dwarfs, and do not injure the lame, do not sneer at a man who is in the hand of God of sound mind. A suffering person is not to be left without help. Go to him, and do not abandon him"

Wow! What happened, Egyptian physicians were trained how to respect patients 2,000 years ago, so how did the physicians looking after Julian be so careless as to lose their caring skill in 2008?

A photograph of Julian in his typical pose in a listening tilt
with his nephew George.

Not only did Julian listen to others he was also a great listener of his own body, he recognised what is body needed before seeking a medical opinion.

Another type of listening he did; he would always take notice of his pain, pain he said is our natural alarm bell installed in us from birth to let us know something is not right. He never believed in 'no pain, no gain' paraphernalia. We could all take a leaf out of his book and "listen" to the message your body sends us. "It's our body; we shouldn't let others abuse it!"

My body has always spoken to me but I have chosen not to listen, I realise its importance now. I call it my 'Body talk' I've noticed if I've eaten refined sugar I almost instantly suffer from hot flushes. I've noticed if I drink wine with sulphur dioxide in I have a heavy head next morning. I've noticed if I've eaten hidden synthetic fats or oil, I develop a dull headache above my eyes. I've noticed if I've eaten anything with artificial sweeteners I have to make emergency trips to the toilet. I've noticed if I've eaten white refined flour or sugar I instantly feel and look bloated.

All my coincidences

When you lose someone who's been your guide for many years, I can only describe it as being like a child lost amongst a crowd of people or a blind man without his dog.

You don't know what direction to take, your very foundation has been whipped from underneath you and your five senses of sight, smell, hearing, taste and touch appear to have become sharpened as a form of defence or animal instinct. I don't know why, maybe it's because in case one misses an opportunity of re-tracking oneself back on to one's original life path.

While I was in this re-tracking mode I have been puzzled since Julian's death, why I had experienced a lot of unusual happenings in the house. Which I found strange because Julian used to say "I don't believe in any of that witchery pokery stuff, I'm a Christian through and through"

How strange that funny and unexplained things only started to happen after his death. I don't feel I had provoked them or encouraged them.

Having said that, he was no stranger to the 'supernatural' himself, when he was a teenager living as a boarder in a private school he used to pop home occasionally in the evenings on his Vespa Scooter, I realise I'm splitting on him now but he's beyond punishment from the school authorities. Any way this particular evening he rode the scooter home, and ran up two flights of stairs to his attic bedroom. Baring in mind he was the only one with a key to his bedroom, he unlocked the old fashioned lock and to his horror found all the bedroom furniture in the centre of the room and the carpet folded neatly from each corner over the furniture in the centre.

He called down in anger to his grandmother who was child minding his younger siblings at the time. "Nan! Who's done this to my bedroom?" His grandmother called up, "I didn't, you're the only one with the key, but there was an awful row going on up there last night."

I don't know how old the house was, but he told me there used to be a psychologically disturbed relative who lived in the attic before they moved in, hence the lock and key. Knowing that didn't faze him, but having a bedroom that could be locked when he was away certainly appealed to him.

Recollecting years later he used to say, "Funny enough, my dog would never climb the last flight of stairs to my bedroom no matter how many times I called her."

I wonder why? Coincidence maybe!

There was another occasion, when I was at work and Llewela was at school. Julian needed to transport some old fashioned heavy computer screens out of the house to the shed at the top of the garden. He thought; if he slotted his wheelchair table into the arm rests in front of him, relay all the monitors one by one on the table top up the steep slope to the shed that will and did work.

He'd managed all but one, when he was half way up the slope the table suddenly shunted forward, down slipped the screen, wedging itself in a diamond shape between his legs. Still holding the screen with one hand, he now only had one hand free to finish the second half of the slope. His mathematical head told him, if he pushed the wheelchair one handed he would turn round in circles. As he stayed still for a moment thinking what the next best move was, he suddenly felt someone push him in a straight line up the remainder of the steep path. When he arrived at the top he placed the screen down then quickly spun his wheelchair round to see who had helped him.

Knowing the front door was always locked on the account we never used it the back gate was just in front of him, with no other access into the garden; who could have possibly helped him?

He was obviously disturbed about his mysterious little helper because that evening he hardly spoke a word, I eventually coaxed it out of him. I jokingly said, "It was probably your Grandmother, seeing you in trouble and giving you a helping hand" Was this divine intervention, we will never know as the subject was 'never open for discussion' ever again. Another coincidence, probably!

After Julian's death Kevin true to his word had been a brick to Llewela looking after her when I couldn't as she was so far away in Oxford, he encouraged her with her studies even when she felt like flagging on occasions. On a few occasions Kevin spoken to Llewela with a stern voice saying something similar to what Julian would have said, but more than that both of them would mistake Kevin's voice for

Julian's. Kevin saying, "Purr, did I say that", and Llewela saying "Yes, you're voice sounded just like Dad" Strange or coincidence!

I mentioned earlier, from the first night I came home I was woken at 3 o'clock every morning by a noise that resembled the bedroom door handle rattling. I would soon settle and go back to sleep after saying, "Is that you Ju?" then the noise would stop. This went on every night for a long time; even though I tried different tactics of making sure it wasn't the wind. In the end I just left the door ajar and the door handle continued rattling just the same at precisely 3am. Before going back to sleep each time my thoughts would always go back to the entrance hymn I had chosen for Julian's funeral, 'Here I am Lord, I have heard you calling in the night' I wonder, was this my wakeup call did I like Samuel in the Bible mistake Eli his teacher for our Lord, could I have mistaken the door rattling thinking it was Julian when in fact it could have been my 'Maker' directing me towards my life purpose. Nickodemas also went to visit Jesus in the middle of the night, was I like Nickodemas secretively trying to seek an answer to my future path in the depth of the night? But Jesus did once say, "Ask and it shall be given; knock and it shall be opened" And didn't I beg God to help me on the road to Telford early one morning, when the sky was 'lit up like a flame'. Three o'clock in the morning is quoted in the Bible as the 'morning watch hour' when Jesus was praying in the garden of Gethsemane, before the cock crowed three times.

I have since heard that 3am is referred to as the healing hour, it's also considered to be the hour that gives us the strongest urge for peaceful prayer! Of course there are fewer disturbances at three in the morning. Maybe we are all given signs, but don't connect them to our calling or was the rattle just another coincidence!

On another occasion I was woken at 3am and heard a bang in the airing cupboard, worried something had happened to the emersion tank I got out of bed to investigate, only to find I'd forgotten to turn the heater on before going to bed. Coincidence do you think, but what about the bang?

When I was first called to attend Telford Police Station to make an additional statement to answer some allegations made against me, this was before Id realised who had. I had no first-hand experience of how to conduct myself in these situations, I had no idea how serious the allegations were, or if it entailed being charged. Worst still, if they were going to keep me there and how long for. If I thought life was intense while Julian was struggling with the insulin issue, it wasn't faring much better now without him.

I had been caught short once before with Julian, having no medical back up at his bed side, I didn't intend to be caught short at the police station repeating a similar scenario with no answers to their questioning. I did my homework; I had all the paper work all laid out all over the table, the floor and the settee, when suddenly I heard a noise upstairs. I ran up to investigate only to find Julian's battery toothbrush going off in his toilet bag. I had not touched the content of his toilet bag since the day he died. I opened the bag and switched it off; as I was coming back down the stairs I heard rustling of papers. As I entered the lounge I found all the orderly papers in disarray. One could argue it might have been the wind, but that day was a particular cold winter's day and all the doors were shut tight and the gas fire was on, so no there was no draught at all.

I took it as a sign that everything was fine and that I wouldn't need any of the documents including my overnight bag. And sure enough none of the paperwork was needed.

The flying sheets of paper might be considered a coincidence, but how do you explain the battery toothbrush buzzing nine days after it was last used on Remembrance Sunday by Julian? Was that a coincidence too?

On another occasion one of the young men who we used to take to France with us called round on his scooter late one night. I told him off for coming so late, it was after all 11oclock at night.

We had a chat over a cup of coffee; I was asking him what tools needed replenishing in the house in France? He mentioned that the grinder needed replacing, and that they were on special offer at the local DIY that week. At that the light dimmed, hissed and frazzled he jumped up and said, "Wow what's that", I said Oh! I expect that's Ju agreeing that it's a bargain, take no notice it often happens. He got up and put his mug down and said, "I'm off, that's really spooked me."

I'm sorry John if it disturbed you, but was this regular occurrence of light interferences a series of coincidence?

Sometimes I would forget to set the alarm clock, but on those occasions I would here a voice calling very sternly, "OLWEN". I'd jump out of bed realising it was five thirty in the morning; time to get up, was someone was watching over me or was it just another coincidence?

There were many, many occasions when I would smell logs burning and still do, like a smouldering smell. This was usually when I'd been talking to someone about Julian's case. I asked someone once about this, the only explanation she could offer me was that maybe Julian was agreeing with me, hence the old saying "There is no smoke without fire" was there a possibility that this could be true! It would even happen in the middle of the night when I was fast asleep. I would wake up frightened the house was on fire, after checking the house and finding it to be sound I would realise on those occasions I had been dreaming about Julian. I eventually recognised the smouldering smell to be identical to the incense used in church. Coincidence or not, it still left me wondering.

During that first winter month between darkness falling and the time to go to bed, in the silence of the lounge I would hear Julian's wheel chair spinning round on the wooden floor up stairs. It was easy to distinguish; it was a sound I'd heard for nearly 30 years. Since I didn't watch television any more it wasn't possible I'd mistook the noise from the television or, do you think it was my imagination or possibly another coincidence?

Quite soon after, I attended the funeral of my Uncle in mid Wales we were all gathered in the hall having refreshments my sister-in-law made a beeline towards me and in a loud'ish voice said she had a message for me when she attended a "psychic supper". This is the sort of thing Julian used to protest most fiercely about, and would not tolerate in the house at all. I don't mean its practice I mean the subject could not even be mentioned. So when my sister-in-law proceeded to inform me that the lady had told her, the man was healed now and walking, but she would not have known him walking while he was living. My sister-in-law realised straight away she was talking about Julian. He had a message to give to me, "Tell her I am five foot nine" it took my breath away because he used to tell me this, but I never believed him until the pathologist report arrived after his death stating how tall he was. I had to believe then, so was this confirmation the message maybe from Julian? As I never discussed his height with my sister-in-law ever, I had no reason to. My sister-in-law then relayed what else the lady had to say, "He's very insistent, he's yakking in my ear" She made the motion with her finger tips close to her ear.

The message was, "I fought very hard at the end not to come over but tell her I'm alright now. Also tell her, they weren't listening then, and they aren't listening still. Tell her she needs to write a book and then she will be healed" On the strength of this message, this book came about. If the above was true and Julian has asked me to write a book from the other side then I find it doubly strange, when he was so against anything to do with the spirit world why would he be trying so very hard to make contact with me through others.

Do you think this is another coincidence?

Another strange phenomena's I experienced, after returning from my Uncles funeral I set about writing this book but to my irritancy Julian's laptop wouldn't work, no matter what I did to try and get it to function. It wasn't just my laptop I had a problem with I had a problem with all computers, a friend of mine called Julie Thorp recommended I should buy a CD. Whilst I was at a checkout trying to order the CD three of the computer screens crashed and I left without ordering. Then one afternoon while I was visiting my sister, her friend called for coffee and as we were chatting I asked her why she thought my laptop wouldn't work. Her reply was, "Julian will let it work when the time is right" Then on the day I received the last set of Julian's medical notes, and suddenly the computer came on of its own accord. Coincidence again?

Now I had access to the computing world, I set about my new task of writing his book. After I had been typing for a few days with some intent, an arrow appeared at the bottom right hand corner of the screen. It started to move upwards in a jerky movement. Once it reached the top right hand corner it turned direction and started to point in a jerky movement across the top of the screen just below the icons. I quickly pulled away from the laptop thinking I might have been touching the key board somehow. The arrow stopped mid screen, still at the top. I thought that was a bit strange, so I asked in a normal voice, "Is that you Ju, if it is and you've got a message carry on." The arrow restarted again in jerky movements still moving from right to left along the top of the screen. It went as far left as it could, I thought it was going to go off the screen when all of a sudden it started to change direction now it was pointing down wards towards the left hand corner of the screen, once it reached the corner it started to go frantic. The arrow became bigger, and was dancing up and down pointing at a white square icon with the words "Read page 7" inside. I couldn't believe it, was this really Julian contacting me? I'd never seen this square on my screen before, was it an instruction? I quickly went back to the pages I had already written, it took me a while to detect page 7 as I hadn't even numbered the pages at that stage. So what did this instruction know that I didn't? Unbeknown to me I had written nine pages, I hurriedly returned to page 7. And there it was as bold as brass, the opening sentence at the top of page seven read "On the 7th day a Doctor told Julian he was not a diabetic" By the way it's not on page 7 anymore because I've written so much more since.

This was spooky; if this really was Julian then I guess he had a bigger picture from where he was.

I have never seen that icon from that day to this, so come on you, 'Computer Whiz Kids out there' what earthly explanation can you offer me, unless you're telling me it was one of my coincidences.

There were other times when Gweno and I would hear a buzzing interference our telephones, it only appeared to happen when the truth was being spoken, especially when we were talking about Julian's case, never when we spoke about mundane things. As if Julian was joining in with the conversation. Sometimes we would say "Shush Julian", and then the noise would stop. On other occasions Gweno would say, "What do you think Ju"? Then it would start again. I thought it might have been my phone at first, but I have since changed my phone twice, then I noticed it would happen on my landline, my mobile phone, and even on Julian's mobile phone. Gwenos landline and her mobile, she has also changed her mobile phone and on top of that she's also moved house and it still happens at her new address. It even once happened when I was speaking to my mother, we were speaking about Julian at the time when she asked "What's that noise?" Coincidence again, I don't know it never used to happen.

Crackling on the radio was another one, when the song appeared to be giving me a message this would happen either on the house radio or car radio even if I was in someone else's car. People used to say I don't know how you can put up with that crackling, turn it off. I never told them what I thought it was, but I appeared to get the appropriate answers to whatever was troubling me through the lyrics of the songs.

I found comfort in what appeared to be my answers to my troubles. Coincidence, I don't know! You'll have to humour me on this one.

Just over twelve months after Julian's funeral on New Year's Day 2010 I arranged to go to Bridgenorth on the Severn Valley Railway. As I said my prayers the night before I asked God if Julian really wanted me to continue with this book could he make it snow the very next day. I woke early and the sky was as blue as can be with brilliant very warm sunshine not a single cloud in the sky a most unlikely day to snow, it felt like a hot spring morning. I became dis-heartened as I got into the car thinking maybe the beautiful sunshine was a sign to stop the book. But before I had left the estate the whole sky suddenly went dark and down it came, huge flakes of snow. Coincidence! Still not convinced that was a sign, I made another deal thinking if I could just see a robin that very day that everybody else seems to have seen since his death, that would clinch it, I think I would then be convinced. As we walked round Bridgenorth Castle my friend took a photograph of me, it just happened to be three o'clock as the church bells rang. Note the sky at three, just like the lyric again; "Light up the sky like a flame"

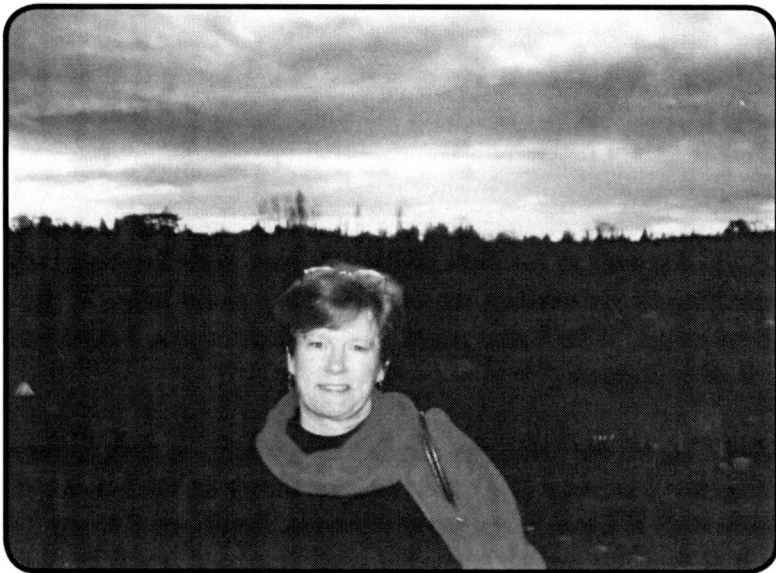

The sky went from sky blue at 11am, to grey clouds and snow at 12 noon to raging flames at 3pm

As we were waiting for the train to take us home out of nowhere bobbed this Robin, jumping round my feet in a playful manner. I was ferreting in my handbag for my camera, I thought if I could just take a photograph to show others that there really was a Robin at my feet. But my friend called out "Come on, you know it's the last train to Kidderminster" so I had to leave my little 'Robin' perched on the bench at the station platform as if he was staring me out. Bye-bye Robin, now I believe the book needs to be published. Thank you God, I tested you and you supplied me with snow, then you 'lit up the sky like flames' and finally you sent your divine little helper the little robin red breast. All on New Year's Day the very day we used to have our Christmas get together.

But let me set the record straight that was the only time I had provoked the Devine to give me proof. Feeling guilty about asking for proof and putting heaven to the test, on the train journey home I quietly remembered the "Story of Bernadette" the miracle of Lourdes in the Pyrenees in South of France, a young girl called Bernadette Soubirous went out colleting fire wood, when she saw the apparition of the Virgin Mary at the grotto. When she told the Priest that the lady had called herself the Immaculate Conception he was astonished that an uneducated girl could say such a thing and remember the words. The Priest asked Bernadette to relay a message to the lady in the rock by asking to make the wild rose bush in the grotto bloom today out of season in the month of March.

Of course the rose did bloom in March, but the comparison I'm trying to make is, if a Priest in 1858 was allowed to ask the Devine for proof without any earthly criticism from the church, then maybe I too could be excused this once.

Incidentally Bernadette's miracles may have taken place 162 years ago, but people all over the world still pilgrim to Lourdes in their thousand on a daily basis. There can be as many as 20,000 some days taking part in the candle light procession.

I do feel, there is a fine line between faith and the supernatural, for example when devout prayer's witness marks of stigmata, when others see the vision of Mary, or smell flowers in unexpected places. Then there are some acts in churches which to some resemble pagan ways, such as burning incense like Frankincense to cleanse negative spirits and luring holy ones.

Since that first sighting of the Robin on the train station platform, I have only sited a Robin on special occasions since, one every New Year's Day and two robins on St Valentine's Day. How strange Julian started taking diabetic treatment on Valentine's Day in the year 2001, should I file this under 'Strange but true?' or just another coincidence.

Coincidence or not I was slowly beginning to be convinced that Julian was guiding me to soldier on with this diabetes dilemma, telling me that something was still not right.

The Lodge Julian once belonged to in the Buffalo movement once considered starting a 'Robin Appeal' in his memory, to raise money for their chosen charity.

Guilt's?

Seventeen months after Julian died, my ward Sister pulled me to one side and said, "Olwen what's happening to you, what's the matter with your memory"

We spoke at length that afternoon and as I broke down she said, "I think your hanging on to too much guilt, your hanging on to too much facts and figures, and there is no room left inside that little head of yours for any more."

It was true I didn't want to let go of the facts and figures in case I needed them one day, to either defend myself or get justice for Julian but as far as guilt was concerned I had no guilt as to how I'd taken care of Julian.

It was not so much of a problem of forgetting things at work, but more of a problem of not being able to get it registered in my mind in the first place. I couldn't file it under "Remember" so how could I possibly recall something that was not even recorded. My personal filing system was failing me.

She had several suggestions, go off sick or reduce my hours or be shadowed by a colleague at all times until my memory improved. I decided to do the decent thing and take time off to sort out my head once and for all. Being shadowed was degrading; staying at work could be detrimental to a patient if my complaint was connected to 'memory issues' the third choice was not practical for my colleagues either. After all I didn't want to be caught out trying to defend Julian's case at the same time inflicting harm on others, that would make me no better than Julian's carers. Then his last word to me would become much more meaningful to me, "You're no better than them"

We have a prayer in church in which we ask for forgiveness, "in what I have done and in what I have failed to do" In Julian's case I had to forgive them for what <u>they did do</u>, in my work place it was more of forgive me for what I <u>failed to do.</u>

That evening I thought; how can I best deal with my problem, this was serious, my career was about to ebb away. If Julian was here he would say "Olwen make a plan" I didn't think I had any guilty hang-ups but I decided to make two separate lists 'guilt verses no guilt'.

To my amazement I discovered I was burdened with eighteen guilt issues.

1. I felt guilty that I had buried Julian, when he specifically asked Llewela and I to cremate him, he did not want us to be tied down to Kidderminster for the rest of our lives in order to maintain his grave, the other reason he did not want us to endure a large cost for the headstone.
2. I felt guilty that I hadn't been able to stop the medical profession giving him Insulin when he was begging every day not to have it.
3. I felt guilty about getting rid of his cloths, what would he wear if he came back.
4. I felt guilty I had not been to see his Father since the funeral.
5. I felt guilty about not being able to support Llewela educationally at University, like Julian did.
6. I felt guilty I was no closer to preventing someone else suffering in the same way as Julian did and I promised him I would do something about it.
7. I felt guilty that his Mother and half-sister hated me with such vengeance and that I couldn't put their hurt right. I don't know how to.
8. I felt guilty for not answering the phone in case I felt the wrath of his mother's tongue.
9. I felt guilty for not going out visiting people who were kind and caring towards me.
10. I felt guilty that I hadn't finished the book that Julian asked me to write.
11. I feel guilty when I am happy in someone else's company.
12. I felt guilty that one person had the courage to call me the "Merry Widow".
13. I felt guilty I had not managed to convince the panel enough at the Inquest of Julian's plight to change the death certificate.
14. I felt guilty that I was off work sick and my friends had to cover my shifts.
15. I felt guilty that my nursing qualification did not save Julian.

16. I felt guilty that I was hogging his wheelchairs instead of putting them to good use.
17. I felt guilty that I was getting rid of traces of Julian on earth.
18. I felt guilty that I had not put a headstone on his grave.

Dealing with them

The realisation I was suffering from these guilt's came as a shock to me on St George's day, I don't know if this had any significance or not?

His sainthood stands for "Good over evil." The dragon symbolises the devil, and he is often depicted carrying the shield of protection and the sword of truth defending the faith.

I feel as if I need this guy more than ever, especially his shield of protection and most of all his sword of truth regarding Julian's diabetic dilemma.

I decided to look up the definition of the word guilt, to see what I was suffering from.

I was horrified at the explanation; I took it personally and thought the ward Sister is right I need to ditch these feelings if I was to believe the definition.

It states, "Guilt = Deserving of punishment, condemned to pay, own fault, having done wrong, responsibility for criminal or moral offence." Wow! I don't feel guilty to this degree.

What I need to be able to tell my manager before returning back to work was, that I was travelling light after reliving myself of all these guilt's, because I cannot be seen to be attached to such things as these.

Gweno rang me that evening as usual, she comforted me by reminding me that my married life with Julian had been a very colourful one. With Julian dying so young it left our colourful tapestry of life unfinished and frayed at the edges. She agreed with the ward Sister that it was a good idea to take time out to tidy my frayed edges. Then carefully and lovingly roll it up, leaving the remainder of the canvas to continue with the remainder of my life.

So in order to move on I needed to firstly deal with my guilt's.

Confrontation

I've never been good with confrontation but I realised I needed to confront this little lot one by one. My first guilt I mentioned was burying Julian, instead of cremating him. Because of the complication surrounding his death, I felt I had to heed the comments of the Detective Inspector who advised me to bury him rather than cremate him. Even Julian sometimes made u turns in his life after he was better informed. This was my u turn, after all I had been to several funerals recently where many of the deceased had complained of similar complaints as Julian; it didn't make sense to me to cremate them. If there was the slightest doubt about their final days; to me it was like burning the evidence. I was sure Julian would agree with me if he was alive, after all he had asked me not to let it happen to someone else. This reasoning cancelled this guilt trip.

My second guilt was witnessing Julian being forced to take prescribed drugs which was a type of 'drug pushing'! This guilt I will have to learn to live with, but to try and cancel that out I will have to endeavour to research; why he couldn't tolerate their drugs. If I fail, I will have to beg Julian's forgiveness.

My third guilt was about getting rid of his cloths, I had no problems with his regular cloths it was his working cloths I couldn't get rid of. When that task was completed, then this guilt can be put to rest too.

My forth guilt was about not visiting his Father; I was worried in case his family mistook my genuine visits for greed for Julian's inheritance. Time lapsed and I never made my visit before his father died too. I should accept that it was just as difficult for his father to visit me as it was for me to visit him and file this guilt under 50/50 blame.

My fifth guilt was about supporting Llewela at University the way Julian use too. She comforted me by saying, "Don't worry Mum, Dad taught me everything I need to know." So that cancels that one out.

My sixth guilt was about preventing further suffering; I can't until this book is finished, and maybe not even then. I need to wait and see what I discover.

My seventh guilt was dealing with the hatred his mother and half-sister has towards me.

I don't think our paths will ever cross again, but if they ever read this book I hope they will come to understand Julian's difficult journey, but above all, they will understand that I loved him and never harmed as much as a hair on his head. I also understand that when we are born we are all on our individual paths of life. We can accompany others, but we must not cross each other's paths or divert them from theirs. With this thought in mind, I feel comfortable cancelling this guilt knowing they are on their path and I'm on mine.

My eighth guilt was my phone phobia. I know I was missing out on my friend's kind words and wishes. But Id starting to feel more confident answering the phone, realising if I don't like who's on the other end I can always replace the receiver. Changing the number was not an option, that's just creating another hiding place.

My ninth guilt was not visiting friends, but the book has taken so much of my time. One day soon I will come knocking for my cuppa, mine is Welsh medium brown with no sugar thanks. I hope I will still be welcomed and when I start visiting then this guilt will also disappear.

My tenth was about how long I'm taking writing the book. It never was a quick fix book. You could not explain Julian's life in a sentence or his condition. I also think Julian would say, "Don't rush it Olwen, just get it right." So that cancels that guilt.

My eleventh guilt was 'being happy in front of others'. I don't feel so guilty about laughing in public now, I realise now it's one way to honour the dead. I'm sure he's pleased to see me happy; the dead don't want to see us wasting our precious lives being miserable when theirs was cut short, besides none of us are here for long.

My twelfth guilt gave me a heavy heart, wondering how many people thought I was the 'Merry Widow', when in fact I was the 'Sad Widow' trying to be happy. It's not easy finding courage to socialise when you're feeling down. I've come to the conclusion that they are entitled to their opinion and I'm entitled to mine. That guilt stops there.

My thirteenth guilt was about; not being able to change the death certificate. On re-reading the inquest report, the Coroner did say to the Consultant Physician, "Do you agree that Julian was reluctant to take Insulin and Antibiotics whether or not you could put your finger on the allergic effects that he was suffering." I feel I did get confirmation off the Coroner that day that clearly something was not right. The death certificate is still not changed in its content only in its order; the Coroner recognised Julian's difficulty with Insulin and antibiotics, that's enough for me **for now**.

My fourteenth guilt was about being off work sick. But then I recollect how I had covered for many of my colleagues over the years, they are just doing the same for me right now.

My fifteenth guilt was about what a poor advocate I was for Julian during those last five weeks of his life. I will now try to put it right in death. I realise in writing this book it may raise cause for concern about others who are suffering like Julian did. That thought is easing my guilt.

My sixteenth guilt was about hogging his wheelchairs. The issue was solved one afternoon when I impulsively sprayed one pink, one lilac and one bright yellow then I donated them to a retired paediatric consultant who volunteers his service by operating on children in India.

The chairs served as work horses for Julian, and he would be pleased they are serving a similar purpose in his absence.

My seventeenth guilt was about; getting rid of marks Julian had left here on earth, like the polish off his shoes on the stair case as he went up and down on the stair lift. I cried as I painted over them. Sanding down and filling gaps in skirting boards made by his foot plates on the wheelchair. Saying a silent goodbye to a broken down old fridge that was being towed away, taking with it the scratch marks made by Julian's wheelchair. It felt as if I was erasing the last few traces of Julian's existence on earth like a rubber. I then took strength from the fact I was recording his existence in these pages, not forever maybe, but at least in forming a bigger picture.

My eighteenth guilt was about not erecting Julian's headstone, but I didn't want the head stone laid if something developed at the Inquest that required Julian to be exhumed. As the Inquest didn't take place for ten months following his death, and nearly one year before I was in possession of his final death certificate! It was difficult to find a closure until then.

My next mammoth task was to decide what type of headstone would depict his short but interesting life.

Most of my guilt's are now laid to rest, I am now guided by these words written by Reinhold Niebuhr who wrote in 1942 'God grant me the serenity to accept the things I cannot change, the courage to change the things I can, and wisdom to know the difference'

The head stone

I feel the headstone deserves a chapter of its own; after all it's often the only thing that's left of us in the end. I would like to tell you a bit about how the headstone came about. I knew I had a hard task ahead of me to do the right thing in memory of this brilliant man, who died before his time. First of all, he always put education above everything else; because of this I wanted it represented in stone.

I went to view some headstones with my friend Joanna, Llewela's God Mother, who had recently lost her own Mother a short time after Julian's death. She had also gone through the same difficult decision of choosing a headstone for her loved one. It seemed like a very important task to me, because this is your last gift to them. As we entered the reception area of the funeral parlour we both went "WOW" to this one particular headstone. There in front of us stood this column in dark grey flint garnet. Stacked on top of this column were three brown leather cover look-a-like books, also in garnet. We were shown a collection of catalogues with a variety of shapes and sizes of headstones. Nothing jumped out at us as we were looking at simple open prayer books. Llewela had suggested getting something low down and inexpensive with low maintenance. The lady enquired if we needed help, we explained we couldn't find anything that had the same wow factor as the column on show in the foyer. We both assumed that it was more of an advert statement rather than a stone that could be chosen. She replied "Oh! No we could order that one if you wish"

I took the price list home and thought blow it I could spend the rest of my life paying for it after all there was no more presents for Julian after this one.

I then spent some time thinking what would be most fitting for this well-loved man.

I wanted his name, date of birth, date he left our company here on earth and I wanted something a bit different engraved on the front, a verse or a poem that told Julian's life or what he'd left behind.

In the finish these were the words I eventually choose after much deliberation—:

Life was no mere candle to you.
It was a splendid torch which you got hold of for a moment,
And you wanted it to burn as bright as possible.
Before handing it over to the next generation.
Our lives were made brighter by your presence.

The torch to me symbolised two things, firstly the <u>enthusiasm for life</u> he was handing over to the next generation, and secondly <u>the quest</u> he handed to me to decipher; why he suffered like he did.

I decided to have the inscription on the front of the column with the impression of a Roman impeachment as a back drop. He would have liked that, he loved the Romans. The impeachment was then going to be sand blasted leaving the letters of his memorial raised rather than engraved. In effect it was going to be the reverse technique used on this headstone as most lettering on headstones is carved into the stone. When the stone mason heard what I had ordered, he was exited and very keen to get every detail correct.

On the top left hand corner I requested a picture of Julian in his cap and gown, as a reminder to everyone who come to his resting place, "Here lies a learned man."

This was to be finished in beautifully oval shape porcelain. In the centre of the base I asked for the Worcestershire crest, with the Worcester City Castle walls at the top of the emblem with the Worcestershire black pear tree in the centre, I insisted that the pears on the tree were black not green or yellow. The blue at the base of the tree represents the river Severn. I'm guessing the green represents the Malvern Hills, I could be wrong on that presumption.

I chose this emblem as a reminder of his involvement with the Buffalo organisation, where he held the position of "Web Master" he was also responsible for designing the original World Wide Web Homepage of the Worcestershire Provincial Grand Lodge of the Royal Antediluvian Order of Buffalos. On the left hand side of the base, I chose a red breasted Robin with a glow radiating from his breast standing on a terracotta flower pot surrounded by a flurry of snow.

I chose a Robin as a reminder that it was he who instigated the Robin as a theme for our Christmas gathering, which took place only six weeks after his death. He found a legend about the robin that he wears his red breast as a 'badge of honour' after he sat on Jesus's shoulder and sang softly into his ear to relive his pain and suffering, then while plucking the thorns from his crown he stained his chest from his blood. Because of this legend Robins are considered to be Devine little messengers of God. I asked for the snow, to remind me in years to come that it snowed the very next day after he died. On the right hand side of the base you will find an old fashioned Bee Hive because he expressed a worry about the depleting honey bees just before he became ill, his words were "This is very serious Olwen, we must do something about it." Sadly due to lack of time his quest was left un-tackled, but I felt his concern had to be set in stone. Ironically our town has just had its coat of arms changed; incorporating a 'Bee' on its shield symbolising industry and two shuttles commemorating the buzzy carpet trade that once graced this community.

On the 28th July 2010, I was asked to view and proof read the head stone before they started to sandblast it, this had to be done on site at Bilston, near Wolverhampton. I took fright when they said where. I thought, Oh! No, I'm still a country girl at heart and I don't like driving in big cities, and definitely not on my own. But sometimes when your back is against the wall, when you have no choice but to face the music you have to confront your fears. I decided to take Tom with me. (Tom-Tom) he tends to take me miles out of my way and occasionally get me lost, but I thought I'd take my chance. I travelled about four miles out of Kidderminster when my mobile rang; I pulled over into a lay-by like all good citizens should, to answer my phone. It was Clive, asking if Id rung him on Julian's mobile phone. I said No, but the Tom-Tom is asking me to turn round when possible. He said, "No carry on; he's trying to take you on the motorway." So who rang who, I don't know, it was a mystery to both of us, as we both thought the other had rung. Spooky! I can only assume either Julian or Devine Intervention was offering a helping hand by contacting both of us at the same time so we could speak to each other. Never the less, I did as Clive told me. Things got really complicated then, all the villages and the towns seemed to merge into one mass of buildings. Sometimes I was in built up areas then trading estates then housing estates. Just when I thought my Tom-Tom had let me down I said "Please God help me" I suddenly went through a village called Gospel End. (Thank you, God.) Many more roundabouts and miss-shape crossroads later, I was sure I was traveling in the wrong direction this time I prayed "Please Mary can you give me a sign that I'm on the right road?" At that I passed a side road called Saint Mary's Place. (Thank you, Mary) A bit further on I felt as if I was heading in a completely different direction, this time I said, "Please Julian help me" at that I passed a road called Saint Paul's road, as this was Julian's middle name I took this to be a sign off Julian this time, and sure enough a few seconds later I found myself outside the Stonemasons. How was that for Devine help? As I always say never under estimate the power of prayer. There to greet me was a gentleman called Phil Wilkins. He was the only one dressed in a smart shirt and trousers. I took this gentleman to be the boss; just as Julian insisted dressing smart beckons respect, and demands attention. What lovely people they all were, the young man called Christopher Wilkinson was a very talented Mason, he draws free hand what he thought you wanted on paper. He then proceeds to copy free hand the art work required then sets it in stone in time and memorial. He sculptures such things as angels to rest on top of head stones. He makes the wings bigger, smaller, taller, and fatter no detail is too small or job too big. It just left me wondering; when did this young man and others like him get up one morning and say, "I want to be a Stonemason when I grow up, and what's more I want to be a good one" it's such an unusual job. At times like this, where would we all be without their skills? Our loved ones would be just a blur in the past attached to forgotten memories. Definitely a very moving day for me I was so fascinated with it all. Phil Wilkins gave me a guided tour round the old fashioned plant, It had been going since 1900 or there about. The pride in their work had obviously cascaded down the ages. The roof was made of glass panes, I presume to let as much light in for their accuracy in Stonemasonry, but of course today the ornate glass roof has a preservation order on it. They have also deliberately saved a lot of the old fashioned equipment in case a museum would one day be interested in displaying them. The building boasts of an old saw mill upstairs, that was once used to cut the wood for the coffins on sight. The large doors once accommodated horse drawn carriages to enter the building. The place is massive compared to the front of the establishment. I'm so glad I went in person to see these characters, not only was there a lot of changes done to the layout of Julian's headstone I also got an insight in to the life of a Stonemason. "Thank you gentlemen" Besides, Julian was such a stickler for the smallest of detail to be correct, I could not afford for any detail to be incorrect. He used to say, "People who can't do the job any better, have great joy in telling you, 'you made a mistake there'. The secret is, don't give them the opportunity to humiliate you" That is why such a lot of proof reading went on in our house to avoid such painful remarks.

Photograph of Julian's head stone,
erected 16ᵗʰ September 2010.

Trying to let go

Now the head stone was in place I had to learn to finally let go, time was moving on and I knew I hadn't grieved like I was supposed to. Maybe I was putting too much restraint on myself, my first 'don't greave yet' until after the funeral, my second 'don't grieve yet' until after the inquest, my third 'don't greave yet' until the book is complete. Was I ever going to allow myself to grieve?

I felt sad inside but strong? As Julian had found such comfort from 'sound healing' towards the end of his life I wondered if music really did have the power to heal, and if it did, could I too possibility draw strength from such an experience.

The next day I made arrangements to meet Gill, Julian's latest friend who introduced him to sound healing and the beauty of tranquil angelic music at his bedside.

Gweno and I met Gill at Llanfaircaeirion, in Mid Wales there the three of us went for lunch, we had intended to meet once a month, but family commitments often upset arrangements Gill usually said "It was not meant to be" she has a such a lay back disposition about life its quite lovely to witness. We then made our way up into the mountains as I call it; the last mile at least is a dirt track to a farm called "Hiros Ganol"

The young couple, who moved to this old farm house practiced alternative therapy but were constantly on the lookout for an alternative building. After spending several years looking for this wondrous place, one day they stood still and thought were already in possession of this 'Grand God Given View' their perfect plot was on their land sharing the same view.

This is when the idea was born, to build a purpose built alternative therapy log cabin just above their family home, both sharing the same view that acted as a beautiful back drop.

They called it "Central Harmony Centre" for wellbeing. It doesn't matter which window you look out of, there is a stupendous view. Everyone finds this setting breathtakingly magnificent, when the centre was first opened Carol said that her first few visitors commented, "There was something missing" They didn't know what until one day someone said, it's something simple like birds. And sure enough that's what it was.

Some bird feeders and bird baths were installed now not only does it feel like paradise but it now sounds like paradise.

Before I left home that morning I was still a tad worried that the church might think unkindly of me meddling with something other than Christianity. I wanted to be quite clear that I was not confusing the word meditation with hypnosis. Because I had been told that I would be lying down on a couch for this sound healing and I would be so relaxed I might drift off into a meditated state. First I looked up the definition of the word meditation. Meditation means to quiet the mind, a skill most of us have forgotten how to practice in our fast modern day society.

Then I read there are two types of meditation, one based on Easton Religion where one empties the mind and the other is Christian meditation, this is a kind of prayer where one tries to reach the depth of Gods message. The word meditation apparently derives from the word medicine, the difference being modern medicine costs and carries side effects whereas meditation is a free healing agent, possessing no side effect.

While I was at it, I also looked up Reflexology too, something else Id given Julian while he was recovering. Was this accepted by Christians? I found on 26th November 2003 Reverend Eugster had massaged Pope Paul 1l's feet and when asked what he thought. The Pope answered "At least now other people realize that there is nothing wrong with foot reflexology"

The third topic I looked up was taking part in healing, I concluded myself that the Scriptures clearly indicate that healing is something appropriate for Christians to be involved with, as Jesus led by example by using his hands and palms to heal others. I was comfortable with all these explanations. As I approached the cabin I felt comfortable in the surroundings, the cabin had this American feel about it, with its substantial veranda offering shelter from the hot sun or torrential rain, in fact it reminded me of the 'Little house on the Prairie' Then amidst this rugged exterior was this beautiful bevelled and engraved glass front door that one would normally associate in with a beautiful traditional gypsy caravan. As one approaches the door the visitor's first view is of the reception desk, at the same token the receptionist can't help but notice whose calling.

You're greeted with hugs and a heartfelt 'lovely to see you' greeting whether you're a new comer or a long standing friend. Its common practice for visitors to remove shoes as you enter, I thought when I first went it was some sort of custom, but it's not. Ahead of you lies yards of cream carpet and the act of removing your footwear immediately makes you feel at ease because it mimics bare feet on your own bedroom carpet. As you enter you're offered a hot drink and usually led into a communal open plan kitchen to the left of the entrance, just to chat while the kettle boils.

To the right of the reception is a large relaxing room, the cabin has been designed to accommodate a gathering of folk in large numbers. This large sitting area is furnished with lovely leather sofas.

The tranquil atmosphere is bathed in beautiful angelic background music, low light with flickering candles and delicate incense. Once we'd finished our drinks, Gill invited me into one of the three cosy side rooms which again branching off the reception area. She asked me to lay fully clothed on a tall couch positioned in the middle of this small cosy room, allowing plenty of access for the healer to circle the couch. She placed a blanket over me for snugness, I soon started to feel relax. I decided to direct my meditation to prayer, that God would help and heal me.

As I lay down I felt the need to close my eyes, and before long Gill started to sing, she sounded like a Native American Indian lady chanting, my thoughts went back to when Julian was so ill and he told Gill that the Native American Indians had the best idea of how to live and die.

I recalled what he'd said to Gill when she asked him, "What can you see Julian?" With his eyes closed he said, "I can visualise an Indian who is preparing himself for death by retiring to a mountain top, he is sitting there cross-legged on the grass cocooned in a Buffalo skin over his shoulders, surveying the land and the mountains beyond."

Leaving my memory of Julian's visualisation behind I tried to concentrate on my own experience instead, it was strange that she was drawn to sing in this style of music. Gill unaware of my private thoughts started to sing in a deep female voice. With my eyes still closed, I visualised this middle aged woman dressed in traditional Indian attire, she wore her hair in two long thick black plats. She stood alone on the hill top with her arms out stretched upwards towards the sky wailing with such deep, deep sadness in her heart. She was staring at a burial scaffold with a dead person wrapped in buffalo skin, suspended high on stilts. Although I felt this deep, deep sorrow, I could not sob out loud, only cry gently. I could feel a trickle of tears cascading past my temporalis onto

377

the pillow. When the song finished I sensed Gill had moved to stand by my midriff, this time the tone of her chant had change completely, now she sang with a very young girls voice, the tone was lighter and more cheerful but still in Native American Indian style chant.

With my eyes still closed I visualised a young squaw had joined me now, and was singing beautifully beside me, her arms however were down beside her. As the song came to an end another song began, this time I sensed Gill had moved to my feet, and the older Indian lady was chanting again, this time the song was not so sad. The older woman was returned down the hill slowly constantly looking back and longing to be at the young squaw's side wishing it was her staying with the dead body not her.

The young squaw stood motionless and did not return the older woman's glances.

I appeared to join the path below (I had evidently become this older lady now, in my thoughts)

The singing stopped and slowly I opened my eyes and felt so relaxed as if I had been sleeping for 100years, I got up slowly thinking I wonder what all this meant.

Gill asked "What did you get out of that Olwen?" I told her about what I visualised.

She deciphered the visualisation as I was the older Indian, but I was also the younger Indian who had stayed with the dead, she represented the youth in me who will stay with Julian for ever along with the memories we shared together, while I must venture on the remainder of my journey to make new memories. Sad as it sounded, it did make sense.

I wondered if the experience would truly help me in the future, I'll have to wait and see. Although I already like the idea that Julian was keeping company with the younger version of me. I realised this was not strictly a dream, but deciphering dreams is nothing new the practice has been going on for centuries as far back as the Biblical times. In a strange way I did feel healed, but it seems that parents have been involved in this 'sound healing' for centaury's, when they pucker up their lip to kiss their injured child after a bump, the sound of the kissing makes the child think it will get better instantly just like when they have unknowingly they have administered 'hands on' healing, when parents rub the injured area after a fall, convincing the child it will soon get better.

Once it was explained to me in these simple terms, I felt more at ease with this 'mystery therapy' called sound healing and our faith was our privet concern or affair.

Evidently it's the oldest form of healing, we use sound vibration through voice, music and rhythm to create changes in the way we feel in our emotions and how it affects others around us. At the other end of the scale bad sounds can just as easily create the opposite such as the voice of a violent man, high pitch house alarm, an inconsolable crying baby, loud construction site or a hysterical screaming woman. Compare these noises to angelic music like the sound of a harp, birds singing in the woods or a beautiful singing voice, I'm feeling better already just thinking about it.

As I went to sleep that night my mind was still occupied with the word 'meditation' which reminded me of the lyrics in a song sung by a popular group in the 1970's called 'Boney M'who sang in one of their songs, "Let the words of your mouth and the meditation of your heart be accepted in thy sight here tonight" And as I drifted off I concluded if the treatment was harmless enough for Julian, then it was harmless enough for me.

But just like the older Indian, I <u>still</u> found it hard to let go of the connection of the past. One such incident I recall when I was out socialising one evening at a cheese and wine party, when one of the gentlemen came over to talk to me. His opening sentence to me was, "I'm very surprised that you're still wearing your wedding ring Olwen" I tried to defend myself but I felt as if I had been pushed over in a sense and in the process I'd lost my balance.

I wanted to shout stop, stop I don't want to carry on with this conversation, but the room was full yet again I felt I had to keep my feelings contained and not behave like a hysterical woman. After I had gathered my thoughts, I had the courage to say to him "I'm a widow not a divorcee"

He continued "I know, but the wedding ring you're wearing symbolises a contract you drew up with Julian on your wedding day, you have honoured that contract in sickness and in health till death do us part." I agreed quietly, but was very upset, something else society wants me to give up, my wedding ring! That night I rang my sister, who I thought was going to give me some sympathy. Gweno over the last few years tells it as it is, she thinks there's no point hiding behind white lies only to be confronted with the truth later. She listened intently then said

379

"Is this man a churchgoer?" I replied "Yes, that's what's shocked me". "But he's telling you the truth, you have honoured your contract, I don't know why you're getting so upset!"

A few evenings later I thought I better get to grips with these suppressed feelings, but where did I start? I decided to go back to where my sadness began. That was the morning the Ambulance men came to pick Julian up, at five thirty in the morning on the 9th October 2008. Silently that morning I wanted him to say good bye to his home, in case he didn't return.

This is the sort of memory I had shoved hard to the back of my mind, as I allowed myself to ponder on this moment, I started to sob uncontrollable it was ten o'clock at night when I started to cry and near eleven thirty when I finished. At last I realised I needed to do this with every painful sequence of events I had crushed to protect my feelings.

My next experience happened the very next day when I went into the garage while reaching over I came across his CD player. Julian used to listen to it when he was usually repairing or engineering something new. I decided to take it into the house to clean and to my surprise I found a tape in the recorder, I turned it on; the words were so poignant I thought Julian was speaking to me. I started to cry and I quickly turned it off, I didn't like being out of control and decided I would listen to this when I knew I wouldn't be disturbed.

That evening I locked the back door and took his CD player upstairs to listen to in private, but as I opened the bedroom a most gorgeous orange sun set awaited me yet again those lyrics came to mind, "Light up the sky like a flame" It was so dramatic I wanted to savour the moment forever so I impulsively took a photograph of the this beautiful evening sky before settling down to listen to his tape, then I nervously switching on the tape.

Photograph of the evening sun through my bed room window
as I listened to Julian's unlabelled tape.

My suspicions were well founded, the words were poignant.
Ironically the titles of the song came in this order, just as if he was having
a conversation with me. Could it be that Julian was speaking to me
through music; every title tore at my heart strings.

1. "It's five in the morning, and sorrow in your eyes"
2. "Lady, are you crying, do the tears belong to me?"
3. "I have to say, it's been a good life"
4. "I'm sorry to be leaving you, but I have to go!"
5. "We have memories that can't grow old"
6. "Hold me like you'll never let me go"
7. "If I could give you one day"
8. "Our lives became in twined"
9. "I'm as close to you as I can be"
10. "Why do we have to fight, when I have to go?"
11. "When my day is done, I'll still be friends with you"
12. "Let me die in your arms"
13. "What a friend we have in time"
14. "The mountains will teach us to be free"
15. "Seek the wisdom of the children"
    And the last one was,

16. "How nice it is to sit a while by the fire and watch
    my friends and lady sit, and pass the pipe around.
    How nice it is to love someone, how right it is to care"

Most of them don't need an explanation, but I wonder about number seven, what would he say or do if he did have a day to give me?

Number ten of course disturbs me greatly, because of the last words he spoke to me, why do we have to fight, but then number eleven gives me new hope, that he will still be friends with me. Number twelve states let me die in your arms; he did die in my arms from 'natural causes' Number thirteen of course generations have been telling us since time began, time is the only healer. Number fourteen, Well!, it was in the mountain at Carols Cabin while having sound healing I found my freedom. Number fifteen; I listen very careful to what Llewela has to say to me now, as she is wiser than her years as the song suggests 'seek the wisdom of the children'

Listening to those words were so painful, they made me realise I had just exposed the tip of my nerve endings I realised now I wasn't totally healed, what if I heard one of these songs in 20 years from now? How would I cope? There was nothing for it I had to listen to this tape all day every day until I didn't cry any more. Then I knew I would be healed; from this episode at least.

The next few days were tough, answering phones calls or talking to people without telling them what I was going through was hard. Was this tape a coincidence or are we attracted to words, melodies and sentiments that appear to contain massages for us. Incidentally I don't know where the tape came from, because it was defiantly not his style of music. More to the point, I'd never heard him play the tape as I constantly took cups of tea to him into the garage.

My second most painful experience was dealing with his working clothes. Although Id managed to get rid of his best clothes, I just couldn't bring myself to throw away the clothes he actually worked in. This was proving to be more difficult because of what they represented. I was on a roll now, I was sad anyway so I might as well get on with it. The next day happened to be a beautiful hot summers day so I decided to open this taped up box on the lawn containing his work cloths. I couldn't believe it, after 18 month of not wearing them; bearing in mind I had washed them before putting them away, the smell of Julian jumped out at me. I sobbed; I didn't know how I was going to throw these away while they still smelt of Julian; that was like throwing Julian away, secretly I was thinking; what would he wear if he came home? It's what the clothes symbolised that made me sad, when he wore them there was either great engineering going on or something new was been designed and produced or returning an old useless thing into its former glory. To overcome this stumbling block in my life I decided to put the clothes back in the box and pull them in and out of the box as many times as I liked every day until I didn't cry any more. After a couple of weeks of doing it daily, the realisation came to me one morning after I dreamt I saw him standing tall and looking slim wearing tight white trousers, white shirt and a white cricket type jumper. When I woke I realised this world had no further use for his clothes, not now or ever, not now their owner had left. His working days was now over I could make the trip to the tip to discard them at last. You have to understand these were his old working cloths that could not be recycled they were full of grinding holes, sever scuffs from saw damage, dried lumps of wood filler, welding burn spots, paint dribbles, wood glue marks, blobs of sealant, oil finger prints all tattered and torn. I made my long overdue trip to the tip and ceremoniously dropped each article in the skip, still with a tinge of sadness that I would not see these clothes in action ever again.

This next experience was going to be tough, trying to make sense of why my own kind had let me down so badly and embarrass me like they did in front of Julian. But much worst, how could they let Julian down. Why didn't the nurses question the many side effects he was suffering and become his advocate along my side?

Confronting this issue was going to affect me greatly, I felt as if I was running my own kind or family down. Why Oh! Why didn't they listen to him when he begged them to stop? It is this very topic I didn't want to pursue with the NMC and GMC because I didn't want to point fingers causing others to jeopardise their job. But at the same time; if I excluded this part in my book, how could I rest easy knowing others could suffer and endure the same end? I asked myself how would I like things to be differently in the future. In a fantasy world I would like the entire medical profession who dealt with Julian during those last five weeks of his life to be placed in a mirrored dome to reflect their actions on how they treated him. In a realistic world I would like them to develop a deeper understanding of this modern Type two Diabetes, secondly I would like them to recognise the suffering he endured at their hands following the administration of their medical treatment, thirdly I'd like them to re-consider that his Adrenal Tumour must have had an effect on his glucose levels, fourthly I would like to remind them that all patients have the right to refuse treatment, fifthly I would like to remind them that they don't have the right to disrespect his opinion when they felt their treatment was harming him, sixthly I would like to remind them they did not have the right to continually bombard him into taking treatment once he had been offered informed choices. And finally, now they know his outcome would they still have treated him in the same manner or would they conduct themselves differently by reconsidering the abuse he suffered in their care and the lack of attention they gave him regarding his consent to refuse treatment?

I don't know, some of them might; all I'm asking them to do is place themselves in Julian's position, and ask themselves, how would they like to be treated with drugs that they knew was harming them to the point of excruciating pain and impounded on them every four or six hours.

At the same time I wouldn't want anyone's career destroyed on the strength of a mistake following a long line of good service, but this was not one mistake this was repeatedly giving someone drugs that the patient believed was harming him. This was not a one off slip-up; this was an on-going deliberate drug admission that lasted for five long weeks. I can't begin to express the anguish he felt each time someone came towards him to either persuade him to take the drugs or to take the drug he knew he'd suffer physically within minutes. This was nothing short of adult bullying followed by adult abuse of the very worst kind.

Adult Abuse

Albert Einstein once said, "The world is not dangerous because of those who do harm, but because of those who witness harm and do nothing about it" I saw this quote on a teaching board at a Hospital. The topic was on "Adult abuse".

The teaching board stated that there are four types of adult abuse, Physical, Psychological, Sexual, Financial and Neglect. If onlookers who do nothing are considered more dangerous than the abuser, then where does that leave me if I was to do nothing about Julian's suffering at the end? Can you all now see why I have to raise concern!

I feel the abuse Julian suffered at their hands were physical, psychological and neglect.

'Physically' when the syringe punctured his skin and he begged them not to administer the drugs.

Secondly 'Psychologically' when he lived in fear of the medical staff approaching to persuade him to take the drugs, when he knew he would always loose the battle of wits against them and the nurses psychologically belittling him further by informing him that they have old ladies who inject their own insulin.

And thirdly; 'Neglect' when they failed to respect his entitlement to refuse treatment by law, never mind maintaining his hydration by allowing him free oral fluids forcing dehydration on already a dry crisp body. Then worsening a sad situation by insisting he accepted diuretics.

Poor Julian, his wisdom on every topic in life had always gained him respect in every walk of life, how sad for this respect to be snatched away from him at his time of life, when he had struggled all these years to maintain it.

Question is who's responsible for reporting adult abuse?

Adult abuse is everyone's concern, warning signs to look out for are-.

Vulnerable adults appear uncharacteristically frightened, withdrawn, distressed, agitated, anxious or aggressive in the presence of another person.

Julian was frightened of the staff, he was always saying to me, "Please don't leave me alone Olwen, someone might come and give me something while your away." I barely had time to go to the toilet, that's how frightened this man had become; this description does not depict Julian Davies at all.

<u>Another sign</u>, significant and unexplained changes in his mood or behaviour!

Julian's normal behaviour had defiantly changed; he was now constantly looking round checking all the time to see who was about, as if he was on guard a truly pitiful sight.

<u>Another sign</u> was they have Difficulty in getting to see the vulnerable person or seeing them alone.

That's true; nursing staff might agree with this, and his family, because of my presence, but Julian was using me as a human shield to protect himself from further drugs and from his mother who was constantly begging him to take the drugs. Ironically, she detested taking prescribed drugs!

<u>Another sign</u> was vulnerable adult defers all decisions to another person.

This I can relate to, Julian was always asking me to ask the staff and Doctors to stop the Insulin instead of insisting himself. This was so unlike Julian, he was always the strong one who 'knew it all' in our partnership. He was as they say, very much his own man.

<u>Another sign</u>, unexplained deterioration in a person's physical health

Julian always predicted that his skin would break down beyond belief if he carried on with the treatment. How true his fears were! He also lost four and a half stone in five weeks.

<u>Another sign</u>, vulnerable adult seems overly eager to please carer.

When the medical staff were telling him his only course of action, Julian would always try to please them in other ways so he could be let off the drugs. I'd never seen Julian stoop so low, on occasions he looked like a 'beggar in the street' with outstretched arms begging the medical profession to stop the treatment; he normally treated them as equals. He was well known for calling a 'spade a spade' before this last admission

There is another form of neglect, with vulnerable adult and that is failure to ensure adequate medical treatment. I would go further by stating 'failing to ensure adequate nutrition and fluid' as neglect. In some cases medicine can be considered as, 'Food that harm and food that heals' food can sometimes be the best medicine especially if the patient is starving.

In those last five weeks of Julian life the two of us lost nine stone in weight between us; if we'd gone to weight watchers I'm sure we would probably have made the news headlines.

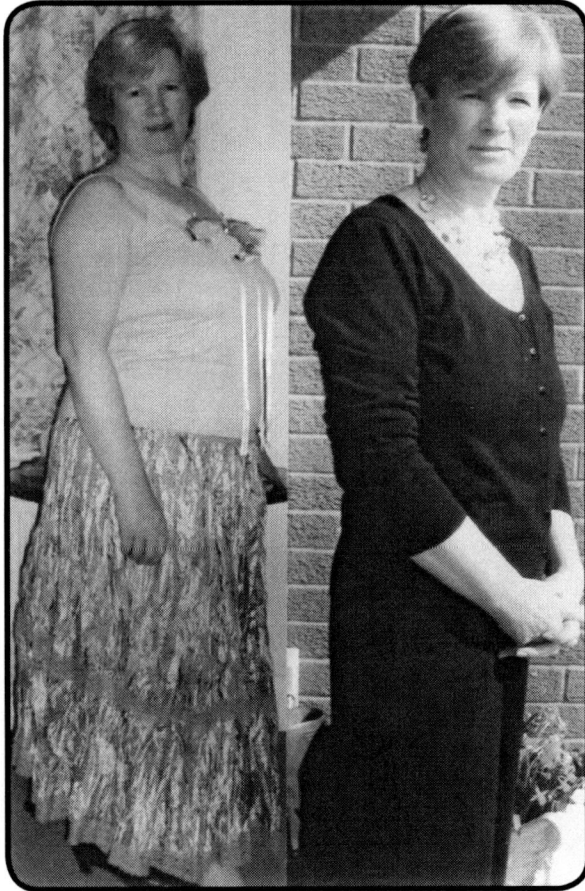

I don't have a photograph of Julian after his weight loss, but this is a 'before and after' one of me.

Abuse is a violation of an individual's human rights and civil rights by any other person.

He didn't have the choice to die in his own bed in his own home.

It can also be an omission to act.

Nursing staff did this by not raising people's awareness of Julian's difficulties.

A vulnerable adult is a person complaining of illness and unable to protect themselves against significant harm or serious exploitation.

Julian was unable to get people to understand that the treatment he was receiving was causing him server pain which he also felt was also harming him.

<u>Whose duty is it to report abuse?</u>

Whatever position you hold in life, we all have a duty to report any allegation or suspicion of abuse of a vulnerable adult.

<u>What are my responsibilities?</u>

It states, "Safeguarding a vulnerable person is everybody's responsibility".

That is what I was trying to do, safeguarding Julian's life but sadly I failed.

What a failure I turned out to be!

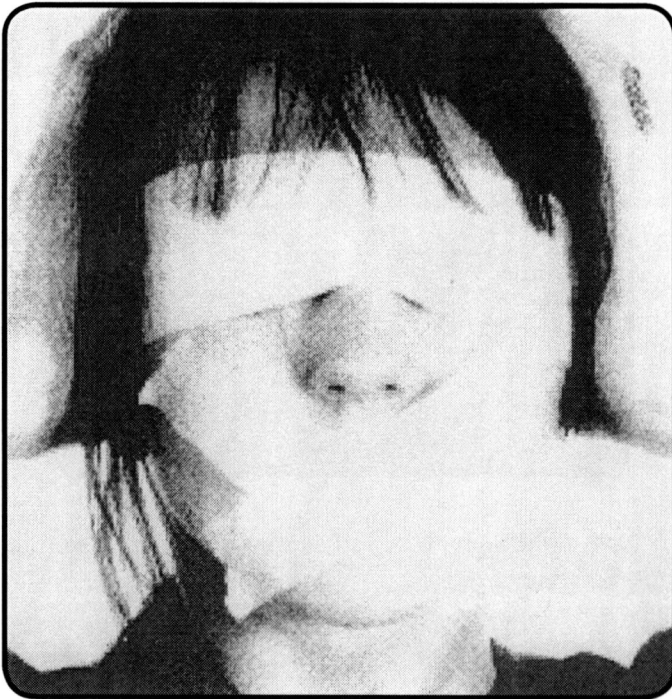

Hospital poster informing society, '
Abuse is everybody's businesses'

This photograph is meant to depict how a patient might feel if they are abused, but in actual fact this is exactly how both Julian and I felt for five weeks bound, gagged and blindfolded.

<u>Under Code of Professional Conduct it states nurses must—</u>:

- Respect the patient as an individual
- Must obtain consent before giving any treatment.
- Must act to identify and minimise the risk to patient.

<u>Under Standard for Medicines Management, it states nurses must—</u>:

- Be certain of the identity of the patient to whom the medicine is to be administered.
- Must check that the patient is not allergic to the medicine before administering it.
- Must know the therapeutic use and side effect.
- Must administer or withhold in the context of the patient's condition.

<u>Under the Physical Abuse it states—</u>:

Any physical contact which harms the patient or is likely to cause them unnecessary and avoidable pain and distress, example includes giving medication inappropriately.

<u>Under Verbal Abuse it states—</u>:

- Any remarks made to a patient which is sarcastic or using condescending tone of voice

<u>Under Neglect it states—</u>:

Failure on the part of the registered nurse to meet the patients' needs examples, were fluids, medical aids and assistance.

<u>Under Staff Attitudes it states—</u>:

The practitioner who seeks to control clients.

<u>Under when Consent is Refused it states—</u>:

Legally, a competent adult patient can either give or refuse consent to treatment, even if that refusal will shorten their life. Therefore you must respect the patient's refusal just as you would their consent.

There are many more rules and regulations of course but I have only highlighted the ones that Julian was directly affected by.

For this man to survive allergies, reaction and serious side effects like he did, he must have been in possession of a will of iron.

The man with a will of iron

I hope in reading these pages you have experienced the pleasure in meeting Julian Paul Davies and that I have done justice to his memory, recognise the courage he had in dealing with his disability, admiration in his endless charity work, determination to follow his dreams, his persistence in trying to make the diabetic treatment succeed but most of all for showing dignity when dealing with the medical profession when others would of raised their voice and displayed verbal aggression. Sadly in the end, his self-control cost him his life.

This title reminded me of some ancestors Julian told me he belonged to, who also experienced psychological abuse but lucky for them, they like Julian were blessed with a will of iron also.

At the beginning of 1982 while we were waiting for the contracts to be completed on the 'Off Licence shop' quite soon after we were married, I embarked on a small project of Julian's family tree in the hope of finding out some interesting facts. Although Julian carried the family name of Davies, one set of his Grandparents were descendants of the 'Christian' line from Manx on the Isle of man, the other female line were the 'Kelly's' from Ireland. Unbeknown to me Julian had already researched as far as he could on both sides while conducting a family tree during a school project, years previously.

On the Christian side of his family he was convinced he was connected to Christian in the 'Mutiny on the Bounty' Fletcher Christian, was born on 25th September 1793 (189 years before Julian)

Fletcher's father died when he was only four years old, Fletcher was known to have been educated with William Wordsworth and proved to be an excellent scholar and chose a Naval Career. His widowed mother fled from England with her three children back to the Isle of Man, after running up a huge debt. Luckily for her she was a descendant of a Gentry line. Following the mutiny on the ship called 'The Bounty', Fletcher docked and on the 16th June 1789 he married a daughter of a local chieftain while out in Tahiti. He is said to have fathered three children leaving his Christian descendants on the Island. It's not quite clear if he was murdered in 1793 at the age of 29 on the Island or he escaped to the British shores, where it is said he was sighted several times on many docks.

His other claim to fame is he was seen on a shilling 1/—stamp in 1940 with King George V1.

Julian claimed on the Kelly side of the family that he'd made a link with a certain 'Ned Kelly' the Australian outlaw. Ned was the head of the family at the tender age of 12, he was originally wrongly accused of hitting a Chinese man with a bamboo stick, which he claims he was protecting his sister from being molested by this china man. Sometime later he was accused of cattle steeling and served 3 years imprisonment, a crime he again claimed he did not commit. He is described by his countrymen as a man unwilling to bend to injustice, no wonder. Australians feel he was hounded into crime, but in death feel little short of martyrdom. He was hunted down for 2 years which drove him to have an iron 'suit of armour' made for his extraordinary "Last stand" Poor Ned was caught, convicted and hanged on 11th November 1880. When Ned was about to be garrotted, as he stepped forward onto the platform it is said he uttered these words in a low voice, "Such is life"

In the year 2000, Australians were asked to vote on whether they felt Ned Kelly had received a fair trial before he was sentenced to death, 91% voted against. Ellen Kelly his mother out lived all her children and grandchildren and was asked in 1923 at the grand age of 93 what her last words on her son Ned were? Her reply was, "Mind you die like a Kelly son"

You may ask, "why have I mentioned these two ancestors of Julian", well if it was true that Julian was truly a descendant of these two characters in history then maybe he had more in common with them than I first thought.

- All three had a will of iron.
- All three would not bow down, if they felt they had been wronged.
- All three had their freedom threatened.
- All three felt they were wrongly punished.
- All three felt their cause was worth dying for.
- Ned wore his metal amour for protection, where as poor Julian was caught short although he'd possessed a metal helmet and

was in the process of making his chain mail armour, sadly not finished in time.

- Ned's life ended by hanging on the 11th November, discussion took place on the 11th November 2008 to terminate Julian's life. The ventilator wasn't actually turned off until the 12th November in other words both nearly died on Remembrance Day; I wonder if both will be remembered for different reasons.

- Fletcher and Ned have had books written about them, Julian has one now too.

- Fletcher and Ned have had films made about them, I wonder if Julian will one day?
  Mel Gibson was portrayed as Fletcher Christian and Orlando Bloomer was portrayed as Ned Kelly.

- I feel Julian died like Ned, both quietly going to the gallows before their time. After all Julian did say on many occasion it felt as if he was forced to commit suicide each time he was given the drugs.

- They all lived lives we only dream about, by being extraverts and living life to their limits but in the end all three of them paid dearly for their 'free spirit' because in death all three were forced to become outcasts in society, one was hunted, one was impounded and Julian was imprisoned.

None of them were allowed to live or die as they wanted, or as free men in the end. Julian valued life above everything; I read a quote by Mother Teresa who once said, "Abortion is murder in the womb. A child is a gift from God, if you do not want him, give it to me" This is what I felt Julian was in possession of, the wonderful gift of life so why would he want to give up on it? But rest assured Julian, in the end you did exactly what Ned's Mother asked of you which was, "Mind you die like a Kelly's son"

I admire what Julian's father wrote in his last birthday card "You have borne your suffering with such valence" I will add to that, "He fought death silently"

Some people might say because of his 'will of iron' Julian was difficult to reason with on occasions, but a weakling could not have survived or achieved what he did in his number of years if he had been a mouse. Not to colour too colourful a picture of Julian for those who did know him,

393

although he was a wise man he did not suffer fools gladly. As Llewelas teacher and guide, she inadvertently picked up his traits and like him, will not be down trodden easily.

Even in death Julian like Ned and Fletcher are still touching the lives of people they never even met. That is quite powerful, don't you think! People who never met Julian are still saying to me even now, "It's a pity I never met Julian, I'm sure I would of got on with him" They're right they would have, he always managed to get the best out of every body, and fire up some passion in either them or for his cause. I feel it was Julian's wild imagination people loved and admired the most; he always looked outside the box and always with a sense of humour. Another quote I found by Albert Einstein, "Imagination is more important than intelligence" I suppose not even Professors can invent without a wild imagination.

To the man who once said to me after Julian's death, "It must have been like looking after a baby" I can assure you I never nursed him for a single day out of pity, but I did care for him out of love. He was twice the man of most able bodied men I know.

He had such a huge personality and as a character he was a force to be reckoned with, and of cause he was nearly always right. I miss his right choices in life right now. But I have to make do with my own decisions in life and live with the consequences. But it was definitely not like nursing a baby! It was more like being in the army and being a valet for a Major. Nothing babyish about our setup, to be truthful I miss his military-ness. But his Major-ness helped him to be single minded with all his tasks, in other words his will of iron helped him overcome every obstacle. He never allowed his Disability to cripple him; it was not in charge of him, he was in charge of his ability. In fact he could have been a good Rehabilitation officer. He had the intellect to outwit them, he had the stamina to keep up with them and he had the empathy to push them to their limits, but most of all he had the excitement, humour and originality in his expectation of them. In other words, they would have had a lot fun!

Question of Diabetes

On a more serious note, I need to get to the root of why Julian could not tolerate modern drugs.

In the words of a Chines philosopher called Lao Tzu who once said, "Every journey begins with a single step" The first step of 'Julian's Diabetic' journey started when his GP rang him at home informing him of his new diagnoses. The rest of the mysterious journey is about why his high blood glucose could not be controlled and worst still why he couldn't tolerate the treatment he was forced to take! Ofcaurse my other triumph will be when I reassure the doctor who managed to make me feel so 'stupid' when he mockingly said, "Be reasonable Mrs Davies, how can your husband possibly be allergic to something as natural as Insulin, when we all need it to survive. After all, what we're giving him is Human Insulin"

I agreed with what he said was correct, but something was defiantly not right in Julian's case!

I understood the management of Diabetes Type One which is diet, exercise and insulin injections. To confirm this I came across a physician called Dr. Elliot P. Joslin, who described it in a similar way in 1935 as a man manipulating his horses. I quote "I look upon the Diabetic as a charioteer and his chariot drawn by three steeds named Diet, Insulin and Exercise. It takes a strong will to drive one horse, intelligence to manage a team of two, but a man must be a very good teamster to get all three to pull together."

I felt this was a good parable on how to manage Diabetes Type One successfully.

However Julian was not diagnosed with Type One he was diagnosed with Type Two Diabetes, but no matter how hard the medical profession tried to treat him he didn't fit into any of their medical text-book descriptions. It was like trying to stuff a round cog into a square hole, Julian did not or could not conform because his body did not respond to treatment and worst still it reacted to it.

I used to think that taking care of Type Two Diabetics was reasonably simple, just a matter of feeding the person with a controlled amount of carbohydrate, sugar free diet with plenty of fruit and vegetables not forgetting adequate exercise, failing that oral anti-diabetic medication accompanied by regular blood glucose monitoring. That's simple enough, don't you think?

Thinking back I recalled a Doctor at Oswestry once referring to Julian's troublesome diabetic case as 'Julian's Diabetes'. He was obviously troubled enough to refer to it as Julia's complaint otherwise he would of called it either type one or type two. He did say it in a light hearted manner, but they do say, 'never a truer word spoken in jest'.

I knew there was more to this miserable situation than met the eye. There was something sinister lurking under the surface just as the retired Chief Inspector said at my parent's house a few nights after Julian died, "Clearly something is not right"

So now I intend to do some detective work of my own, my mission is to find out what's clearly not right, if anything at all!

When Julian was alive I mentioned before we both were television-addicts, more of documentary addict's really. Since his death I have watched next to nothing of television, but one program we both enjoyed when he was alive was 'Brother Cadfael' the blend of both historical and fiction monk detective based ironically in Shropshire around 1137. Little did I think when I followed the series, that one day I may become a modern day Cadfael studying how and why Julian suffered and died like he did in Shropshire of all places.

My first thoughts were how grateful I was for those 15 months grace when I was blessed with Julian's extended company, after he had been allowed by some medical professor to discontinue his diabetic treatment, between the summer of 2007 through to the winter of 2008.

This Detective work is not just about how and why Julian died, it's also about should the rest of us be worried and are we heading in the same direction as him?

Maybe if we choose to ignore what's going on, it should be at our peril. If the scientists are correct in thinking it's only a matter of time before we are all diagnosed with Type Two Diabetes in the near future in that case I need to work 'flat out' on finding out what's going on and how it can be halted. As professors and learned men could not successfully treat Julian, could it be possible they were looking for a too complicated an answer in which case I needed to keep it simple?

This brings to mind, a disagreement Julian and I often used to have when the postman arrived with a reply from 10, Downing Street. He used to shout from the front door, "Olwen, will you stop sending letters to Number 10 they will be getting fed up with you; they know how to run the country". I used to snatch the letter out of his hands spinning round saying, "Well they don't; they need a simple mind like mine to work some things out. People at the top don't always know the answers; it's often the people on the shop floor who can see what's causing the problem"

Looking back I can't help thinking that maybe Julian's 15 months of treatment free might have happened for a reason. Could it be that, I <u>had</u> to witness his survival without treatment in order for it to stir up enough passion in me to investigate Julian's unusual case after his death.

As Julian did not have a history of Diabetes in his family, I thought I'd look to see how serious this complaint was becoming. Statistics from Diabetic UK revealed that there are 1.8 million people with diabetes in the UK today, 1.5 million of those have Type Two Diabetes. That means there are only .3million people registered with Type One. So where have all these Type Two come from? This reflects an increase of 400,000 people in just 8 years. Why?

Ten million pounds a day is spent on treating diabetes. (That's a good money spinner)

Diabetes UK seems to think, that's it's because we as a nation are putting weight on our mid rift, which is indicative of bringing on Diabetes. Why has this come about? I read that eating carbohydrates containing white refined flour and products containing white sugar causes sudden and unusually high spikes in the blood levels and stimulates the pancreas to produce insulin. A constant over stimulation of our pancreas, year in year out causes the "internal machinery" to wear out prematurely.

In other words the pancreas cannot produce enough insulin so when it hears the frequent "Dinner Bell" ringing it gets tired of hearing it and stops running to the blood sugars defence. Consequently the exhausted pancreas requires extra help, which is additional insulin. It's at this stage a person gets labelled Type 2 Diabetic. Although the explanation above makes sense to me, there is still something lurking in the back of my mind telling me "There is more to this that meets the eye"

Before I go any further, I wish to apologise to anyone I may have caused distress to over their Diabetes treatment, but if your treatment is trouble free there is no need for you to read any further. Do you remember I mentioned a nurse telling Julian once, "One should feel <u>instantly </u>better once you start taking diabetic treatment whether it is tablet or insulin"?

My only concern is that everybody deserves the right to be treated equally, and should be offered appropriate treatment with harmless medication that others have access to.

This Insulin 'malarkey' can confuse the brightest of people including a simple minded person like myself. I do however feel that over the years the medical profession namely Diabetic Nurses or Specialists keep moving the goal post when it comes to Diabetes.

In years gone by patients had to weigh everything they eat, potatoes, meat etc. All their food was manhandled onto a set of weighing scale before it was transferred on the plate to be eaten.

Yak! How appetising does that sound? Of cause, one definitely was not allowed sugar or alcohol.

Modern day diabetic type two are educated differently, they can have a little bit of this and a little bit of that as long as it's in moderation. Frankly I think this 'moderation diet' confuses people, I don't wish all diabetics to hate their life style I just don't see any constructive guidelines.

Then there is a huge confusion about Type 1 and Type 2 Diabetes.

Traditionally Type 1 has been around since time began. Found at birth and referred to as a juvenile or congenital Diabetes, they do not produce any Insulin at all in their Pancreas and they rely solely on an emergency alternative donation of Insulin and without it, it can be life threatening.

That one is pretty clear, the Diabetic person is in total control of its own body; a little bit like a scooter that runs on a two stroke mixture, which is petrol with a few drops of oil needed to function properly.

Type two Diabetes on the other hand, produces some insulin but not sufficient. Originally it used to affect adults between the age of 40 and 50 years of age. Sadly in recent years the condition is now affecting adults as young as 30 and even younger. This type of Diabetic person used to be successfully treated on diet alone but in recent years General Practitioner's felt forced to prescribe anti-diabetic medication. In no time at all Type Two Diabetes appears to be even more out of control and suddenly they had to be treated with additional anti-diabetic treatment.

Soon Type Two Diabetics had no alternative but to commence on Insulin, but mysteriously these Type Two were still experiencing raised glucose levels. "Why"?

Something is definitely not right; to me they look pale faced, unwell, exhausted, unable to sleep at night and constantly cat napping in the day. Are we sure we are not soaking them in drugs to no avail? This is where the confusion sets in, people who were once diagnosed as Type Two Diabetics are now fast becoming Type One and psychologically the sufferers feel they are switching sides and turning red coat as the saying goes. Why isn't everybody asking the same question as myself, "How can a Type Two Diabetic suddenly jump to Type One Diabetic, how can this be right"?

They were never juvenile diabetics, so what has changed in their body function for their pancreas to suddenly produce very little insulin to no insulin at all.

Something must have changed in our environment for them to stop producing insulin altogether!

I once said to Julian at his bed side, "Wouldn't it be funny if it was something as simple like a vitamin or a mineral your lacking" He got very angry and said, "For goodness sake Olwen, if it's something as simple as that try and find out, because right now it's not very funny at all, I'm in absolute agony in fact it feels as if the treatment is killing me" So what was going on?

As Julian didn't have any family history of Diabetes I thought I'd latch on to this word <u>History</u>, how long has diabetes been around?

History of Diabetes

Firstly I looked up the definition of the word History; it stated 'History is a recording of a memory of past experience, which can later be recovered to study previous knowledge'

What I understood from that is history should be used as a tool to reflect on the past, in order not to repeat the same mistakes in the future. Military and Navel men through the ages have learnt from past battles, recorded by their ancestors in order not to fail in future battles. Maybe I should take a leaf out of their book and do the same.

Recently I've heard Diabetes being referred to as a Disease, in my mind it defiantly not a disease it's a disorder. I looked up the definition of both descriptions; it stated Disease is <u>contagious and infectious</u> whereas a Disorder is a <u>disturbance of order</u>. That definition concludes that Diabetes is not contagious. Maybe people are getting mixed up with the phrase 'Diabetic Epidemic', which could then misleads some into thinking it's a Disease! Well! We all knew we couldn't contract Diabetes from each other. I digress my plan is to go back in history to find when Diabetes started and was there ever a time we didn't have diabetes?

It appears the world has been affected by Diabetes Type One since before the year of our lord, how long before I don't know.

The earliest diagnostic tool I found was recorded in 1920.

1. In pre 1920's they only had the Ants test.
2. In 1921 the first diabetic dog was treated.
3. In 1935 they discovered Type 2 Diabetes Mellitus.
4. In 1935 we were introduced to Pork and Beef Insulin.
5. In the 1950's the first oral anti-diabetic tablet was given.
6. In 1960 urine dip strips were introduced.
7. In the 1970's Glycalside oral anti-diabetic came on the market.
8. In 1982 they manufactured Genetic Engineered Insulin.
9. In 1995 Metformin oral anti diabetes treatment came on the market.
10. In 1999 Avandia was introduced on to the open market.

I will enlarge on these historical events in order.

The original test I could find was the 'ant test' recorded in pre 1920's. Where a physician Dr. Thomas Willis would collect a patient's sample of urine and leave it outside overnight. If the ants congregated over it by the morning, he concluded the patient's body was 'honeyed'!

The second discovery was made in 1921 when a young surgeon treated a dog with some murky mixture of pancreas extract; he then administered the first sample to a young boy who survived. Up until then, patients went into a comma and would gasp for air; they called this, 'Hunger for air' or 'Internal Suffocation'. At this stage families were allowed to pay their last respects. (Sorry to mention this one, I found this one very disturbing myself.)

The third discovery was in 1931 when it was recognised and then later reconfirmed in 1936 that Insulin Resistance was the underlying cause of Type 2 Diabetes Mellitus. Remember this small fact I will recap on this one later.

The forth discovery was in 1935 when two types of insulin was introduced, and mass produced for the growing need of life saving insulin. The insulin was extracted from Swine and Bovine Pancreas, otherwise referred to as Pork and Beef insulin.

The fifth discovery was in 1950 when a Diabetic oral medication was discovered called Tolbutamol. This was discontinued when it was linked to bladder cancer and cardiovascular problems including death. It carried side effects of weight gain, hypersensitivity to Sulfonamide including drug interaction.

The sixth discovery was in 1960 when urine dip strips were introduced to detect Glucose, Ketenes, Specific Gravity, Blood, pH balance, Protein, Nitrogen, and Leucocytes.

This testing was strictly adhered to up until the late 1970's but has been eradicated completely in recent years.

The seventh discovery was Glycoside, a bit of a mystery drug. I was unsuccessful in finding out who discovered it or who produced it or in which year it was brought onto the market. Thought to be second generation drug of Talbutamol !!!!!!!

The side effects of Glycoside were mainly gastrointestinal problems causing nausea, vomiting, diarrhoea and in some cases meteorism which is flatulent distension of the abdomen leading to bowel necrosis. The most obvious side effect was flushing of the face after intake of alcohol.

The only thing that disturbed me greatly was; one can purchase this drug on the internet with no restrictions or questioning of proof if the user is a diabetic. I'm not talking about ¼lb of sweets from the corner shop here; this type of online purchases could well be life threatening if its administration was abused.

The eighth discovery was in 1995 when Metformin oral Diabetic treatment came on the market. I found an interesting write up in the Oxford medical journal about this one "They would like to remind the Prescribe (Doctors) of a commonly fatal complication of Metformin therapy in patients with liver or renal disease and cardiac problems leading to developing multi-organ failure with poor prognosis and die."

Quite soon after Julian's death I worked with a German Doctor, who informed me it was their hospital policy to withhold Metformin for 2 days prior to surgery and 7 days after surgery as they believed it lead to Myocardial Infarction (heart attack)

I am not aware that Hospitals in this country take the same precaution!

Metformin now carries the FDA warning for Doctors to be more cautious when prescribing, but I don't know how serious they are taking their advice.

Metformin is still widely used in this country often unbeknown to patients under generic names such as Glucophage, Glucophage XR, Glumetza, Fortamet, Riomet and Glucorance.

I read Metformin does not produce Insulin; instead it blocks the liver from releasing sugar! I wasn't comfortable with this word 'Block' it felt as if this was going against nature. Concerned about my findings I contacted a Hospital Pharmacy, who felt 'The Medical Information Centre' would be more helpful. After contacting the centre, she said the topic was too complicated and she would ring me back, which she kindly did. She explained that Metformin reduces the amount of glucose that is produced by the Gall bladder; therefore less insulin is required for the body to function. But she didn't mention any measuring technique available to gauge how much or how little insulin an individual was producing? So it stands to reason if the body is still not producing adequate amounts of insulin after taking the Metformin then the glucose reading will still remain high; Correct or incorrect?

One of its many side effects is diarrhoea which was proving very popular with female diabetics as a weight controller. But more worryingly it seems some prescribers are giving Metformin to non-Diabetic obese young adults to aid losing weight, which may lead to anorexia. I understand the dilemma the GPs have with a surgery full of overweight children and they all have the potential of developing diabetes, but this does not sound like a good medical practice to me. My worry is; if this drug carries a multi-organ penalty with diabetics, why would you risk giving it to a non-diabetic youngster, isn't this taking an unnecessary risk?

If it doesn't feel right or sound right shouldn't we be questioning these practices?

Beware non-diabetics, scientists now claim Metformin can prevent cancer and slow down ageing. I expect it can if one dies of Lactic Acidosis first.

The ninth discovery was Avandia oral anti-diabetic tablet. Introduced on to the market in 1999, this one caused a lot of controversy into its safety in recent years. I saved a cutting from the Guardian newspaper regarding its safety after Julian had suffered the near-multi-organ-failure in 2007, this s was the newspaper Julian and I craved for, to offer as evidence to the Physicians at Shrewsbury. It was of little help to Julian when the two of us were stuck by his Hospital bed miles away from the safely saved cutting. On my return home I re-read the much needed Newspaper article in the Guardian. Splashed on the front page bearing the headlines "Scientists link Diabetes drugs to heart failure" This article was dated 27/07/07 It revealed that one in every 50 patients taking the drug over a period of 26 months will have to be hospitalised for heart failure, causing substantial burden on the hard pressed NHS. Most patients in the study did not have heart failure prior to starting the treatment. This drug was taken by 7 million people at the time in the USA. At the same time a British owned company boasted that European sales had grown by 20% and Avandia was their second bestselling drug.

This diabetic tablet was taken off the market in America and reported to cause Fatal Myocardium Infarction, (hole in the heart leading to death) but the GP`s in the UK were asked to be vigilant of its affects. When I asked Julian's GP about it, he said, "I haven't heard any such warnings about it". Avandia is otherwise known as Rosiglicazide.

My concerns were, how can GP`s be vigilant of a patient's condition when the GP is in the surgery and the patient is at home.!!! What's more it's even more difficult for the GP if they are not even aware of the warning that had been issued in 2007.

In another daily newspaper called the Daily Mail, three years later, it reported the same message but a different newspaper dated 20th July 2010, the head line stated, "Should you still be taking Avandia?"

In America, Glaxo Smith Kline paid out more than £330 million in compensation to US patients who suffered heart attacks, strokes and heart failure as a result of taking Avandia/ Rosiglitazone.

A Doctor Ralf Abraham of the London Diabetes and Lipid Centre said, "We have had serious doubts about the safety of Avandia for a number of years.

Then why have they allowed it to go on for so long? These are people's lives they are playing with.

I read in the Daily Mail of a, Doctor Karet, who advised Diabetes UK, "Ask your GP why you're on Avandia. In my opinion, the only reason would be if you also have a condition such as polycystic ovary that makes you insulin resistant. Ask if you should be on Actos or taking another diabetes drug altogether. You should be pushing your healthcare professionals to get up-to-date with the data".

I want to point out to all readers; the above is not my advice, but a quote from the Daily Mail. Avandia was found to have 43% increase risk of heart attacks and 27% increase risk of strokes, fractures of the upper arm, hands and feet, Macular oedema leading to blindness and hepatitis.

Europe has not yet taken it off the market, as the drug is under review. Why not, I ask myself?

I can't believe what I read next, they recommended a natural alternative to Avandia.

'Cara-Health-Blood-Sugar' it contains cinnamon, nettle, milk thistle and bilberry. It prevents the sharp rise and fall of blood sugar and reduces sugar craving on the receptors on the tongue. The cinnamon slows the rate of the stomach emptying after meals which prevents slumping of energy. I have nothing against herbal remedies, but it sounds as if they have gone from the ridiculous to the sublime.

America eventually banned Avandia in 2010 but Britain used the 'wait and watch' policy before following suit by banning it in 2011, by which time many people had suffered at its mercy.

I assume or trust, no one in the UK is taking Avandia any more, since its ban. Commission on Human Medicines (CHM) voted unanimously for Avandia's withdrawal from the UK but the recommendation was not made public. Why all the secrecy?

I read on line that if a patient demands to be on Avandia in America they have to sign a consent form to accept responsibility for any side effects. That's what you call consent in the reverse.

Patients in New Zealand were asked to contact their GP's to discuss alternative treatment to Avandia as soon as possible, and the drug was withdrawn off the market in on 29th April 2011.

When I read findings like this, with hindsight I can now see how Julian presented himself at Worcester Hospital with severe chest pain.

The drugs were then stopped just in time preventing him going the last lap into fatal multi organ failure, his recovery was exceptional. Julian was saved by a very clever Doctor who had the presents of mind to send that blood sample to the Poison Unit in Birmingham to be analysed.

He may of sent the blood samples for the wrong reasons (suspecting me of poisoning him, but lucky for me it proved it was the diabetic medication that was causing the toxicity) for me it turned out to be for the right reasons, clearing my name in the process. Fortunately for Julian too, the clever Doctor discontinued his treatment but he was not clever enough to document his findings in his notes or informing his colleagues verbally preventing the repetitions happening 15 months later, sadly causing Julian's fatality.

By not documenting this in the medical notes, his lack of attention to detail eventually had serious consequences on Julian's survival.

The tenth and most resent treatment introduced in to the Diabetic world is 'Synthetic Engineered Insulin'.

I thought that can't be true. So I decided to look into it.

I was shocked—I thought pork insulin came from pork?—Correct.

I thought beef insulin came from beef?—Correct.

I thought human insulin came from humans?—Incorrect.

Human insulin is made by man, in other words it's synthetically Genetically Modified **BY** humans, and hence this is how it gets its name, 'Human Insulin'. I was still not convinced, so again I rang a local Hospital, and asked to speak to the pharmacist to find out if this was true or not. To my surprise she said, "Yes, all NHS Insulin is genetically modified now." She then went on to ask why I was enquiring. I informed her I was trying to find out why my husband became so ill while he was taking human insulin, and wondered if it was the synthetic insulin that might be causing him to have such bad reactions. She then realised she was speaking to a member of the public and not to a member of staff. She advised me to take my husband to see his own GP; I informed her it was too late he died a year ago. The conversation came to an abrupt end.

Do we know enough about this Genetic Modified product, not only is it secretly producing our food but now I see its producing our life surviving medicine as well? It might have been proved safe, but I still don't know enough about it!

Genetic Engineered Insulin was introduced in to the world market in 1982. For anyone who is not sure how many types of insulin's there are on the market, here's a shortened list that has been compiled by a pharmacist.

Human Insulin comes under various names; they also vary in their length of action.

Short Acting Insulin's
Regular Insulin.
Humulin R.
Novolin R.

Medium Acting Insulin's.
Humulin N.
Novolin N.

Long Acting Insulin's.
Lantus. (Contra-indicate with diuretics, and any allergy)
Levemir.

Rapid Acting Insulin's.
Humalog Mixtard. (Contra-indicate with Diuretics, Thyroxin
and Growth Hormones found in pesticides)
Aspart/Aspart Protamine.
Novolog Mixtard.
Actrapid

I decided to look up what the content of some of this modern man
made Insulin contained just to see what Julian could have been allergic
to. I randomly chose Actrapid Insulin, as this was the one Julian was
prescribed the most during the last five weeks.
Actrapid Insulin claimed to contains

Hydrochloric Acid.
Zinc chloride.
Sodium hydroxide
Metacresol
Glycerol
Water.

I decided to look up each one individually. Firstly <u>Hydrochloric Acid</u>
can be found naturally in the stomach known as gastric juices. This acid
is powerful enough to breakdown a large slab of steak. It would have
to be, bearing in mind the stomach does not have a set of dentures or
teeth. I recall an Aunt of mine felt nauseas once, her husband asked her
to put her head through the car window as they were stuck in traffic.
She promptly vomited and immediately felt better, after arriving at their
destination it was discovered that where the hydrochloric acid in her
stomach had made contact with the passenger door it had striped it down
to bare metal. So I have always known how strong this hydrochloric Acid
was. It also derives from sulphur-uric acid, used in a household cleaning
product for de-scaling.
   Some of you might think, why, am I making an issue with this, it's
found naturally in the body. Yes I know, in the stomach not running
through my veins!
   The next one was <u>Zinc chloride</u>; although we need Zinc and
Magnesium for insulin to function adequately I could not find any
information to indicate the human body requires 'Zinc chloride' to

function. In its raw form its Toxicology is corrosive when inhaled and can destroy the upper respiratory tract, cause headache and vomiting. Contact with eyes can cause blurred vision; contact with skin can cause burns and ulceration.

No wonder Julian's sixth sense told him that his skin would break down beyond all recognition if he continued on Insulin plus his short stint of blindness.

The next was <u>Sodium hydroxide</u> otherwise known as Caustic Soda used as a drain cleaner.

No comment I can't even be bothered to go there I'm just sickened

The next was <u>Metacresol</u> this little blighter derives from coal tar, petroleum and creosote.

In its raw form it carries a health warning labelled as Health Hazard—Carcinogenic. (Cancer)

Blood Toxicant.

Gastrointestinal Toxicant. (Julian complained of severe abdominal pain)

Liver Toxicant. (Julian had raised liver function tests and swollen, painful liver area but only when he was on Insulin)

Kidney Toxicant (Julian complained of very painful kidney area when on Insulin)

Neuron Toxicant. (Julian complained of his brain hurting, tingling in his hands, loss of coordination, finally his mother had to help feed him. It affected his IQ and his social behaviour at the end)

Respiratory Toxicant. (Julian had difficulty breathing, and developed plural effusion when on insulin)

Sense Organ Toxicant. (Julian complained of freezing cold and painful organs)

Skin Toxicant. (Sadly Julian suffered total breakdown of the flesh, to the extent of a decomposing body accompanied by a decaying order while still living)

Last one was <u>Glycerol;</u> thankfully this appeared to be an organic component the only ingredient that was safe and free of any nasty side effects; With the exception of <u>water</u>!

Trying not to cause hysteria with the reader I realise these chemicals I have mentioned in the production of man-made Human Insulin are in their raw form and in minute quantities but I still find the 'recipe' very disturbing, it mentions very little natural products!

I fear our bodies are not yet immune to such harm.

Although I said I was surprised that Human Insulin was man made, now I have discovered what chemicals that have gone into it the word 'surprise' is too calm and I feel the word 'horrified' more fitting. Is there any wonder people, male or female, posh or poor, colour or creed is affected by these chemicals!

I also found under Precaution on the Actrapid insulin pamphlet, "Care should be taken when taking Actrapid, if you have problems with your **liver**, **adrenal gland** or **thyroid gland**."

Julian should never have been offered this insulin never mind insisting on administering it. A friend once said to me, "You don't want to take any notice of everything you read on the medication pamphlet, otherwise you won't take anything" but that's my point, we **<u>should</u>** take notice. Wake up Nation; it is dangerous to think like this. These money grabbing drug companies don't write about possible side effects for no good reason. To start with, it's not good sale technique to mention side effects, but it is cost effective to mention side effects if it gives drug companies a get out clause if a law suit might be pending.

We should all wizen up and heed their warnings, and act on them accordingly even to the point of demanding an alternative drug prescribed from the GP, it's our body not theirs.

My anger continues because I then discover that Human Insulin was allowed on the market after only a short trial. Approved process should take 2 years; the study involved a small number of 51 Insulin dependent diabetics from September 1983 to November 1984. That is only 13 months, 11 months short of the recommended 2 years. They suffered hypoglycaemia attacks with no warning of symptoms. It was licensed in Switzerland in November 1984 before the study results were known. In 1995 ten years later at a Diabetic Association Conference a Physician asked the Guest speaker Dr. D.M. Nathan, "When Human Insulin is not compatible, what should be done?"

The answer was "Animal Insulin needs to be available" But this is not possible as there is only artificial man-made human insulin available today.

Even Diabetic UK states, "Some people are not able to manage their condition effectively with Human Insulin"

Sadly I say to the Doctor who took me to one side behind closed doors at Shrewsbury Hospital in a condescending tone "Be reasonable

Mrs Davies, how can your husband or any one for that matter be allergic to something as natural as human Insulin?"

Well it seems that both of us had been hoodwinked in to thinking human insulin was from Humans therefore it was more natural and more compatible to humans than the old fashion pork and beef insulin. How misled we both were, nothing could be further from the truth, this insulin they held in such high esteem, which they used to humiliate both Julian and I is in fact choked up with chemicals.

I was right to be concerned about the make-up of this product called Insulin, I then started to wonder where it came from, my hunches were right there too, some drug companies now import Chinese and Japanese impure insulin.

Human Insulin is then manufactured by adding a small amount of this synthetic insulin to E.Coli and yeast, this method is used which then multiplies the insulin more rapidly, as we live in an allergy awareness world, not that anyone took any notice of Julian's allergy. It begs the question if the recipients are allergic to yeast, could it cause unrecognisable reactions. Additionally is there any research to indicate, if one takes sufficient amount of synthetic insulin that they might contract E.Coli?

I found another compound in Human manmade Insulin called, Protamine Sulphate. It has been associated with numerous clinically significant side effects including hypotension, pulmonary vasoconstriction and anaphylaxis. Does this sound safe to you?

Protamines derive from Salmon sperm and culperine from herrings. Shouldn't people who have fish allergy be made aware of this? Sulpha can be found in some antibiotics as well as diabetic drugs. Surely any one allergic to sulpha should also be made aware of this too.

I trust that everybody these days questions everything concerned with their treatment because it's your body, don't let others abuse it.

My heart goes out to people who are struggling to put what they believe to be wholesome food into their bodies to enable them to better control their diabetes only to chase their diet with these chemicals. How can they possibly gain glucose stability?

Others who experienced difficulties

I read of a couple of young men corresponding with each other on the internet, stating how they had experienced a near death experience after taking NHS insulin. When the other asked how he now managed his diabetes, he explained he imported all his Insulin from America. The response was, "I expect you live in fear of running out of Insulin, don't you?" The answer was, "Not as much as being involved in a car accident in this country and not be able to express my wishes not to have NHS Insulin, it will be like committing suicide." Suddenly it sounded like disavow, Julian expressed the same fear to me each time he was given Insulin his words were, **"it's like committing suicide"** and **"near a death experience"**

About 20 months after Julian died; I looked after a post-operative patient on the day care unit.

Written in big letters on the front of her notes were, 'Allergic to all diabetic medication' I quietly pointed this out to a colleague and my colleagues reply was, "Don't question it Olwen, her husband is a Consultant" I realised then that Julian didn't have a chance, because he didn't have a Consultant for a wife to act as his advocate, he only had me, a mere nurse!

The difference is; **I** respected this lady's wishes implicitly and of cause did not give her the drug or even try to coax her into taking it. If I had, I would have been in breach of something very serious.

I also read about a distressed wife who was beside herself with worry, she was asking on line if anyone was suffering with the same complaints as her diabetic husband and what advice could anyone offer her. She went on to say that her husband was complaining of frozen organs, the room was too hot to bear, he complained of painful abdomen (This sounded too familiar I thought)

A silly reply came from someone advising her to, "Tell your husband to keep up with his blood sugar monitoring" I was full of rage with this advice; it was not the monitoring that needed increasing; it was the cause that needed investigating. She made me feel cross because I didn't even feel qualified enough to answer this lady's plight, not even with my professional opinion or my identical personal witnessing my loved one suffering in the same way, yet this lady's answer felt flippant and unhelpful.

To the little 'Miss Know-it-all' who answered, "If you haven't lived with someone who has this complaint and tried to breath this disgusting stifling hot air that almost burns the inside of your lungs as it enters your nasal passage, PLEASE don't make stupid comments about a complaint you blatantly know nothing about.

Now look what she's done, she's made me angry on paper.

My Father once told me when I was a child; "Olwen, if you haven't got anything sensible to say don't say anything at all." My twin sister and I took this teaching literally as we didn't consider our thoughts sensible, consequently the two of us never talked much in public when we were children. People used to say to our Mother, "Can the twins talk?" She used to say "Oh! Yes, they don't stop at home"

Maybe my Father should have had a word with this lady too when she was a child, then maybe she wouldn't make such stupid remarks as an Adult.

Before I venture further I would like to mention a comment a friend of mine made while I was out socialising. I was discussing a few of these points when she suddenly said, **"The phrase scare mongering comes to mind, Olwen"** The remark took me by surprise and I felt compelled to think she was indicating that I should 'shut up' as I might scare people with my opinion, so that is exactly what I did. I sat there for the remainder of the evening in a "shut up" mode just like my Father told me to all those years ago. For days I pondered and struggled over her comments, and wondered if I should abandon the book?

After some deliberation I thought she was right, I was scaring people but what's more I wanted to scare them into thinking for themselves.

The rest of us have managed to take care of our allergies for decades, why couldn't we be like sensible citizens and look into this diabetic dilemma?

Delving into the history of Diabetes didn't satisfy my curiosity of the cause of Type Two Diabetes at all. I'm still left abandoned with unanswered question,

- Why has the world witness such an explosion of Diabetic sufferers amongst us?
- Why did the retired Detective at my parent's home say, "Clearly something is not right?"
- Why did Julian die such a horrific death?

Because of these very questions I decided to plod on and find out exactly how many other causes that could inflict, raised glucose levels.

Another mystery Julian tried to understand was the fact his Hba1c results were always in reasonable ranges, when his Blood Monitoring Readings which he conducted himself were always so high. Why was that, unless he wasn't your regular Type Two Diabetic?

No wonder the Doctor at Oswestry said to me, "I don't pretend to know anything about Diabetes it's far too complicated for me"

I too confess it is easier to wash your hands of it, but not when lives are at risk.

I'm sure if the same Doctor who uttered those words had a member of his family suffering the same consequences as Julian, he too would develop the same obsessive interest as me towards Diabetics and possibly say the same as the retired detective friend "Clearly something is not right"

Twenty other causes

I was sure at Julian's bed side there was more than one reason to have raised glucose levels in the blood, and I was right to keep harping on to the Doctors to try and find out what they were. Once I got home I found twenty causes.

1. **Diabetes type 1** - The obvious one is referred to as Congenital or Juvenile Diabetes. Treated by Insulin due to no Insulin been produced in the Pancreas.
   Interestingly Type One has been found to have low vitamin C levels; the transport of vitamin C into the cells is facilitated by insulin. In recent times it has been postulated that due to impaired transport of vitamin C the deficiency can lead to vascular disturbances in diabetics resulting in leg ulcers and poor healing. A patient who

suffers from Neuropathy which is nerve and sensory impairment has also been shown to have deficient vitamin B6.

2. **Diabetes Type Two** - Onset in adulthood known to develop after the breakdown of the immune system, causing the Islets of Langerhan to malfunction resulting in producing reduced amount of Insulin. Type Two manifested during the Second World War.
3. **Addison syndrome** - It's when there is too little Adrenal hormone called Cortisol causing reduced stimulation messages to be sent to the pancreas to release the insulin to deal with the glucose in the blood supply leaving the body with raised blood sugar.
4. **Cushing syndrome** - is the opposite to Addison syndrome it's when the Adrenal gland produces too much Cortisol hormone causing reduced levels of glucose in the blood supply.
5. **Gestational** - Diabetes in Pregnancy can produce high glucose levels. Once the birth takes place, the sugar levels usually return to normal. No treatment required.
6. **Hyperthyroidism** - thyroid dysfunction causes increased insulin resistance.
7. **Acromegaly** - is a disorder causing enlargement of parts of the body, when excessive growth hormones are produced it can have a direct increase in glucose levels which lead to Diabetes
8. **Medication** - such as Steroids, Chemotherapy, Diuretics and Antibiotics abuse are known to affect the immune system. I confess Julian took part in antibiotic abuse throughout his adult life.
9. **Pain** - can elevate blood glucose levels. To the Doctor who mocked me at Julian's Inquest; when I told him analgesia was the only thing that reduced his blood sugar readings. I say to him, "On oath you claimed to be an expert in your field, yet you belittled me in front of my family"?
   He must agree that one would not attempt to perform a blood sugar reading in the middle of a cardiac arrest for the same reason—pain. It would be inaccurately high!
10. **Constant Stress** - can cause Adrenal Gland to burn out and without adequate Adrenal Hormone it can lead to excessive untreated glucose in the blood.

11. **Illness** - repetitive infection such as urinary tract infection, chest infection anything that raises white cell count would raise glucose levels.

12. **Surgery or Injury** - the fight fear and flight puts stress on the adrenal leading to raised blood sugar levels.

13. **Dawn Effect Diabetics** - this can occur in Diabetic and non-Diabetic. This is when blood sugar dips 2 hours before waking, and then they wake up with high blood sugar readings. But in the evening find their blood sugar readings low. They refer to this as 'Dawn Diabetes' I called it 'Back to front Diabetes'

14. **Depleting Magnesium** - a number of drugs can reduce magnesium levels Antibiotic being one of them and Diuretic is another. Magnesium is needed to transport insulin from the pancreas to other organs, without this it leaves the circulation saturated in glucose.

15. **Depleting Copper** - can double glucose readings, how interesting! Copper function is to aid the thyroid gland to secrete thyroid hormone, it also synthesises Adrenal hormone. Low level copper causes cells to suffocate from lack of oxygen. Is this why Julian obtained unexplained infarct (holes) in his spleen?
    Raised Alkaline inhibits copper, Julian's Alkaline levels were as high as 275 when normal range should be 43-114. The other side effect of low copper is hallucinations which Julian suffered from on the date his alkaline was at its highest. There is no evidence he ever had any copper levels done.

16. **Depleting Vitamins** - especially vitamin C, B12, B6, E, and D prevent the absorption of Insulin. Wow! So the myth that vitamin supplements don't help isn't true then, I should have given Julian a daily multi-vitamin after all.

17. **Prolonged sugar intake** - eating re-fined white sugar products for a long time can cause the Pancreas to get fed up of answering the dinner bell and say no more I'm exhausted and refuse to dispense much needed insulin. So it wasn't a myth that 'too much sugar can cause Diabetes'

18. **Chromium deficiency** - normally found in soil which filters through the animal chain either milk or meat, chromium function is critical, without it the hormone insulin will not work.

19. **Diuretics** - dehydrate the body which can cause a higher concentration of blood glucose in the blood.

20. **Low Potassium** - can interfere with glucose metabolism leading to raised glucose levels.

I recall a haunting episode shortly after Julian died when I came across a chain in Julian's jewellery box; Llewela had bought it for his birthday when he first became a diabetic. The sight of it made me cry, how serious he had taken this new condition he'd been newly diagnosed with, to ask his daughter to buy him this chain called 'SOS chain' with her hard earned money at a young age of 16. With his name, post code, date of birth, telephone number, diabetic on insulin, B rh neg, Tetraplagic C6/7 engraved on the back. He wore it faithfully until he realised the treatment was making him very ill. He once said to me, "I better stop wearing this in case I'm involved in a car accident, and they may think I need insulin, it will be the last thing I need while I'm copping with any other injuries." It grieved him to stop wearing it because it was a gift off Llewela. Why would any loving father deliberately not wear his daughter's birthday present unless there was a very good reason? There are some medical professionals who recognise that something in the Diabetic sector is not quite right. When they see patients reacting to insulin, they refer to it as the systemic allergy. In more serious cases it can cause them to have breathing difficulties and rapid heart rate.

In recognition of their allergy they are prescribing long term anti-histamine along with the diabetic treatment. "Does that sound right to you?"

Sadly it seems we are living in a world of "Take this medication and I'll give you another drug to combat its side effect" we need to join forces and change this to "Thank you for the prescription that won't make me feel worse" "Something is definitely not right"

I may have nursed Diabetics through ignorance in the past, but I can no longer ignore their difficulties through 'wonder' anymore! I need to know why they are having difficulties on behalf of everybody else.

What tests were available

So what test could have been conducted to confirm Julian did in fact have Diabetes?

I mentioned earlier that Gaj my old time superior had given me a list of questions to ask at the inquest. The majority of those questions enquired what tests had been carried out to discredit Julian's signs and symptoms after he was given some medical treatment.

I rang the Biochemistry department at Worcester Hospital to enquire if there were any tests to confirm insulin allergy. He informed me that there was a blood test available and it's simply called '**Insulin test**'. I asked if this test was done systematically on all newly diagnosed diabetics. The answer was no, only if the patient had suffered a hypoglycaemic attack. That ruled Julian out twice as he would not be offered it as a newly diagnosed diabetic and what's more he never suffered hypoglycaemic attacks, he was always hyperglycaemic. Had they conducted this test they may have discovered he was producing enough Insulin but had some difficulties making the connection between insulin and glucose. "That could have been Julian's number 1 test"

Another blood test I asked for on several occasions was **Albumin level**, due to his past medical history of often slipping into low protein levels. They said; the investigation would prove to be of no value in his diabetic treatment. The reason I was asking if his albumin was depleted then I could ask my family to bring in high Protein powder just like I'd done on previous hospital admissions. I felt they were missing my point when I was asking for this blood test, but with hindsight they might have discovered his low Albumin and in correcting his levels, Julian's glucose balance would have returned to normal because his proteins had been corrected allowing the protein to become the transporter of magnesium once more unlocking his pancreas allowing the insulin to make contact with his high glucose level. How sad, he could have got better by accident.

"That could have been Julian's number 2 test"

There were many occasions when I brought up the subject of his **Adrenal Tumour**, so they were all well aware we were both concerned about this complaint, although the Pathologist behaved surprised when I mentioned it at the inquest. I used to frequently ask could his high glucose levels be connected but there was never a forth coming reply. Now I realise Julian could have had a test called 'Insulin sensitivity' a test used to differentiate Diabetes Mellitus from Pituitary or **Adrenal Diabetes.** A test dose of Exogenous Insulin could have been conducted, which would have produced a rapid decrease in blood sugar if the Pancreas was not secreting sufficient Insulin.

But a much less dramatic response would be produced if hyperglycaemias were due to excessive secretion of the Pituitary or **Adrenocortical Hormones** rather than insufficient Insulin production. I can see now why Julian had problems taking any diabetic treatment, just as Julian's 'gut feeling' told him; he was producing enough of his own insulin but not enough Adrenaline hormone and when he suffered stress to stimulate the pancreas to create sufficient insulin into the blood stream, in fact taking more insulin for him was like over-dosing on it. So when he used to say to the Doctors on many occasions, "Enough is enough" he wasn't too far from the truth. All he ever wanted was confirmation from previous CT scans conducted at Worcester that he did have a tumour on his Adrenal gland, but as the medical notes did not materialise we could not convince them otherwise. Sadly this blood test was not made available to him either.

"This could have been Julian's number 3 test"

I discovered another test that Julian could have had which I found on the internet dated July 2003 by the American Diabetic Association. It reports the first case of **Insulin allergy test** to the New Human Insulin was confirmed by using skin-prick tests on Asparc and Lispro Insulin otherwise known as Novo Rapid and Homolog.

Although Julian felt he had adequate insulin, he suffered a double whammy as they say, not only did he have to receive additional insulin which he felt he didn't need but he then had to endure the allergy reaction to this modern day BIO-SYNTHETIC Human Insulin.

Tests for this allergy were made available way back in 2003, why wasn't Julian offered this test five years later in 2008. Could it be because it was an American test? Is the medical sector so anti-American that the

British people have to suffer? However I would like to remind you it was eventually through American research that I have been able to make sense of Julian's unusual case.

"Could this have been Julian's number 4 test?"

Another test that is always conducted during most hospital stay is **potassium levels**, because perfect balance of potassium maintains a steady heart rhythm and prevents heart attacks. When they talk of potassium imbalance it could be either too high or too low, both abnormal readings could cause the heart to stop. Although Julian did not suffer a heart attack as such, he was so close to one on several occasions when he complained of severe chest pain. An ECG was always requested but always told his ticker was sound as a pound. He seemed to be plucked from the brink of death each time he complained of chest pain, all drug therapy would be stopped and as soon as he was hydrated in the nick of time his pain started to ease. The nursing staff would frequently tell him after the event, "You must eat" but because he felt his other organs was crushing his stomach they would persuade him to sip food supplement drinks instead, which contained magnesium and potassium I can see now how these drinks would have speeded up his recovery, unfortunately the recovery was always short lived, because the insulin treatment would start again because of their high sugar content. I feel this part of his treatment was not a well thought out plan, but more of an accident.

"This could have been Julian's number 5 test"

I remember one afternoon in Shrewsbury Hospital a Doctor asking me to escort him into the office to discuss Julian's care. Behind closed doors I begged him yet again to take a fresh view of Julian's unusual case, asking him if anyone could do some research on Julian's behalf.

His reply was, "I hope you're not suggesting we should take heed of any American rubbish." I was constantly made to feel supressed, deflated and speechless by this man's comments.

He was right, on my return home there was very little English research available and because of that I had to rely on our cousins across the water in America for any literature on this topic.

To be fair it's the Americans who take a leading role when it comes to removing medicine off the market, whether it is because it's due to any human harm or if there is a law suit pending.

America took Avandia off the market in 2007 after complaints of 100,000 heart attacks, Britain eventually followed suit in 2010. America has also removed Ciprafloxacillin antibiotic from what they call 'Feathered Meals' I think they mean poultry intended for human consumption.

Is it because Ciprofloxacillin should never be given to any one below the age of 18, it's considered by some to be the silent assassin. Bayer's confess they don't know which mechanism in 'Cipro' is crippling people and the FDA isn't biting on this one. If you're harmed by it, compensation is not an issue they will defend themselves with, 'read the small print' I suspect they will soon ban Cipro, but the British jury is still out on this one too, in other words it's still being prescribed to Jo Public in the UK.

Metformin was another drug Julian struggled to take when he was diagnosed with near multi-organ failure. I see it's banned in America, Germany, France and Austria because of causing severe muscle injury, leading to Lactic Acidosis or Multi organ failure but I don't see no such banning in Briton. Co-amoxiclav antibiotic otherwise known as Augmentin is banned in the USA and Europe from use in the domestic animal food chain. They mean cattle and pigs.

Julian was prescribed this little blighter at home once; within hours it had fetched all the skin off his bottom, his lower back and the back of his upper thighs. He looked like someone had douched him in a bath of acid or scolding water. The reaction was so severe we had to have a bed down stairs in the lounge where he remained on bed rest until it had all healed. District nurses were assessing his dressing daily. Incidentally it contained penicillin.

We do eventually tow the line and follow suit with the Americans, but not until we have exposed the British public to further harm; why?

So without repeating an expensive CT scan, they could have conducted <u>any one</u> of these simple tests to better manage Julian's diabetes.

Although this chapter is about 'what tests were available', I confess there were many other blood tests that were conducted on Julian. I've highlighted the deranged ones.

On the 16th October 2008 his sodium (salt) levels was well below normal at 29, normal range should read133-146. On the same date his Potassium was raised to 6.4 the normal range should be 3.5-5.1. Another test that was conducted was Alkaline his was raised to 195 the normal range should be the 43-114. His Gamma GT (liver tests) results were 146 normal ranges is 0-45. Again on the same day his Lactate was raised to maximum level, normal range should read between 0.7-2.2 his was smack on 2.2

I realise all these results were only slightly abnormal, but two days later they were considerably elevated. His Alkaline rose to 267, his Gamma GT rose to 298, there was a definite trend that clearly things were on the increase. Unfortunately the next sets of blood results are missing; but there are only so many times one can request the same copies, only to be charged again and again.

"So what could these deranged results mean?"

Raised Potassium may indicate adrenal problems as the adrenal glands are regulators of potassium levels. Potassium levels can also be influenced by such drugs as diuretics, penicillin's and insulin. Early signs of potassium imbalance are chest pain and heart palpitations, very raised or very low potassium can lead to cardiac arrest.

Low sodium may indicate adrenal problems. When investigating Addison disease (Adrenal Tumour) the first test that's investigated is low sodium. When the liver is affected by adrenal malfunction the toxins are forced to be excreted through the skin, this is achieved through prolonged sweating in the process excreting large amount of salt, equally diuretics could cause the same effect by shifting sodium out in the urine.

Raised Alkaline may indicate adrenal problems and could also confirm liver disorder.

Raised Gamma GT may indicate adrenal problems when toxins are not converted by the liver due to its disorder.

Low Protein levels may indicate adrenal problems when proteins are excreting into the urine in an attempt to rid toxins from the liver when it's not functioning adequately, another cause could be due to wound healing.

Raised Lactate results signifies increase risk of morbidity and mortality, a condition Julian scathed with his life once in 2007 but sadly was struck down for the second time fifteen months later, talk about been struck by lightning twice.

With hindsight, all these simple blood tests could have indicated he was suffering from some form of 'Adrenal Malfunction' so he didn't strictly need further proof and confirmation from the other hospitals that he did in fact have an Adrenal Tumour?

I think the tell-tale signs were there, their answers were in the blood results, but sadly the medical team couldn't see because they were wearing 'Insulin Blinkers'

Another test I wish I could have conducted but I do realise now is too late, 'was there E.coli in the beer pumps that night he became ill'. Inside my head; the jury is still out on this one but if there was E. coli there and it did cause the abscess to manifest itself and it was later treated with Insulin that is derived from E.coli, it beggars belief. You never know, I might have to write a sequel book on this subject in twenty years' time based on the effects of E.coli in our medicines.

It appears the only investigation that was done and was worth its salt was conducted by Ben Calder, the Kinesiologist who visited Julian in Hospital during his last few days of his life to assess his allergies. He stressed before he came that his advice was not intended to replace the advice of a medical physician only to support and enhance natural health. After his visit I felt his recommendation was rather feeble, I hope he will not be offended by these remarks but now with hindsight I can see Ben was bang on target. When he advised Julian to eat bananas in an attempt to increase his magnesium levels, which I now realise could have helped him transport his adrenal cortisone to stimulate his pancreas, to shift his own natural insulin, in conjunction with the Magnesium he also recommended another supplement called chromium which would of further assisted the magnesium to perform his much needed rapid reduction in sugar levels consequently, relieving Julian's need to partake in the synthetic insulin.

I don't know what I expected of Ben, because I imagined he was going to come up with something powerful. But why should he? Modern medicine has been making man sick with its powerful drugs for so long, so why would I wish Julian to have something even more powerful off Ben. Ben and people like him offer kind genital therapy to aid and compliment health, not harsh drugs that often make already the vulnerable attack their own immunity.

In fact he suggested looking into a herbal remedy called 'Bio-superfood' I promised myself I would as soon as I got Julian home. Sadly Julian didn't return home and after his death I veered away from Ben's recommended therapy only to spend two years and come up with the same conclusion as Ben. "Magnesium and Chromium replacement"

Sadly while I was at Julian's bed side I didn't have the courage to tackle the 'cloth eared medical team' and informing them of Ben's findings, my fight was ebbing away and I was sure they would have enjoyed ridiculing me.

"Well done Ben, and thank you for showing such kindness and patience towards Julian"

It's been a hard balancing act trying to be the neutral party with Julian's care at all times, sometimes with my wife's head on and sometimes with my nurses head on, at the same time trying to show respect to the medical team especially on such occasions when a doctor called out to me in the corridor, "No more requests for his notes, do you understand"

I understand this much; there was documentation in his notes by more than one medical professional stating, 'treatment must be stopped'

Whenever I felt like laying this book to rest, I would be encouraged by some unexpected party. On one occasion it was a patient, I was advising him what to be on guard following discharge from hospital and when to seek medical advice

—If he had a fever or he felt unwell
—If he had difficulty or an inability to pass urine
—If he had pain in his kidneys, back or surrounding area.

He interrupted by saying, "This could be difficult, I have been suffering from all of those things you just mentioned since I became a diabetic, but not just my kidneys but all my organs. In fact my organs always feel frozen. He admitted when his Doctor reduced his diabetic tablets and Insulin his signs and symptoms did improve but I still feel cold, feel my hands nurse.

Once again I found myself gagged unable to say, I knew someone who felt like you once.

After this incidence I read an article written by Dr T. Rinpoche printed in April 2007 how Tibetan medicine described Western Diabetes. It's when diabetes affects their kidneys; they become cold and cannot function properly, in turn it disturbs the circulation causing some diabetics to refer to their organs as frozen. Tibetans refer to it as "Cold blood" It appears Tibetans don't suffer from this new 'Diabetes Type Two' we suffer with the west! How is it; they recognise the symptom of 'frozen organs' but have no need to study the complaint as their culture doesn't even suffer from Type two and yet we who suffer with it, have no one with the slightest bit of interest in finding out on our behalf. It makes me wonder if this is done on purpose, the phrase 'a good money spinner' comes to mind after all Diabetes does involve ten million pounds a day!

Talking of money, the N.H.S. carried out over 4,000 weight loss operations between the year 2008 and 2009 a 9 fold rise from the year 2003 where only 480 were done.

Peter Sedman a spokesman for the Royal College of surgeons says, "There is something in the order of 500,000 people who might be eligible for surgery" There are 300 million people obese in the world. My thought on the subject is,

"Don't keep cutting them up, find out why they are so obese"

I'm worried that most of these raised glucose levels are linked to the endocrine system which makes me wonder that Julian may well have been telling the truth about his Adrenal Tumour!

'Did Julian have an Adrenal Tumour'?

Once I discovered that Julian did indeed have correspondence in his medical notes that he definitely had allergy to all diabetic treatment I now question myself did Julian really have a Tumour on his Adrenal Gland or was it a figment of both our imagination, because no one else seemed convinced he had such a thing!

Backed up by the letter I received in June 2009 from Oswestry, in reply to my enquiry 'did Julian have a tumour on his adrenal glands'. Their reply was; they could not find any abnormalities on his kidneys in his notes.

Then the fact the Pathologist appeared surprised in the courtroom when I asked him about the Adrenal Tumour, made me doubt myself, but why did Julian repeatedly tell me and the medical staff that he did have a tumour?

Who was I to believe the Pathologist or Julian? and furthermore why did the Pathologist make a 'shrugging shoulder gesture' to the Consultant Physician sitting behind me in the courtroom at Julian's Inquest saying "I wasn't aware he had a tumour"

"Why not"? He of all people should have been able to tell me and everyone in that courtroom whether he had a tumour or not! Every one kept reminding me a Pathologist holds the highest position in the land; they can even override the Royals if a crime has been committed.

I recalled a letter that was sent to me stating, before the Post Mortem, that Julian's body belonged to me, but as soon as the Post Mortem started his body belonged to the crown, when he'd finished his investigation he became my property again. Firstly Julian didn't belong to anybody, he was his own man and secondly while Julian was in his possession the Pathologist certainty had full access to confirm if he 'did or did not' have a tumour, whereas Julian only had a verbal confirmation. I didn't feel it was my place, the deceased widow to inform the Pathologist on the stand about a possible tumour, certainly not during the eleventh hour of the Inquest.

This was defiantly unfinished business for me, it became a 'did he or didn't he have a tumour quest' It seemed to me, if I do discover he really did have an Adrenal Tumour; it will have a lot to answer for.

Why Oh! Why didn't I look in to it more thoroughly when he first informed me about his tumour? Why did I let Julian dismiss his tumour as a bit of nothing to worry about, because someone else was keeping an eye on it, because it certainly wasn't me?

As I didn't receive the scan results until the day before the Inquest I wasn't able to study them to elaborate any further in the court room that day regarding the existence of a possible tumour. I had a choice here, the Inquest was 'done and dusted' and my window of opportunity to prove whether he did or did not have a tumour was long gone. Therefore there didn't seem to be much point in giving this topic much more attention.

While I was pondering on what to do next I did what Julian used to do best, and that was to make a cup of tea. As I was filling the kettle I quietly whispered, "Oh! Ju, do you really want me to carry on with your Adrenal Tumour Issue?" As I placed the kettle on the gas ring with one hand I turned on the radio in passing with the other, the radio came on full volume and out blasted The Bee Gees singing, "Staying alive." With these poignant lyrics,

> Staying alive.
> Life going` nowhere.
> Somebody help me.
> Somebody help me.

I sobbed over the sink feeling a Disavow coming over me, something similar to this had happened to me before; I didn't hear the rest of the words from crying. I've listened to the whole song since, and it didn't make the slightest bit of sense, except for that small chorus for those few minutes. That's all poor Ju wanted in those desperate days. Somebody please help me! I'm trying to stay alive. There was my answer, the 'whys and wherefores' of Julian's Tumour was about to begin. That night I received a phone call from my sister informing me that her friend had received a message off Julian, the message this time was "Go back to the beginning" My heart sank when I heard this instruction, only because I'd written so much. Whatever did this simple message mean, beginning of what, beginning of the book, beginning of Julian's life, beginning of Julian's illness, beginning of our relationship, beginning of the Bible, beginning of the world, how far did he want me to go?

With this simple instruction 'Go back to the beginning' I decided to stay focused on Julian's case from when his health began to deteriorate.

I decided to view the investigation I hadn't had time to study before the Inquest regarding his Endocrine system, the CT scans, MRI scans and the Ultra Sound and their matching written reports. I just hoped I'd find what I was looking for, I realised without all the medical notes from all five hospitals, including his GP notes and his scans I had no hope of finding that missing jigsaw piece, that is if there was a missing piece!

Then I saw it, dated June 2006 Julian was diagnosed with Angiolipoma (Adrenal Tumour).

BINGO, just as Julian had tried to convince both myself and all the medical profession that he had a tumour, this letter proved he was in fact telling us the truth. "I knew he wouldn't lie to me"

To try and make 'head or tail' out of Julian's second medical mystery I was keen to find out when abnormalities were first detected and to work out why his health suddenly plummeted so suddenly at the end. This could be a long chapter.

I tried to retrieve as far back as I could into his medical history as to when he first started to develop any Endocrine symptoms. The earliest I could find was in August 1982 when Julian attended one of his regular Spinal Injury follow up appointments, he mentioned to the Doctor about two recent episodes of sudden excruciating abdominal pain attacks he had accompanied by a severe bout of sweating attacks and a pressured headache. The Senior Registrar suggested it would be better if they could see him during one of these attacks! This was going to prove a bit difficult as he lived over 60 miles from this clinic.

Looking back Julian started to experience body perspiring in the mid to late 70s, because of this in 1978 he was prescribed Probanthin tablet which he took orally for 17 years.

The drug was originally intended for bladder and bowel spasms, but one of its side effects was it caused body dryness. In other words he was taking the drug because of its side effects. Years later it was noted at one of his follow-up appointments that Julian was experiencing low blood pressure and light headedness and on the strength of these symptoms the drug was eventually stopped and he was commenced on a similar drug called Oxybutynin. Unfortunately both these drugs are not recommended for any Hepatic sufferers and as Julian had contracted Hepatitis C in the mid-70s it might not have been the best choice of drug to take long term, without risking suffering some form of liver disorder later on in his life. One of his liver blood tests known as Gamma GT was first noted to be raised in 1986, but they may well have been raised prior to '86 but those blood test results are not included in the notes. Three years later in 1989 an ultra sound scan revealed he had a multitude of gallstones in his Gallbladder, for ten years his Gamma GT blood test remained high, with Julian still suffering from bouts of body perspiration and periodic Epigastric pain radiating to the tip of his right shoulder. Evidently one of the long term side effects of Hepatitis C is formation of Gall Stones! That explains that one then.

After 13 long years of suffering attacks of Epigastric pain, in 1999 he underwent his much needed Cholecystectomy operation, to remove his troublesome galls stone. It turned out to be more than one stone; the gall bladder was impacted and exploded as the knife was shone. After the Gallstones were removed, one would expect his Gamma GT levels to return back to normal and his body sweats to be eradicated, but they didn't!

So what was going on? What else could have kept his Gamma GT elevated when I thought the cause had been removed?

During one of his 'Pre-annual MOT' as Julian used to call them at the Spinal Injury Unit in 1999, he underwent an ultrasound on his urinary tract there they discovered he had also developed a Fatty Liver. At the same time they discovered a cyst on his left kidney, although an indentation to the cortex of the left kidney had been noticed three years previously in 1996. Could this have been the start of his Adrenal Tumour?

From the year 2000 to 2006 Julian endured a multitude of minor ailments, such as umpteen urine infections, chest infections, small leg ulcers but nothing to write home about just irritating low immunity complaints.

Then in January 2006 a Trainee Doctor requested an ultra sound scan of his abdomen due to the fact he had experienced excessive sweating in the previous five months, coupled with the fact he was complaining of central abdominal pain and was still harbouring raised Gamma GT results. The scan revealed that both his Spleen and Liver was enlarged which would explain the centralized pain he was experiencing. Less than six months later in June 2006 a Gastro Surgeon requested another CT scan, this time revealing not only an enlarged Liver and Spleen but also an enlarged right kidney with Angiolipoma (Adrenal Tumour).

A month later on 25ᵗʰ July 2006, Julian went like a 'lamb to the slaughter' as they say, when he agreed to have a Bone Marrow trephine which is another name for biopsy that is taken from the sternum bone. I only say this because it's not a very pleasant procedure to have done, but he wanted to feel well again and if it was a means to an end he would do anything. This test was to exclude lymphoma which is cancer of the lymph nodes, which proved negative.

I wasn't surprised at this stressful time in his life, while waiting for Bone Marrow results his blood sugar readings became more and more elevated and 28 days later on the 22ⁿᵈ September 2006 he was commenced on an additional diabetic tablet called Metformin.

With this many tablets on board, Julian's body started to feel the strain. Altogether he was taking Glicozide, Avandia, Co-dydramol, Levothyroxine, Lisinipril, Asprin and now Metformin.

Christmas kind of merged into sickness at our house that year, he struggled with his treatment for four months then when his body couldn't take much more he asked me to take him to the GP surgery. On the 12ᵗʰ February 2007 I drove him to the surgery because he said he wasn't well enough to drive himself. His purpose that day was to tell the Doctor that since he'd starting taking Metformin he'd felt much worse and wished to have a second opinion. While he was there he was offered his annual Influenza Vaccination, I remember him declining saying he was not even fit enough to drive let alone struggle with flu like symptoms, he often suffered following his other flu vaccinations.

I mentioned previously that his Gamma GT readings had remained high since 1986, but less than three months later he was admitted with 'near-multi-organ-failure' and in May 2007 his Gamma GT on that occasion had elevated to 612, but when his medication was discontinued eight days following his admission, he was well enough to be discharged home two days later. His Gamma GT starting to recover instantly, on the day of discharge it was already down to 507.

Once he was home he started 'detoxing' as it were, taking no prescribed drugs at all. I introduced his body to a herbal remedy called

'Milk Thistle' to help rejuvenate and heal his poor exhausted liver. Astonishingly his GGT levels came down even further to 135. Pleased about its decrease, I was aware that something was still not right, for the reading to remain in the three figure bracket; it should have descended even further to between 0 and 45.

I pondered long and hard as to why it wouldn't come down further, I eventually resigned to the fact I must have been doing something wrong!

I say, I was doing something wrong because there was no one else involved in his care at this stage.

Without all these investigations and results I would not have been in a position to make 'headway' with Julian's second medical mystery, Diabetes of course being his first mystery.

Different tests were now merging, causing confusion amongst the medical profession as to why his organs were deteriating so badly!

Between 2006 and 2008 it appeared Julian's Endocrine system was well on its destructive journey as most of his Endocrine organs had either become enlarged, developed large holes or lesions in, or had growths growing over them.

This next paragraph is just 'hear say' did his Hepatitis C originally cause his Gamma GT results to elevate? Then following 48 weeks of treatment, his Hepatitis C was cured, but, could the condition have left painful scaring on his Liver inflicting low grade constant pain leading to permanent sweating? As I mentioned before one of the side effects of Hepatitis C it can cause Gallstones to form in the Gallbladder, it stands to reason after thirteen years of periodical Gallbladder blockage and waves of excruciating pain it would have put a strain on his flight, fear and fight hormone in his Adrenal Gland.

At some stage his right Adrenal Gland developed a tumour and the left adrenal became Atrophic (shrivelled up) this non-active Adrenal gland then becoming inadequate in supplying sufficient amount of cortisol hormone to stimulate the Pancreas to release the insulin. Hence he was labelled 'Insulin Resistance'

In these situations the body produces an adequate amount of insulin, but lacks the ability to transport the insulin to metabolise the glucose. The excess glucose is then converted and stored as fat and accumulates in the liver, which then renders the diagnosis 'Fatty Liver'

Incidentally there is more evidence available these days that Non-Alcohol-Fatty-Liver-Disease (NAFLD) can be associated with Insulin Resistance.

So Julian was right to question if the two were connected, when and what he wrote in his unsent letter in 2006.

When I first heard this diagnosis 'Fatty liver' I considered it to be an offensive label to those who suffered with it, but equally offensive to myself who took the diagnosis personally in that others might think I was feeding Julian a high fat diet for him to have globules of fat deposited in his liver. I didn't possess a chip pan and I didn't buy oven ready chips either, I grilled or boiled most of his food. To look at him you wouldn't think so, so what was making him look so over weight?

"After some research this is my interpretation of how 'Fatty Liver' develops"

To start with; a healthy liver can deal with any amount of saturated fat in a normal diet. That is why God gave us gallbladders, so the bile can break down the fat.

Between the Hepatitis C, the Gallstones and 17 years of taking Probanthin followed by Oxybutynin Julian was not in good polling position to start his healthy race of life. He was already at a disadvantage, but Julian being Julian was not perturbed.

I realised if the liver was not working adequately then these fatty deposits in the liver had not yet been detoxified by the liver either. These toxic fat deposits are sometimes referred to as tumours or nodules which can later develop lesions.

Once his liver become full of these toxified fat deposits, he needed to find somewhere else to hoard them. So where was Julian hiding his fat globules full of toxins, using Julian's medical notes as proof, I discovered he was hiding them in seven different hideaways.

In January 2001 he was diagnosed with Lymphoma in his groin, referred to as Inguinal lymph nodes.

In January 2006 he was diagnosed with a fatty infiltration in his right kidney referred to as Angiomylipoma.

In May 2006 he was diagnosed with Fatty liver referred to as Hepatic Stenosis, benign fat deposits.

In May 2007 he was diagnosed with Adeopathy of his right adrenal gland which means the gland was enlarged with a Myeloipoma, this is a benign tumour with a lesion, wound, cut or slash on the surface. Benign

431

Adrenal Tumours are harmless unless they press on vital structures such as blood vessels or nerves in which case it's more serious. At the same time he was diagnosed with <u>Atrophic </u>left adrenal gland, which means shrinking. The Adrenal Cortex had suffered destruction, in Latin it's described as 'ill fed' or 'ill-nourished'. Who would have thought that of Julian?

In other words both his Adrenal glands were in fact affected, one enlarged with a tumour and the other shrunken.

In August 2007 he was diagnosed with a round plural nodule at the base of his left lung called <u>Pulmonary nodes</u>.

In 2007 he developed 11 nodes measuring 13mm in diameter located near the bronchial tree, where the tube separates into the right and left lung called <u>Bronchial Adenomas</u>.

He also had a slow growing large fatty nodule on his forehead camouflaged by his fringe and another one on his bicep called <u>Sebaceous Adenoma.</u>

So really this was enough evidence to prove he was in possession of more than one benign tumour! So why, couldn't any of these diagnoses be faxed to the appropriate hospital to prevent him being given Insulin?

I felt much more positive about trying to find out what affect these tumours had on his health, at the same time being constantly aware I needed to go back to the beginning of every problem.

As his Diabetes appeared to start in the summer of 2000 in Pompeii in Southern Italy twelve months after his cholecystectomy, I was intrigued to see if his Adrenal Tumour had any bearings on that attack in Pompeii.

I decided to go down the avenue of the Adrenal Tumour first, to investigate and exclude any red herrings. With hindsight I would of been better equipped for those Doctors at Shrewsbury had I known more about this condition?

So far I've established he had a tumour, I've established it caused him to develop fatty liver, but I haven't established what caused him to develop the tumour in the first place!

I felt I failed Julian miserably in life at the end, now I intend for him to be proud of me after his death. Maybe Julian's message was more helpful than I originally thought; with anything that is mysterious you have to start at the beginning. I decided to recap on what healthy Adrenal Glands are responsible for first and then I will be better equipped in understanding how a Myeloma (Adrenal Tumour) might have affected him.

Healthy Adrenal glands are responsible for the balance of-:

Stress.
Fasting.
Temperature.
Infection.
Drugs.

I wondered if Julian's Adrenal tumour affected the balance of these five points to start with.

In other words, did Julian's life style change at all, after he was diagnosed with this tumour.

Let's look at <u>stress</u> first, prior to his trip to Pompeii he used to thrive on stress. He loved coming face to face with confrontation and defusing problematic situations, but at the start of the Millennium even a simple task like a public speech had become too much for him to handle, it would affect him physically and psychologically. His visits to the toilet were very frequent before leaving the house. Psychologically he would go over the same thing over and over again in a nervous state. This was not the Julian I knew, normally a powerful character who was nearly always right. Things had definitely changed there.

Let's look at <u>Fasting;</u> he couldn't manage this anymore. He had to have regular meals otherwise he would complain he was in danger of fainting. When I first met Julian he lived on a 'Warrior's Diet' resting his digestion all day and 'Feeding for battle' in the evening. In other words he only had one meal a day and that was late at night. Things had definitely changed there too.

Let's look at <u>Temperature.</u> Before the Pompeii trip his temperature was always normal, unlike most spinal injury victims who suffer from extreme temperature ranges. Of cause when he had an infection his temperature could go as high as 40 degrees, but that's expected of anyone.

It was only when he was taking diabetic treatment his temperature would react and plummet to as low as 34 degrees (hypothermic levels) but once he was off the anti-diabetic treatment his temperature would return back to normal once more. Things had changed there too.

Let's look at <u>Infection.</u> Paraplegics and Tetraplegia are notorious for attracting infection; it's a small weakness they acquire. But could this tumour have exhausted Julian's immune defence hence making it easier for the abscess to develop and take hold like it did?

Let's look at <u>drugs.</u> When we were first married Julian used to be able to eat tablets like sweets. But during his later years it became more and more difficult to tolerate prescribed drugs, ultimately in the final weeks of his life it became impossible to tolerate any drugs. I recall a Doctor once mocked me by saying at Shrewsbury Hospital, "What are you trying to say Mrs Davies, that your husband cannot tolerate any medication at all?" My reply was, "Stupid as it sounded, No he can't! Not anymore." Now I know what goes into some of the medication he was trying to tolerate Im not surprised.

When a researcher in the 1950s called Hans Sdye discovered the flight, fear and fight reaction with the Adrenal hormone. He explains the sufferer goes through three stages; first he goes through the 'Adaption stage' secondly he goes through the 'Alarm stage' and thirdly the 'Exhaustion stage' Looking back I can see now when Julian had his first experienced of 'Adrenal Exhaustion Stage', when I recall Julian's face amplifying PANIC at the top of the high slope in Pompeii way back in the summer of 2000.

Although I had looked into what the Adrenal glands were responsible for, I was aware that the Adrenal glands are only a small part of the Endocrine system and the Endocrine glands are very intertwined with each other. My next step was to find out; could Julian's Adrenal Tumour have been affected by any of the other Endocrine glands?

There was only one way to find out and that was to recap on what I had learnt years ago in my biology lessons during my pre-nursing course.

The Endocrine system is composed of eight glands distributed throughout the body; each one is responsible for different functions. I read in a book called 'Healing our Hormones' written by Linda Crockett who fondly described these glands as 'Hypothalamus' the Consolidator, 'Pituitary' the Organiser, 'Pineal gland' the Time keeper, 'Ovaries and Testacies' the Life givers, 'Thymus' the Protector, 'Thyroid' the Energiser, 'Pancreas' the Balancer and 'Adrenal' the Defender.

In more detail they are responsible for—:

1. **The Pituitary gland**. These are situated in the pituitary fosa, at the base of the brain behind the bridge of the nose. They are responsible for normal temperature, thirst, sleep, emotional behaviour and memory. They are sometimes referred to as the master gland, as it produces a hormone that stimulates other glands to function, they are the cortical hormone in the adrenal glands, thyroid hormone in the thyroid glands, oestrogens and progesterone hormone in the ovaries, and testosterone in the testacies.

2. **The Thyroid gland.** These are found at the front of the throat and produce a hormone called thyroid. They are responsible for metabolism, over active thyroid causes too slim a figure, under active thyroid causes obesity, thyroid production increases with exertion, stress, fear and illness.

3. **The Para-thyroid gland.** These are found just behind the Thyroid gland and they produce Para-thyroid hormone. These are responsible for calcium balance, when it is imbalanced it affects our personality, nervous system, bone density and can contribute to kidney stones forming.

4. **The Adrenal gland.** These glands are found sitting on top of each kidney and they produce cortical hormone one of their functions is to activate the pancreas into releasing Insulin.
    They are also responsible for maintaining blood pressure, pulse, sodium in the urine, immune system, natural anti-inflammatory, controls fat proteins carbohydrates and converts glycogen into glucose.

5. **The Pancreas gland.** This is partially sandwiched between the stomach and the spine and produces an enzyme called Insulin. This is responsible for the balance of glucose in the body.

6. **The Testicles**. These are found between the upper thighs, in two scrotal sacks. These produce a hormone called testosterone, and are responsible for reproducing.
7. **The Ovaries.** These are found in the lower abdomen, above the womb and produce female hormone called Oestrogens for the first two weeks of the month and Progesterone for the third week and during the fourth week it sheds its lining that is if the egg has not been fertilised. These are responsible for the female monthly menstrual cycle.
8. **The Gastro Glands**. These can be found in the Gastro-intestinal tract. These are responsible for braking down the food in the gastric tract. There are two dozen of these hormones. One of these is called Ghrelin and is responsible for triggering hunger, eating compensates this feeling. If too much of this hormone is produced, then an excessive eating disorder can occur, causing obesity.

I might mention this Ghrelin hormone again; it's an interesting little fella, as my friend Jo Green would say.

All these glands produce hormones necessary for normal bodily function. When functioning properly, the Endocrine system is likened to a fine tuned Orchestra. If comparing the system to an Orchestra and one instrument is out of tune then you would agree the music is not worth listening to. All are meant to work in unison with each other, as they are all so intertwined with one another, the imbalance of one can cause the others to suffer.

I wonder if this is what is meant when we hear of yet another old wives tales when we say,

"One should be in tune with one's body!"

When you consider what this system is responsible for, is there any wonder why we are often complaining of minor ailments that we often can't put right because of lack of knowledge, instead it leads to yet another complaint. How many times have you heard people say, I only went to the Doctor with one complaint and I've returned with a shed full of drugs?

I remember saying at the beginning of this book, "I hoped my studying days were now over", it seems to me I'm looking up more facts and figures now than ever before.

This has become a bit like compiling a family tree, I have to be careful to stay focused on the Adrenal Tumour trail and not get to side tracked with the whole Endocrine system.

I wonder if Julian was displaying obvious signs when he was suffering with the Adrenal Tumour, there is only one way to find out and that's to look it up.

Signs and Symptoms of an Adrenal Tumour!

Fatty liver - can be caused by adverse reaction to drugs, exposure to toxic chemicals or viral Hepatitis. (There is proof in his medical notes he had fatty liver)

Plural effusion - is excess fluid in the plural cavity surrounding the lung, can be caused through low protein or drug allergy. (He once had three litres drained off his lungs)

Enlarged spleen - can be induced by prescribed medication or drug allergy. (Julian's spleen weighed in at 800g, normal spleens should weigh 150mg.)

Abdominal pain - as the tumour grows it can apply pressure on surrounding nerves leading to abdominal pain. (When he took analgesia his glucose levels reduced)

Feel full quick - if the tumour is enlarged it can shift other organs towards the stomach.

Feel a mass in their abdomen. - On occasions a lump could be felt, and sometimes it was very visible. (I felt and saw it on many occasions)

Weight loss - brought on by excessive stress (He lost four and a half stone in five weeks)

Salt craving - Adrenal gland is responsible for sodium or salt balance in the body. (Blood results confirmed his Sodium levels were below normal range. Julian immediately recovered when he was given Normal Saline Intravenously)

Muscle wastage in upper trunk - reduced Potassium can cause muscle destruction, when accompanied by depleted protein levels it's difficult to recover. (Protein found in urine every time he was unwell)

Heart palpitations, - increased potassium can cause heart arrhythmias. (On occasions he thought he could hear his heart beating)

Eye symptoms - low blood pressure reduces blood volume which can cause blurred vision, and drug allergy can cause sudden blindness. (He complained of both)

Hair loss, - due to lack of Cortisol, the Magnesium cannot transport the vitamins and minerals such as Zinc to the hair follicle. (His hair loss returned when he stopped medical treatment and took Zinc and Vitamin C)

Breathing difficulties - Zinc and Copper imbalance can causes poor liver function leading to an accumulation of toxicity. (His breathing difficulties only recovered when drugs were stopped)

Ear symptom - allergy to some prescribed drugs can induce sudden deafness.

Runny nose - brought on by drug allergy. (His never materialised into a cold)

Larynx symptoms - can result from immune deficiency causing Thyroiditis leading to difficulty swallowing and a hoarse voice. (This was very evident in the end)

Increase in systolic blood pressure reading - induced when placed under undue stress. Julian's escalated to 228/80 when he was given Insulin against his wishes.

Mental changes - mood swings can arise from reduced Cortisol but mistaken for bad temper.

Diarrhoea and constipation - can occur when Cortisone is too low.

Decreased Potassium - potassium is stored in muscle and retains its bulk. Heart is made of muscle. (X-ray reported his heart was enlarged just before he died)

Weakness and muscle cramp - can result from Electro imbalance.

Fluid imbalance and Dehydration - caused by low sodium (He was on restricted fluids and Diuretics at the same time, his lips were crisp and dry)

Enlarged Liver - can indicate Adrenal Tumour, and mineral imbalance can cause the organ to stop functioning. (He had Raised liver function tests, and localised swelling)

Clay coloured stools - this goes hand in hand with liver disorder.

Sweating - indicate Adrenal Tumour and the body is excreting toxins through the skin when the liver becomes incapable.

Spleen infarct - indicates Adrenal Tumour and bouts of oxygen starvation can cause the tissue to die. (Positive Scan results indicates this)

Tingling of face and parenthesise of the hands - potassium imbalance exacerbated by Diuretics. (He complained of this when he asked his mother to hold his cup)

Skin tanning. Julian had this brown pigment over every scar line.

Decreased tolerance of the cold - caused by drug allergy. (He complained of frozen organs every day he was on diabetic treatment)

Fragile skin and slow-healing - only when on medication otherwise he had good healing skin.

Adrenal Tumour can inhibit the effect of insulin - deficiency of the Cortical in the Adrenal Gland is inadequate in stimulating the Pancreas to excrete insulin.

Delirium can be brought on by multiple drug reaction (Julian's body was shutting down after prolonged drug abuse)

Peripheral vascular collapse - prolonged low blood pressure induces low blood volume making phlebotomy difficult. (Taking a blood sample)

Lactic acidosis - deriving from imbalance of Acid and Alkaline in the body otherwise referred to pH balance. Lay man's term for this is multi-organ failure.

Separate diagnoses of all the above conditions when not grouped together can be misdiagnosed as individual conditions, which would warrant a multitude of different treatments but once re-grouped and re-diagnosed can lead to appropriate diagnosis of Adrenal difficulties.

Incidentally did you notice that the words, 'Drug Allergy' were mentioned nine times in the list above? It is known recognised that some drugs can block the production of the corticosteroids, for instance long term antibiotics can cause Adrenal gland damage. It can lead to elevation of sodium and retention of potassium causing dehydration resulting in slumping in energy, low blood pressure and raised glucose in the blood.

Although the above list is about the signs and symptoms of Adrenal tumours, the two main Adrenal conditions physicians are taught to recognise these days are the two extreme conditions called Cushing syndrome and Addison syndrome.

Cushing syndrome - this is when the Adrenal gland produces too much cortisol hormone. This can interfere with the body's immune system predisposing a patient to unusual infections

Addison syndrome - this is when the adrenal glands does not produce enough cortisol hormone.

Cushing and Addison syndrome are as different as black and white; unfortunately Doctors often refuse to recognise the grey areas in between.

Those middle of the road Adrenal malfunctions vary slightly but they remain much of a much ness. They are sometimes referred to as Adrenal Exhaustion, Adrenal Insufficiency, Adrenal dysfunction, Adrenal Burnout or Adrenal fatigue. It appears that prolonged attacks on the Adrenal Glands can hamper their function enough to cause the above so called mild Adrenal conditions to lead to full blown diagnosis of either Adrenal Cushion syndrome or Addison syndrome which may further lead to tumours that simply remain benign or sadly become cancerous.

So why go the whole hog and develop these more serious conditions when we can avoid them in the first place.

Most Physicians opinion about Adrenal glands are; they are either working or they are not working. Although GPs are well aware that other glands function to different capacity such as thyroid, pituitary, ovaries and testes. Adrenal glands are the same they can also be partially functioning.

If someone has partial loss of adrenal function they can appear well until they are faced with crises such as physiologic stress, infection, burns, surgery or allergy.

President J.F. Kennedy suffered from Adrenal disorder one day he was subject to a sudden shock after witnessing the whole of his platoon being blown up in front of him during the Second World War. This sort of shock can bring on Adrenal crisis; patients who suffer from reduction of cortisone hormone need extra cover over stressful periods following such things as shock, before, during and after surgery as well as during illness, infection or injury.

Unfortunately Adrenal malfunction is considered by some to be a "Too-well-a-kept secret"

It is also believed by some, that Adrenal insufficiency is the starting line in a race of complaints such as Polymyalgia, Fibromyalgia, Asthma, Rheumatoid Arthritis, Hay Fever, and Inflammation of the Bowels such as Crohn's Disease. These conditions are aggravated by abuse of substances such as alcohol, tobacco, caffeine, sugar and artificial sweeteners.

A Doctor Lawrence Wilson MD wrote in January 2011 for the 'Centre for Development', that Adrenal Malfunctions are caused by toxic metals and toxic chemicals as well as nutrient deficiency. His belief was if the toxic metals as well as the toxic-chemicals were removed from the body, the entire body would then nourish. The Adrenal glands would begin to function normally and energy would return, but it is a lengthy process and can take up to two years to heal. It cannot be fixed with one good night's sleep.

Sadly children who are born into families who live on poor nutritional diet can reach 'Adrenal Burnout' by the time they are five years of age. They usually crave sweet and high salt diet which can lead to recurrent infections. Impounding these already emotionally burdened children with already low immune systems with constant verbal aggression can lead to suicide.

Did you know the term 'the straw that broke the camel's back' is often referred to as nervous breakdown but in fact can also be mistaken for Adrenal Fatigue? It's a common occurrence these days due to lack of relaxation and other factors such as chronic pain, inducing allergies and sleep depravations can kick start Adrenal problems.

Fifty years ago, physicians were far more likely than modern day counter parts to correctly diagnose an Endocrine ailment.

Now I discover that there are two types of non-evasive tests available to diagnose Adrenal Malfunction, they are 24 hour urine collection and a 24 hour Saliva test.

Question is how can we recognise the start of Adrenal fatigue?

These are some of the Signs and symptoms to look for.

- Morning fatigue - don't feel fully awake until 10am.
- Afternoon 'low' could easily sleep between 2pm-4pm.
- Burst of energy at 6pm if you managed that afternoon lull.
- Sleepiness again between 9pm-10pm.
- If you resisted your bed at 10pm—you get second wind from 11pm until 1am.
- Salt craving.
- Mild depression or sadness.
- Lack of energy most the time.
- Decreased ability to handle stress.
- Muscle weakness.
- Increased allergy.
- Light-headedness when standing up.
- Frequent sighing.
- Inability to handle food high in potassium or carbs unless combined with protein or fat.

<u>Safe home tests.</u>

- Pupils should dilate, if a torch is shone in to the mirror.
- Pain on pressing over kidney area.
- Perform the 'Raglans sign' this is a simple blood pressure test. Take blood pressure sitting down first, then stand up and sit down again. Repeat the blood pressure in sitting down position. The systolic should go up, but if it's gone down then you really need to see the GP to conduct a more thorough investigation into adrenal imbalance. This is not a diagnosis these are three simple tests to be used as guide lines.

The same Dr Wilson advises these 18 steps to help yourself if you feel you are suffering from Adrenal fatigue.

- Try to sleep in until 9am as often as you can.
- Try to power nap mid-morning for 10 minutes.
- Try to exercise more.
- Try to avoid junk food.

- Try to eat five organic fruit or veg a day and exclude all GM food.
- Try to eat regular meals.
- Try to chew your food well, don't stress your digestion.
- Try to combine carbs with proteins and fat.
- Try to take calcium and magnesium supplement.
- Try to take vitamin E with tocopherols.
- Try to take vitamin B-complex high in B6 and panthenic acid.
- Try taking vitamin C, we can't produce vitamin C but we do store it in the adrenal glands-but not if they are malfunctioning.
- Try exchanging your existing salt for sea salt in your diet.
- Try adding liquorice root to your diet.
  (I like the next four)
- Try minimizing stress.
- Try something fun each day.
- Try laughing a lot.
- Try removing negative people out of your life.
  (By telling yourself out of their ear shot, "Sorry but you're not good for me")

Dr Wilson states that if you take his treatment plan seriously one could expect ones Adrenal Fatigue to heal within 6 to 24 months. He refers to this treatment as, "Taking back your life."

I've mentioned his advice purely because it's pretty non-evasive treatment; I hope to goodness no one feels worse after trying it. I am aware Doctors prescribe and Nurses are only allowed to Nurse, having said that I am <u>quoting</u> Doctor James L. Wilson ND, DG, PhD <u>not advising</u> you.

You may be wondering how qualified is he on the subject; he has three Degrees, two Masters Degrees, a PhD in human Nutrition, Minors in microbiology, pharmacology, toxicology and psychology. He is listed in the 'International Who's who in medicine' He's published a book called 'Adrenal Fatigue, the 21st Century Stress Syndrome'

He sounds like a good all-rounder on the topic to me; the only thing I would add to his advice is check with your pharmacist if it's safe for you to take these vitamin pills with any regular prescriptions you're already taking.

Other tell-tale signs I should have noticed, but didn't

On the subject of going back to the beginning I recall another occasion when Julian felt drained and very unwell, he went to town shopping with Llewela. He later described this sudden gush of energy leaving his body, as if he had a big hole in his stomach and if he didn't have a drink and something to eat immediately he would fall into this hole. (Of course it was only a sensation he felt) On that occasion he sent Llewela into the shop with some money and said, "Quick, get Dad some pop and a bar of chocolate and tell the lady that Dads very poorly outside, hurry" Poor Llewela, because she was so shy, the till lady ignored her for some time thinking she was with one of the other costumers. It was some time before she got served, but eventually returned to her father with his bag of goodies.

Thinking back it was one of those very rare hot English summer days. Dehydration comes to mind, as he was perspiring from pushing himself around in the wheelchair, in addition to this the hot sun was bearing down on his body without his usual free flowing tea. Following this episode he tried not to be caught out again without a bottle of diluted squash in his possession and a packet of crisps, even for the shortest of journeys he always made sure he transferred his bottle of squash from the car into his rucksack. It became his fashion accessory in the end, anything to avoid the repeat of that escapade. Unbeknown to him he may have kept his Adrenal signs and symptoms in check by keeping himself hydrated. It may have been the little man inside of him advising him, after all Julian was very good listener to his own body. The rest of us tend to ignore our body instinct and carrying on regardless, continuing to inflict more harm

So with hindsight Julian may have been suffering with Adrenal Fatigue long before it developed to full blown Adrenal Tumour!

The second tell-tale sign which I've mention before was in Pompeii when I may of miss took the incident for a sugar depletion where in fact he could have been suffering from an attack of Adrenal Crises.

There was a third tell-tale sign; unbeknown to most. Julian had two, Sebaceous Adenoma on the outside of his body. One was in the form of a large lump on his forehead camouflaged by his hair, the other on his biceps neither of them bothered him only if they were accidently pressed. He'd asked for them to be removed on a couple of occasions but he was told they were only fatty tissue. But just these two lumps could have acted as evidence for the doctor's at all three hospitals that he may have had one on his Adrenal gland; while we waited patiently for news of his medical notes to confirm that he did have an Adrenal Tumour.

I like most did not pay much attention to them, lymphomas are raised fatty lumps which homes a store of excess toxins that the liver has been unable to process. Patients are often told that they are nothing to worry about but in fact it's like ignoring a smoke alarm. A lymphoma is like a red warning flag that the body is out of balance. Removing the fatty tumour does not address the original problem; only removing the cause will prevent the lymphoma from reappearing.

There was one tell-tale signs that steamed back to when he was 14, when he first developed Boils as a teenager, suggesting his immune system was already starting to show signs of decline even then. Later when he was in his mid-twenties he developed Septicaemia hours after sustaining burns to both legs, the following year he developed a Sinus over his right hip, ten years after he developed osteomyelitis in his right hip and six months later he contracted MRSA all in the same hip. In 2008 he developed an Abscess again in his right hip a month later he suffered Necrotising Fasciitis which is a flesh eating bacteria caused by toxic shock syndrome.

Toxic shock syndrome is caused by 'Drug allergy' firstly causing the skin to peel away then leading to Necrotising Fasciitis, coupled with the fact that staph-infection were fast becoming resistant to most antibiotics.

If Toxic shock is caused by drug allergy Medical advice is <u>stopping the drug as soon as possible is imperative</u>. As we could not convince the medical profession he was suffering from any allergy, consequently the treatment could not be stopped. So when his mother had her 'outburst' in the Court room during Julian's Inquest regarding how she wanted him to take all prescribed antibiotics, it was in fact the Antibiotic Allergy that had caused his catastrophic Necrotising Fasciitis in the first place so it was more of a case of 'Less not More' antibiotics that was going to heal him.

They say bugs behave like cowards and attack the weakest spot; it's obvious to me now that Julian's Achilles heel was his immune system, his right hip taking the brunt of the attack almost every decade.

What I'm saying is from the early age of 14 his Adrenal glands had been bombarded with only a low immune system to fight back. When I consider all the other minor ailments he suffered in-between these more serious conditions, I don't know why I didn't stop and think "I need to heal this man's Immune system" I was so stupid!

It is possible to die from undiagnosed Adrenal Tumour if one slips into Adrenal Crisis, if one does not receive treatment. But Julian was very lucky he knew he had an Adrenal Tumour the problem was he couldn't convince any of the medical team he had one!

I didn't realise ex-Hep C sufferers should never be given Erythromycin or Aspirin; it can cause the Adrenal gland to become over worked.

The last tell-tail sign that I also did not connect to Julian's tumour was his insomnia. Evidently if you suffer from hormone imbalance it can cause malfunction in the neuro-transmitters in the brain leading to difficulty sleeping.

Cynthia Perkins, M.Ed has researched toxins effects on our physical and mental wellbeing.

Surprisingly she did not recommend sleeping tablets; she felt they caused additional stress on the nerve impulses in the brain.

She claimed the six main causes for insomnia are-:

1. Diet—all white refined food and junk food.
2. Excessive stress.
3. Genetic-born deficiency of magnesium, calcium, iron, B1, B5, B6, B3 and excessive level of copper and Chromium.
4. Food sensitivity.
5. Physical signs—restless legs, the need to urinate often, sleep apnoea, worry, working shifts and chronic pain.
6. Chemicals—herbicides, pesticides, perfumes, air fresheners, cleaning supplies and metal—poisoning.

Recommendations were; address all of the above including being tested for Adrenal fatigue and learn deep breathing techniques and how to meditate just before sleep.

Diagnosing Adrenal burnout can be a blessing in some cases. Once it's diagnosed, it can act as a wakeup call, even if it does take two years to cleanse the body of its toxins.

I was once told we all need a low level of stress to survive. How else can we jump out of danger if we don't suddenly experience a healthy amount of stress? It's when we experience too much of it and too often that causes the problem leading to the Adrenal glands being in a permanent state of stress leading to crisis.

I often used to ask Julian, "Are you sure that tumour shouldn't be removed"?

Since his death, I've read about a surgeon who claimed after he performed key hole surgery of removing the benign Adrenal Tumour, all his patients claimed that all the unbearable signs and symptoms had disappeared by the following day, including the relief they felt of not having to endure the treatment for diabetes they felt was harming them.

The terminology the Doctor referred to was "cured".

Admittedly the patients would have to take hydrocortisone cover periodically at such times as, before-during and after surgery preventing suffering from steroid crisis but only until the body was able to produce sufficiently steroid cover of their own.

Although our body is a wonderful piece of machinery and incredibly wise it is our poor personal judgment in a stressful society that is one of the reasons for exhausting our adrenal glands causing them to malfunction. We need to learn to chill out and respond to stress in a healthier ways.

Most Doctors feel the answer to the multitude of Adrenal malfunction symptoms is drug therapy, but there are a minority of Doctors who feel the answer is not more drugs but the opposite— elimination of all drugs including removing all toxic chemicals from the body.

I understand now, when Julian said to his friend Gerry at our family home while he was waiting for a bed at Oswestry, "I feel as if I'm dying" the anguish he was experiencing during those nine days before he was admitted into hospital, of being given drugs that he knew would harm him sent him over the edge into Adrenal crisis, which would have made him feel as if he was dying. The sad thing was there was no need for him to feel like this, he should have been introduced to cortisone treatment then educated on how to increase or decrease his own treatment according to how he felt. This adrenal crisis is very much a live or die complaint but not if your trained to manage it. Maybe, we need to become a better informed population?

His GP wrote in his notes the day his friend visited, "Patient does not appear Septicaemic" which meat he didn't have a temperature or was delirious as if he had Septicaemia or blood poisoning. As his GP confirmed, he was not in a sick or confused state. Yet Julian still uttered those few words to his friend the day before he was hospitalised, one can only surmise he was on the brink of Adrenal crisis!

When I realised Adrenal hormone insufficiency can lead to plural effusion, raised blood sugar and sepsis I could almost hear the tapping of the nails going into Julian's coffin.

Then finding out that replacing his absent steroid, could totally recover his ailing body, as long as he was given steroid boost during infection period, also prior, during and after operation.

Today's Addison sufferers could have normal life expectancy! There I rest my case.

Pandora's Box

In my last chapter I re-capped on what the Adrenal glands are responsible for and the signs and symptoms of Adrenal Tumour, now I intend to go back a little further to find out the second half of Julian's diagnoses and concentrate on the word 'Tumour'.

My question is; how is a tumour likely to develop?

Why did Julian have one and am I likely to have one or may be I've already got one.

This is when my Pandora's Box burst open, hence why I've called this chapter "Pandora's box"

For those who are not totally familiar with the fable or myth of Pandora's Box, I'll remind you of the story. According to Greek mythology Zeus gave Pandora a box containing evil. Tempted by curiosity Pandora opened the box and evil immediately flooded out and filled the world.

In terror she shut the box trapping only 'Hope'

The moral of the story is, don't let curiosity get the better of you by taking part in evil deeds.

This is the list I discovered that could trigger tumours.

- Hydrogenated oils.
- Processed foods.
- Exposure to toxic substance.
- Environmental factors.
- Artificial sweeteners.

At first I thought, they don't sound dangerous enough to cause a tumour to me but at the same time I did know we should air on the side of caution with some of them and not over indulge with the others. The only trouble was I was now beginning to feel uncomfortable because the list mentioned things I had either fed Julian or exposed him to throughout our married life.

Could I have been the main culprit for causing Julian's tumour, unknowingly I might have been.

I started to feel sick thinking others had accused me of harming him, could it turn out to be true! What I needed to do was to put my feelings to one side and research each topic mentioned in order on the list, and try not to be bias.

But I had to be honest with my findings even if it did put me in a bad light regarding what I exposed Julian to.

Hydrogenated oil

As instructed by Julian, I will go back to the beginning to see how Hydrogenated oil came about originally and was there a suspicious history attached to it. I wanted to know how, when and where it was introduced into the food chain.

First of all **how** did it get its name? Its name evolved because of the way it's treated, hydrogenated gas is pumped into it, hence its name 'hydrogenated oil'

My next question was; **when** did it come about? It was first invented by a French man in 1813 as mechanical oil, not much was done with it commercially other than using it for oil lamps up until 1914 when during the First World War it was used mainly to lubricate machinery in the front line. Things went quiet again until the Second World War when all nations experienced butter shortage. My third question was, **where** was it first converted into a buttery substitute. It appears it was the Germans who took the leading role by mass producing hydrogenated oil and converting it into margarine, it continued to be used in the rationing years following the war. It took a second wind and increased its popularity again in the 1960s due to diet fads, when we the consumers were made to believe through advertising, that margarine was healthier for us than butter. Before the margarine era, food production used coconut oil to get that buttery flavour and texture in our food. When coconut oil was replaced with this hydrogenated vegetable oil that's when we witnessed the explosion in worldwide obesity.

I wonder was this a coincidence or was there a connection?

My next question was, is it safe? If it was originally designed to be used in a dirty machine it seems to me, it's jumped from the engines on to our tables!

This didn't sound right to me; I needed to investigate the make-up of this oil further.

A friend of mine at work called Alison once told me that she always tried to made sure she included Tran's fats in her diet, after hearing this I started to wonder if Trans-fat was good or bad for us, I was a bit confused as to which oils were safe and which oils were not so safe for us.

I became increasingly suspicious when I discovered these alternatives substance to butter carried similar alarm bells. What was going on?

There is a variety of them on the market, but which ones are safe?

- Hydrogenated oil.
- Trans fats
- Rape seed oil.
- Mono-and di glycerines.
- Canola oil (Mono-unsaturated fats).
- Poly-unsaturated oil.
- Vegetable oil. (Check this one for hidden Rape seed in the ingredients.)
- Saturated fats.

First on the list was Hydrogenated oil, this contain high levels of Tran's fats. I read one scientist claiming, 'Tran's **fats are poisons, just like arsenic or cyanide.** They interfere with the metabolic processes of life; our body has no defence against them because they never existed in our two billion years of evolution—so we have never had the need or the opportunity to evolve a defence against them'.

These were very powerful statements, I wondered if he was qualified enough to write so boldly.

I took this quote from a book called, 'Fats that heel and Fats that kill' by Udo Erasmus. The writer was born in Poland to Latvian parents and at the age of 12 he immigrated with his family as a refugee to a 112 acre bush-land farm in Canada, this was during the Second World War. In adult life he received his B.Sc Degree in Honours Zoology with a Major in Psychology. Then in 1980 he was poisoned while carelessly working with pesticides, unfortunately medicine could not help him, but he managed to survive by burring himself in literature on nutrients and health. He concluded, his health was his responsibility and started to study and stumbled on an area that was the least understood, which was 'Fats and Oils' and in 1986 he earned himself a PhD on the subject. His nick name from then on become 'The Fat man' or 'His Royal Oiliness'

Sadly this hydrogenated oil he studied is hidden in nearly everything we eat these days. When we dine out our prepared food is soaked in it and he recommended we avoid deep fried foods, cooked in restaurants for this reason.

I quote another person Walter H. Schmitt. DIBAK and DABCN compiled notes on clinical nutritional products in 1990 in the North Carolina Chiropractic Journal,

"If its labelled hydrogenated or partially hydrogenated don't let your family eat it, if its labelled hydrogenated or partially hydrogenated don't let your friends eat it, if its labelled hydrogenated or partially hydrogenated in your friends kitchen then get out of their kitchen"

When we hear the word unsaturated fats, it means it's only had half the treatment of the 'hydrogenated gases' pumped into it. When they say the unsaturated fat interferes with the metabolic system they are referring to hormone imbalance such as blocking the secretion of the thyroid hormone and it also knocks out the immune system by killing the white blood cells necessary for fighting infection.

Polyunsaturated fats are similarly treated with only half the hydrogenated gas.

Not only does heating Hydrogenated oils alter protein it also changes into abnormal toxic fatty acids and destroys all vitamins and minerals. I'm sorry Julian; it seems I destroyed all your vitamins and minerals when I fed you this toxic oil.

Trans fats. The second one mentioned was Trans fats an artificial fat made by chemical process of partial hydrogenation. So my friend had been misled into thinking Trans fats were good for her.

To be fair it has a lot going for it from the producer's point of view, it has a long shelf life, it's cheap, it tastes good and is addictive, but the downfall is, it is higher in calories than most.

So it's no good going on a diet with this one then its other downfall is, we can't get rid of it, it lingers in our blood vessels it actually raises cholesterol readings, increases heart disease and has no nutrient value at all. Opposite to what I was led to believe years ago. Am I scaremongering?

In 2007 'McDonald's' fast food began to use 'Trans-fat-**free**-oil' in their cooking, why would they bother if Trans Fat is a good fat? Denmark has managed to totally ban Trans-fat successfully from their country. The Mail newspaper wrote on 1 July 2007 "Trans fats are STILL lurking in your weekly shopping" the article concluded "Government is letting us risk our lives through ignorance, there's not enough publicity about its dangers not like alcohol and tobacco"

A Nobel Prize winner V. Euler of Stockholm warned us in 1949, "The fat lacks the ability to integrate in the living tissue; Trans fatty acid is the name of the fat that lacks this ability. It is a bad fat" How ironic the country that first developed Trans Fasts was also the first to ban it in 2008, now in Calgary Canada Tran's fats have been banned in Restaurants and fast food establishments. Switzerland followed suit in 2008. Not UK though, we will wait a bit longer as usual. The FSA are asking for better labelling although eight leading food stores in the UK have removed it out of their own label food, but it's still found in leading brand names. I'm sorry I gave you this destructive bad fat Julian.

Rape seed oil. Third one mentioned was "Rape seed oil" I'm talking about the bright yellow fields that most British people say, "Ahhhhhh! Don't the fields look lovely" as they drive past with their windows wide open, then wonder why they have difficulty breathing when they arrive at their destination!

Not only was it originally manufactured as a lubricant and for engines, it is still used to make soap, synthetic rubber base, and as an illuminate to give colour pages in magazines a glossy slick look. In short it is Industrial oil that does not belong in the human body. It is typically referred to in the light industry as penetrating oil. It is also used to free rusty mechanical parts; I don't think we suffer with internal rust do you?

It forms a latex-like substance that causes blood corpuscles to clump together. Aw!

Rape seed was widely used in animal fodder in the UK and Europe between 1986-1991 but because animals went blind, mad and started attacking humans the Rape seed was removed from their feed and the attack and blindness stopped. So if it's not good enough for our livestock why would it be good enough for us humans? I'm not suggesting it was mad cow disease, but strange how it took place about the same time.

If we humans consume this rape seed oil could this be why youngsters are behaving in a 'thumping mad' behaviour towards other humans similar to the cows?

It then made me wonder about human eye complaints. A more recent popular eye complaint that one hears more about these days is "Macular hole" a condition that strikes people suddenly causing blindness (Reported in Wall Street Journal on 7th June 1995)

I found that study's had been conducted at Tufts University on 90,000 people over the age of 50 to see if fat intake had an impact on "Macular degenerative changes" Apparently people who ate Trans fats were much more lightly of developing this condition. These studies were done and published in 2001, there must be more recent studies done somewhere!

Researchers could not understand why saturated fats (once considered bad fat) did not cause Macular Degeneration. They mean butter and lard.

It appears that rape is a member of the mustard family plant, and the source for the chemical agent **mustard gas,** which causes blindness, blistering on the skin and chocking of the lungs when in-haled. Mustard gas was banned after World War One for these reasons. It has been rumoured that it was used in the Iraq v Kuwait in the Gulf war.

So why would we think consuming something similar in our diet would be safe 96 years later, haven't we grown wiser with the years, evidently NOT.

Rape seed oil protesters are claiming that, **rape seed is the most toxic of all food oil plants**. When I read not even insects will eat it, something is very wrong.

Wynn Stay Stores boasts in a 'Country and Border Life' magazine dated May 2010, that they sell bedding for animals from ponies to poultry, which has a pleasant citronella smell reducing insect's. It's made from the straw by-product of the oil seed called RAPE plant. (No wonder, insects don't bother it, they know better)

Rape seed oil is widely used in thousands of processed foods.

We need to be careful with some of this so called safe food, for example peanut butter. Some companies are removing the expensive peanut oil and replacing it with cheap **rape seed oil,** obtaining a better price for peanut oil. If it is not interfered with, it should only say peanuts and salt listed as ingredients on the label. It could have devastating effect if you're allergic to rape seed oil.

More to the point what could it cause?

The most worrying side effect, it can dissolve the myelin sheath of the nervous system, which can lead to numbness and tingling in extremities, heart arrhythmias, hearing problems, tremors, shaking, palsy, in—coordination with walking and writing, slurred speech, detrition of memory and thinking process, blurred vision, difficulty in urination, allergic to smells, breathing difficulties and unexplained exhaustion. It is often miss-diagnosed as Multiple Sclerosis.

The above makes sense to me now if mustard gas destroyed the nervous system then it stands to reason a small amount of it could still affect the nerve endings or its protective layers.

On the other hand if this vegetable rapeseed is safe, why can't I buy it as a raw vegetable in the supermarket, boil it and present it as an additional vegetable to grace my table to impress my guests? It sounds as if it's too dangerous for the housewife to handle it in its raw form, surely the big boys must have thought of this one already, anything to make a fast buck but not at the cost of being sued. Imagine all that pollen buzzing around the kitchen while Mothers were trying to get this beautiful yellow flower into their boiling pot while her children were running round her feet. One could almost imagine the rest of the family gasping for breath, at the same time squabbling over the inhalers.

I hope no one is taking the above paragraph seriously; I'm only mooching or summarising.

I found these statistics published in 1965 on world-wide Rapeseed production when 5.2 million Metric ton was produced, by 2005 the production had risen to 46.4 million metric ton.

The top Rapeseed production in 2007 was in China with 10.3 million metric ton.

Canada—9.5
India—7.4
Germany 5.3
France 4.4
Poland 2.13
British Isles 2.10
Australia 1.1
U.S. 0.7

Total world production this year was 50.5 million tons and the figure is still growing. That's a lot of pollen. There is a lot of controversy as to whose pollen blows over whose crop especially organic crops. When I see for myself how the seeds have blown onto motorways and are growing wild on motorway embankments, I can appreciate the organic grower's concerns.

But I'm not the only one worried about this synthetic oil, according to a Doctor Mary Enig from Silver Springs, Maryland an expert in fats and oils, with a PhD in Nutritional Sciences in 1984, she has health concerns with rape seed oil and has written 14 scientific papers including several books on the subject such as 'Dietary Sense and Nonsense' in1984, 'Know your fats' in the year 2000 and 'Eat fat, lose fat' in 2006.

A lay person called John Thomas wrote a book called "Young again" he believes to, "Give Rapeseed to a sick person they are doomed, to give Olive oil to a sick person and their immune system recovers" the book was recommended by Doctor Ralph.

I thought the Adrenal gland had a lot to answer for but I think this one tops the bill.

Protesters were worried what was going to happen if the consumer begins to become aware of the dangers of hydrogenated oil and Rape seed oil? Are the consumers going to stop using it?

They felt the answer would be "No" the companies would be devious enough to get in there first and change its name.

Well! It appears the worst has happened; they now call it Mono-di-glycerides oil but don't forget to keep up with them because they are sure to change it again now were on to them! Julian I'm sorry again, I fed you this toxic oil, further destroying your immune system.

Mono-di-glycerides (other name Rape seed oil)

Forth one mentioned, sounds like something that's about to blow up. Manufactures have now moved on to using the word Mono-and di-glycerides as an alternative name to Hydrogenated oil. Protesters are hoping that the law will step-in, in the next 10 to 20 years to stop this practice. Although the scientific knowledge has been available since the early 1990`s, so there is no doubt the Governments are aware of what they are doing. They have been ignoring the health effects for the sake of profit. The protesters believe such behaviour is both unethical and immoral with any luck one day soon it will be illegal as well.

It was a David Lawrence Dewey a journalist who first raised awareness of the dangers of Trans Fats. In 1996 the FDA asked for Trans fats to be labelled, but the manufactures then changed the name to Mono-and-di-glycerides. David Dewey then published in 1998 "It's just a new name to disguise an old silent killer"

If you do happen to find it labelled on your food package it will probably be printed so small you will find it difficult to read without your glasses. Possibly that's the idea, I fear they will continue to hide behind small print, then constantly re-invent the name on a regular basis which will no longer be pronounceable, and by the time you get to the Super Market you will have forgotten the name to look out for. How clever is that!

These are very sobering thoughts. Julian, I can't believe I fed you this silent killer.

Canola oil.

Fifth one mentioned was Canola oil, another genetically modified oil its name derives from Canada and oil. This one was produced on a grand scale in Canada, again for industrial use mainly a substitute for petrol and diesel for motor cars. I remember people jokingly years ago saying "What will they think of next, they are running cars on cooking oil now"

Allegedly the FDA did not pass Canola oil as safe until the Government paid the FDA a sum of $50 million dollars. (My source of this was book called Young again by John Thomas)

A licence was obtained by a scientist of the Canadian government to produce Rapeseed in 1954 but in 1956 the Department of National Health Welfare for Canada ruled Rapeseed not edible but in 1964 after a lot of controversy it was re-licenced and by 1974 Canola oil was produced after being extracted from Rapeseed.

As a matter of public record the Canadian Government and Industry paid the Food and Drug Administration $50 million dollars to have Canola otherwise known as Lear oil placed on the GRAS list 'Generally Recognised As Safe' as part of a scheme to sidestep the other lengthy and much more expensive approval process. No medical human research was completed for its safety before money was spent on promoting the oil. They did however conduct tests on rats that developed fatty degeneration of the heart, kidney, adrenal glands and the thyroid. When the Canola oil was withdrawn from their diet the deposits dissolved but the scar tissue remained on all the vital organs. The producers or farmers were amazed how quick the crop grew, how cheep the crop was to produce and lastly how low maintenance it was. But more surprisingly how pests did not touch it, consequently farmers did not have the expense of purchasing pesticides.

Canola oil is produced from Rape seed and the latest name for Canola oil is Mono-unsaturated fat.

I did find some write-ups about Canola oil in their defence, that it is healthy but none of the defenders had any letters attached to their names such as Doctor, PhD, MD, to support their theory's. I try only to quote highly qualified researched findings. I'm sorry Julian I know you liked tinkering with engines, but I didn't realise I was feeding you engine oil as well.

Polyunsaturated fats. The word poly means several, indicating many pairs of hydrogen atoms are missing which makes it incomplete and chemically unstable and prone to oxidation. Oxidation is when it's exposed to oxygen it becomes rancid, but it will have already started its rancid journey in the food shop when it is exposed to light, then further exposure to moisture increases the process. Heating it to high temperature finishes the process off causing a 'Jekyll and Hyde' effect especially when oxidation comes into play

We're looking at liquid peroxide travelling through our body, pillaging at every turn causing premature aging, skin diseases, liver damage, immune dysfunction, weight gain, inflammation even cancer.

With this insight into its behaviour, I'm concerned that the health sector are advising us to fry with it as it is meant to be healthier than lard for us. It leaves me wondering did Grandma know best, our ancestors didn't have peculiar conditions and diseases with strange lumps and bumps growing all over the place like our modern day society do.

Doctor Bruce Fife recommends if you want to prevent Diabetes, Alzheimer's and Cancer "Throw the Polyunsaturated out now, I know too much about what it can do the body" He recommends that the only fat one should use in high temperature is lard, butter or coconut oil; he claims these are the only ones that are stable when exposed to high temperature. I guess what he means is, 'fry less but fry safe' I confess it's hard to change a way of life when you've been brain washed into thinking the opposite!

Sadly I discovered prolonged use of polyunsaturated fats on a liver that's suffered previous Hep C can cause obesity. Milk Thistle is considered a good healer of damaged liver, but if the toxicity is allowed to continue then checkmate occurs with its repair. I'm sorry Julian I contributed to your obesity, when I fed you this oil believing it was safer than lard.

All these modern manufactured fats or oils appear to be much of a much-ness really; they all have some harming influence on our bodies.

<u>Saturated fats</u> was the seventh one mentioned, I think of this one as a word on its own, unattached to any other letters. When it's deranged and latches on to such beginnings as mono, poly and un then rest assured it has been tampered with, just like the product itself it has suffered genetically modified interference.

Examples of saturated fat are butter, coconut oil, animal fats and olive oil.

In most parts of the world heart disease escalated when the world started using genetically modified cooking oils. Prior to these oils, butter was used in Europe, ghee in India, pork lard in China, beef tallow in America and coconut and palm oil in the Tropics. That would explain why our grandparents were raised on bacon and egg every morning and yet lived to a grand old age.

We were brain washed into thinking Butter was the villain in the quest for good health in the 1960s, prior to this era heart disease was rare. After ditching the butter out of our diet, heart disease became our number one killer but our consumption of synthetic fat escalated.

When I realised the above, I took fright and started buying butter but just using small amounts of it. I soon discovered it contained polyunsaturated fat and monounsaturated fats, I then exchanged this butter for organic butter only to find it also contained polyunsaturated fat and monounsaturated fat.

I was Perplexed, how it could be called organic? Evidently organic means the soil the cows grazed on has not been contaminated with pesticides, the herd has not been given growth hormone and the stock has not been injected with antibiotics. The label organic is not free from synthetics.

All I wanted was pure and simple un-interfered with butter, just as it says on the wrapper!

When I was a child visiting friends and relatives in neighbouring farms, it was customary to be asked to take a turn at the butter churn so not to discontinue the continuous momentum of the churning. The only thing that went into those churns was cream, no interference such as hydro, mono or trans in those churns. How can they advertise modern butter as pure butter then?

By the skin of my teeth, I found a butter on the market that did not contain these unwanted interferences. The butter was made in my homeland Caerphilly, South Wales and is simply called 'Welsh Butter' I contacted the company asking them to confirm what I understood from their wrapping. If I had not discovered this butter, my next project was going to be to purchase a butter churn and make my own.

I'm not such an idiot to think it's fine to apply lavish amounts of butter on my bread, but it was interesting to read that Health promotion organisations say in the UK that 'children under the age of two should not be on fat-restricted diet because cholesterol and fat are thought to be important for brain development'.

What about me, my brain is important to me too!

There must be something good in butter if we should not deny our younger generation it. Evidently it contains vitamin A, D, Iodine and Butyric acid. Iodine maintains thyroid function; vitamin A prevents blindness especially in children. Butyric acid helps absorption of vitamin D for strong teeth and bones. The cows access this through the grass, passing it into the milk supplying the butter with ant-inflammatory, anti-cancer, anti-Chrohn's disease and other immune diseases. Finally butter is a good antitoxin that protects young developing brain-cell membranes from damage. Our babies are born innocent and pure, what are we giving them to eat?

I feel the 'take home message on this one' is; if you're scared of this fat called butter, study the alternative you're taking right now!

All this talk about bad oils, left me wondering how does this coconut oil fare up? It appears to be a multi-purpose oil 'a friend amongst enemies'. It can aid Fibromyalgia sufferers, if ingested it can prevent your skin from burning while sunbathing, what you might call a 'protection from within' and it can also fight infection.

On the olive oil front according to Doctor Kiritsakis a world renowned oil chemist in Athens who says in his book called, "Olive oil, from the tree to the table" second edition 1998. The myth that adding olive oil to vegetables when roasting destroys their nutrients is not true on the contrary he claims it adds taste and is a healthy anti-oxidant, this style of cooking is found mainly in a Mediterranean diet.

How confusing, I first understood years ago that saturated fats (e.g. butter, lard, coconut oil, palm oil) were bad for us; now at the age of 55 I understand differently that too much saturated fat is still bad for us but the most shocking news of all I've discovered is, 'all man made artificial fats' are not only bad for me, but downright dangerous because I can't get rid it.

This hydrogenated oil has taken a terrible beating in the press lately, referred to as 'bad fats', 'man-made fats', 'evil Tran's fats' and I think the worst one was labelled by David Lawrence Dewey who raised the aware ness of its danger in 1996 by calling it the 'Silent killer' If what all these protesters are saying is not true then why aren't the Hydrogenated oil companies taking these accusations to court for liabilities?

No wonder my friend Alison Tranter and I were confused as to what fats were good and which ones were bad, it's taken me months of studying the above to condense it to only a few pages.

It leaves me wondering about the people who boast of losing weight using these synthetic fats, are they putting their insides at risk by developing pockets of toxins leading to internal lumps, bumps and tumours at a later date?

After many years of the scientist studying the 'pros and cons' of which ones are healthiest for us, the dust is still settling on the battle fields between the good and the bad fats.

I think they have established that, the only question remaining is which one will turn out to be the ugliest for our long term health? Now you can see how easy it was for me to unwittingly feed Julian's tumours.

The good, the bad and the ugly fat stories.

I have recently found very disturbing stories of other peoples experiences connected to these oils and fats, I trust they are true stories otherwise I'm in trouble.

A son wrote about his father who bred birds, he was always checking the labels to ensure there was no Rape Seed in their feed. He said, "The birds eat it, but sadly they did not live very long after".

Another story tells of two factory workers where Canola oil was used for frying, the two of them developed health problems. Loose teeth, grey nail beds, numb hands, cramps, swollen arms and legs, cloudy vision, hearing loss, easily skin tears, lack of energy, hair loss.

One night the two employees took the waste product home and fed it to their baby calves. The calf's hair all fell out. After stopping the feed, their hair grew back.

Another tale was of a Mum who was telling a joke, tapped her daughters arm with the back (flat part) of a butter knife, in a gesture. The daughters skin on her arm split open as if it was rotten. The Mother said, "I bet you anything that you're using Canola oil". Sure enough there was a big gallon container in the pantry. I am now worried that I might be accused of advising people to revert and indulge in a 'butter eating' diet, when their GPs have advised them to eat only margarine and cook in hydrogenated oils to lower their cholesterol.

I came across a lady called Zoe Harcombe who graduated at Cambridge University and wrote a book called 'The Obesity Epidemic, What causes it, How can we stop it?' it was published in 2010. But was she qualified enough to give advice on the subject? Well! She has conducted 'Obesity Research' obtained a Diploma in 'Diet and Nutrition' and gained another Diploma in 'Clinical weight management'

What she writes about cholesterol makes sense, but is it true?

I quote her claims, "We will die instantly without cholesterol, so why do we try to stop the body producing it? There is no good or bad cholesterol. Cholesterol is cholesterol. Cholesterol is transported in the blood by tiny 'Couriers' called lip-o-pro-teins. There are five lipoproteins formed in the body in different sizes with different density.

They are—: Extremely Low Density Lipoproteins (ELDL), Very Low Density Lipoproteins (VLDL), Intermediate Density Lipoproteins (IDL), Low Density Lipoproteins (LDL) and High Density Lipoprotein (HDL) All five carry triglyceride, proteins, phospholipids and cholesterol. All five cholesterols play a vital role, and together they actually repair damaged vessels.

So why do GPs pick on one of them informing patients there are good and bad cholesterols in our bodies? Stopping any of these cholesterols doing their job, is like accusing the police of committing a crime or trying to shoot the Samaritan.

I found another Self-help advice recommended by Stephen Stiteler, LAC, OMD, NMD, D.Hom, FBATCM and FOHAI.

Who suggests exercise three times a week, eat plenty of fruit and vegetables a day, eat 30% of your daily required saturated fats, eat organic diet, never drink tap water unless filtered, relax and play, lastly obtain prescribed herbal supplements from your GP, avoiding Statin drugs with their side effects.

I wondered why he mentioned fruit and veg, and this is why. He asks us to imagine the LDL as a weak person walking inside our blood vessels carrying cholesterol, but it's too heavy to carry so it drops it on the way like litter and it manifests itself into a plaque and sticks to the wall of the blood vessel. But if we were to eat plenty of fruit and veg the work load of the LDL would be made much easier. Whereas the HDL is stronger and can be relied on to deliver the goods to the liver for the gallbladder to break down the fats. Don't forget that's why we were given a gallbladder in the first place, at the same time don't abuse the poor liver by eating excessive amount of saturated fat e.g. butter. Also remember the liver cannot tolerate, deal with, digest or dispose of any synthetic fats.

Daily intake of Vitamin E is essential to act as an anti-oxidisation.
To clarify the difference between the two—:
Oxidation harms our body where as
Anti-oxidation protects us against bad chemicals and radicals.

When I told Julian he was suffering from was BIG, I had no idea its roots may lie across the water in America and Canada. But my quest of finding out exactly 'how and why' he developed these tumours, are still not completely clear yet.

I'm holding on to Pandora's hope, hoping that one day I will be able to say, "Julian, I've cracked it, I've found out why you suffered like you did"

Processed food and Additives

The second cause they gave for triggering tumours was processed food, once again I went back to the beginning to find out <u>why</u>, <u>where</u> and <u>when</u> it came about.

I knew in ancient times the Romans preserved their food in salt, but that's not the same as processing food. During my childhood days on the farm I was familiar with the way my ancestors preserved seasonal foods using natural methods such as salting, jamming, pickling, smocking, fermenting and sun drying process.

Food processing has evolved away from these simple practices of preserving, to much more complicated and dubious processes with some devastating effect on our health.

The modern method of preserving food today is pasteurising, sterilizing, canning, freezing and irradiating not forgetting chemical additives.

Most processed food today can be recognised as either 'Boxed, Bagged or Canned'

My first question was <u>why</u> it came about? Food manufactures would argue it was to feed the world, but I suspect it was more to do with their financial gain. But I fear we the consumers are a bit at fault here too, we were suckered into buying these convenience foods because it freed us from the chains of the cooker and the sink. We used to prepare all our food from scratch using only fresh produce. Today we prefer to opt for fast food allowing us more time for recreation and becoming keep fit fanatics.

My second question was; <u>where</u> did its journey begin?

I don't know exactly who first invented its process, but people in high authority have known about the effects of this type of food on our bodies since after the Second World War.

I was then horrified to discover a Doctor Potterger who in 1940 financed his own research on the influence of processed food in cats. He studied 900 cats and divided them into five categories.

The first two groups were fed raw food and they remained healthy throughout the experiment.

The remaining three groups were fed processed food.

The first generation developed health conditions such as arthritis, allergies and diabetes in their later years.

The second generation developed the same conditions during the middle of their life span.

The third generation developed the same condition again, but this time very early on in their life.

One has to ask is the same pattern reoccurring in humans!!!!!!

On the account of this test alone, Doctors and Scientists should have been on the lookout for this new complaint now called Type Two Diabetes after the release of processed food into our worldwide markets.

If the above is true where have all the Endocrinologists been all these years, why haven't they been looking into third generation Type Two Diabetes, and connecting it to processed food like Doctor Potterger did in 1940? **Wake up sleepy heads, do something**

During the process of producing Processed foods it destroys the natural nutrients in our diet, evidently there are nearly 40 nutrients that our bodies cannot produce; they include 15 vitamins, 14 minerals and 10 amino acids. If we need these 40 nutrients to function normally, then it stands to reason if the process of producing processed food has destroyed these nutrients, our bodies are going to fall short of a healthy outcome.

Last question was <u>when</u> were we first exposed to this new style of food industry? Food adultery started just after the Second World War but it took off in earnest between 1960 and the 1970s. I've just learnt there are nearly 6,000 additives and chemicals used to preserve our food today.

Each year Food industry uses 3,000 tons of food colouring and 2,000 different types of flavouring.

These chemicals are also known to cause such conditions as, asthma, nausea, vomiting, headaches, migraines, cancer, brain damage, trigger allergies, high blood pressure, high cholesterol, impairing liver and kidney function, **tumours** and are toxic to the nervous system.

There are 12,000 babies born each year with deformities, is there any wonder?

I have known for a long time that too much processed food was not good for me, but the question was how much was too much, and how bad was too bad?

I'll deal with the 'too much' first then 'how bad' after, I have established that the technique they use to process the food destroys the natural vitamins and minerals. To compensate for this, the food manufactures replace the vitamins but unfortunately we still fall short of the missing minerals. Discolouring and altering the taste in the process forces the companies to replace colour and taste with synthetic additives in order to make it attractive and tasteful once more. The food additives consist of such things as flavourings, colour agents, texture enhancer agent and preservatives to extend their 'shelf life' such as nitrites and sulphites which may cause adverse health effects.

To me that covers 'too much' because that's too much messing with my food, it also covers 'too bad' because it's left me with robbed nutrients type food.

My discovery of food additives were not yet over, I looked up another two additives found on most of our processed foods called Guar Gum and the other Xanthan Gum. They are both registered under GRAS, which stands for 'Generally Regarded as Safe' this means it was once under suspicion but allowed back on to the market until they found enough finance to conduct further research! Does that sound safe to you?

Xanthan Gum derives from a bacterium, which causes black rot on vegetables a synthetic sugar called corn growth a medium is added along with isopropyl alcohol which is known to interact with parasite in the body. This one is not suitable for anyone who is corn sensitive or is a celiac sufferer and especially if one suffers with complaints such as bloating, gas, diarrhoea or migraine headaches.

Question is; are you experiencing Xanthan reaction?

Although its counterpart is considered to be a plant grown mainly in India, people are advised if they have any history of colon cancer in the family they should be cautious when consuming large amounts of Guar Gum.

Guar Gum used to be sold as a weight loss agent, but the tablet was recalled and later banned following several hospitalisations and in one case death. I ask myself why is it allowed in most of our food in small quantities, where are the food safety laws here? I wonder if they mean its ok for us to die slowly but we must not do it quickly because that would raise suspicions!

Both act as a laxative, both are able to absorb toxic substances including bacteria which can later cause infective diarrhoea.

I'm just pondering if I should enlist a double entry here of Pesticides as I feel it also comes under additives; after all they have added it to our food and that makes it an additive in my book.

If all the above mentioned carries the risk of inflicting allergies I have found two Doctors who are willing to lend a sympathetic ear to the cause. They are resident Doctor Hilary Jones from ITV `Day break` who was in agreement with a patient taking an interest in food allergy, he is quoted saying; "For years the orthodox medical profession has neglected the role of food intolerance in ill health, this includes a range of symptoms including eczema, IBS, bloating, fatigue, migraine and many others.

The other doctor was Doctor Chris Steele MBE, who also appears on ITV `This Morning` Resident Doctor and is quoted in the same pamphlet saying "I'm a GP and to be honest, I would not think of food intolerance initially, but I think we should be more aware of it.

Discovering all these things about our food could easily turn some of us to drink, but I'm not so sure that's safe now either as nearly all our wines contain a preservative called Sulphur Dioxide otherwise found under E220. The word Dioxin refers to a chemical that's has a negative effect on our health. International Lab Organisations asked us to avoid this one as it destroys vitamins and minerals causing untold effect on conditions such as asthma, hypertension, conjunctivitis, bronchitis, emphysema or cardio vascular conditions. Something else to destroy our already depleting vitamins and minerals, I can't believe I'm almost vitamin sterile!

Apparently red wine produces its own sulphur naturally and does not need this additional Dioxide chemical, but the producers put it in any way. Sweet wine has the most as the grape skin is removed early on in the process. This is my new 'did you know' sulphur dioxide contributes significantly to 'hangovers'. Look out for organic wines that state no added sulphur dioxide on the bottle, I will enjoy researching this one myself thank you just to see if it gives me a hangover.

I then felt some thought should be spared for our Pet Food? Guess what, they dont have a governing body looking after their food at all, so I allocated someone and called him 'Mr Nobody' that's who's looking after man's best friend. We should be worried that the pet food industry has no controlling body to answer to; because it seems to me the same low standard eventually sneaks into our food chain.

Anything goes in the food industry so it seems. I don't understand because when it comes to catering standards we have to be squeaky clean, whereas it's a different matter when it comes to the cooking pot, nothing changes until it's challenged. So let's challenge them!

It is still sad to see written on some food packaging, "no additives", there shouldn't be any anyway.

How can I set about banning food additives in our food?

I decided to see if there was any advice I could find on the net of how we as a nation could legally protest. The first step they recommend was to learn as much as you could about the issue first, then sign petitions, write to your government and local government, even the food stores themselves so they can pass on your concerns to the manufacturers.

Martin Luther once wrote, "If you want to change the world pick up your pen and write"

And my recommendation to you is similar, 'Don't break the law, let the pen win the war'.

Let's start by writing to the companies of your favourite foods and ask them to have a bigger print on their labels, so we can read them in the supermarket stores, and then ask them what are they trying to hide behind their small print?

What else can I do to prevent these additives entering our food?

Some customers are already effectively using boycott strategies, when they come across foods such as hydrogenated oils in them, they place them at the back on the shelf upside down and back to front, especially if it's found on the healthy shelf (surly this is false advertising.)

I must confess I have become a bit of a rebel and joined forces with the boycotters by doing the same in the big supermarkets turning the content label out wards for other costumers to take note of the ingredient label.

The biggest food additive we consume each day, that we may not be aware of is Mono-Sodium-Glutamate otherwise known as MSG. How did it come about?

MSG was originally discovered by a Japanese Professor Ikeda in 1908.

He loved his wife's soup so much he decided to reproduce her soup stock, which she made from seaweed. After spending six months studying, the Professor published his findings. A company approached him but informed him that extracting kelp from sea weed was not realistic because for every 10kg of kelp only 0.2 g was obtained.

Originally MSG was made from wheat, soybean and seaweed; later MSG was made from bacterial fermentation of sugar water and sodium. Professor Ikeda's original fermentation used to take six months to complete but modern MSG has additional ingredients and contains harsh flavours and chemicals and now only takes two days to produce.

To be fair a MSG company conducted their own safety test, using a 'Plaebo'.

Unfortunately the 'Plaebo' was Aspartame, an artificial sweetener which gave the controlled group the same result. They were confident it would give them the result they wanted before they even started!

Don't forget MSG is another ingredient that cannot be cooked using high temperature without some chemical reaction. I suspect that's why when you buy some oven chips it states oven bake or grill but no instructions on how to cook using high temperature as in deep frying. Why not it's only supposed to be potato!

Unfortunately for us, we the consumers cannot find the letters MSG on our food labels, but it will be hiding under such names as yeast extracts, caseinate, cutolyzed plant protein, whey protein, hydrolysed oat flour, textured protein, 'natural flavours' and 'flavours'.

Evidently MSG can play havoc with our body by causing side effects such as instant diarrhoea, but more worrying MSG is believed to go through the brain barrier, unlike other agents such as analgesia drugs which can't. These MSG can lead to such complaints as insomnia, headaches, and more seriously Alzheimer's. Once in the brain, it picks on a random area and sends the body hyperactive, it also disrupts normal appetite and function preventing us losing weight. I'm concerned that most Governments don't mind that these chemicals are rammed in nearly everything we eat. The problem is once were on the MSG trail, the more we eat it the more we crave it—just like a drug addict craves their drugs.

You may be thinking; if MSG food has been used widely in Eastern Society for such a long, why doesn't the Eastern society suffer from the same complaints as headaches, insomnia, obesity and Alzheimer's as us in the West? The answer is the Easterners eat sea weed in abundance in their diet which combats the chemicals and acts as anti-toxins. The problem we have here in the West and in fact in the rest of the world is we don't include sea weed in our daily diet, because it's not to our pallet.

MSG is responsible for such a lot of disruption in the body, for one it mimics sugar causing an insulin response which stimulates the pancreases to produce more insulin, telling the cells in your body to absorb sugar and within an hour or two we are low in sugar again. Our body then says, "Feed me, I'm hungry"

So we eat, but the food we eat has more MSG in, so we produce more insulin than we need so we eat again, and again and so on.

Hmmmmm . . . . Sounds a bit familiar or suspicious to you?

How many times have we eaten a meal and said; I could eat that again, I know I have. My tummy can be ready to burst but my brain tells me I'm still hungry.

Allegedly MSG is another one that does not belong in the human body, it can disrupt the normal appetite and function of our body preventing us losing weight. If we have **adrenal problems**, and we eat MSG food our fight, fear and flight should kick in to compensate the chemical reaction. Instead the brain rationalises the problem, but does not tell the gut to hold tight so your gut panics and suddenly you have diarrhoea or tachycardia and possibly heart palpitations.

I think everyone needs to make their own mind up about MSG food whether it is good or bad for us. What I wanted to know is; is it time you all take responsibility in finding out for yourselves what's gone into your food, instead of listening to all this 'brain washing hype' of what others think is good for us. You know the familiar phrase we often use, "Do I have to do everything myself, round here" The answer to that question is "Yes" you do, because you can't trust the big companies to stop medalling with your food. It has now become your responsibility not mine or others, <u>YOURS.</u> Not for the sake of your body but for the sake of all our 'tomorrow's children'

In short we need to become DIY'ers in spotting what food contains MSG, the problem is most of us aren't even aware were eating it, because it's not a requirement in this country to include it on the food label.

What examples of 'processed food' are we to be on guard against?

- Homogenised dairy products, such as milk, cream ? yogurts.
- Sterilized milk.
- Processed cheese.
- All canned foods, 'processed peas' spell it out for us.
- Bread made with white refined flour.
- Pasta made with refined white flour.
- Crisps
- Sweets
- Frozen dinners
- Cakes made with white refined flour and sugar.
- Biscuits made with white refined flour and sugar.
- Breakfast cereals
- Processed meats

These brand names contain Monsanto MSG products—
Kraft, Knorr, Kellogg's, Natural Valley, Hellman's, Hunts, Pepsi, Green Giant, Uncle Bens, Pringles, Proctor and Gamble, Coca Cola, Ocean Spray.

My new rule of thumb now is, 'if the food is boxed, bagged or canned think twice'!

I also have some other worries about what is put in some of our food, these are just random examples of what I found on some food labels; they are—:

- Anal glands of a Beaver in Raspberry sweets and some vanilla ice cream!
- Lanolin from sheep's wool in bubble gum!
- Coal tar in some sweets!
- Sand in some anti-caking agent and in pre-grated cheeses!
- Mashed chicken carcass in hot dogs—you know the odd crunchy bit!
- Anti-freeze in low fat ice cream.
- Titanium dioxide in skimmed milk.

The above list might be legitimate, but do they sound right to you?

Hence why this chapter has two titles, 'Processed food and Additives' I didn't realise the additives were so serious. The producers claim the additives are so small in quantity, they don't have to list them under ingredients, but why is it necessary to include them at all, I ask myself?

I am beginning to get a bit angry now, how dare they hide such things in our food, its dishonest not to disclose these unnatural farm and mechanical products in our food chain. I don't want to sound paranoid but are they laughing behind our backs, I fear they are? What I wanted to say is "Take me to your leader" let me tackle you face to face. But there doesn't seem to be one person in charge, it's an organisation that has the ability to change disagreeable situations at lib, but nothing more. The organisation is called FSA which stands for Food Standard Agency that was introduced in the year 2000 to act as an independent watch dog for the UK. Now ten years later FSA are going to be disbanded and its responsibility will be shifted to the Department of Health and the Department of Environment and Food and Rural Affairs, otherwise known as DEFRA for short.

Exposure to toxic substance

The next topic that was mentioned lightly to triggering tumours was exposure to toxic substances. This could turn out to be a short chapter as neither Julian, Llewela or I had any connections with toxins. But I soon discover we didn't have to be naughty teenagers and sniff glue to induce toxic substances.

I thought I'd go back to where we all started to tox-ify ourselves; history of manufacturing toxic chemicals can be traced back to 1825, but didn't seriously affect us until the 1960s with such contamination as DDT which affected our wild life to start with. Secondly the Toxins and synthetic chemicals started to threaten and affected our environment by poisoning our water supply, our air, land, oceans and our future. Luckily for us in 1971 Green Peace came about and one year later in 1972 Friends of the Earth was founded and both have been fighting our chemical wars on our behalf for the last 40 years.

The only toxin I could recall handling was normal household washing up liquid, it might say mild on the bottle but still toxic. I'm nearly sure it was Trevor McDonald the ex-news reader who did a documentary about how bad caustic soda in washing up liquid was to our health. Since that day I have when I wash up, rinsed every surface of any crockery that is going to have food or drink resting on its surface. For example surfaces of plates, cups, mugs, cutlery and glasses.

Previous to this program I once poured myself an orange squash into a tall tumbler at work when I noticed a large collection of bubbles on the top. I stupidly mistook them for the gush of water from the tap causing the bubbles to form on the top, I hurriedly drank half the tumbler and instantaneously felt a burning sensation in my throat. I soon realised someone had failed to wash the tumbler correctly and inadvertently left some washing up liquid in the glass. How do I know this, because the bubbles remained on the top of my squash with its shiny multicolour froth? That burning in my throat remained with me for two whole days.

The other harmful substance I was vaguely aware of was the rumour that white bread contained bleach. I wondered if this was true or false and if it was true, could it be classified as some sort of toxin. Guess what, it can and is!

I used to worked with a Consultant for some years who used to get distressed if he caught the nurses making his patients toast using white sliced bread. He used to argue that it was only a matter of time before his patient needed further surgery on their bowels if they continued to eat white bread. We used to plead with him, saying we have to respect the patient's choices and wishes.

I remember once someone telling me how the American soldiers used to complain either during the Second World War or just after the war that British bread looked grey unlike there's back home, which was white and sliced.

I don't know how much truth there was in that tale but I was aware that our famous sliced white bread did come about around that time.

To back up some of these possible theories, I remember offering a patient a choice of either brown or white bread after his surgery, he went off on a tangent screeching why would he want white bread? It transformed he was a retired pharmacist, because of this flair up I asked him to enlighten me. He did by telling me it was a product called Benzyl Peroxide that was used to whiten the flour in white bread.

Other common use for Benzyl Peroxide is hair lightener; it is also an active ingredient for teeth whitening. It is potentially an explosive component in its raw form hence it can cause a fire without external ignition. We ingest this stuff, it's frightening isn't it, by the way it is more commonly known as "Bleach"

I now discover 9% of the flour used to make British bread comes from Canada.

Why can't we produce our own flour? We throw plenty of it away; I don't see the sense of carting food halfway across the world. What a waste of fuel then we throw half of it away once it arrives here or worst still feed it to the ducks, poor ducks! No wonder people complain of distended abdomen after eating white refined flour with all that bleach inside them, it stands to reason our insides are going to expand or ferment.

Our modern diet of refined sugar and flour further depletes our chromium levels which we so desperately need to maintain glucose levels. Is this why Diabetics are told to eat brown bread, what about the non-diabetics wont they fast become diabetics without chromium?

I then recalled a study day I attended after Julian died with my friend Gill, Gweno and my Father on how to make simple herbal medicine. When we were offered some refreshments one of the ladies' that day declined saying she was allergic to the polystyrene cups. The conversation unravelled that she had an allergy test done which also indicated she was also allergic to white refined sugar and was advised to recognise sugar as 'poison'. At the time she was due to have her tonsils removed a few days later, she immediately excluded the sugar from her diet and was able to cancel the surgery and announced her childhood complaint as cured.

This word poison sounded like a serious statement to me, I then looked up its definition in my Collins English Dictionary, it stated "To exert a harmful influence"

Scientists knew about the danger of this product refined sugar as long ago as 1957 when a Doctor William Martin said that refined sugar was worse than nothing in nutrient value. In fact he said that refined sugar strips the body of its vitamins and minerals such as salt, potassium, magnesium and calcium.

He said; initially the excess refined sugar is stored in the liver in the form of glycogen. When the liver capacity is full the liver expands like a balloon. The sugar is returned into the blood stream as fatty acids and is forced to be stored in inactive areas such as the belly, buttocks, breasts and thighs. When even they become full, the sugar then seeks shelter around the heart and kidneys causing such complaints as high blood pressure and malfunction of the immune system. In other words our bodies have become hoarders of sugar.

But I digress again; my question was how did our sugar become white? In 1929 in Panama, Sir Fredric Banting witnessed amongst sugar plantation owners who eat large amounts of refined sugar, suddenly suffered from Diabetes.

Whereas the native Cane Cutters who were only allowed to chew the raw cane, did not suffer from Diabetes at all!

I'm still asking the same question, how did the sugar become white?

At the last stage of the refining they add either Carbon Dioxide or Sulphur Dioxide in order to bleach the discoloured cane juice. So I was right all along refined sugar is bleach after all.

I see there are books available on how refined sugar can de-rail your health and how absence of refined sugar can put your health back on track!

Another product I've recently started buying is organic tea bags, but wondered why the bags had a brownish tinge to them. The answer is the bags are not bleached; it leaves me wondering what chemical reaction happens in my cup with ordinary tea bags when I pour boiling water on the bleached bag!!! Yak!

How much more bleach can my body take?

For Lent I gave up white re-fined sugar and to my surprise my menopausal hot flushes nearly stopped. But once Lent was over and I dropped my guard and indulged in the occasional sugar intake, back came my 'hot flashes' not flushes as they call them now. I don't claim they are scientifically connected, I'm only telling you what happened to me.

I realise I've already brought up the subject of margarine in the last chapter but I find myself drawn to talk about it again, this time from a toxic point of view.

My sister once frightened me about what went into margarine, so I stopped using it then thinking at least butter is natural. Now I intended to find out exactly what frightened me, and what ingredients do go into manufacturing margarine? The content contains an oil blend, water, milk, salt, soy lecithin, citric acid, artificial flavours, vitamin A, beta carotene for colour and veggie mono-and-di-glycerides (try to remember this long name when you're out shopping)

That was the recipe now here is the method.

Margarine starts with cheap poor quality vegetable oil(often Rapeseed oil or Cotton seed oil) by using high temperature and high pressure it changes it into rancid oil, causing cell damage and premature aging in our population and a host of other problems in humans. More however some of these oils are not fit for human consumption to begin with. As mentioned in previous chapter's rape seed oil was designed originally to run motor cars. The cotton seed crop used to make the cotton seed oil is the most heavily chemical sprayed crops there is in the world, in other words cotton seed oil may be highly contaminated with pesticide residues. The raw oil is then steamed cleaned thus destroying all the vitamins and antioxidants. It is steamed cleaned for the second time to remove the odour. The oil is then bleached to get rid of its grey colour; if this wasn't done it would remain grey and smelly grease.

In fact, originally American margarine was whitish grey and resembled lard. The product was left in this state to protect the consumer, so it wouldn't get mixed up with butter. How interesting, should we still be keeping them separate too and if so why? Why are they trying to camouflage this grey smelly grease? The process is not yet finished synthetic vitamins and artificial flavours are then added.

A George Caldwell wrote on the 10th November 2010 that "Cardiologist, Doctors, Hospital Dieticians, Pharmacists and Pharmacological Industry have been misled for 50 years, into thinking that margarine was a healthy option. It was originally used to fatten turkeys but unfortunately all the turkeys died"

I originally intended to stay focused on Julian's Diabetes and not get side tracked onto other topics. But as I fear I would have a case to answer for, if I was seen discredit margarine when their GP's had advised them to do so to reduce their cholesterol.

I know I've already mentioned how important the five cholesterols are for our body to function adequately, but there's something not right about this cholesterol, why are we suffering from these abnormal levels and what causes some peoples cholesterol to spike like they do? I read on 25th May 2010 of Byron J. Richards a Board Certified Clinical Nutritionist who wrote about derange cholesterol levels, ". . . it has only one purpose in public health dogma and that is to scare people into taking toxic-statin drugs to lower their cholesterol!" A new study shows that people with high cholesterol taking statins have increase rates of chest pain, heart attacks and death. He describes the system as the low cholesterol as a truck delivering fat, antioxidants and other products around the body, it only becomes bad when it's insulted by been overloaded with toxins. The high cholesterol is like its tow truck towing it back to the liver to be recycled. If this scenario is left to continue the body starts to suffer from 'Toxic Stress' it's up to us to recognise our raised cholesterol levels and change our diet to heal and balance our cholesterol. He claims taking a toxic drug to try and suppress high cholesterol is like taking away the tow truck!

Evidently the true culprit for their rocketing cholesterol is tap water and homogenized milk. I'm shocked! So can homogenized milk alter cholesterol levels more to the point what is homogenized milk anyway? How I understand it, during the process of producing homogenizing milk it is beaten up and put under such high pressure that the fat particles are broken down into such minute globules that it is fine enough to enter the blood stream.

While milk from cows that are not exposed to this 'high pressure technique' called homogenized, contains natural cream particles floats on the top and believe it or not are not harmful fat because the larger fat molecules pass through the digestive system to be later defecated (down the toilet) Whilst homogenised milk is so pulverised the fat globules are small enough to entering the blood stream lingering in the blood vessels. This is opposite to what I was made to believe years ago, which would explain why our ancestors lived longer without complaints of high cholesterol while banqueting on full fat diet of butter milk and cream.

But what about this culprit number two our tap water, evidently the chlorine in the water reacts with the oxidize cholesterol in our body causing plaque to clogs up the arteries.

I wondered how I could confirm if we still receive chlorine in our drinking water?

I decided to write to my water supplier regarding my concerns. My reply was prompt; he categorically assured me there were no pesticides, toxic waste or hormones in my drinking water. He also enclosed a further water quality summary report which claimed their drinking water standards in the UK are the toughest in the world. In the report that was sent I was pleased to find no traces of Aluminium, Colour, Iron, Lead, Mercury, Nickel, Nitrate, Sodium, Chloride and Sulphur. Concussively in my district, unfortunately, there is no Chromium either, which we need to help us with our glucose balance. He said he could not vouch for other districts.

Even though I received 128 results, the report did not include Chlorine and Fluoride the very two products I enquired about. To get this information I decided to save time and I would ring them up. The answer was; yes there is Fluoride in our water supply. Quality control over this one is in the hands of each local district council, they dictate how much Fluoride is put in daily. He also confessed there is Chlorine in the water, one part per million. Is this I wonder enough to cause high cholesterol along with the Hydrogenated milk amongst our population? I do remember one water supplier on the news not so long ago accidently pouring too much chlorine into water causing untold death to the fish population, and if chlorine is another word for bleach no wonder they died. The other place you hear the word chlorine is at the public swimming baths, how many times have you come away from the pool with red or pink eyes and feel nauseas because you've swallowed some water. And what about having difficulty breathing in the steamy atmosphere, as if your lungs are closing up whilst you are getting changed? Is this because swimming pools are heated and heating bleach causes fumes?

My next question was, are there any adequate filters on the market to filter these two little horrors, namely Chlorine and Fluoride from my drinking supply. The answer is, "Yes" for a price you can buy anything but check it says on the box it filters chlorine and fluoride most don't. Of cause the more elaborate the filter the more flamboyant the price. You get what you pay for in this world. The question is how serious is your cholesterol problem at the moment.

Also avoid distilled water as it contains the wrong Ionization.

There appears to be two types of Fluoride natural and synthetic man-made. It's the synthetic Fluoride that's added to our drinking water that derives from Industrial waste, Fertilisers, Nuclear weapons, Mining waste and Chimney scrubbers. This next fact is interesting; in 1952 Germany conducted an experiment to fluoridating their drinking water. But it was forbidden after two years in West Germany and when East Germany joined forces once more in 1990 it was abolished altogether over all of Germany. Austria has never implemented fluoride. Why? When the entire world was told it was good for our teeth!

Was it because they knew it was cariogenic, I don't remember giving them permission or consent to add such toxins to my drinking water. I do pay my water rates you know.

I also wrongly assumed if I boiled my tap water I might destroy the two chemicals my water board was adding to my supply. Wrong, boiling it doesn't get rid of it when chloride is heated up it can then be absorbed through the pores into your skin, from such things as steam in your bath or shower. The kettle left to boil its head off in the kitchen can have the same absorption.

To counteract this effect, there are companies out there who cater for our needs. They sell shower head and bath tap filters to help reduce the risk of absorbing chlorine. Again not all equipment achieves this, so be on your guard if you decide to buy.

Let's look at concentrated chloride; this is general household bleach that we all use. It's a toxic chemical and it releases gasses continually into the air. Notice your reaction next time you open a bottle of bleach, how you turn away from the smell, maybe crunch your nose! This is our natural body reaction our bodies are aware it's toxic to us. Then watch your pets sneeze, squint their eyes and then stay away from the product if overzealous housewives decide to put it in their mop bucket. It seems to me we're not as intelligent as our pets?

Do you remember where I told you where we store our toxins? 'In our fat' Why burden our bodies with these chemicals, soon we won't be able to move with them.

What can we do to help ourselves?

We could take cooler baths or showers, maybe bathe or shower less often, spend less time in the bath or shower, so not to over expose our pores to the chemicals and we could turn off the shower when lathering.

In the 1960's a Doctor Joseph Price wrote a book called "Coronaries/Cholesterol/Chlorine" The title almost covers the above chapter.

The book concluded that he fed several 100's of chickens on chlorine water; they developed heart and circulatory disease and poor growth. During winter conditions they shivered dropped feathers and displayed reduced activity. While the non-chlorine water fed chickens grew quicker, larger and had better health and kept their feathers.

If non-chloride water is good enough for a healthy foul, then it should also be good enough for us? This study was done 40 years ago. It begs the question; what's taking so long for someone to put it right. Furthermore what's the point of conducting these long and laborious studies only to file them away for 40 years or more? I used to be constantly involved in collecting data for some Doctor or other, not much point if they're not going to be acting on their findings.

I attended a course once on adult abuse.

The lecturer quoted an incident when a victim was stabbed 26 times, and no one called for an Ambulance because every spectator looking on assumed someone else had made that call. Is it the same with the British Water Board, do we all assume that the Government is looking after our best interest but in fact they are totally unaware of the fact that we are all consuming bleach in our drinking water. ????

My Father has known this fact for many, many years. His water supplier puts bleach in his drinking water every Thursday. He knows this because his taps reek's of bleach on a weekly basis, I mean really STINKS of bleach. Needless to say he has to use a filter before drinking his water from the tap and before he boils it for a cuppa.

Most housewives use this little blighter freely in its neat form in the home, kitchen, toilets and drains. If you turn your bottle of bleach round can you see the orange square on the bottle with a black cross? This symbolises danger or toxins. For a start it says seek medical advice immediately if you get it in your eyes and take this bottle with you. Another worrying comment it states, "Do not use with other products, it may release dangerous gases—chlorine" Should we be using this without a mask for protection? I remember a Domestic worker once putting bleach in her mop bucket; to ensure her ward was extra clean she added boiling water to the bucket. To her disbelief, she felt her lungs close up and she collapsed to the floor, luckily a colleague saw her in difficulty and with the help of others got her into a wheelchair and rushed her down to the Casualty Department. The gas that was produced had in effect eroded the lining of her lungs; it left her with long term Bronchial problems. Her condition was so chronic she was unable to return back to work. It affected her voice box, I remember this because she brought in her sick note on one occasion and she spoke with a hoarse voice. This lady told me she did not have any respiratory problems prior to this accident. I call it an accident because she did not intend to harm herself in this way.

To this tale and many like it I say "Ditch the bleach" it's not good.

All these 'man made' problems seem to intertwine with each other. Who would have thought talking about margarine would bring you to the effects of Chlorine/Bleach and Fluoride.

While on this toxic topic I started to wonder who was in charge of chemical regulations in this country, it's the same company I mentioned in the last chapter its DEFRA again, short for 'Department of Health and Department of Environment, Food and Rural Affairs' All I can say is, they better be good at their job because we the tax payers are paying one of the employees £161,110 a year, that's more than the Prime Minister is picking up which is £142,500 a year according to the Cabinet Officer figures. I hope this big money doesn't mount up to a 'kwango' position. I wanted to know what we the tax payer are getting for our money, from what I can work out DEFRA are trying to reduce junk mail, provide guide lines on how to bring dogs through quarantine, advise on how to raise pigs and how to move them, policies on Bovine and TB, exotic diseases, fisheries, flood defences and drinking water inspection. A mixed bag really, sounds to me they've got 'too many irons in the fire' to get a top quality result in every department. I also found that they are responsible for chemical regulations, pesticides and Nano-technology. I still don't understand why they are investigating their safety now, all this work should have been done before they came on the market. What's this, 'not guilty until proven—policy'? Wake up every body!

This DEFRA needs to drop all these side lines like 'how to move a pig' and concentrate all its efforts on guarding us against any chemicals that we are unknowingly ingesting.

Why does our Government allow these companies to put these chemicals into our water supply when other countries such as Germany have banned them? Surprisingly these countries didn't find an increase in tooth decay but in fact less, most Dental Practices agree it's the sugar intake that causes tooth decay. Our local water boards claim they will continue to add the fluoride not only to prevent tooth decay but also to give it that clear sparkle! Australia now has to label 'Fluoride' on their drinking water bottles! Why if it's safe?

For years I was under the impression that Gallstones were caused by too fatty a diet, after taking Julian's advice of 'going back to the beginning', I realise stones are formed when the liver has been constantly battling to rid itself of processed food, chemicals and toxins and it's the toxins that cause the formation of stones. When the stone or stones suddenly block the bile duct it hinders the bile from pouring out of the Gallbladder to break down fat in the digestive system. It tries and tries to push the bile out by performing this peristaltic spasm action, which results in excruciating abdominal pain.

I can see now, how I wrongly assumed a person suffered from gallbladder attack was associated with pain following eating a fatty diet for a long period of time, when in fact the original problem stemmed from a more sinister culprit, which were undiagnosed toxic stones.

Our bodies have been over oxidised for such a long time, anti-oxidising may take a while but not impossible to recover if we stop inflicting the same harm now.

I'm banking on Pandora to keep that lid shut on this one to preserve hope long enough for us to deal with the toxins.

Environmental Factors

This brings me to the forth topic which is environmental factors, and as I've become a bit of a townie I didn't think this one would affect Julian and I much either. Wrong again!

My earliest memory of what was the best way to take care of our environment was when I was about eight or nine reading the Bible in my bedroom about crop rotation, how the method prevented disease and didn't rob the soil of the same nutrient year after year.

I hastily ran to my Father to explain my findings, to which he replied, "Farmers have been doing that since time began Olwen" I walked away thinking well how did they know that, then thought better of it they must have read the same book as I was reading, the Bible. What a handy little book this was tucked under my arm. To try and understand why something was not right with our environment I decided to go back to the root of the problem, if you pardon the expression.

The risk must have always been there otherwise it would not have been necessary to mention it in the Bible as a guide.

It appears we got fed up of being so poor for such a long during the Second World War that once peace was declared our hunger for bigger, better and 'I need it now' era started even though the rationing years still remained until the early 50s. Supermarkets started to buy farms, ripping up hedges in order to have massive fields to bring in greater yields, of course this way of farming did not lend itself to crop rotation. Unfortunately this style of farming disrupts our link with nature; once the hedges were torn out we witnessed the disappearance of most of our wild life. We all have a role to play in life and that includes the animal kingdom, once the birds were discouraged from homing on the land then there was nothing to eat the insects, consequently the farmers were plagued with them so they were forced to use 'Pesticides'. Each year the insects required stronger pesticides but at the cost of our health. It seems we have been temporally blinded for 66 years regarding the dangers of pesticides and the importance of crop rotation which returned essential nutrients back in to the soil.

Have you seen how a pesticide employee dresses these days? They usually dress in an 'all in one white suit' with face mask, eye protections and sometimes with breathing apparatus. One could mistake them for men out of space, but joking aside that's a lot of protection their using to spray my food. That's one way of spraying; another is from the air from a light weight aircraft. These toxins are renowned to cause birth defect and brain damage.

The first environmental hazard that I came across was something called Roundup. I was vaguely familiar with this word but not what the substance entailed. I continued my research to see if I had ever been in contact with it in the past. It appears it's a pesticide used in most countries including the British Isles, so 'Yes' I have been in contact with it

On the 3rd of May 2010 a reporter stated in The New York Times that—

'Just as the heavy use of antibiotics contributed to the rise of drug-resistant super germs, American farmers near Ubiquitous use of Roundup pesticide has led to rapid growth of tenacious new super weeds. Farmers throughout the East, Midwest, and the South had been forced to spray fields with more toxic herbicides. Some of them had to resort to pulling the weeds by hand and return to more labour intensive methods like regular ploughing as a result of the super weed'

"We're back to where we were 20 years ago" said a farmer from Tennessee. Who would only plough a 1/3 of his 3,000 acres of soybean fields that year?

Farming experts say; such efforts could lead to higher food prices, lower crop yields and more pollution of land and water.

The first resistant species to pose a serious threat to agriculture was spotted in the year 2000 in Delaware. It has now spread to 22 states infesting millions of acres in short this Roundup no longer works. "What they are talking about is Darwin evolution in fast forward"

Now Roundup Resistant weeds like Horse weed and Giant Ragweed are forcing farmers to go back to more expensive techniques they abandoned years ago. Today farmers are witnessing Pig weed growing 3 inches a day and reaching 7 foot or more, choking crops.

The supper weed can be so sturdy it can damage harvest equipment or even roll tractors over. In an attempt to kill the super weed before it becomes too big the farmers are combining old banned pesticides with the new then instead of spraying it on the land they are ploughing it into the land as well. The big weed killing companies who once <u>reassured</u> farmers that resistant would not become a problem are now saying, "It is a serious issue, but it is manageable" Friends of the Earth say, "Highly Toxic herbicides, some of them banned in other countries, (which glyphosate was supposed to replace,) have had to be brought back into use in addition to Glyphosate.

On the 28/07/11 in the National magazine called the Article published an artical 'The Politics of food' by director of the food centre for food safety. Ann Foster a spokesperson for Monsanto in Britain was quoted saying, "People will have Roundup Ready Soya, whether they like it or not"

Wow! That doesn't sound as if the subject was open for negotiation to me!

Most people have issues with pesticides on their food let alone increased amounts. Studies now show exposure to Glyphosate and Roundup increases the risk of Non-Hodgkin's lymphoma. (This is a cancer of the lymphatic system so called "none" as it is made up of different cells types which can later present themselves as tumours.)

Your probably thinking why is she going on about America's problems, they don't affect us. Well! actually they do, if you eat breakfast cereals which are grown mainly in South America this being one of the areas that was the most affected with this super weed; then we are affected.

But we don't have to worry about our cousins in America supplying us with food grown and treated with pesticides. We too can keep up with the 'Jones's', we don't fall short of toxins in this country either. We have been producing, spraying and contaminating our own crops for many years now. (We should pat ourselves on the back for keeping up with the big countries)

This pesticide spraying brings to mind a tale my friend once told me about when she took her son for a stroll in his pushchair one a sunny afternoon. This happened to be in Shropshire but it could have been anywhere. A farmer who on his tractor was spraying his field came too close to his hedge when a puff of wind came and my friend and her son were covered in some sort of liquid spray. On contact, their skin immediately reacted and became raised, red, hot and an irritant rash. She immediately turned the pushchair round and ran towards home. All I can recall from this true story is that she scrambled upstairs and stripped both down to their underwear and doused themselves in a bath of cold water. Who did what after, I don't know but a GP was summoned to the house and the only treatment he could offer was carry on with the dousing until the angry skin has subsided then to use the "watch and see" policy. My friend enquired what was meant by this. He replied, "We'll have to see if there is a long term after effect from the crop spray."

That young boy is grown up now and has suffered with his chest ever since his last episode took him to a Specialist in Birmingham who enquired where and when he was exposed to this toxic substance that is banned in this country. Luckily his mother was there to confirm there was an incident years ago with pesticide spraying. This spray had evidently lay dormant in his lungs all those years, but not trouble free because he has suffered all those years with Asthma. Sadly burdened with his chest complaints he may be asked to abandon his career before he's actually completed his long and arduous training.

Do famers have any idea how much they are effecting the health and life of their own community never mind their own family.

Because of this next true story, is there any wonder why we never hear parents saying to their children at weekends in the summer, "Come on, grab a bowl each we're going blackberry picking so your mum can make a crumble later"

How dangerous does that sound now after hearing that story? How doubly sad that parents have been robbed of quality time they could be spending teaching them about nature, not that there is much nature left in hedgerows nowadays.

I came across another study that had been done on patients who had cancer. Tissue was taken from the cancerous tumour and also from the same patient a sample or biopsy from healthy tissue to compare. The result was both contained toxic pesticides but the cancerous tissue had a higher concentration of toxic chemicals of pesticides!

There it is again, I don't go searching for this word, IT comes to me.

What do others say about Pesticides?

I read of a young girl who had her hair analysed, the result was she was harbouring way above safety levels of mercury, arsenic and lead. Her Doctor informed her if she did not get rid of these toxins in her system she could not recover from her short term memory loss, low concentration, fatigue and exhaustion. I wonder if such patients are often misdiagnosed as ME sufferers, when in fact they are suffering from high toxin levels.

In another sighting in the 'Royal Society', they published that Pesticide spray has hormone distrusting chemicals and recommended a precautionary approach in particular with pregnant women exposed to these chemicals. But what about young children, can they be effected?

On the 12th July 2006 the EU Commission confessed "Long term exposure to pesticides can lead to serious disturbances to the immune system"

Oh! Julian I might have stressed your Adrenal gland that often with my pesticide food, that it led you to developing an Adrenal Tumour, I'm sorry.

Farmers are up against another chemical called Bovine growth hormone, that's injected into cows to increase their milk production; the growth hormone passes into breast feeding mothers who then pass it onto our babies. The baby then develops into a 'quick growth infant' but that's not all sadly the growth hormone later harms the mothers by settling in the tissue causing breast cancer. The only way of buying hormone free milk is to buy organic, it possesses neither growth hormone, pesticides nor antibiotics.

In 2008 Monsanto started to apply pressure on farmers who label their milk that had not been injected with artificial Bovine growth hormone by advertising the fact on their milk cartons, which made them look bad.

On this occasion the Federal Trade Commission did not side with the big boys, Monsanto.

The farmers defence was "The public have a right to complete information about how the milk they buy is produced"

What else is Monsanto responsible for? It produced Nuclear weapons, atomic energy commission, pesticides and lastly with its end products creates Aspartame or Nutria—Sweet as an alternative to sugar.

Did you know this Canadian company called Monsanto carted tons of toxic waste and illegally dumped thousands of tons of highly toxic waste in the UK landfills between the years 1965-1972, knowing their chemicals would contaminate wild life and our ground water for 30 years?

According to the Environmental Agency it cost £10 million to clean up a site in Cardiff, South Wales. Locals were unaware the land filled site was accepting toxic waste. It was referred to as one of the most contaminated sites in the UK. Monsanto first gained access to Europe by opening a chemical works at Cefn Mawr, Ruabon North Wales producing vanillin, salicylic acid, rubber and Aspirin. It is worldlier known for producing Bovine growth hormone; it was also the first to produce 'Agent Orange' for nuclear weapons in the Vietnam War, DDT and Aspartame and the first to manufacture Genetically Modified Agriculture Plants in 1982.

In 2007 France fined Monsanto $19,000 for claiming that their pesticides left the soil clean after use. Other countries were not happy with Monsanto either for example Germany, Brazil, China, India, UK, USA and India not to mention employing child labour.

Monsanto Company has been employing workers with a conflict of interest such as a Justice of Attorney, Food and Drug Administration (FDA), Assistant Administrator United States Environmental Protection Agency. It seems they will stop at nothing to get their own way.

Indian farmers have been committing suicide in their thousands because of Monsanto applied pressure to the farmers to producing more crops. American Farmers are now referring to Monsanto Company who uses bullying tactics as the 'Gestapo' or the 'Mafia' because the little farmer cannot afford the law suit. A David Nobles wrote in 2011, "Don't let the future belong to the likes of Monsanto, choose health and freedom over food slavery"

This company must be wondering where it's gone wrong recently, because for years it's been collecting awards for being the best for producing these dangerous products. In 2011 Monsanto was named as the 'Worst' company in environmental health and its consequences.

It seems to me that Organic farmers cannot co-exist side by side with GM farms it's not practical. What Monsanto wants, is to eliminate all organic growers so they can have total monopoly.

We the consumers can be powerful allies to the Organic growers, for more than 10 years we have been waking up slowly to ditching the 'Fast-fatter-bigger-cheaper food' in exchange for 'Slow-sustainable-local-healthier food' for the benefit of our bodies, more preciously our children, fondly man's best friend our animals and lastly our planet.

When will we shout stop contaminating our food, water supply, environment, and life threatening medicine. Will we say 'No more' when our babies are born with two heads, a tail or even worse?

Wow! Maybe it has started already? The other day I noticed in a national newspaper that girls are entering puberty at the tender age of six. I found this statement in The Mail newspaper it goes on to say that toxic chemicals were widely held to blame.

They questioned, should powerful drugs (normally used to treat cancer) be routinely prescribed to young children to block the hormonal changes taking place in their bodies. In America, they are considering bringing down the age of puberty to as young as seven.

It makes me feel sick, that were doing this to our little girls.

How can we stop growth hormones entering the food chain, how often do we hear people say, "Well it must be safe because the government allows it." Think again folk's our Government is too busy fighting each other to worry about what's safe on our table, even their own tables I fear.

I must confess I am not that learned in politics, but when I have voted in the past I have never given the Green Party a second thought, and why not.? How could I have made a balanced choice in voting if I have not studied what each and every party has to offer? The Green Party claims if they ever got into power, they envisage an organic nation.

I'm not asking you to vote for the Green Party, I'm asking you to consider asking your own party to have some of the same clean living values and laws passed. Have you ever wondered why we have taller, bigger, fatter children?

I repeat the question "Does the government know what they are doing" The answer to that is YES they must know what's going on, but choose not to do anything about it.

I've just had a horrible thought; if our children are reaching puberty at the age of seven, could it be that everything else will speed up too? Will they look 90 when in fact they are only 40? Sounds ridiculous, but can I trust them anymore with our very basic commodity for survival, that being food, water and medicine.

My motto for this one is, "Stop interfering with our children's Endocrine system" It is disgusting and should be against the law. I consider it to be on the same levels as child abuse. You are robbing them of their innocent childhood; if a single man abused a child he would be imprisoned. Think on.

In Victorian times, puberty age was 15 for young girls and 17 for young men.

It saddened me to read that most primary schools these days have sanitary bins in girl's lavatories, what a thing to deal with at such a young age. On top of that, some schools feel they need to supply counsellors, to help these children psychologically because these children are confusing and find it difficult to deal with. (I'm not surprised, I would have been too)

There are studies available in some areas to prove that environmental factors can affect human hormones.

The pollution of drinking water in some areas has a certain amount of oestrogens derived from the contraceptive pill and HRT. These small levels of hormones in the water supply have been known to cause hermaphrodites in fish. Not necessarily yours, but my water board stress that very little oestrogen remains. (But could that small amount be enough to upset the balance affecting our children hormone levels. It shouldn't be there at all in the first place.) Twenty five years ago during my nursing training a Doctor on the ward had just completed a study on tap water; he discovered a percentage of drugs in the water supply. He had a long list of his findings but I remember two that stood out the most, Diazepam and Morphine. This was not acceptable then and it's not acceptable now. Today medical staff are not permitted to discard dangerous drugs down the sink, but I cannot account for how house holders discard their dangerous drugs whether it's down the sink or flushed down their toilet? It begs the question are our children taking drugs unbeknown to them? May be the water boards should plough more money in to preventing such things happening instead of giving themselves large pay outs for saving money at the end of every financial year. Surly that's part of their job, and it's our money not there's to help themselves to as a golden handshake.

I mentioned before that my local water supplier assured me this is not the case in Worcestershire. I can only suggest you write to your own water supplier to get the same confirmation.

Going back to this word "Hermaphrodite" it's been bothering me, what does it mean? The word derives from Hermaphrodites, the son of Hermes and Aphrodite in the Greek mythology. The son possessed physical traits of both sexes.

What are they trying to suggest, that this might happen more often to our future generation? I'm not worried now, I am very, very angry how dare they mess with our children's hormones.

The Sunday times stated that scientists believe the phenomenon could be linked to exposure to chemicals in the food chain. A study revealed that young girls developed breasts at an average age of 9. A number of artificially produced chemicals have been blamed for interfering with sexual development notably 'BISPHENOL A', a plastic found in the lining of tin cans and babies feeding bottles.

Also include a group of industrial chemicals called PHTHALATES, which are linked to early puberty and have recently been banned from a vast range of cosmetics and household products, such as sun tan creams for children even baby shampoo, but be careful they are still out there especially in baby products including big name brands.

This would explain the state of our children today who are much taller, born to parents who may be short, with all these growth hormones soaked in their food.

The Mail newspaper amplified my worries by saying, "It's hardly surprising that the burden of chemicals are affecting the growth of our children. Will our civilisation go down in history as the one that poisoned itself to death"

It's not all about what we intentionally give to our children sometimes, it's about what we mothers unintentionally pass on to our children. I found this one under "Toxin 12 Beauty" this Toxin was found in 22 leading high street lipsticks. They all had one product in common, that product was LEAD. If this is allowed to build up in your body over a period of time it can pass into our unborn child then through breastfeeding, which can lead to delays in developing or learning difficulties. Not what you want to hear if you're pregnant, but now you know you can at least stop using the products. That is not to say all lipsticks have lead, only 22 of them that were tested you need to find out which ones they are or even campaign to stop them using lead.

On 12th February 2011 in the Daily Mail Louise Eccles writes, the average woman uses 12 products a day that contain 168 ingredients; eye shadow is the worst offender. In particular heavy glittered make up, mascara with kohl and anti-aging creams can have an effect on fragile skin.

Laura Rudoe from London set up 'Evolve Beauty' an organic company, after becoming alarmed at the chemicals in moisturisers and hair care products. She said, "There is very little awareness about the potentially harmful chemicals in every day beauty products."

There is still some research going on into excluding carcinogenic fears attached to Parabens.

This is something you, 'new mums' could research and campaign against while you're on maternity leave for the sake of all our children. Nothing happens unless we object, so let's. It's <u>not impossible</u> for women to have their say, women managed to run this homeland for five years when their men folk were fighting other men during the Second World War. I'm sure we can investigate how much lead is put into our lipstick during peace time.

I'm not sure to file this under diabetes or here under environmental health problem.

There used to be another mineral found in our soil which is often missing these days, it's called Chromium. Historically it used to be absorbed from the soil into the plants, we later consumed it and our bodies gratefully received it saying, "Thanks, the insulin will really appreciate this, it can't function without it"! Unfortunately modern man has sprayed pesticides all over our soil destroying most of the chromium worldwide. These days the body probably reports to the pancreas on a daily basis, "Sorry pancreas, still no chromium available" consequently the pancreas has to declare itself a 'Diabetic type two'. Some call it 'Insulin Resistance' and others call it 'Insulin Deficiency' but if you want my opinion it should be renamed as 'Gross Chromium Deficiency'

So is the answer to buy chromium replacement from herbal shops to compensate its shortage, or should we be worried about the question of imbalance of taking too much replacement without supervision. It sounds to me as if the best answer is to eat organic food that contains it in its natural form and is balanced.

We worry about human abnormalities, but should we be concerned about our food abnormalities? Have you ever seen an egg like this? The shell was so thick and irregular could this be a sign of nature retaliating or could it be a sign that something is very wrong with what we feed them.

Photo of an irregular egg nestled amongst some
overgrown potatoes.

They might look funny to you, but they're not normal are they? I call it my Dragon egg, and next to it are these larger than life potatoes. I have a sack full of them all averaging the same size most of them measure 10 inches long! Does the words 'growth hormone' come to mind?

There is a new potato out on the market called Bt potatoes. When questioned by a New York Times reporter were they safe, he was told by Monsanto Director of Corporate Communications, "Monsanto should not have to vouch for the safety of biotech foods, our interest is in selling as much of it as possible, assuring its safety is the FDA job"

Well that statement says it all, Monsanto Company doesn't care and the FDA says anything goes!

Where does that leave the consumer?

What can I do to prevent bad chemicals entering our bodies, whether it is food supply, water supply, absorption through skin or our lungs?

Originally I understood farmers were losing 30% of their food product to the perishable factor. Allegedly now they are using chemicals such as pesticides and they are still losing 30% of their food produce. So why bother contaminating our food at all?

What I need to do is to convince the crop growers of my plight. Maybe I need to go round speaking to Young Farmers to convince them of the dangers to their consumers and their own family, I realise the older generation might be more difficult to convince. My other option is to visit a technical college and question the lecturers, what they are teaching our young farmers about in how to take care of our farming community and challenge them to feed this country well with good wholesome food.

I need to convince them that they are the most important link in this reshuffle of the food chain. Just like I consider the Domestics to be as important as the surgeon in a Hospital, if the ward or the theatre is dirty then the surgeons skill is of no value to the patient at all.

It's the same with the farmers, just like the animal kingdom we all have a job to do and the jobs intertwine like links. The chain will break if one link is missing.

I'm thinking more of the ladybird who eats the green fly, the green fly who eats the . . . . and so on.

Allegedly there are 14,000 man-made chemicals in our food chain. So joking aside, it's hard to detoxify when you're up against these sort of figures.

I saw a harsh quote about our food producers the other day called, "Killing for profit" I don't want to go down the line of accusing our food growers, but I do want man to try and help himself from a kamikaze attitude. But is it greed, ignorance or pressure the farmers are enduring?

Maybe the farmers get bombarded with companies sending them glossy magazines and pamphlets through their letter boxes enticing them to use their product. With the emphasis on benefits of purchasing their harmful product, maybe the poor farmer can only see one side of the coin. Maybe we need to portray our needs for good wholesome food on our table. I'm sure the little man inside his heart has been saying the same thing to him for a long time. And I'm also sure he has been thinking, this isn't right what am I doing to the food production. Maybe the grower has learnt to switch off because other farmers knocked his sixth sense out of him, or in lots of cases young farmers work with their fathers, their attitude might be "get on with it, we have been doing it like this for years" and there ends the possible clean up trail.

Someone is bound to point out to me that we have to use pesticides and GM food in order to feed the world. That's a load of rubbish, did you know we throw away 1/3 of the world's food each year. It's estimated that we in the UK discard £10 billion worth of food in money terms, just because it has expiry date on it. I realise now, food with preservatives in it has to have an expiry date on because of the chemical reaction it may have on the food and our insides after that date. If we insisted that the companies were to remove the chemicals out of our food then we could then rely on our own common-sense when the food was going off.

Maybe there is something in what Julian said at his bed side, "The Native Americans had the right idea about the way they lived and died" Unlike us westerners, the native Americans only took from the land what they need, hence they don't have our problem of vast food wastage because of a hunger for greed to over produce, package it, transport it at least 1000 miles laden with preservatives in order to make us ill the other end of the trail. In the process we have defaced the earth, contaminated it, half covered it in concrete and tarmac, dug landfills then to top the lot disregarded nature. How can we possibly expect a balanced life style?

The Native Americans would consider us to be no better than Vandals; do you know where that name came from? I'm going to tell you anyway. Vandals were a Germanic tribe that rose to power in the fifth century described as the rude Northern race better known as Barbicans. We don't need invaders to destroy our country thank you; we can do it to ourselves. Well done us.

I need to boycott these toxic companies somehow; the trouble is they are so powerful.

I'm joking now, but if they should advertise that toxins need to be released into the atmosphere to kill any floating bacteria I'm sure millions of television addicts would fall for their false advertisements. Because we have become so accustomed to their hypnotic tactics! There is no getting away from the fact the biggest toxins to mankind have surly got to be pesticides on our food crops. This product called pesticides seems to overlap with such topics as exposure to toxins and environmental factors.

Our daily immunity is challenged by the face of an environmental toxic world which can affect our bodies with such complaints as viral bacteria, parasites, fungal infection which can lead to fatty tumours or worst still cancerous tumours.

Poor Julian, I along with others made you so ill with all these chemicals, exposing you to such harmful products daily, your immune system went down unable to fight with poor equipped Adrenal glands. My motto for this one is "Stop making us sick with your chemicals"

Ironically Julian had an affinity with a Saint called 'St Francis of Assisi' who was born in 1181 and died in 1226. He was born in Italy but raised in France, he started the Franciscan Monks. Francis had a burning desire to travel amongst the Crusaders, especially their enemy the Saracens to try to convert them to Christianity. He was captured and imprisoned, but he begged an audience with the Sultan, surprisingly he was not harmed but released instead. When Francis returned to Italy, whilst out walking late one night he came across some shepherds guarding their flock on the hillside. In the light of the moon and the flickering light of the camp fire he reminisced of how the Knight Templers who called themselves Christians; year after year the Knights battled with the Saracens over the cradle and the tomb of the 'Prince of Peace', his companions that night remembers Francis's eyes filled up with tears. St Francis died aged 45 on 3rd October (our wedding anniversary) and exactly ten years younger than Julian, and in the year we were courting 1980 nearly eight hundred years after his death, he was proclaimed the 'Patron Saint of animals, birds and the Environment' isn't strange how someone felt it necessary to appointed a Saint in 1980 to protect us from all its toxins in our environment!

The Native American Indian first rule is, "Treat the earth and all that dwell there with respect" and I hope Pandora you still has enough hope trapped in your box to help us get rid of all the chemicals from our environment.

Artificial Sweeteners

The fifth one they gave as a cause for triggering tumours was Artificial Sweeteners. It may be the last one on the list but its certainty not the least.

Sadly I was guilty of giving Julian a shed load of these little chappies, once he was diagnosed with diabetes I did what was expected of me I threw away all the sugar in our house and replaced it with artificial sweeteners. That included all his hot drinks, gallons of unsweetened squashes, all foods and treats including beer. I didn't stop using this little blighter not even after the medical profession advised him to discontinue all diabetic treatment.

If I thought for one moment that these artificial sweeteners were dangerous or harmful to his health I would have conducted my own investigations while Julian was alive, not now after his death.

I can feel another trail of investigations coming on. I dread to think what I was going to discover next, it appeared that all the healthy things I thought I was giving Julian and Llewela were now being questioned and discredited. I was beginning to feel cheated, how could I have been so gullible in thinking that all these healthy products were harmless!

First of all I needed to find out how many types of sweeteners there were on the market, so I went back to the beginning of this one too. There appeared to be five groups and I will look into each one in order that they came on the market.

1. First one was Saccharin, discovered by accident by a scientist who was studying coal tar at the time; this was way back in 1879. Due to his poor hand hygiene and before he dined one evening he noticed his fingers tasted sweet.

In later years it was introduced and manufactured on a grand scale to feed the forces during the First World War due to sugar shortage. When it was realised Saccharin was 500 times sweeter than sugar it was reintroduced into the food market in the mid 1960's when dieting became a fad.

America and Canada wizened up to its side effects and it was banned when they realised it caused bladder cancer. They also discovered it increases blood sugar levels, which is something Diabetics should be aware of.

2. The second one to appear onto the market was Splenda otherwise known as Sucralose.

The name has a nice ring to it I think, sounds as if it derives from the word splendid.

Unfortunately this is another one of those once upon a time story, this time in 1975 an Indian Graduate Student in London was trying to invent a new insecticide. Due to a language barrier he thought his adviser had asked him to taste it. The student tasted it and found it to be sweet and this is when Splenda was born and it replaced Saccharin. In actual fact the student adviser had requested him to <u>test</u> it not <u>taste</u> it. I trust it is now used for what it was originally intended for and that was to kill insects.

Splenda has been sued by the sugar industry for misleading the public into thinking its more natural than it is. In a survey 57% of people thought Splenda was natural.

To say Splenda comes from sugar is like saying carbon dioxide comes from air.

Eight years after its discovery in 1983 a study was conducted on 3,000 products that contained Splenda. Data showed that artificial sweetener users were twice as lightly to develop Diabetes.

How horrifying, why would you want to continue to give someone something that was the cause of their complaint in the first place? Further tests showed that, when patients consumed artificial sweeteners they had a higher fasting glucose level, in other words their blood glucose levels were raised. How did Diabetic Type One manage in the old days? Easy, they used the strategy of either abstain or die.

As the saying goes, there are some things in life worth dying for; as I see it Splenda is not one of them. Continue to watch out for this little horror, now we the public are aware of its dangers they have given it a different name and it is disguised under the new name of LIPITOR (lip-it-or) what, I say. The product may have a new name but it sound more like a threat to me.

The Inventor of Splenda admits himself that around 15% of Sucralose is absorbed by the body with no guarantee of what % leaves the body. They have yet to conduct that study. I don't know which year they are thinking of conducting this study, this year, next year, sometime maybe never?

I thought everything had to be safe before we the consumers were allowed to buy it, wrong again!

I'm well aware that every public building and most private homes have sugar alternative. I am just surprised to see Hospital and health care institutes which specialise in improving people's health continue to offer vulnerable people products such as squashes with artificial sweeteners that contain Splenda. When sucralose is excreted, the compound is unchanged in the faeces and in the urine. There are no known studies showing what happens to this chemical when the raw sewerage is treated and then released back into the environment. Research on animals who were given sucralose have however shown to have 40% shrinking of the thymus, enlarged liver and kidneys, atrophy of the lymph glands, follicles in the spleen and increased weight, reduced growth, decreased red blood cells, hyper plasma of the pelvis, diarrhoea and extension of pregnancy period. (Extended pregnancy rings bells with modern mums who are left unindicted past their expectant date only to hear of frightening fatality stories of babies born after nine months pregnancies.)

If the body is fed an indigestible product such as plastic found in margarine, then it is incapable of dissolving through normal digestion. It will pass through undigested just like the sucralose is indigestible due to its laboratory component, then we have yet another serious health problem! Because if it is not dealt with in the sewerage plant, then I presume it gets re-introduced into our water supply again and again at a greater strength each time.

Splenda is 600 times sweeter than sugar.

I still don't see anything splendid about it.

3. The third that was released on to the open market was Aspartame. I don't know where they get these names from. In order for me to remember how to spell it I have broken it down like this, As-part-a-me. This one too was originally developed as an ant poisoning substance. It was denied approval into the food industry in 1975 and was told in 1980 further studies were needed before it was licensed for human

consumption. However in 1981 it was introduced into the food chain on the strength of a Japanese Brain Tumour study. Lots felt it was an 'un-qualifying approval' and that it had sneaked in via the back door as it were. Several objections took place, but to no avail

An Investigation was done into whether Mr G.D Searle had falsified Aspartame studies.

Searle did submit a report and blamed the findings on computer error. They also found the medical researcher in charge was, inexperienced in conducting studies of this nature. He had only attended one seminar on the subject. Searle made deliberate decisions to cloak Aspartame toxic effect. One of them was surgically removing tumours from animals to mask the effects of Aspartame. Based on the dangers of saccharine which were 600 times sweeter than sugar, Pepsi Cola switched to Aspartame to put in their drinks, which was only 200 times sweeter than sugar.

I don't know where our health concerns lie now, because as you know Aspartame is out there on the open market, the horse has bolted and no one is worried.

I can only base this story on trust, but a Canadian Doctor forbids his wife to consume Aspartame in her diet after it was approved by the Canadian Government. Years later they divorced and with her new found freedom she drank gallons of Diet Pepsi. She suddenly went blind, but when she remembered her ex-husbands warnings, she stopped the sweeteners and she recovered. Some years later she started to feel a burning and stinging sensation in her eyes, silver flashes and floaters. Remembering her ex-husbands warnings again, she was horrified to find her usual brand of yogurts had started to put in Aspartame as one of the ingredients, she threw them away and the symptoms subsided immediately.

Aspartame is a bit more worrying, because it is a neuro-poision which means it interferes with the nervous system, attacking the optic nerve, nerves in the heart and killing the senses of taste and smell. Doubly dangerous because it's not suitable for high temperature, in other words you can't bake this one without having a chemical reaction. I wonder if poring boiling water on it has the same effect. Some people are lucky, they feel the effects immediately, others are not so lucky.

In 2004 Justin Dumais an athlete in Athens, an Olympic Silver Medallist was diagnosed with Grave's Disease. It's a condition that affects the autoimmune system, causing the thyroid to become twice its normal size. Fearing the condition was going to put an end to his career he did some research himself and read a book called "Sweet Poison" by Doctor Janet Hill. He later contacted the author and she advised him to remove all Aspartame out of his diet.

In six weeks he was fully recovered from a 'false' diagnosed Grave's Disease.

Don't be miss lead into thinking if it doesn't say Aspartame on the product it's not in there; believe me it could be hiding behind E954 or E951 code.

The Aspartame company feels it is a slur campaign when its products are being run down.

But can anyone explain to me why in 2007 Indonesia banned Aspartame; in 2008 the Philippine's banned it as well as New Mexico, in 2009 California and South Africa banned it. Some British supermarkets namely Sainsbury's, Marks and Spencer's, Wat-Mat and Asda announced in 2007 that they have removed Aspartame from their <u>own</u> products not leading brands. Why, if it's safe and harmless? UK has not banned Aspartame because were doing the British thing and holding out until the bitter end. We don't rush when it comes to health issues.

Going back to its name, it might be called As-part-a-me but I defiantly don't want it to be—**a-part-of-me.**

4. The fourth one mentioned was Acesulfame discovered in 1967 but didn't come into general use until 2003. I struggled with this pronunciation but wondered if they were aware I was a bad speller so I broke it down like this Ace-su-l-fame, sounded a bit French to me.

I couldn't find any history for this one, except it provokes cancer cells in lungs and breasts and frighteningly it causes hypoglycaemia in diabetics. No wonder diabetics find it hard to control their diabetes when one sweetener will raise their glucose levels while another will reduce it. But if they are not aware which one does what, how can they possibly predict their treatment. It's like having an invisible pig in the trough.

Other side effects it can cause is mental confusion, headache, dizziness, nausea, liver and kidney problems and eventually takes you down the road of Alzheimer's, Parkinson's and other neurological symptoms. The only thing it had going for it was it was only 200 times sweeter than sugar. Not much to boast about then really.

5. The fifth and latest one on the market is Neotame.

I've broken this one down into two syllabuses. Neo-which means new in Greek and tame-speaks for itself. No unusual history of how it was discovered but it appeared in the food chain in 2002.

Only difference is this one is more toxic than Aspartame. It is known to cause brain tumours and cannot be used in meat products. **It is 13,000 times sweeter than sugar**, so shouldn't we be advised to take only microscopic amounts of this sweet dust rather than the same amount of sugar in our beverages. The amount of times I have had patients say to me over the years, "Are you sure this is suitable for diabetics its seems much sweeter than normal puddings" I recently coupled the echo of what patients use to ask me with the recollection they often suffered with frequent diarrhoea. In conversation I mentioned this to my sister who then suddenly wondered if that is why her residents suffered similar toilet habits. On her next shift she made it her priority to investigate what sweeteners the kitchen staffs were adding to the diabetic puddings and how much of it was being used? There was no strict regulations into the quantity used, but since the topic was raised no blame was attached only concern raised. They now abide by universal measures in the kitchen.

It appears the artificial sweeteners are getting sweeter and more dangerous each year.

This sweetener Neo-tame might be <u>new</u> but it's definitely not <u>tame</u>.

Some might feel I have been a bit one sided in my research especially after I read the Aspartame company felt that it was a slur campaign to discredit them. In their defence I decided to randomly choose one of the sweeteners to find out its content, in other words its recipe.

I chose Splenda to fight their corner, listing the content

Acetone. (Nail varnish remover)
Acetic acid. (Vinegar)
Acetic anhydride. (Odour of vinegar)
Ammonium chloride. (Dry cell battery)
Benzene. (Dangerous deadly chemical)
Chlorinated sulphate. (Bacterial cleaner)
Ethyl alcohol. (Pure alcohol)
Isobutyl Ketones. (Hazarders solvent, production resins, paint, varnish, lacquers)

Formaldehyde. (Found in insulation this one is cariogenic)
Hydrogen chloride. (Corrosive toxic gas)
Lithium chloride. (Drug used for bipolar)
Methanol. (Antifreeze, varnishes, paint remover, and toxins.)
Sodium methoxide. (Kills human nerve cells)
Sulfuryl chloride. (Toxic and reacts violently to alcohol) I
know it states there is Alcohol above!)

I don't feel the content of this concoction has done them any favours. Still in their defence I realise the amount of the products that I've mentioned above, might only be miniscule. Sadly I still feel they have lost both the battle and the war in my opinion because chemicals such as these should not be in any way shape or form entering our bodies.

By keeping stump instead of defending themselves, in my book, spells guilty as charged. But it doesn't end there the worst charge of all is; they are not being frank, open and above board with their customers regarding the chemicals they have placed in the sweeteners. In facts its worse, they even advertise it as 'sugar free' hoodwinking us into believing that they are in actual fact healthier than sugar. I better stop there before I discredit them even further. Looking at the above ingredients, no one should ever be ashamed of questioning the content of the food they are expected to eat.

Manufactures were banking in the 1970's that we the consumers would not be absorbing a large quantity of artificial sweeteners, but as it is now in 4,500 of our food products, it's difficult for any of us not to consume as much as we do. Worst still it states it has a split personality, which weakens our immune system, and can cause irregular heartbeat, enlarged liver, shrunken kidneys and thymus glands, birth defect, blindness, and mimics Multiple sclerosis.

They are 'Mixing and Matching' chemicals at the expense of our health.

I wonder if Columbus realized what he was doing when he first brought sugarcane from the New World and introduced us to the sweet taste of sugar and years later Scientists are taking us down the chemical trail of sweeteners to satisfy our sweet needs, which is now called sweet poison.

The phrase 'Dying to be thin' might not be too far from the truth.

In the diet market, the healthy diet campaigners are fighting the 'artificial sweeteners war' on our behalf, but the big companies are not playing fair with their false advertising. The consumers are not in with much of a surviving chance if they don't know who to believe, the big boys with their advertising power or the poor Health Campaigners with our health at heart. If it's true that excessive intake of these five factors hydrogenated oils, environmental factors, toxic substances, processed foods and artificial sweeteners cause the Adrenal Gland to be under prolonged stress and can lead to Adrenal Tumours, then not only should we be worried that us the grown-ups are likely to grow tumours but our children are even more at risk.

We already know they are developing out-worldly and up-worldly but do we know what is happening to them in-worldly?

A friend of mine recently informed me she was out of circulation for a while, her niece had been rushed to Birmingham's children Hospital to have a tumour removed from her chest; it turned out to be the size of a grapefruit. Does anyone consider this normal, the child was only 7 years old when she underwent this surgery? She endured 5 hours of surgery, so this was no quick fix keyhole surgery. I ask you again, what are we doing to our children?

Britain has just been introduced to a new sweetener called Truvia, which claims to be healthy, but if this one is healthy why did Canada, America, Australia, New Zealand and Europe ban it in 1990 as a food additive due to 'lack of long term safety research'?

Silver Spoon is currently launching 'Truvia' in the UK in a bid to take a major share in the £50 million sweetener market. This sweetener is in 55 products in the UK already, including Coca Cola who helped develop Stevia. The countries who have banned it say, 'more testing needs to be done on the rest of the leaf extract to determine its safety'

Since discovering how harm full refined-white-sugar is to us and more frightening how toxic the alternative sweeteners are to our frail bodies. What safer alternatives are there out there for us, children only consume what we make them eat; do you remember our childhood when parents used to say "Clear your plates"

It begs the question what alternative can we offer our children other than refined sugar and artificial sweeteners? How can we satisfy their already developed sweet pallet, we could be introducing them to such things as organic dried dates, figs, apricots, raisins, pineapple, cranberries, liquorice root, organic sugar, Palm sugar, Coconut sugar and coconut sweetener not forgetting local pure honey as long it <u>doesn't</u> contain refined white sugar from the bee keepers as one of its ingredients or alternatively Maple syrup which contains vitamins and minerals, organic honey which contains vitamins and minerals, Yawn syrup as a sweetener which is suitable for diabetics. Pure gold raw honey contains natural antioxidants, enzymes, amino acids, vitamins and minerals and one could use Manuka honey for the more affluent amongst us.

Surprisingly there are more healthy sweet alternatives out there than I originaly thought.

My new shopping trolley rules are NO artificial sweeteners, No Fructose corn syrup and No products containg white refined sugar. I know I will fall off the 'Band Wagon' from time to time but I must learn to get straight back on, how else do children learn to ride a bike unless they keep trying? I know I will eventually conquer this unhealthy craving I have of consuming products with refined sugar and artificial sweeteners and one day I will triumphantly claim that I have 'Zero Tolerance' over these sweet poisons.

My sweet, sweet Pandora, I hope you haven't been tempted for the second time to try these artificial sweeteners or re-fined sugar? Julian was right, something has gone horribly wrong!

Genetic Engineered Food

All this discussion about interference with our food raised my suspicion about another type of food that I had heard about in the past and to be perfectly frank I hadn't taken any in-depth interest in. Genetic Engineered food, Id obviously chosen to bury my head in the sand with this one and deliberately ignored it over the years, but could this have contributed to Julian's ill health too. As always I went back to the beginning, to see in what year were we first subjected to Genetically Modified food and did it matter anyway?

The trouble with abbreviations is they can sometimes be misunderstood, so to make it quite clear in this chapter I will refer to Genetically Modified food as GM food.

The first GM product introduced into the food market was called soybean this was in 1990 followed by corn, canola oil, cotton oil, sugar, and then rice. Tomatoes however was not introduced until 1994, incidentally none of these foods carried the GM label then, and still don't today. We the consumer purchased these goods because 'the price is right' not because were making informed choices. I, like thousands of other housewives was ignorant of the fact I was buying, cooking and eating and worst still offering GM food to others. Whether it was good or bad for me and my guests I should have been informed of what I was partaking in.

My first question was; when did this country start to get concerned about child and adult obesity. Guess what, world obesity was officially recognised between 1990-91, how bizarre the same year GM food flooded the market. GM companies might defend themselves by saying this is a coincidence.

My second question was what does GM food really mean?

I read an article written by a Doctor Ashu Goyal who explained that "Genetically Modified seeds are modified by DNA alteration which will be a mixture of plant DNA and animal DNA"

That does not sound right to me, he confirmed what I understood by saying it is a curse for anyone who wants to live a vegetarian and natural life style. Stop this practice immediately, he says and file it under URGENT and give the topic MAXIMUM EFFORT. He asks us to spread this message to friends and influential people. I hope I'm doing my bit by including this message in my book.

Thinking about it, if it's not fair on the vegetarians then was it fair on Julian and Llewela?

We have been a part of the Genetic age for some time now since the cloning of Dolly the sheep, but as I understand it we the public have very little knowledge of any possible consequences of the scientific interference with nature. Have we gone public before our time?

We all remember Albert Einstein who was instrumental in developing the Atom bomb during the Second World War. Before he had time to assess the consequences he was pressured into using it.

Einstein once said, "Nothing will end war unless the people themselves refuse to go to war"

Just like us, if we are against eating things that we don't approve of but don't do anything about it, nothing will change. Just as Einstein stated all those years ago, only we the people can change things. Are scientists of today travelling down the same road as Einstein? Obliviously!

I wondered should I be worried about GM food products and is it in many of the things I eat, if not I won't lose any sleep over it.

Then I was shocked and horrified to discover it's in 65% of all our food we purchase already.

'Organic Consumers Association' and 'Green Peace' say that GM foods have not yet been investigated thoroughly enough before offering it to the consumer, so why are these foods already out there on the street for us to buy. WOW! This sounds huge! What's going on?

Evidently this is how it is, GM supporters are telling farmers that they stand to reap enormous amount of profit from growing GM crops. They are brain washed into thinking that animals that are given GM feed can be leaner, grow bigger faster, have greater milk production, but actually need to eat less food. Is that why I see thinner cows in the fields, with udders so massive the cows are almost unable to walk?

Salmon that are fed GM food are capable of growing almost 30 times faster than normal Salmon. My concern is, if the Salmon is caught and cooked before the growth hormone has left the fish does that mean the growth hormone is then passed onto us humans when we consume it and are our bodies finishing off the growing process, probably sideways as I'm too old to grow upwards, but our children aren't.

Food under GM trials at the moment are apples, strawberries, pineapples, sweet peppers, bananas, coffee, cabbage, melons, potatoes, rice, sunflower for oil, corn, soya corn, soya bean, sugar cane and sweet corn, they might be under trial, but in the meantime it appears we are eating them unknowingly right now. Something is not ringing true hear!

If you're a farmer all this talk about bigger production must be music to your ears, but to us the consumer it sounds like a living nightmare.

I was further horrified to read that bribes were offered to Indonesians so that their crops could pass the controls of screening of GM cotton crops. Why am I worried about this one, it's because we use an abundance of cotton oil in our cooking. Studies were also suppressed when GM potatoes were deemed "unfit for human consumption" but were also passed by the said controllers.

I read of a journalist who had her freedom of speech suppressed on hazards of Genetic Engineered Bovine growth hormone. It's hard to escape this GM food if it's found in animal feed which then cascades down into animal products such as milk, eggs and cheese and finally our meat. Then when scientist further meddle with the makeup of its DNA in fruit and vegetables, what's left that's safe to eat?

Questions I then asked myself are; If there is a risk, one day a mix-up could take place between animal feed and food intended for human consumption; Too late its already happened, humans were inadvertently eating food that contained GM products meant for animal feed, the difference is animal GM feed usually contains a heavier percentage of growth hormone to bulk up the livestock. On the other hand, why should, the animal kingdom be exposed to such wickedness? We along with the animals just want simple food that does us no harm.

I then looked up the side effect of Genetic Engineered Food, the explanation was a bit erratic, "It's like performing open heart surgery with a shovel" I understood that comment to mean they haven't got a clue and they don't care even if the effects are colossal? It sounds to me that we the public are the Guinea pigs performing on stage as it were with no rehearsal, without even knowing we are been studied from afar for any side effects? We're living in the research stage as it were.

Friends of the Earth are demanding, "Mandatory labelling' of these food products, independent testing for safety and environmental impact and liability for harm to be assumed by biotech companies" It's going to be hard for us to spot them when they're not even on the labels.

If they were on the labels, these would be their abbreviations—:

> Genetic engineered =GE
> Genetically Modified = GM
> Biotech-companies =Bc.
> Trans-genic =Tg.
> . . . but they're not on the labels!

Have you heard the phrase, when GM food is cooked or heated it becomes unstable, what do they mean by that? I heard a similar explanation when I took a friend to see a Kinesiologist not so long ago, as he was complaining of this dreadful irritating itching on his chest. He had suffered with this for about five years. When he questioned his GP about it on several occasions he continually prescribed anti-histamine, my friend once asked his GP if he could have an allergy test. The reply was, the complete test could take years to complete. After suffering for five years and religiously taking the medication, he started to conclude that he could have had that test by now. I suggested he paid my Ben a visit, the same Ben who recommended Julian needed to step up his potassium and magnesium levels in an attempt to try and absorb the toxins that was being produced in response to the drugs he was having a reaction to.

My friend's appointment was for one hour, immediately after the session he was able to tell him exactly what he was suffering from. To his amazement he was told that he had an allergy to 79 products mainly food additives, PVC plastics, but the most prevalent ones were pesticides on fruit and vegetables. He was advised if there was no organic choice of salads and vegetables available, he recommended he should chose salad over the cooked vegetables. One would initially think the obvious choice would be boiled vegetables not the salad. Evidently the salad has not had its chemicals impregnated into the food like the vegetables would have when cooked. Is this what is meant when GM food become unstable when cooked?

A Doctor Arpad Pusztai explained in a correspondence on the internet, how GM foods could trigger new allergies from toxins that are harmful to our bodies. I admire this gentleman for informing us on line and also for appearing on the 'World in Action' program for 150 seconds declaring his scientific findings on GM food, which was already on the British food shelves. He felt the British tax payer had a right to know as we had already paid 1.6 million pounds on the research, but Jo public had no access to his findings. Why do I admire him, he risked everything by going public because he went against his 'code of practice' for our safety sake. Thank you Doctor Pusztai, were not totally on our own then we do have some allies by the sound of it.

If the last chapter is not kosher and GM food is not harmful to us, then why aren't the GM companies taking everybody who is discrediting them in public to court, in addition to that, why did over 8,000 scientists from 84 countries sign an open letter calling for a ban on GM seeds and food? I have already mentioned the concern Doctor Goyal had about crossing DNA of seeds with animal DNA. One such study was done with tomato gene crossed with the fish gene, which evidently have unpredictable behaviour "inside our bodies" One report indicated this was fed to laboratory mice; the mice refused to eat it.

No wonder scientists have to meddle with the end product, who wants to eat a tomato that smells of fish? How can you trust them not to medal further and possibly produce a square tomato to fit your sandwich.

Japan claim independent research into GM food is systematically blocked by GM corporations!!!!!!

Punch line or insult, farmers who grow organic food may have to pay to have their produce certified. Whereas GM crop farmers do not, their excuse for not labelling GM food is "restraint of trade" that means the cost of labelling. What they're saying is, if your selling GM products you don't have to 'pay and label' but if your produce is <u>GM free</u> in other words Organic and you want to reassure the customer of its content you have to 'pay and label' for the privilege of informing us the consumer its safe. No wonder organic food is more expensive, the government is forcing it to be so. That's absolutely crazy; surely it should be the other way round. No label should indicate 'no toxins'. Labelling should indicate exactly how the product has been interfered with. But in all honesty who would buy a jar of something that states on the label, 'GM in this one'

I still feel the Government is sheltering the bad guys on this one!

On the other hand I wonder if it's not written on the box, can we still get them for trade description; surely they are misleading the public by being economical with the truth.

Something is not right here; this process of farming is not natural. What happened to the Biblical guidelines, have they been ignored?

Someone raised the question; what if the public one day black listed previous GM Farms?

A young student at one of the GM labs wrote on line asking us, "Not to over react!"

Its ok, we are trying to keep calm about all of this, but it's not easy when one feels all choked up with abnormalities sneaking into our bodies unseen and our loved ones dying all around.

Is there any wonder why the world is experiencing obesity? It seems to me that children of today cannot help looking fat and suffer with diabetes, because we their parents have interfered with their insulin levels so often in the course of a day, never mind all their young lives. We are the naughty ones not them when they appear to be behave badly, were are constantly offering them sweets and chocolate as a 'well done' treat, we are secretly punishing even torturing their body's at the same time telling them "we love them" but do we? I don't think so when we're shovelling rubbish down their throats.

In other words; its DIY time for all of us if we want to remain healthy! I think it's about time we cleaned up our act as guardians of the next generations and put some wholesome food on the table for our children and our loved ones? We must not be fooled by the 'pro-GM or MSG hype' that they are safe; they are bad news for ourselves, our family, our environment, the poor and hungry in the developing world not forgetting our pets.

How can I set about banning genetic modified food? Well! May be it is too big a subject for me to deal with on my own and by buying organic or growing my own is not enough to make the change the world needs or to make the big boys sit up and listen. If anyone is willing to join me, then we need to be seen to be singing from the same hymn sheet.

They claim; New Zealand is a healthier nation without epidemic of obesity, type 2 diabetes or food allergies! Where are we going wrong? It seems New Zealand is doing something very right, is it because they are proud to be a 'nearly all organic nation' and could 'the proof of the pudding be in the eating'? Evidently organic agriculture in New Zealand has provided evidence as part of the standardizing global food system for the world. New Zealand has a vision of reaching total organic farming by 2020, comparing these figures to such countries as Taiwan who only boosted 0.1% organic food production in 2006 hoping to double its % to 0.2% by 2008, these figures sadden my soul beyond belief.

I feel like standing up and becoming a cheer leader for New Zealand chanting, 'Well done NZ'ees well done' unlike my home country, I'd probably remain sitting down out of shame chanting, 'Poor show UK, poor show' In fact UK appears to be one of Europe's most vigorous cheerleaders for the expansion of GM crops along with Spain and the Netherlands. Although I'm glad to see some European countries have not behaved like sheep and were easily led. In 2009 Germany banned all GM crops along with France, Austria, Greece and Hungary invoking a "safeguard clause"

Having said that, in our favour, when a British survey was done for public opinion on GM food, only 2% of the survey said they did not mind eating GM food so can I presume that the remaining 98% did mind!

I wonder if things would have been different if the UK hadn't joined the EEC in 1973 and continued to trade worldwide dealing with the likes of New Zealand, instead of dropping her like a 'hot potato' like we did. Would she have influenced us to be as organic as her? I don't know, it just leaves me feeling, we slapped her in the face saying 'No thanks to good food and good practice'

Of cause I could be under educated on this topic, I was only 16 when we entered the EEC.

Generally speaking, I don't think we as a nation ask enough questions, unlike children who constantly ask "why, why, why?" But of cause that's how they learn. Are we too big to learn, or too proud to ask or too stupid to look into things, or do we suspect something is not right but are too frightened of the truth or sadder still, leave it up to someone else to look into it? I suspect it's the latter.

To bring about change I still think my strength lies in the quill, by writing to my local supermarkets, the government and my local government expressing my fears and concerns over genetic modified food. I intend to write to all the labels on my favourite foods I use regularly, asking individual companies if they have considered producing the same brand in the organic line, GM free and MSG free. Don't forget how the market works, on the basis of supply and demand. We demand they supply. If I bombard them enough they should get the message eventually, that I'm not happy with my food being tampered with like this. Don't forget they don't like complaints, complaints don't sell products.

Apart from writing letters I have created these 10 useful tips for myself, now I understand the consequences of eating these foods. I could on the odd occasion consider eating GM and MSG foods as treats but the difference now is; I'm making informed choice knowing they are not going to enhance my health.

These are going to be my new 10 baby steps towards healthy living, they are—:

1. I need to avoid buying food that I don't understand what's on the label or too small to read.
2. I need to make a list of 'poor quality' foods that could harm me, put it in my purse for when I'm out shopping.
3. I need to avoid eating and buying food cooked in hydrogenated-Trans fats oil.
4. I need to avoid all foods with artificial sugar substitutes.
5. I need to avoid all products with long shelf life.
6. I need to avoid all processed food that is enriched with added vitamins. It means they have destroyed the original natural vitamins.
7. I need to avoid all Genetically Modified Foods and Mono-Sodium-Glutamate (MSG) food.
8. I need to avoid all 'Added Natural flavourings' and 'Added Natural colourings' same again they have destroyed the original flavouring and colouring.
9. I need to avoid all added refined sugar.

10. <u>But I do need</u> to ADD Garlic and vitamin E to my diet to protect my body from hidden harmful effects of eating refined foods which will cause toxins in my body.

I may study which 'foods that harm and which foods that heal'.

Now I've ascertained the food I gave to Julian was not enhancing his health, I'm now left wondering did I prepare his food correctly. After all the Doctor at Worcester did ask Julian who prepared his meals, I don't intend to leave any stones unturned on this topic.

I knew raw food was considered best, then steaming comes second, boiling comes third, grilling comes forth and frying last of course. But where does that leave the microwave, its safety has been hovering for years. How and when did this peace of cooking apparatus become available to most householders? Microwaves were originally invented by the Nazis with some Russian input; it was developed for convenience when the army were on operations. But in 1976 Russia banned the microwave issuing an International warning they were a health hazard to humans. They were originally called 'Raider Ranger' because it radiated food, this 'space-age cooking miracle' first become available to most of us in the early1970s I wonder if this is where the price of convenience started to compromised our health? As the Russians were 'chucking' them out the rest of the world was thinking what a fantastic piece of kitchen equipment this was.

Then on 25th September 1998 a case was heard that the European Court of Human Rights felt there had been a violation of justice committed in 1993, when a court decision took place placing a 'gag order' prohibiting Hertel from declaring that microwaved food was dangerous to our health. Contrary to the rights of freedom of expression the opposing party had to pay F400, 000 in compensation.

Over the years Scientists have started noticing a condition called 'Microwave sickness' which starts with low blood pressure, slow pulse, headache, dizziness, eye pain, sleeplessness, irritability, anxiety, stomach pains, inability to concentrate, hair loss, cataracts, reproductive problems, cancer eventually leading to Adrenal Exhaustion.

An additional survey was conducted by Doctor Lurie and Doctor Peror who give ten reasons why microwave ovens should not be used. 1. Can cause brain damage, 2. The body cannot break down the unknown by-product created in microwaves. 3 Male/female hormones stop functioning 5. Distroys vitamins. 6. Minerals in vegetables become cancerous free radicals. 7. Cause tumours 8. Increases cancer cells 9. <u>Causes deficiencies in the immune system</u>. 10. Causes memory loss.

For many years I was brainwashed into thinking harmful 'microwaves effects' were a myth! But at the same time I wondered if the radiation used for x-ray was the same used in microwaves. Answer is yes they are similar they both produce radiation, so why does a Radiographer department need two layers of brick work and then sandwich a thick layer of lead to prevent radiation penetrating through a layer of bricks? Whilst in our kitchens all we have is a flimsy glass door to protect us!

In the early years they used to recommend standing a foot away from the microwave, and never look through the glass door as it could cause eye complaints such as cataracts or poor vision. In 2010 Doctor Mercola is still recommending the same 40 years later, surely they should have conducted some more vigorous studies by now, although if previous scientists were issued a 'gag order' from courtrooms then it didn't encourage others to conduct further studies. Doctor Mercola emphasised while the apparatus is in progress, children certainly should avoid standing near as well as expectant mothers; it has a firm link to leukaemia presumably due to poorly shielded doors.

What about the rest of us?

What's also frightening is industrial microwave repairs, this is 'hot businesses these days, but is it safe business? Safety apart, if the nutrient in microwaved food is destroyed, then it's like eating 'dead food' there's not much point buying good quality food in order to destroy it before it arrives on the plate.

How many foods does it actually affect, evidently it affects cholesterol if the microwave destroys vitamins, it then helps to kick start malnutrition virtually automatically and we don't have to be thin to be malnourished. But wait a minute, if it destroys vitamins which we need such as vitamin B, C, and D for our insulin to operate correctly it stands to reason it's yet another step in the direction of becoming a self-made Type Two Diabetic.

The microwave further exposes our bodies to toxic chemicals when we heat processed food.

It seems to me that microwave prepared food can only serve as a 'warm comfort food' with no nutritional value. I now tell myself when I eat microwaved food that this is as nourishing to me as cardboard and I must remember to replace my destroyed vitamins otherwise I will be diagnosed with Diabetes like Julian.

On a lighter note I would like to quote once more my Hero and Heroine, Robert Jones and Agnes Hunt the founders of the Orthopaedic Hospital, from the book called 'Healing and Hope' that was produced 100 years after of caring at their foundation for compassion. It states when the Hospital was first opened in 1900 a new Cook was engaged on average every two months. The only one with any talent had to be removed to an Asylum. Then Mrs Aldis came along, the perfect cook. Robert Jones once took a group of visiting Doctors into the kitchen and introduced them to Mrs. Aldis and announced the secret of their success. He said with an out stretched arm, "Miss Hunt may think she cures the patient, but there stands the real healer" pointing to Mrs. Aldis.

Robert Jones and Agnes Hunt believed the Hospital ethos was that 'good food' was part of the treatment.

So if Sir Robert Jones the Consultant had worked out over 100 years ago that good food was the only way his patients would get better. Where have we gone so wrong!

Incidentally this Hospital grew all its own fruit and vegetables on site in the vast green houses at the back of the Hospital until the late 1970's when one day the Head Gardener was wondering why the kitchen staff hadn't been to collect the vegetables that day. When the suspense got the better of him, he hurriedly marched to the kitchens to see what the hold-up was only to be escorted in to the store room and with a proud out stretched arm displayed an array of tins of vegetables, packets and frozen foods. A lorry driver was going to be their supplier from now on. All the food he had laboriously grown was left to root. One can only wonder is this when the true root of our society set in? The early 1970's certainly had something to answer for.

The Gardner from then on was employed to tend to the upkeep of the lawns and pruning of the roses. How short sighted, unhealthy and unproductive was that unwise decision from the higher Achy. Strange they called the book "Healing and Hope" that's exactly what Julian longed for when he was taken there. In the early days he always used to say, "When I'm wheeled through the doors of the Spinal Injury Unit I know they will make me better"

That's 'hope' for you and he believed he would be 'healed'.

My motto for this one is, "Self-preservation at all cost, stop radiating and GM-ing our food"

Agnes Hunt and Pandora had something in common, Agnes had hope in her book and Pandora had hope in her box.

Organic Food

Organic food is a modern name for 'Old Fashioned Farming' In the past all our food was grown in the natural way in the ground, on small farms with no toxins or fed with any fertilizer stronger than compost. It's sad that we have to choose between organic and conventional when minerals found in organic food are hundred times higher than that of Farmed in chemical soil.

I wonder if this is a wakeup call for us all as I recap on Agnes Hunts philosophy, that we won't heal without good food, fresh air and plenty of laughter. I think what she meant by good food was organic food, but in her day the word organic was not fashionable or possibly even thought of. I'm not ashamed to say I have started to buy organic food, but when I've mentioned this to young Mums they say, "I can't afford organic prices". I agree with them, neither can I but now I only buy what I need. Going organic is a big challenge, but at first it does appears more expensive. My answer was to 'shift my money' instead of buying unnecessary treats like confectionary or go bargain hunting I put it towards organic products.

I will explain what I do different, instead of buying a large pack of cheap carrots, which I only used to consume some of them and then throw the rest away because they'd become rotten and soggy.

I now buy fewer organic carrots, but consciously make sure I use all of them. If however I am not able to, I then make vegetable soup with them. I'm even wiser now; I buy them at reduced prices as they begin to look past their best. I imagine it could be a fun family thing to do, searching for the cheapest organic produce not to mention more educational than staying at home watching television or playing on computer games. The other thing I've noticed is the organic fruit and vegetables are sweeter, you might think that's a likely story. Help me conduct an experiment, try one organic apple and one GM and pesticide sprayed apple and see if you can tell the difference. The second experiment I'd like you to do is try one organic carrot and one GM with pesticide sprayed on, see if you can taste the difference but not just you; ask your family to try. If you're not convinced, then I thank you for trying. If my taste buds are to be relied on, the organic apple and carrot are sweeter? Could it be because the additives and the pesticides are not camouflaging the natural taste we used to know?

I did go back to eating normal fruit and vegetables for a spell, guess what; my constant headaches returned. Was it a coincidence or fact?

We have such a lot of advertising pamphlets through our letter boxes these days, but one of them was from Abel & Cole offering a weekly home delivery box of organic seasonal fruit and veg including organic milk, eggs, meat and bread. Well done to them for trying.

My sister rang me one day to ask me if I had watched the six o'clock news.

It was a lady passer by being interviewed at the Three Counties Show outside the organic fruit and vegetable tent, she was asked if she ever bought organic produce, she confessed that she didn't on a regular basis but when she did, she noticed it lasted longer, which made it more cost effective. When I thought about it, she was right it does not rot as fast as GM fruit and vegetables.

I have since performed my own mini test by deliberately purchased organic apples and carrots and non-organic apples and carrots. Once labelled, I left them to their own devices to see which rotted first. The answer was the GM fruit and veg.

As I was struggling with all these interferences with my food I came across a Doctor Alan Greene a Paediatric who felt our food might be affecting his patients. He decided to go organic for three years at home, on the road and at restaurants. He felt if fruit, vegetables and animals could be 100% organic, why can't we? He confessed it hadn't been easy but more surprisingly he couldn't believe some people had never heard of organic food. When he asked for organic choices, they would often say "Do you mean vegetarian"? It proved to be so difficult on some days that he had to go without. He's written a book called, 'For three years, every bite organic' compiled by Tara Parker-Pope, it was published on 1st December 2008 twenty days after Julian died.

After reading the above I thought it would be nice to go out for a meal one evening, but after going through the trouble of preparing my own organic cuisine, I was grieved to go out and pay never mind eat non-organic food. I wondered how difficult it was to dine out in organic restaurants locally so I decided to look it up on the internet to see if there was much to offer locally. Bingo! The organic facilities are on the increase, they are too numerous to mention individually but I have grouped them together. There are Restaurants, Café's, Bed and Breakfast, Hotels, Farm markets and Shops with next day delivery, Public Houses, Inns, Bars, Tea rooms, British cuisine, Organic Horticulture movement, Fish restaurants, Mail order, Beer, Cider, Wines, Cocktail Bars, American Bars, Tapas, Sushi, Mezzo, Chinese restaurants, Take away, Restraints Guide Book, Bistro, French, Brazilian, Caribbean, Indian restaurants and a Delicatessen and last but not least Pet Food.

How about, next time you go out for a meal test the water by asking the waitress if they have an organic alternative. After all a vegetarian always has an alternative choice, a diabetic has a choice; glutton free has a special menu why not the organics. I don't need to be rude, I could ask this once and maybe next time I come I may find an alternative they may have sneaked on to the menu. I might appeal to the chef's better nature as I leave the restaurant, or ask the waitress to extend my request to the kitchen for your future visit! I know I won't win the war overnight, so I intend do it nice and steady.

From what I read in the British Food Journal in the UK, the British community deserve a pat on the back because we topped one billion pounds turn over in organic sales for the first time this year. Well done, but I feel the above industry must of contributed to those figures. We still have a long way to go to compete with New Zealand. I don't know if I can offer the Government the same congratulations, I'm still not convinced they have our health at heart yet!!!!

And what about our next generation! There is no need for us to offer sweets to our children especially if they don't ask for it? Let's not stress their immune system unnecessary leading them to suffer untold minor ailments. I like this next short organic true story, a father out of passion for his daughter's health and lack of nutrition while babysitting her felt there was nothing suitable in the house to feed her, and was inspired to produce organic baby food. He went into production and named the product after his daughter, 'Ella's kitchen' so in a small way he is making a difference.

We will always have GM farmers defending themselves by saying, "You cannot grow a huge abundance of food with organic techniques to feed the world"

They're right, they can't but if you deduct the amount of food the world is throwing away because it's gone past its sell by date due to its chemical reactive process with the added additives, then one should arrive at a much reduced figure needed to feed the world.

All we have to do is just be less wasteful and stop throwing so much food away.

I've worked out in an ideal world if the organic produce got sold first, then what's left on the shelf is GM or MSG food which will either perish or expire then hopefully the Supermarkets will stop stocking the shelves with GM and MSG food.

It's not good business to have what they call dead stock on the shelf, in other words we could have the power to change what's available, by how we conduct our purchasing. For the organic producer, the more they sell the cheaper the produce becomes. Maybe we should abide by an old saying, 'let's vote with our feet' and the other old saying is 'money talks' no shopkeeper wants to list his stock under wastage.

I recall what an American farmer said in the Pesticide chapter, "Were back where we started"

I just feel, if this country survived on so little during both wars, they say we were at our healthiest then with no greed, overindulgence or obesity.

In a Homely (sermon) once at church the Priest asked the congregation to think of their bodies as temples for our souls to dwell in, this way we would not be tempted to dishonour it by shovelling greed into its shelter. Julian and I used to jokingly say to each other if the other had an extra dollop of cream, "Are you dishonouring your temple"?

On a more serious note in 2001 the Government set up a watch dog and met up with 'Soil Association' who published that organic food was safer and better for us than non-organic food which directly contradicted the 'Food Standard Agency'

We are famous as a nation for not making too much fuss, but I think these topics GM and MSG deserves a lot of fuss and there are some famous people making a fuss out there on our behalf.

I'm glad I'm not the only one worried about what's happening to our food before it enters our body.

For a start there is Carol Vorderman from Count Down program, she wrote a book called, 'Detox for life' to get away from all of these food additives, pesticides, and other toxins. She has also included a chapter on going organic. I love the way she entices the reader to be converted into an organic way of life. She suggests we buy one organic fruit or vegetable in our shopping ever week and buying seasonal and support our local organic grower.

Another famous person Jamie Oliver in a television program referred to the dining table as the family Alter. We should treat it with respect regarding what we put on it. (I like that a lot) I must say he has more faith in the Government than I have, when he was quoted saying, "The British Government also pledges to address the issue" What I was pleased about was in an RSPCA article Jamie Oliver cooked, their Patron Prince Charles, an organic meal using produce grown at High Grove from the Princes estate. Jamie served guests such as Sting, Stephen Fry and Jasper Conran.

Charles Windsor has more insight into how harmful pesticides and GM produce are to the human body than all the politicians put together. Tony Juniper and Ian Skelly have produced a book called, 'HRH, the Prince of Wales Harmony' Prince Charles has been involved in an ecological movement for 30 years.

Another famous person who wanted to shout STOP to his increasing waist-line was the singer Tom Jones. I read in The Daily Mail on the 21st June 2011 that he had taken stock of his overweight and by announcing publically "This has got to stop" so he turned to a 'Caveman diet' Which sounds a bit ancient, but all you have to do is imagine your ancestor as hunters and gatherers. Eating only what you killed like meat and game, only what you could catch like fish, only what you pluck like fruit off the trees, only what you could dig from the ground like vegetables, only what you can forage on the ground like mushrooms, salads and herbs.

No mention of fast foods soaked in pesticides here smothered in additive sauces, then garnished with GM trimmings and finally washed down with aspartame fizzy pop in this cave.

I could just imagine, Tom opening an organic Restaurant and calling it 'Toms Cave'

I read that in pre historic times mushrooms were eaten by early hunter-gatherers. Unbeknown to them it supplied them with vitamin B, which acted as an antitoxin and enhanced their immune system. I think the trick is, not to go hunting for sugar but burn what we have.

Incidentally Tom did lose his tum and became a leaner and lighter looking man for it.

These celebrities, like me want to attempt to make this world the second Garden of Eden. I know the rule of thumb in society is, don't talk politics, don't talk money and don't talk religion

But I feel this next story deserves a mention.

I remember once when I used to teach Liturgy at our Church for the young children, (Sunday school) the topic that Sunday was "Are we ready for the second coming?" I wasn't allowed to teach or chose my own topic the teaching had to run parallel with the Gospel reading the Priest was reading in the Church, the topic was already mapped out for both of us every week in every country all over the world. I spent some time trying to think how I could make it simple for them to understand. This is how I handled it in the end.

I asked them to imagine a Mother and a Father who wanted to go on holiday with their teenage children, the children protested and said they wanted to stay at home on their own, they argued that they were old enough and responsible enough to take care of them self and the family home. The parents eventually gave in, on the understanding that they trusted them with all they had.

I then asked the children "If they had been those teenagers how would they have behaved when left on their own? Would they have cooked sensible food every day? Would they have taken extra care when cooking, so not to burn the family home down? Would they have washed up after each meal? Would they have made the bed every day? Would they bath or shower every day? Would they have kept up to date with the washing of cloths every day? How would they shop for food, sensible food or fast foods? Would they have kept the house including the bedroom tidy? Would they have bothered to vacuum? Would they invite friends round, and what sort of friends good ones or bad ones? And would they have asked them to tidy up after themselves?

If not, would they have made a mad rush at the end to tidy everything up just before their parents returned? There was a mixed response, but then I reminded them if they had left it until the end and the parents had come home early, how could they explain their behaviour and how could they possibly trust them again? I was then able to compare the situation to God and how we need to be ready at a moment's notice. No good being sorry when it's too late.

To me this is how God has handed me his world to live in, but in his absence I haven't been a wise caretaker of his property. In fact I haven't even practiced what I preached to those children that Sunday morning he holds the deeds to this world and one day I need to hand his property back to him in mint condition. But now I've worked it out, I must not pretend it's not happening. With hindsight, if I had known what harm the pesticides, chemicals, toxins and the effect the interfering with the DNA was going to have on our society I would have started the clean-up long ago.

I'm not going to listen to any more comments like "What I can't do on my own" I know now I have seven serious world issues on my mind and I need to address them before my life is finished and join forces with someone who is willing to help correct the error of my ways. I hope that someone is you!

I once mentioned when I was a child what a handy book the Bible was that I was carrying under my arm. I have since discovered not only did it have the 10 commandments, but also other handy hints of healthy living too, these are my ten healthy guides,

1. Rest on the 7th day. That means recharge your immune system, release nervous tension, to rejuvenate and be ready for the following week. (Isaiah 58, v 13-14)
2. Bread of life. Bread strengthens a man's heart. (Beware of today's white bread, with its chemicals and preservatives, it is robbing people of life giving strength and polluting their bodies) (Psalms 104, v-15.)
3. Contaminated meat. Don't eat animals that have died, or anything you believe to be bad for you. (Daniel 1, v 8)—Meat with growth hormones and antibiotics.
4. Eat and drink in moderation—wine should help us to be joyful not drunk and food is for energy not greed. Psalm 104, v14-15) Drink Natural spring water. (Proverbs 5, v15-18) not full of fluoride and chlorine and other additives!
5. Be happy. (Proverbs 17, v22) Being cheerful keeps you healthy; it's a slow death to be gloomy all the time. It also releases endorphin's which is a natural painkiller.
6. Be active—We should learn lessons on how ants live. (Proverb 6, v 6-11) I think it means exercise and keep buzzy.
7. Sleep—ensue a proper night's sleep and rest. (Ecclesiastics 5, v12) Old wives tale while we are sleeping we are healing.

8. <u>Grow your own food</u>—eat food grown in good soil (Luke 13, v6-9) Crop rotation prevents build-up of harmful organisms and pests in the soil and keeps the crops vigorous. Encouraging and accepting wild life's helping hand, using tried and trusted farming methods. If we don't look after the environment in our life, in time there won't be one for our future generation. Also in Matthew 25:v15 "I have given you every herb that yields seeds which is on the face of the earth; and every tree whose fruit yields seed; to you it shall be food"

9. <u>Keep your body clean</u>—by purifying ourselves, body and soul. Bathing, dieting and meditating keep's your body cleansed inside and out. (Corinthians 2 chapter 7, v 1) hence the old saying, Cleanliness is next to Godliness

10. <u>Be healed</u>—ask the Lord to heal you if you become sick. (James5, v14-15) and massage the limbs with olive oil.

Sounds like modern day alternative therapy to me!

I'm looking forward to returning to these wise ancient ways.

How ironic I discovered these 10 guide lines in the Bible on St David's day, and how even more ironic I converted to Catholism on St David's day in 1996. St David was a man who lived a simple life on a diet of bread, olive oil and herbs and water for hydration. He walked bare foot from town to town aided by a staff to steady him-self.

Possibly finding these ten guidelines on St David's day meant he was leading me by example. I don't mean I intend to live this poor, but I do need to reconsider my eating habits.

What has this got to do with Julian, you may ask? Do you remember that 'Good Book' I had tucked under my arm as a child, it also says in that the book called Ezekiel chapter 47, v12. "The trees will provide food and their leaves will be used for healing people" My question is, "Why aren't we using them"? By the way there is a stained glass window dedicated to this very verse in St Peters Church in Bromyard, Worcestershire, depicting Jesus with a bunch of herbs and a mortar and pestle at his feet. How many different ways can he send me the same message, through the Bible, through perching and through the image seen in stained glass windows! He's probably thinking I've sent you all the antidote to all your ailments, what more can I do!

We're so blind some times, modern man thinks he's just re-invented the wheel with alternative medicine when in fact it's been around since Biblical times. Considering the above verse which quotes "herbs and healing" then shouldn't we insist that more research should be done into 'Organic Amygdalin' or Apricot kernel for the treatment of cancer. And I don't mean its synthetic man-made toxic alternative 'Laetrile'.

Which scientists try to fool the public by calling theirs, vitamin B17, of cause their toxic alternative treatment won't work you can't successfully treat toxins with toxins. Calling it vitamin B17 makes Jo Public think it is harmless because it carries the name vitamin. Later Jo Public then discredit it, by saying it doesn't cure cancer. Consequently patients are then forced to have expensive chemotherapy and long term medicine. Does the word 'profit' come to mind?

Hippocrates expressed in 377 BC, "If we could give every individual the right amount of nourishment and exercise, not too much and not too little. We would have found the safest way to health"

Instead modern man has opted for processed food, frozen, canned, dried and in the process destroyed valuable vitamins and minerals causing imbalance in the blood supply creating such a vast array of medical conditions which needs more expensive treatment. Somebody is making a lot of money at our expense somewhere!

Not only has the Devine supplied us with natural medicine but he's also supplied us with local food to keep us healthy in the first place. Example of this is when we see Eskimos in Alaska, Greenland and Siberia where the sun only shines for three months of the year for them to get their vitamin D. When this source of vitamin is finished, in order for them to replace the missing vitamin D nature has supplied them with an abundance of fish rich in vitamin D. Sadly when other nations invaded their status quo and interfered with nature, introduced them to such modern product at Coca-Cola they suddenly suffered tooth decay and before long they were growing a second set of teeth. Prior to this, Eskimos only ever had one set!

We all enjoy continental feasting these days Chines, Indian, Italian, French, Mexican and many more and nature has chosen local plant for local people worldwide. The Indian cuisine is highly salted which is fine if you're living in the heart of India perspiring like a good one. A doctor once told me when he went home to India it was so hot, he had salt granules forming on his forehead and had to take salt tablets to compensate his salt loss. But I don't think we need that much salt in our cold British climate!

In china and Japan they eat a lot of soy but to compensate any negative effect it may have on their thyroid gland they eat an abundance of seaweed, the problem is we don't in the west because it's not to our pallet consequently we suffer from thyroid problems.

In Italy they have an abundance of olive oil in their diet which seeps through their skin leaving it oily preventing the hot sun from burning them, hence the term 'olive skin'

The French eat an abundance of garlic in their diet which seeps through their pores acting as a mosquito repellent.

You see horses for courses as they say.

Organic organisation suggest, we should buy food like this, "Buy it with thought, cook it with care, use less wheat and meat, buy local, buy seasonal, serve just enough and use what's left over".

As I listened to a Welsh CD called 'Parti Cut Lloi' by singers from Dyffryn Banw in Montgomeryshire, one of their lyrics tell of the passing of the old ways. How our old way of life is disappearing. It seems in modern days we have to attend the gym to stay slim. But in the old days, shear hard work kept those pounds off on such events as the humorous 'sheep shearing' days, with its sweating and it's back bending manoeuvres, moving in a gang from one farm to another helping each neighbour in turn. It describes the sound of the clicking of hand shears, young men chasing and catching the sheep in their pen, the skill of trimming and cutting hoofs off the sheep and pitching your mark on their rump. Then later in the year 'harvesting the hay'

The comradeship it brought it when fifteen hands or more sat down together round a table to banquet and feast, on what they'd grown in the fields. The noise of the butter churning and the smell of the home baked bread is only a reminder of how things used to taste. They of cause are referring to the old fashioned organic way of life. The ones who remember, are now dwindling, it's up to the rest of us to rebuild and rekindle the old way of life that was once so free from harm. Good lyrics if you can understand Welsh!

Let's exchange that modern treadmill for an allotment garden, and then exchange those MP 3 players that are stuck in our ears for the sound of birds in their natural habitat and lastly exchange the artificial light and the stifling air surrounding the computer games for natural sunshine and the pure fresh air! I think sometimes it's alright to move back in time, we don't always have to shoot forward into the future.

By going organic we heal our bodies and the world we live in by simply cleansing both.

Ann Frank wrote in her diary while in hiding, "How wonderful it is that nobody needs to wait a single moment before starting to improve the world" Sadly poor Ann never had that chance but maybe we could on her behalf.

I fear this is such a big topic I just hope Pandora has enough <u>Hope</u> left in her box for all of us to put things right.

Genetically Engineered Medicine

After discovering that our food had fellen prey to a Genetic Engineered commodity, it set my mind racing about all the talk about genetically modified medicine.

It disturbed me greatly to re-read a comment I wrote at the beginning of this book, when a Doctor asked me at Shrewsbury Hospital, "Are you telling me that your husband cannot take any drugs at all now?" at the time I replied "Yes, stupid as it may sound, it appears that he cannot tolerate any drugs anymore, but I don't know why" I intended the 'don't know why' comment to mean can you help me find out. Nobody volunteered any such assistance, even though they could see we were both in such distress. The comment I made to Julian so many times while he was so ill was, "I don't know why you're reacting so badly to their treatment Julian". These comments were not very helpful to him at the time I know, but at least he knew I was on his side in that I recognised something was not right.

Today I decided to look up everything and anything Julian was having difficulty tolerating.

If only to try and find out how this Doctor managed to make me sound so stupid that day?

I recalled his comments because this was unfinished business for me I needed to know had anything changed in the medicine world, and did any of these drugs interact badly with each other to make him feel so unwell and suffer such terrible reactions. When in previous years he had been able to take tablets and eat them like sweets. It used to be one of my big tasks in life, to make sure he had adequate supply of his repeat prescription. So I can't see how anyone could accuse me of encouraging him to withhold on his treatment.

I decided to venture on this trail of Genetic Engineered medicine, to see if this may have been the link I was looking for in the medication Julian could not tolerate. This could be a long chapter, but as usual I'm going back to the beginning.

My first port of call was to look into Antibiotics in general, mainly to see if their history had changed which might explain his recent intolerance! The answer was 'Yes' they do produce genetic engineered antibiotics and what's more, they're on their third generation of Genetic Engineered Antibiotics. How do I know this for sure? I rang a Hospital Pharmacy to find out before I started this chapter. The pharmacist informed me that, most if not all Antibiotics were now genetically engineered. Now, the can of worms has just exploded and what a mess! I wanted to know why they'd gone down that line. Originally antibiotics were necessary to sap serious infection such as gangrene or full blown pneumonia. As the NHS developed so did affordable health care and prescription come about and so we all developed a hunger for "Inappropriate use of antibiotics" either by our GPs over prescribing and giving in too freely to patients demand who expect a course of antibiotics before leaving the surgery and often for very minor ailments. This was the world's first medical mistake; we the public should have been better informed about the dangers of over prescribing making us better equipped about reserving our 'trump card' for such life threatening conditions as pneumonia and gangrene.

Did you know that a single dose or a broken or incomplete course of antibiotics can lead to a greater risk of resistance to that particular antibiotic in a person, for up to a year?

I need an explanation for this one, because I don't understand how a two day supply of antibiotics for a urine infection can quantify a full course of antibiotics, without causing resistance to that drug. Can you?

When it was discovered that the original antibiotic could no longer treat infections, scientists then had to engineer their own, hence the name Genetic Engineered Antibiotics came about. I found a correspondent by a Doctor Narash Harang on line saying, "One of the primary reasons for his interest in looking into Genetic Engineering antibiotics causing resistance pathogens, was simply to protect his family and friends from the day when antibiotics became useless due to ignorance, apathy, and business driven imperatives". That day may come sooner than we expect, he feared due to the way genetic engineering is done it may cause all of us unknown danger. How many are truly aware of this problem I wondered. So I wasn't the only one worried about antibiotics either. We were both worried for different reasons, he for their length of protection and myself for their safety.

I've already touched on the subject of GM tomatoes in the last chapter, but now I want to know what about crops that are modified using DNA from viruses and bacteria crossed with Antibiotic resistant genes, will we see new diseases as a result of impregnating these viruses and bacteria into the seeds cascading into our crops not to mention were unknowingly accepting additional antibiotic in the crops.

Then there is the worry of GM feed given to live stock that are also given GM antibiotic routinely which can then be passed from the stock into the human food chain such as cows, pigs, fish, chickens and would you believe it Honey Bees. It then begs the question, are our meat, milk, eggs and honey safe. We already have a problem with ineffective antibiotics do we need to develop further antibiotic to fight these brand new human-made viruses and bacteria's?

What about people eating meat injected with penicillin, what if that person happens to be allergic to penicillin can that person be indirectly affected by the drug? And shouldn't the packaging say under ingredients 'may contain Penicillin?' We are advised to take some antibiotics on an empty stomach, is this because some GM food such as tomatoes contain genes that is resistant to antibiotics could they alter the drug's effect? These are not facts, these are just my questions.

I looked up what formula went in to producing modern day antibiotics which might have upset Julian's system. The fact that we are on a third generation antibiotic alone could have been enough of a change to upset his insides, but that was not the only issue.

The first ingredient that caught my eye, which didn't have a good ring to it, was Titanium dioxide. What was it? I certainly hoped it wasn't what it sounded like, sadly it was. It was discovered in the 1800`s and was mined for its light weight properties. It is the same titanium that Julian used to rave and get all excited about when he purchased his first lightweight aluminium wheelchair. It made his life so much easier; little did he think he would be eating it unknowingly years later?

It is mined all over the world but mostly in southern India by a company called Tata, it has a history of sparking opposition and violence at its plants. In January 2006, 13 people were gunned down for protesting against their land being taken over. Some 10,000 farmers have committed suicide as a result of a debt-ridden situation. This is in the most prosperous agricultural area of India. Any communities, who live in the paths of these companies live in the shadow of despair.

Do we want or even need this Titanium in our medicine and food bad enough to be prepared for others to die for us? I don't think so.

It is not proven, but it is being questioned that Titanium dioxide in medication destroys the autoimmune system. So if that turns out to be true, then Doctors are prescribing antibiotics to people who are feeling unwell, and the side effect of modern day antibiotics could cause your immune system to suffer even further, that doesn't sound helpful to me.

I happen to know someone who cannot tolerate any medication that has a plastic coating in the form of a capsule. She used to tell her GP, "I can't tolerate those plastic things; can you prescribe me tablets instead of capsules"? Maybe there is something in what she's saying, in years to come we might find the joke is not on her, but has back fired on us for laughing at her comments.

You will be pleased to know that Titanium has excellent corrosion resistance and high strength to weight ratio. Thank God, at least we won't rust or weigh heaver as a result of taking antibiotics.

The "Common-sense test" asks this question, did Titanium dioxide occur naturally in the indigenous human food supply? The answer to that is, of course absolutely not.

That's why holistic nutritionists are increasingly seeking to avoid this ingredient in anything we eat or swallow. It is not part of the food supply in nature, and has not been proven to be completely safe for human consumption.

Would you believe Titanium is also on its second generation as a drug; its new formation is called Nano-titanium just as the name suggests it consists of much smaller particles except this new product has now been introduced into our diet. I found in 2004 the United Kingdom Society had recognised serious early warning signs of Nano-toxicity, there are many distressing letters on line to support this. Scientists are still researching its safety, but it's as if the horse has already bolted and it's out there like a rash. It's hidden in food under E171; it's in most of our food packaging like plastic milk bottles, baby milk bottles and beer bottles. To be fair titanium has been around a long time, it's only when they decided to produce Nano-titanium that it became our biggest problem to our health. Some concerns about potential health risks have been raised by an Environmental Working Group, when these particles of titanium are inhaled, absorbed through the skin or gut. When I mean inhaled I mean when it's added to building material which later disintegrates in to fine dust which we then inhale.

When I mean through the skin I mean when used in products such as sun tan screen creams, with no requirements to disclose potential harm.

Health concerns are worried that Nano-titanium can be absorbed directly into the blood stream; chemicals are more dangerous when absorbed through the skin than by digestion as larger partials of titanium travel through the digestive system to be excreted. During this process of digestion they are at least neutralized by the acid in the stomach and detoxified by the liver before entering the blood stream and other organs. Whereas when it's absorbed through the skin it is absorbed untreated directly into the blood stream.

Titanium dioxide has recently been classified by the International Agency for Research as a possible Carcinogen to humans.

How strange that skin cancer has been on the increase since the fad of using sun tan cream came about in the early 1970's.

Did you also know that sun screens that contain Zinc oxide and Titanium = Aluminium. The human body is incapable of flushing out this toxic metal called aluminium without intervention. For decades we have been told to stay away from Aluminium but they are hiding it behind these two products.

Nano-Titanium can cause unexplained dysfunction for example allergies and impairment to the immune system. In that case, maybe we should be thinking, should we be putting anything on our skin that we're not prepared to put in our mouth especially now we know that skin is capable of absorbing chemicals.

I seriously think if the jury is still out on the safety of both Titanium and Nano-Titanium, shouldn't our safety be taken into account until it's proved absolutely beyond possible doubt that it is safe?

I thought everything had to be safe before it was introduced onto the open market. Evidently not, it seems to me all products are innocent until proven guilty so now it's not just our food that can harm us, but our medicine as well as anything that touches our skin.

If it's true that Titanium is not yet deemed safe, why are companies allowed to add it in their building materiel when laying drives? It's not a problem until the product starts to break up in years to come from general wear and tear becoming fine dust. Who will suffer then? The home owners, the children playing outside, the postman, the milk man, or the paper boy the list is endless even the double glazing man won't be safe. These innocent parties' lungs should not be put at risk.

In another article it mentioned side effects of Titanium can cause nausea, diarrhoea/ loose stools and dyspepsia. That was exactly what Julian suffered from when he was on Antibiotics. Could this be a contributing factor to Julian's allergy the Nano-titanium? Both of us used to say to the Consultants at Shrewsbury, Oswestry and Telford that Julian was not strictly allergic he just couldn't tolerate them, we confessed and realised he did not lapse into Anaphylactic shock each time he took them. Our argument was when he suffered from diarrhoea and vomiting, what value were they to him if the drug was shunted through his system in this manner down the toilet?

Was it his body language telling him, stop giving me this stuff otherwise I will get rid of it for you. If this was the case was there any wonder Julian was so very ill every time he took modern day medicine? It goes on to say that at a later stage one can see the liver getting swollen and irregular bumps known as nodules can be felt.

On the occasions Julian was on antibiotic treatment, he used to point these nodules out to me, and they did feel like small marbles under the skin. During the last five weeks of Julian's life I spent day and night massaging his swollen liver area. Even when the Doctors and Consultants were present, I sometimes used to stop out of respect, but Julian would say, "Don't stop, that's soothing" What I find odd now is; not one nurse or Doctor ever questioned what I was doing and why. It must have looked odd to them; other visitors did not conduct this practice on their relatives.

Could his fatty liver be due to the genetically modified antibiotics?

What other ingredients are there in Antibiotic? The two ingredients that appear to go hand in hand are Methyl-paraben and Propyl-paraben. It is also found in water based cosmetics such as moisturizers, shampoos, shower cleansers, conditioners and sunscreens. It is even used in lipsticks, foundation, mascara and eye shadow sometimes at levels as high as 25%.

In the pharmaceutical industry it is now a common preservative for certain drugs. Studies have created fear in some consumers, a group of British researchers tested tissue samples that were taken from women who had cancerous breast tumours. They found traces of paraben's in the lumps of all the 20 women. How could it get in there unless it was put there?

I've mentioned these parabens before under the Environmental Toxins chapter. While discussing cosmetics a study was done in September 2008 on 20 girls between the age of 14 and 19 and on those using cosmetics containing Propyl-paraben. Propyl-paraben was found in every girl!

The fear is, that parabens mimics oestrogens in the body and there for increases a women's risk of developing breast cancer and that is very concerning for everybody. Each woman or young girl has a father, boyfriend, husband, partner who would be traumatised when the female sector are at risk.

Does this sound a safe product to be swallowing, when it doesn't even sound safe to put on our skin? I didn't set out to find out what is corrupt in the medicine world, neither did I think that I would find chemicals that other people should be concerned about for the well fair of their health, just like these females mentioned above.

Taking antibiotics knowingly is one thing, but taking them unknowingly is devious on someone else's part. How and when do we do that?

Apparently Genetic Engineered crops contain genes which confer resistance to Antibiotics; these genes may pick up bacteria which may infect us.

This is only a peep into the corrupt world of Antibiotics. Question is, will Antibiotics eventually become so distraught in their makeup that one day our body will not recognise them as our saviour but more as our enemy, in other words the treatment might be more harmful than the original complaint. Was Julian's body our first example to display revulsion towards these 'non-human-invention' in the medicine world.

Then I came across something called the 'Black Box' warning label, something I now feel I should have been well aware of during my nursing days!

Black Box warning label

Have you ever heard of it? I hadn't until now, evidently it means when a drug is classified as Black Box it carries a dangerous warning label.

I wondered when did it come about, it came about in the year 2008 when there was a big review in America on the medical front. In this big shake up, some drugs were withdrawn from the market completely while others were issued with the Black Box warning label because of their safety. One such drug that was withdrawn while been investigated was Avandia otherwise known as Rosiglitazone and in October 2010 the Avandia Company had their licenced withheld.

Avandia was one of the drugs Julian had been taking before he suffered his near multi-organ failure. Other drugs they decided could remain on the market but must be prescribed with care, and they were the ones that were labelled with the 'Black Box warning' they were Metformin, Gentamicin, Metronidazole, Ciprofloxacin, Levothyroxine, Lisinopril and Furosemide.

The USA government refer to these drugs as the big 'Bad Boys'

Unfortunately yet again this 'Black Box' system is only recognised in America, not in Britain or Europe for that matter. Doctors are still being asked to be <u>vigilant</u> of the side effects, I read this word <u>vigilant</u> in our National newspaper in 2007 and now I'm reading the same message again in 2013, in other words nothing's changed.

I'm sure we will eventually follow suit, and will give out worrying drug with similar labelling as the 'Black Box Warning', but at what cost? The years are rolling by and our people are suffering while they wait for news of any ban.

I was discussing extensive drug side effects in general with a friend one evening when he said, "Olwen, Everybody knows about the interfering that's going on with our food and medicines" My very angry reaction was, "If everybody knows, why hasn't everybody done something about it before I have got to hear about it?"

He asked me to calm down, and reminded me once again I couldn't change anything single handed. "Why not" is what I wanted to know? I am willing to have a go; all I need is a bit of help from someone who is willing to listen.

HELP ME, SOMEONE!

As I discover that most if not all antibiotics are second and third line generation Genetically Modified drugs, I am still on my quest of finding out why, did Julian go blind, deaf, suffer limb dysfunction with his hands, become aggressive, hallucinate, suffer chest pain, unbelievable muscle and flesh break down and finally lost his mind before he died?

These were not mild side effects he was experiencing, but a complete body and organ breakdown.

This is a list of the antibiotics Julian was prescribed during the last five weeks of his life. Metronidazole, Gentamicin, Ciprofloxacin, Vanclomycin, Flucloxacillin, Erythromycin, Trimethoprim and Silver Nitrate Wound Vacuum System.

To stay focused on Julian's case, and not to make this book sound too much like a medical encyclopaedia, I've decided to just look up these eight drugs. I hope the detective in you is still hanging on in there.

Metronidazole Antibiotic

The first Antibiotic I looked into on behalf of Julian was Metronidazole. It states unnecessary use of this drug should be avoided. It should be reserved for conditions such as venereal diseases, intestinal dysentery, liver, ovarian, brain, and lung abscess.

Even though Julian did not suffer from a lung abscess he did have a hip abscess, it could be accepted that he might warrant this type of treatment.

Metronidazole should only be given when culture information is available. In the absence of this data pharmaceutical opinion should be sort before selecting this therapy.

I assume there were blood samples taken for this reason but blood reports for these dates appear to be either missing or not taken prior to prescribing this drug. I'm exhausted of repeatedly asking for missing documents.

But how widely is this drug used? If you are familiar with the name of this drug and have not suffered from the above, ask yourself were you over prescribed?

One of the ingredient in Metronidazole is Colloidal Silicon Dioxide, when I looked this up it stated when used with titanium dioxide it can be used as a coating agent for wood, metal, ceramic, glass, paper, tiles, wallpaper, fibre optical lens and paint. It doesn't make sense that we should be talking about medicine in the same breath as the above. It's as foreign as saying, "I fancy a wood and glass sandwich for my lunch" I was still confused, because if Metronidazole did not contain penicillin why did Julian feel so unwell on it? Metronidazole confesses to having 94 side effects. The one side effect that caught my eye was; caution should be taken if giving to a patient with raised liver function tests. Evidently if the liver is not functioning adequately the effect of the drug is increased in strength, due to a slower removal of the medication from the body resulting in body toxicity.

. I now understand why Julian felt the need to refuse this antibiotic, saying my body is not yet recovered enough to handle the next dose. His last dose had not yet left his body before been offered more. On top of that I knew the Metronidazole recommended dose was 500mg every 8 hours, but to my horror I discovered Julian was given 500mgs every 6 hours.

. I now understand why Julian's body felt the 'drug round' was coming round too often, in his case it was.

Julian was then given a diuretic at the same time as the Metronidazole.

. I now understand why Julian would say that Furosemide made him feel so ill, but would not confess that he was allergic to it. In effect what was happening, the diuretic was getting rid of his body fluid which then further concentrated the side effect he was suffering from the Metronidazole.

Still not convinced that the above explanation was making Julian as ill as he appeared I looked up the possibility of any contra-indication, and sure enough there it was.

Metronidazole **should not** be given to patients who suffer from hypo-adrenalism.

. I now understand why Julian became so stressful when he knew it was time for this antibiotic; it was hampering his fight, fear and flight with his malfunction Adrenal Tumour.

Oh! Ju, Ju, Ju I just want to cry, my poor poor Ju.

Gentamicin Antibiotic

My second Antibiotic I looked up on Julian's behalf was Gentamicin.

I always recognised this as a powerful drug; I always felt it had a 'sawn off shot gun' effect on infection. But I was also worried what else it was doing to the rest of the body in the process.

On 23rd October 2008 Julian was given 600mg of Gentamicin in one dose. The International best practice has withdrawn high dosage from circulation since Julian's death. There appears to be a big mop up from circulation going on, to date they have allowed 20mg 40mg, and 80mg at the most to be administered at any one time, as you can see Julian was given a massive 600mg dose. Fourteen fold overdose if 40mg is what is considered the new recommended dose.

High doses were withdrawn from the market due to toxicity mainly because of these three terminologies, ototoxicity = inner ear poisoning, nephrotoxicity = renal toxicity, endotoxin = lead to septic shock if **immune system is severely pronounced**.

. I now understand why Julian reacted so badly to this drug that day and why the pathologist report stated that the right kidney was somewhat enlarged weighing 180mg, while the left appeared rather small in size and weighed only 100g. When prior to this last hospitalization he had two healthy plump kidneys of normal size, we knew this because of his regular IVPs.

. I now understand why Julian became deaf on this day after he suffered ototoxicity from the high dose in quick succession.

. I now understand why Julian started to develop septic shock when the gentamicin affected his already hampered immune system.

It also stated that Gentamicin should not be given in conjunction with some other drugs one of them being a Diuretic. Julian was on his sixth day of Furosemide 40mg twice a day, when he was given this large dose of Gentamycin.

. I understand now how Julian suffered the night he was given a seven fold dose of the Gentamicine, as well as suffering at the hands of three other drugs he was given intravenously at the same time, they were Flucloxacillin, Metronidazole, and Human Actrapid. These effects was then exacerbated by many fold because of six long days of continues diuretic.

. I can understand why Julian used to say, "Why are they giving me all these drugs at the same time, I can't work out which one is affecting what in my body"?

What a concoction, if a druggy took four drugs he knew he was going to react to one in one session; we'd all say 'What an idiot!' Julian was no idiot, just over whelmed with pressure.

I can barely take in what chemicals his body took on board that day. He also felt he was bullied into taking the insulin because his glucose reading was too high. Staff would not take into account he had been coaxed into drinking three High Calorie Ensure Drinks a day, which would have obviously contributed to elevating his readings. He drank 20 cartoons in total; he was constantly asking the nurses if he could see the dietician to discuss the high content of the sugar levels in these cartoons.

They were obviously dealing with one tough cookie in Julian. Sadly on 23rd October 2008 these drugs took a toll on poor Julian's body, because it was during that night Julian had his most horrendous night mare ever. The reason it was so horrendous was because he had an insight into to its horrors, in other words he was fully awake and remembered everything the next day. He was always strong, but this particular night he was extremely strong.

I used all my strength and wit to reason with him without restraining him. Just the very thought of what he went through that night makes me shudder as he described those ferocious dogs chasing him with their dribbling saliva and bad breath.

Some of the side effects of Gentamicin are Insomnia, anxiety attack, depersonalisation, cognitive disorder, and gastro intestinal damage, brain, heart, liver, kidney, pancreas and blood disorder and endocrine disorder. The last one will sadden me for ever, muscle damage, how the Anaesthetist described it to me in such detail, I almost felt he was decomposing while he was still living. I say decomposing because the pungent smell of decay that came from his flesh after this night stuck in my throat and nostrils.

Gentamicin was given its 'Black Box' warning label in America in Feb 2008 because of its potential toxicity sadly the American 'Black Box' warning label did not extend it self across the water to Julian's aid nine months later. If you're ever offered Gentamicin be sure it does not exceed the 80mg maximum dose.

In America patients are offered 'support groups' for anyone who has suffered from Gentamicin toxicity, or poisoning that has affected their balance long term, or kidney damage warranting kidney dialysis.

. I can now understand why Julian suffered this horrendous nightmare, accompanied with the depersonalisation, anxiety attack coupled with insomnia. Because of the high dose he'd received, the effect would have been eight fold. No wonder he said the next morning "Don't let anyone suffer like I have"

Sadly three years after Julian's death, I now read of a 91 year old lady named Mrs Audrey Evans on 22nd September 2011 who was given 400mgs of Gentamicin on four separate occasions even though the same Doctor wrote in her medical notes that she required 40 mgs not 400mgs. The Post-mortem revealed, after she had been administered ten times the recommended dose "There was evidence that acute damage to the kidney was caused by the overdose" sadly this took place at the very same Hospital where Julian was treated, which is Shrewsbury. Her son however said, "It was an error and should have been picked up, but we do not wish to attribute blame. That's very decent of her son, but history is still repeating itself in the same place!! Remember Julian received 600mg not 400mgs like this poor lady did.

Vancomycin

The third Antibiotic I looked up on his behalf was Vancomycin.

Again totally unrelated to Penicillin and as he didn't receive this one until he was on a ventilator the day before he died, I don't feel this contributed to his early death.

Not much point going into great detail about this one because of that reason.

Erythromycin

The fourth one was Erythromycin. Another one that is Penicillin free, but unfortunately Julian always suffered from chest pain, nausea, loss of appetite, low temperature, stomach pain and vomiting when he took this one. I couldn't understand why he reacted so badly if it did not contain penicillin. There must have been another reason. They were not life threatening side effects that's true, but extremely unpleasant if he was expected to take it for two weeks.

The abdominal pain and the chest pain I think were the worst to witness. Julian agreed to start this other drug called Erythromycin under duress on the account he knew it would disagree with him, on the condition the minute the drug started to cause a reaction the doctor had to agree to discontinue the treatment. I've already mentioned in a previous chapter that he asked me to summon the doctor to give him an antidote minutes later.

The doctor documented in Julian's notes on 15th October 2008, "Patient requested to see a Doctor and an antidote to Erythromycin, I informed him to my knowledge I don't know of any" and "Patient found it difficult to finish sentences, due to burping" I looked up any contradiction to Erythromycin, advice was—should not be used with any liver dysfunction, it may also interact with other antibiotics. He was given Metronidazole at the same time as having raised liver function results. The next piece of advice was, contact your Doctor immediately if you suffer from chest pain, nausea, stomach pains or low temperature. His temperature was 34.5 at the time.

Julian did exactly what it said on the box as they say, he summoned the Doctor but to no avail.

Shrugged shoulders' isn't much of an antidote when you're having a survear drug reaction. On this occasion I'm forced to write <u>I still don't understand</u> rather than I now understand why Erythromycin was prescribed especially when Julian had predicted he would become very ill if he was given it. But to give someone a drug that may have a devastating reaction on a Sunday afternoon with skeletal staff and no pharmacy staff available for advice regarding possible antidote beggar's belief! We were left to our own devices to ride the waves as he advised. But at last I can now write <u>I understand,</u> patients who have suffered with Hepatitis C in the past should never be given Erythromycin; it can have adverse reaction on the liver. That was my long awaited answer; he couldn't tolerate it because he would suffer adverse reaction.

Another antibiotic he was given was Augmentin its other name is Co-amoxiclav, this should not be prescribed to an ex-Hepatitis C sufferer either including some over the counter drugs Ibuprofen, Naproxen and Aspire which he could not tolerate either.

Trimethoprim

The fifth antibiotic was Trimethoprim, again Penicillin free and another 'I don't understand' why Julian was only prescribed this one orally for only 72 hours two weeks before he died. This was the one he was prescribed by his old GP on numerous occasions for years.

He used to call it his old faithful antibiotic; he never had trouble with this one.

. I now understand that Julian's blood results indicated he was sensitive to trimethoprim so he could have tolerated this one. How strange that this one comes in tablet form not a capsule.

It does leave you wondering about the titanium and the Nano-titanium in the plastic coating in the capsule which is so disagreeable to our bodies.

Flucloxacillin

The sixth was Flucloxacillin, I don't know why he was prescribed this when Julian always told them he had difficulty with penicillin. Although Julian was not strictly allergic to Penicillin it was quite obvious to both the Coroner and I that Julian had difficulty with penicillin. If he was not allergic to it he was defiantly sensitive to it. So I decided to look up the definition of sensitivity.

'It is a state of altered reactiveness in which the body reacts with an exaggerated immune response to what is perceived as a foreign substance. There are two types of reaction immediate and delayed. Immediate speaks for itself, but delayed could be as long as 72hours after admission of the drug. Immediate is caused by antibodies which are fighting cells, whereas delayed is caused by lymphocytes which have long lived memory cells and react when exposed to the same agent again.' I looked up signs and symptoms of hypersensitivity to penicillin.

Numbness, neurovascular changes, nervousness, apnoea, hypoxia, severe agitation, dizziness, hallucinations, mottling, headache, abnormal liver function tests, gangrene, coma.

. I understand now, how Julian was right all along. The terminology we both had been searching for at his bed side all that time was hypersensitive to penicillin. Hence why he always managed to tolerate it for 72 hours then he would start begging for mercy, but sadly no one listened.

. I understand now why Julian complained of numbness in his hands when he was no longer able to hold his own cup when his mother visited that one afternoon.

. I understand now why Julian's character had changed from being the confident person to this nervous person.

. I understand now why Julian had those mysterious holes develop in his spleen, caused by hypoxia which is oxygen starvation causing death to tissue.

. I understand now why Julian had out bursts of severe agitation.

. I understand now why Julian suffered hallucination.

. I understand why Julian had raised liver function tests, causing his liver to swell. To be fair these were raised periodically at home usually when he had to go on bed rest and was prescribed antibiotics. I have photos of his abdomen extending so badly on these occasions he would find, it was difficult to bend at the midriff.

. I understand now why Julian developed huge purple mottling rings on his lower back, bottom, hips and upper back of his legs during the night of 24th October 2008. These large purple areas had a lasting effect on me, they never recovered, in fact they eventually became black and crusty; the flesh and muscle had to be removed surgically two weeks and four days later when he was a patient at the Intensive Care Unit.

Poor Julian, neither of us thought he would be taking his last breath 18 days later!

Ciprofloxacin

The seventh I look up was Ciprofloxacin. This one Ciprofloxacin is no longer recommended as first line treatment for urine infection, prostatitis, and respiratory infection like pneumonia or sinusitis. I have already mentioned a trend in Julian's s GP notes that his old familiar GP used to prescribe him Trimethoprim, but when he sadly died before retiring may I add. A new young breed of GPs came up the ranks prescribing such drugs as Ciprofloxacin.

In the year 2000, when the three of us went to Pompeii, Julian was prescribed seven courses of antibiotics on different occasions that year. Three of those courses were Ciprofloxacin, one course for seven days, the other two courses on concurring fourteen days.

Twice during that year he experienced loss of vision, starting with tunnel vision then complaining of looking through rippling water peripherally. Following these two antibiotic courses, on both occasions he had suffered server dehydration, one from scorching mid-day sun in Pompii and the other occasion when he was suffering with a severe urine infection causing him to feel nauseas and vomiting preventing him drinking leading to dehydration.

Julian did not have this antibiotic again until the day before he died. Out of the ten side effects it carries Julian suffered from nine of them, acute liver failure, heart problems, confused state, anaemia, drug induced psychoses, abdominal pain, hypertension, muscle breakdown, loss of vision and breathing problems that may require ventilating.

<u>. I understand now</u> how dehydration can cause such havoc on its own, but when coupled with drugs that need hydration to flush out the toxicity from the body, it proves to be catastrophic when the kidneys and liver prove to be inadequate to filter the toxins on their own; it can cause untold reaction in the body.

Two years and three months after Julian's death, on 25th February 2011 ciprofloxacin was certified with the 'Black Box' warning label in America, in response to complaints of spontaneous tendon ruptures, **muscle breakdown and breathing problems leading to being ventilated.**

Disavow! Julian suffered from both while on this drug. Not to mention two other separate occasions he took this drug when he ruptured tendons in both biceps when getting out of the bath, but did not attend GP practice for either injury. On one of the occasions we were late for a Christening because he was stranded in the bath. Not easy getting out of a bath when you're paralysed from the chest down then finding one of your arms not only won't help you but is excruciatingly painful. Needless to say he did not go to the GP about it, but when he did mention it at a later date, the GP told him there was nothing that could be done at that late stage.

The window of opportunity had been missed.

There are still no such warnings as the 'Black Box' warning on this drug in this country yet. But one day maybe, one day!

Ciprofloxacin should never be given to anyone who has suffered from Hepatitis C in the past!

Silver nitrate

My eighth is Silver Nitrate vacuum pump. Out of all the seven antibiotics I've looked at, at a glance this one sounded the most dangerous. But in fact I found myself making a U turn on this one. Hippocrates, the Greek Father of medicine taught that silver healed wounds and infection in 400 BC during the middle ages. Silver utensils and goblets were used amongst the affluent in preference to gold table wear because of the healing power of the silver. Because of this, silver wear was used to provide bacteria-free table wear. It has now been proven that silver is toxic to E.Coli and Bacillus typhus. On the other hand, over use of silver caused the upper class to have a bluish tinge to their skin resulting in commoners asking if they were of a 'Royal blue blood' family. There is also another phrase that we are familiar with, 'Were you born with a silver spoon in your mouth' when babies were given a silver spoon on their baptism day. The gift was intended to keep the child healthy while feeding from it. Modern day thinking conjures the meaning to be, the baby was born to a wealthy family. During the Pioneering years the Americans would place a silver coin in the milk bucket to keep it fresh preventing it going sour.

I am aware that just because it was good in days gone-by, it wasn't necessarily good to day.

But I've already quoting what the Tissue Viability Community Nurse documented in Julian's medical notes, "Wound bed clean and granulating" Verbally she also commented that she hadn't seen healing at such a speed as this, since she had been implementing these pump apparatus. I can vouch for her disbelief because I too witnessed these bunches of grapes like granulation taking place inside the wound. It's a shame this old 'Silver Nitrate' treatment couldn't of continued its course, without the additional reactive antibiotic he was so desperately trying to abstain from.

The sad thing was, she could not foresee any problem if Julian wished to go home with the equipment, she said other patients often did and especially if I had used the pump equipment before.

A Doctor Toby Richards, a vascular surgeon of University College Hospital London, was quoted on line stating about the Silver Nitrate Vacuumed System, "Because of its portable and its disposable factor, it is cost effective in that it frees up an NHS bed" that's exactly what Julian wanted. The company boasts of its healing power, and I can vouch for that.

I was familiar with the system but some readers might wonder how does the system work? With deep cavity like this they place a sterile sponge in the wound, and then place a sterile tube on top of the sponge, sealing the cavity with what appears to be cling film. The tube is then attached to a suction machine which draws the exudates into a drained bottle which is disposable.

It states that while modern day antibiotics kill about half a dozen different organisms, silver nitrates kill 650. It appears the old fashion silver is emerging as a wonder drug of modern medicine. More wonderful than anything its virtually toxic free. Fantastic someone had just reinvented the wheel.

I now understand why Julian's wound responded so well to the Silver Nitrate dressing, because he was not persuaded to start the insulin until 17ᵗʰ October 2008 that was eight days after admission. In that eight days the tissue Rep commented and documented how well the new growth in the cavity was progressing. So how could 'not having insulin' be detrimental to his healing, his wound did not deteriorate until he was persuaded to take a host of drugs.

In fact, Julian was constantly coaxed into taking antibiotics because of the threat of osteomyelitis, and wound infection but in fact when I read his notes there was no proof or evidence he had osteomyelitis. The MRI scan result dictated 10 days before he died, the written report used the word 'suggested' to have osteomyelitis three times, and 'possible' have osteomyelitis once.

Given the reaction Julian was having to every antibiotic he was offered, except to the localized silver nitrate dressing, why was the psychological pressure so great?

Because of this insistence for oral and intravenous drugs through his system caused him to suffer kidney pain and damage, chest pain and cardiac damage, hearing damage, temporary blindness, possible brain damage but definitely pain in his brain, loss of function in his arms, destruction of skin, muscle, tendons, and excruciating abdominal pain.

We have travelled far since Alexander Fleming first discovered Penicillin in 1928, but have we become endangered of travelling too fast and spinning off the road, and left wondering how to get back on tracks?

At the beginning of this chapter I wrote, "I don't understand why your reacting to the treatment like you are, Julian" one chapter later I have written "I now understand" 20 times, which means Julian was right again. In order for me to heal I needed to write the book so that I could understand why he did react like he did, how else could I work out this complicated scenario if I didn't put everything in order?

On recapping I feel most of the medical staff, nurses, doctors including his Mother and his half-sister indicated that I had tried to prevent Julian receiving medical treatment hampering his recovery leading to his death.

During those five weeks Julian received—Gentamicin x 1massive dose of 600mg.

> Metronidazole x 36 times.
> Vancomycin x 4 times.
> Flucloxacillin x 24 times.
> Erythromycin x 12 times.
> Trimethoprim x 6 times.
> Ciprofloxacin x 2 times.

Total antibiotics admiration given was 85 doses.

He had an additional 50 doses of Human Actrapid Insulin, plus 6 interrupted days of sliding scale Insulin, including 1 dose of Lantus insulin which he was extremely allergic too.

A further 36 doses of Furosemide, which is a diuretics prescribed for water retention, some he took in tablet form and some in injection form. (A medication he <u>wasn't</u> prescribed at home.)

That's enough to pickle most of us. He also gave-in into 20 high in glucose 'Ensure drinks' which must of helped raise his glucose readings.

My quest at the beginning of this chapter was to find out three things, they were

.   Why did Julian insist he had different insulin on the 20th October 2008, causing him to complain that it was his worst night ever?
.   Why did Julian go blind and deaf one lunch time on the 5th November 2008?
.   Why did Julian's flesh break down as badly as it did after one horrendous night on 23rd October 2008?

In short the explanation I have for these three questions is—:
First one being what he considered to be 'The worst night ever'.

To recap on the morning in question on the 21th October 2008 Julian said to me, "Olwen, I don't know what insulin they gave me last night, but I'm not taking that again" When he made this comment I presumed he had his usual Human Actrapid Insulin the night before. Thinking it might have been a build-up of the insulin. Although my nurses head told me that short acting insulin should be out of his body in four hours. So whatever he had the night before certainly lasted all night. I was shocked Julian was right as ever, no one could ever pull the wool over his eyes. On reading his notes he had indeed been given a different insulin the previous night on 20th October called 'Lantus' an insulin which he had been diagnosed as been allergic to by the Diabetic Nurse at Worcester. Although it was documented clearly on his medicine chart under allergy, "Allergic to Lantus'

Lantus

Why was he prescribed this by the Doctors and worst still why was it given by the nurses who should have noticed from the front of his medication chart, under allergy and secondly on his red armband stating allergic to "Lantus" before administrating it, insisting he took it will remain a mystery to me.

On the strength of this discovery I decided to look up the signs and symptoms of Lantus insulin.

The most obvious first advice was; Lantus should not be given to any one allergic to Lantus. The next one was not such a well-known fact. It should not be administered to anyone who has any allergy at all! In other words Zero tolerance, if one sufferers with <u>any other</u> allergy.

Most common side effects of Lantus are difficulty breathing, tightness of the chest, confusion, fast heartbeat, fast shallow breathing, headache, stomach pains, nervousness, thirst, increased hunger and sweating. Lantus is also an ACE inhibitor which means it lowers blood pressure. Another side effect of Lantus is; Diuretics can interact with ACE inhibitors. More upsetting of all was; Lantus can harm the heart and brain.

<u>. I now understand why</u> as soon as he was given this insulin why he started having breathing difficulties, complained of tightness of his chest, his pulse rate went up to 140 and remained high throughout the night, his respirations was over 30, he described his headache as if his brain was swelling inside his skull, constant abdominal pain, abnormal perspiration, come day break he said "I feel the poison leaving my body". Then he had this sudden hunger about 5am and could hardly wait for breakfast. He also said, "I need to finish soaking up this poison" Unfortunately he was not able to finish the porridge because he said, "My other organs are so swollen they are crushing my stomach". He still had the chest pain, shortness of breath and the profuse sweating when the Doctors conducted their ward round the following morning at 9am. His blood pressure at that time was 225/80, his oxygen saturation was 77% and he looked ghastly, grey and dark around the eyes.

Julian begged, "No more insulin please"

Even in this dreadful state, the Doctor insisted "This is nothing to do with the insulin, be reasonable how can it be, its human insulin found in every body's body naturally which we all need to survive"

The only other drug Julian was given that night 20 minutes prior to the insulin was his second dose of 40mg of Furosemide, which dehydrated his body further causing the effect of the allergy of the insulin to be exacerbated. No wonder he'd never felt this bad ever before.

Breathlessly Julian bowed his head and shook it saying to the doctors, "I don't know why I'm reacting to all the medication like this, but I'm telling you I am".

As far as pain was concerned, this was truly Julian's worst night I ever but to add insult to injury the following morning the hive of Doctors round his bed didn't believe him. I searched in his notes for a record of this episode but very little was written, not even a record of the Doctors request for an ECG due to his complaint of chest pain throughout the night. They did document however, "Patient wishes to go home to die" They didn't even act on that.

If nothing else, <u>I now understand why Julian</u> had the worst night ever. Was this the night his heart was under such strain from the side effects of the Lantus which caused him to develop Hypotrophy of his left ventricular because they allowed his blood pressure to remain so high for so long. For a man his age a normal heart should weigh 300g, Julian's heart weighed 600g that's twice the weight it should of been. Up until this episode his heart was as strong as an ox they said, so what went wrong that night?

Poor Julian, he always had a big heart in life now he can boast of a bigger one in death.

Furosemide

The second question was, 'Why did Julian go blind and deaf one lunch time' after receiving four Intravenous Injections in quick succession, while I quickly ran to the toilet. On arriving on the other ward and discovering his blindness I was concern the speed the Intravenous drugs had been administered had contributed to both affliction blindness and partial deafness. As well as the speed the drugs were given, I was also concerned that their combination might have had a contradiction effect on each other. On research it turns out that Metronidazole can cause blindness, if one has deranged Gamma GT readings, Julian's fluctuating between 261 and 298 normal range should be 0-45. Then to further exacerbate the effects of the Metronidazole, he was given Furosemide a diuretic which would of strengthen its dose. To make matters worse his body was further impounded with fluid restriction of no more than one and a half litres of fluid total in for 24hours.

This dehydration not only drained his body of its hydrated states quo but it caused the aqua fluid in his eye ball to drain away too. There was my answer; the drug concoction had contributed to his 27 hours of blindness.

Sadly one of the side effect of Furosemide is it can cause tinnitus at best or at worst it can destroy the inner ear and cause permanent and total deafness if the drug is given in haste.

On arrival to the ward he was given a further dose of 40mg of Furosemide injection. I don't know if the staff on this ward were aware he'd only just been given Furosemide in haste just before leaving the other ward but one signature was on the inside of the drug chart and the other signature was on the inside of the chart, consequently his dry body had receive 80mgs of diuretics.

Yes at last I have an answer to why Julian went deaf and blind at the same time that lunch time. These diuretics have something to answer for. They have their uses in their proper place I know, but I once heard of a young girl being prescribed diuretics for a right swollen ankle. She became so off balanced with the drug she nearly sprained the left ankle; yes I mean the 'left' ankle because she was suffering from a sprained right ankle not an oedematous ankle.

. I now understand how he became blind and deaf on the 5th November 2008. Poor Julian, he had been involved in organising so many Bonfires' over the years dressing the Guy up in his old work cloths but on this particular Bonfire night there was no fireworks for Julian, he could neither see them nor hear them that night.

Gentamycin/ Flucloxacillin/ Furosemide/ Metronidazole

My thirdly quest was to find out why did Julian suffer such destruction with his flesh, when he used to have such good healing skin.

On the morning of 24th October 2008 Julian's skin had become mottled after receiving the night before three antibiotics two of which carried the 'Black Box' warning, if we are to credit the American guidelines. Gentamicin, which can cause such toxicity if given in high dosage, it can lead to severe muscle damage.

Hypersensitivity to Flucloxacillin which can cause neurovascular changes leading to gangrene accompanied by Furosemide that dehydrating the body causing a more intense effect of the drugs on a body that was already low in the immune department unable to fight back because of his Adrenal Tumour. The Metronidazole caused slow build-up of the toxins as his dysfunctional liver could not rid the previous dose; causing further concentrations of all the drugs in effect he was suffering from 'unintentional overdose'. It was this Mottling of his skin that started him on 'the rocky road of non-return' as the Coroner referred to at the Inquest. The Coroner was also right in Julian's defence, when he insisted to the Physician on the stand at the Inquest, when he said, "Julian definitely had a problem with antibiotics, **whether or not you and your colleagues could actually particularly put your finger on the allergic effect that he was suffering from**" to me these comments confirmed to me that the Coroner at least recognised Julian's struggle.

Do you recall when I called out from the pitch dark waiting area to Julian's Consultant, "One day I will find out why Julian can't tolerate your medicine, mark my words dead or alive I will still find out and when I do I'll come back and let you know why! Do you hear me? Something is not right here"

By following Brother Caedfals footsteps in faith, and with some knowledge into medicine and a bit of detective work I think at last I've deciphered Julian's complicated issue.

Although the medical staff wrote some very unkind things about me in Julian's medical notes during those last few days of his life, I would stand up for the vulnerable again and again if I felt some one was been wronged. Not only was he suffering the physical reaction, the worst anguish we both experienced was 'No one was listening' I'm sure this inflicted un-measureable stress on his Adrenal Tumour causing devastatingly high glucose levels.

With hindsight I can now see what Julian was up against, his once strong will and body had become defenceless due to his Adrenal Glands, they once acted as his armour. Now his Tumour had weakened his immune system and was letting him down. He was in fact fighting solo in the face of three antibiotic fronts. They were the modern synthetic genetic engineered antibiotics, secondly the fact he reacted physically to penicillin and thirdly he had to contend with often more than two 'Black Box Warning' drugs at the same time.

Indecently the Pharmacist at Shrewsbury Hospital did a spot check on the medication charts one afternoon and to our surprise she crossed off the Ciprofloxacin, Flucloxacillin and the Human Actrapid on Julian's chart and wrote 'See allergies, patient has listed under drug sensitivities'

How was it possible for her to acknowledge Julian's difficulties with some drugs and act on it, while the Doctors and nurses would not budge on their opinion what they considered what was best for him.

Would you believe it, after the Pharmacist discontinued the Human Acrapid on the 3rd November 2008, it was 'definitely' re-prescribed on the 4th November 2008 and poor Julian had to endure 8 more doses of this allergic Insulin and then commenced on sliding scale insulin before he took his last breath. Julian's blood sugar reading was 1.4 at the point of death.

Thyroxin

This is a drug I intended to leave out on the account Julian had not taken it since his near multi-organ failure. He had found it very difficult to tolerate it when he was originally commenced on it, but impossible after he suffered the near multi-organ failure in 2007. The drug was called Levothyroxine. Again I wanted to know why he couldn't tolerate it!

As I'm quite aware that there has been an explosive epidemic of the population diagnosed with thyroid problems in recent years, this next chapter bothers me greatly and I would rather bury my head in the sand that mention it, but I won't sleep easy if I do.

As per-norm I will venture back to the beginning of this condition too. I was shocked to discover that although Diabetes Type Two is on the increase, thyroid diagnoses have vastly exceeded diabetes statistics for some time, did that shock you as much as it did me? I wonder why?

I was not sure what caused thyroid disorders in the first place, I discovered there were many reasons for this disorder, Graves disease was one of them this is a disorder of the immune system, it was the adrenal tumour in Julian's case, smoking was another, stress, steroids, food containing soy was another, too high or too low iodine intake in the diet another.

As well as Amiodarone medication which controls the heart rhythms, localized throat injury such as contact sports, whiplash injury in an road traffic accident, dental brace or surgery such as tracheostomy.

Julian did used to enquire at different Doctor's appointments periodically, if they thought the Tracheostomy might have damaged his thyroid to warrant thyroxin. They use to ridicule him by saying, "No! Where ever did you get that idea from?"

The product Soy surprised me the most, because I thought most vegetarians eat this as a safe substitute for meat. Evidently soy mimics toxins to the thyroid gland, if that is the case no wonder our ACTH thyroid hormone is out of balance when we have our blood results.

Julian loved his soy sauce on his home made Chinese dishes but I know very little about its origin. It is grown mainly in Asia and they eat about two teaspoon full of it in their condiments on a daily basis, but to compensate its effect they eat a diet rich in Iodine to support their thyroid function. You see this is where we westerners are going wrong and that is why we need to eat local, we don't eat a lot of fish soup or seaweed soup like they do because it's not to our pallet. Soy oil was also originally an industrial waste product, in other words it's not real food. The FDA refused to approve it as safe! Yet we were allowed to eat it, why? I wasn't even aware there was a problem with it.

Going back to the diagnosis of thyroid problems, regarding its treatment natural thyroid hormone was first discovered in 1914 and extracted from pig thyroid glands, it was called Amour thyroid. This contained T1, T2, T3 and T4 a good all-rounder, as they say.

In 1926 Sir Charles Harrington MRC of London, isolated thyroxin from thyroid hormone and twelve months later in 1927 the American Goitre Association was formed and for years, removing the goitre was the only treatment for thyroid problems.

Then in 1980 synthetic Levothyroxine was produced and manufactured on a grand scale by Sandoz. I recently came across a test for thyroid antibodies and wondered what this was about. Evidently when thyroid antibodies are high it's like an alarm system indicating they are going into battle, because something is not right. In other words the antibodies are getting fired up to defend their homeland the thyroid gland, but the physicians recognise this as some sort of invasion and prescribe synthetic Levothyroxine.

Common-sense tells me, it would be better to correct whatever is affecting the thyroid complaint rather than giving a drug to stop the natural thyroid antibodies from fighting on our behalf.

From what I understand the body needs the correct the amount of iodine in the diet for the thyroid to function properly. What's frightening is the body mistakes fluoride in our water supply for iodine, so when this happens it can cause thyroid disorder. In other words fluoride mimics the action of Thyroid Stimulating Hormone. (TSH).

I hope I've understood this next part correctly, bear with me it's a bit complicated.

We were told for years that Fluoride was good for us, whereas now we are told its bad for us? Until 1970 European Doctors prescribed Fluoride tablets to patients with over active thyroid, the condition is called hyperthyroidism it's when the thyroid hormone in the thyroid gland is suppressed. Are you with me so far?

So when the rest of us with normal thyroid levels are given an abundance of fluoride in our tap water supply and such things as tooth paste, it stands to reason our thyroid levels will also decrease hence why we will all eventually be labelled as hypothyroidism which will make us warrant additional thyroid hormone. Without it we suffer fatigue, depression, weight gain, muscle pain, disarrayed levels of our five cholesterol and heart disease.

What worries me is; if this happens to strapping adults spare a thought for the younger generation especially babies in arms! So not only do sufferers have thyrotoxicosis brought on by fluoride in our water supply, but now they have to contend with Genetically Modified Thyroxin Replacement.

I need to slow down here, what they're saying is our drinking water supply containing added fluoride is getting rid of our natural thyroid hormone, then we are offered synthetic thyroid replacement by our GPs which may react with other drugs.

How can we tell which one is making us ill, the tap water or the synthetic thyroxin?

Why bother messing up the natural system in the first place?

In countries that have had Fluoride discontinued in their water supply for this very reason, one would imagine increase in dental decay to take place but surprisingly it actually decreased, it leaves me wondering why aren't we following suite?

Who said we needed to add Fluoride in the first place? Adding fluoride to our drinking water supply came about during the Second World War, inflicted on the Prison of War to supress any agitation in the camps as a crowd control. The more fluoride they added to the water the more subdued the people became, evidently the levels were increased in Ireland during its troublesome times when Maggie Thatcher was in power? Are we to believe this, or not?

There is NO such thing as a universal measure of fluoride that's put in our drinking water, it's on the basis of heavy rain fall and if the water is unclean there will be more added.

Dr Bonner a nephew of Albert Einstein, who was himself a prisoner of war, wrote on the subject. No wonder Hitler and Stalin fully believed and agreed from 1939 to 1941 that, quoting from both Lenin's Last Will and Hitler's Main Kampf, when they said "America we shall demoralise, divide and destroy from within" they were talking about the fluoride!

A Doctor Limeback DDS PhD a leader in authority in Fluoride publically apologised for misleading the people of Canada for 15 years on the issue of fluoridation. He was not the only one, there were other leading experts changing their minds. Some Doctors have even lost their jobs for daring to speak out against fluoride. They have now retrieved to their original beliefs that the causes of tooth decay is high refined sugar diet which also destroys vitamins and minerals as well as creating a diet absence of calcium, zinc and vitamin D.

But most of all, the refined foods that our children eat have a deficiency in vitamins and minerals before they start. To add to this worry that too much Fluoride lowers their IQ.

Another worry I ponder over was when the Adrenal glands are not working to full capacity they **can appear to have thyroid symptoms**. In fact when any hormone is off balance it can easily affect other glands. For example if the Adrenal gland for some reason produces too little cortisone the Pituitary gland senses this and increases the release of the ACTH (thyroid hormone) which then stimulates more cortisol hormone to be released, but if too much cortisol is released it will then switch off the release of the ACTH (thyroid hormone) then does the opposite, and reduces the cortisol hormone, if this cycle becomes repetitive it can lead to Adrenal crisis which could be serious.

Because Julian's thyroid levels were low he was first prescribed Levothyroxine in July 2004. Question is, how can one differentiate one condition from the other? In other words was Julian suffering from genuine low thyroxin levels or was it his Adrenal malfunction causing him to have low readings of the thyroid hormone?

This is the test, when people with low thyroid levels and are prescribed 'thyroxin' and responds positively, all well and good but if people with low thyroid levels are prescribed thyroxin and they respond negatively, then one could presume they have consistent <u>hidden</u> low adrenal hormone production.

Worse still, if thyroid hormone is given to such a sufferer, it may exacerbate the already low Adrenal hormone. This would explain why Julian used to say he **felt much worse on thyroxin**.

The good news for such sufferers are; often correction of the Adrenal problem can reverse what appears to be <u>hypothyroidism</u> and the second piece of good news is; sometimes this condition can be reversed through dietary life style changes along with detoxification.

According to Doctor Mankhyman in Utra-Metabolism, New York Scriber, published in 2006. When hormone replacement is required, contrary to popular myth, it may not be needed for life.

I mentioned previously that soy mimics toxins, fluoride does the same but to add insult to injury the condition is then treated with a synthetic drug called Levothyroxine which could further cause an additional allergy. We have to remember all chemicals don't suit everybody.

Things I didn't know about Levothyroxine?

- Did you know, due to some side effects, Glaxo Smith Kline sent a letter to Doctors and pharmacists advising patients never take Levothyroxine on an empty stomach and the tablet must not be cut, split or broke! (No reason given—just don't do it)
- Did you know one should not take Ciprofloxacin if you are taking thyroid replacement, and that's a warnings?
- Did you know Levothyroxine should not be taken following a recent heart attack, but I don't know how recent, is recent?

- Did you know there are many complaints of serious eye complaint that Hospitals could not explain, but felt it came about when the NEW thyroxin drug called 'Levothyroxine' was introduced onto the market. Patients were advised to continue with the treatment, on the account there was no alternative because they had discontinued the production of animal thyroid hormone.
- Did you know other complaints with the drug is memory loss, blinding headache, vomiting, diarrhoea, shaking and joint pain?
- Did you know' that if you are allergic to 'Whey' it states you should NOT take Levothyroxine, (if that is the case what alternative thyroid therapy, can they take?)
- Did you know if you're allergic to maize starch you should not take Levothyroxine.
- Did you know there are some over the counter medication that can affect Levothyroxine; they are calcium supplement, Iron and some medication for the common cold.
- Did you know that the contraceptive pill can affect absorption of Levothyroxine?
- Did you know in 1997 Levothyroxine was submitted under 'new drug' application for drug safety effectiveness and consistency policy **for the first time.** Does that mean it hasn't passed any tests yet deeming it safe? When will they conduct these tests this year, next year, maybe never! However some batch numbers have been recalled on different occasions.
- Did you know Natural thyroid hormone replacement has never been recalled?
- Did you know Natural thyroid hormone is not dangerous for pregnant women?
- Did you know there are no herbs that contain thyroid, but there are some plants that have high concentration of iodine for example seaweed and kelp to help support the thyroid hormone?
- Did you know if you have an allergy to any dyes, Levothyroxine contains many colour additives, patients should be aware of that.
- Did you know according to Lita Lee PhD there are only three types of fats that are good for the thyroid; they are olive oil, butter, coconut oil.
- Did you know herbicides and pesticides are toxic to thyroid glands.

- Did you know Levothyroxine is a generic drug, the term generic means the drug is not protected by a trade mark! If that's the case, is the drug protected by anybody if the person takes the drug then has an adverse effect? My motto for this one is, "Stop palming us off with cheap substitute alternative medicines that make us take risks with our body that have not yet been tested for their safety"

- Did you know if the Adrenal gland for some reason produces too little cortisone the Pituitary gland senses this and increases the release of the ACTH (thyroid hormone) which then stimulates more cortisol hormone to be released, but if too much cortisol is released it will then switch off the release of the ACTH (thyroid hormone) then does the opposite and reduces the cortisol hormone, if this cycle becomes repetitive it can lead to Adrenal crisis which could lead to serious consequences. Did you know Levothyroxine should never be given to patients who have untreated Adrenal gland problem? This is probably why Julian always felt worse after taking Levothyroxine because his wasn't treated. People with Adrenal Insufficiency should be treated with glucocorticoids. This is what Julian probably needed following surgery or when he was exposed to stress and infection.

- Did you know Levothyroxine has 67 drugs it interacts with, Diabetic and Diuretic treatments were just two that was named?

Sadly I fear nearly all of these complicated complaints are man-made, it makes me want to take a sharp intake of stressful breath and roll my eyes.

I confess this is such a big, big subject, please research it yourself and form your own opinion.

While researching I found many disturbing letters, but feel one especially disturbed me the most. It was from a lady who claimed her GP thought her body was shutting down every time she took Levothyroxine, but did not understand why?

Could it be because she was allergic to the Synthetic Levothyroxine, or was it because she was suffering from an undiagnosed adrenal complaint or simply an allergy to the colour additives used in its production?

This is why Julian could not tolerate Levothyroxine, he complained of the same side effects just before his multi-organ failure. He once said, "It feels as if my organs have come to a standstill"

Julian was not the only one making such crazy statements then!

Green Party health spokesperson lady said, she had received 571 reports on problems with Levothyroxin drug with adverse reaction in 2009, and it was only January then.

I don't know how I can make the whole medical WORLD sit up and listen, that there are people suffering and in some cases dying because they cannot tolerate these Generic so called alternative man-made chemicals, disguised as medicine. When people say they feel so much worse on treatment, why are they forced to continue to take them? In some cases they may have taken that drug for years, and then suddenly they can't tolerate it anymore, now we discover drugs are periodically reformulated without informing the patient. That means changing their make up!

I say to all pharmacy assistants, "Please don't fool us the public or lie to us by saying, they're just the same lovey, just a different brand name"

I beg you don't be so-condescending towards us, by camouflaging the whole issue using such phrases as "LOVEY" it won't wash. Surely medication is there to make us feel better, not worse!

As I was just reading this, my body was displaying small but clearly visible spasms in my muscles, the same sensation I had when Julian was on the ventilator during the last few hours of his life. Except these were not in my thumb this time, these were all over my body, in both my thighs, my calves, my upper arms. If this was Julian again, then he was going berserk I can only assume he was agreeing with me.

It was pointed out to me at work one day by a colleague, that I should be careful not to imagine door slamming, windows rattling, lights flickering as a sign from Julian. I hope other people don't think the same, but people have witnessed the movements in my muscles when I have shown them. No matter how clever one is, one cannot spontaneously revoke these movements on command, I also sometimes get these spasms on my tongue, which makes me chuckle this usually happens when it appears I need to speak up or defend this huge subject I now feel so passionate about which is Julian's diabetic issues.

On this thyroid topic, I do want to avoid negative-ness towards all the medical profession; I'm just concerned about the 'not so well informed doctors' in the update of medicines. I feel fewer physicians are trained to detect this secondary hyperthyroidism.

If the companies who produce the synthetic thyroxin drug DO worn the medical profession that, 'it should not be given to patients who have any Adrenal malfunction and doing so could lead to Adrenal crisis' then why do the medical profession prescribe it? Why! Was Julian prescribed it?

In an ideal world it would be helpful if all the General Practitioners in all the land, all the Prescribed Drug Barons in all the land, all the Medical Physicians in all the land, along with all the Pharmacists in all the land including all the poor people who are having difficulties with their Thyroxin levels to attend a massive multidisciplinary meeting to seek a solution into this complicated issue of thyroid problem to improve their quality of life. If we can meet halfway and agree that synthetic thyroxin might suit some, but natural thyroid hormone might better suit others, then we can achieve harmony in the medical world regarding synthetic thyroxin at least.

Note I refer to the synthetic one as thyroxin and the natural one as thyroid!

It's not impossible for the medical profession to access natural thyroid hormone, they can still prescribe the natural thyroid treatment the difference is the patients often don't even know there is a choice available. If some patient finds the synthetic treatment impossible to tolerate, it raises the question, "Why should some patients suffer at the hands of the synthetic treatment when there is an alternative natural treatment available?"

To me it displays a total disregard towards the patient who tries to explain to them what they feel is happening inside their body.

There are a lot of patients out there who feel passionate about trying Natural Thyroid extracts but the Royal College of Physicians has recommended exclusive use of synthetic Levothyroxine for the treatment of ALL hypothyroidism in this country, in other words it's become a 'state of Fate de comple' on their behalf and the subject is not open for further negotiation, but why can't it be a question of balance for the highest good of all?

As time has evolved, the use of Natural thyroid hormone has become associated with complementary and alternative medicine. Those prescribing it were considered unscientific and irrational practitioners, they mean alternative medicine.

Don't forget, this is what was used before we went synthetic, but maybe the GP's are being cautious about embracing alternative medicine due to lack of studies conducted. On the other hand I am now left wondering how much study has been done on prescribed drugs.

However there is a growing number of Doctors who are working towards better understanding of herbal therapies. In fact there is a number of Doctors leaving the traditional medical practise in preference to the Private Herbal sector. You hear of more and more of National Health Practitioners re-training and becoming Natural Health Practitioners or Holistic Doctors or Holistic Nurses who although have medical qualifications are capable of addressing standard medical needs, as well as adhere to holistic principles of promoting physical, emotional and spiritual health.

A Holistic Medical Doctor will draw wisdom from both treatments, for example surgery will only be recommended when all other avenues have been exhausted.

I will give you an example of a combined treatment if a patient required thyroid treatment or may need Adrenal treatment. Natural pig thyroid hormone extract could be used for a patient suffering from hypothyroidism and natural Cortisol hormone could be used for a patient suffering from a malfunction of Adrenal gland. Although both treatments are natural, both treatments would require a medical prescription.

Diagnosis and treatment is the same, but in some cases only natural treatment could be tolerated in preference to popular Genetically Modified substitute.

There are quite a few such practitioners but you might have to travel to find them.

By the way I am sensitive to the fact that vegetarians or some Religious dietary laws would object to 'Amour' Natural Thyroid hormone due to its origin is from Pork.

But horses for courses as they say, and it's down to individual choice, bearing in mind at the moment there is no choice. It's their freedom of choice that's being denied, of what suits them best actually I'll correct that statement not their choice but their body's choice. These people are not being finicky about their tolerance; their non-tolerance is out of their control!

To the doctor who made me feel stupid at the beginning of this chapter, I now say to him 'Thank you' for inspiring me to go on this journey to prove my worth. I now understand why Julian became so ill on modern day drugs.

Not only have the business driven Drug Barons been clever enough in hiding the consequences from the patient, but they have managed to brain wash the medical sector as well.

Fancy me thinking Human Insulin came from human and thyroxin came from thyroid glands, how gullible have I been these last few years? Worst still all the Doctors who dealt with Julian were also hoodwinked into thinking the same!

Not only do I understand a lot more about the medicine world now, but I also realise Julian did not have a sad life, but a very sad end. Sorry Julian, as a nurse I should have known about the underhanded makeup of these drugs.

I'm not alone in my 'Concern Crusade' in my defence a pharmacist put a note in the window asking any Levothyroxine users to the alert staff of any problems.

There are other professionals now worried too, thank you God for sending me some support.

Another patient wrote to the Med-safe company asking, "I'd like to get the drug analysed"

He evidently didn't get a reply, but I'm not surprised he didn't get an answer. Because Levothyroxine appears to be the world best guarded secret when it comes to its content, I can't find its make up or recipe anywhere. What have they got to hide? They might as well blindfold the patient and ask them to trust them regarding what they're sneaking into their bodies!

Julian might have been labelled as a 'free thinker' once by his physician, but I'm labelling him as not able to tolerate 'free radical' before his death, because just as the Doctor who ridiculed me when he mockingly said, "Are you trying to say that your husband can't tolerate any medication any more Mrs Davies"? I could not boomerang a sensible medical answer at him that day, but today four years later, the answer to that question is, "Correct, Julian's body could no longer tolerate any of his synthetics medicine any more, only pure natural products"

And what's so wrong about that?

I've saved this last 'did you know' until the end. One of the side effects of hypothyroidism is anxiety, it has been known for Doctors to prescribe antidepressants as strong as Lithium which can lower Cortisol in the Adrenal glands causing conversion of T4 to T3. In fact this psychology drug would not help the complaint, only exacerbate it.

The Native American Indian rule on this topic would be, "Look after the wellbeing of your <u>mind</u> and body"

Sadly in 1978 1.5 million people in America were hospitalised because of medical side effects alone. In 1991 72,000 people died due to doctor-induced causes, compare that 72,000 to only 24,073 people who died of firearm shooting in the same year!

Does that make doctors sound more lethal than guns?

I read recently in a book called 'Grandma's Remedies' by Cherry Chappell who explained "Orthodox medicine in the west tends to treat patients with a 'one size fits all' principle, offering predominantly drug therapy, surgery, physiotherapy, radiation and dialysis" Thankfully there are a few orthodox doctors around who believe that the personality of the patients is often the key to the quality of their lives, whether they have optimistic or negative attitudes towards their life and conditions. In other words thinking positive will help bring about positive health!

It was interesting to read that the Greek physician Hippocrates who is considered to be the 'Father of modern medicine' and after whom the Hippocratic Oath was named, he used many herbal remedies. He wrote around 400BC "Let your food be your medicine and your medicine be your food" How interesting, that his belief as a physician and as a herbalist was necessary to combine both in order to treat a patient as a whole. Why can't we take a leaf out of his book for today's modern living?

Although a NHS doctor did once recommend that Julian should visit his local herbalist and buy some Horse Chestnut tablets to aid a healthy circulation following a lumber chemical sympathectomise injection to improve circulation to his lower trunk.

I discovered another Doctor called Dr Henry Bider MD who wrote in his book, ". . . I stopped using drugs in treating my patients when I began to re-examine an old axiom which is, that nature is the true healer, using the body's natural defence. The physician's role is to assist in the healing in co-operation with natural and not replacing nature. Natural cures slowly like trees grow slowly; not suddenly like the chemical drugs market claim . . ."

He discarded drugs in treating his patients after his own health broke down; he gave up the use of drugs and relied solely on food for medicine.

He mention's a Chinese book of medicine that says, "What cannot be cured with medicine can only be cured with food"

Next question is "What direction should we take now?"

If we have exhausted the 'modern-day-man-made-medicine' then we need to look elsewhere for our treatment. Do I need to go back to the beginning of this topic too or just put my 'simple head' on and think lateral for an alternative?

May be we should concentrate more on preventing rather than treating. So how can we prevent developing such conditions unless we balance ourselves like space age people in a sterile bubble by avoiding all these cross contamination of viruses, infectious, diseases, injury, insect bites and many more conditions?

May be that's it, may be the key word in that last paragraph was 'balance' Did our ancestors stay healthy and in fine tune because they ate simple food, drank pure water, took heed of old wives tales, practiced their faith therefore maintaining perfect balance?

Have we lost sight of our perfect balance, I recall when I first started nursing, nurses were expected to test all urines for pH balance.

What it is all about; well pH balance dictates if our bodies are too acidic or too alkalised. I think of this balance like the wings of an aeroplane and without perfect balance it cannot fly safely neither can it land perfectly.

How strange I used to teach student nurses years ago to draw an imaginary line down the centre of their body from the tip of their forehead to the floor, explaining that in orthopaedics everything needs to be symmetrical. In other words both sides of the body must be balanced, for example if a patient has a painful big toe he will lean to one side to avoid the pain, developing an awkward walking gate then later finds himself at the doctor asking for pain relief for his bad neck, bad back or bad knee. I wonder could it be this simple with our ailing bodies?

If we make a conscious effort to keep our bodies free from toxins such as pesticides, additives, GM, MSG products it stands to reason we will not over work or exhaust our endocrine glands, our liver, our kidneys our lungs, our gut, our spleen and lastly our circulation causing us to think we need to take additional heavy duty drugs to fix our ailing bodies.

If that is the case then surely we won't need Antibiotics so often either, so we could possible return to the non-vicious Antibiotic avoiding the first, second or even third generation synthetic genetically modified antibiotics that most of us cannot tolerate any more anyway.

Balance of Acid and Alkaline

Now I've hit on the idea of balance I feel as if I've reinvented the wheel. I'm not taking credit for this but I do intend to recognise the original scientist who first discovered it.

It was a Swedish gentleman by the name of Svante Arrhenius who originally became a Physicist but later studied and became a Scientist; he theorized the dependency of Acid and Alkaline in our lives. On the night in question 13th May 1883 he was later quoted saying,

"I could not sleep that night until I had worked through the entire problem"

One year later he published his Ph.D. thesis on the subject and obtained a grade of, 'approved without praise' certificate. Which must have been disappointing for him, incidentally I looked up the definition of the abbreviation Ph. It stands for 'Philosophy' which means 'love of wisdom' in Greek.

His work on the Acid/Alkaline was not truly recognised until 1903 when he was honoured with the Nobel Peace Prize. So what does this Acid and Alkaline balance mean to Jo public?

Why do we have to have it? How can we detect when it's not balanced? How do we know if we're suffering from it? How can we balance it once it's imbalanced?

Our first detection of the problem is, if we have abnormal body temperature, hence why the Doctors have asked since Egyptian time, has the patient got a temperature?

To remain well we must maintain normal temperature. Neutral pH is a bit like looking after a pet fish; the water has to remain balanced if it becomes too acidic the fish goes belly up. We take a bit longer but we too quickly become sick.

First of all what does pH stand for? The abbreviation derives from the words Protenial Hydrogen. It measures from 0-14. Zero is the lowest Acidic reading, 7 is the neutral reading in the middle and 14 is the highest Alkaline reading.

So what does this Acid and Alkaline balance mean to us? We use it to measure the balance of urine, saliva and blood and even soil. They should all carry a neutral reading of 7 to be balanced.

So how can we keep a check on this Acid and Alkaline reading with our own bodies?

One can purchase from the pharmacy a pH. Hydrion lab sticks to dip into your urine or a lab stick to measure pH in your saliva. A healthy balance should read between 6.5 and 7.5 if you find your readings are out of balance there are books available on what foods are best to eat and what are best to avoid to maintaining this healthy pH balance. Basically foods that affect pH in a good way are green vegetables, in other words 'Go green'. On the other hand foods that affect the pH in a negative way are all refined food such as white flour, white sugar, white rice white pasta and unfortunately <u>to much</u> alcohol including <u>too much</u> red meat and <u>too much</u> dairy products.

In other words 'High-living-foods' or someone described an over Acidic person as a 'Human toxic wasteland'

This steady intake of toxins causes an imbalance leading to an array of disease and disorders.

There is a book called "Warning" by John Ossipinsky he claims an undetected Acid and Alkaline imbalance is slowly killing us and severely hurting our children! The problem is the pharmaceutical companies would prefer not to hear of any simple treatments, it entails them losing out big time financially to lack of drug turnover.

Ossipinsky claims if we use these five points to aid our correction of the imbalance we could be home and dry. 1. Learn to recognise toxicity. 2. Adopt an Acid Alkaline diet. 3. Exercise deep breathing. 4. Manage stress. 5. Do something about your toxicity.

There is another book with a disturbing title called "Alkalise or die" by Doctor Baroody.

So once I discovered that I'm out of sorts with our balance and I decided not to add to what I've already got, how do I get rid of my existing toxins? I'm glad to say the answer is inexpensive but personally taxing. Its exercise, the more I sweat the more I will get rid of my toxins. You'll never guess where I'm hiding my toxins? In my fat! The more medication I have on board the more toxins I am lightly to cling onto. It seems I have more medicine than health in my body at the moment. I need to learn to swap one for the other.

I've mentioned a few Nobel Peace Prize winners in this book, but sadly 100 years down the line we haven't heeded their discoveries. I don't want to admit it's been a complete waste of their time and effort on their behalf, working into the depths of the night often by candle light, for modern man to flippantly disregard their toil. I'm referring to the likes of Svante Arrhenius who discovered the balance of Acid and Alkaline.

I'm going to re-cap on Julian's pH situation, to see if he was balanced or not.

Our bodies are in constant battle to be slightly Alkalised balanced. If one is too Acidic one can be diagnosed with Diabetes, but Julian was in an Alkalised state.

So why was this then, well there are three reasons for been alkalised.

—Body immune system becomes destabilized causing it to be vulnerable to infection.

(This was true he did have Adrenal Tumour and developed an abscess)

—Dehydration due to lack of fluids through fluid restrictions or diuretics.

(This was true he was often inflicted with one or more of these)

—Respiratory problems leading to difficulty oxygenating other parts of the body.

(This was true when he periodically suffering from plural effusion and holes in his spleen)

This would happen when his Buffers were imbalanced.

What are Buffers?

In the blood steam there are substances known as buffers that act chemically to resist changes in pH Balance. The four most important of this component are known as—;

- Bicarbonate,
- Albumin (Protein)
- Haemoglobin.
- Globin.

Bicarbonate

Sodium Bicarbonate possesses the property of absorbing heavy metals and dioxins, in other words it detoxifies the body.

A study conducted in 1986 showed when the body is hit with a reduction of Bicarbonate; it also affects the urine output. The kidneys and the Pancreas then have a build-up of acid which then begins its deterioration journey leading to kidney failure and Diabetes.

Sodium Bicarbonate is sometimes given to people suffering from lactic acidosis (organ failure) it's given to reverse the acidity. I have no recollection of Julian ever having it after he was diagnosed with near Multi Organ Failure, nether could I find any medical records that he received it, except this was the occasion he excreted black urine?

In fact I could only find one biochemistry result for Bicarbonate done, and that was in 2008 at Shrewsbury his bicarbonate readings then were 23, national recommend average should range 22-30. Maybe Julian's was not low enough to warrant active treatment but not adequately high enough to fight the toxins that lay ahead of him either?

Albumin

The other buffer mentioned was Albumin otherwise known as Protein. My first encounter of Julian ever having low Albumin was in the autumn of 1989 the same year Llewela was born. He was Hospitalised that particular time when he had a Gerdalstone operation, and I recall a doctor informing Julian that his Protein levels then was only 3. Normal national average should range 36-48. I remember walking the streets in search of this High Protein powder to correct his poor depleted Protein level. It was the most revolting substance I'd ever mixed; it had a thick grey consistency. I admired him as he diligently swallowed every slimy mouthful, but he consumed this gunk just to get home quicker to be with his new baby daughter.

Now I'm in possession of the medical notes, I see he was excreting an abundance of protein in his urine at the time. Consequently the protein he was retaining was hanging by a thread.

Once he was diagnosed with Diabetes in 2000 I periodically tested his urine for glucose, I never once found glucose but I often found plenty of Protein.

So Julian was getting rid of Protein for at least eight years to my knowledge, he would not be affected by it until he became ill, then it wouldn't take much to tip the scales into imbalance.

Signs and symptoms of low Albumin or Proteins—

Shortness of breath, pulmonary oedema, chest pain, palpitation, and as-cites which is swelling of the abdomen.

These signs and symptoms just pluck at my heart strings as I recalled what Julian was complaining of so often but especially on the morning in July in 2007 when he asked me to ring for the Ambulance.

The shortness of breath could not be relieved by oxygen therapy.

The chest pain could only be relieved by morphine.

The palpitation, he said "I can't believe you can't hear my heart banging away".

The As-cites he often suffered from when he was ill.

When Julian was well and sitting in his wheelchair, to me he just looked like any other man sitting down, but the minute he became unwell and took to his bed his abdomen would almost immediately swell up beyond belief and become rock solid.

One of the Albumin function is to maintain the 'osmotic pressure' which is exchange of fluid in the tissue. When the Albumin is absent then inadequate fluid exchange occurs causing the fluid to remain in the tissue leading his abdominal to become 'Ascites' and general oedema.

Low Albumin can also be exacerbated if the person becomes dehydrated but at the same token return to normal when dehydration is corrected. On these occasions the last thing he needed was diuretics and fluid restrictions.

I now feel this is what happened to Julian in Pompeii, when he became dehydrated from the hot sun, to such an extent it affected his vision which only returned when he was given the two cans of pop and not because of the sugar content in the drink.

Basically it means instead of the fluid entering the body orally or intravenously travelling in the circulatory system then execrating the body via the bladder in urination. Instead it escapes into the tissue cells and lingers there making the body appear full of fluid. I recall his fingers looking like five fat sausages and his legs looked like big tree trunks and most uncomfortable of all, his abdomen looked as if he was 12 months pregnant.

Too often the medical profession mistake this for oedema and prescribe diuretics to get rid of the fluid (water tablets) although water tablets have a place in cardiac condition, but not in these unusual low Albumin cases.

The knock on effect, is the diuretics cause further dehydration resulting in lowering the blood pressure and the patient appears to have inadequate urine output. At the same time excreting even more Protein in the urine, the doctor then thinks, Oh! urine output is still poor still, let's give more diuretics and the patient becomes even more dehydrated but still remains oedematous (swollen) Which is understandable because the fluid is not round the heart and lungs but trapped in the cells, with no Albumin on board for energy to escort it out.

Albumin is also essential in transporting such substances as drugs and toxins in the blood stream to the liver for it to excreted in urine.

If the Protein is not allowed to carrying out its duty, it stands to reason the vital organs will start to retain drugs causing the body to become toxic and inevitably extremely ill.

When Protein has been allowed to complete its function of transporting vitamins, minerals and toxins to their appropriate organs the excess Protein cannot be stored as Protein, but gets converted into fat deposits which contribute to weight gain. Unless of course one burns it off before it's converted into fat. So discovering Protein in urine can be potentially dangerous to your health! It's like watching a stolen car making a getaway.

It leaves me wondering did Julian escape these signs and symptoms because he drank such large volumes of tea. By keeping himself hydrated and having adequate amount of salt in his diet he avoided a lot of complications. To him being hospitalised, meant fluid restrictions, compared to what he normally drank. At home he drank tea from a 500ml cup, as soon as it was finished he was pouring another, unlike when he went into Hospital and only offered a 180ml cup off the trolley at their allotted times. The only treatment I can see to correct this complaint is to rebalance the Albumin levels either by high protein diet or by intravenously administering Albumin fluids.

In the comfort of my own home, I now realise how important pH balance is along with normal Albumin (Protein) levels which enables transportation of drugs, bilirubin, hormones such as Insulin, vitamins, minerals such as magnesium, potassium, zinc, copper which would have serviced his organs and maintained his good health.

Photograph of Julian on one of his bed rest stints, see how swollen his abdomen has become.

This would happen every time he went on bed rest long term. Looking back at this photograph his ascites is so obvious to me now. How wrong the Doctors were when they said to me, "Taking blood samples to assess his protein levels would be of no use to his Diabetic care" It would have, they would have seen his transporter was missing.

The old saying goes, 'sometimes its the obscure we need to seek not the obvious'

Many Doctors, Herbalist's and Nutritionists believe that most common diseases in our society today are 'Acid and Alkaline Imbalance' in our blood.

When excess Acid needs to be neutralised our alkaline reserves are depleted leaving our bodies weakened. It's nothing new in 1933 in New York Doctor William H. Hay published a book called 'A new Health Era', based on self-poisoning due to Acid accumulation in the body. Evidently no one took any notice of its publication otherwise the topic of conversation in public would be, "How's your pH balance these days"

What we probably need these days is a 'pH clinic' rather than a Diabetic clinic, Blood Pressure clinic, Cholesterol clinic, Ulcer clinic, MS clinic, and Parkinson clinic.

A pH clinic could probably cancel all these 'supply and demand' clinics out.

It appears the body cannot be healed unless the pH is balanced.

Julian's Diabetes appeared very complicated at his bed side. But after much soul searching it appears it was a simply question of balance that held the golden key to Julian's perfect health.

I suspect each family has a tendency to be neutral, acidic or alkaline depending on what the cook of the house puts on the table. If the family is shovelled 'fries and preservatives' on to their plates their pH is lightly to be Acidic but if the cook gives her family raw mainly green vegetables and fruit on to their plate then the family is lightly to be Alkalised. On the other hand if the cook produces organic cuisine and graces the table with plenty of raw fruit and vegetables then the family is more lightly to be in perfect neutral balance.

Julian's medical notes showed that his alkaline phosphate was abnormal previously in July 2007 when he suffered his near multi-organ failure. Blood results are missing for the April 2008 admission when he suffered a severe reaction to medication, Insulin in particular while under general anaesthetic.

His Alkaline phosphate was raised again when he was an inpatient at Shrewsbury to 267 normal national readings should range between 14-43.

One might think; if I feel Julian's illness stemmed from imbalanced of Acid and Alkaline then why have I bothered to mentioning all the other topics. It's because now I have become wise to all that's going on in our body, our environment, our food, our water supply, our medicine I can only now see it all had a knock on effect on his pH balance including disturbing his glucose levels. So yes they do all deserve a mention because by reverting back into his ailment I could not have arrived at the answer of Acid versa Alkaline.

Before we start allowing our bodies to be treated medically we must have total assurance that there isn't an underlying cause to our complaint first, in other words the root of the cause is being treated, for example in Julian's case his Endocrine system needed treating before the array of other conditions he displayed such as Diabetes, high blood pressure, thyrotoxicosis, plural effusion, headaches, chest pain and so on.

I have mentioned the word 'balance' in this book so many times; with hindsight the word was symbolic to his treatment I was holding the Golden Key of not 'wealth but health' in my hand all along when I was giving Julian support by balancing him on the edge of his bed. Metaphorically speaking off course, the word 'Balance' was crucial to his survival.

I physically balanced him on the edge of the bed but now I understand it applied not only to his health but ours too.

It seems the world has misplaced balance for decades and we all need to re-capture it somehow, we can find it hidden in a balanced diet, balanced exercise, balance of time dedicated to meditation and last of all recognise the toxins we either digest or absorb and learn to balance their intake. Occasionally we have to gracefully accept some necessary toxins into our bodies, examples of these necessary short lived intake of Toxins are anaesthetics, antibiotics some antidepressants and analgesia. The difference from now on is we will be making informed choices about if we should take them and how we set about getting rid of their bad effect afterwards by using the 'soak and flush' therapy. I mean soak by eating wholesome food as antidote of the side effect and I mean flush by drinking lots of bottled water to rid the toxins.

Poor Julian couldn't get rid of his enemy from his body because he wasn't aware who the enemy was.

I find it strange now how Julian used to say to every Doctor he encountered after his near multi-organ failure, "<u>Sometimes</u> Doc, the best treatment is no treatment" He probably didn't realise the importance of that small sentence; as they say never a truer word spoken in gest.

Will it be hard to change the way we live? Yes, of course it will and being English we don't like change, but we've done it many times before. We have educated ourselves over the years that seatbelts are safer for us; cigarettes are not so healthy, exercise is good for us so why can't we do the extra mile by considering the importance of the balance of Acid and Alkaline.

I hope I'm not preaching, I'm only asking you to consider!

In considering, we could drop our Hospitalizing appointments by thousands of folds hence removing the heavy burden on the NHS financially, their occupancy, the Doctors time, but more to the point the poor over worked nurses who can give much needed care to their sick patient. Just like private schools, 'the lesser the number to care for, the higher the quality of care'. That's got to be good for everybody. I did see a poster once stating we have a 'National Health in a toxic world' at last I understand what it means now.

How ironic the Doctor who first dealt with Julian 34 years previously had predicted if he didn't take excellent care of himself he would either die of kidney failure, pressure sore or pneumonia. Sadly Julian had all three written on his death certificate, because he like many of us didn't realise how badly our bodies were been contaminated and been knocked off balance by either Acid or Alkaline.

Reflecting how stubborn both parties had become in Julian's care, the doctors who felt Julian needed treatment and I who could see that he was suffering at the hands of their treatment. It brings to mind a story I once read about two friends walking along the road when a gentle man in the other direction walked between them. After exchanging greetings and parting company the one referred to the gentleman who strolled between them wearing the white hat, while the other insisted the stranger wore a yellow hat.

A heated argument ignited, but luckily a fourth person appeared and he was asked to oversee the disagreement. He calmly explained he had seen the gentleman they were referring to and that they were both right. The stranger was indeed wearing both colours, half white and half yellow hat. But as the two friends could only see one side of the stranger's face both wrongly assumed the other half was the same colour. Moral of the story is; I feel the same way about Julian's case. The medical profession insisted that Julian needed to have the insulin and other drugs.

Whereas I on the other hand could sympathise with Julian and could see he was suffering some dreadful reaction, and desperately needed further investigations.

What we all needed was an independent party; unfortunately I met this person after Julian died. That very person was the Coroner at Julian's Inquest, who said to the Doctors on the stand, "Whether or not you and your colleagues could actually particularly put your finger on the allergic effect that he was suffering"

My Conclusion

When I started this book I felt very confused about Julian's Diabetes, now I've untangled the complicated web of his imbalanced pH, brought on by his toxic way of life eventually applying permanent stress on his Adrenal Glands causing it to develop into a tumour. I now visualise his tumour as a fuse blown in a plug.

I realise now his Adrenal Tumour had a big part to play in his illness towards the end, causing him to be inadequate at fighting toxins. I feel his last bout of illness could have stemmed from any one of these three possible causes.

. <u>The First possibility</u> which occurred on 20th September 2008 was at that social event only four days after his 55th birthday and two weeks after becoming a God Parent to his new niece, whether it had something or nothing to do with that unfavourable Beer he drank that night, it is something I will never know for sure? But it raises the question did the Beer taste as awful as it smelt because of bacteria, virus, parasite, yeast mould, spores or fungi in the keg pipes? Coupled with the fact Julian's Adrenal immune system was so shot allowing an abscess to manifest itself in his weakest spot, which was his hip?

. <u>The Second possibility</u> did the surgery he had back in April five months previously heal too quick sealing the surface of the wound leading to a sinus to develop at a later date?

Was Julian too quick to express his excitement about the prompt healing of the wound when his surgeon showed concern that a sinus may develop at a later date leading to an abscess formation.

. <u>The Third possibility</u> could his Gerdalstone site which he was operated on 18 years previously, it may have harboured something which had lied dormant until his body was triggered into reawakening and without a good immune system to fight it off.

All this is just, 'here say', but all three complaints did take place in the same region which was in his right hip!

With a good immune system in place no sad end should have taken place, I will try to simplify this 'rocky road' as the Coroner referred to it at Julian's Inquest the one he was forced to travel just before he died.

Julian's toxic journey

It was true to say Julian enjoyed 15 years of reasonably good health from 1980 right through to 1996 suffering from only minor ailments and I feel that this was mainly due to the fact his liver was actually coping. I say coping because evidently the scaring on his liver following his Hepatitis C in the mid-1970s may have caused him internal discomfort leading to constant stress on his Adrenal Glands. This inflicting pain on his liver caused him to endure a bodily perspiration which he was prescribed Probanthin to dry his damp body, a drug he took for 17 years followed by Oxybutynin for another 16 years. I then further stressed his Adrenal Glands by unknowingly feeding him a toxic diet for 28 long years. This led him to develop a tumour on his Adrenal Gland and it was this tumour that finally took its toll on his exhausted body causing him to present himself as a Type Two Diabetic.

I have established that the endocrine system is such a complex network of services acting up as a work horse and a much needed transporter. Here I have compared it to a busy city centre in rush hour, are you ready for this journey, it is very intense.

Once I understood Julian's Adrenal Gland was not 'firing on all cylinders' "as it were" I could see how it could cause him to suffer a medical tragedy.

His rocky journey started long before his abscess burst, he may well have been able to battle it out but as he was suffering from insufficient immune backup the puss started to build up and his normal pH balance see sawed and tipped his Acid/Alkaline scales off its pivot point. I liken the pH balance to an old fashion kitchen scale, with the centre balance reading as negative the Alkaline balancing one end and Acid the other end. As the scales see sawed back and forth a bad man called 'Toxins' started to create havoc, a taxi firm called 'Protein' was called to escort this bad man 'Toxins' off the premises to a place called 'Urinal' but in the rush to get rid of his passenger called 'Toxin' he forgot to secure his hand break and over the edge they both went crashing down into ravine.

Now Julian's body didn't have 'Protein' to transport his other much needed vitamins, minerals, hormones and toxins to and from his organs.

'Protein' knew his duties; his daily routine consisted of picking up 'Cortisone' from his Adrenal Gland who possessed the golden key to open the door to his friend's house in 'Pancreas' street his friend was called 'Insulin'

Normally the taxi firm called 'Protein' would dash over and pick up some minerals called 'Magnesium' and 'Chromium' these little fellas known as the twins knew the combination numbers to release the 'Insulin' out of the safe, so it could go out to socialise with its best friend called 'Glucose' When these two got together they would joyfully skip around, jumping from one muscle to muscle another supplying the whole body with abundance of energy. This went on all day long everybody was very happy, all the organs, the vitamins, the minerals and all the hormones even the bad guys called toxins was always glad of a lift.

But when this taxi firm called 'Protein' stupidly allowed itself to go over the edge, it created a critical situation. For a start the 'Cortisol' Hormone in the Adrenal Gland becomes housebound and is unable to leave its home to help anybody.

The chain of events break down, the 'Insulin' can no longer make contact with 'Glucose' which means they can no longer produce the abundance of energy, instead it caused the body to suffer a sudden 'Adrenal Fatigue' and the body slumps. Unfortunately this frightening state can often be mistaken for a Hypo-glycaemic attack (Low blood sugar) but in fact the body is saturated in glucose. This low energy high blood glucose reading confuses both patient and carer.

Even if 'Magnesium' and 'Chromium' had managed to thumb a lift they still needed 'Cortisol' to let them in through the front door. So the 'Insulin' still couldn't be released and this is when people are referred to as 'Insulin Resistance' Insulin is resisting coming out to play. It was at this point Julian was diagnosed with 'Type Two Diabetes' The medical profession mistook Julian's body as not producing enough 'Insulin' but in fact he was, he just didn't have a network of transport he could rely on to carry his important cargo of 'Cortisol' to his 'Pancreas'.

'Magnesium' is normaly a very busy worker it holds down two jobs, he works very closely with another mineral called 'Potassium' it acts up as a bodyguard, together they escort the bad boys called 'Toxins' to the liver to be detoxified which the liver later releases for excretion.

At this stage Julian's body was beginning to feel a bit choked up; he had no further use for these end products such as used drugs, pesticides, additives, processed foods, artificial sweeteners, hydrogenated oils, GM and MSG products but at the same time he didn't have a 'Taxi' service he could depend on to reshuffle the system. He was also worried the bin man had forgot to call or worst still, was he on strike? or maybe has no intention of coming at all. Can you see how quickly a body can become out of tune?

Although the liver is normally a very forgiving organ, it tries to keep the body in a harmonising state but without the 'Protein' to bring the toxins to him; Julian's liver was of no help to him at all. (The liver was like a Baker calling from his door way, 'I'll bake you some bread, but you will have to bring me the flour first')

To try and improve this serious situation, a 'Do-gooder' called 'Doc' came along and offered to introduce him to an Antibiotic called 'Penicillin' Julian wasn't keen about getting reacquainted with 'Penicillin' he remembered falling out with 'Penicillin' on more than one occasions before. He dug his heals in and said, 'No thanks I'd rather not, I've met him before he didn't like me then and I don't suppose he'd like me any better this time round. But the 'Do-gooder called Doc continued to apply pressure and eventually he managed to persuade Julian to meet this 'Penicillin', within minutes of clapping eyes on each other Julian's body immediately recognised him as bad man 'Toxin'. Obviously Julian tried to defend himself but the fighting was vicious, 'Doc' had forgotten to inform Julian's body an 'ex-Hepatitis C' sufferer that he should never, ever of been introduced to his friends Erythromycin, Augmentin, Ciprofloxacin, Ibuprofen, Naproxen and Aspirin. He had no idea this little gang would have such a devastating effect on his deteriorating body. Julian was angered that he'd trusted this 'Do-gooder' called 'Doc' he thought he was going to help him instead he'd tricked him into arranging a rendezvous with these undesirable drugs.

Once they made contact the battle of wills began with a most vicious combat taking place, Julian soon realised this was worse than being in an arena with cheering crowds, this was a more sinister place he was down a dark alley without any ammunition for protection.

Suddenly he felt isolated and outnumbered with this vicious gang of villains, it's hard to defend yourself when your all drugged up, what he needed was some comrades from his beloved Buffalo Mother Lodge called the 'Embassy Lodge' to hire a Brinton's van to make his getaway.

Ahh!! How he wished for that!

Just when he thought things couldn't get much worse, the gang started inflicting insulting abuse at his beaten body and the war of

'Reactions' started, he suffered such afflictions as low blood pressure, raised pulse rate, increased respirations, low temperature, chest pain, breathlessness, decreased cola coloured urine, profuse perspiration, extreme abdominal pain, kidney pain, liver region pain, high glucose levels, excruciating pain in his head, blindness, deafness, unable to sleep, unable to lie down, plural effusion, skin breakdown, muscle and skeletal detrition and finally hallucinations and brain dysfunction.

Can you imagine the chaos that was going on inside his body, his poor injured Adrenalin Gland could do nothing but look on thinking, how can I help this poor battered body with no transport.

He couldn't even call the Emergency services, but there was worst to come, all these new 'Reactions' behaving as unwanted guests had to be treated individually with some more drugs.

As more and more drugs were being brought on sight it felt like a rubbish tip with lorry load after lorry load unloading their unwanted cargo of 'Toxins' to an already over loaded body.

There was another friend in the equation now called 'Circulation' he decided to become a 'Vigilante' in all of this by taking the situation into its own hands. With no training at all, he started frantically shovelling urine out of Julian's body faster and faster in an attempt to get rid of this unwanted 'Toxins'. But unbeknown to him, his friend 'Circulation' was making matters much worse by further depleting the very thing he needed the most to recover, which was his best friend called 'Protein'. In the old days it was referred to as 'Throwing the baby out with the bath water' I mentioned before that 'Magnesium' had a second job, well I forgot it also has a third job working with 'Potassium' sustaining muscle bulk. As the body became more dehydrated it started to affect the balance of 'Potassium' it wasn't so much of a problem losing muscle bulk around the skeletal frame, but it was becoming a problem now it was starting to affect the muscle of his heart which is imminent of causing a cardiac arrest!

At this stage the only treatment that could have corrected this dreadful chaos, was to replace his missing Protein otherwise known as Albumin Intravenous.

To exacerbate the problem further, he was introduced to a troublemaker called 'Diuretics' which further dehydrated his already crisp body. As his body was forced into a state of dehydration Julian was holding 'Prescribed drugs' as hostage due to lack of 'Protein', because of this they doubled up in strength causing him to appear to be entertaining 'Illegal Drugs'. It was at this stage on looker's thought he was loaded with Illegal drugs!

Don't forget Julian always protected himself with 'Plan B', if his liver couldn't get rid of his unwanted toxins then he was going to make a stand and force the toxins out through his skin, and that's exactly what he did. For four weeks, day and night he perspired profusely forcing the toxins though his pores soaking up big bath towels every ninety minutes in the process.

We all know we need a balanced amount of salt on board, not too much and not too little. But when he was getting rid of so much salt through sweating, no wonder he was craving salt he was desperately trying to retain his body fluid by the only way he knew how and that was by making sure his salt intake was high. The trouble was, the more fluid he excreted in urine and perspiration the <u>higher</u> his glucose concentration became, don't forget **Adrenal Tumour Diabetics** don't excrete glucose in their urine. As the glucose was not excreted the glucose became more and more concentrated miss-leading the Doctors into thinking he needed more insulin. When he was given more Insulin he not only became more toxic, but was actually taking part in 'Unwilfully overdosing on Insulin'

Needless to say when this repetitive vicious circle was allowed to continue, his condition spiralled out of control. Yes he was definitely down a dead end alley with no one offering a helping hand, dying in the street all alone with only curtain twitching nurses watching, too frightened to help. He didn't want to give up his life, but some thieves had stolen his credit card, which he always carried round with him called 'Cortisone Hormone'. He used to use this card when he needed a little extra fight, fear and flight. How did the thief find them, he always kept them safe in his Adrenal pocket? The immune system is our internal army that distinguishes friends from foe, unfortunately Julian got caught up in a friendly cross fire; the medical profession didn't mean to harm him they just chose to ignore his begging.

Do you the reader, now understand when I say Julian was a good listener of his own body, he knew he didn't need more drugs but he couldn't defend his case or himself. Julian may have been a friendly militant family man once, but in the end he didn't know who his enemy was. He was dealing with snipers trying to gun him down from

585

all directions. To me he was a hero among men in the arena of life, fighting with his very last breath, but sadly he lost his battle of survival to something I failed to supply him which could have been his only shield of protection, 'organic diet' and because of that he had to endure years of drug taking, slowly destroying his organs and finally, being humiliated into being made an example of in front of nursing staff, young impressionable medical students and lastly his family with these words etched in Llewela and my memory,

"We are not forcing him; we are just going to keep asking him until he agrees to take it."

As in the lyrics of the song 'The Flood' sung by Robbie Williams which echoes his inwardly struggle says,

The Flood.

Although no-one understood,
There was more of them than us,
Learning how to dance in the rain,
There was more of them than us,
Now they'll never dance again.

Sadly not just Julian, there are many others who will not dance again. In memory of those who appear to have died in similar circumstances may God forgive me for not doing more to save them! May they all now rest in peace, John, Charles, Julian, Derek, Yolanda, Michela, Eurwyn, Phyllis, Bill, John, Margaret and Shirleys brother, Jim.

I hope I haven't managed to make Julian's scenario sound too childlike, but the Endocrine system is so complicated and I don't know how else to explain it. I hope you're not confused.com! Unfortunately this is as simple as it gets, and this is why most doctors refer medical patients to Endocrinologists as they are called now, so called because they are the experts in the endocrine system. You would think to an Endocrinologist these signs and symptoms would scream out at them, after all Julian was on a special Endocrinologist ward and not misplaced on a maternity unit due to shortage of beds, which often happens these days. I suddenly realise when I read another article by a Doctor Sarah Myhill who stated, 'People who have been exposed to chemicals such as pesticides, become highly sensitive to other chemicals such as diesel fumes, perfumes, cigarette smoke and alcohol and wait for it DRUG INTOLERANCE'.

These people smell things long before others do, in effect they have become 'human canaries' Is this why Julian could not tolerate modern man made drugs, had he become intolerant of such things as antibiotics, diabetic tablets, thyroxin, and diuretics and of course insulin. Not to mention my perfume, bleach in the home, smell of paint, furniture polish spray and air-freshener, nail varnish smell, hair spray, even his own deodorant spray. All these products made him wheezy after his near multi organ failure incident.

My concern is, "Why are people like Julian abandoned just because the big boys (Drug Company) have so much clout in the medical world. I can only assume that allergies, reactions and side effects don't sell drugs so that's why they don't want the public to voice their pain and suffering.

It will make their statistics look unattractive to the buyer i.e. the NHS.

But without research and proper trials we don't have a chance to convince anyone out there, there is a problem. I think in 34 years of nursing I've only come across 2 people who said they were allergic to Paracetamol. It's hard to believe that any one could be allergic to such a simple thing as Paracetamol, but I could not bring myself to persuade those two people to take Paracetamol. On the other hand it's hard to believe that anyone can be allergic to something as natural as nuts, but can have devastating consequences if given to someone with nut allergy. Allergies are not usually taken so lightly, so I could not understand why no one was taking Julian's reaction seriously.

I know if Julian had realised his body needed detoxifying, he would have been the first to start practising it and in the process he would of healed his ailing Adrenal Tumour even if it did take two years to heal and then I'm sure he'd organise a party to proudly announcing he was "Taking back his life."

No wonder he sent a message to me go back to the beginning, he meant to before all this Adrenal issue started.

I would like to quote another person who has found difficulty in the medical world; I found this filed under Adrenal Diagnosis on line.

"The ignorance, arrogance and incomprehension of the medical doctors I have been subjected to in my search for diagnosis and treatment leaves me incandescent with rage. Even as a qualified health professional working for a major DGH I remain powerless to prevent the cumulative long term health risks associated with lack of treatment. I am voiceless, neutered, patronised and crawling day-to-day through what used to be my vital and colourful life. I would give everything I have for an open minded and creative diagnostician and more for a little compassion but this seems to be entirely beyond the capability of modern medic. God help us all"

The above could have been written by either Julian or I, as Julian waited for death at Shrewsbury hospital. But it wasn't, it was written by an ailing health professional; does this letter amplify anyone else's sentiments?

I suspect the entire world is now suffering from some degree of either Adrenal Malfunction or Liver problems toxicity the question is how much?

I understand

I've written <u>I now understand</u> several times under the Genetically Modified Medicine but I have some more general ones regarding the small but mighty Adrenal Gland, when it's out of synchronisation with the rest of the body.

<u>I understand</u> now why Julian experienced so much pain when he was given GTN spray way back in April 2008. I now realise Insulin allergy can cause breathing difficulties, so when he was given an additional drug called GTN spray to help relive his chest pain, which at the time mysteriously increased his pain. I now can now see he was well on his 'DRUG INTOLLERANCE journey' brought on by his over exposure to toxins, mainly from such things as pesticides which inflicted terror on his Adrenal Gland evolving him into the 'human canary'

<u>I understand</u> now why Julian suffered such hypertension and high glucose readings when he was given Insulin against his will, while exposed to unnecessary and unplanned general anaesthetic in April 2008. His Adrenal hormones were inadequate in managing his fight, fear and flight while under psychological and physical trauma of the Insulin and antibiotic Reaction.

<u>I understand</u> now when Adrenal Tumours are pressed they inflict pain, and as Julian kidneys were constantly receiving pressure from the canvas on the back of his wheelchair, it would have caused him considerable discomfort if not constant pain to his adrenal tumour. This pain or stress inhibits the Adrenal Hormone from been produced consequently it failed to stimulate the insulin to engorge the glucose in the blood stream. Leaving Julian with a high glucose readings!

<u>I understand</u> now how adrenal hormone also acts as an anti-inflammatory, sometimes referred to as the 'anti-pain hormone' which helps us be pain free. During its absence it's hindered in supplying the Pancreas with the hormone to stimulate the insulin to convert the glucose into energy, hence Julian was left with a sugar surge in his blood. So yes, in Julian's case taking analgesia did aid his anti-pain hormone, consequently it helped him to bring down his glucose reading.

To all the Doctor who rolled his eyes during Julian's Inquest, embarrassing me and making me feel stupid in front of my family and friends when I reminded him that, "The only time Julian's glucose readings came down was when he took Analgesia" These experts should have recognised these alarm bells, it should have been their 'second nature question' to ask Julian if he was he suffering from any sort of Adrenal malfunction

I understand now how Adrenal Insufficiency can cause hypothyroidism

I understand now why Julian could not tolerate any Diabetic treatment. Because of the assumption that they felt Julian was a 'Type 2 Diabetic' consequently they impounded diabetic treatment on him, which led Julian's body to react to their treatment most violently. Julian tried to convince everybody including myself, that he was sure he was producing enough Insulin of his own. His gut feeling was right, he didn't require their additional insulin, his body tried to tell them 'if I don't need it, I will reject it' but sadly in Julian's case it was more of a case of 'rejection often offends' and the medical profession were certainty offended. What he needed instead was an array of vitamins and minerals such as magnesium, zinc, folic acid, chromium, vitamin Bs and Protein in particular as their transport to release the Insulin out of his Pancreas.

I understand now why he suffered with low temperature, chest pain, freezing internal organs, high pulse, drop in blood pressure, sores developing on extremities, low oxygen levels, splenic infarcts; high respirations between 30-40, breathlessness, and bubbly chest immediately following taking prescribed drugs. It was just as Julian suspected all along, it was caused by drug allergy and toxicity.

I understand while Protein and magnesium was missing Julian was not receiving his full quota of vitamin D, which makes sense to me why Julian's skeletal pelvic region disintegrated like it did.

At the same time I'm not totally convinced yet that the artificial insulin did not have a helping hand in speeding up the destruction, when I consider what preparation goes into its makeup.

I understand why he could not tolerate the drug he should not have received after Hepatitis C.

I understand now why he used to say, "My organs need more time to recover" it was because of his dehydrated state, the drugs strength had doubled. In effect he was over dosing with the drugs causing 'drug toxicity' before he was coaxed into taking additional doses.

I understand now why he said, "I need to soak up this poison" after he experienced a night of horrendous hallucinations. It was his gut feeling, to call them poison not mine.

I understand now that metal toxicity can also lead to panic attacks, bipolar disorder and schizophrenia

I understand now if physicians place patients on diuretics who are already suffering from already exhausted Adrenal glands; it acts as a further stress on the endocrine system causing them to tip from Adrenal Exhaustion to Adrenal Crises.

I understand now why he was offered such ferocious third generation antibiotics, because he unbeknown to him had been taking unknown quantity of antibiotics in his meat, poultry and dairy food for years. In other words, he had consumed erratic quantity of constant broken courses of antibiotics for years, causing him to become an antibiotic abusers eventually leading to multi-resistant.

I understand now that those who can tolerate third generation antibiotics need to consider de-toxing after completing each course. Julian's problem was, he couldn't tolerate any drugs at all because in his rush for life his body had reached saturation point long before the rest of us, he was in desperate need of cleansing before he could undertake anymore of man's modern day medicine. Had he lived, I think he could have tolerated modern medication in small doses eventually.

I understand now when he pleaded with the Doctors, "Why can't I tolerate your treatment, I am really trying"

I understand now a Spleen can be enlarged if there is Adrenal malfunction present.

I understand now someone suffering from Adrenal malfunction can develop enlarged liver.

I understand now when he was working on a difficult project involving high stress, his sugar levels would then be sky high because of the Adrenal malfunction was having difficulty coping with his fight, fear and flight.

I understand now when an array of signs and symptoms of the Adrenal disorders are not grouped together they can be misdiagnosed as individual conditions, which would warrant a multitude of treatments causing further stress on the Adrenal Gland leading to a vicious circle. 'More complaints, more drugs, more complaints, more drugs . . . .'

I understand now why people who suffer with any Adrenal problems should avoid all refined food, caffeine, artificial sweeteners including **all** Genetically Modified products.

I understand now how normal secretion of cortisone hormone keeps our energy levels constant in-between meals. But when inflicted with Adrenal malfunction, it interferes with the status quo of the glucose balance in the blood supply and can lead to inappropriate emergency eating, which is often mistaking for hypoglycaemia.

I understand now that during the Second World War it appeared the introduction of refined food along with many other food products such as preservatives, pesticides, Genetically Modified food appeared in our diet caused untold damage to our Endocrine system. Twinned with this change came an explosive new diagnosis called 'Type Two Diabetes'.

I understand now when Diabetic UK states that diabetes has a connection with obesity around the mid-rift have they considered that our Toxic World might be responsible for our Liver De-fault leading to 'Mid-rift Obesity'?

I understand now why this present generation have become so obese, when we are inadvertently eating 'growth hormones' in our food chain.

I understand now why the liver cannot digest synthetic oils and fats, which lead to obesity, when we were given gall bladders to deal with butter and natural fats. Why are we abusing this organ?

I understand now when Julian used to complain of freezing organs. When I read of Tibetan culture that recognises the symptom, but doesn't suffer from either the complaint or the Western condition called 'Diabetes Type Two' possibly because they don't indulge in our 'substandard western diet'

I understand now how Julian was miss-diagnosed with irritable bowel when it was one of the Adrenal traits, constipation alternating with diarrhoea.

I understand now the body can't produce its own Zinc, but we need it for the immune system to function to aid wound healing, breakdown carbs for energy we also need it for our sense of taste and smell and to help with antitoxin. (Word of warning, care should be taken when taking additional zinc mineral with antibiotics, ACE inhibitors, HRT and Steroids.)

I think I now understand how if any of the other endocrine glands have tumours they also have an effect on the release on insulin. For example pressure on the pituitary gland would reduce the hormone needed to stimulate the cortisone in the Adrenal gland that's necessary to prompt the hormone insulin to maintain normal glucose levels. The same goes for the thyroid gland, polycystic ovary, and the Testes glands.

I understand now without Magnesium none of us can retain Potassium; they go hand in hand like Siamese twins, derangement of either too low or too elevated Potassium can lead to a heart attack.

I understand now when Julian became severely dehydrated, and then was prescribed diuretics it robbed him of fluid from every corner of his body including from his poor eyes causing him to go blind, his vision only returning when he was hydrated again.

I understand now if we continue to hinder the liver by bombarding it with toxins it will be doomed to create a condition called 'Fatty Liver' and we will increasingly start seeing strange lumps and bumps develop under our skin. Of course it will eventually be too occupied to breakdown our natural fat intake.

I understand now how helpful Julian's comments were when he constantly drew attention to his lumps and bumps, one on his forehead and another on his biceps. Sadly these Angiolipoma could have indicated to the medical professionals that he was in possession of Adrenal tumour.

I understand now adrenal rebuilding is a corner stone to a lot of conditions such as chronically ill, constant pain, Diabetes, long term stress and poor eating habits.

I understand now how other complaints can stem from Adrenal malfunctions such as Myalgia Encephalopathy, Chronic Fatigue Syndrome, Polymyalgia and Fibromyalgia.

I understand now why he kept informing, all the medical sector including the nursing staff, "I never have glucose in my urine, not even when my blood glucose readings are very high"

As Adrenal malfunction don't excrete glucose in urine, he was right to raise this alarm.

I understand now why he always had protein in his urine; he was execrating it because his Adrenals were in difficulty, nothing to do with urine infection. Leucocytes in urine indicate infection not Protein. Finding Protein in urine should be considered more serious than urine infection.

I understand now how Adrenal malfunction can indicate high glucose readings due to toxicity, pain and stress especially when negotiating with the medical staff for reprieve from the drugs.

I understand now as he was been transferred to one of the wards he said; "I can't heal here" because he knew he'd have to encounter a particular Medical Physician who he had to negotiate with and refused to recognise his allergies which was going to lead him to great stress.

I understand now when a Diabetic, a ME sufferer, a Fibromyalgia, a Polymyalgia and other Adrenal dysfunction sufferers, admit they are having a good day for no reason at all. It's very likely they are not putting their adrenal glands under stress that day?

I understand now how exhaustion and fatigue are often undiagnosed 'Worn out adrenal glands'.

I understand now how an adequate level of cortisone keeps us free from auto-immune illness. That includes any illness ending in "itis"

I understand now when a patient has partial loss of adrenal function they can appear well until they are faced with adrenal crisis such as physiologic stress, infection, burns, surgery or allergy. If the ACTH cortical levels are border line and adrenal insufficiency is clinically suspected, due to a known adrenal **tumour** particularly if a patient is to undergo surgery and there is no time for testing, then hydrocortisone is needed to cover the stress period. There were many occasions when Julian was in need of something to raise his low blood pressure.

I understand now why Medical professions especially Anaesthetists should be on the lookout for a drop in blood pressure following surgery or trauma, whether they are a diagnosed or undiagnosed Adrenal malfunction sufferer, they should be mindful of steroid crisis.

I understand now and recognise others who may suffer with Adrenal Tumour, when they display tell-tale sign of large lumps of Angiolipoma just like Julian had on his body, then hearing that their GPs are dismissing them as mere harmless fatty tissue. When in fact they are harbouring toxins, and if left alone could mature into carcinogenic tumours.

I understand now that too much Insulin can make you look obesity, it can panic cholesterol reading, it can raised blood pressure and it can cause water retention and eye problems.

Please re-read the last sentence, I didn't say diabetes with inadequate insulin causes the above I said too 'much insulin' meaning additional injected insulin.

I understand now how Statin drugs stops liver producing balanced groups of cholesterol, and that low cholesterol diet imbalances the cholesterol that we need to maintain a balanced health.

I believe now I understand that Type Two Diabetics appear to produce sufficient Insulin; they don't need more Insulin but adequate natural vitamins and minerals to transport their insulin.

I understand now why Julian said to the Doctors, "I will die if you carry on giving me this medication" He was offering them a way out, relieving them of their duty to give him any more drugs. He was even willing to sign anything preventing him chastising the medical profession.

We're not without Hope

I understand we all need to exchange our white refined wheat flour for organic oats. Because during the refining process of wheat 14 vitamins, 10 minerals and protein are lost in the process and often only 4 vitamins are replaced. During the bleaching process it leaves chemical residue in the flour which creates gluten which also occurs in barley and rye and it's this glutton that many are allergic to. It's the bleaching that impounds toxins on the Adrenal Glands causing unnecessary stress leading to diabetes. Globulin is another found in corn and rice.

I understand now we the non-diabetic who eat white refined sugar activates our Insulin to instantly devour our high sugar intake. But very quickly it leaves us famished, tired and emotionally sensitive. This leads us to over eating consequently over weight; it's this constant yoyo eating of refined food that will lead us to being diagnosed as Type Two Diabetes.

I think I understand that we like Type Two don't need low fat diet, what we all need is small amount of natural fat such as butter to aid the transport of vitamins, not the modern clogging synthetic spreads.

I understand now the curse of both Diabetic and non-Diabetic persons, is the array of artificial sweeteners in nearly all our food that leads one group to become a Diabetic and the already Diagnosed Diabetic to be lumbered with uncontrollable and erratic sugar readings.

<u>I understand</u> now we all must have adequate amount of Magnesium, Zinc and Vitamins to help transport insulin, avoiding us becoming diabetics.

<u>I understand</u> now we could all benefit from adding some natural herbal remedies to our diet to help reduce (not cure) high glucose levels in both already diagnosed diabetics and non-diabetics.

<u>I understand</u> now the myth behind sweet fruit and raw honey is bad for Diabetics, may **not** be true. The two are loaded with natural vitamins and minerals which enables the cells to process those sugars immediately unlike refined sugar.

<u>I understand</u> now it's the refined sugar and wheat that's the biggest demon in our society not saturated fat.

<u>I understand</u> now when the Adrenals are weak the things that are harming it are winning, but if we want to turn the tables round then we need to minimise the harm.

<u>I understand</u> now adrenal rebuilding is a corner stone to a lot of conditions such as chronically ill, constant pain, Diabetes, long term stress and poor eating habits.

<u>I understand</u> now when Julian was alive my original belief was to radically remove the offending tumour, but since his death I now see an alternative treatment to surgery, although more time consuming but long term more beneficial to everybody concerned, which is—abiding a detoxing diet, engaging in additional exercise, deliberate act of de-stressing and ensuring time for adequate sleep.

<u>I understand</u> now the importance of wearing a lifesaving medical alert bracelet as an 'Adrenal insufficiency sufferer' which is not emphasised enough and further more people should carry a pre-packed kit of hydrocortisone for emergency use, being fully educated on how and when to administer it.

<u>I understand</u> now why Adrenal malfunction sufferers should be more vigilante of prescribed and over-the-counter medication.

<u>I now understand</u> how crucial Ben's advice was to Julian's survival, when he conducted that allergy test at his bed side. How important it was to increase his magnesium and chromium intake and the shame I now feel for keeping stump about his findings. But had I tackled the topic, would the Doctors have listened to me; I don't think so do you?

I understand now that most modern medicine is ideal in an emergency situation, but can be very taxing on the Adrenals Glands long term. In most cases we need to fix the cause not the symptoms.

I understand now Insulin works better when the tissue is at its optimal neutral pH balance, according to Doctor Wolgang it should only take six months on low carbohydrate (that's excluding such things as cakes, biscuits, pastry's anything made with white re-fined flour and re-find sugar) to heal the insulin resistance in Type Two Diabetes, along with a GPs supervision of controlled intake of Magnesium and Chromium and regular checks on Potassium and other Minerals.

I understand everything now, without this book how else could I have pieced together this little lot without starting at the beginning of every subject then putting everything back in order? As the Priest once said in the film of 'The Song of Bernadette' when he was asked to attend to a sick girl, "It was very dark when I was asked to come last night but now day break has broken, everything seems much clearer" This is how I feel about Julian's case.

This last four years I have felt as if I've been imprisoned in my own home trying to defend Julian's unusual reasoning at the same time trying to clear my own name. Ironically I came across a book Julian bought from our church the Sunday before he became ill, called, 'Persecuted and forgotten' it's about Priests who have been wrongly imprisoned in third world countries and placed on death row. It's hard to imagine innocent people been wrongly accused in this day and age, but at the same time it's hard to believe that Julian's wishes could not be respected in modern day nursing either. Considering we are meant to be living in a multi-cultural tolerating world, I feel there are many pit falls in our modern day society.

Stepping back and looking at the bigger picture and armed with all my facts I can now understand why the Doctor at Worcester originally suspected that I was poisoning Julian, but fortunately for me he conducted some blood sampling investigation and the results proved me innocent.

I can also understand why Shrewsbury Hospital staff felt I was trying to prevent Julian from having what they thought was their appropriate treatment and I can understand why my Mother-in-law and her daughter was persuaded by the Doctors that I intended him harm. In turn it's understandable why they felt it necessary to bring allegations against me. Looking back I can understand towards the end of Julian's life, why some staff felt he looked as if he was taking illegal drugs and why blood tests were taken, possibly when the doctor locked eyes with Julian and he said, "I have to" the investigation that was requested that day, was to clarify if Julian's body was harbouring Amphetamines, Cocaine, Methadone and Opiates. Physically his poor body had become so thin, his neck looked so scraggly, under his eyes had become so dark, his pro-fused sweating had by then become his norm, his eyes appeared bulging, his lips were so swollen. He didn't look like Julian anymore and finally as he sat on the edge of the bed head bowed forward dribbling uncontrollably from his mouth and sadly robbed of his marvellous brain.

The difference was, they all felt I was harming him, the truth was Julian felt the treatment was crucifying him. I only ever relayed how he felt, and acted as his advocate by standing by him even in his darkest hour. I now realise I was only able to accomplish this heavy task, through the power of love. No wonder I was having difficulties remembering to document things at work, I was left in limbo saying to myself constantly "I don't understand" which I didn't but now I do "I understand everything"

The sad thing is; it didn't have to be like this at all!

I can't believe I've hardly diverted from Julian's case in this book, no wonder I said to Julian I think this is really big, but in my heart of hearts I felt it might be something very simple like vitamins and minerals. I was right all along; all he ever needed was an old fashion way of life, to eat wholesome food that was not robbed of its natural nutrients like vitamins and minerals!

It wasn't rocket science after all; it just needed a simple mind like mine to figure it out. Do you recall what I used to say about 10 Downing Street!

My conclusion on this matter is, this book might have been about Julian's life, but this is 'my life now' and I cannot stand by and pretend nothing happened, because something very serious most definitely did

Shall I tell him

This last paragraph has just reminded me of an incident that happened in the summer of 2007, a couple of days before Julian had been admitted to our local Hospital with near multi-organ failure.

Some might feel this is a dangerous confession, but it's a means to an end and I hope you can appreciate how serious the situation had become.

On the afternoon in question I popped out to our local shop to get some groceries as I came out I spontaneously went into the pharmacy next door and randomly asked for some insulin. The pharmacist asked, "Who is it for"? I replied, it was for myself! He informed me, first of all I needed a prescription and secondly what type of insulin did I normally take. I said I don't normally take insulin, and I was not a diabetic either.

His eyes widened with horror, then he said, "Do you know how dangerous it is to take insulin when you don't need it, it could kill you"

I answered, "Yes I thought it could, I just needed confirmation" turned on my heels and briskly walked out.

Incidentally I didn't need any insulin; I had an array of different ones at home left over from Julian's attempt to find out which one would suit him.

Some months later I re-visited the same pharmacy and as I was paying for my goods the same pharmacist ventured from the back room enquired about my health and to reminded me how I had frightened him and his assistant last time I was there.

I apologised and explained briefly that my husband had been rushed in to hospital the very next day and ten days later was diagnosed with near multi-organ-failure. His diabetic treatment was stopped and he was now home enjoying perfect health, although his glucose levels were still elevated.

The next time I went in, he struck up a conversation yet again but this time he expressed concerns that my husband was not taking any treatment at all for his diabetes. I assured him he was still enjoying very good health.

It was some sixteen months later in the December of 2008 I returned to the same chemist, again he engaged in conversation but this time I informed him that I was now a widow. Shocked he asked, why what happened?

I briefly explained out of the customer's ear shot that he had gone into hospital with an abscess and was given insulin over a period of four weeks, which he knew he was allergic too and consequently died. He then expressed his concern because he too had become a diabetic now. I reassured him, "Please don't be worried, I'm going to get to the bottom of this" His reply was, "When you do, I will be very interested in your findings"

One day I will return, to let him know what a rocky road poor Julian travelled and if we don't change course we too may travel down the same path. Although it was Julian who asked me to write the book, in essence I feel its journey really started with this pharmacist's concern for my safety and Juliann's 'Non-Treatment-Diabetic' dilemma. I now feel I have done a full circle by returning to the echo of this man's voice when he said to me "Do you know how dangerous it is to take insulin if you don't need it, it can kill you" Throughout Juliann's illness there were other strange cryptic advice given to him, by other professionals amidst the jungle of events. One of them was when the Ward Sister called out as she waved to Julian in the ambulance "Don't forget to take everything they offer you Julian" So when Julian used to whisper to me quietly, "I feel as if I'm committing suicide, when I'm forced to take all of these drugs" He would not have made this statement lightly; the whole idea of suicide went against his faith.

I wonder if one day I will have enough courage to tell my local pharmacist face to face that I no longer believe there is such a thing as 'Type Two Diabetes', but a breakdown in our Endocrine system. He's bound to ask me how can I make such an outrageous statement, then I will ask him to restock his shop with abundance of good quality Vitamins and Minerals as our society has become depleted in Magnesium, GTF Chromium, ...

This is just my observation now, if 'Type Two Diabetes' affected people in their 50's during the 1990s, then at the turn of the millennium it started affected people in their 40s and by 2010 people in their 30s. One could only assume, if left to our own devices by the year 2020 people in their 20s will be affected. Before we know it, world population will be born diagnosed as either Type One or 'Type Two diabetic' but definitely one or the other!!!!!!!!!!!!

Using the same words Gweno uttered to me on the phone towards the end of Julian's life she said, "This has got to stop!" She said this in a stern voice and I intend it to be received in the same tone by the reader today.

My Mother used to shout at my Father when he used to play 'rough and tumble' on the floor with my two brothers years ago, with her hands on her hips and waving a wooden spoon she would shout, "Now, stop this right now, before someone gets hurt" maybe we should do the same and stop tormenting our poor Pancreas with refined food especially refined sugar before we hurt our Pancreas beyond repair.

Julian like others were searching for all sorts of explanations including looking into Type Four Diabetes for an answer, I can see why such books have been published because they like me were searching in the dark for an alternative Diabetes. I feel finding another type was not the answer, but questioning the ones we already had, should have been our quest.

How ironic, one of the Doctors treating Julian at Oswestry referred to Julian's condition as, "Julian's Diabetes" he obviously didn't feel comfortable calling it 'Type Two Diabetes'!

Now I don't believe that Type Two Diabetes is out of control I believe our toxic world is out of control making us think there is such a thing called type two. Were still behaving like Adam and Eve eating the forbidden food in the Garden of Eden still tempted by the serpentine. What we need is someone like St Patrick who once banished snakes out of Ireland. It was of course a figure of speech when he said this, because evidently there never were any snakes in Ireland in the first place. What he meant was, he was banishing temptation out of Ireland. We need someone just as powerful in this day and age, to banish toxins out of this world. But I fear one person can't do this on his or her own, so maybe we need to join our quills and use the Musketeers motto, 'All for one and one for all' and see if the intertwined feathers can gain strength for the cause? I re-cap on the words of Albert Einstein, "Nothing will end war unless the people themselves refuse to go to war" I'm afraid we all went to war against our own bodies the day after the Second World War ended. It's about time we raised the flag of surrender on our ailing bodies and then exchange it for the flag of peace.

Writing this book has been a huge learning curve for me, studying Julian's medical notes, researching, talking, discussing, phoning pharmacy's, reading medical books including looking into herbal remedies.

Sadly Julian's intellectual head could not make any sense of it while he was here in the land of the living, it was only when he could see a bigger picture from where he is he was abled to guide me by sending me a message instructing me to, "Go back to the beginning" and in doing so

I have been able to see how the condition has evolved and become more of an epidemic each decade.

Sometimes in life we have to do a U-turn and this may well be one of them. No one likes doing U-turns it's like admitting defeat but sometimes we need to do it in order to get back on track.

If we're big enough to do a U-turn with our diet and environment, why can't we do a U-turn with our medicine too and try to use less aggressive treatment and lean more towards gentler treatments. I don't mean totally, surely the medical world and the herbal one could learn to live side by side offering a more holistic approach, isn't that what the Coroner was asking all the Doctors one by one on the stand at Julian's Inquest asking 'Did they feel they had treated Julian in a Holistic manner?'

We consider modern medicines to be poles apart from ancient Egyptian medicines 2000 years BC with its practice of massage, spiritual healing and herbal medicine. But I think we could co-exist by taking an interest in the more genital therapy of herbs as prevention avoiding ailments getting a grip on us, but giving in when we have too, to stronger prescribed drugs. After all it was a Doctor who once prescribed Horse Chesnutt tablets to Julian, after he'd undergone a lumber chemical sympathectomises injection. He obviously regarded the local herbal shop in high regard in high enough esteem to recommend such supporting therapy at his follow clinic.

There are more and more scientific proof these days that 'Old Wives Tales' are beginning to gain credibility at last. I spent years asking people, "How did the old wives know" I now realise it was probably cascaded down by word of mouth from Egyptian times.

As children, we were rarely sick, was it because our parents used the herbs in our garden?

Medicinal herbs are quoted in both the Bible and in the Koran. In the Old Testament Moses taught the Israelites after they left Egypt to keep their premises clean, wash their cloths and bodies, and discard harmful articles including the lustful diet but to live simply on nourishing food and to use herbs as their medicine! As the Bible was often the only book in the house, so it may well have cascaded down from Moses's time through the pages.

The old wives tales weren't all about herbal remedies they also recognised food that harm and food that healed. For example can carrots really help us see in the dark? Apparently so, Beta Carrots is converted into vitamin A which is imperative for healthy night vision.

When we went to school with an apple every day, the old saying goes "An apple a day keeps the Doctor away" Apparently the skin of an organic apple contains antitoxins, so if were free of toxins then we can assume we won't suffer with minor ailments resulting in multitude visits to the Doctor it can also maintained cholesterol balance and body weight. When older folks say, "I think bad weather is on its way, I can feel it in my bones" they have now scientifically proved a drop in low atmospheric pressure can increases arthritic pains. And when our parents used to say, "Wrap up warm and wear a hat or you'll catch a cold" It's true, when we feel cold, it reduces our immune defence and encourages the common cold to develop. My father always claimed the best place to catch a cold is in a cemetery on a cold winter's day, standing still in a draught, especially if unprotected with inadequate clothing.

So what are we to think, did Granny know best! May be we should watch out for other proven facts about preventative sayings in the future then.

Talking about going back to basics Gweno my sister who is a Nursing Sister at a Nursing Home occasionally feels the need to transfer some of her residents to a ten bedded bungalow, situated at Newtown a neighbouring town in the heart of Wales. This place is called 'Fan Gorau' translated it means 'Best Place' Nice name for a house don't you think, what happens hear you may ask! Well, it's a 10 bedded accommodation assessment unit for a very short stay, two weeks at the most. Patients or residents come here first of all to be taken off all of their prescribed medication. Then reflecting on their original diagnosis, making sure they still require the same treatments. The treatment then entails re-introducing them on a very low dose of the medication that was first prescribed, one prescription at a time. They then thoroughly observe for any contradiction with other drugs. People often re-emerge from here on very little medication and with fuller faculties than they did on entering this 'Best Place'. (Better Place) But don't you think there is a need for such a place in our modern day society in every County, Province and State. A place to 'start over again' as the Americans would say. To me its another form of 'Detoxing' our bodies, when we stop taking drugs we no longer need. There are two sayings that come to mind here, 'Nothing is sometimes the best treatment' and 'Less is some times more.

I now understand what's meant when they say, 'modern man is referred to as a Canary' Since he's been exposed to so many toxins, his human instinct has become sharpened to reject further toxic substances such as the chemicals found in the human insulin and other drugs. This is probably why Julian reacted so badly to all drugs he was offered and forced to take. If Julian had of known of this place he would have begged to be transferred there. I'm convinced that poor Julian is as nearly intact as he was when he was laid to rest, because of all the preservatives I fed him over the years.

Sadly I now feel if we didn't live in such a contaminating world, Julian would not be where he is today, consequently there would be no need for me to compile this book. I fear his land slide began at the turn of the millennium, now the echo of what my Grandmother said to me before she died comes to mind, "Olwen I don't really want to live to be very old, but I should like to see what the new millennium has to offer" I realise now why those words have haunted me, maybe her little voice of conscience told her to utter these few words to me. Maybe we are enjoying the 'wealthiest of time' but her generation enjoyed the 'healthiest of time' did things alter on the stroke of midnight on the eve of the millennium. After all it was in the year 2000 Julian had his first attack of something in Pompeii!

I'm now exhausted of saying the same old thing, our organs are failing, our babies are damaged and our bodies are decaying, our eye sights are deteriorating, our memories are shot, we are growing tumours inside and outside our bodies at an alarming rate, cancer is fast becoming our modern plague, not to mention suffering from diseases that we've never heard of before.

If this carries on, our future appears grim. I don't want to sound as if I'm right and they are wrong. But I do feel betrayed; I have trusted the Government to supply us with good safe food, safe water, safe medication, and safe environment. I'm beginning to think now that children's toys undergo more scrutiny before entering the market place, compared to the food we feed to our children.

It's true when they say, some people have the most profound effect on us Julian was one of those who changed mine. Another such man was Martin Luther King, who over the years must have changed many people's lives just by this small phrase he once vocalised in front of thousands of people gathered before him, when he called out to the crowd saying "I have a dream" Well I too have a dream. I hope one day we will all live longer, healthier lives without the contamination of our basic needs of food, water, air, and medicines. I read that Raphael instructed 'The reward for making good changes in our diet will effectively allow us to spend more productive hours devoted to our dreams, desires, health, family and our life purpose' Makes sense to me!

The retired Chief Detective Inspector was right, something is definitely not right. If I do 32 miles an hour in a 30 mile an hour area, I have to face the consequences and serve my punishment. I don't see any punishment here for the food companies or for the Government that allows it to go on, so the crime continues. Bribery in the food industry, allowing food not fit for human consumption onto the open market should carry a heavy penalty. It seems the sector we trust with what matters the most to us don't care less any more. Some might dare to go as far as to say, "Why not, if they can get away with it"

No, not anymore!!!! The buck must stop here, right now.

All the questions I've asked in the entirety of this book have been on behalf of the living.

Julian your right something has gone very wrong!

And I hope Pandora has enough 'Hope' left in her box for all Nations to wake up to what's going on!

I remember; my Uncle Ifan years ago was obsessed with eating cold food in case the hot food gave him stomach cancer. You guessed right, he died of stomach cancer.

With hindsight I wonder if Julian's secret phobia was about being caught out without a plan 'B'

because it was ironic he lived by the strict code of plan 'B' always at the ready, but when he needed it the most he was too weak and too poorly to plan one.

Was this what he was secretly afraid of all our married life, to be caught out when his defence was down without a plan 'B'? Throughout our married life every single morning over breakfast we would discuss the plan of the day, then we would discuss if that plan fell apart he'd always conjure up a plan 'B'. A bit like being in the army, it was a nice safe feeling though, we never wasted time halfway through the day wondering what to do next; we just went straight to plan B. At the end of the day we would reflect on the day's activities and discuss which plan worked best was it plan A or did we have to rely on plan B. Was it Julian sixth sense to be constantly on guard about his plan 'B' I wounder!

I hope Julian's looking down on me now, and saying like he used to, "Olwen, when you get a Bee in your bonnet you won't let go until it's sorted, will you".

Well things haven't changed down here much Julian, and 'you're diabetic' issue definitely needed looking into. How strange I called it 'Your Diabetes' do you remember a doctor once referred to it as, "Julian's Diabetes"

Talking about plan B, I haven't forgotten the Bee you had in your bonnet just before you died either.

Disappearing Bees

Although Julian and I had this long relationship of helping each other, Julian with his wit and inelegance and I with my physical contribution, between us we made a good whole one. We tackled each project or task 50/50. I suspect this would have been our next project together and as a last gesture to Julian's memory I will attempt to give this dilemma my 100% effort.

It started one the evening before Julian became ill, while on his lap top he suddenly turned to me and said, "Olwen, there is something terrible happening to the Honey Bee Worldwide" I flippantly asked, "O! Yes what that then"? In an almost agitated state he said, "No, I'm serious there dying in droves, we must do something to help them" And because of his worrying words, I now feel duty bound to do something or at the very least look into the problem that was causing him so much concern and then maybe do something constructive to help. I hope 'Old Man Time' will be kinder to me than he was to poor Julian.

I don't know how much Julian had read up on the topic that night, but it was enough to pull at his heart strings to say to me what he did.

Up to that point the only Bees Julian had been in contact with, was when he was involved in fund raising for Llewelas primary school. The school was named after the Patron Saint of Bee keepers. Julian was a member of the school parents committee and like other likeminded parent's their sole reason for volunteering their services was to raise money to enhance their children's education. The committee chose a 'Bee' as the theme for their fundraising and Julian went ahead and built a three foot tall Bee hive out of fibre glass in our back garden, then asked all the pupils to construct a second skin to the hive with 2p's, I think it raised in the region of £500 for the school kitty. He was also involved in instigating the naming of the Bee Mascot Competition, a pupil named Luisa Butera won with her entry calling the mascot 'Bee-trix' In his garden shed he made bronze medals for the school sports day depicting the new 'Bee-trix mascot' He also designed the emblem of a Bee Hive for the school sweat shirts, peaked caps and the school bags.

This is a Photograph of Llewela age seven standing next to the impressive 2p fundraising Bee Hive.

Other than this, Julian was not involved with any real Honey Bee situation at all, with Julian's instructions I thought I'd go back to the beginning to find out how a hive operates.

Each hive has a 'Queen'; the Queens responsibility is to reproduce the next generation of Bees by laying hundreds of eggs.

There are 'Drove Bees', these are the male worker Bees and they have no sting.

Then there are the female 'Worker Bees' these are sterile females, and don't reproduce any young.

The older Bees are called 'Field Bees' these Bees are very unlikely to sting because once they do, their jagged prong rips out their abdomen and the poor Honey Bee dies.

Lastly there are the 'House Bees', they are the young Bees who stay at home and are busy tidying up the pollen in the hive when it's brought home.

Now I understand the basic fundamentals of how the cast works, in what appeared to be a top secret society. My first query is if they belong to such a highly organised organisation, why are their numbers depleting'?

As the Inquest had taken so much of my time, I confess I hadn't given the Bees much attention until I came across a cutting from a newspaper Gweno had sent me from her local newspaper about the Honey Bee crisis. I had carefully filed the cutting in my diary so I would not forget the date. The venue chosen for this discussion was in Newtown Cinema, in mid Wales. I promptly requested the day off, to make sure I did not miss the lecture. As the day approached I rang Gweno to make arrangements to meet her somewhere. She seemed perplexed about the plans and had no recollection that she had sent me the cutting. On viewing the cutting again she asked what's on the back of the cutting? I chuckled and said, "It's about diabetes". She said, "That's the article I sent you, but I'm sorry I can't come with you to this Bee lecture, I'm working". Well that was the end of that. Then on the morning of the lecture in question I thought, it's no good, there was something inside of me so strong drawing me to attend, with or without Gweno. Was this artical a coincidence or was it guiding me to be educated on their plight. On the day of this lecture Llewela and Kevin visited, I apologised and explained I needed and had to go, the feeling was over whelming. The lecture didn't start until 8pm, so it was evident it was going to be a late night. My friend was concerned that I was traveling on my own in the dark at such a late hour on isolated back roads; he offered to drive me there. He volunteered to come and listen for a few minutes, but if he found the topic boring he would be coming home immediately with or without me. I took a chance and decided to let him drive, he would be company and hoped to goodness the lecture was going to be interesting and informative.

All four of us were nearly ready to leave the house, Kevin was in the bathroom, Llewela was in the bedroom, my friend was in the conservatory, and I was in the lounge. When, all of a sudden we all heard this terrible noise. It sounded like someone was falling down stairs with hob nail boots. We all rushed to the bottom of the stairs, all thinking it was one of the others who had fallen the length of the stairs. But to our surprise it was the big arched mirror that had fallen off the wall onto the floor, simply face down. Broken into bits of course, but none of us could explain why we all thought the noise had travelled the length of the stairs and not just simply off the wall. The mirror incidentally had been hung there since Llewela was ten. I know that, because it was Julian and Llewela who bought it from an Antique shop that was closing down just outside her school. They thought it would look good in the house in France. By the way, the school she was attending at that time was named after the patron Saint of Bee keeper. Was this another coincidence or a connection? Was this a sign from Julian to say this honey business was serious or did the wire simply give up the ghost that day anyway! I don't know.

We arrived at the Cinema in plenty of time, and instead of complaining of how bored my friend was, he kept saying, "This is fascinating" I kept saying, "Hush" I think that night it opened both our eyes to how serious the situation has become. Julian was right to take fright like he did when he discovered the world's plight and its future. There were several speakers, all of which were very enlightening about the catastrophic possibilities of human surviving. Most of the evening was taken up by a film show, emphasising the problem worldwide.

The first to be mentioned was the Bees habitat. Our country side has lost 92% of the wildflower meadows in the UK, they vanished between 1980` and the 1990`s. Farming on a large scale ripping up hedges to produce greater crop yields and this has not helped the situation. Farms owned by supermarkets are largely responsible for this practice.

The second to be mentioned was disease, which has killed nearly 70% of the Bee population. They know what it is, but not why. It's a virus mite, a tiny rust-coloured crab shaped parasite. It has spread across the world over the last 10 years sucking the blood of our honey bees.

When the Varro mite lands on the Honey Bee it sucks their blood and weakens their immune system making them more susceptible to viral infection before they die.

The third to be mentioned was pesticide, it interferes with the Bees electric and chemical signals, causing problems navigating home; in other words it affects their memory. If by chance they did find their way home they then delivered pesticide in to the hive making the young 'Home Bee' suffer the same immune plight. They are like us humans, rely on a good diet to sustain a good immune system to survive. Unfortunately in this process they then suffer a double whammy they pesticides cause them nerve damage as well as immune breakdown. Farmers are using a pesticide called Neoicotinoids which is 7,000 times more toxic than DDT! Germany, France and Slovenia have banned it, good old UK is only just considering such a ban at the moment. UK always holds back at all costs when it comes to health safety, why can't we be world leaders in something other than wars, toxicity and ditherers?

The forth mentioned was Genetically Modified crops. Unfortunately most crops in this country are GM insect resistant.

I was not too ofay with this so I looked into it. Originally Bacillus thuringenis (Bt) was sprayed as pesticides on to crops. Scientists then used Bt bacterium to transform the DNA of crop seeds to GM seeds, now the Bt is in every cell of the plant including the pollen. When the insects either eat or pick up the pollen they digest the toxins produced by the Bt. It causes crystallisations in the gut leading to death.

Government claim there is no risk of GM crops affecting the Bees, but John MacDonald a Bee Keeper with a background in Biology proposed and asked if he could conduct a test on two Bee Hives, one hive feeding on GM crops and the other on GM-free crop.

His request to conduct the test was denied, but he went ahead and conducted his test anyway as his own independent study and under his own cost.

First of all, he made two hives out of new wood to ensure they were given a disease free environment to start with.

He distinguished between the two by calling one hive 'Farmland Bees' and the other as 'Non-farm colonies' The Farm land bees failed to gain weight, while the Non-farmland Bees did. The Non-farmland Bees produced 200 lb of honey and 150 lb per hive for over the winter brood supper. While the farmland bees had not even started to work the honey and would need to be fed, well before the winter set in.

I wonder are the Honey Bees as wise as our ancestors say they are, are they too frightened to indulge in picking up pollen from the GM crop and think this is like 'committing suicide' and worst still if they take the toxins back to the hive it might feel like aiding euthanasia amongst their own kind, maybe they prefer the other option and chose the 'starve to death policy'.

You don't know how close I am to crying right now, over these little vulnerable creatures.

The biblical fifth commandment says, "Though shalt not kill!

It's like saying, shall I drink this dirty water and die or shall I go with out and die anyway?

I could not find any Government approval nor if a licence was issued for agriculture to grow GM crops, but what I did find was a Government

611

Consultant agreeing with a survey conducted by 'The Mail' online, the findings was; that UK publicly made their opinion clear on GM crops. 37,000 people voted against eating GM food. Don't forget the rule of thumb is, for every one vote of protest, there is ten who wished they had.

Even Professor Malcolm Grant the chairman of GM Nation confessed the public's mood ranged from caution, doubt, suspicion, scepticism, hostility to rejection. There doesn't seem to be anything positive in his statement, and he's the chairman!

I then wondered who was in charge of our Food safety, it appears it is European Food Safety Authority referred to them as EFSA, it was reported that even they were corrupt, because they failed to report conflict of interest and until amendments are undertaken the public cannot have confidence in the EFSA regulatory process. So what are the EFSA responsible for regulating anyway, they are in charge of food handling, food preparation, food storage and food contamination which included bacteria in food and food poisoning.

So when GM food toxins was found in the blood of 93% of unborn babies, doesn't that indicate that this FOOD regulator EFSA is not doing its job properly by not protecting the public from food toxins, if it's found in miniature humans not yet born?

This is what you call going back to the beginning!

Why is this corruption allowed to go on, Julian was wrong on this small point when he used to say the Government doesn't need simple minded people like me to interfere with the running of their affairs, with my letter writing?

This simple minded person, (meaning me) still feels, how dare our Government send British envoys out to third world countries dictating how to take care of their crops and communities.

Who do we think we are? We don't even know how to take care of our own crops and communities?

The poor Bees have got such a lot stacked up against them, and look at their size compared to us. And after all they are only trying to help us and look how man repays them. These defenceless little creatures work so tirelessly above the call of duty to preserve mankind at their own risk, with no reward for themselves.

I only learnt about the Bee's plight in 2008, but it seems that the poor Honey Bee has been poorly managed for at least 25 years at the hands of those who depend on them the most for their survival?

(It feels as if the scenario resembles—children who suffer neglect and are taken from their natural parent and placed in a family who abused them.)

Could it be they are in fact insulted and harmed at the hands of man's greed? I fear their extinction maybe the result of un-appreciating or ignorant human race. I am not surprised at all surprised everything else man touches, seems to be destroyed or be contaminated. The fact that they are dying in droves all over the world is saying something is not right; they are nearly becoming an endangered species. It's sad to think such a lot of things in our world are not right any more.

The famous Albert Einstein once predicted that "The human race will cease to exist four years to the day following the death of the last Honey Bee" No more Bees = no more humans.

On February 13th 2011 I had a text from my friend Louise Walker, urging me to buy a Sunday newspaper called The Mail on Sunday. So it wasn't just Julian that was concerned about the stripy little fella then, the article was written by the TV chef called Valentine Warner, he was raising awareness about the de-pleating Honey Bees in Britain. The headlines read "Save the Great British Bee." He was reminding the reader that our Bees are responsible for pollinating one third of the food we eat. They are vital to the success of 90 crops grown worldwide. Most of our fruit, vegetables, nuts and seeds, not to overlook crops like cattle feed, who then produce milk, butter, cheese, cream and yogurt extract.

It's not just that jar of honey we should be worried about disappearing off the food shelf, imagine our supermarket without a host of other by-products that we take for granted, such as candles, furniture polish, soaps, saddle soap, waterproofing for shoes, car wax, canary past, sealing wax, lipstick, eye shadow, mascara, hair condition, hand creams, face creams, bath oils, cotton crops that give us cotton for our cloths. I expect there are many more, the list is endless.

These by-products are not much use to us if we fail to survive along with the Honey Bee. Suddenly this cute little furry thing has become the focus of attraction. I haven't even mentioned how important it can be in the herbal and medical capacity.

The old saying, busy as a bee is accurate, if the poor Honey Bee was to be eradicated from the face of the earth and it was left to me to pollinate every single crop in the world, how would I fair? To start with

I'd have to give up my day job to replace their industrious activities. It wouldn't take long for us to realise we could not possibly pollinate the amount of plants they do in a day. To collect a pound of honey a Bee has to fly more than 50,000 miles that's equivalent to twice round the world. It would involve visiting tens of thousands of flowers, travelling at 22mph. I could not keep up with that sort work load or that sort of speed, so you could count me out.

My mother used to say there is good and bad in every walk of life and it's the same with Bee keepers. The good Bee Keepers produce organic honey, the alternative honey is produced by unscrupulous bee keepers, they feed their bees refined white sugar syrup over the winter months, and we all know how that can affect our immune system never mind the poor Bees. They allow their bees to collect pollen from rapeseed and GM crops who then feed it to their young; it later acts as a slow killer. Some bee keepers even place antibiotics under their hives as a preventive treatment, why if their bees are healthy? It's evident that the bees have now become as sick as the human race and they now need man's modern medicine in an attempt to cure them. Instead the third generation antibiotics are making them even sicker, further attacking their already weak immune system.

This elixir called honey used to be thought of as pure, pure in the sense that bacteria **could not** grow in it, and this is how it could be used for wound healing!

All this contamination has saddened me, but how glad I am to discover that there are some good Bee Keepers out there who have a good conscience and strive to keep the honey pure as it was originally intended. They are the 'Organic Honey Producers', I used to think all honey was organic, apparently if it does not boast it on the jar, assume it is not. Care should be taken also when reading the label; if it says pure honey on the jar then it should not have sugar labelled under the ingredients. If it lists sugar in the small print that means they have been feeding the hive with white re-find sugar over the winter months to keep up their honey production. But people like my sister who are allergic to white refined sugar will have a reaction immediately. She doesn't have to read the label, her body will tell her.

I rang up a honey company while I was compiling this chapter and spoke to the manager who informed me that labelling regulations are very strict these days. If it says Pure Honey on the label with no mention of sugar in the ingredients, one can assume there is no sugar in its production. So on this gentleman's say so, I have decided to trust them on this one, but low and behold if I ever find out they are lying on the jar.

I recall not so long ago when I visited my sister; she randomly asked if I was still keen on preserving the Honey Bees. I told her my enthusiasm hadn't faltered; she offered to ring a friend of hers who lived in a farm house next to her old farm. I was all for it, Gweno made the phone call and lucky for us Mary the Bee Keeper was home alone, she was so excited about our unexpected phone call. Gweno drove both of us to her old stamping ground and on knocking on her front door she quickly ushered us through her home on to the patio at the back of the house, where this beautiful quaint dwelling opened up into a magical old fashioned English garden. I thought Peter Rabbit was going to pop his head round the corner any minute. We made ourselves comfortable while she busied herself making afternoon tea for the three of us on the raised wooden patio. As she was pouring the tea I smiled inwardly thinking how lovely it was to see her so excited our visit, she quickly explained how she'd originally inherited the hives off her brother years ago when he decided to go on holiday. Before embarking on his holidays, she reluctantly agreed to look after the hives but to her surprise he transported the hives from down south to her home in mid Wales. On his return he congratulated her on how well she'd taken care of his Bees but he no longer wanted them. And here started her passion for Bee Keeping.

While sitting in this tranquil setting, bathed in beautiful warm sunshine, we became aware of the humming of Honey Bees and the presence of butterflies amongst this abundance of wild flowers in her colourful garden. Mary went on to explain how she visits schools and educated school children on Bee keeping. Then in turn they informed their parents of the plight of the Bees, and often the parents would become Bee Keepers in the true sense.

The problem she had was; the children attempt their Bee keeping experience wearing adult Bee suits, which was not very satisfactory. Her aim one day was to obtain somehow child size Bee suits. It wasn't strictly about the funds; firstly she needs to find a manufacturing company to design a 'One size fits all' suite, then they would have to produce them for the right price. Ideally purchase a collection that she could either take from school to school or for each school that showed an interested to own their own.

Although Mary, my new Bee Keeper as I called her had an abundance of butterflies in her garden we won't find them in abundance in the rest of the country.

It was reported that 44% of caterpillars have vanished from Britain in recent years, so butterflies are also on the decline too. Did you also know that 46 wildlife species associated with broadleaved woodlands have become extinct in the last 100 years? Which means Einstein's theory may well be on its way.

We have to accept that we all have a job to do in life that includes the animal kingdom. Once that link is broken, the chain of events cannot always take place and the race of life gets mixed up.

I wonder, when did this chain start to perish? In order to find out I need to go back and delve into the history of Bees.

History of the Honey Bee

I wanted to find out; when did this sweet sticky substance called honey begin? It appears to have been here pretty much since time began, we know it's steeped in ancient history. Pre-historic man took honey from wild bees, long before bee keepers were even thought of.

It is written in many places that Bees are thought to have originated from Paradise and are traditionally known as "little servants of God" or "Divine Messengers" In ancient times they believed they had knowledge of the future and all secrets.

It is mentioned in the Bible 38 times, in such context as "The land of milk and honey"

The Egyptians traded honey and bees wax along the East African coast for a long time, and Ancient Greeks claimed it was the first stable food.

Remarkably honey has been found in perfect condition in an Egyptian tomb from 3,300 years BC. Hippocrates the 'Father of modern medicine' used honey for treating ulcers, a practice that continues in modern day Hospitals today.

People with great importance choose the emblem of the Bee as it symbolised high status. It has been seen on paintings, coffins including Egyptian King Men-Kau-ra 2,500BC, and the 239th Pope Urban VIII chose it as his emblem and it can be seen on the Basilica of St Peters in Rome. Napoleon, also choose images of Bees to decorate his robes and flags.

I would like to point out at this stage that when I chose the image of an old fashioned Bee Hive to be engraved on Julian's head stone I did so before I discovered how our ancestors revered the humble Honey Bee. I simply chose it because it was Julian's next quest, to remind me to preserve its future.

We don't have to go back very far in history to hear when the Bee keeping 'land-slide' started. In Victorian days, it is estimated that one in every three British households used to keep bees for sweet supplements for the table. Our modern day society is way off beat on the ratio of Bee keepers compared to our population. How many Bee keepers do you know? I confess I didn't know of any Bee Keepers at all before I started looking into this dilemma, I only know of two now, after developing an interest.

It is evident from the above that people for centuries have respected this industrious little worker, who are we; to be so careless as to destroy this important link in our chain of survival. I'm worried we will we go down in history as the generation who destroyed the Honey Bee and all it entails.

If we don't all take action now, Einstein's theory just might be put to the test.

They also say honey, is an intelligence food, informed food and miraculous natural substance. I see this sort of mystery writing about our honey Bee in lots of different places, I don't just mean the internet but in new and old books as well. What else don't we know about the honey bee?

I recently read it was traditional to inform the Honey Bees of the Beekeepers death. I asked my sister if she'd ever heard of such a thing, it inspired her to tell me of a true story a friend of hers told her. Her friend was attending a funeral of a Beekeeper up North, if you can visualise this scene of back to back houses and cobbled stoned street. As the funeral procession began, down came this swarm of honey bees and they hovered behind the funeral hearse all the way to the church and then suddenly dispersed just as quickly as they appeared when the coffin was taken in to the church.

Was this a coincidence or were they paying respect to their Keeper just like the mourners.

It leaves me wondering are they wiser than we give them credit for and are they truly intelligent, informed and miraculous. These days, our generation are more worried about being stung than they are about preserving their life saving insect. The very mention of the word bees makes some people automatically think of the killer bees' The film called 'Killer Bees' was first shown in 1974 and four years later in 1978 another film called 'The Swarm' graced our screens. Such films haven't helped our psychological phobia with the possibility of been sting. But is it fact or fiction, do killer bees exist? Unfortunately they do, it's yet another man-made mess. He's interfered with nature once too often; no wonder nature is turning on him. It's like teasing a dog once too many times, then wondering why it's turned vicious. Man then has the audacity to demand the death sentence to be handed out on 'man's best friend' I think there appears to be a bully in the equation somewhere here. It looks as if man is now handing out the same death sentence to 'man must have to survive' our furry little friend the Honey Bee. So how did the Killer Bee come about?

The Africanized Bee had already evolved into an angry breed some time ago in the wild, because its home or hive was constantly been invaded and destroyed by the 'Honey Badgers' but when they were crossed bred with South American Bees, the American Bee character changed and evolved into a much more ferocious bee which kill. They were originally scientifically and deliberately cross bred, but accidently released into the environment by a Brazilian Biologists in the late 1960's. I cannot find any proof that this vicious Bee has ventured onto the coast of Britain yet. The only information I could find was this vicious breed of bees cannot survive cold winters. If that's the case wrap up warm and start hoping for cold winters.

Although scientists have been involved with nearly all of our food interference over the last sixty years, they haven't yet managed to go so far as to reproduce honey in a synthetic form.

Thankfully medical scientists have **given up** on how to reproduce honey chemically, but not because declined but because they failed.

Some say only the Bees know the precise ingredients that go into producing this golden elixir, although man has identified 200 of its components he has only been able to replicate six of them. No wonder they call it a miracle elixir, maybe they truly are Gods divine little helpers, if it's beyond man's conquest.

But in trying to decipher the code they did discover one thing accidently, that bacteria can't live in pure honey, but bacteria will multiply and breed if refined sugar is present. That would explain why modern day bee keepers need the assistance of antibiotics to heal the bees after they have fed them white re-fined sugar after becoming sick. Problem then exists, if the bees have been given antibiotics, are we later inadvertently taking antibiotics in the honey? Worst still what if it's an antibiotic we happen to be allergic too!

A question that's often asked by Diabetics is; can they eat honey? I don't want to be targeted, for misleading the public regarding the safety of consuming this golden food, but instead, I will quote a book called "Honey Revolution"—Restoring the health of Future Generation, written by Ron Fessenden MD, MPH and Mike Mclanes MRPS. Dec 2008, sadly printed just one month after Julian died. He stated that the opinion amongst the general public, doctors and other health professionals is 'No.' it's not safe for Diabetics.

The conventional question is that, honey and diabetics don't go together. He states the question Diabetic sufferers should be asking their Doctors is; "If fruits are permitted in their diet, a tablespoon of organic honey consists of the same carbohydrates as a quarter cup of raw apples". He also says that Diabetics can be <u>assured honey contains significant lower blood sugar response than the equivalent amount of refined sugar</u>. In fact he says; if honey is consumed regularly over a period of weeks and months, Honey will lower blood sugar levels.

Research has shown; using Humans it reduced the glucose readings.

They know honey is directly converted to liver glycogen and does not raise blood sugar levels the same as sucrose.

This could also explain why Diabetics find that some honey reduces their blood sugar readings while other honey elevates their glucose readings! Is this winter sugar feed a contributing factor? In similar words of Shakespeare 'Too sweet or not too sweet that is the question'?

You will always come across a diabetic die-hard who believe that honey is a bad food. I'm not recommending diabetics should take it, but if you are like most diabetics (not all diabetics) who indulge often in white sugar treats because your cravings get the better of you, exchange it for a safer and more natural product, preserved for you since pre historic man.

How ironic my first Christmas without Julian I was given a book on how to become a Bee Keeper, the last chapter discussed 'Bee Keeping for Disabled'

Of course Julian would not have needed to read this chapter to inspire him or give him confidence to have a go. I'm sure if he had survived we both would be avid Bee Keepers by now. Raising money for charity by selling jars of honey, but he wouldn't have stopped there I'm sure, we'd be in full production with the by-products of honey as well. The money would not have been crucial to him, but more of a 'I can do it just as well as the next man can, if not better' attitude to the task.

But he doesn't have to prove his worth anymore; his work was done and set aside just as the lyrics in the song says.

How can I become a Non-Active Bee Keeper?

That's contradiction in itself, isn't it? One would think either I am or I am not a bee keeper, but I'm probably like most other people and don't feel I can commit myself to such dedication as a good Bee Keeper. Mostly because of the constraints it puts to one's life style. That does not mean; I'm not willing to support their cause in other ways. For those who are keen to have a go; I came across one recommendation for beginners that they should firstly be made aware of the workload that's involved. The article suggested starting an apprenticeship in Bee keeping, by working alongside a person with a wealth of knowledge in order to learn from that person's mistakes, learning from your own mistakes just hinders you from moving on. Alternatively it also suggests going on a beginner's course.

But how can I become a Bee Keeper for others without the daily commitment?

I could 'Bee-Bug-friendly'!

By avoiding using bug killing pesticides in my garden, I did read an article recommending using organic ways to manage pests instead. One such product was called Enzyme, it stated it can be used in organic gardening without causing harm to our Honey Bees, but it stressed to be careful what type of enzyme one buys. There are other enzymes used for, drains, septic tanks and swimming pools which are toxic.

In my opinion 'None' is the best choice, because it doesn't make good environmental sense to kill all insects in our garden if they are beneficial to each other, they can keep the balance of nature in check. If I used pesticides on my plants, it would then cascade onto the soil causing the soil to be toxic for my next plantation.

By eradicating pesticides it allows the Bees to collect non-contaminating pollen keeping their memory sharp allowing them to find their way home and what's more, take 'safe food' home to their hive? I remember seeing in French vineyards, farmers planting rose bushes at the end of each row of vine to entice insects like green fly to land on the roses instead of his vines. That what I call working with nature.

How else can I become a Bee Keeper for others?

I could conjure up a 'Bee-live society'.

I didn't know it was illegal to kill a Honey Bee in this country, because of the consequences on humanitarian grounds? They say it's unnecessary, selfish and will ultimately destroy our future generation and eventually our planet. There is also an old superstition, it is considered unlucky to kill a Honey Bee. We know why now, we lesser our own survival chance if we lesser theirs.

I hope history does not document that our life time was the "Era of the missing Honey Bees"

But not to worry even if someone does document it, there will be no one around to read it.

Not swatting the honey Bee policy ensures both of our survival.

How else can I become a Bee Keeper for others?

I could educate people on the 'Bee-re-homed' service.

Let's think big; to start with do you know what to do if a swarm of Bees come into your garden? For a start it is considered to be a sign of good fortune. Once you've got over the shock of good luck being bestowed upon you, contact your local Environmental Health or the

Police Station. Both places will have a list of local Bee Keepers who will come to your aid and skilfully remove the hive for you and rehome them. (Have your local Environmental Health telephone number handy.)

Photograph of Mary my Bee Keeper in her Honey Shed
holding a Hive Transporter.

How else can I become a Bee Keeper for others?

I could instigate a 'Bee-voice' organisation by being their advocate or mouth peace in society ensuring contamination free pollen is made available to them.

In their defence, folk like you and I need to fight on their behalf to eradicate all that's harmful in all our crops world-wide at all cost, if not the cost could be very personal.

How else can I become a Bee Keeper for others?

I could 'Bee-friend' a local producer by buying his honey.

I discovered that eating honey from your local environment acts as a vaccine? It introduces a dummy virus into the body then tricks it into believing it has been invaded, triggering the immune system to respond.

This produces antibodies to fight foreign invaders. When the body is exposed to the pollen, the antidote is then ready for them. The pollen in the honey is very low compared to sniffing a flower directly. Ideally the honey-eater will not have any reaction at all. Consequently you're less lightly to suffer from hay fever.

A study was done on three groups of people at Xavier University, New Orleans they all suffered allergies, the ones who showed the most improvement were the ones who ate local honey for only six weeks, compared to those who took supermarket honey harvested from around the world. The third group were not given any honey at all; no change in their condition was recorded. So eating local honey really does help or eradicate asthma, the local pollen that caused the asthma in the first place is the same pollen the honey bees collect to take back to their hive and magically converts it into the golden elixir called honey, which acts as the antidote to the dreaded asthma. Isn't nature fantastic! (Don't forget baby's under 12 months should not be given honey on the account their immune system isn't fully operational yet.)

How else can I become a Bee Keeper for others?

I could 'Bee-prepared' for emergencies.

What we all worry about the most is "What happens if I get stung?" If we have to have the Bees in our lives to survive then we need to learn to live side by side with them, like our ancestors did.

Some of us might need to get our defences up, against any invasion. So how are we going to arm our self against any possible danger? Julian always invested in plan 'B' this one can be ours. Let's not behave like Ostriches, whether we are allergic to Bee stings or not we should all know how to treat any sting. In case you're stung accidently, what's your plan?

First thing first; is it a Bee sting or a wasp sting we are dealing with and would you recognise the different species?

Honey Bees have a rounded body, usually hairy with hairy legs and feeds on pollen and nectar.

Whereas wasps usually have a more slender smoother body, they are predators or parasites of other insects, basically scavengers? To confuse you, they both have a thin junction between thorax and abdomen and have a waist like appearance.

Are you better informed or more confused? Try this one to help you differentiate between the two.

If you're out BBQ'ing in the summer and you appear to be plagued with one of these little specimens, place an old jam jar with some Strawberry jam diluted with water somewhere in the garden preferably away from the guests.

If the sticky water attracts the little fella's one can assume you have a wasp in your presence. But if it shows no interest in the jam it's quite possible you have a Honey Bee as an unexpected guest, Honey Bees do not like strawberry jam. Now you've recognised it lets get back to the sting.

I have already mentioned it's only the older Honey Bees that sting and they only sting once, then they die. They don't really want to die; they have a busy day ahead of them, the rule is they only sting when provoked, if we leave them alone they will leave us alone so that removes any hysteria from the equation. While were all still very calm the first aid treatment for a Honey Bee sting is to remove the sting by pulling or scrapping it with a knife, it's not a tweezers job. You are more likely of squeez the venom further in to the skin if you're using a pair of tweezers. The act of removing the sting is to prevent causing a secondary infection. Household immediate remedy consists of either making a paste of Baking Soda or dissolving an aspirin and dab it on to the local area to help reduce the inflammation. There are non-herbal believers who discredit this treatment.

Carrying Anti-histamine tablets or cream is useful and observe the person closely for 24 hours. Looking out for hives, itching, shortness of breath and if there is any difficulty breathing, seek emergency medical attention immediately if this occurs.

If you know you are at risk of developing an allergy you should carry an Epi-pen at **all** times. I mean at **all** times it's not fair on others who cannot help you if you have left your pen at home. If you live close to any Honey Bees they recommend a regular intake of Zinc, it is meant to inhibit the Bees from stinging Humans. Check with your pharmacy first in case Zinc is contradicting with your prescribed drugs.

Wasp stings are slightly different, this little might has two prongs, they stab with one sword like a jabbing action then the other, when it's deep enough the wasp injects the venom. Immediate first aid treatment for this one is bath with a diluted solution of cider vinegar or lemon juice to neutralize the venom. First Aid recommends a cold compress, but dis-courage ice therapy with both Bee and wasp stings as this constricts the skin surface, therefore helping to retain the venom. For after treatment dab with calamine lotion to sooth the area. If the pain persists take Anti-histamine orally or apply anti-histamine cream locally if that fails to ease it, seek medical advice. If stung in the mouth or throat, minimise the swelling with ice therapy, ice is permissible in this instance by sucking Ice cubes or sipping cold drinks slowly and seek medical advice. Again the same applies watch for 24hours for any problem breathing. See! To 'Bee-fore-armed' is better than to 'Bee-frightened'.

You might be thinking why does the two of them need such different treatments? Allegedly wasp stings are alkaline so it needs acid to be neutralized by using vinegar. On the other hand Bee venom is acidic so it needs alkaline to neutralise it, example that's given is sodium of bicarbonate.

Scientifically the jury is still out on these handy kitchen treatments, but scientists do accept that human psychology comes into play with pain relief and that if we believe these kitchen cabinet remedies will work, they will. They obviously recognise the saying 'Mind over matter' really can work. <u>Will</u> it work or can we <u>will</u> it to work, that is the question?

I consider the glove compartment is as good a place as any to keep Anti histamine cream, taking into account we are never too far from our vehicles usually. Take extra care when hiding it in the glove compartment, if you are lightly to have small children rummaging.

How can this help the Bees? We're learning to live side by side and accepting them back into our lives like a long lost prodigal relative.

How else can I become a Bee Keeper for others?

I could 'Bee-suit' little ones.

I haven't forgotten Mary the Bee keeper who took over her brother hives and is still looking for a company who has the skill to produce a child friendly garment, if that person is you then I would be willing to match your commitment by fundraising to pay for these suits so enthusiast's like Mary can continue to create an interest in our next generation of Bee keepers.

How else can I become a Bee Keeper for others?

I can create a 'Bee-awareness' amongst these pages.

Although the future of our Honey Bee is hanging in the balance, thankfully there is a hive of activity going on in the Bee keeper's world.

We're starting to see Bee-Fanatics out there, who are willing on behalf of others to take care of new Bee hives; they all have different catch phrases like 'Adopt a Bee Hive'. They intend to start a new Bee colony by offering a twelfth share of a Hive. In return for your money you receive a shareholder certificate, wild flower seeds to attract more Bees and a 1lb of honey for around £30, or an entire hive for £350. This is generally the total running cost of a hive for 12 months.

Someone did say to me recently "You can buy a hives cheaper than that"

After some thought, what I would of like have said to that person is, I'm sure he could, but the above cost is for working the hive not buying it. In fact, if he was worried about cost he could build one free of charge if he down load a pattern off the internet accompanied with instructions on how to assemble one, and if he used recycled wood from his garage or garden shed. But if he had no knowledge of how to maintain the hive, how to handle the bees, how to look after the Queen, how to keep the hives clean, how to fumigate the hive, how to re-home colonies, how to harvest the honey, how to treat the honey, how to jar it, how to label it legally, how to produce other by-products such as bees wax, how to deal with a swarm of bees, how to care for them in different seasons, how to sell it, but most important how to keep himself safe. What I'd be paying for was their years of expertise on the subject, not a cheap possible infected second hand wood empty hive!

How else can I become a Bee keeper for others?

I could be part of the 'Bee-honest' with Bee keepers.

I have this year dug up all my plants and recycled them by giving them to others and planted wild flowers instead, to my amazement I have witnessed the return of the Honey Bee in my garden, the dotty little lady bird, lots of butterfly's and caterpillars. To my surprise I have not been plagued with green or black fly. Why is that then? Could it be, I left my garden for nature to take care of itself? For once I stopped interfering with nature. How lovely to hear the sound of the Honey Bee back in my life once more and the sweet smelling fragrance of wild flowers as the sun warms the perfume in the air.

Monty Don a well-known gardener on the television suggests we should create a garden with a gentle disorder so that we can enjoy the privilege of hosting a vibrant Bee population by planting open flowers, **not** closed tight petals.

The Bees thrive best on open petal flowers such as British bluebells (not the robust Spanish blue bells that threaten to take over the delicate English ones), and crocus's in the spring. Honey suckle, lavender, thyme, geranium, buddleia, rosemary, cornflower, hollyhocks and evening primrose in the summer and Daisies and salvia in the autumn. Heather in the winter, 'Heather Honey' is so highly prized. Bee keepers love their Bees to collect pollen from heather; it provides colonies with a good store of food for the winter when bees cannot forage. So go ahead get some heather in your garden to aid their survival over the winter months.

By ensuring the garden has bloom throughout the year the Bees stand a better chance of survival. Bee keepers believe if you hear buzzing in the garden it's a good sign, as a child I found the sound of summer was defined by the sound of the humming bees.

They say we would not think twice of giving a bunch of flowers to a valid friend, so why not say it with flowers to the Bees? That's alright for the summer, but what about offering them a Christmas present by planting heather in the garden so they don't have to dine on refined sugar syrup on Christmas day.

Another lady who has stirred a lot of enthusiasm recently is Sarah Raven who appeared on BBC2 program called 'Bees, Butterflies and Blooms' she is on a mission to inspire all of us whether we live in the country side, village, towns or cities to get planting nectar rich plants. She believes in 'people power' making small changes to stop extinctions and secure a stronger helping hand to our little pollinators. You could have witnessed this lady's handiwork at the 'Pollination friendly landscape at the Olympic Park' in London and other city centres in Britain.

Photograph of wild flowers I grew in my garden for the sake
of our local Bee Keepers.

How else could I become a non-active Bee keeper?

I could encourage non-Bee keepers to actually become fully fledged
and much admired 'Bee-Keepers' Mary my Bee keeper in Welshpool,
now sells new flat pack Bee Hives, and offers evening classes on how to
take care of the much needed Bees.

By sharing the responsibility of Bee Keeping, it ensures more colonies
for the future.

Our future is already sounding a bit sweeter, but I fear we may have
treated this little creature very badly in recent years, who's only purpose
in life was to supply us with the precious golden elixir of life. Thankfully
it has transpired that I can do a lot more than I originally thought to
help these little furry friends without actually keeping Bees myself.

Suddenly I feel like an important link in the honey production, and
I hope it will turn out to be a sweet success story as long as we all pull
together.

Native American Indians fourth rule is, "Work together for the
benefit of all mankind"

I also read of a quote by Edward Everette Hale who once wrote,

I am only one, but I am one.
I cannot do everything,
But I can do something.
And I will not let what
I cannot do interfere
With what I can do. Reminisce

As one, I joined up with my sister Gweno and as two we organised a party and called it 'Gathering of the clan' we invited all our extended family armed with their old black and white photos to reminisce over the good old days. The idea of this party was to raise awareness that up until now we have been able to organise family get together since time began, but if we fail to take care of the Honey Bee then there won't be a future generation to enjoy such party's as these.

To further aid the cause we organised a raffle, which incidentally raised exactly £350. Our intention that day was to buy a 'Family Hive' then ask Mary our friend the Bee Keeper to take charge of our hive. But sadly she informed us that nature had taken a turn for the worse, and the Bees had been starved of their normal abundance of pollen due to an unusual dry spring and fierce beating rain storms had destroying the pollen they had enjoyed in previous years. So although she agreed the world needs many, many more hives there is now a more pressing crisis and that is the inadequate amount of pollen. Because of these disastrous freak weather conditions; consequently the honey production has plummeted leaving the Bee keepers with no choice but to leave the small amount of honey in the hives for the Bees to feed on over the winter months in order to survive for next year. Because of this crisis we agreed that our fundraising money would be better spent purchasing bushes for this autumn, heather for the winter, flowering trees for next spring and wild flowers for next summer.

Because of the 'Gathering of the Clans' success, Gweno and I are thinking of organising an annual 'Clan' event, hoping it will inspire others to do the same with their family tree in their own village or town. Wouldn't it be lovely to create an orchard for the 'love of the Bees', with benches and bird baths dedicated to past ancestors as a place of rest and to enjoy nature at its best! With maybe a summerhouse for reading or tranquil music and fluttering butterfly's, but isn't that what the Victorians used to do in days gone by? They might have been financially rich but we can be just as rich appreciating nature.

What a mess we humans have created, I'm afraid it's not just about trying to survive with the depleting Bees, it's also about all the other factors I've uncovered in these chapters.

Detoxing needs to be every body's business and possible priority, especially expectant mothers; they are passing on such things as 'Nano-particles-titanium-dioxide' to their unborn baby's causing them to become very ill in the womb or just after birth, then when they are exposed to their first dose of antibiotics or second helping in their case of Nano-particles-titanium-dioxide the little things accept it with often catastrophic consequences. All this before the defenceless little things have even starts to live. Think on, our future is not just at risk because of the depleting Bees, NO humanitarians are at risk of not surviving because we can't seem to get past the infant stage.

My twelve world issues

I do realise I can't correct these twelve on my own, but I'm willing to start on my own.

If it's true that these five contribute to causing tumour's, then my intension is to take steps in eradicating them out of our environment by attempting to—:

1. Banning Hydrogenated oil
2. Banning Processed food.
3. Banning Toxic Substances.
4. Banning dangerous Environmental Factors.
5. Banning Artificial Sweeteners.

No small task I know, my other causes for concern are the remaining seven that can also lead to all sorts of ill health. I intend to take steps in eradicating these too by—:

6. Banning Pesticides from our food chain.
7. Banning food additives.

8. Banning Genetic Modified food including MSG ? is this right Olwen?
9. Banning growth hormones in the food chain.
10. Banning genetic engineered medication.
11. Convince the medical world, that deranged minerals affect Diabetic.
12. Help prevent further de-pleating Bee Connolly's

It appears to me that the12 issues above have one thing in common and that is; they are all man made problems. If that is the case then man has the technology to repair man's damage.

Something a past employer used to say to me years ago "Don't bother coming into this office complaining if you haven't got an alternative answer in solving the problem Olwen, what do you want me to do about it?"

If I didn't have an alternative approach he would say "Exactly! Nothing" All I had achieved was making my boss cross, myself unpopular and the situation remains unsolved. I hope I don't get trapped into that predicament with my 12 issues, in which case I need to plan a strategy of how these man-made issues can be reversed!

What have I achieved single handed, so far?

Something lots of people took great pleasure in telling me over the years was,

"Don't bother Olwen, you cannot change the world single handed."

I know I cant, I just need a little helping hand and if everybody contributed just a tiny, tiny bit my striving for correction can be achieved much sooner rather than never.

If I take leaf out of Mother Teresa's book when she said, "Don't wait for leaders—do it alone person to person"

So what have I done on my own person to person so far?

. I have received an answer from Kellogg's food company regarding producing organic cereal.

The reply stated, "It's something they have been considering in recent years and may occur at a future date" I feel it's a step in the right direction towards removing toxic pesticides from our food chain.

. I received another letter from Aldi food stores on the 6th April 2011 regarding rapeseed oil in their Mayonnaise. They will be forwarding my concerns to their buying office for their attention.

. I also received another letter on 18th August 2011from Aldi stores regarding rapeseed in their baked beans assuring me my comments would be forwarded to their buying office for their attention.

. I need to continue my letter writing seeking reassurance; when will GM food be deemed safe for human consumption, and why was I hood winked into believing GM food was produced to feed the world, when in fact it was for financial gain. I will continue to bombard them by thinking global but acting locally writing to local Supermarkets, local MP, and local newspaper.

I need to watch out for **brutal policing** in this country when 'good living people' try to protest against lack of GM labelling, as they were in Canada not so long ago. **Is** this the way we want our country to go?

. I wonder if one day I will have the courage to fill a supermarket trolley full of GM food and demand to see the Manager by the till, one busy afternoon so he can explain to me how he/she can allow GM food to be sold in his/her store. My dream will be to see this country boast it's a 'GM free country'

. I found a leaflet promoting Splenda sugar substitute, the leaflet was asking if anyone was interested in holding a fundraising tea party, called "Care for a cuppa" It sounded harmless enough and so friendly, except it was promoting Splenda low calorie sweetener. The event was to mark Diabetes UK's 75th anniversary. I wrote to them asking if they could assure me that these artificial sweeteners were safe to give to already vulnerable people who are suffering with insulin insufficiency. (My thoughts were no wonder Diabetics always appear to be so unwell!)

I received an answer from Diabetes UK on 12th August 2011. Sadly they misunderstood my concerns for the multitude of artificial sweeteners, and instead they sent me a diabetic web page bosting what sweeteners they recommend for their Diabetic patients. To be fair to them, they did warn diabetics not to take **Aspartame** if they were suffering from phenylketonuria that contains phenal-al-nine which exacerbates the phenyl-ketone-urea.

. I did became impatient while waiting for my reply from Diabetic UK, so I rang them on the 0800 number asking the same question verbally if they felt the product they were supporting namely Splenda was a safe product for people who had Diabetes and were already at their most vulnerable state? The answer was very woolly, but I was asked if I wanted to discuss the matter with someone else. I declined, but informed him as he could not assure me it was safe, could I then assure him that if he looked into the history and content of Splenda he would find his findings most interesting.

Unfortunately these companies are so clever, once they realise the public are on to them they secretly move the goal posts by exchanging their trade name product to a code numbers. For example Splenda has now become E954 and E951. Before long we will need to go shopping with a little book full of these codes so we can cross reference them in the supermarket isles, in fear of accidently placing an undesirable food product into our shopping trolleys.

. On the Honey Bee front I have planted wild flowers to encourage the survival of the honey Bee and other wild life such as butterflies. I produced 'Seed bombs' to enhance wild flowers to grow in spaces that would appreciate country colour which would attract wild life like butterflies. It sounds dangerous but all it is; is a mix of compost, clay and wild flower seeds rolled into balls then I tossed into my favourite haunts. Word of warning, most local councils need you to seek permission from them to do this!

. I have also replaced the use of white refined sugar in exchange for organic unrefined cane sugar.

. I've tried to satisfy my sweet pallet with honey when possible. And of course only buy honey that is labelled pure and organic, not with added sugar filed under ingredients.

. I need to persuade the UK to remove chlorine and fluoride from our drinking water just as France, Germany, Belgium, Netherlands, Denmark, Norway, Sweden, Northern Ireland, Austria and the Czech Republic have. According to Professor Joni Jaakkola of University Birmingham, he claims that chlorine in the water supply has doubled the risk of birth defects; it was published in the Daily Mail UK. I need to be on this case too, not to mention untold damage it creates with the thyroid gland.

. On the Pesticides issue I haven't actually done anything constructive yet, but I'm still coming across a lot of sad issues connected to pesticides. One such finding was a book called 'Silent Spring' by Rachel Carson it was written as far back as 1962 about a prediction of a season without the sound of birds as a result of agriculture toxic contamination. A biochemist wrote later on the book, "If man were to follow the teachings of Miss Carson we would return to the Dark ages" He was trying to ridicule her book, nearly fifty years later her prediction in her book came true when on 16th Feb 2011 a French wine-grower became the first farmer to have his death linked to pesticides the headlines read 'The face of a poisoned man-the human cost of pesticides'

The biochemist needs to eat his words!

. I have written to 10 Downing Street asking for an alternative to synthetic human insulin. I'm still awaiting an answer, only because they have no alternative to offer me or the Diabetics of this country.

. I wrote to the Government about alternative to synthetic thyroxin. I'm still awaiting an answer to this one too. As there is no natural alternative yet again, I'm not lightly to get an answer.

. I once grew my own vegetables and I intend to do it again one day, even if it entails renting an allotment plot.

. I did have my own hens once, and supplied the house hold with free range eggs. Next time, I fancy the Japanese bantam short legged breed. Apparently they are the ideal breed for children due to their placid and trusting nature. They're also perfect for the smaller garden as they need very little space. The cock crows relatively soft, and both male and female cause little damage. I'm sure they provide a wonderful talking point too. I'm excited already and I can't wait.

. One wet afternoon four of us, my Father my Sister, Gill our friend and myself attended a study day on how to make simple medicines from the garden. We had to dig our own herbs, prepare our own and label our own then take our own home. I must confess these study days are not cheap but very interesting and educational. You do feel you know what went into the bottle before you administered it. There are many books on the market these days, such as Hedgerow medicine.

. I avoid Hydrogenated oils and fats like the plague and when I'm feeling brave I confess when I'm in supermarkets I give cooking oil containing Rape seed oil a quick twirl so that the customer can see the ingredients label. The other idea being the recognisable label is not on show, hoping other shoppers will consciously not, or buy non-rapeseed oil.

. I've also tackled take away restaurants asking them if they use Rapeseed oil in their cooking, so far they all have proudly announced

"No we use vegetable oil" at which point I've asked them to check if there is Rapeseed listed as one of the ingredients hiding as a vegetable?

It's hard to believe that all this rubbish has been allowed to enter our food and environment, and why the Government hasn't insisted that the Scientists haven't towed the line on their Hippocratic Oath. But guess what! They haven't got one, they don't live by a 'Universal Code of Conduct' like other professionals such as the Doctors and Nurses.

It all makes sense now, anything goes. Thank God someone else has thought of it before me, but his worry was not raised until 1992. It was Sir Joseph Rotblat who suggested in his acceptance speech for his Nobel Peace Prize in 1995 by saying, "The time has come to formulate guidelines for the ethical conduct of scientists, perhaps in the form of a voluntary Hippocratic Oath"

I question the word 'voluntary' why not compulsory?

The UK did heed his recommendation, but not for 12 years, it was as late as 2007 before they devised a seven code principles. Briefly they are—1. Act with skill and care. 2. Prevent corrupt practice. 3. Respect rights of others. 4. Own work must be lawful and justified. 5 Minimise adverse effect on people, animals and eviroment. 6. Listen to the concerns of others. 7. Be honest and accurate in your findings.

But who was Sir Joseph Rotblat; he was a Ashkenazi Jew born in Poland and due to the first world war was uneducated. But he rose up the ranks with evening study to University level and went on to study in Paris with Mari Curie, then Liverpool University and later St Bartholomew's Hospital in London. In his early years he studied the invention of the Atom Bomb but after 1955 he became one of the prominent critics in the Nuclear Arms Race. In 1995 he won the Nobel Peace Prize, and in 1998 he was knighted KCMG. He was involved with 'Stockholm International Peace Research Institute' and also the 'World Health Organisation'. He died in 2005 a widower, after his wife died in Poland during the German occupation when she was only 24.

May be I have bitten off more than I can chew with these twelve issues of mine. If it took Joseph Rotblat 45 years to get a bit of attention over one topic he was passionate about, I can't even think how long it's going to take me. Never mind, maybe others can take over my plight if I get too weary.

But if we are the caretakers of our own bodies, our children and the world we live in, we should be held responsible for becoming 'doers' as well as 'not-doing' something.

I quote another Native American Indian rule, "Take responsibility for your actions"
Hawaiians have a similar saying too,
"Whatever you do, do it for the sake of the next seven generations"

If you think there is nothing the matter with this nation's health then you have nothing to do, but I ask you to go to your nearest town and sit quietly on a bench one afternoon and 'people watch' and see how healthy or how pale all the passers-by look. Some of them look so pale faced, I don't even know how they have the stamina to put one foot in front of the other never mind work.

Incidentally if you have decided to become a doer and are planning on protesting against the things you hold very dear to you, such as one of my twelve world worrying issues let me recap on what I have mentioned before. Let the pen do the talking, that's where the power lies. It's the pen not the sword that will eventually win the war. If you decide to do any peaceful demonstrations, appeal to any 'hot headed' protester who may cause trouble to think again. Don't let their hearts rule their heads. It will not aid the cause but will destroy any additional support you may have gained already.

Let Peace go with you, if or when you decide to go on any marches.

When I first became a widow I approached six different organisations to help me defend Julian's case, they were a Solicitor, who specialised in medical negligence, Action Against Medical Accidents (AAMA), Court of Human Rights, POhWER, ICAS, and lastly PALS, but as a result of all their negative-ness I decided to push on single handed against all odds with Julian's book instead. They say everything happens for a reason; in this case I'm glad no one took me on. I could never of given them this much information in a letter or in a quick chat.

I hope in Julian's defence I haven't excluded anything, as they say 'exhausted all topics'

As one comes to the end of an evening one extends gratitude for their hospitality, now as I'm coming to the end of Julian's book I feel the need to extend my gratitude for Julian's company on my life's journey, also for the things he taught me, the outstanding things we did together, things that I might not of experienced had I married a boring man.

Even though we had those last five weeks together, at the very end I didn't actually say 'Good bye' properly, not while he still had his faculties about him, but does anybody? My biggest regret is I didn't **thank** him either.

Thank you

So now I would like to extend a belated thank you to him in his absence, I hope he can hear me where ever he is! To start with I'd like to thank him for the 29 wonderful years of happy memories he gave me. He worked so very hard to create a normal life here on earth for Llewela and I to enjoy.

The day before Julian's fever broke I asked him to research something on the computer for me on behalf of the Brownies; he agreed to do it after accusing me of being a 'last minute dot com'. His next comment has haunted me ever since, his words were "One day you will miss me" and that I certainly have done that, just reminiscing those few words makes me want to cry because although he was in a wheelchair, I know plenty of people who live very boring existences even though they have been blessed with a strong strapping body. Life's not all about what you've been given, but more about what you can do with your life once it's been given to you. Not to paint to Romanic a picture of him, he always displayed an edge of aggression in his tone. He had to be this way, otherwise society could easily mistake his physical 'low down sitting position' for mental inadequacy which could beckon 'Patronisation' His loud vocal-ness accompanied with in-depth knowledge on every subject, forced people to stop and take notice of his intellect. Consequently he was quickly accepted as 'One of the people' he treated life very much as, we only have one stab at it, so he attacked it swiftly then moved on.

My first thank you I'd like mention is, for teaching me the value of 'Don't think about it, just do it' even if it seems impossible, at least have a go. My first experience of this was in the summer of 1980 when he first drove the 900 miles down to the south of France. The very next morning he made me push his wheelchair through very hot soft sand (do you know how difficult that is?) to the sea edge, he then asked me to push him right into the sea, waist high. With a rubber ding-gee in tow dancing on a piece string behind us, he shockingly asked me "Now tip me into the sea" I refused protesting, "I can't the beach is packed, someone might think I'm trying to drown you, and they might call the police" His reply was "Just do it" and as I did the whole beach went, "Ahhhh" but to my surprise no one intervened, not even when I was struggled to pushed the rubber ding-gee under his 'butt' You'd think someone who was paralyzed from high chest down would be too frightened of jumping out of this safety zone into potential dangerous deep water.

It felt as if he was committing kamikaze, but not to Julian his motto was 'get in there and experience life'.

Photograph of Julian; achieving the same thing in life as others, only done in a slightly differently manner.

My second thank you is for teaching me the magic of spontaneity, I recall one such incident when he did an emergency break again in France and turned to face Llewela in the back seat and randomly asking her, "Do you fancy a camel ride, Llewela"? Llewela of course said yes. He quickly did a three point turn with the camper van and then suddenly pulled into a layby. And sure enough, there they were all huddled up in the shade a herd of camels all roped together waiting to be hired.

A photograph of Llewela and I trying to balance on
this poor camel.

While the two of us went on our unexpected jaunt, Julian decided to have a little experience of his own. He courageously or stupidly transferred himself across from the driving seat to the passenger seat then spun the passenger seat round 90 degrees enabling him to transfer himself into his wheel chair. He then opened the sliding door and very gingerly dropped himself still sitting in the wheelchair in a reversed position onto the car park. Imagine our horror when we discovered the van empty on our return only to find him precariously balancing on the edge of the marsh land 'fishing' What if he'd fallen into the water? Llewela and I wouldn't have a clue where to start looking for him!

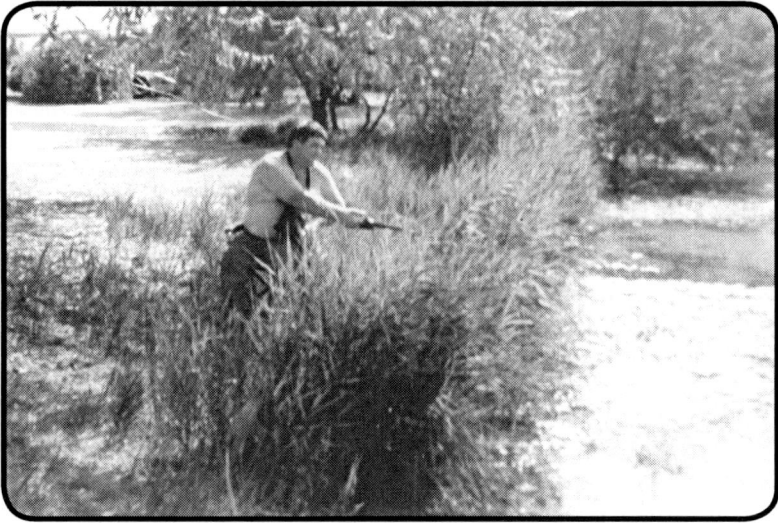

Photograph of Julian with both front wheels sunk over their
heads in marshy ground.

My third thank you, I'd like to extend, is to one of the young men
who came to visit me just after Julian died. He told me that Julian
had said to him one hot and sunny afternoon in France that "No one
appreciated him like Olwen and Llewela did, so when he shouted at us,
it hurt his feelings very much."

I'm grateful that Anthony shared those few words with me, I can take
it he loved Llewela and I very much because we both experienced his
short fuse of high explosive temper towards the end. At the time we both
assumed it was his high standard of workmanship but I now I realise his
Adrenal tumour must have played a big part with his fiery but short lived
quick temper, his character had been affected by his fight, fear and flight
mechanism. It was nice to discover in the after math what we both knew
all along that 'He truly did love us' I have recently read about 'conflict',
by an assistant Professor Tabitha Holmes who wrote in her book, that "A
conflict a day is about the right amount of rowing necessary" to keep a
healthy relationships going.

She was surprised to discover in her research that teenagers
themselves found 'locking horns' with parents brought families closer
together. She was more worried that teens that don't get involved in a
heated argument may develop into 'yes' men or women. She also felt
conflict must be positive and parents need to listen to teenager's point of

view and then modify their own opinion. Off course she also relayed that constant on-going arguments are not healthy either.

Shouting aside I would like to thank him for all his teachings, he taught me that every job must be done to the highest perfection.

There was no point asking him to inspect a task he set me, if I knew it was open to criticism.

My first encounter with his teaching was after we had just met, he asked me if I knew how to change a wheel on a car? I confessed I didn't, but I didn't own a car either or drive one. That didn't seem to matter he was going to show me anyway. Once he showed me, he then said, "Now you do it" luckily I had paid attention. Proud of my accomplishment he said, "Now do it again, and if you ever get a puncture as a passenger you'll know exactly what to do"

That was my first introduction to surviving skills, many more were to follow. They ranged from simple ones to near impossible ones, simple like putting air pressure in to tyres, from not too much and not too little, whatever it said in the manual book.

On the DIY front, I needn't bother to start sizing up a job without a tape measure. A teenager said to him once, "It's the width of a finger nail" Julian went berserk shouting, "Whose finger nail, yours, mine the babies, who's"? Being accurate at all times mattered to him, including visiting the DIY ware house, he considered it a stupid practice not to go armed with a tape measure, he claimed no one would ever lend you one, "It was the tool of their trade".

The second tool I had to be familiar with, and was made to use on every surface was a set square. Who did I think I was, to be more accurate than this tool!

The third tool I had to respect was a level, I had to take care of this clumsy thing, and making sure I never dropped it or damaged it in anyway. I had to make sure it was kept clean, ensuring no cement dried on it making it uneven next time I needed it. I admit I didn't have an eye for level, so it was common sense to treasure this tool.

I was warned never to drop a chisel or a pair of scissors, he used to say, "Dropping a chisel destroys its sharpness, and did I fancy sitting up late at night sharpening the chisels like he did?"

Storing a hand saw in a safe place was imperative; otherwise I would be reminded of how difficult it was to sharpen its teeth, and did I want to stay up late sharpening each tooth?

Another thing I learnt early on was be careful and don't break anything, replacing it meant time spent away from the job. Working in a clutter free area prevented a lot of damage, even simple things like standing on a three point plug; it could deem the equipment useless if you didn't have a new plug to replace it immediately. If you had to go out and buy a new plug, then again the job came to a standstill. That's time wasted.

Of course if the tools did become damaged precious day light hours would have to be sacrifice for the sake of the job, that's what evenings were for, repairing and planning next day activities.

These were tools of the trade he was teaching me to looking after, how could I possibly do a good job with useless tools. I'd only end up blaming bad workmanship because of poor maintained tools.

He taught me to always think one job ahead to save time, time was precious to him, and it should be for me too. He would spend hours planning the next day's task the night before, questioning himself did he have the right tools for the job, did he need to buy something before that day ended, did he need help, did he need to pick some ones brains who knew how to do the job better than him, there was no point been proud, but most of all could he look it up on the computer, and educate himself beforehand no point repeating other peoples mistakes. Preparation was everything.

Those are of course the practical jobs, but the same rules applied to any studying.

I'm sure Llewela will vouch for that, all those years he trained her to be methodical and focus on the task until it was finished. I look at Llewela and I see a miniature Julian, he's left all his traits behind with her. He used to make her a 'home made diary' for term time at school, pointing out when she should start what project, when it should be finished, when it should be handed in, when she should expect the results, when she should start the next one, where she should be looking for research. This tough training started when she was 11, but she still used the same format later at university. He knew what he was doing all those years ago putting himself through university life for four years so he could recognise the pitfalls, the highs and the lows of Uni life. So when the time came he was better prepared to give her guidance and support. As things turned out he wasn't there for any of her Uni life but she had, good grounding. I know because she never once rang home to say, "Mum what shall I do?" She probably thought; what would Dad do? And there was her answer. Thank you Julian!

Llewela was not the only person Julian supported. There were lots of other people who have approached me since he died, saying Julian taught them this or that, put them on the right track for their career. People who I had no idea had been to the house for computer lessons while I was at work. I'm sure it was free of charge, because he often used to say, "I don't deal in money, I only deal in favours and when I'm desperate I cash in my favours" In other words he traded in favours, but I don't suppose any one realised what his game was.

I'd like to thank him for all the hours he gave me supporting me with my Brownies with his computer skills, his bright ideas, hours on end producing pamphlets, craft items used in teaching brownie skills. He always had a simple but clever angle on getting things over to them. It all helped the future generation understand the quirkiest of tasks. He did endless research on facts and figures so I would not be caught out on a limb without an answer for that odd question. He put himself in their position and thought; what I would want to know about this subject if I was a child. This did not include umpteen trips to packed holiday sights to check out their health and safety, what was happening locally and what 'Theme' would best lend itself to the sight. Thank you Julian!

I want to thank him for originally organising the Jones's gathering for the Annual Christmas bash. He was always conscious about over burdening Mum and Dad with extra work, so he encouraged all of us to share the load with the idea of the 'Bring and Share table'. This then extended to Easter gatherings, with the grand children first spending the afternoon doing Easter crafts followed by the Easter egg hunt. Summer would bring the Strawberry tea party with its Crocket, Badminton, and Table Tennis on the lawn.

Late summer, we would have Barbecues for different family birthdays, in the orchard on sunny days under the shelter of marques on rainy days. Autumn would bring Guy Fawkes Night, with a great big bonfire and the stuffed Guy on top.

Gweno and I might have organised the food and negotiated the dates but it was always his idea in the first place. With or without good weather it still went ahead. The idea of sitting at a banquet table with all the immediate family breaking bread together appealed to Gweno and I. Now in Julian's absence we continue this tradition, recently my parents celebrated their 55th Emerald Wedding Anniversary, 95 of the extended family turned up to celebrate and reunite. It started at four in the afternoon; we shared a cold buffet, followed by Welsh cakes and Bara Breath not forgetting 'digon o de' plenty of tea. Gill and her friend Brenda accompanied by her daughter Eilwe . . . . who all sung with such angelic voices. How strange that Gill has become so involved in our lives when she only knew Julian for four weeks. You notice I didn't mention a disco; discos are fun when you want to dance, but when you want to talk and be able to hear what's being said, you just need the sound of chatting and the odd song here and there.

Thank you for teaching me how healthy it is to remember our roots, it can help to ground us. This happened when I discovered such a story of my Grandmother contracting Diphtheria while at school, 13 children in her school class was infected and 12 out of the 13 died. The sole survivor of that sad episode was my grandmother. Without her survival none of us would be around to celebrate that big family get-together. Thank you Julian; for reminding me that family trees are fine, but meeting the people behind the name is so much nicer.

I think the biggest lesson in life he ever taught, me was, 'never grumble'.

I never once caught him grumbling about his health, his disability, but most of all his poverty. You would never hear him say, "Why does it always happen to me" but he did used to say, "Why shouldn't it happen to me, it happens to everybody else". Thank you for putting things into perceptiveness Ju.

His cousin Lynn once sent me a letter from her Hospital bed when she had to spend a short spell on bed rest herself. The letter was full of admiration for Julian's stamina for sticking it out on bed rest for months

645

on end, never knowing when it was going to end. He used to tell me the exercise taught him patience, and he treated the punishment as time out to mentally work out his future plans. I used to look on and think, this man never wastes a minute. I too, like his cousin thank him for teaching us by example.

Sometimes we all have; days when everything seems to go wrong, when I had them he would say, "Can you do anything about it"? If I said, "Yes", he would say "Do it then" if I said, "No" he would say, "Stop worrying about it then, wasting time and energy over something you can't change" Thank you for teaching me, worry never helped anyone only made them ill.

Do you remember at the beginning of our married life he told me not to be house proud!

I recently asked a patient if he had any hobbies, he pondered a while then said "None, I've just spent all my life keeping the house in good condition. Decorating, checking the guttering, gardening, maintaining and polishing the cars every weekend" The conversation soon dried up, my mind drifted to Julian's instructions all those years ago. I then started to think what had this man done for others? How had he improved the world we live in? What had he contributed to charity? This poor man's life echoed emptiness, I then realised what Julian meant.

I mentioned this tale to a friend, she replied, "But he will leave a house well kept" True, I thought, but the garden still needs tending along with all the other jobs the following year, what lasting imprint has he left in this world? Ironically that morning I read in an angel guidance book

'Some people become so fixed on order, that they lose their spontaneity. In such cases, tidying up is a delay tactic to avoid working towards their life purpose and happiness. There should be a balance between enjoying and needing organization'.

It made even more sense now. It also brings to mind what Mahatma Gandhi once said, "Be the change you want to see in the world".

Yes, another big thank you there Julian we sometimes need to stay focused on our purpose in life and let unnecessary tasks slip by, and Mother Teresa once said, "A life not lived for others, is not a life" That described Julian to a tee.

Another lesson he taught me was, try to see life from other peoples view point. I used to look at him some times and secretly admire him doing what appeared like simple jobs for you and me. Things like washing up, cooking, ironing, sawing a piece of wood, drilling, grinding, welding, mechanics, carpentry, carpet fitting, tiling, wine making, beer making, lawn cutting, painting, decorating or a simple task like pulling a door towards you on a slope. The list is endless but all these tasks he conducted from a wheelchair. When you're bored one evening instead of watching television, sit in a normal chair and attempt to do one of them, it's not easy living life sitting down.

Here's a good one to attempt with your family, sit in a chair near an electric wall plug. Then from a sitting position try to bend forward to switch an electric plug on and off. Do this with every wall plug in the house and see how many obstacles such as lamps or ornaments you have to lean over or you have to move to get to the plug. Once you've done that silly exercise, trying pulling a three point plug out of its socket without pulling yourself off the chair. Don't forget he was at risk of tipping out of his wheel chair because his foot plates were 2 to 3 inches off the ground. Standing up and reaching is a great asset.

Someone once said to me, "I can only use my right hand to use a screw driver." But when you have to use both hands, you have too. Needless to say, Julian might not have been able to use his legs so consequently he taught himself to be ambidextrous. He taught himself to be a craftsman with both hands using a hammer, screw driver, a saw and power tools in both hands. It's called making the best with what you've got. What's the lesson here, I think he was teaching me 'you don't know what you can achieve until you push yourself to the limit.'

When I was at the Post office not so long ago, an elderly lady in the queue in front of me started to complain about old age and all the ailments it brings. "I know" I said, "But aren't we lucky to have it, lots die young." She still wasn't having it, she continued with her complaining. I then said something that I don't usually tell a stranger "My husband would have liked to have seen old age and all the baggage it brings." She said, "He wouldn't"

I stopped there and thought I cannot reason with this stranger. But he would have, he suffered 10 times more than most of us from the age

647

of 18 and at the end, he was still begging for more life, his hunger for it never stopped.

What did he teach me, he taught me how important it is to hold on to life with both hands and grip like mad and don't let go until you have to. Hence why I mentioned it on his head stone engraved in time and memorial.

Thank you, for teaching me that nothing is impossible; I recognise you had the same drive as Mother Teresa. In September 1946 she had a calling within a calling to serve the poor and the dying; by 1996 the year she died she had created 517 missionaries with 4,000 sisters taking care of them. That is what she achieved in her life time, but she didn't start this impossible task until she was 36. So it's never too late for any of us to turn our dreams into reality.

I remember coming home from work one day. It had been a particularly hard day. On top of that we had very heavy rain. By the time I got home I was soaked to the skin. Julian was waiting for me at the back door, eager to go voting. I said, "No, no, no I've had it, I'm too tired and too wet to go"

He turned on me and said, "People like you make me mad, when women like Emily Pankhurst were willing to die for the likes of **you** to have a 'woman's vote' in the 20s, and you can't even be bothered to get a bit wet for the sake of her sacrifice"

I felt I had to go then, so off I went in dry cloths, to get wet first and vote after. The following week Julian took great pleasure in reading aloud the headlines of our local newspaper. The party we had voted for had won by two votes. The sealing statement was "You see Olwen, you can make a difference"

Some people say the smallest of sentences, but it has the most profound effect on us long after they have left our company. I wonder if that haunting sentence was meant to make a lasting impact on me, could I possible make a difference in improving the world we live in today?

I mentioned before that Agnes Hunt was my first heroin, who nurse against all odds. Emily Pankhurst is a close runner up, refusing to give up when all those around her were begging her too. Marie Curie plodded on in a world where women were not welcomed. Mother Teresa opened all those missions without a single penny. Bernadette Souborou managed to erect a Basilica at Lourdes while still in poverty, where thousands of pilgrims still attend 150 years later. These five women gave me the inspiration to struggle on, in an attempt to change things. Was it possible these five women could give me second wind to my sails to push me on further with this book for the sake of Julian's case and others?

Incidentally one of these ladies, Emily Pankhurst, a leading figure in the suffragette movement, played a vital role in securing the right for women to vote and on the 24th January 1912, she addressed a packed public meeting at Kidderminster town hall which she enlightened a large audience of local female carpet workers.

Thank you, Julian for teaching me the power of the pen.

I extend another thank-you to you Julian for been so long suffering and patient about my repetitive 'last-minute-dot-com' request from you. No matter how big the task I begged of you or how impossible it seemed, I like Llewela always knew you'd turn up trumps and deliver the goods on time. Sadly my last recollection of such a big project I begged of him was when I asked him to help me prepare the Brownies Annual Strawberry tea party which took place on June 28th 2008.

It entailed the Brownies serving their parents strawberries and cream, scones, tea or coffee and to obtain their badge they also had to entertain their guests. That summer it happened to be 50 years since the death of a local Kidderminster hero called Peter Collins the Formula One Racing Driver who was on the verge of becoming the First British World Champion. At the time, he was racing for an Italian called Fangio. He married an American lady in 1957 and lived an enviable life-style on a yacht in Monaco Harbour. Sadly in 1958 at the Grand Prix in Nurburgring he lost control of his racing car and died a few hours later of head injuries. He raced at such places like Silverstone at the age of 17 at Reims and Monza. He was buried at 'Stone'village just outside Kidderminster. Sterling Moss and Murray Walker the racing commentator attended his funeral, there is also a stained glass window dedicated to his memory in the church.

Sadly Julian himself died 17 weeks after helping me put this event together. Why have I mentioned this episode of his life, do you remember I mentioned earlier that Julian had given Llewela permission to marry her boyfriend on his death bed; ironically this was the same church they were married at and it was this man Peter Collins who my brother Glyn was reading about when Julian was dying. Even though

Glyn hadn't finished reading the book, he requested that the book should be placed in his coffin with the inscription 'enjoy the read' Later I read in our local newspaper of a Peter Collins enthuses who was preparing to set up a memorabilia display commemorating our local hero in one of the disused carpet factory which will be converted into local museum. I contacted the organiser and he took away Julian's hard work on the research Peter Collins life. The display including some of Peters wife's contribution can be viewed from 2014 onwards in Kidderminster.

Thank you for teaching me about the importance of passion in everything you did. In your creativity, in your teaching, in your faith even passion in getting your point of view over to the extent of ranting and raving while I was whipped up like a tornado then at its peak you'd say, "Fancy a cup of tea" later I would try and rekindle the topic, but you would always say with no eye contact, "It's finished, it's over now let's get cracking with the job in hand" and life would return to normality instantly. No long psychological silence to endure for days on end destroying our relationship.

My next thank you is a bit long winded, but it stemmed from a haunting phrase I wrote earlier that we were suffering from "Darwin evolution in reverse" What did it mean? It keeps echoing in my mind. I decided to recap, who was he and what was he responsible for. I had an inclination he had something to do with evolution of monkeys to man, but other than that my recollection of his theory was a bit vague.

If you feel you cannot remember what he looks like, look on the back of a ten pound note to see the image of the aging Charles Darwin.

Charles Darwin was ironically born in Shrewsbury, Shropshire on February 12th in 1809 and died in 1882. (126 years before Julian time.)

Charles mother died when he was only 8 years old. Charles was then raised by his Father and his older sisters. At the age of 16 he attended University in Edinburgh, Scotland as a medical student. He was revolted by the brutality of surgery, so he dropped out after two years in 1827. His Father then sent him to Cambridge University and in 1828 he started to study theology. Following his graduation in 1831 Darwin secured a berth on a British Navy ship and went on an expedition around the world which took him nearly 5 years. Darwin was only 22 at the time. It was on Galapagos Islands in the Eastern Pacific Ocean that he made the observation that plants and animals evolve. He first noticed that Finches differ from each other in beak size and shape on different islands. This he noticed was due to diet, he realised once they developed the variation; they had the advantage of staying alive longer to reproduce. The bird's diet varied from cactus eaters, nectar eaters to seed eaters.

Another species he studied was peppered moth, which evolved their colour as the trees changed from dark to a lighter colour.

By the late 1860's Darwin referred to this process as "survival of the fittest" but often felt that the phrase was frequently misunderstood. Many assumed that "the fittest" meant strongest, biggest or smartest or the most cunning. In fact the survivor may be small and even weak, but if it changed in accordance with the environment it would have the greatest success of survival. Darwin did not rush with the publication of his findings due to the fact he could have been charged with blasphemy in the Christian sector regarding his unpopular theory.

After returning from yet another voyage of the Beagle, Darwin eventually settled down in England, married Emma Wedgwood, a daughter of a wealthy pottery manufacturers and raised a large family and quietly continued his research 16 miles south of London.

He didn't publish his theory of evolution for another twenty eight years, not until he was 50 years age. The first edition came out on 24th November 1859 and was sold out on the same day.

So what connection has Charles Darwin with Julian Davies?

If it is a question of evolution, could it be that we have started to develop illnesses following consumption of pesticides, preservatives, and digestion of food that does not belong in the human food chain.

Could it be that our bodies have not yet evolve enough to tolerate the high quantities of these toxins and poisons causing such complaints as high blood sugar levels, high blood pressure, thyroid'isem, cancer, tumours, diabetics, obesity and possibly Multiple Sclerosis, and even more worryingly haven't evolved to tolerate the toxic treatment of these conditions?

It appears that Julian had evolved enough to tolerate his conditions but none of the treatments. That appeared to be just too much to bear and in his case it proved to be fatal

With hindsight it seems to me the best cure is to remove the original offender which is the toxins and poisons that is causing the explosive epidemic in our society in deed the world. The treatment seems simple to me. Just as Julian instructed me, "Go back to the beginning" I now feel he meant, before we started to contaminate our world.

I read this somewhere, but for the life I can't remember where so I hope I don't get done for copy right. If the comment is going to save humanitarians I hope I shall be forgiven for pledurisam. "Now is the time to be fully accountable for the state of our lives and the state of the world we live in"

I file this one under 'thank you' for sending me on this journey, asking me to write a book and then go back to the beginning.

Maybe faith and scientist are much closer in their views than they think. I realise I have quoted many times from the Bible, but I don't think it's a such a bad thing, maybe we should take the Bible off the shelf dust it down and read it! It has a great deal to say about nature and the environmental conservation, social justice and voice of conscience. To me it's like an antique computer full of answers, but sadly most people are too proud to be seen reading from this ancient book.

One of my last thank you is for being such a good teacher to Llewela through those education years. Because when you left our life suddenly, I was as much help to her as a chocolate fire guard. Without your input and training she may have found University life difficult. I can now say to the Head mistress who said to Llewela 11 years previously, that all the right buttons have now been pushed. In three weeks after leaving University she was presented with her certificate for her degree at Oxford Brooks University, secondly she was successful in an interview and accepted a permanent full time employment and thirdly she was told the contract was ready to sign for her new three bedroom house. And yes she did get married to the same young man Julian gave permission to, to wed his daughter days before he died.

Julian would be so proud of her; she made it on her own with his guidance in the early years.

I wonder what the rest of her life holds for her. Thank you, Julian.

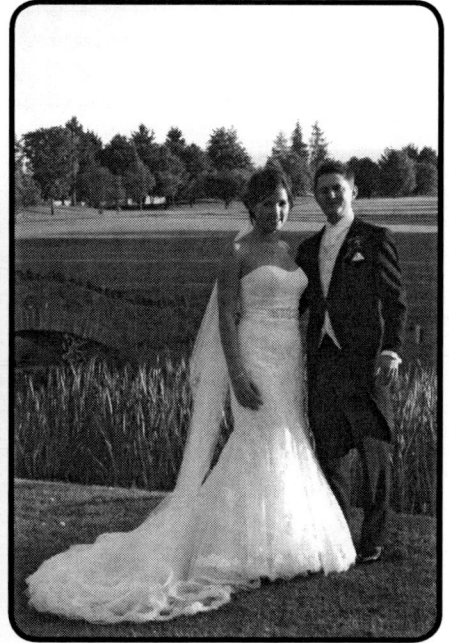

A Photo of Llewela, in her cap and gown in 2011 and on her wedding day in June 2012.

I'm glad Julian did take an interest in Llewela's education, because on June 17th 2010 Nick Clegg made a speech in Parliament about children and families in this country. He said, "We have built a Britain not fit for our children to grow up in" I agree with him, growing up should be about discovery, learning and adventure not stress, anxiety and insecurity. In fact on National news five months later on 3rd November 2011 the Government feared our children were becoming 'Feral' I confess I was not familiar with this word, so of course I was eager to find out in case Llewela was suffering from the condition. I'm proud to announce she's not, it stated a 'Feral child' is a human child who has lived isolated from human contact from a young age with very little experience of love, social skills, language or corrective behaviour. How sad for our Government to be reduced to confess to such a thing publically about his own country!

There is an old Chinese proverb that says, "Children owe obedience to their parents, but parents have a responsibility to their children and must put their interest first."

Well done Ju, you did well there!

But just because Llewela's education was nearly completed he was not intending on putting his pen and ink away, he was getting ready to help his niece Molly tackle the difficult road of University life. In his absence Molly Jones is doing just fine, well done Moll. I'm sure Julian's very proud of your efforts.

It would be remiss of me not to thank Glyn Jones for not obstructing Gill's path to come at a moment's notice to Julian's bedside. Another thank you to Elwyn Jones for being so understanding, letting Gwenno attend to Julian's needs.

My final thank-you to you Julian, is for being my private teacher but most of all for being my very best friend and constantly making me see the best and the most positive things in life and of course for making me laugh and lastly for tolerating my silly female ways; I know I possessed them I just chose not to recognise them when you were around.

Since you've been gone, my life has not just been about going to work, running a home and completing this book. I have continued to be involved with charity work, something we both used to enjoy contributing to mainly driven by your sense of giving back to society what society had given you over the years. There's a saying, 'One can feel energized when donating time to charity work' and I think it's true it can give you a buzz doing something for other asking for nothing in return!

My fund raising days after Julian

When Julian was in Shrewsbury Hospital I mentioned he'd uttered these words from the heart,

"I wish I had cancer, then you'd let me go home to die".

Looking back with sadness those words still cut me to the quick; I consider it to be verging on a psychological criminal act the way the Doctor conducted himself that day, to reducing a fellow man to these depths, as he begged him to let him die peacefully in the comfort of his own home. But to further make him wish he had what most people dread, in order to get out of his grasp was despicable. I would go as far as to say they obstructed his dying wish.

This conversation must have disturbed me much more than I thought, because on my return to home the following summer I found myself involved with many fundraising days.

I recalled how Julian was so involved in the school parent's committee, and how he dedicating his time to such fundraising as BBQ, which firstly entailed a lengthy engendering design to form a four large barbeque area from two empty 500gallon drums. By cutting, grinding and welding its detachable legs for transporting them from one venue to another.

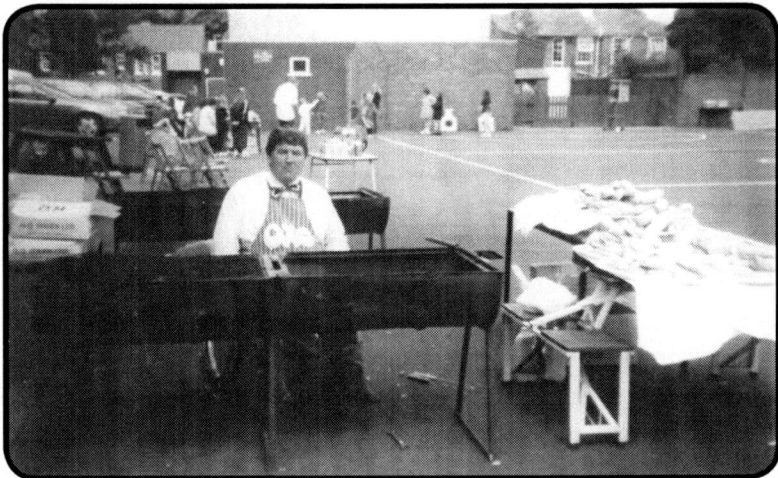

Photo of Julian after feeding what felt like the five thousand,
at one of the school fetes.

I've mentioned previously about the games he made, the Bee Hive, the Jumbulance not to mention organising 'Cheese and wine' tasting event at the Town Hall which was no mere task I can tell you, the venue was chocker block. Then there was a sponsored wheelchair push, a 'Big toys for Big boys' day on Hagley playing fields which was also a big event. A Promise Auction was a huge money raiser the list goes on.

But in April 2005 he was initiated in to Buffaloism, and from then on all his fundraising days was channelled into the good of the order. He loved belonging to this order because he used to say, "It what can I do for the order, rather than what can the order do for me"

When I returned home I felt this huge void in my life, not just the fact that this big personality had been wrenched out of my life but the constant on going fundraising activities wasn't active any more. This military organisation that used to be present was now gone and I needed to replace it somehow. I didn't want to be involved in any mundane fund rising; this hadn't been Julian's style. Looking back, I had subconsciously chosen charity funds that were connected to either Cancer research or Local Hospices.

My first encounter was a Ladies Day called "Heels on the wheels". It gave ladies the opportunity to drive vehicles that they would not normally have access to, they entailed a Bus, a Paramedic car, a Double Decker Bus, a16 wheeler articulated lorry round a circuit three times then another 16 wheeler lorry reversing it backwards between two parallel rows of orange bollards without jack knifing the lorry. The most difficult or should I say the most moving vehicle for me to drive that day was the Ambulance. Why you may ask, well the size was not the issue, I was used to driving a camper van which was of similar in stature. But the Ambulance flooded back all the anguish that surrounded Julian's early death.

The Ambulance lady driver was very sympathetic when I told her of my many recent Ambulance journey's to and from different hospitals. She coaxed me through the experience.

There were other fundraisers I joined in with which was "The mid night walk" dressed in something pink where I accompanied some 600 lady's through the Wyre Forest walking from 12 midnight, raising money for the local Hospice. Later in the year the same Local Hospice organised a Santa Run, where 320 of us dressed up in Santa outfits ran a circuit round Kidderminster district. With just those three events alone I raised £300.

In one of the Marie Curie pamphlets they sent me, it stated "We give everyone the choice of where to die." It goes on to say that, "Asking someone where they want to die is not easy. We're here to help with that sort of conversation".

No one had that terrible job with Julian, he was begging to go home to die, but still they didn't listen; in fact I still stand by what I believe, they obstructed his last wish.

Was there any wonder I was drawn to raising money for people to die peacefully at home, after Julian had been denied the same care others were offered.

In August 2009 I attended an event organised by the Buffalo's, an Annual Dinner event presented by the Provincial Grand Lodge, at the event there were many speakers but amongst them was the Grand Lodge of England Officer Aden Bennett, who announced that his chosen charity that year was "Brain Tumour research," to that date he had raised £8,000. Well done I thought, but why did he feel the need to draw attention to this particular cause, I wasn't aware that many people suffered from this condition. I was intrigued and wanted to know what drove him to choose this charity "Brain Tumour"

As he was mulling round each table after the meal and speeches were over, I asked his wife why he chose this charity, she signalled him over and introduced himself but he did not enlighten me on why there so many suffering.

The following morning I decided to do a mini research to find out it's possible cause, in the New York Times dated 29/091997, Scientists suspect modern chemicals as a prime suspect for causing brain tumours. Environmental Research wrote, 'Cancer patients had a higher pesticide residual in their body fat'. Another Journal of Neuropathy stated in 1996 'Aspartame was one of the causes of brain tumours' (As it derives from pesticides, it may well contribute)

The British Medical Association (BMA) has refused to acknowledge the health risks of pesticides and played down any link between pesticides and chronic disease. (Off course they refused, they're British) On 12th July 2006 the European Commission stated, "Long term exposure to pesticides can lead to serious disturbances to the immune system, sexual disorder, sterility, birth defects, damage to the nervous system, genetic damage and cancer". Why are we the British people put through these unnecessary exposures, when organic farmers manage without these chemicals? Who are we to believe, The British Medical Association (BMA) or our European neighbours and our American cousins?

The following year in 2010, I decided to raise money for Reg Smith the PGP for Worcestershire. Trying to think of something different I rang my sister to see if she could think of a different fundraiser. She's excellent at plucking ideas out of the air, she suggested asking Gill, Julian's best friend who lived on a farm in the heart of Wales to ask her husband to teach us how to shear sheep.

I thought why not, how I could call myself Welsh, if I couldn't boast of speaking Welsh, making good Welsh cakes and shearing Welsh sheep!

We chose a very hot summer's day in wet Wales for our sheering lesson. I went first, only because I was the most nervous. I was biting at the bit in the kitchen saying, "Let's get going, the longer I'm waiting here drinking tea the more agitated I'm getting." I recalled Gweno saying, cool as a cucumber, "Just chill out Olwen, there's plenty of time" I remember my first attempt; the poor sheep looked like a white poodle with tuffs of missed wool sprouting out where I'd missed. I confess the others did looked better, practice does make perfect. In the cool of the evening we had a nice spread of old fashioned welcome in the shelter of a Marquee on the Farm yard. Our parents joined us later bringing with them a relative from Australia. I'm sure she would like me to mention her name. (Ethel Jones) Ironically she used to work on the Spinal Injury unit with another relative of ours called Ann Cook ne-Thomas. The two of them are still great friends. Julian was always pleased when the two of them were on duty together with Carol to look after him.

In addition to the welcome, my sister and I were presented with a certificate each.

That afternoon, my sheering experience raised £50 for Multiple Sclerosis.

Photograph of Gill hosting her first 'Female Sheering' banquet.

Whilst out socialising at another fundraising function, a Hogg roast affair I asked the host Reg Smith for no reason at all, if he knew of someone who had a JCB digger, I fancied digging a hole. He said, "Whatever for?" I said, "You never know when the skill might come in handy!"

He laughed and asked, "Do you know what I do for a living Olwen?" I replied "No"

"I dig holes all day long, and I own my own JCB" how spooky was that?

So one cold November morning I took off towards Alverley and met my new instructor Reginald Smith and his wife Josie Smith who taught me how to operate a JCB digger.

After an hour or so practicing operating knobs, I managed to dig a very deep hole. I jumped off to inspect my handy work.

For a split second I thought that's the very hole I sometimes imagine I'd like to crawl into when the brown envelopes keep come through the letter box and I don't know how to pay for them. That's one thing Julian doesn't have to worry about any more, only the living have to worry about the brown envelopes. Other types of people who don't have to worry about bills are prisoners. All their bills are taken care of; by the likes of you and me! I soon pulled myself together, and continued to take photos of my freshly dug hole, so that the whole exercise was not a complete waste of time, I asked the farmer if I could burry a time capsule tin?

He laughed and agreed I could, I opened the tin to let them see what I was burying. I chose an empty chocolate tin of Roses to represent England, a Welsh tea towel and a silk daffodil, a selection of coins ranging from 1p, 2p, 5p, 10p, 20p, 50p and a £1. I placed the coins in a box that looked like a tuxedo suit to remind me of the posh events the Buffalos held, a card with a note explaining what I was raising the money for 'Multiple Sclerosis', a Halloween mug as it was Halloween weekend. My sister suggested a fire work to remember Guy Fawkes, I declined in case it blew the tin up and lastly I placed in a poppy in remembrance of Julian as he died on 12th November.

Reg being the gentleman he is, offered to jumped into the freshly dug hole on my behalf and ceremoniously placed my Time Capsule in the burial hole in time and memorial.

We all laughed after the burial of the tin, the hole was so deep we thought only Alien's from another planet will ever excavate this tin, unless of course "Time Team" came across it in years to come. After arriving home, I wondered why I was drawn to raise money for Multiple Sclerosis. So yet again I conducted a mini research thinking, was Julian yet again leading me to this cause!

Would you believe it, like an old record that had got stuck the same old answers came up again? Why does this topic keep raising its ugly head, I don't go looking for it, it just jumps out at me.

It stated Pesticides can be the biggest trigger of Multiple Sclerosis. To be fair it did not say it definitely caused it, but triggered it. The Pesticide companies were infuriated that their product was mentioned and not enough emphasis was placed on the amount of bug free fruit and vegetables that was produced. The point is; these sprays kill little animals, and it stands to reason it will do people some degree of harm to their nerve endings too. Tests showed that rats suffered damage to areas of the brain and nerve damage to the same areas involved in Multiple Sclerosis.

One letter dated in 2006 from a lay person "I wonder if the Industry spokesman who claims there is no link to human health from breathing these pesticides, would he be willing to have his home sprayed inside every day for a year" My opinion is "Why not if it's safe enough for us to eat on our food all our lives it should be safe enough for them to breathe in for just one year. I think they would be willing to stand by what they believe to be safe".

Another person wrote in from Nottingham, saying he had been suffering for 10years from pesticide exposure causing unexplained neurological symptoms.(I'm not saying this gentleman had MS, but it was found on a MS site) No Doctor had referred him for further investigations despite his constant requests, he said he was always brushed aside. He claimed he had several photos of himself before and after exposure and says he was unrecognisable.

How many more like him cannot get medical professionals to take them seriously and recognise there is a very serious problem out there?

If Doctors refuse to '**note and report**' then there is no way of knowing the true amount of people who may be affected!

It's just another sad Pesticide story floating away in to space, with no means to an end! What a waste of an existence for these people, because you can't say it's a life.

This is a sad but true story, I heard today of a young girl age about 15, who suddenly suffered unreperable neurological nerve damage to her lower body. After several visits to the GP she was eventually referred to a Professor who ran a few blood tests and discovered she had an elevated amount of pesticide in her blood stream. The Medical team questioned the Parents to find out how this could have happened; to the Fathers horror he discovered the very chemical that was found in his daughter blood sample was the same as in his pesticide. This young girl was not only his only daughter but his only child. He is now campaigning against pesticide sprays at the cost of his daughter's health. What a high price to pay! Was it worth it getting rid of those little might's in exchange for his only daughter to suffer long term neurological damage? I think not.

As I was still attending the Buffalo functions, in 2011 the newly elected PGP Sean Mcvicker announced his chosen appeal for The Queen Elizabeth Hospital Teenage Cancer Trust.

As I had raised funds for the past Provincial Grand Primo, I decided I would do the same for him. On my return home I wondered, why did Sean feel the need to make people aware of Teenagers suffering from cancer, was it on the increase? They hadn't yet lived, the circle of life was all wrong. Some thing was out of order; I tried to think back to my school days to see if I could recollect any of my friends who had cancer. I drew a blank, not a soul. My secondary school had 500 pupils attending the school. So what's changed in the last 40 years or so?

I decided to look up cancer amongst teenagers, and according to a Richard Wiles who directed the Environmental Working Group stated, that children born today are exposed to chemicals from birth if not before. They accumulate between 25% and 35% of their life time cancer risk from several carcinogenic pesticides by the age of 5. I felt that was a big percentage in a small body.

In Virginia, 276 juvenile delinquents at a detention facility, particularly hardened adolescents, were put on a diet for 2 years that removed chemicals, additives and reduction in sugar. During that time the incidence of theft dropped by 77%, insubordination dropped by 55%, hyperactivity dropped by 65%. If this is a fact, what are we doing to our young generation?

Could this have been the reason why we witnessed such violence in the streets in Briton in August 2011 was 'wicked food, producing wicked adolescents'?

Should we all vote with our feet by buying organic food to help 'heal our youth'?

I decided to raise money for the existing suffering teenagers but we should be looking at preventing future teenage suffering not curing.

Thankfully the word "organic produce" is the buzz word amongst chefs of today, keep it up chaps. Getting back to Sean Mcvikers charity, he directed his money at a different angle to his predecessors, instead of cancer research which I'm sure they must have enough funds by now.

He chose something practical that touched my heart, the money raised was to renovate and refurbish a room for family and friends of the young cancer victims to spend quality time in pleasant surroundings trying to create a 'home from home' feel about it. To me, this part was just as important as fighting for life. I could relate to this from personal experience, I know what it was like to start the day tired after no sleep and sitting on a plastic chair all night, without offer of a drink or breakfast, without a wash, clean teeth or clean clothes for near on five weeks. With very minimal bed space in between each bed, and the same strict visiting time for the living and the dying. Dictating only two to a bed, at a time in your life when time might not be your best friend, in an environment so far removed from home. So, yes this was a worthy cause, and it wasn't going to be a bottomless pit. Still thinking of something different to do as a fund raiser I rang my sister to ask her yet again did she have any good ideas, she suggested making a horse shoe! She made the appropriate arrangement to meet up with this Farrier at Welshpool, in Mid Wales. When we arrived, HE turned out to be a She, a young 24 year old petite female Farrier. What a good teacher she turned out to be. These quirky charity events have given Gweno and I such an insight into how difficult other people's occupations are. Not to mention what we have learnt on a personal level.

This small event raised £50, I also donated to the charity a horse shoe as a gift from the heart, for them to nail to their door as a reminder that others are thinking and praying for them. The horse shoe I made, I gave to Llewela on her Wedding day.

My fundraising days I hope are not yet over, as long as there is a worthy cause and not a bottomless pit, with no further advancement towards a means to an end, I will continue to fundraise.

How strange my fund raising events seemed to be connected directly or indirectly to Julian's plea, "Don't let others suffer like I have" all these sufferings seemed to have come about, because of our dreadful life styles.

I have no bow to my bundle

Do you remember I wrote at the beginning of my investigation, if ever I found out that Julian had an Adrenal Tumour it will have a lot to answer for? Well it did. The other comment I made at Julian's bed side was "Julian I think what you're suffering from is really big, but the answer might be very simple like a vitamin or mineral deficiency" What an odd thing to say, was it my little voice of conscious speaking out on both occasions?

You would think I'd be happy with the discovery that Type Two Diabetes doesn't need Insulin, but I'm not! I'm still un-nerved about the state of this world and the directions were all heading, I want, I insist and I demand a quick fix to our ailing world. But who can heal us, something is still not right, the book is not coming together, there appears to be a gap in my findings. I understand how our food and medicine has been interfered with but why, who, would want to do such a thing? Question is did it evolve or was it committed deliberately?

It's as if I'm in possession of a bundle of loose clothing without a piece of string to secure them together. What would Julian do if he was in my situation? Well, he'd probably abandon the book and make a cup of tea. After completing his brew he would probably sit quietly with his eyes closed then listen to his voice of conscience. And that's exactly what I did, I let my mind meander over the content of the book to see what common factor would jump out at me and guess what, something did.

It was a signal word that's been repeated over and over again and that word was 'Pesticide'

So who was responsible for inventing this toxic product called 'pesticide' and more worryingly who went ahead and produced it? I feel as if I'm on the brink of finding out about two little boys, one who thought about doing something bad, and the other for carrying out the dreadful dead. The question is which one will be the naughtiest, the thinker or the doer? I feel as if I'm entering uncharted waters here so I'm going to take a chance and recap. It worried me greatly that I couldn't find one genuine governing body that sounded trust worthy enough to be in charge of our food safety in this country, except for a watch dog called Food Safety Agency that was set up in 2011, but they seem to have a conflict of interest with our food safety, because they approve of GM Food production.

Do I need to look further afield to find an overseer I can trust?

Thank goodness there is one and it's called 'United Nations' or UN established by Rothschild and Rockefeller in 1946. Two years later Rothschild and Rockefeller formed another food regulator called 'World Health Organisation' otherwise referred to as 'WHO' they were established in 1948 in Geneva.

Concerned that strange things were happening to our food supply; I was heartened to read that in 2002 'World Health Organisation' or WHO published an article called 'Terrorist Threats to Food' these guidelines were issued as a matter of public health policy. I was glad someone was raising concerns over the quality of our food. But instead of pacifying me, it just aroused my suspicion, why would they make such a statement if they were in charge of the world health.

What was going on, if all these bodies were watching out for us worldwide, who is inflicting terror on our food chain, is there an enemy within?

Wait a minute, I mentioned another one in Environmental Toxins chapter called 'Codex Regulator' this is another one that was formed and controlled by Rothschild and Rockefeller. Codex joined the food regulators in 1962 bringing the total number of food protection organisations to five. But who is this company? I've hardly heard of before called Codex! It appears 'Codex Aliment-arius Commission' is an American regulator responsible for the standard of processed food, raw foods, additives, contaminants, labelling, analysing, sampling and pesticides. These regulators are multiplying; it should be more music to my ears discovering more people interested in our healthy food control. I'm drawn to going back to the beginning of this new regulator called Codex! It appears the word codex was first used in 300 AD when scrolls started to be replaced by books. To establish how the word codex was reinvented in the 21st century I will go back in our modern day history to the Second World War, when a German Chemist by the name Fritz ter Meer was convicted of Nazi War Crimes after being involved in the planning of Mono-witz concentration camp and Auschwitz. His crime was to 'invent nerve gas' for the gas chambers, he was also found guilty of conducting human experiments and holding 25,000 forced labourers under horrible circumstances prior to their death, including adding fluoride into their drinking water to lower their IQ, acting as a crowd controller. When asked at his trial; didn't his conscience prick him when he conducted such atrocities on his fellow human beings? He showed no remorse and said "No they were due to die anyway". He was sentenced to seven years imprisonment at the Nuremberg Trials in 1948 for which he only served four of those years, due to his influential and powerful friends. When he emerged from prison in 1952, like the phoenix out of the ashes he re-established himself with the chemical industry.

You're probably thinking, so what has this Fritz ter Meers a 'gas man' got to do with our food chain!

Well, when he was serving his sentence in prison and was fed substandard food the idea came to him, 'if one was in control of the world food supply including its quality, one could be in control of the world health'! Instead of inflicting 'Manslaughter' in the gas chambers like he had been, he could have inflicted long term 'Malnutrition' instead. Inflicting malnutrition on any living thing could quietly attack the immune system and render death without obvious proof that it had been done deliberately. All this set his mind racing, four years after his release in 1956 he was invited on the Board of Bayer AG and in 1958 he became the chairman of the company.

Four years after that, in 1962 'Fritz ter Meer' and 'Bayer' formed a commission called 'Codex Aliment-arius Commission' this very same company called 'Bayer' was responsible for producing gas for the gas chambers at Auschwitz. So one of them invented the lethal gas and the other produced it. What a dangerous combination I thought! Not only were they on the same team then, but they were now working together!

But they say with friendship 'like attracts like' don't they!

So I was right, about 'the two little boy's theory' except they were not two naughty boys, they had become two, dangerous men plotting once more.

Within ten years of his release from prison he had risen through the ranks and by 1962 he'd approached the Food and Agriculture Organisation and World Health Organisation to take them under their wing. The two organisations acted as their 'Parent Company' treating Codex as their 'Son Company' in other words the FAO and WHO financially funded his scheme.

But Bayer's had other connections; he was also in partnership with a company called 'Monsanto' a world renowned chemical company responsible for producing pesticides and its end product commonly known as artificial sweetener such as Aspartame.

Four years later in 1967 Fritz ter Meer died leaving behind a well-established commission with a company philosophy 'Whoever is in control of world food and water supply is also in control of the world' Bayer company later claimed Fritz ter Meer had nothing to do with its company, but it continues to openly refuse to distance itself from the convicted war criminal. When on the eve of Halloweens day 'Bayer's' company continue lay a wreath on this German born Chemist's called Fritz ter Meer grave, which is now over 40 years since his death. Why would they conduct this small act of compassion, if he was unknown to the company?

I digress, in 2002 the 'Food Agriculture Organisation' and 'World Health Organisation' had serious concerns about the direction Codex was going and hired an external consultant to investigate Codex. The Investigation concluded that 'Codex' should be immediately discontinued, and they should exert their powerful influence to do so. Instead they cowardly asked 'Codex Aliment-arius Commission' to politely address 20 of their concerns. Why? When Codex openly admits what their company philosophy was based on "If we control food, we control the world"

Why should **I** be worried about Codex? What other things does Codex intend to bring about if it controls the world? This is one disagreeable trick they have conducted so far, 178 countries voted for 9 very dangerous pesticides to be banned. Codex on its own strength re-introduced 7 of those dangerous pesticides successfully. What happened to the 178 countries opinion? It boils down this! The rest of the world has no power against Codex! My next question was; what else do they intend to do? Evidently if they get their own way, they intend to make it compulsory by law that every animal intended for food consumption <u>has </u>to be injected with antibiotics and <u>has</u> to be treated with growth hormone. If they get their own way, they will insist all food <u>must</u> be radiated, killing all vitamins in the process. If they get their own way, they <u>will</u> make vitamins and minerals as illegal as Cocaine. Therefore, making it impossible, to replace the destroyed vitamins. If they get their own way, they <u>will</u> make it law that everybody must to be vaccinated with the flu virus or be imprisoned. If they get their own way, Police acting as Food Safety Officers <u>can and will</u> raid premises without warrants, using any equipment they deemed necessary. (Could mean guns) If they get their own way, Monsanto employers <u>can</u> also raid premises and Non-Codex complying producers like organic farmers <u>will</u> be shut down including small cottage industry food growers, they will also stop self-sufficient gardeners from supplying their local communities even your personal allotments. If they get their own way, they <u>will</u> make it illegal for us to help feed third world countries. This <u>will</u> be the law, if we allow ourselves to be comatose to their bulling. On the vitamin issue alone, health concerns envisage three and a half billion deaths through mal nutrition once Codex laws are put in to practice, because if the radiation of all our food is permitted it will eradicate all natural vitamins and it will be illegal to buy vitamins and minerals to replace the lost nutrients including herbs and garlic. It stands to reason as our bodies cannot function without them, one can almost visualise Bellson

How stupid and naive of me to think MSG food was developed to feed the world and not to harm us by using culling technique!

I don't know if I'm scaring you, but I'm scaring myself.

If this company is still practising under Fritz ter Meer's philosophy 'one can have power over people according to how you feed and water them' then this is scary!

<u>If</u> Codex Regulator was founded by this man called Fritz ter Meer, do you consider this man's credentials to be sound, considering his past reputation of wanting to depopulate the so called second class citizens of Jewish people, Gypsies and the Disabled who he referred to as 'useless eaters' Has every one forgiven his past, enough to allow this man's philosophy to live on long after his death in 1967 and then his founder company, to be in charge of all worlds food safety?

This man did not have good people skills before he was imprisoned, why was he allowed after his release to still be honoured with the title Doctor? Don't all Doctors have to undertake the Hippocratic Oath worldwide to 'save life at all cost?'

Why is it that all modern teenagers these days jeopardise their career if they have the smallest police record, never mind commit such atrocities like he committed!

What a contrast, following the Second World War Agnes Hunt was buzzy working out the best technique on how to improve health, up until her death in 1948, while Fritz ter Meer in the same year was buzzy plotting the opposite, calculating how best to destroy life by depopulating the world through food and water supply.

It is believed by some, that 'Codex Aliment-arius Commission' is the single most virulent assault on human freedom in recent times.

It then begs the question, if all these food regulators were instigated by these two men called Rothschild and Rockefeller with their vast wealth have their aims in life been about look after our welfare, lining their own pockets further or have they joined forces with the likes of the Fritz ter Meers to depopulate the world like he intended all those years ago? I realise money talks but have these two billionaires joined forces with any other billionaires? Actually NO, it seems it's the other way round; Rothschild and Rockefeller are pretty high up the ladder of this organisation which they privately call the 'Billionaire's club' but publically they refer to themselves belonging to the 'New World Order' run by the 'Elite' the name 'Illuminate' often appears alongside these two secluded circles, basically they all mount up to the same namely Power, Greed and Money.

When I first heard of this 'New World Order' I originally thought maybe that's what this world needs, a new order of things. It certainty had a nice ring to it, a breath of fresh air, new ideas, new beginning and calling it new world order might be the answer to all our troubles!

Who else belonged to this 'New World Order', well there is Bill Gates a man Julian admired for years for his forward thinking in computing engineering skills. Sadly I watched a clip of film where Bill Gates was talking openly about this 'New World Order' which he claimed his father was once head of 'Planned Parenthood'

This is a branch of the 'New World Order' that believes most human beings are "Reckless breeders" and were "Human weeds in need of culling"

Wow! I wasn't comfortable with this word culling, being a farmer's daughter I thought I knew what culling meant, but I double checked the definition anyway in case it had a double meaning. Culling is another word for 'killing' and killing is another word for 'murder', so what's going on?

Years ago I used to think Bill Gates could feed the world with his wealth, I never dreamt that one day I would hear him talking of 'culling instead of feeding' the human race!

In 2010 Bill Gates stated at the 'Technology, Entertainers and Design Conference' otherwise referred to as TED, that they intend to compulsory vaccination all children in the world, secondly compulsory produce GMO crops and thirdly compulsory vaccination adults by rendering selected individuals infertile.

Bill Gates mentioned his 'world aim' of culling, by compulsory vaccinating and enforced planting of GM crops when he was President of the 'Technology, Entertainer and Design Conference' but I have no idea why he mentioned it at TED's conference it has no connection at all in my opinion, unless he was so obsessed with the topic?

By the way, before Bill Gates was the President of Technology, Entertainer and Design there have been other well-known Presidents such as Bill Clinton, Gordon Brown, Nick Clegg and David Cameron. Which is fine, but are these Politicians' drip fed at such conferences that culling of Nations through vaccinations and producing GM crops are acceptable? Don't forget, if a child hears swearing in the family home, often enough, he too will accept it as the normal behaviour.

It left me wondering had Bill Gates been brain washed by his father into thinking that MSG food is the 'be all and end all' to feeding the world or was there something more sinister regarding this troublesome word 'culling' My suspicions were further raised when in 2010, I read, Bill Gates had purchased 500,000 shares valuing at $23 million dollars in the MSG industry? To date he is in control of technology, medicines and now he has an added interest MSG Agriculture. Just as 'Codex' had predicted, the 'New World Order' is already setting things in motion by starting with three of the topics on their list and they intend to enforce them as soon as possible. To date they have successfully financed and distributed Polio vaccination to thousands of children in India; unfortunately the vaccine used was previously banned in the USA on the grounds it caused the very physical disabilities it was meant to prevent. Over 47,500 Indian children who were given the vaccine developed polio-like paralysis! Their second program is to give poorer countries Monsanto GMO crop seeds that have inbuilt pesticides. These seeds will be distributed free of charge, unfortunately they only produces low nutrient value crops. When the farmers request seeds for a second crop the following year they have no choice, but to **buy** off Monsanto, that's like returning to a drug dealer after receiving its first freebie sample! Thirdly World Health Organisation or 'WHO' have been injecting women between the age of 15 to 45 in Nicaragua, Mexico, Philippines and Africa with tetanus, laced with Gonadotropin, when the two are combined they impose a state of permanent sterilization.

This has been going on since 1972. Isn't that a bit hypocritical coming from the Rothschild and Rockefeller dynasty when allegedly they have been producing illegitimate children all over the world and then placing them in positions of power for years!!!!! Double standards come to mind! What's good for the goose should be good for the gander, surely! The New World Order organisations have denied these people the privilege of experiencing parenthood 'once'.

It's been bugging me why people like Bill Gates, a parent himself didn't hear his own voice of conscience whispering to him in the dead of the night 'This isn't right'? I've studied the definition of the phrase, 'The Voice of Conscience' at great length, and found it to be too deep a subject to decipher, except people who are in possession of it can decide for themselves what is morally wrong and what is morally right. But to understand the word 'moral' it's easier to grasp if one has a faith, and more difficult if you haven't, but not impossible.

Martin Luther once said, "It is neither right or safe to go against my conscience"

I then started to wonder who else belongs to this 'New World Order' apart from Rothschild, Rockefeller and Bill Gates. I knew it would be people with financial status, but I did not prepare myself for this list of famous household names. Winston Churchill, Roosevelt, Kissinger, Nixon, Onassis, Robert Murdock, David Attenborough, Arnold Schwarzenegger, Richard Branson, Tony Blair, Gordon Brown, Three generations of the Bush Presidents, Clinton, Obama, David Cameron, Hitler and Prince Phillip. That's a lot of "I want to be in charge men"

I quote what Prince Philip said in his own words on the topic of depopulation at an anniversary meeting he was chairing for World Wildlife Federation, which incidentally, he has been involved with, since it started in 1962. The guest speaker was David Attenborough from 'Planned Parenthood' (heard of that before) who said "Depopulation was the answer to the world problem of hunger" He explained we have a choice of either having 2.2 families or accepting a more destructive technique of controlling world population through famine, disease and war. But these people are not talking of slowing down on reproducing the human race over a period of generations; they are talking about a sudden depopulation right now. For example they believe British population needs to be reduced from 60 million to 30 million right now, for us to sustain ourselves, otherwise we could find ourselves living in a 'Battery chicken world'

Going back to World Wildlife Federation; what they intend doing is to set aside pockets of land, mostly farm land and converting the zoned-land into game reserve for the preservation of animals and calling them 'Park Reservations' I did feel his plea was more about saving the nearly extinct breed of animals in preference to fairly distributing food around the World to save human population. Although as a child I used to think, I'm sure God had supplied the world with enough food, the problem was it wasn't evenly distributed. Waste being the worst culprit leaving others to starve.

If the likes of Prince Philip who believed very strongly that couples should only have two children in this New World Order, think on 'Your Royal Highness' you have four children which two would you consider culling first? Once the point is made personal, it doesn't sound so attractive any longer does it? If we go along with this New World Order will we Secom to making life cheap like them? Culling today's population can't be morally ethical, by treating current population with chemical medicines, feeding them with pesticide infiltrated food, artificial additives, hoodwinking them into thinking that mechanical engine oil is edible and putting fluoride into drinking water to dim their IQ into submission that the Elite know best. I understand now why Prince Charles is growing his own organic food, is he growing it for the Elite with self-preservation in mind?

Are we their Subjects too late, it seems it's been going on for years, they have been controlling famine in Africa, creating constant world wars, and developing new disease's we've never heard of?

How dare the media pull at our heart strings with pleading adverts on our television informing us that 22,000 children die needlessly every day in Africa? Then they say "It doesn't have to be this way" Begging us to cough up £2 a month to save these starving children's live's, while they are the ones purposely inflicting it in the first place with 'Depopulating through controlled starvation'

I fear I'm getting in too deep here, all I was looking for was, why Julian couldn't tolerate Diabetic treatment, I feel as if I'm swimming further and further away from my life saving ring. But as Julian's message continues to ring "Go back to the beginning" I decided to venture even further out of my depth and ask myself, have I been going about my business with my head bowed forward instead of raising my glance into the distance, checking for the advancing enemy!

As Julian's motto was "Think big and aim high" it started me thinking was this 'New World Order' only involved in tampering with my food or are they meddling with any of my other life dependant topics that I should be aware of?

I don't know how to explain this next life changing paragraph I came across, it's called the 'The Pyramid of Manipulation' and it describing what the 'The New World Order' are in control of?

This next exercise would probably be easier if you could find a pen and a piece of cardboard then draw a pyramid in the centre of your card, on the right hand side of the pyramid write these five words down one under the other—Banking, Business, Military, Politics and Education.

Moving to the left hand side of your pyramid write these six words down one under the other—Organised Crime, Intelligence Agencies, Religions, Media, Illegal drugs, Medicines and Drug companies. Now use this card as your book marker and a reference as you read the next few chapters.

These two lists depict everything I consider to represent my freedom of choice, in other words my democracy. I need to wake up, where have I been all this time? All the alarm bells have been ringing for years, especially when I recall my Mother constantly saying,

"I don't know what this world is coming too"

Before I finish I intend to find out who's at the pinnacle of this pyramid.

The pyramid mentions eleven fundamental topics, manipulating my very freedom of choice.

Banking

I will start with Banking, I realised from my childhood that the Rothschild's were a very rich family because if I chose the most expensive thing in the shop my mother would ask, "Who do you think I am Olwen, Rothschild?" But I wasn't sure what position the Rothschild's held in today's day and age. All I knew was, I couldn't manage without a

Bank Account in order to conduct my private affairs such as paying my mortgage, paying direct debits for house hold bills and receive my wages and later my pension.

As I delved into this German family's past, I discovered their financial business started when Moses Amschel Bayer the head of the family, started his small empire by opening a money lending shop and placing a red hexagon shield above his door. Red in German is translated as Rot and shield is translated as Schild. It is thought he wanted the name 'red-shield' for his shop to signify his ancestor's roots in Georgia and their faith the Ashkenazi Jew who were referred to as a Red Jew due to their descended red hair line.

His Banking technique is I likened to cheating at 'Monopoly' because what he did next was unacceptable. This is how it was explained to me, once he'd collected one million pounds, he'd then lend the same one million pounds to ten people, over a period of time they paid him back one million pounds each including a high interest rate which would total to ten million pounds including the additional high interest. Does that sound legal to you; after all he only had one million pounds in the first place.

I haven't finished yet, because if one of the ten faltered with his payment the Banker then seized all of his property, his home and declare him bankrupt. Sounds very unfair to me, as the Bank didn't have a million pound to lend the bankrupt man in the first place, neither did he have it to lend to the other eight either, but try telling the homeless man in the street with his wife and children, that his lender was a corrupt operator?

What I want to know is; are todays Banks operated in the same way? In other words is the money in the bank that people borrow real money or myth money like Moses Amschels money?

This system is believed by some to be the largest, the most colossal theft ever prepared in the history of mankind and it is so slick, so unpublished by the media that the victims (that's us) are not even aware of what's going on. What a devious way of creating an empire.

But he wasn't content with his new found wealth, greed set in and he wanted even more after marrying a sixteen year old girl and producing ten children five daughters and five sons. We don't hear much about the daughters but the sons became well known Bankers.

To increase his empire he set about sending his sons to establish Banks in different European capitals in an attempt to grasp a firm hold on the Europe's gold. But first the sons changed their surname from Bayer to Rothschild

His first son Mayer Amschel Rothschild stayed home in Frankfurt to control the German Banks, (he was also allegedly involved in instigating the Illuminati order.) His second son Salomon was sent to Austria to control the Banks there (it is believed by some that he was Hitler's Grandfather?) His third son Nathan was sent to control the Banking system in London, (he made Royal connections and was often a guests at Sandringham Palace, his descendant Baroness Kitty de Rothschild offered the couple Duke of Windsor and Mrs Simpson refuge at their Castle in Austria after the abdication.) His forth son Karl was sent to Italy to control the banking system there (he was entrusted with the Popes treasure) His fifth son Jacob was sent to Paris to control the Banking there (also famous for the Chateau Mouton Rothschild wines in the Bordeaux region) All five sons were Bankers foremost and specialised in their side lines second. To further keep the money in the family the sons were encouraged to marry their cousins.

I mentioned his eldest son Mayer Amschel Rothschild the one who stayed in his home land in Germany, who also formed the Illuminati. What is this Illuminati, in 1773 he assembled 12 of his most influential friends and convinced them, if they pooled their resources together they could rule the world. Mayer Rothschild chose Adam Weischaupt to lead this organisation and on 1st May 1776 Weishaupt code name 'Spartacus' established a secret society called 'Order of the Illuminati' they seek to establish a 'New World Order' Their object was to abolish all orderly governments, abolish the owning of private property, abolish inheritance, destroy patriotism, breakdown of family unity, cause chaos amongst religion then create a New World Government.

Because of these predicted turmoil's President Jackson is supposedly to have said about the Rothschild's "You are a den of vipers! I intend to rout you out, and by Eternal God I will rout you out. If the people only understood the rank of injustice on our money and banking system, there would be a revolution before morning"

The Rothschild's have continued to finance the Illuminati and the New World Order by joining forces with the 'Elite' of this world.

The central banking system today are the Rothschild's descendants and they run the Financial Empire that spans the world over not just Europe but Australia, USA, Canada, Mexico, Rio-de-Janeiro, Tokyo, Hong Kong and Singapore.

There are however three nations not yet under the control of the Rothschild's Banking system and they are North Korea, Cuba and Iran. Not surprising they are troublesome countries because they are fighting to maintain their financial independence which the rest of the world failed to do years ago.

There are many examples of how the Rothschild family inherited sudden vast wealth, it goes as far back as the Russian Revolution days, when the Romanoff's the Tsar of Russia entrusted his wealth to the Rothschild Bank, but when the Rothschild were refused access to establish a central Banking system in Russia the Rothschild sent in some Jewish people to drum up a revolution. The Rothschild's next clever step was to finance the Russian Revolution and then order the execution of the Royal household through the Bolshevists, even though the Tsar had been forced to abdicate on March the 2nd, his his family were still executed four months later, the firing squad were made up of Hungarian soldiers to avoid any Russian soldier suffering from an attack of conscience. At midnight on the 17th July 1918 the Royal family were woken and taken down to the basement to sit on chairs to be executed. Some had to be shot more than once; one of the Princesses had to be bare net because her corsets forbid its piercing point. Following the murder of the Romanov's family the Rothschild demanded their millions back off the Russian Bolshevist government, not only did they want their money paid back in full, but with huge interest. The Rothschild then picked up a cool 50 million dollars from the Tsar's account. (What I call blood money, does Prince Philip know about this? He was blaming the Russians recently not the Rothschild's Dynasty) Rothschild learnt early on that it was much more profitable to lend money to Royals or a titled person than a commoner, not only to pick up a fatter return but often to gain power. The message here is clear; don't mess with the Rothschild's! It seems the world has to learn to toe the line when dealing with this family, especially when it comes to world banking, in the past two Presidents have lost their lives opposing the Rothschild Banking. They were President Lincoln and President J. F. Kennedy. Abraham Lincoln once wrote, "I have two great enemies, the Southern Army in front and the Bankers at the rear. Of the two, the one at my rear is my greatest foe" Lincoln was assassinated in 1863. A hundred years later in 1963 J. F. Kennedy signed to give US Government the power to issue currency without going through the Rothschild's, six months later he too was assassinated!!! Same message; don't mess with the Rothschild's. And have you ever thought why the Vatican is protected by the 'Swiss Guards?' Allegedly in 1527 the Imperialists didn't have enough funds to pay the soldiers, blaming the wealthy Vatican for their shortfall for their wages. The soldiers decided to seek revenge on the Pontiff Clement VII by storming the gates of the Vatican. The death toll that day was 12,000 and the Bounty amounted up to 10 million ducats. This attack is referred to as the 'Sack of Rome' following that event, 200 mercenary soldiers or 'soldiers of fortune' were commissioned to guard the Vatican's Bank and as the Pope's life had been saved that day by the Swiss Guards, only they were entrusted to protect the Pope. Is this why the Papal Treasure was allowed to be stored in Switzerland as a precaution, preventing a repeat of the '1527 theft'? This would explain how the Pope allowed the Papal treasure to be taken out of the Vatican to Switzerland to be guarded by the Swiss Bank, by now it is owned by the Rothschild's. Which means; they are now holding the 'Papal purse strings' the other oddity is, why during both World Wars, was Switzerland allowed to remain neutral? Are the Swiss citizens exempt because they are a special race or is it because of another reason? Why did the Rothschild Bank operating from Switzerland during both World Wars, lend money to both sides of the conflict. Even though it might have been a situation of 'Dog eat dog' on the war front, it was certainly the 'Don't bite the hand that feeds you' scenario behind the scenes in Switzerland, a country that became a sanctuary to many and remained unspoilt by war.

Another disclosure of how they got 'rich quick' was when Rothschild confided in the Apartheid President P.W. Botha of South Africa during the 1980's, when he was offered an extensive loan, explaining there was massive wealth available in the Swiss Banks Accounts which once belonged to the German Jewish people who suffered under German Nazis regime.

To further increase the wealth of the Rothschild dynasty in 1987, Rothschild created a 'World Conservation Bank' for the third World countries to cancel their debts. I took this to mean the debts would be wiped out and they could make a fresh start. I even signed a petition at the back of our church supporting their debt clearance. I didn't realise, in return for their 'debt clearance' these countries had to give up their land to the Rothschild Banks. I don't feel this is debt clearance; this in my eyes this is compulsory purchase!

It sounds more like 'You don't owe us any money; neither do you own your own land either'

The 'third world' land represents 30% of the land surface of the world! Guess who's hurtling ahead to buy, grab or claim that 30% of the World Wilderness. You've guessed it the Rothschild's with the help from Global Environment Facility which totals to 30 billion over three years, as well as the help from World Banking. They then returning the land back to 'Home Countries' leaving the locals without crop land, causing food prices to rise which is exactly what the Rothschild's want to create with this 'New World Order' thing. Adding to this humanitarian insult, Edmond Rothschild sometimes referred to as the 'CO2 Man' or the 'Global Warming Pusher' who tries to convince the world of the 'non-existent man-made' or more lightly the 'Rothschild-made' Global Warming Catastrophe that's about to bestow us, but in fact the scientist are telling us, its cooling not warming. In 1989 he conned the World Wildlife Congress with his scam, that this CO2 needed to be 'caught' and transported to the North Pole in order to maintain the temperature in the Sahara Dessert, but of course this needed money so the tax payer paid! How did they catch it, was it bottled?

By the way, the World Central Bank has other titles too, Bank International Settlement, International Monetary Fund and World Banking!

The Rothschild's have been making a killing through 'Diabolic Genius' ideas for centuries. To me, it's like a rich man claiming off the DHSS and getting away with it.

Business

I wondered, how could, the Rothschild's possibly be involved with world business!

I understood employers supply employees with employment to keep the wheels of economy turning. I couldn't believe the name Rothschild was about to reappear once again, but I was saddened when I read that some believe that they have contributed to manipulating bouts of unemployment for many decades. The most memorable example of this was in the late 1920's when the Rothschild Bankers were responsible for deliberately 'constricting money flow' in order to create the 'Great depression' was it called Great because they made great wealth by causing it?

My next question was; are the Rothschild Bankers about to play with our lives once more, by deliberately destroying the British economy when they advised the British Government in 1985 to privatise British gas, British steel, British coal, Electricity and British Water board. Was there a hidden agenda here I wonder, the word power comes to mind! When these companies are in private hands anything could happen.

I often hear the man in the street saying, "This country has gone to the dogs, it doesn't own anything anymore; the Government has sold the family silver" which make me wonder are there Rothschild's within the Government?

Rockerfell once said, "The way to make money; is to buy when blood is running in the street" Is this what he considered to be good business sense?

Think on and take a stroll down any high street in Britain today, and what do you see? Empty shops for rent, the only thriving shops open are the charity shops, but they are not helping the British economy they are run by volunteers and managed by high salaried managers with extremely expensive 'freebee' cars.

I don't know why each town in Britain doesn't re-name their high street 'Charity Street', what do you think? Whatever profit that's made, we assume is either sent to third world countries to either feed their army or to buy their ammunition. Is that helping British economy, I think not! On the other hand if the money is not sent abroad, it's usually fed into a bottomless pit in the name of research! And we've all heard that charity such as 'Cancer Research' has so much money in their pot; they are just looking for ways to waste it!

Many a word spoken in gest, when my friends husband said recently "Jo, don't give away any more cloths, soon the only clothes we will have are our old ones" I can see what he means if the price of petrol and diesel escalates as Rockerfell intends, then clothes trafficking across the world will cease to exist.

Military

Military or War, it's all the same thing to me but I couldn't believe the Rothschild's could possibly be in control of 'War and Peace'

But then I read that the Rothschild's have deliberately created every war since the 1800's, shockingly they finance both sides then later collect the borrowed money in peace time from both sides, making puppets out of every country involved. Very clever don't you think, but very wicked! How have they achieved this you may ask, when Mayer Rothschild first instigated the 'Illuminati' its sole purpose was to 'divide and conquer' by encouraging Government and Nations to tear each other apart with war, causing political, financial and Religious unrest leading to ruination of countries. The Rothschild's then stepped in, calmly to piece together the chaos they had caused in the first place, yet again lining their own pockets. Example of this can be seen during the Napoleonic war at the battle of Waterloo, which was the beginning of the Rothschild's great fortune. When Napoleon appeared to be winning on the battle front, the secret military reported their findings to London. On June 20th 1815 Nathan Rothschild informed the government, but the politicians did not believe him. Rothschild immediately began selling stocks on the English stock market and every one followed suit causing the stocks to plummet to practically nothing. At the last minute Rothschild began buying the stocks back at rock bottom prices, which then gave the Rothschild family complete control of the British economy. Bank of England was set up and Nathan Rothschild was placed in total control, two years later in 1817 the same technique was used on the French Government.

Their next move was to create unrest against the Bores, which became known as the 'Bore War'. The Bores were a combination of German, French and Dutch settlers who emigrated to the Cape of South Africa in 1600's, but when the Rothschild's discovered they were digging up gold and diamonds in the 1800's, the Rothschild's had the British army wage a brutal and cruel war against them, starving the women and children in diseased ridden concentration camps and destroying their farms.

Instructions were to kill all the Bores just like they'd done with the Native American Indian Tribes, in 1770's.

Incidentally the destruction of the Native Americans at 'Wounded knee' was to clear the way for the Rothschild financed Railways, to carry European immigrants across America. A US journalist once wrote this about the Native American Indians "Why not annihilation?" Because their glory has fled, their spirit is broken, their manhood effaced, better that they die than live the miserable wretches that they are" My response to this is "Nations of the world be still for a moment, because one day the Native Americans may rise up and remind the world of the Rothschild sins"

But I digress, the Bores finally submitted and accepted English rule and were not permitted to leaving the British Commonwealth until 1961.

Their next big money spinner after the Bore War was the First World War which started in 1914, better known as the 'Great War' nothing great about this epic event either. Why do the Roth's refer to hideous events they have caused as 'Great' they caused nothing but misery?

This war came about because King Edward VII became financially embarrassed and borrowed money from the Rothschild Bank. It's documented in many places that the Rothschild ignited this war not to just make money but to gain power. Winston Churchill was in power at the time, question is had he been placed in prime position to direct this war or was he there by honest election. If he was contently placed there, was it because he was beholden to the House of Rothschild to safe guard his reputation avoiding scandal leading to ruination of his political career over his hidden secrets which included huge gambling debts, drinking problems, whoring bills and a special interest in young boys. But there appears to be an illegitimate connection to the Rothschild's blood line. Winston's family tree seem a bit unclear, it is alleged that Nathan Rothschild was Queen Victoria father. Winston Churchill's mother was already three months pregnant when she married Randolph Spencer-Churchill, but she had previously been keeping company with Edward VII a friendship which lasted for two years. So if Edward VII was Winston's biological father then Nathan Rothschild may have been his great-grandfather! Even if Edward VII was not Winston's biological father, Randolph Spencer-Churchill supposedly real father was in debt to the tune of £66,902 to the Rothschild Bankers. So the family was either beholden to the Rothschild financially or related from the other side of the blanket. If the above is true there are some moral issues there, but not as much as Winston's growing up years.

The House of Rothschild knew creating war created money, so the Rothschild deliberately instigated unrest between Poland and Germany to create more wealth and of course gain more power. To safe guard Rothschild's bets, they split the lending money between the British, the French and the Germans to enable them to finance the war on all fronts.

(No loyalties there, just a board game to them.)

Winston Churchill was desperate for the Americans to join his war, but the Americans would not join unless they were provoked. Then on 7TH May 1915 a British ship called the 'Lusitania' was carrying 159 American passengers from America bound for England, then just off the coast of Ireland a German submarine deliberately torpedoed the civilian luxury liner and she met her fate at the bottom of the Irish channel. It is rumoured by some, that the German submarine was a captured U-boat manned by British men, used as bait in a bid to anger the Americans into joining the war. That day 'Lusitania' lost 1,201 of her passengers and crew to the raging sea.

A Colin Simpson described it as "The foulest act of wilful murder ever committed on the sea"

Twenty years after World War 1, violence raised its ugly head again and in 1939 another World War was declared. Churchill was quoted saying before the Second World War started, "We will force this War upon Hitler, if he wants it or not"

It seems to me that the Rothschild's achieved their power by placing their heirs and illegitimate children into war-mongering positions then forcing them to instigate wars, turning Nation against Nations people against their own people, black against white, black against black, families against families and friend against friend.

But are these people in power warmongers or just puppets with 'Monsters' controlling their strings, are they forced to dance to their tune?

Winston Churchill found himself once more at the helm of another World War, how convenient to be at the right place at the right time yet again, or was he placed there? Again Churchill wanted the support of the Americans at his side, (almost like a play mate) but they were still not willing to join unless they were antagonised yet again. But on the quiet, Roosevelt was a warmonger himself and was secretly jealous of Churchill's involvement with the war. To cajole things along Roosevelt gave the Chinese one hundred million dollars to bomb Japan, the attack was called 'JB355' or 'Fire Bomb Japan' just to double secure his ticket for the war he ordered a Freeze on Japans assets and the Brits joined in with the ban as well by cutting off the Japanese oil supply. The Japanese were outraged when they saw their oil being shipped right pass them to Russia. Japan was dying a slow death from 'economic war' Roosevelt and Churchill got their beloved war with both barrels, in retaliation the Japanese bombed Pearl Harbour.

At the end of the war Churchill was quoted saying, "We butchered the wrong pig" Who was the pig he was referring to, was it Adolph Hitler?

Hitler apparently didn't want to fight the British, he sent Rudolph Hess to secure peace in May 1941, but Churchill locked him up for 27 long years and he was found hung in his cell in 1968 at the grand old age of 93. Which raises the question, could a 93 year old man really have hanged himself? I don't know, but adding to his punishment no guards were ever allowed to speak to him during those 27 years, he was forced into a world of silence. Were these two wars worth it, I don't know. Roosevelt was poisoned on 12 April 1945 by a Nazi agent and the Nazi agents were employed by the Rothschild's. Hitler was supposedly instructed to poison himself on the same day 12th April 1945 and Joseph Stalin was poisoned on 1st March 1953. That only left Churchill to live to a grand old age, but why was he allowed to when other leaders weren't? I have mixed feelings about this man who many admire; a man who demanded so many to die for him, there is so much said about him that doesn't sound like a balanced citizen. Some claimed Winston Churchill held political meetings in his bathroom while he was naked in the bath! It's well documented he was a high ranking Freemason and a Druid, even the Romans were sickened by the Druids practice of burning humans in wicker chairs. After reading such rubbish, I cannot bring myself to honour him with the title 'Sir' when he was responsible for killing millions of innocent children worldwide including mothers, the elderly not to mention unwilling soldiers who had no wish to kill Churchill's enemy, much less an unknown stranger. How could these survivors go to church on their return to their homeland with a happy heart knowing they had broken one of the Ten Commandments, which is 'Thou shall not kill' What are they say at the gates of heaven, 'Sorry but Winston made me do it'?

Jean-Paul Santrc once said about war, "When the rich wager war, it's the poor who has to die" how true that is. And a British Labour leader also said, "Whenever there is rumours of war, you may be sure Rothschild is near the region of the disturbance"

It is said by someone, the reasons the Second World War came to a sudden end, is that the Rothschild Bank pulled the financial plug on Germany. The Rothschild's then had the audacity to draft up a treaty called the 'League of Nations' to secure peace amongst Nations. It was Max Rothschild who was one of the eleven who took part in the signing ceremony.

Some believed this was the war to end all wars, but Rothschild not happy with the money they'd made from both World Wars started to lurk in another under-cover war, a modern day deadly game of genocide on a scale Hitler would have been envious of, the test case study was Rwanda.

When the world thought it was their neighbouring Uganda who had caused the invasion, sadly it was later discovered to be the 'Club of the Isles' who were also in control of 'World Wild Federation for Nature' they instigated the war between Rwanda and Uganda. As a result of this war the Rwandan's were genocide and virtually wiped out off the face of the earth. The Rwanda's were deliberately killed through famine, starvation, war, disease and inoculation. Over 800,000 lives were lost through torture and soul destroying tactics and in 1994 in such countries as Angola, Rwanda, Southern Sudan, Ethiopia and Somalia were part of this vast culling, to clear central Africa of their population to make way for 'The New World Order and the throne of the Antichrist' this massacre was paid for by the Rothschild. All the cruel lies have been printed by white-owned Rothschild media, stating that Africa is too poor and over populated and diseased with Aids and HIV but in actual fact, Africa's population density is 15% per square kilometre in comparison to Europe which is 89% per square kilometre. Never mind watching out for wild life extinction, the African people should be more worried about, their own extinction and losing their identity in the process. Maybe Africa needs to shut the door on the outside world for a while and make peace with her own people and spend some time healing relations with their own kind. Stop this black killing black and rekindle your brotherhood love. In my mind, Africa could survive on her own, I think she could feed herself and I think she has enough wealth to trade when she finally opens her door to the outside world once more. If only she could unshackle herself from the clasps of the oil grabbing tentacles of the Rockerfell and the Rothschild financiers.

An unknown author once wrote this about war.

War is a waste of muscle, waste of brain.

Waste of patience, waste of pain.

Waste of work, waste of wealth.

Waste of beauty, waste of health.

Waste of blood, waste of tears.

Waste of youths most precious years.

Waste of ways the Saints once trod.

Waste of glory and a waste of God.

George Patterson, who you'd think would love war, once said "No man ever won a war by dying for his country. He won it by making the other poor man die for his country" How true that is!

Going back to 'World Wild Federation' when I discovering Prince Phillip was its Chairman I was not convinced he would have any dealings with this unsavoury family the Rothschild so I decided to investigate further. I went back to Prince Philips roots, I discovered Prince Philip's <u>Father</u> was tried and convicted of treason in 1921 for disobeying army orders and jeopardising his own country Greece, when Turkey were invading. He was sentenced to death by a firing squad, but a British Arms Merchant paid off the Greek Government and he managed to escape to the UK.

Although Philip was only six months old when he left Greece, he spent his youth in France and his teenage life in Germany where he was trained in the Hitler youth. His three sisters became members of the Nazi party and all three married German high ranking Soldiers. One of Philips brother-in-law became chief of Goering's secret intelligence and were frequent guests at the Nazi functions. In later years Lord Louis Mountbatten, who was Prince Philips Uncle and Princess Elizabeth's second cousin arranged their marriage. Before the wedding, Prince

Phillip renounced his Greek Citizenship and was granted a British Citizenship.

He also changed his faith from Greek Orthodox Church to the Anglican Church.

Going back to the topic of WWF, in Jan 1961 a few months before the launching of the WWF Prince Phillip killed an Indian tiger in India then killed a very rare Rhino leaving her baby Rhino to fend for itself; to me a person who enjoys a blood thirsty sport does not qualify for a Chairpersons post in the World Wildlife Federation! Prince Philip still shoots, but prefers to calls it culling, not killing. All across Africa WWF Mercenary Armies carry out brutal population war, Park rangers armed with helicopter guns, infantry weapons and light missiles functioning as death squad's conduct cold blooded killing, referring to the natives of their own country as 'Poachers'. When 70 murder charges were brought forward to a Zimbabwean parliament, they rushed through a bill called, 'The Protection of Wild life Indemnity Act' What this act stood for was a licence to kill any black African on site 'in the name of duty' sadly, at the same time 'World Wild Federation' was running an operation to save the Black Rhino. So Black Rhinos have more protection than Black Africans. Surely not!

I don't condone any killing and that includes, Africans killing Africans or Royals killing for fun.

Today the same plan of genocide is directed by 'Club of the Isles' against East Africa. The WWF is said to be involved in a 'Human Zoo' where people are kept in en-forced backwardness.

I mentioned before the WWF are in the process of setting land off limits, this means they intend at the end of this decade to set 80% of the state of California as off limits, that means not to be used by humans. Their future plans are to carve up the United States into nine Nations and Australia into two, east and west ensuring semi-permanent state of underdevelopment. Beware if WWF have moved you from you native or ancient land to create a Wild life Park, and if one day you decide to re-visit your old homestead you could be shot on sight on suspicion of Poaching.

What I'm discovering is; all this killing in the world is not necessary, we could live peacefully together, but how can we possibly reason with this 'House of Rothschild's?'

Is this what they mean when they talk of 'New World Order' they are prepared to kill until they mould the world to how they want it?

What we need to do is have a 'pow-wow' and share a peace pipe on this topic. Although I've often wondered if the American Native Indian way of life was so good, why did they smoke? Evidently their tobacco didn't have additives like modern day cigarettes do. In an attempt to cull the world the Tobacco companies have added additional ingredients too deliberately to cause ill health, with which they later cash in with medical costs. Don't let them win, don't suffer at their hands and definitely don't line their pockets. Their tobacco contains Lead, Copper, Mercury, Aluminium, Acetone, Ammonia, Arsenic, Butane, DDT, Toluene and Naphthalene (which is moth balls) igniting these chemicals causes formation of Nitrogen oxides, Hydrogen cyanides and Carbon monoxide to be present in the smoke, and it's these toxins that passive smokers inhale!

All Tobacco companies belong to the Illuminati, one of them being the Rothschild and because they inter marry, it's a small world at the top.

Strange that John D. Rockerfell totally abstained from smoking, why what did he know?

In 1812 Mayer Amschel Rothschild said on his death bed "Remember my children, that all the Earth must belong to us Jews and the Gentiles being mere excrement of animals, must possess nothing" (although he was a Ashkenazi / Khazar Jewish Jesuit mislead the world into thinking he was of the original Hebrew Jewish faith)

Waite a minute, he was referring to me as a Gentile, how dare he compare me to animal excrement!

Years later in 1849 Gutle Schnaper Rothschild said this of her five sons on her death bed,

"If my sons didn't want war, there wouldn't be any"

Could all of the above be true about the Rothschild involvement with war through the ages, maybe so because when I read of one of the Baron Von Rothschild credited saying, "The time to buy is when blood is running in the streets" His friend replied, "Do you mean to say you're buying real estate with the gutter of Paris running with blood and the city in the hands of a mob"? His reply was, "Yes my friend, that's the only time you can buy at 50 cents on the dollar"

I'm not certain which Barron said this, as all five brothers were granted the Nobel Status of Barren hood by the Emperor of Austria in

1816 two years later they devised the emblem of five arrows in a fist symbolising their strength as a family lay in their unity.

But there are three well-known quotes made by two famous men about war, one was said by President Kennedy, "Mankind must put an end to war or war will put an end to mankind"

The other was said by Albert Einstein, "It is my conviction that killing under the cloak of War is nothing but an act of murder" Maybe we should heed both these men in history, because all this talk of war has suddenly made life sound and feel very cheap.

Politics

Again I couldn't believe the Rothschild's were involved in politics, but when I read that Nathan Rothschild is supposed to have once said, "I care not what <u>puppet</u> is placed on the throne of England to rule the Empire on which the sun never sets. The man, who controls Britain's money supply, controls the British Empire. And I control the British money supply".

My next discovery is totally dis-believable; it's a secret that's been kept for exactly 100 years.

In 1909 there were at least five very wealthy men who had made it abundantly clear that they were not in favour of Federal Reserve System in America (American Central Banking). To remove these men from power, their fortune had to be taken from them. Shooting them would be too obvious; a meeting took place on Jekyll Island just off the coast of Georgia to establish how to establish Central Banking in America. These seven men represented three Dynasties they were Rockerfell, J. P. Morgan and Rothschild Dynasty. These three financial families did their bidding for the Jesuit Order, at the meeting J. P. Morgan, who owned the White Star Liner company, was ordered by the Jesuits to build a ship and call her the Titanic. To them this was just a 'game of destruction of the super-rich' they undertook this expensive project just too safe guard their own wealthy position in order to delete their competition. The idea of creating this red herring, took the heat off any suspicion of committing murder on a grand scale by their opponents the Jesuits. These wealthy men with their total of eleven billion pounds worth of today's money were coxed aboard the floating Palace at Belfast docks in Ireland. Constantly reminding in the press, it was an unsinkable vessel, in actual fact it was designed as a 'tomb for the wealthy'. Edward Smith their Captain who was more than capable of steering the ship on a safe course was under orders from the Jesuit to sink this luxury liner and take these wealthy men to their wintery grave. The Captain was a 'Tempore-co-agitator' this is a Jesuit who wears a short robe.

The remaining crew and passengers were made up of characters from France, Ireland and Italy. The five very rich families did board the ship that day, along with a total of 3,447 very cheap expendable souls to vanish and perish at sea on that fateful night, leaving only 606 survivors. If the above is true and not an accident as I've been led to believe all these years, then I'd like to say "May perpetual light shine upon them, and may they all rest in peace. Amen."

Was this deliberate act of destruction just 'here say', but was there any possible proof that it could be true? For one thing was it a deliberate act or carelessness that they had only supplied enough lifesaving boats to save only the women and children, leaving the men on board to perish as planned?

Secondly the nearby ship claimed they only saw white flairs jettisoned as a sign of celebration, not red flairs to signal they were in distress, so was it an oversight that the ship only possessed white flairs that night! But why then was the beautiful polished box containing a 'Flared Gun' with an unused flair taken off the ship by a crew member, which survives to this day? The other question is; did it contain the red flairs which they all so desperately needed on that icy cold night, and why remove this essential piece of equipment anyway?

Also was it a coincidence that the Titanic went down on the 14th April the very Anniversary of Abraham Lincolns assassination? It appears to be the most perfect crime ever committed, has it taken 100 years to be exposed or did the Rothschild's think it humorous to leak the truth out on the very anniversary of her sinking a hundred years later? Lastly why did several survivors claim they heard an explosion first, and then hit the iceberg after?

And why was one survivors explanation of the explosion trivialized and told it must have been the other way round, it must have been the chimney's she heard cracking. What she should have said was! 'Was he there' to witness it?

And lastly why was Father Francis Browne a Jesuit given a camera and a ticket for the maiden voyage on the Titanic costing £4, sailing from Southampton via Cherbourg to Queensland in Ireland paid for by his Uncle, himself a Jesuit Priest. He was to board the Titanic on the 10th April and take as many photographs of the rich and wealthy on board the ship before disembarking at Queensland in Ireland. But not before Browne had briefed the Captain one last time, exactly what he was to do in the Atlantic waters, as instructed by the Jesuit General. But why would the Captain behave like a lamb going to the slaughter unless he was a Jesuit himself following orders from above and under oath. It now transpires that Father Frances Brown was the 'Jesuit Master' and one of the most powerful Jesuit in all of Ireland, who answered directly to the Jesuit General of the Order in Rome!

Witnesses reported that the Captain was not capable of giving his usual strong commands that night, why? And why did the White Star Liner company deliberately keep their other ships away from the Titanic that night? When questioned they claimed it was to save coal!

But it has still left me wondering, why would even a wealthy man part with $7.5 million of his money so easily to finance the building of the Titanic and then deliberately allow her to be sunk? Unless she was insured! After 100 years in 2012 an insurance document has been released for the first time revealing that the Titanic's hull and machinery was valued at £1 million pounds, but insured for £5 million pounds. Mr J. P. Morgan had hundreds of other different insurers; can you imagine us insuring different parts of our car with different insurers?

Why did he do this? Unless he was safe guarding his <u>expected</u> loss, the difference is, we insure <u>in case</u> of our loss. Seven large insurance companies took nearly 40% of the risk between them.

So Mr Morgan didn't lose out at all, in fact he probably made a small fortune and the insurance companies paid up within seven days. How prompt! Guess what the first claim was for? It was for a $5,000 25 horse power Renault car which was declared as 'Lost at sea'!!! Cargo pay-out first, life pay-out second. Interesting, maybe it was all intentional after all then! And why did J. P. Morgan cancel his passage at the last minute, even though he had a purpose built cabin on board?

This next story is meant to be a strange but true tale; in 1912 an American Politician Senator Alden Smith became the Chairman into the Inquiry of the sinking of the Titanic. He claimed he carried with him a yellow tarnished newspaper cutting in his wallet for ten long years, of a poem which read like this—"Then she the stricken hull, the doomed, the beautiful. Proud to fate based, her brow Titanic"

What a strange poem and why did he keep it in his wallet for ten years, then revealing it to the world after the famous Titanic sank. Unless he was one of the seven who met up on Jackal Island just, off Georgia.

This is not a statement; I'm just questioning what others believe. The 'Jesuit Zionists' ordered the attack on the World Trade Towers in 2001 to teach the Americans a lesson???

Again in 2003 some believe the 'Jesuit Zionists' instigated the invasion on Iraq because they wouldn't accept Central Banking

I don't know, I don't trust the Rothschild's who represent the Jesuit anymore.

The mistrust goes on; 19th May 2011 Monroe County Daily interviewed a vice chairman of the Liberal Democratic Party of Russia. His name is Vladimir Zhirinsky, a Kazakhstan (non-Hebrew Jewish person) when asked how he felt about Georgia and the USA who were trying to block Russia's entry to the World Trade Organisation (WTO) he claimed they had a quiet and peaceful weapon that could put the whole continent to sleep for ever, if anyone interferes with Russia's claim on Kuril Island.

He then referred to the Tsunami in Japan, suggesting it was caused by the new weapon which has been intensely studied by both the US and the Russians since the 1950s. Moscow has been routinely controlling the weather for decades to ensure sunny skies for military parades to take place, including National holidays; the process is called 'Cloud seeding'

The above was substantiated when in 1997 the US Secretary of Defence spoke of a threat of, 'Eco-type of terrorism where they can alter the climate by setting off earthquakes and stimulate volcanoes to erupt, through the use of electromagnetic waves'

In that case I think we should take this Russian man very seriously, at the moment we are dealing with a Christian Russian Prime Minister called Valdimir Putin, but if Vladimir Zhirinovsky comes to power we should question his conscience, and ask ourselves does he recognise right from wrong? Already he's made two worrying quotes, "We will surely stop the work of all Western Christian, Eastern and Islamic faiths" the other quote he made was "There is no problem with the opening of new houses of prayer for Lutherans" Does he mean devil and Satan worship?

This man once advocated dropping a Nuclear Bomb over the Atlantic Ocean to flood the whole of the British Isles. Does it make you wonder about Hurricane Sally in America in October 2012, was that an act of God or did the Elite, the Zionists, the Illuminati the 'New World Order' interfere with nature?

When a wild teenage party gets out of hand the police are summoned, and the trouble makers are asked to leave, but unfortunately were not dealing with harmless teenagers here, are we?

We're dealing with power-crazy politicians on both sides who have their finger on the button ready to go, and we their subjects have never asked them to inflict any world terror on our behalf.

They certainly don't have to kill on my behalf.

So they can STOP it right now!

Education

When did part of the education board come under the influence of the Rothschild's?

Luckily Protestant schools are not under the Rothschild canopy yet, but some Catholic schools operate under the Jesuit ethos.

So how and where did the Rothschild's get involved? A man by the name of Cecil Rhodes was born in Herefordshire in 1853, but he was a sickly asthmatic child and at the age of 16 his parents dispatched him off to South Africa to join his brother Herbert, hoping the sunshine would improve his health. In 1873 at the age of 20 he returned to England to complete his studies, at Oriel College Oxford where he was first initiated into the Freemasons.

After only one term, he went back to Africa and did not return again. It was noted after he joined the Freemasons, to harboured disturbing ideas of how he viewed the world, he wanted to create a 'Master/Slave Society' through select breeding by reducing the inferior race by 'Human weeding' (heard of this before) through famine, planned biological warfare, environmental poisoning, suppression of knowledge, suppression of invention, planned wars to de-populate and generally cause a disorder. This man was a Jesuit first, educated at Oxford second, a Freemason third and a 'Culler of mankind' forth.

After only 17 years in South Africa, in 1889 he had gained a reputation as a 'Diamond Baron', by buying up all the small diamond mines, sealing the world's monopoly on the diamond trade. He also manifested other titles, such as a 'Cheifton' who incur 'Hut taxes' on the Zimbabwe's tribes. Another title he acquired was 'Prime Minister' of Cape Colony, voted in by white members because the black people weren't allowed to vote. He introduced an act to push black people from their land, he once said in a speech "Africa is just lying ready for us, it's our duty to take her" and what easier way of taking it than through a secret society of Freemasons. In other words Rhodes instigated the first 'Land Grab' in Zimbabwe and once made a prejudice remark "I prefer land to niggers" The death toll in the slave trade was 100,000,000 and 1,000,000,000 black people were killed in Colonialism. In Britain he is better associated with Scholarship, not with mass murder; I can now see why Hitler was a fan of this man. Winston Churchill, Robert Baden-Powell and Cecil Rhodes were once overheard saying, they enjoyed their outing, and saw the slaughtering of Africans as a sport and adventure. To confirm their association Robert Baden-Powell was often seen sketching Cecil Rhodes amongst the natives. Even his friends termed Cecil as a 'race patriot' and the 'most evil man' Before his death in 1902 Cecil had already set up a secret society called 'The Round Table' in South Africa, with the intention of introducing it into Britain. Rhodes was the format of the round table but Lord Nathanial Rothschild was to be the financial controller. In Cecil Rhodes 'Last Will and Testament' he bequeathed a gigantic fortune to the Freemasons with the understanding that it would finance the continuation of the Round Table in Britain, to secure his dream of 'New World Order' and the remainder of his estate went to the Rhodes scholarship at Oxford University. The money was to educate a select number of overseas students, who would then return to their own country as world leaders and install the idea of 'New World Order' Their extra curriculum at Oxford was to introduce them to the secret society of Freemasonry and also a man called George Estabook who taught the use of hypnotism and mind-control to British Intelligence. This is where Cecil Rhodes was first introduced to mind manipulation. This type of education must have had powerful influence on Cecil because he emerged from a childhood of a sickly weakling with asthma, to possessing ideas of grandeur of conquering the world long after his death. He was once asked, how long did he think his memory would endure? Rhodes replied, "I give myself four thousand years" He envisaged a world where British would occupy Africa, Middle East, South America, Pacific Islands, China and Japan. He entrusted the likes of the Rothschild's and the Freemasons to continue his dream. I'm British myself, but I have no desires to control other countries, I veer other culture and their individualities, why would I want to live in a world with one uniform of clothes, language, food and beliefs.

Other 'Rhodes scholarship' schools are located in Gordon's town in Scotland, Salem in Germany and Annarrighta in Greece. Prince Phillip and Prince Charles were both educated at Gordon's town, the head master was Kurt Hahn the founder of the Hitler Youth Movement, which would explain why Charles once compared it to 'Colitz in Kilts'

I don't know what tone this was meant to be received, but it still remains to be said they were educated in a Jesuit school! Another famous name which appears on the Rhodes scholarship list was Bill Clinton, he won a scholarship to be educated in Oxford University in the UK, and later went on to Yale University for his degree.

After Rhodes death in 1902, a conference took place on the 4th, 5th, 6th of September 1909 in a house called Plas Newydd at Lord Anglesey's estate near the village of 'Llanfairpwllgwyngyllgogerychwynrodrobwylll lantysiliogogogoch' in North Wales, Anglesey. (It should contain 58 characters if it's spelt correctly) The original Round Table referred to themselves as the 'Elite'a group of 'twelve wise men, and considered themselves as respected English Freemasons who were the 'Think Tans' of their organisation. There were such names as H. G. Wells, Georg Bernard Shaw, Rudyard Kipling and Lord Rothschild who modelled themselves on the Jesuit movement. They boosted of a 'Race of Supermen' who had been bread in preparation for the Millennium. Years later the Round Table branched off, forming the 'Council of Foreign Relation', 'Royal Institute of Affairs' and others. The Round Table we are more familiar with today, are the very outskirts of its core known as the 'Association of helpers' working for the good of others in the name of charity. Going back to Rhodes, have you ever wondered why Zimbabwe changed its name to Rhodesia? Well four years before he died in 1898 it was renamed after Cecil Rhodes! Not surprising a hundred years on, the name 'Cecil Rhodes' has become a British embarrassment and his name has been branded as the 'Bad man in Africa' so much so, an application has been forwarded by some Africans for Cecil Rhodes bones to be excavated from its carved rock grave in Rhodesia, and taken back to his birth place to rot there! Not that I'm taking sides, but can you blame them? We all want to see monuments raised in memory of people were proud of. There is a statue of a naked man on horseback in front of Kensington Palace and also in Rhodesia commemorating the life of Cecil Rhodes. The Queen Mother went out to Africa with Princess Margaret on her 16th birthday in 1947 and again in 1953 to view Rhodes memorial. Princess Elizabeth and Princess Margaret's cousin, who was also called Margaret (Elphinstone) married one of the Rhodes; they met while she worked as a secretary for the MI6. I'm assuming were talking about the same Rhodes family, I could be wrong.

With hind sight as far as Africa is concerned, maybe Cecil Rhodes should have concentrated more on recuperation in their beautiful sun bathed country rather than brutally trying to take over the world. We all need to stop poaching on other peoples territories, could it be considered a sign of weakness or jealousy when countries invade others, in which case we the British must have been very jealous of others possessions over the last 700 years, to make false claims on land, minerals, oil, money and even diamonds. It sounds like 'Men, behaving badly' to me, thieving land that doesn't belong to us.

It's true, Cecil Rhodes did not directly affect my education, but he did affect our world leader's education, which indirectly affected me.

Now brace yourself for this next educational lesson, to start with it is said we learn more in the first five years of our lives than we do during the rest of our lives. In that case it's very important what we're taught in those precious years regarding the difference between truth and lies, right and wrong, safe and unsafe, moral and immoral. This next paragraph reduced me to tears; it was referred to as "Manipulation of Consciousness, and Thinking"

Rockerfella, also a 33rd degree Freemason was once quoted saying, "The entire reason the bloodline allowed the women's liberation movement to move forward was for various reasons. 1. It takes the children away from their mothers to be taught by their teachers and to be more dependent upon others other than their parents. 2. It doubles the taxes that can be collected by a single family.

3. It allows for corporations like McDonalds, Burger King and the fast food companies to control our diet because the women are no

longer willing or able to prepare good nutritious food for their children. 4. It is easier to control and manipulate the woman that controls and manipulates their husbands if they work for your business. 5. It destroys the home, and children and men are not being taken care of like most want and it creates opportunities for people to cheat on their partners because things are lacking within their relationship.

I know this is the way of the world, but the fact it didn't just evolve, but was actually deliberately created-it not only educated me but crushed me!

Religion

I cannot imagine that the Rothschild's would interfere with our individual faiths, tackling this topic worries me greatly, thinking I might expose myself to extreme criticism, but with Julian's encouragement I will venture back to the beginning to find out why so many 'Non-Church goers' feel that nearly all faiths are corrupt! In their defence, I will say this 'At least they are questioning their concerns, whereas up until now, I have accepted it at face value'

I hope this chapter won't sound too much like a history lesson, as I'm not qualified to teach. But this is how I capsulate Christianity in one long breath, ready? Jesus was born a Roman citizen, was raised in the Hebrew Jewish faith and because he was born in Judea was a naturalized Judean; at the age of 30 he started to preach, when he was only 33 he was crucified and died. Before he died he spiritually or symbolically handed over the keys of his Fathers Heavenly Kingdom to Peter one of his Apostles. Jesus referred to Peter as "The rock on which I build my church" in effect Peter became the first Bishop of Rome. (Take a breath and full stop) There have been two hundred and sixty six Popes since Peter; but in 'mid-term' the continuation of the Papal link in Rome broke, when in 1305 a French Pope called Clement V was elected. This Pope didn't actually set foot in Rome, partly due to the fact he was so involved in the Trials of the Knight Templers in France, consequently his Papacy was conducted from Avignon in the south of France and continued there for the next seven reigning French Popes. These 67 years spent away from the Holy City of Rome are called the 'Babylonian Captivity of the Papacy' they are referred to the Babylonian years because of the 70 years the Israelites spent in captivity in Babylon. But in 1376 the seventh Pope of Avignon, Pope Gregory X1 was persuaded by St Catherine of Siena a young 29 year old mystic woman to visit Rome, even though the Pope had been handed a letter written by a Friar who was reported to have second sight warning him, if he went to Rome he would be poisoned. He didn't heed the letter but took Catherine's advice instead and travelled to Rome, he died not long afterwards at the aged of 49, the cause of death was 'unspecified' bearing in mind it wasn't unusual for Popes to be disposed of in those days. Allegedly over the years there have been 18 murdered Popes and 14 Martyred Popes. Because Pope Gregory X1 died at the Vatican, it meant Rome once again could elect a new Pope at Rome! To understand why and when corruption started in the Christian faith, I need to go back even further in time to when the Vatican became nervous about Christians losing their visitation rights to the Holly Land. I've had to go back as far as 637AD when Jerusalem was captured and the city was surrendered to the Saracens, even though the Saracens were ruthless Non-Christian Knights, Omar their leader was kind enough to allow the Christian pilgrims' a safe passage into Jerusalem to pay homage to the Christian Holy Sites. But in 1065 Jerusalem was taken by the Turk's and 3,000 Christians were massacred.

As a result of this barbaric act 54 years after this Christian slaughter, in 1119 a French Nobel man from Champagne region collected eight holy and willing men mostly related to protect the pilgrims on their journey to and from the Holy land.

When the Turks retreated from Jerusalem, they left King Baldwin in charge of the Holy City. He knew the Christians didn't have a church or a place to live so he allowed this 'poor order' their visitation rights once more and also allowed them to set up their headquarters on the ruined Temple Mount, the old site of King Solomon's Temple. These eight men formed a new order known as 'The Knight of the Temple of King Solomon' later abbreviated to the 'Knight Templers'. In 1139 Pope Innocent II recognised their good work and allowed these Holy men to carry swords to safe guard the pilgrims on their journey. From then on they were referred to as the 'Warrior Monks' He also gave them permission to pass freely through boarders and exempt them from paying taxes, in return for these privileges the Pope expected them to owe their allegiance to no-one other than himself. To join this Holy Army, the new Templers were expected to give up their wealth for the good of the order;

they were also expected to live a life of poverty and chastity. And because of their obedience, the 'order' not them personally, quickly grew rich. Not only were the eight original Knights of Nobel descent, they were also well educated and could easily control their own finances. As a result of this pooling of their wealth they were in a position to lend money to affluent people in financial difficulties.

They were wealthy enough to leant money to such people as King Edward VII of England and King Philip IV of France, Philip worried about his debts, made an agreement with the Vatican prior to the election of the next Pope, regarding the possibility of electing a candidate who was neither Italian nor a Cardinal, but in fact his childhood friend. His friend was successfully elected and was anointed Pope Clement V in 1305 in Lyons France, not in Rome like all the other Popes before him. The day was not uneventful, because it was marked by a wall collapsing on the Pope during the procession, he lost his balance and his crown fell to the ground.

The reason why King Philip was eager to entice a Pope to take root in French soil was because he knew of the Papal wealth, and as Philip was suffering financial embarrassment himself he thought if he could borrow from his friend the Pope it could solve his problems. In the meantime he asked the Knight Templers for a further loan to fight the English and the Flemish in Flanders. The Templers declined his requests, possibly because the Templers had now built their headquarters in London in 1184 called the 'New Temple' and supplying money to a King to fight against their headquarters wouldn't have made sense!

On the other hand it might have been an unwise decision to insult the King of France like this, knowing the Kings reputation for always wanting to have his own way not to mention his arrogance in conducting unscrupulous activity when he was driven by greed.

As a result of the Templers refusal, the King started pressurising the Pope to take action against the Templers, as a way of freeing himself from this dreaded debt. But soon after their denial, Christendom was driven out of the Middle East, and the Templers lost their foot hold in the holy land to the Emption Mamluks. The Knight Templers started to flood back in full force to France and their overwhelming presence in France just fuelled the Kings jealousy over their wealth. As Pope Clement V was constantly under the thumb of King Phillip IV, he eventually gave in and allowed the arrest of the entire Templar Order to take place. It was to happen swiftly across France and their arrest was to take place at a Dawn raid on Friday 13th October 1307, including the seizing of all their land. (Hence why, Friday 13th is considered unlucky even to this day)

On their arrest the Templers were excommunicated from the church and secondly, charged with false accusations such as financial corruption, homosexuality, and heresy and for conducting magic.

The King sent word to all catholic practising countries in Europe to arrest all Templers for interrogation. England arrested and questioned the Templers but could find no wrong with the order including no evidence that they had any knowledge of magic, consequently they were released. The only secret they could find the Templers were in possession of was, that they were introduced to knowledge and wisdom of the orient, such as the stars, medicines and architecture. And with this wealth of knowledge they were able to build superb buildings such as our spectacular Cathedrals. Needless to say a large number of Knights confessed to these vile accusations in France, but only under terrible torture, even after their confession they were still burnt at the stake for their supposed crimes. The trials took place between 1307 and 1312 and their execution went on until 1314 and the last execution took place in Paris. The Knight Templers last execution was their leader, the Grand Master Jacques de Molay who was to suffer the same fate as them, except he was to be burnt at the stake in the shadow of Notre Dame Cathedral in Paris. It is reported he requested to be tied in such a manner that he could face the very Cathedral his own Knight had built and that his hands should be tied in prayer. As he was burning it is said that he called out above the flames, that he had remained faithful to God throughout and that anything he confessed to was due to torture. But because of this injustice, King Philip and the Pope would be knocking on heaven's door before the year was out for their false accusations. And sure enough his prediction came true; both were dead before the year was up! So King Philip didn't live long enough to enjoy his ill-gotten gains. The Templers wealth was ceased and their land was donated to the 'Order of St John of Jerusalem, Knight Hospitallers'

I have to admit that these Knights were now scattered and were operating without a leader, with no boundaries or rules to adhere too. They were once of Nobel ancestors, which made them very learned, these men were highly skilled in every aspect, these men were highly educated, these men were very holy men, these men were very well respected at all levels, these men were very trusting. Pilgrims put their lives in their hands as they walked a complicated network of paths leading to holy sites in Jerusalem, these men gave up their wealth, their luxury life style to join a life of poverty and hardship, these men bowed down to every 'whim' of the Pope and the Vatican. So when they were betrayed, humiliated in public, stripped naked, tarred, shackled by their hands and feet and forced to walk bare foot to be burnt alive in front of a mocking crowd, it stands to reason that one day there would be a degree of repercussion.

Why did I fear this, well there is <u>nothing</u> more frightening than the wrath of an 'unjust man' but imagine the wrath of an 'unjust army' an army as vast as the Knight Templers?

Especially when I recall how angry Julian once became, when he was caned for a crime or prank he knew he hadn't committed, and the excruciating pain he not only endured at the time but remembered for the rest of his natural days, all because he knew he had been wronged.

The question is, were they capable of revenge? Well even Jesus lost his cool once, when he witnessed 'Money Changers' and 'Selling for profit' taking place in the Temple accusing them of creating a 'Den of Thieves' in his father's sacred house. It is true the Templers would of developed defending skills against the Saracens these were Muslim warriors of Arab Tribes, who led their men into battle after being tricked into partaking, inhaling or chewing Hashish (its other names are Cannabis/Marijuana or Weed) causing them to hallucinate.

They described the hallucination state as being taken into a 'Secret Garden of Paradise' and in order to re-enter this Paradise permanently they would first have to serve the Assassin and fight to the death. The Saracens also used another fighting technique, which was to operate in the dark and strike when their enemy were asleep, hence the name Saracens which evolved to 'Assassins'.

Did I need to mention the Saracens at all, yes I did because this is what the Templers were up against and that's how ferocious I believe the Templers had become. So when King Philip of France allowed his jealousy over the, Templers expertise in money matters, to 'get the better of him' one has to ask, was this King brave or foolish to attempt to destroy this 'Army of Holy Men' or did he allow a loose Cannon to escape that day?

The King of France must have been furious on that same dawn morning of October Friday the 13th following the dawn raid when he heard that when the vaults were opened in Paris their headquarters, to discoverer the Templers vast fortune had disappeared.

One could imagine some of this powerful order to immerge underground to fester like a cancerous tumour waiting to erupt and destroy the very organisation they were prepared to give up their life for, after all it was the Roman Catholic Church who had violated their reputation equally the French Royalist. The big question is, did these holy men get their revenge?

I don't know, but what happened to this vast order no longer called the Knight Templers? Did the Templers go into hiding because they weren't all burnt at the stake in France!

This is just hearsay, could their Banking skills have been taken to Switzerland, because how else can one explain a sudden expertise in Banking in a country that once was not. And why was this country allowed to be tax exempt arousing further suspicions, when such phrases as tax haven is used, including money laundering, underground economy, off shore banking, including secret banking accounts. I might find out differently later.

There had been 15,000 'Templers Houses' including an entire fleet of ships! These Templers fleets were used to carry pilgrim's part of their journey to and from the Holy land; Kings would even hire their fleet for a price to go into battle. It was reported that on 12th October 1307 the day before the mass arrest, that 18 ships were anchored in the port of La Rochelle in France. But on 13th October the following morning their 18 fleet of ships had mysteriously vanished, some believe they'd scattered to various parts of the world taking with them a wealth of sea faring knowledge.

Could it be that they were forewarned did the exiled Templers taken their navigation skills with them onto the high seas? The world should have been worried when Jacques de Molay was burnt; because when Pope Clement V was seen to support King Phillip IV they must have felt he'd turned his back on their Mother Church, who they felt they had defended with such ferocity.

I was beginning to realise they were a force to be reckoned with, they were well known to possess the 'heart of lions on the battle fields and hearts of lambs at the heart' at last I know what chivalry means, to behave ferocious in defence, but kind and gentle in the presence of a lady. These Warrior Monks did not hate other men, but man's wrong doing. Their order had obtained their fortune fair and square, but now they had been robbed of their leader, their vast lands, vineyard's, farms, churches, even castles but not their ships evidently. They were once considered the cutting edge of society with their high standard of practices, which are still regarded in high esteam today.

To be fair, they had all lived by strict codes, 76 of them to be exact but one Knight among them named Admiral Roger de Flor was once caught breaking those rules by pilfering for his own personal gain. He was thrown out of the order by the Grand Master Jacques de Molay himself, Roger de Flor later purchased his own Galley and turned Piracy. He hoisted a plain red flag which the French called 'Joli Rouge' which meant pretty red but he intended it to signify attack. (As we still recognise red for danger today) Roger de Flor died in 1305, which was nine years before Jacques de Molay was burnt at the stake in 1314.

Legend has it, that some took to the sea hoisting a similar red flag with the symbols of Jacques de Molay's skull and cross bones of his two femurs. The 'Joli Rouge' was quickly nick-named by the English as the 'Jolly Roger' the red background of the Jolly Roger was later exchanged for a black background. They chose black as a symbol of death and a warning to others that they never took prisoners, but fought to the bitter end. In defence of the Pirates, it appears, they were the first to practice democracy, as each shipman had a vote and all votes were equal! They were the first to recognise 'retirement if hurt on the job' the first to use psychological warfare by shouting abuse at their opponents, they were known to fight rough because they were already marked for execution.

We have good and bad in every walk of life, so it might have been with the Knight Templers; they were now leaderless, fugitives seeking escape from torture and execution. Those who did not turn Piracy is believed to have fled by sea and sought refuge in Scotland, taking up residence with the 'Scottish Stone Mason's' after all the Templers did have great stone masons amongst them, they had already built Westminster Abbey in London, Notre Dame Cathedral in Paris, York Minster Abbey in York and Chartres Cathedral in France and many more fine looking buildings.

But why Scotland one might ask, well in 1127 after the Templers had excavated some artefacts in Jerusalem, the Grand Master who was also a senior advisor to the Pope, travelled with one of the nine original Knight Templers to England to meet up with the King to seek a safe passage. Having obtained a Royal Safe Conduct from the King they travelled directly to Roslyn Castle to stay with the St Clair's who were related by marriage to the Grand Master Hugh de Payne of Champagne I.

On arrival Lord Rosslyn immediately granted them land to build a Chapel to house the Templers artefacts. After the dawn raid in 1307 some of the Templers knew that Roslyn Castle in Scotland would be a safe haven for them and, by 1314 the Templers felt they needed to create a new order. They chose the name 'Franc' meaning French and 'Mascon' which is French for builders or masons, these two names might have evolved to Freemason. Two more modern explanations of the name Freemason is, men join the order of their own free will or men who are free thinkers, does 'Franc-Mascon' sounds more plausible to you? More to the point did one evolve into the other?

The modern Freemasons aren't mentioned until 1381, that's nearly 70 years after the Vatican dispensed of the Knight Templers, although some believe, the 'Franc-Mascon' formed an alliance with the local Scottish Stone Masons and using the Templers expert skills went ahead and built 'Rosslyn Chapel' as was originally planned.

The chapel was not started until 1446 and it took 44 years to complete in 1490. Strangely enough there are many Templer symbols, images and traits carved throughout Rosslyn Chapel.

The other point to consider the new order called the Freemasons didn't have time to evolve enough, to create such exquisite architecture, unless they did tap into the Knight Templers in exile masonry experience.

The Architecture is magnificent, its interior has been described as 'White stone lace' and the Masons pillar and the Apprentice pillar have outstanding carvings too.

One of the prominent families mentioned were the Stuarts who later became the first 'Scottish Rite Freemason' considered by some to be the 'Inheritors of the Knight Templers' but I'm not yet convinced! But guess who became the first 'Grand Master of Masons of Scotland?' it was non-other than Earl Sinclair. So it seems both orders have become intertwined somehow.

There is another riddle; apparently there was another Rosslyn in Rennes-le-Chateau near Roussillon in Southern France. Twelve months before the Templers were arrested; the 'Templar Order' lent Pope Clement V's nephew a large amount of money to extend his Château into a Fortress with eight towers. My question is; did the Pope intend to have some treasure stored here, or was it secretly transferred to the Rosslyn Chapel in Scotland?

We will never know if there was ever a connection, but it leaves me wondering, what was the big mystery with both Rosslyn's. My other concern was didn't the Pope feel any guilt that the Templers had injected such a large amount of wealth into his nephew's chateau, yet he still went ahead and pulled the plug on their organisation on Friday the 13th

It seems this new Freemasons order has been obsessed with rebuilding King Solomon's Temple for a long time, but I could not find any desires of the Knight Templers to rebuild Solomons Temple. Solomon's Temple was after all destroyed 434 years before Jesus was born. To a Christian 'King Solomon's Temple' is an interesting piece of Ancient History, but for the pagan Freemason it has become absolutely crucial part of their order. Christianity is rooted in the New Testament; Freemasonry is rooted in the Old Testament devoted to the foundation of Solomon's Temple. It appears the Freemasons in present times are erupting events in the Middle East to make way for the Freemasons to re-build Solomon's temple. In fact it even looks as if the Anti-Christ is planning World War three to get what they want; it leaves one wondering if all Arabs are targeted.

I have no problem with the Knight Templers 'dissolving' and the modern Freemason 'evolving' from the order, except what's disturbing me is the Freemasons exchanged their Christian Knight order for a Satanic Freemason order.

We hear no more of the Knight Templers holy order, until another Knight appears in history. This time it was a Spanish Knight who fought in the Spanish Inquisition. Their eruption spread as far as northern Italy, southern France, Germany, Netherlands, Mexico, Latin America and Poland.

In 1504 the Pope had the foundation stone laid to start the rebuilding of St Peters Basilica in Rome. In an attempt to finance this huge project he sold 'Indulgence' these were certificates signed by the Pope which pardoned sins without confession and repentance. Martin Luther compiled a list of 94 points against the 'Indulgence' and nailed the list to the church door on 31st October 1517 in Wittenberg

Germany. Those who sided with Luther became known as 'Protestants' because they protested. This lead to many Catholics leaving in droves, consequently it left the collection bowls sparse and soon the Catholic church was in even more financial difficulties because people were no longer paying their 'Peters Pence' to rebuild St. Peters Basilica. The Pope realised he was starting to lose control, because previously he was able to dictate through Kings but now even they were turning Protestant, Henry VIII being amongst the first.

In an attempt to retrieve his lost sheep Pope Paul III was tempted by a Spanish Soldier Ignatius de Loyola. A Spanish Inquisition Knight who had been badly injured in a battle which forced him to end his military career. Ignatius de Loyola was born into a wealthy family, a Crypto-Jew of the Occult Cabala Practice and due to his family wealth was a member of the Spanish Illuminati. While recuperating from his war injuries, he acquired a book about Christian Saints, while studying this book he experienced a spiritual vision which resulted in him converting from his Occult Satanic Worship to the Catholic faith. Following his recovery he decided to pilgrim to Jerusalem, but was sent home by the Franciscan Monks. Why, I don't know? He travelled to Rome and eventually became a priest. While he was there he formed a new order called the Jesuits, it was at this point he offered his destructive arm to the Roman Catholic Church, to deal with the ever increasing Protestants. And in 1540 Pope Paul III officially sanctioned Ignatius as the head of a new order called the Jesuit, Ignatius was recognised as the first 'Black Pope' and within four years of being accepted into the Vatican in 1545, the Jesuits were given specific assignments to convert the protestants back to the 'mother church' either through theology, deception, torture, or Inquisition. The Jesuit oath contained a pledge—if the Protestants did not convert back to catholic faith they were to be exterminated from the face of the earth and to spare neither, sex, age nor condition.

They vowed to hang, waste, boil, flay, strangle and bury alive those infamous heretics, threatened to tear open the stomachs and wombs of their women and crush their infants heads against the wall, in order to annihilate for ever their excretal for the purpose of infiltration and controlling the Catholic Church. He devised an elaborate spy system which not even his own order was safe from. If there was any opposition, death was met swiftly. This period in history is known as the 'Roman Inquisition' The Dominicans worked in public while the Jesuits worked undercover. They were sent out as 'double agent missionaries' posing as Protestants as well as Catholics, which ever was needed in order to sabotage the Protestant movement. They also took on most of the Catholics religious roll, including taking confession from the poor, Rulers, Nobility, Kings and Queens. (Question is could these confessions have put them in a position of knowledge, which they later used to empower themselves) This Jesuit order demanded obedience, if they said black was white so be it, if they said it was right to kill, then it was not considered a sin.

They were later involved in creating the Council of Trent which consisted of 25 doctrines, it condemned freedom of speech, freedom of press and freedom of conscience.

By 1572 they had secured the right to deal in 'commerce' and Banking, a right that had not been granted to any religious order of the Roman Catholic Church since the Knight Templers time 260 years previously, they must have managed the finances successfully because in 1626 St Peters Basilica was finally completed. And needless to say because of their spy techniques they created several secret intelligence services.

More than two hundred years after the Pope had sanctioned the Jesuits into the Vatican, in 1764, the French Catholics smelt a rat and told Pope Clement XIII that the Jesuits were "Immoral and a menace to the Church and her Faith" and they expelled the Jesuits from France for their Satanic behaviour and five years later in 1769 the Spanish Catholics did the same and are still banned from Spain to this very today.

Evidently other Nations cottoned on, and sent the Jesuits packing back towards Italy and this is what a later Pope had to say about their home coming, "The soil of Italy was polluted by this unclean slime, which Nations have rejected and sent back to Rome, the fountain of all creation"

No wonder the world felt invaded by the Jesuits, Pope Leo XII had earlier placed the Catholic Education System under the control of the Jesuits who used this motto 'Quod divina Sepientia' but I failed to understand what the motto means!

History states that Napoleon was born on the Island of Corsica, an Island where the Spanish banished the Jesuit to in the late 1760's.

These 'Jesuit Fathers' had Rasputin like powers over women and specialised in seducing them through confession. Some believe this was the case in the birth of Napoleon, as in adulthood he subsequently declared war on all the Kings who had banished the Jesuits.

Napoleon was born a Catholic, but later attended a Jesuit school, where it is claimed he lost his faith at the tender age of 13. What happened to him at that school? Napoleon was also a practicing Freemason which would explain his non-committal to faith in later life, supported by the fact that all his Portraits showed him with one hand always in hiding, this suggests further he was a Freemason. Pope Pius VII was totally at the beck and call of Napoleon and on 7th August 1814 Napoleon finally restored the Jesuit order back into the Vatican. That explains why the Jesuits are still attached to the Roman Catholic Faith today and are a permanent resident in the Vatican grounds.

Even Earl Shaftesbury said years later in 1859 of them "We have got to get rid of these Jesuits, England is swarming with them" To confirm there was a satanic connection to the Jesuits the 'Secret A Monita' was discovered (Secret Instructions of the Jesuits) and is still on file in Brussels. There was a warning in the document for the order to remain a secret, as the people might get the wrong idea about the order.

Once the order was banned from most of European countries they continued to operate secretly by moving their headquarters to Russia, hiding behind Masonic Lodges.

This would explain why Russia is predominantly a non-Christian country.

Still struggling financially the Pope asked the Bank for a loan and in 1835 Mayer Rothschild stepped in and lent him a large sum of money.

Here enters the Rothschild Dynasty connection, under the topic of Religion!

Question is, why mention the Jesuits at all? I've mentioned them because the Rothschild's are Jesuits, not Jewish as I first thought. I now discover there is more than one type of Jewish sector. The name Jewish derives from the name Judean, one who resides in Judea regardless of religion, race or nation. Does that mean every resident born in Palestine is Jewish?

On the other hand, does that mean Jewish people born abroad are neither, Hebrew or Jewish by birth or religion, but a different type of Jewish person? (The next paragraph would be easier to understand if you had a world map at hand) The non-Hebrew Jewish sector were created by 'man' originating from the land between two seas called the

'Black sea' and 'Caspian Sea' in the land known as Khazaria, today we know it better as Georgia. It had five neighbouring countries which were Russia, Poland, Lithuania, Hungary and Romania. The ruling King of Khazaria at the time felt vulnerable with Christians on one side of him and Muslims on the other, worried about invasion from either side, he tried to convert his Idol Satanic Worship country to the Jewish faith, as both faiths traded with the Jewish people.

They became known as the 'Ashkenazi' Jewish race or 'Khazaria' named after their country of origin today known as Georgian, they speak Yiddish which became their official language in 1934. The other two Jewish sectors are called, 'Asiatic' and 'Sephardi' Jew. 'Asiatic' Jewish race originating from Asia and they speak Tadzhik whereas 'Sephardi' Jews originate from Spain and Portugal and they speak Ladino.

That only leaves the original Jewish people who are born and bred in Judea; they speak the old Hebrew language and are known as a 'Hebrew' Judean. In 1948 the 'United Nations' which was created by the Rothschild's, had a law passed called 'Law of Return' guaranteeing every Jew worldwide the right to dwell in Judea (Palestine) this gave them permission to exercise their 'Right to return' even though most of them had never before set foot on Judean/Palestinian/Israel soil, their ancestral homeland lay 800 miles away in Georgia.

Does this sound like 'permission to cause aggravation' to you?

When the United Nations gave the Ashkenazi Jewish 'resettlement rights' to migrate in droves to 'Palestine' it is said, the Rothschild started to rule them with a rod of iron. The migrating Jewish people started to challenge the Rothschild's by asking them "If you wish to save Yiddish, first take your hands from it and for once, permit the colonist to have a possibility of correcting for themselves, whatever needs correcting" Baron Rothschild's reply was "I created the Yiddish, therefore, no men neither colonists nor organisations have the right to interfere in my plan"

This migration of the Non-Hebrew Jewish people consists of the 90% of the world's Jewish population today.

Incidentally did you also know the name Nazi derived from the name Ashke**nazi**? The next question is, how did the Rothschild's get involved, well they were originally the Ashke-nazi Jewish from Georgia but later converted to the Ignatius de Loyola order called the Jesuit order.

Allegedly today the Rothschild's own 80% of the land of Israel, which means their plan is working out quite nicely for them, don't you think!

My suspicion was strengthen when I started to notice some connections with these countries through their flags. The original National flag for Georgia was a red cross on white background, funny it's the reverse on the Swiss flag but the same as the First Aid Red Cross emblem, which incidentally, was started in 1859 to protect the wounded in battle, but recently First Aiders were forced to change their emblem because it was protected by the Geneva Convention. So now we have a white cross on green background!!!!! Strange after all these years, don't you think?

The Protestants religions continued to branch off from the Vatican but unbeknown to them, they were all financed by the Rothschild Dynasty. One of the first protestant faiths to emerge was in 1830 called 'Mormon' started by Joseph Smith. Thirty five years later in 1865 the Rothschild's financed another religion, this time called the 'Salvation Army' This new faith did not claim a denomination of its own, but went under a banner of Christian charity; sadly the Rothschild's found it amusing to insist, they used their emblem of the 'Red Shield' a symbol of Satanism as their logo.

Five years on in 1870, Rothschild financed another religion called 'Jehovah Witness' this time it was Charles Taze Russell who became their leader and he produced a magazine called the 'Watch Tower' Does this sound a bit like Big Brother is watching? Because, the Rothschild's controlled what is printed in this pamphlet.

There were many other protestant's, who further splintered off the Catholic Church, the Pentecostals, Baptists, Methodist, Reformed, Anabaptism, Anglican, Eastern and Oriental Orthodox.

I can understand the Protestants disagreeing with the wealth of the Vatican and, their disagreeable actions through the centuries, but I'm under-educated when it comes to the Anti-Christ.

I need to go back to the beginning of this Satanic and Lucifer origin, "I hope Julian knows how far to push me on this topic?" In Revelations 12 v7-9 Lucifer was originally the highest classification of angel; he was a 'Cherub' and described once as the perfect one. It was his job to bring light, but he became proud and sought to take the place of God. He led a third of the angels in a revolt against Archangel Michael for the control of heaven. There was a big battle and Lucifer was cast down to earth and became known as Satan and his followers became his demons, ever since Satan has been carrying out his plan to corrupt the earth, starting with the temptation of Adam and Eve in the garden, disguising himself as the serpent.

Satanism is what Christians fear the most; it's the worshiping of Satan and the spread of the occult that enables the Illuminati to create the New World Order and eventually one world government. They are the descendants of the underground Druids, or Men of the Oak, who they veer as their oak god. Their biggest night of their year is 31ˢᵗ October, a ritual that involves sacrifice. Mmmm!

Is that why the Bayer's have always placed a wreath on Fritz ter Mear grave on this very anniversary for the last forty years?

In Revelations 12 v18 under 'falls prophets' it predicts Christians will be forced "Anyone who refused to worship the statue of the beast will be put to death" but somehow I need to interpret the number 666 in the last verse!

Who is this false prophet, could it be the Jesuits?

Does it sound as if I'm talking piffle again or is Christianity truly under attack? I read on 23ʳᵈ Jan 2013 of a court that sentenced a widow and her seven young children to 15 years imprisonment for converting from her husband's faith Islam, to her birth faith Christianity.

And a Korean refugee summed up the situation in Korea saying, "People are simply killed if they say they believe in Jesus"

Going back to my question, 'Did Ignatius de Loyola forget to let go of his satanic and occult past, when he converted to Christianity?' No I don't think he did forget, he had no intention of letting go, he retained his Crypto-Jewish roots of pretending to be a Christian, but secretly continued with his occult and satanic practices. I'm worried, how will the likes of me who renounce Satan every Easter when I renew my Baptismal vows and reject his work and his empty promises.

Will I in the near future be killed because of my faith?

And why did David Spangler, Director of Planetary Initiative say, "No one can enter the New World Order unless he or she makes a pledge to worship Lucifer"!

Writing the above paragraph has made me feel as nauseas as I felt when I sat at Julian's bed-side willing for someone to listen to his plea, that the drugs he was given were harming him.

In need of a breath of fresh air, I remember a true film I once watched about how the Devine sent a heavenly message to three innocent children who were shepherding in Fatima, Portugal. It was 1912 when a ten year old girl called Lucia and her two younger cousins witnessed an apparition of 'Our Lady' Mary the Mother of Jesus. Here on the hill side, Mary divulges to them a three part secrets, two were to be revealed in thirty years in 1942 and, the third was to be withheld and disclosed on either Lucia's death or in 1960 whichever came first. The Bishop at the time insisted the third secret should be written down and placed in safe keeping. The secret entrusted to the children however was not read out in 1960 as agreed, but remained locked up in the Vatican Archives until the 13th May 2000 when it was retold 88 years later on the anniversary of the apparition. The Vatican had withheld this third secret for forty years, assuming we the people were not ready. This is allegedly the third vision Sister Lucia wrote down for the Vatican's safe keeping and was read out (in her words) by the Pope in the year 2000.

"An Angel cried out, Penance, penance, penance! Bishops, Priests, Religious men and women going up a steep mountain. At the top was a big cross, the Holy Father passed through a big city, half in ruins, afflicted with pain and sorrow. He prayed for the souls of the corpse's he met on his way. Having reached the summit of the mountain, at the foot of the cross, they were all killed by a group of soldiers who fired bullets and arrows at them. Beneath the arms of the cross stood two Angels, each with a crystal Aspersorium (a holy vessel) gathering the blood of the Martyr's!

After the 'Pilgrim Pope' Pope John Paul II had read out the document in Fatima, a Convent Nun asked Sister Lucia, did the Holy Father (Pope) convey her massage as instructed to the congregation? Sister Lucia wavered her finger saying, 'No! We need more men like St Pius XII, St Benedict and St George the Great" (who were once the bishop of Rome.) Sister Lucia died five years later on 13th Feb 2005 aged 97 in a Convent in Portugal.

Some believe the document had been tampered with, because there were supposedly two sheets of paper handed over to the Bishop at the time. Some witnesses also claim Pope John Paul II nearly fainted with fear when he first read the script originally, so did someone remove some horrific details from the original written secret? Others say the Pope may have misinterpreted the prediction of the assassination of the Bishop as his own assassination, but could the assassination of the Holy men have been the assassination of Christianity meaning the assassination of 'God?' It has been criticised that Pope John Paul II had ample opportunity to avert the coming event, instead he freely chose to be popular with the world rather than with Christ. If this document had been read out to us in 1960 instead of the millennium in the year of 2000, then it could be said we have wasted 40 years of valuable time to mend our ways.

Why have I mentioned Sister Lucia at all, well I feel the vision of the three children might have been referring to Armageddon.

But do I have enough knowledge about Armageddon, I fear not and because it's such a controversial topic I will ask the reader to conduct their own research on the topic first. But this is how I understand it, the Bible describes it as a natural 'gathering place' due to its surrounding hillsides situated sixty miles North East of Jerusalem. It also says King Solomon once housed several hundred horses for his fleet of chariots there. To support this, there still exist enormous archaeological remains of the stables there even to this day.

Armageddon is associated with the end of time; I looked up 'End of Time' in the Bible and found a reading about it in Daniel chapter eleven and twelve. If you can read those two chapters first, then you can pick up on a few points I found interesting after.

— He will invade the land of Splendour! (Does the Bible mean Palestine where King Solomon's temple of splendour once stood?)
— Gold and Silver treasure will lie in his power. (Does the Bible mean the Elite, the Rothschild's, Rockefella's, Vatican and the Jesuits riches?)
— Pitch the tents of his Royal headquarters. (Does the Bible mean Royal David's City?)
— Michael will stand up. (Does the Bible mean Archangel Michael, who once led against Lucifer and his fallen Angels and will lead again as Gods commandments rise against the Antichrists at the end of time, with his shield of protection and his sword of truth?)

— There will be no help for him. (Does the Bible mean the Antichrist can't possibly expect help from the one he is against, which is God?)
— Those who lie in the dust will awaken, some to everlasting life others to shame and everlasting disgrace. (Does the Bible mean Judgment day!)
— These words are to remain secret and sealed until the end of time. (Does the Bible mean until disclosure of the third secret, once revealed to the three Shepherd children in Portugal?)
— From the moment the perpetual sacrifice is abolished and the disastrous abomination eradicated. (Does the Bible mean, on the day the satanic clubs and orders who worship Lucifer and Satan condemning human sacrifices, then three years and ten months later the world as we now know it will change for the better and 'The world will know only love'?)

There are rumours that the third world war is in the making, but not as we've experienced before. Some predict this time the Anti-Christ's armies of the world will march to Christ where he treads the Mount of Olives; there they will meet him face to face, outside Jerusalem!

Does this mean at Armageddon, where non-Christians will challenge our Lord?

I desperately tried to make sense of who the Holy Land belongs to, and 'when' and 'who' changed its name over the centuries.

After pages and pages of complicated research I realised in the end, the right to that territory was forfeited long ago when Jesus was nailed to the cross. The land no longer belongs to the wondering Jews by divine right, but to all spiritual nations of any ethnic background who crave peace, just like our Messiah, who on the cross, died in the name of peace.

In the meantime it's difficult for good, kind, clean living people to recognise good from evil.

As I see it, if God represents the vine and we are his branches and the Jesuits have grafted themselves on to the vine bringing with them their satanic practices, how can we differentiate between the good and poisonous fruit of the vine, while their satanic behaviour continues? Now Palestine is proposing handing over Temple Mount to the Pope, which once offered sanctuary to the Knight Templers. Do they mean the Catholic Pope or do they mean the 'Black Jesuit Pope'?

I can't believe that the Black Pope is so powerful, when I've never heard of him before!

Could it possibly be true this powerful man the General of the International Military Order of the Society of Jesus (Jesuit) commonly known as the 'Black Pope' could have ordered the attack on the World Trade Centre and the Pentagon on September 11th 2001. Was it carried out by the slaves of the Jesuits? But why I ask myself?

Apparently the appointed time has arrived for the Jesuit General to destroy both the 'Dome of the Rock' otherwise known as the 'Temple Mount' and 'Al Aqsa Mosque' both building are adjoined on the same holy ground in Jerusalem. But I ask the same question again, why? Is it because many believe the Ark of the Covenant lies under these two buildings, so do they intend to destroy both holy buildings, find and raise the covenant. Then with the Vatican's wealth, the Jesuits wealth, the Elites wealth, the Illuminati wealth and the Freemasons wealth rebuild Solomon's Temple? Has the Black Pope nearly created the perfect war between all people he wishes to destroy which are the Protestants, Moslems and the Jewish people by shrouding the world into confusion of a huge aerial war? Is this what the Jesuits and the Council of Trent have been preparing for all these years?

It's been said that the Rothschild's would bring Gentile Kings to heel and Gentile Nations to their knees (that's us) Have I been brain washed into thinking the Jewish Nation have been against us, when in fact they are not, I need to remind myself the Jewish people are like myself, they believe in God, whereas the Jesuits believe in Lucifer and that's where the differences lies. It is they who are against us not the Hebrew Jews?

My Grandmother once scorned one of her sons during the Second World War when he was criticising the Jews, she reminded him "Mind your tongue son, and remember Jesus himself was a Jew"

Julian used to say, "I wouldn't be surprised if our next Pope will be black" but I took remark to mean black skinned, but did Julian mean a 'Black Jesuit Pope'

This chapter has defiantly tested my religion, when I discovered that some holy men were so corrupt, but luckily I realise it was my religion I was questioning, not my faith and there was no need for me to start disbelieving in God, just because our leaders have strayed!

Now I realise what this world needs is, more faith not less, more prayers not less, for a kinder and more gentle way of life, so we can aim for what was once promised in the Bible, that one day the lamb will lie down with the wolf and the lion will lie with the kid.

David Cameron the Prime minister of England said on the BBC 20th December 2011,

"We are a Christian Country and should not be afraid to say so"

At the beginning of this chapter I asked, why do 'non-church goers' feel that most faiths are corrupt? I'm beginning to understand, its 'man' who has corrupted Gods house. In Corinthians 6 v19 Jesus says, "I shall destroy the temple and build a new one inside your heart"

In that case does that mean, God is with us always and we don't always need to seek him in elaborate or exotic buildings? I however like to go to church to hear someone read to me about Jesus teaching, just like my grandmother did all those years ago.

Sadly in 2001 seven hundred years after the slaughter of the Templers, a scrapped parchment was discovered in the Vatican, in the secret archives by a Professor Barbara Frade. The long lost document is a record of the trial of the Knight Templers scribed before Pope Clement V death; it ends with the Papal Absolution from Heresies, stating "We hereby decree that they are absolved by the Church and may again receive Christian sacrament" concluded their ritual was not blasphemous. The Pope failed to make this statement public, because it would entail incriminating the King and himself for falsifying the accusations made in 1312 against the Knight Templers.

The parchment had been hidden or misplaced in the 17th centaur archives.

It's not clear to me if six years after the discovery of the parchment in 2001, whether Pope Benedict XVI apologised on 11th October 2007 on behalf of the Vatican for the decision to burn Jacques de Molay and his men, which was two days short of the 700 year anniversary of his death.

But the Daily Telegraph did write this, 'For 700 years we have been made to believe that the Templers died as <u>cursed</u> men.'

It would have been easy for me to wrongly accuse the 'un-just men' in the order of the Knight Templers for the second time in history, holding them responsible for all the world atrocities' when in fact it was the Satanic Jesuits. Luckily for me I was guided by a message of 'Go back to the beginning'

Because try as I might I could not find a connection between the Holy men of the Knight Templers and the Satanic Jesuits except they both accepted a wage from the 'Vatican'.

I too am a Catholic and take great exception to the fact that this order called the Jesuit was connected to my church, but exposing the Jesuit order is not about discriminating against the 'church member's faith' who know nothing about the Vatican's connections with the Jesuit order.

Organised Crime

So who's in charge of crime, one would think it is the 'law of the land' but is the 'law of the land' corrupt and considered to be above the law?

Organised crimes are still rife worldwide, weather it is human trafficking, human smuggling of migrants, kidnaping of children, illegal business, drug trade, organised paedophilia or gambling.

But who's operating the nucleus and who's pressing the buttons?

When we think of organised crime, we immediately think of the Mafia, but in fact it's the 'Rothschild Zionist' that's behind the Mafia so are they behind every other highly organised criminal activity too. But who's behind the Rothschild's? It seems; it's the Jesuits who are pulling their strings!

The organised crime, have a masterful army of spies and have assassinated and disposed of people in power who try to obstruct their evil antics for decads. They have even made whipping boys, of the 'Jewish people' by placing them in powerful positions and when fault or blame needed to be distributed, it can be neatly placed in their lap.

I was wondering if I was becoming more shock proof to any new findings about the Rothschild's.

My next paragraph deserved to be filed under Banking, but on recapping the topic and if my discovery is accurate, it's right that it is filed under crime.

Their criminal activities go as far back as the reign of Tsar Nikolas II when I mentioned before when the Tsar and his wife the Tsarina Alexandra Romanov's of Russia were slaughtered on 17th July 1918 along with all their five children, including the cook, their footman and their Doctor. They were all taken, transported to their forestry grave to show the world what happens if Nations who refuse to let the Rothschild's open a central Banking system in their country.

I've already mentioned about how many Popes have been disposed of in the past, but this is a recent Popes sad end. In August 1978 an honest, holy and totally uncorrupted man was elected Pope but he soon found himself on a collision course heading for a corrupt Vatican. Once in this post he discovered that 121 members of the Roman Cardinals were Freemasons. He felt invaded and, duty bound to act on his findings.

After being in this new position for only 33 days, Pope John Paul I said at the dinner table to his two companions "I'd like to take a retreat to prepare myself for a good death" both guests were shocked to hear him speak like this. Especially when he appeared so well, they both recalled, he'd said this at 8:45pm and at 9:30pm he bid them goodnight by saying "Until tomorrow, if God wishes" Early next morning at 4:45am he was found dead in his bathroom.

Do you remember I wrote in the last chapter, that Lucia had seen holy men walking up the mountain to the foot of a cross in Fatima? Was Pope John Paul I one of these good holy men?

After his death, the Vatican instructed not a drop of blood was to be shed or any removal of organs to be performed. The room was scrupulously deep cleansed, not a trace of him existed; not even a photograph of his family, just as if he'd never existed. He was quickly embalmed and a Papal mask was taken of him before the police were permitted to see him. He was pronounced dead by a Doctor who never attended him in life; his usual Doctor was not even informed of his circumstance and the time of death was given as 11pm the previous night. Questions were asked at the time, why didn't the Vatican permit a post-mortem or autopsy to be conducted, but the Vatican remained deaf to all these queries. Although this fit man only reigned for 33 days, he is remembered as the "Victim Pope" How strange his Papacy began at the very hour the Holy Shroud of Turin was being placed on exhibition! His only crime was to try and purify and reform the Church of Rome, with which he had to pay dearly, with his life.

But what about our future, Well, the likes of President Obama is surrounded by a tight shoulder to shoulder advisors who are 'Rothschild Zionists' who are edging him on with whispers from behind to clear the way for the Zionists of tomorrow, to let them walk straight in to what they believe is their promised land! (I stress these people aren't Jewish, but Jesuits)

What about the British politicians, is our Government squeezed tight shoulder to shoulder by the High ranking Freemasons, Jesuits and the 'Rothschild Zionists' of this country, guarded where ever they go and supervised by everything they say. There are 350,000 Freemasons in Britain, with the Duke of Kent as their Grand Master with his first cousin Queen Elizabeth II as their Patron.

The Duke's wife formally known as the H.R.H the Duchess of Kent struggled to come to terms with her husband's role in the Freemasons as the Grand Master of England and Wales, while facing gruelling battles against her own poor health. The other high ranking Freemasons include nearly all British judges, Law Lords and Barrister's and politicians such as Tony Blair, Gordon Brown, David Cameron and Nick Cleg just to name a few. Old timers include such names as Robert Burns, H. G. Wells, Rudyard Kipling, and Georg Burnard Shaw.

William Hague is a Zionist and is often said to speak in double Dutch on the Middle East crisis.

I'm learning something new all the time, have you heard of the Frankfurt School it is controlled by the United Nations which was instigated by the Rothschild's. The school for technology and science was implemented to destroy the west by teaching sex and homosexuality to children, under mind teachers, promote excessive drinking, emptying churches, corrupt the courts, depend on benefits, control media, massive migration to destroy identity, daily reporting of violence in newspapers, attack fathers abilities leading to the breakdown of families, create tension but worst of all create subversion technique 'trauma through injustice' by snatching 4,500 children annually from good parents for forced adoption.

The Daily mail is only allowed to cover a tiny number of those stories. Is Madeline McCann's amongst that tiny percentage allowed to be published? And is the roomer true that the McCann's joined the Freemasons just before the abduction and become victims of the Illuminati mind control. Because why did Kate McCann shout "They have taken her" who are they? The MI5, MI6? Is this why they can't talk, only search for their lost child, after all they still have two precious twins they could snatch, so are they trapped in a nightmare? I'm only surmising on this one.

The Jesuits are in control of many organisations, Knight of Malta, Illuminati, York and Scottish Rites, Order of the Garter, Priory De Sion, Rosicrucian's, Freemasons and the Skull and Bones.

The 'Skull and Bones Society' started in 1832 and it came about through incalculable wealth derived from criminal organisations called the 'opium syndicate' and it was operated through the Illuminati. Some years later in 1949 a selection of young men from Yale University calling themselves the Yale Secret Society were given an Island as a favourite summer retreat by the wealthy, called 'Deer Island' to conduct their secret 'whatever they did' The Island comprised of one, half stone and half wooden buildings which contained 15 bedrooms.

They supposedly underwent a ritual, then take up positions in high offices such as politics, finances, media and International Mafia racketeering. It was beginning to sound as if the triangle on my book marker were becoming intertwined. Then Bingo! Two student's names came up as past students of Yale Secret Society of the Skull and Bone, Bush and Rockerfell yet another agent of the Jesuits. I'll say no more about this dangerous society in case someone takes a pot shot at me; you need to look this one up yourself. Some believe they have in their possession the skull of 'Geronimo's' but I couldn't find any proof. Other organisations also use the skull and bone symbols, the Nazi officers used the emblem on their peak caps! Ignatius de Loyola recommended using a skull during meditation when practicing his 'Spiritual Exercise'

It has been said, that the Freemasons are in possession of a total of fifty thousand skulls in the world, which is their official symbol of their occult group. I wonder who lost their heads for the sake of this order. No wonder the Priest who conducted Julian's funeral mass was keen not to have a Masonic contribution in the service, I had no idea what the High Archie order entailed. On ground level the Masonic order seem harmless, it's the High Archie that declares Lucifer as their god with a small 'g'.

Another high ranking Freemason was Nathan Rothschild, he was responsible for forming the Illuminati order. The Illuminati oath mentions to secretly go amongst the enemy like a spy gathering information for the order, planting seeds of jealousy, hatred between communities, create war, revolution, and spy on every class, bankers, teachers, lawyers, merchants and parliament in the pretence of informing the Pope!

Their Oath disturbed me greatly, if what I read was to be believed. When they undertake this promise they say, 'I renounce my own personal views and opinion as well as all control of my powers and capacities. If I become a traitor to the order, <u>I do not</u> hope to find safety wherever I may fly, shame, remorse and vengeance will follow me. Unknown brothers will torture and peruse me' Once this vow was taken, I presume it could not be retracted?

How naive of me, all these years to think evil practice and bad behaviour were just a random coincidence, but it seems it's been orchestrated for years all along!

When I compare the Knight Templers 76 rules and their Oaths, I can now see what a sensible, fair and helpful guideline they were, baring no malice toward any other human beings.

I quote a verse from the Bible found in Act 20 v 29 "I know quite well that when I have gone, fierce wolves will invade you and will have no mercy on the flock so be on your guard" and "Remember how night and day for three years I never failed to keep you right, shedding tears over each one of you"

Was the first verse referring to the Jesuits evil doing? Whereas the second verse reminded us of when Jesus was preaching and protected his flock for the last three years of his life between the age of 30 and 33? I don't mean to be a Bible basher but the book does seem to make more sense to me, the more I try to discover why Julian died like he did.

Intelligence Agency

The more I find out about this 'triangle on my book marker' the more shocked I'm becoming, it now appears that the Intelligence Agency worldwide are corrupt too. In 1914 the Military Intelligence Section 5 referred to as the MI5, was instigated during the Second World War. Are you surprised to hear that Victor Rothschild was an MI5 agent. Years later Maggie Thatcher issued a famous teasing comment, "We have no evidence he was a Soviet agent" but was this Rothschild's contributing to the 'Zionist dream'?

An ex-MI6 agent called James Casbolt claimed the MI6 brings 90% of drugs into Britain. Heroin is from the Middle East, Cocaine from South Africa and Cannabis from Morocco. He also claimed the MI5, MI6 and the CIA were using LSD as a weapon against angry protestors of the 60's and making them into 'Flower power' teens. The trade was worth £500 billion a year, a Mafia boss was once asked in court, if he was he involved in drug trafficking. His reply was "No we can't compete with the government"!!! James Casbolt also claims his father worked for the MI6, but 'Karma' caught up with both of them. His father died a poor man in prison, under strange circumstances and a drug addict. James his son now claims he is drug free and wishes to help others from suffering like he did. An investigative journalist Gary Webb wrote a book called 'Dark Alliance' in which he quoted that Georg Bush Senior was head of the CIA and an American leading drug baron. Garry was later found dead with two gunshot wounds in the back of his head. The case was declared as 'suicide'! (Clever man, how did he manage his first shot through the back of his head, and secondly how did a dead man manage a second shot? I just hope I don't land up in the same situation as him for quoting his suicide)

It appears that all these secret agents are some ones puppets, the likes of MI5, MI6, CIA, FBI, even secret society's such as Freemasons, Nazi, Gestapo, SS are or were all controlled by corruption from above. Question is; are the above controlled by the Illuminati who are under instructions of the Jesuits?

The CIA scientists are all put through a mind-control program to stop them recalling their knowledge, there are other reports when CIA employers decide to suddenly leave they immediately go missing. Or if a task needs completing, a person would suddenly go missing for six hours with no explanation and a crime would then be committed, it is also believed they kidnap children, check their talent then create a genius!

Secret societies also manage other organisations to serve their brotherhood, such as sex slavery, child abduction and mind control.

Could this mean world leaders have been under the influence of mind control, such as Churchill, Stalin, Mussolini and Hitler? Did they all work together for the purpose of war to destruct the Jews to establish the 'Kingdom of Jerusalem' as promised during the 'Popes Dark Ages' (this is when the Popes were so corrupt, they condoned killing, torture and such cruelty such as cutting off noses and removing tong's, tarring and burning live bodies at the stake)

Many writers have commented about Hitler's ability to hypnotise his audience. But was he hypnotised himself before he went out to make his speeches? Lots have said his eyes looked glazed, like a man hypnotised before becoming transformed, and aroused into frenzy if that is the case, who was controlling him?

And what about Churchill, if Churchill was related to Hitler through the Rothschild line, also through the Spencer family tree including Queen Victoria, then it makes sense when Churchill confesses to being on the Agnostic side, then meddling in the occult, it raises the question are all the High Archie in this together?

It sounds as if I've lost the plot? Well! ask your selves this, why did Earl Charles Spencer 'Princes Diana's' brother mention in his maiden speech in the House of Lords in 1993, that Satanism on the Spencer's Allthorp Estate in Northamptonshire existed, and he was doing all he could to eradicate it. Poor Diana was she brought up amongst all this rubbish trying to protect her two sons from any satanic practices. Could the Royal House hold have been exposed to this dreadful practice when one of the Rothschild's (a Jesuit) fathered Queen Victoria? After all, we the commoners weren't even aware that the Royals had Rothschild's children, or had any connections with the Jesuits, which begs the question, is that where the Jewish circumcision practice derives from?

Another question is could Churchill have been 'mind controlled' himself from a very young age by the Jesuits? He was certainty away from his mother for long periods of time! But who did he mix with in adult life, Cecil Rhodes a Jesuit, Prince Philip who attended a Jesuit school, Walt Disney all of which also belonged to the highest level of the Freemasons, the 33rd degree!

This phrase 'mind-control' keeps cropping up, is it what it sounds like?

John W. De Camp wrote a book about mind-control, saying it was not a science fiction but science fact integrating to perform illegal activities such as drug delivery/messenger and even assassination. Talking of assassination Lee Harvey Oswald who is meant to have shot J.F Kennedy; it now transpires that Oswald was hardly a marksman, he was a disaster with a gun, he once accidently shot himself in the elbow and inexplicably fired a rifle into the jungle. I don't know what he witnessed while he was in the army but when he was released he became a 'Freedom fighter' he applied for a six day visa to visit Russia and while he was there he fell in love and married a Russian girl and they had a baby daughter. He was employed at an Electronic Factory where he was befriended by a USSR future head of state who offered to teach him Russian. He received a factory pay as well as being government subsidized, including a fully furnished apartment. Sounds suspicious already, Lee didn't realise the Freedom Fighters were attached to the KGB, and guess who control the KGB and the CIA, yes the Jesuits. The CIA is renowned to inflict MK-Ultra (mind control) could Oswald have been an easy target to manipulate?

These altered states of mind are brought on by stun guns, drugs, torture, electric shocks then hypnosis is used to isolate the memory of their experiences until triggered by a telephone tone, nursery rhyme, dialog, certain moves or hand gesture.

The question is did Lee become a 'brain washed slave' of the CIA? Others have said since, he did express personality traits of mind control such as intolerance of others and being rude.

But why did Kennedy have to die?

Kennedy was attempting to de-escalate the war in Vietnam, but the Jesuits wanted to cash in on the war for a lot longer, at the same time they wanted to continue with the drug trade. Oswald always denied he'd killed the President; he may not have if he was such a poor shot, or he may have attempted but was mind controlled to forget. When Lee was being transferred two days after the presidents assassination from the police station to the County Jail, he called out to the crowd it's a 'Patsy' which is a Mafia word for being framed for a crime you didn't commit. Jack Ruby a Mafia night club owner lurched forward and shot Oswald dead, then immediately gave the Policeman a Freemason handshake.

The Mafia are expert assassins and they were in full force on the day the President was shot.

Jack Ruby was imprisoned and claims he was later injected with a 'cancer causing viruses' before his second trial! It appears no one is safe if you're involved with the Jesuits, if they say kill, you kill and then they have you killed!

This is what I admire about J. F. Kennedy, although he was a Cradle Catholic he refused to allow the Jesuits to cloud his political judgement by giving into to their Mafia like tactics. He put the welfare of his country first at the cost of his own life.

Sadly I feel there were two victims of crime here Kennedy and Osborne, both had a hunger for peace, one wanted to end a war and the other was a Freedom Fighter.

May they both rest in peace, Amen

Media

I feel by now I might be accused of being an 'Anti-Rothschild & Zionist' campaigner, but I'm not I just want to get to the bottom of why Julian died like he did. What else do the media cover apart from newspapers; well it covers books, politics, music, films, radio and television.

Ok newspaper first, evidently there used to be 88 media companies but today there is only six, and ironically they are either owned or controlled by the Rothschild's, which means they have total monopoly over everything that's printed and everything I read.

For example they get rich on other peoples scandal and misfortune, but we don't hear about their scandal, they hush theirs up such as the circumstances surrounding the death of one of the Rothschild, Amschel in July 1996 when he died age 41. Rupert Murdoch was told to instruct all his managers around the world to print, he had suffered a heart attack, when in fact he had been found strangled with his own towel robe at the Hotel Bristol in Paris. Amschel apparently had no interest in the Banking world but preferred a quiet family life, but did have an interest in motor racing. Coincidently he was the winner of 'Peter Collins memorial Trophy Race' at Silverstone in 1996. Peter Collins being the local hero of Kidderminster who I mentioned earlier in the book, sadly 1996 happened to be the same year young Amschel died. Before his death he eventually agreed to join the family banking firm, but within hours of attending his first meeting there was talk of a massive merger. After Amschel was found dead, the French police had determined it was murder, but Prime Minister Jacques Chirac ordered the investigation closed before its completion.

There you have it, some go to prison for their crimes and some don't!!!

But what did Amschel object to at that meeting, which warranted his life?

Still on the topic of newspapers, the Guardian newspaper wrote a comment about human culling, stating "We need to pay more attention to the gender behind the people we place in position of influential power when it comes to culling or depopulation." I couldn't believe we were exposed to such comments! There isn't a good enough or a bad enough person to cull us, Full Stop, thank you.

I thought, we the commoners voted our politicians in, but are our Prime Ministers puppets to someone higher and is the likes of Rupert Murdoch who is told what to print, is he told to lie to the people, is he told to give us enemies to hate, is he told to arrange wars for us to fight and then is he told to stand back and watch us destroy ourselves. (Can the bereaved wives and mothers of young soldiers understand what their implying?) If the Mothers and wives aren't thumping mad, I'm most surly am.

Did you know the aim of control is to destroy genuine culture! Question yourself about the amalgamation of European countries, are we all allowing our separate identities to become a much of a much-ness? Are we all eating, drinking and wearing similar things now? Are we allowing the media to corrupt our decent culture replacing it with merchandized music, scandal mongering, dirty sex and endless conspiracies?

How many times a day do you say or think, "I don't know what this world is coming too?"

It hasn't finished yet, apparently The Rothschild plan to introduce 'Communism' to Britain after creating long term unemployment, starvation, loss of rights, elimination of Christianity, which has already started in some countries such as Egypt and Korea, extinction of all Royalties, and installation of multi-cultures and finally loss of identity by human chipping! We will be reduced to one world, one currency, one world army, one world government called Zionists, but known to us plebs as the 'New World Order' the Russians will appear to be the Trojan horse here. You know the old saying, all roads lead to Rome, but in my case all investigations lead me to the Rothschild's!

I'm not imagining things; the Zionists have already started to inflict their terror on the world.

Does it seem to you that Rothschild Zionist Bankers have already started the devastation with high unemployment sending their politicians in wolves clothing collecting votes to the tune of "Vote for us and we will lead you out of poverty, we will put you back into full time employment, we will rid you of your food crisis, your fuel crisis and your energy crisis." Think about it, isn't this the tactic Hitler used to get Germany to eat out of his hand in 1939, are we going down the same road of allowing history to repeat itself, allowing the 'New World Order' to help us out of the gutter when in fact it was them who shoved us into the gutter in the first place!

I misunderstood and thought Zionist was the homeland for Jewish people, but in fact it's a name given to one world domination called 'New World Order'

Can we stop these Zionists in their tracks? Well it appears two men tried single handed with 100 years apart, Ive mentioned them before the first was Abraham Lincoln who was assassinated on Good Friday April 15th 1865 by a Shakespearean actor John Wilkes Booth, a 33rd degree Mason. He was assassinated because the Rothschild Bank offered Lincoln financial help, but as the Rothschild was already funding the South Lincoln refused on the grounds of conflict of interest and was consequently assassinated.

The other President who refused Rothschild assistance was J.F Kennedy and because of his rejection he was also assassinated this time on 27th April 1963.

Five weeks before JF Kennedy was assassinated he made a 'gobbledygook' speech which went like this—:

"For we are opposed around the world by a monolithic and ruthless conspiracy that relies primarily on covets means for expanding its fear of influence on infiltration instead of invasion, on subversion instead of elections, on intimidation instead of free choice, on guerrillas by night instead of armies by day. It is a system which has conscripted vast materiel and human resources into the building of a tightly knit, highly effective machine that combines military, diplomatic, intelligence, economic scientific and political operations. Its preparations are cancelled not published. Its mistakes are buried not headlined. Its dissenters silenced, not praised. No expenditure is questioned. No rumours are printed. No secret is revealed"

Did you make sense of that speech way back in 1963? Maybe not, can you read it again, but this time, see it through a different pair of eyes. Does this speech fit in with the Rothschild way of operating? These Rothschild and Rockerfella grip their tentacles everywhere; did you know one of the Rockerfella's was trying to date J F Kennedy's sister at the time?

Do you also find it odd that Marilyn Munroe died eight months before this speech! It is alleged there were no traces of drugs in her stomach when she died, but she had a hefty dose of drugs in her blood. So how did it get there? Marilyn suffered from needle phobia, so she could not have injected herself. Accompanied by the fact she didn't have any puncture marks in her skin, she also had difficulty swallowing tablets; she would make a big fuss and need a large quantity of water to swallow them. There was something missing at the crime scene, there wasn't a drinking glass in the room and the main water supply had been off that day. It has been rumoured the only way she could have had such large amount of drugs in her blood that night was if it was administered via a suppository.

Marilyn is said to have been created under BETA program, who are in direct control of the programmer called the 'handler' its mind control again Poor lady. Marilyn Munroe was better known as the 'Queen of Diamonds' but she wasn't the only Queen who had disappeared from public view, there was once another queen known as the 'Queen of the people' her name was Princes Grace of Monaco, she had to go because she discovered too many secrets about the Vatican, the Freemasons and the Illuminati. The Rothschild's were involved with this family too, they go way back with the Prince Rainier family, Rothschild injected large amounts of money into building hotels and casinos in Monaco in 1864. Rainier's grandfather had a daughter with his laundry women called Marie, they named the baby Charlotte. She turned out to be the only heir, so Charlotte carried on the Royal line, she later married a French man and they had two children Antoinette and Rainier. How strange they employed Winston Churchill's cousin a Freemason to be their children's Nanny, was she sent or was it a coincidence! For an added twist Rainer was then sent to Switzerland to be educated! On his return Alfred Hitchcock was involved in finding Rainier a suitable match, he first thought of Marilyn Munroe but chose Grace Kelly instead.

Hitchcock had been educated by the Jesuit which he completed in 1913; he came from a long line of occult generation. He was also known to enjoy psychologically breaking down of his actresses and creating mind-controlled slaves. His relaxation time involved holidaying in resorts suitable for millionaires in Switzerland. He was knighted by the Queen in 1979, although he snubbed a CBE (Commander of the British Empire in 1962)

Grace Kelly stared in three of Hitchcock films, ironically the first one was called 'Dial M for murder' Once Grace married her Prince she was surrounded by Freemasons, Hitchcock for one, her husband and later her son who joined the Knights of Malta.

Grace received Catholic education with instruction from the Jesuit, who also delved in mind control. By now I'm getting worried about the security of Graces mind, was there any one meddling with it?

After her fatal car accident the police reassured her daughter there was no skid marks on the road, trying to make her believe she may have suffered a cerebral bleed! But why would a low mileage car, that was regularly maintained because of the treacherous roads suddenly have no brakes, because her daughter claims her mother's last words were, as she summersaulted 120 feet to her death, "I can't stop there's no brakes"

There was a third Royal who the public loved and fondly called 'Queen of hearts' her name was Princes Diana. She also had plenty of connections with the Rothschild's; some claim she herself was the daughter of one, added to that she may have been married into a Rothschild family.

Sadly Princes Diana knew she was going to die in a car accident; she left written messages informing her close associates of this fear. I recently read that her car had been stolen two weeks prior to the accident and on its return the computer to the steering and breaks were missing. It's now believed there was no Fiat car involved in the tunnel, but the driver was possibly blinded by a laser light by an erratic motor cyclist with a pillion passenger. There are still questions being asked today, why did Dodi's father refuse police protection that night, why did Dodi telephone his father who was advised to contact the off duty Hotel Security Guard Henri Paul to return to the Hotel and drive Dodi and Princes Diana to his flat. But Henri Paul was not a professional driver let alone qualified to drive the Future King of England's Mother (Prince William) in a getaway chase. Why was Diana's 'returned stolen car' requested to be brought to the back to make this fast getaway, why couldn't any one explain Henri Pauls whereabouts for the last six hours before the chase, and why did Trevor Rees-Jones, Dodi's body guard, put his seat belt on when his job description exempts him from wearing one. What did he see in Henri Paul's behaviour to suddenly put his own belt on, but evidently had no time to insist the two he was guarding in the back seat to put theirs on. Why have Henry Pauls family protested that their son would not get behind a wheel of a car while intoxicated, they claimed he was almost tee total, so why did the autopsy revile he was suffering from liver failure through alcohol abuse, although a few days before, he had a clean bill of health to renew his flying licence, and why have they insisted the blood samples were mixed up, why was there extremely high levels of carbon monoxide in his blood so much so he would not of been able to stand up, when security cameras show otherwise! Why, wasn't there any skid marks, was this another case of the brakes not engaging?

Still more questions than answers, could the secret Intelligence have been involved in this plan? If the secret Intelligence is truly operated by Freemasons; did the two back seat passengers have connections with the Freemasons?

Yes, Diana was always cocooned in the high ranking 33rd degree Freemasons, her ex-husband and her father in-law. The British Royals started to join the Freemasons as far back as 1601, when King James VI of Scotland also King James I of England was initiated into the Order of the Freemasons (Our present Royal Monarchy, Queen Elizabeth II is the Grand Patron of the Freemason of England and Patroness and supreme Lodge of the world, which is held in 'Jerusalem Chamber' at Westminster Abbey. The Queen mother was also a 'Lady of the Garter'

Both Mohamed Al-Fayed and his son Dodi were Freemasons, so were they both involved in the plot and was accusing the House of Windsor just a smoke screen? But if that was the case was his father prepared to sacrifice his son for the cause? After all, his father did instruct Dodi to give up his girlfriend and start dating Diana. I don't know, will we ever know?)

Going back to those missing six hours of Henri Pauls life, if he was he placed in a mind-control mode to drive at high speed in order to pile into that 13th pillar in the tunnel.

Was that bright laser light the signal his brain was waiting for to mount the very spot below where Joan of Arc was burnt at the stake on May 30th 1431? How ironic Diana's life was so wrapped up in Masonic Freemasons supposedly descendant of the Knight Templers, who was either assassinated or at the very least died in mysterious circumstances in a dark tunnel away from public view in the dead of the night with Mohamed Al-Fayed son an Egyptian who was a descendant of the Arabic Saracens. Planned or not, it still sounds like 'check mate' to me, two angry families playing a board game with people's lives, or was it human satanic sacrifice to the goddess Diana. How strange she was called Diana, after the Greek mythology goddess 'Diana the hunter' She was definitely hunted, then she died in the Pont D'Alma, meaning, 'Bridge of Souls' pagans used to conduct ritual sacrifices at this very spot, that's why Joan of Arc was burnt there, which is what they did to Witches or anyone who claimed they saw visions.

Still circumstantial, then why did the French Freemason in 1884 present the American Freemasons in New York with the Statue of Liberty holding the 'Torch of Enlightenment' then erect the same occult signature of eternal flame at the entrance of the tunnel where Princess Diana was killed, as well as on J F Kennedy's head stone, Martin Luther Kings, Peter Collins and wait for it at the World Trade Centre!

Charles Spencer described his sister, Princes Diana in his funeral speech in 1997 as a 'Standard bearer for the down trodden' she certainly flew the flag for all of us, but did his speech have a much deeper and different meaning? And could these well-loved ladies have been sacrificial Queens?

And why did Paul Burrell the former Royal Butler reveal to the Daily Mirror newspaper in June 2002 that Queen Elizabeth II had told him "There are powers at work in this country about which we have no knowledge" A strange confession don't you think?

Moving on from media to books, the other day I went to buy a six year old little girl a book for her to read while she was in hospital. Have you been to a children's book shop lately? Go and prepare yourself for a shock, the covers are so gruesome, even if their contents are harmless; the cover alone is enough to give a child nightmare.

There's long been a concern about Harry Potter books playing a part of the Pied Piper, leading children away from a Christian upbringing. One could disregard the ludicrous of it all, but J K Rowling is a Billionaire in her own right and Sarah and Gordon Brown are close friends of hers, who happen to belong to the New World Order. If this is the case, then I beg forgiveness from all parents whose daughters I once took on a Brownie camp, using Harry Potter as a theme.

I would like to stress to every parent, the camp was conducted in all innocence on my part. But please conform this with your, now grownup daughters.

It then begs the question, were books like Alice in Wonderland, The Lion the Witch and the wardrobe with their topsy-turvey story line, were they written in all innocence or were they meant to muddle a child's mind, making it difficult for them to sort out reality from gobbledegook!

I'm not going to look into that possibility any further, but I hope my concern will inspire others to write harmless children's books!

From books to music, the popular musical scene have admitted being made to write lyrics about the occult for a long time, singers such as Jimmy Hendrix, John Lennon, Queen, Elton John, Robert Plant and many more. A lot of these pop groups also use satanic symbols on their album covers. Parents, do you know what lyrics your children are listening too and what are they watching on your TV when your back is turned?

It's been reported that TV shows on average, 18 violent or hostile actions every hour and more than half the films show 35% violence and unacceptable language which are of a sexual nature.

It appears the Illuminati have been heavily involved in the music industry for a long time with mind-control causing split personality and programed slaves. Sounds, far, fetched, doesn't it!

I've just mentioned well loved 'Queens' of our society that we the public have held in high esteem. But there have been other types of Royals who have recently died, 'Queen of Soul' a singer known as Whitney Huston who also died in mysterious circumstances. Why were her family told that the singer was already dead before she went under water, because they say there wasn't enough bath water in her lungs to conclude she was drowned. Her family are now demanding a murder investigation. And why did Whitney slip the singer, Brandy a note during a TV interview while Clive Davies her manager was present, only two days before she died? What was in that note? Brandy's not telling.

Is Clive Davies a gate keeper to the performers for the Illuminati, producing mind-control Artists? I don't know, another thing does he mix in such high places that he possesses power over the LA Police to keep Whitney's body at Beverly Hilton for 11hours after she was discovered dead, until after his weird Madonna performance was over. And why was there two Egyptian statues seen outside her back door when the funeral directors came to pick up her body. Was this a sign or coincidence, a strange thing to find towering either side of your <u>back-door</u> don't you think. What were they symbolising?

There are too many mystery deaths in the modern music Scene, too numerous to mention, but there is one more Queen I'd like to mention, 'Queen of Jazz N' Blues' Amy Winehouse. She attended Ashmole School, which was later promoted to an Academy. I don't know at what stage she became involved with mind control, but she did join the '27 club' just before she died and on the night she died neighbours heard screaming, howling and loud drums coming from next door at 2am, which he said was most unlike her. Amy was discovered by Jay Z at 4am the following morning, a man who was linked to occult practice, Freemason, Illuminarti, New World Order and Satanism. Strange time to discover someone dead don't you think! She was only 27 when she died; her father claims she was drug free for some time before she died and alcohol free for three weeks. In that case why did her toxicology results confirm no illegal substance found at her time of death! So, what did she die from then? They claimed they wrote on her death certificate 'Cause unknown'

What in the 21st century!!!!!!

Talking about make believe royals, there have also been Kings amongst them too. The first one that comes to mind is Elvis Presley the 'King of Rock and Roll'. Another death shrouded in mystery, conjuring up more questions than answers. First question, when Elvis Presley joined the army, why was he being used as testing ground for MK-ULTRA (mind-control) and why did John Lennon say years later "Elvis died when he was in the army, in a manner of speaking" Did Elvis tell him that. And why did Elvis's father insist he was not his father, if not who was? Was it one of the Rothschild? Why did the man Elvis called his father, believe Elvis was murdered. Why did Elvis call his body guards the 'Memphis Mafia'? Why did some people say, Elvis became a liability when he became so obsessed with the two Kennedy assassinations? Was he worried about his own mortality? And what drugs were Elvis given, to make him look as if his liver was packing up? And why did Susanna Leigh who worked very closely with Elvis claim, Elvis was killed by the Mafia the day before he was due to testify in the investigation into the 'FBI Fountain Pen' case! Did she mean his private mafia his 'Memphis Mafia'? And why did, a Freemason called Henry Kissinger laugh and say, "Elvis was like a rusty tin man, ready for the junk yard, then they stopped his ticker"! But guess what, the Freemasons then very kindly erected an 'Eternal Flame' on another young soul's grave, yes Elvis's!

Another Royal in the music world called 'Prince of Pop' was Michel Jackson, unfortunately someone screwed up his mind too. More questions than answers here, what sort of a father would allow his son to be used by older men like Alistair Crowley an occult Satanist, child abuser and a mind-controller for the CIA? What psychological abuse did Michel endure to allow surgeons to do what they did to his good looking black face? What was he trying to scrape off, and why didn't he allow mirrors to be hung in his home? He was desperately trying to recapture his lost youth by creating a 'never-never land' for his children in his 'gold fish bowl' he called home.

Jimmy Hendrix the 'King of Electric guitars' claims he was forced to take drugs originally, as part of the mind-control but eventually becoming dependant. When Jimmy discovered his manager was embezzling large amounts of money from him, Hendrix took legal action. Afterwards Hendrix said "Next time I go to Seattle, I will be in a pine box" and sure enough, he was two days after his death, his manager a former MI6 agent confessed to his murder.

What about the group 'Queen' with Freddie Mercury as the lead singer, he was educated in Mumbai at a Boys Boarding school founded by the Jesuits. The teachers were resident, and it is rumoured that Freddie suffered traumatic childhood rape! My next question is, was Freddie mind-controlled by the Illuminati and did they infect him with a Super-strain of HIV as its rumoured and was John Decon his friend and guitarist life really threatened, including his whole family being wiped out if he ever revealed the truth. Brian May is said to know that Aids was a government orchestrated bio-terrorist attack on the globe, but was he really worried Rothschild's agent might 'Suicide' him like they did Freddie. Freddie's lyrics have spoken volumes to us since his death especially the song 'Bohemian Rhapsody' was this song a bit prophetic about his own death? Why did he call it Bohemian, did he choose this name after the Bohemian Club, at Bohemian Grove, in California. It's a playground for the 'GLOBAL ELITE', Nixon and Regan have been photographed there and possibly Bush and Clinton attended too.

So what was Freddie trying to say through his lyrics in Bohemian Rhapsody when he sang,—'sometimes I wish I hadn't been born at all'—'we will not let you go' (who won't?)—'I got to get out of here'—'nothing really matters to me'. Poor chap, may he rest in peace. The Illuminati might have controlled his mind, but there was no 'Eternal flame' placed on Freddie's tombstone, because Freddie was cremated; he blows in the wind catch him if you can Illuminaties.

Why did John Lennon write lyrics? 'Our society is run by insane people' What had he found out?

I will leave you to see what happened to the likes of Mark Bolan from T. Rex, his son Simon believes that he was on the verge of dropping the mind-controller way of life in exchange for a family life, strange how he died as soon as he was taking control of his own mind! Simon and his mother would not have survived financially had it not been for another pop star called David Bowie. Someone else trapped in the Illuminati world, when he appeared in the film called "Labyrinth" this was a film about the programing of mind control victims at the hands of satanic handlers, on reflection the film has many occult symbols.

Have you wondered why did David Bowie decline the invitation to sing at the Olympics opening ceremony, has he been successful in detaching himself from the Illuminati claws?

Lots of these bewildered celebrity's belonged to 'Scientology' organisations, such as Tom Cruise, John Travolta and Elvis Presley.

But some have successfully broken away such as Lisa Marie Presley, Tom Cruise's former wife and Christopher Reeves. Scientology is based on the belief that the human race is descended from 'Thetans' an exiled race from another planet. The cult was founded by a paranoid schizophrenic called Mr L. Ron Hubbard an American science fiction writer who has millions of followers which included most of Hollywood. The organisation is based on the right to think freely, write freely and have your own opinions, but not if you speak against the Scientology. They sue at the slightest comment uttered against them, so I'll say no more about them in case I suffer at their hands.

Britney Spears is another who allegedly has been mind-controlled by her former manager and handler Sam Lutfi. The singers Nanny went to court to testify he was controlling her life but Britney was not allowed to appear in court, because the judge was concerned it might cause, "irreparable harm and immediate danger" What the judge meant was, mind-control slaves who learn about their true condition are often programed to "self-destruct"

Whilst mass media continues to ignore this issue, we need to be aware that two million Americans have gone through the horrors of this program. My question was; who started this MK-ULTRA mind-control in the first place? Horror of horrors, it was Dr Joseph Mengele who conducted these sickening tests in Auschwitz during the Second World War; he was nicked named 'Angel of death' at the time, but later worked with the CIA to create mind-control as well as multiple personalities and trained unconscious assassination. How could a physician use his healing knowledge to cause so much suffering? It appears 'Mind-control' is exactly what it says on the box.

I never gave these young people much thought before, so I don't know why I'm drawn to their unjust deaths now?

How these poor victims must have craved a normal life, but once they started on this treadmill it seemed impossible to back track or jump off the moving platform, it seemed in some cases if they tried to leave the music world they knew they would be 'followed and eliminated'

It makes me 'cringe' when I hear young 16 year old on X-Factor sobbing "I will do anything to win, anything" They don't mean that, because if they do, one day they might find themselves selling their souls to the devil and lose their self-control, eventually giving up their life to a fake or cover-up suicide! If only they could see the pattern. And tell me, why does, Gary Barlow a Freemason say to some of the singers on x-factor

"Don't let anyone persuade you to change"

Odd, thing to say don't you think! Maybe he's warning them to watch out for the Illuminati offering 'Soul Selling Packs' The rest of us should be on the lookout for people young who use drugs too, are they using them to cover up something! Because why are these celebrities hooked on drugs when they have so much to live for and why are they dying so young?

Is it because, when they have served their purpose, they may be deemed useless and are potentially dangerous in case they start to remember, so Pop! Someone pointed out to me, when a celebrity's voice deteriorates as a result of the Illuminati forced drug taking, the musician or actor is worth more dead than alive.

Drugs, bath-water, fatal car accidents and hanging seem to be the 'norm' ending for these high profile candidates, tragically placed on high rickety pedestals!

Whitney Huston is said to have spoken out nervously just before she died, about dark spirited 'stage and video performances' performed by musicians such as Rihanna, Lady Gaga, Jay Z, U2, and Kylie Minogue with references to Illuminati, New World Order, Devil worship, Freemasons, occult ritual, torture, mind-control, mutilation and pornography.

She concluded, "We need to bring love back into music and on the stage"

Hear, hear I say. And finally, does the program 'I'm a celerity, get me out of here' have a double meaning? Or does this chapter sound like a load of old rubbish to you, may be so!

But what about the exposure of someone involved with a multitude of individuals, Jimmy Saville for one, I didn't invent his secret antics. Jimmy Saville sued the Sun newspaper in 2008 over a series of articles linking him to a boy's orphanage in Jersey, connecting him to allegations of children being tortured and sexually abused. He initially denied ever visiting the home, despite group photographs taken with the boys as evidence to the contrary. Chief of police initially reported, there were child human remains found in the cellars of the orphanage which were charred and cut. Someone high up stopped this investigation, why? Was it due to a politician's involvement, royal involvement, police involvement or high ranking judges? They say one hundred thousand children go missing each year, where do they all go?

I wasn't aware that Satanism practice was allowed in the Royal Navy, so why hasn't Prince Phillip, Prince Charles, Prince Andrew or Prince William stopped it if they claim to be Christian and head of the Church of England? The Royal ships sail under their flag, so what do they stand for?

There was one politician who took action as soon as she discovered young boys were visiting his home. Her name was Margaret Thatcher; she sacked Maurice Oldfield 'Intelligence chief' in 1980 who incidentally was installed on the recommendation of Lord Rothschild. Once in his post he promoted other homosexuals into the service, this is not a slant against homosexuality, only child abusers. And it's not a slant on Freemasons up to the third degree either, and I'm not accusing all Freemasons of paedophilia, but because of its secrecy, it is a good place to hide behind their brotherly oaths for protection.

Moving on from the music world to the film industry, have you ever wondered how an actor became a President? I'm taking about Ronald Ragan; whilst he was in office he kept trying to inform the public of the coming of the 'New World Order' when he repeatedly announced in his public speeches, "The world would come together if there was an external alien threat"

So if there are NO real aliens, do they intend to invent them?

Adam Sightings, a member of the Illuminati wrote "Of all the means I know to lead men, the most effectual is concealed mystery. Once man has taken into his head that there is a mystery in a thing, it is impossible to get it out" Their idea is to create an occult mystery, then make us believe Aliens must be real.

Once the public have been made familiar with these make-believe aliens, convincing us they are real, the rest is made easier. They are already trying to convince children in the school curriculum that UFOs are about and, aliens have escaped, to make it more realistic they have asked parents to take part in this pretence! How frightening for children to be exposed to such rubbish, even worse how deceiving of the teachers to ask their parents to take part in this lie too! I know this is true it's already taken place in Kidderminster!

Nono Hayakawa UFO investigator and lecturer said "There is a 'Project Panic' in the making. High Tec equipment will be used to create an optical illusion of the UFO invasion, this will give the Rothschild and Rockerfella excuse for the United Nations which they control, to call a 'Global State of Emergency' and we will all rush forward begging to join the 'New World Order' then, Bingo we will all be sucked in and trapped like sheep. Bahhhh, Bahhhh.

There was prediction that we would observe a taste of this 'optical illusion' at the opening ceremony of the Olympics 2012. I made a point of watching the opening ceremony with an open mind, but I was left wondering if I was imagining things, or were the Elite and the Illuminati trying to tell me something?

At first it all seemed all kosher, but then some dark even disturbing symbols appeared to reflect the occult side. The all seeing eye appeared in the flood lights shaped like pyramids, then the Glastonbury Tor was relived with people singing 'Green and pleasant land' that was fine at first but then the words 'Among these dark Satanic Mills' Mmmm!. Then there was a Fig tree not commonly found in England, which Jesus once pointed out to be fruitless, this I took to mean it bore no Christian fruit, the flip-side to Christianity is Ant-Christ. Then came the men in tall hats, were they the wealthy Rothschild and Rockerfella of this country, causing 'pandemonium'. A scary baby appeared with his face wrapped in thin muslin, with a separation in the forehead! Did the baby represent new birth of the 'New World Order' and did the split in the forehead represent mind-control? Lastly what about those awful 'one eye mascots' called Wenlock and Mandeville were they representing the all-seeing eye too? My two year old niece jumped with fright when she first saw the mascot!

The closing ceremony was a Gigantic Global Community with the dead John Lennon song sung by children all dressed in non-identity white clothes called 'Imagine'. Then came the phoenix reborn out of the flames an important symbol of the occult culture while 'Take That' group singing 'Rule the World' but the biggest mystery of the ceremony to me was; what did the 70 sheep, 3 sheep dogs, 12 horses, chicken and geese have to do with Olympics? It was the sheep that flummoxed me the most!

It makes sense now, was it their intention to start drip feeding the public by creating mystery in outer space in such films as 'Star Wars' 'Close Encounter of the third kind' 'E.T' and 'Big Foot'?

Someone in the Zionist movement in Hollywood released a press statement, 'The Hollywood digital switch has been pressed and if the world needs to know, we will let them know what they need to know' In that case, do we all need to be on the lookout for secret society symbols on our television, telling us of their presence, such as black and white chequered floors, pyramids, 'V' salute hand gestures, the index and little finger as devil horn salute, the Masonic hand shake, the skulls and many more. For us to assess ourselves if the program was linked to the Illuminati order?

Illegal drugs

Things are getting serious now; is it true that these organisations are in control of all the drug trade, heroin, opium, cocaine anything that's Illegal outward bound from Columbia? It is rumoured that the drug trade is then operated by the Jesuits agents such as the Mafia who also work in tandem with the CIA. The top Illuminati family's divide up the drug trade, including the Narcotic drugs cartel.

How dare these organisations let young people take the wrap at air-ports and Docks for trafficking drugs through customs against their will, when the elite are the biggest traffickers? The wrong people are being punished here and are getting rich at the cost of others. I think the year of the truth has been a long time coming, where the elite, politicians and the royals are concerned and they should not be above the law.

Many journals have reported bombing Afghanistan was a cover up for the Taliban's destruction of Afghanistan Opium Crops thus curtailing the Black Popes International Drug Trade.

I'll say no more on this topic as it would take an honest judge and an un-corrupt jury to sort this little chapter out, and I don't know if either could be found.

Medicine and the Drug Companies

This is the chapter I'm interested in the most; what influences has the Rothschild's had on our modern day medicines to inflict such a terror on Julian's body?

Evidently the medical scientist started its journey in 1901 when the Rockerfella dynasty created 'Rockerfella Institute of Medical Research Centre' in America with Rothschild as their financier. There you have the connection already; in the late 1950s Rockerfell crossed the water and founded 'London University College Hospital Medical School' and the 'London School of Hygiene and Tropical Medicine'.

But I am intrigued as to why these two families would associate themselves with helping people from the 'goodness of their heart' when it obvious they have only ever been interested in lining their own pockets! To name just a few conditions they have been researching on our behalf, High cholesterol, High blood pressure, and Heart disease, Cancer, Tuberculosis, HIV / AIDs, Diabetes and Vaccination.

The Pharmaceutical Racketeering started when the 'Rock and Roth' of this world started sponsoring researchers—but **only** if the research was drug based. The Rockerfell Empire founded the 'Drug Trust' in 1939 and they employed such companies as Imperial Chemical Industries

(ICI) Proctor and Gamble, Welcome, Roche, Carnation, Monsanto, Nestles and Kellogg's with 'Fritz ter Mear' as their board chairman. Do you remember this Auschwitz man who they claimed they didn't know, but continued to lay a wreath on his grave every Halloween night!

I shall never again be drawn in to celebrate these satanic rooted Halloween Parties.

For years now independent pharmaceutical companies have said, Rockerfell Drug Companies were always allowed to win because they couldn't financially compete against them. Their threatening technique obviously worked because today Rockerfell owns all of the drug companies. Having a monopoly over all our drugs, in my opinion can't be healthy?

Doctors and GPs have become yes men to the Rockerfell Prescribed Drug Barron's because they have no other choice.

I've already mentioned how I feel Diabetics, High Cholesterol sufferers, and patients with High Blood Pressure have been misguided in their treatment in the chapter titled 'Question of Diabetes' but the question of the big 'C' has intrigued me for years, especially when my 83 year old mother recalls, when she was a child she over hearing her local GP telling **her** mother, "Once you've shinned the knife at cancer, shh, it just erupts and spreads" That might have been the case then, but we don't seem to have moved forward scientifically much since the 1940's, so who is suppressing the cure? Cancer research, have definitely squeezed enough money out of us fundraisers over the last 100 years. Allegedly a medical conspiracy took place in 1922 when it was discovered that cancer could be cured from a common herb which elevated the immune system. The discovery was shelved until it was exposed again in 1937, it came within 3 votes of being legalised in Canada. Yet again the topic emerged in 1952 by Dr John Richardson published in 'Advocate of Laetrile Therapy' calming 'Cancer was a vitamin and enzyme deficiency disease' which is lack of B17 that's found in Apricot kernel and almonds. When it was leaked to the public, the 'Food and Drug Association' (FDA) started to pasteurise the Almonds adding poisonous chemicals to neutralize the 'cancer curing' element which it normally produces and stored in the almonds. Today the organic Almond kernel is only available through virtually underground outlets at a high price, I say organic because we need to be sure the Food, Drug Association haven't contaminated it first.

It seems to me they cannot afford for us to discover a cancer cure; Pharmaceutical companies rely on ill health for profit. No drug company has a vested interest in curing diseases! Their aim is to maintain ill-health, creating diseases, manufacturing chemicals, promote the need for therapy for symptoms.

Medical drugs industry is a multi-billion pounds industry with ever increasing expenditure on the tax-payers, headed by the Elite manipulators. GPs are no longer free to choose the most reliable or safe therapy they are at the mercy of the drug companies who are often persuade them to buy less effective drugs.

Did you know 'Breast Cancer Awareness Month' was conceived and paid for by Imperial Chemical Industry' or ICI a company that profits by billions from producing chemicals such as pesticides, which is well known for causing cancer. Then the same company, ICI, manufactured a top selling anti-cancer drug such as Tamoxifen. After profiting millions from the sufferers twice over, they then have the audacity to publically beg on television for the Nation to donate just £2 a month to their cancer research. I'm beginning to think, they are laughing all the way to the Bank!

Another mystery virus that came along in the early 70s was HIV and AIDs, the original propaganda theory tried to convince the public it started after an African man ate a monkey, but an American researcher announced in the medical journal called 'Nature' that it was caused by "Mass immunisation Campaigns in Africa, who spread the disease through World Health Organisation or WHO which is a medical wing of United Nations founded by Rothschild and Rockefellers. Another Dr supported this theory calming, "It was not an accident but a deliberate act" Dr. William Campbell Douglas M.D wrote it was first 'Predicted-Requested-Produced finally Induced' It's not a product from Mother Nature, but a product from sick and evil men who in effect are murdering the African population. Once we were amidst the viral epidemic 'Welcome' the Medical Research Council along with the Department of Health used six London Hospitals including NHS staff and their facilities to conduct a trial with three years free health care, using AZT drugs to treat HIV patients. This is a drug that kills the immune system and without a good immune system we can't exist. They administered 1000mg a day, twice the recommended dose by the FDA the patients then suffered serious muscle wastage and anaemia. This drug was once deemed toxic, its side effects bear a striking resemblance to the symptoms they were to <u>expect</u> in the later stage of their affliction. The drug has kept the profits rolling for 'Wellcome' throughout the 1990s to the tune of £400 million a year. There were eight other well-known companies on this board making sure treatment continued.

Which brings up the question, according to the Code of Conduct provided by the UKCC (United Kingdom Central Council) that nurses and midwifes role is to be the patients advocate, entrusted to provide care in the interest of the patient which includes the nurse responsible of administration of drugs, ensuring the correct drug is given, the correct dosage is calculated including being aware of possible side effects. Many terminally ill patients have drawn up 'Living Wills' to arrest active treatment at the last stage of their treatment but the requests are frequently ignored by Drs who continue to pump toxins into dying patients claiming "Following orders from above" (Disavow Julian, how often did we both hear that?) There is too much monkey business going on, "See no evil, hear no evil and speak on evil" Then to add insult to injury AIDs and HIV victims are often deemed as 'dangerous waste' and must be cremated for hygiene reasons almost immediately. No autopsy performed!!!! Treating AIDs patients is a huge money spinner for these companies. Chemical companies don't want the public to know about any findings of AIDs and HIV sufferer's autopsy results, **obviously!**

I would like to state a note of empathy here, to any AIDs and HIV sufferers please accept my sincere apologies if I have offended you, it's your medical drug pushers I'm trying to get at, not you, I'm angry for you—not at you.

. . . .

Dr. John Braithwaite, Trade Practices Commissioner said in his exposure to crime in the Pharmaceutical Industry that "International bribery, corruption and fraud in the testing of drugs, criminal negligence in the unsafe manufacture of drugs, the pharmaceutical industry has the worst record of law breaking than any other industry" Wow! Someone else that's angry?

. . . .

I've copied this quote above and stapled it to Julian's death certificate.

I've never given animal testing much thought in the past except to turn a blind eye, but is Vivisection just an issue for animal rights, or for all of us? Consider this; every medical student must quote the result of an animal experiment before they qualify. How can they match respect for life, compassion and empathy against ignorance of pain, suffering, anxiety terror and death? The two are polls apart, there's no comparison. Dr J Gallagher, Director of Research of Lederle Laboratory wrote on the 14th March 1964 in a Medical Association Journal "Animal study is done for legal reasons and not scientific reasons, the predictive values for such studies for man is meaningless, which means our research may be meaningless"

There is no British or European law that states new drugs, chemicals or cosmetics must be tested on animals, the confusion comes when the legal system call upon these, Vivisectionists for advice in a court of law. But if the studies are meaningless what can the courtroom gain from their opinion?

George Bernard Shaw once said, "Whoever <u>doesn't</u> hesitate to vivisect, will hardly hesitate to lie about it" Mmmmm! Sadly 3.5 million animals die each year in the UK alone at the vivisectionists hands, 75% of the experiments are done without anaesthetic, which are conducted using public money. That means I'm paying for that awful experiment, there are only 19 Home Office Inspectors to cover 20,000 licenced vivisectionists and to top it all the RSPCA has financial interest in vivisections, it beggar's belief.

My last topic is a taboo subject and highly controversial— Vaccination. Am I brave or stupid to tackle this subject? Nobody wants to hear bad press about Vaccination because none of us want to see the return of Polio, Diphtheria, Measles, Mumps and Tuberculosis. But at the same time we only want what's safe for our children and, if slipping the odd bug or two to help cull the world is what they have in mind then of course, us parents are going to sit up for a minute and weigh up the consequences.

Let's go back to the beginning, how are vaccines made first of all. The toxic bacterium is acquired to make a live vaccine; the vaccine then needs to be weakened. This is done by the measles virus being passed through chicken embryos, polio virus is passed through monkeys kidneys and rubella virus through human diploid cell (aborted foetus) The weakened virus then gets strengthened with antibody boosters by adding drugs such as antibiotics, toxic disinfectants, neomycin, streptomycin, sodium hydroxide, aluminium hydroxide, sorbitol and thimerosal. (Mercury derivate) Sadly studies confirm microscopic doses can lead to cancer, neurological damage otherwise known as Shaken Baby Syndrome even death. Spare a thought for all the parents serving a sentence in our Prisons today, for allegedly shaking their baby to death!

Let me recap to see if I understand it correctly, it consists of live viruses, bacteria, toxic substances and diseased animal matter, and then this concoction is injected with a 'gush' into a tiny healthy baby's body.

But if you're questioning, if these tiny babies are strong enough to deal with these vicious vaccinations, spare a thought for the unborn baby when expectant mothers are offered Swine flu vaccination and sadly some suffering the misfortune of a miscarriage the very next day, Why?

The good news is that Thimerosal that was used as a preservative in the vaccine has recently been removed from most vaccines in the UK since 2011. I emphasise on the word 'most' and if I had my time again Id check with my GP what chemical Llewela was given in her vaccines. But I wasn't made aware then that she was receiving any mercury or warned about its danger. The only advise I was given 'She's bound to be unwell for a few days'.

Julian insisted Llewela had all her injections even though she reacted most terribly to all of them.

She suffered High fever, extremely swollen limbs and a formation of a black necrotic area at the injected site. After about a week the black necrotic area would fall out in the shape of a cone, leaving a permanent dip in the muscle. At the time the nurses felt she was allergic to tetanus, but could it of been the mercury derivative thimerosal she was reacting to!

I'm not trying to be the 'Anti-Vax Queen' here, but the FDA openly confessed on 6th October 2012 that cancer cells are the most efficient method for manufacturing vaccines. That might be the case, but it's the drug companies who are pacifying us saying that they are safe, but are they long term?

I'm not sold with this cancer cell theory yet!

I sat up when I read this next comment, when a Scientist said in 1936 "I never saw cancer in an unvaccinated person" In that case I should be asking, why are cancer cells used in the manufacturing of any vaccines! What I found disturbing was; I couldn't find any old or up-to-date data about its safety, and more worrying if the government decided to make it mandatory for every human being to have vaccination or face imprisonment, then where does that leave us? Will we all eventually suffer from cancer? And what about the élite do they have their children vaccinated? No most don't, what do they fear that we're not even aware of or are they too 'posh to jab'?

Others may feel I'm making scaremongering comments about what others feel are lifesaving preventative treatment, but stack my comments against what Bill Gates who openly admits that his vaccinations are used for depopulating the world, which he's already started in Africa and India in a big way and, Prince Phillip and Richard Attenborough openly supports on camera.

I'm not asking anyone to refuse vaccinations, I'm asking that we all don't behave like sheep and take it for granted, what's in the vials is safe for ourselves and our children, 'Check it out first'

At least fifty books have been written questioning the safety of Vaccination, why if it's safe? A Doctor Bonnie Dunbar claimed she observed that her **un**vaccinated children were healthier, hardier and more robust than the vaccinated peers. The **un**vaccinated did not suffer allergies such as, asthma, behavioural and attention disturbances, infectious diseases and their immune system generally handled these challenges very well. Hiding vaccine death statistics under cot deaths is one way of cooking the books, loss of medical notes is a favourite for protecting the vaccine producers from being sued, the other is passing the buck onto the tax payer by expecting the medical profession to fund the nursing care of a disabled child. But is Dr Dunbar qualified to comment, she is a Molecular Biologist Research Scientist and Medical Graduate Student Professor in autoimmunity and vaccine development for the past 25 years. Her brother, Dr Bohn Dunbar developed side effects from Hepatitis B vaccination costing the country thousands in health care to look after him. One of her students also an athletic fit person was partially blinded from a booster injection. Dr Dunbar studies the risk and benefits of any vaccinations.

Did you know flu vaccine can cause immediate risk to our cardiovascular system, which would explain why my father had a stroke one hour after his vaccination! And that would also explain why the Ambulance crew said when they picked him up "I trust you won't be taking that again?"

Why would he say that, unless they could see a pattern forming with patient's they was transporting to various hospitals.

While my father was recovering in hospital in a bay of five other men who had all experienced the same fate of a 'disabling stroke' one hour following a flu vaccination!

In America a Doctor with an autistic son was seeking information on the danger of vaccinations, he had to wait 7 years to hear a judge order the documents be turned over to be viewed, this took place as recently as 20th September 2011. In the UK, the vaccine hoax was exposed by 'Freedom of Information Act' up until then mothers were at risk of being accused of 'Munchausen Syndrome by Proxy' and Fathers were at risk of being imprisoned, accused of causing 'Shaking Baby Syndrome' But at last on March 14th 2012 thirty years of secret official Transcripts were shown to the UK Government Experts, exposing a covered up of 'vaccine hazards' to sell more vaccination which risked harming our lovely children.

I asked myself, do I still want to trade in my healthy immune system for a risky 'Total immune system depression'

There are numerous other black projects on the making, if these vaccine companies are allowed to continue they will vaccinate the whole human race, at the same time inject micro-chip ID and mind control drugs without our knowledge.

Sounds crazy doesn't it, but Gweno and I have been saying to each other for years 'Nothing is impossible'

In Thailand pregnant women are already forced to receive vaccination in order for their unborn baby's to have an ID card, but the vaccine then causes the mother to miscarry!

Other countries suffer too, in Maryland parents are harassed for their children to take the vaccines otherwise $25 of their monthly welfare will be stopped. In Mexico students who return their vaccine consents form early can enter a raffle prize! In Michigan children were offered a free order of French fries! Before Michael Jackson died TV adverts were offering a chance to win free tickets to his concert if they took the vaccine.

Did you know British GPs can earn up to £27,000 bonus if they prescribe a certain number of vaccinations? Its money for old rope, the receptionists do the clerking, the nurses do the jabbing and the doctors do the collecting of the cheque! Think about it, babies receiving drugs into a two month old body with underdeveloped immune system, for goodness sake, why didn't I think that when Llewela was a baby? There not even old enough to have 'Honey' because their immune system are too underdeveloped. Adding to that worry, there has never been any long term safety research into these vaccines. A Doctor Vernon Coleman has been asked **not** to speak to other English Doctors about the dangers of vaccinations, bearing in mind he is a fully qualified GP and fully licenced with the General Medical Council of London himself.

Doctor Len Saputo MD and Stacia Lansman MD are telling us to be wary of 'Big Pharma' when they talk about emergency immunisations like swine flu vaccination. First they scare us, then they convince politicians with worrying signs of questionable science, then they inoculate us on a global scale only to make a fortune in the process!

Doctor Stacia Lansman MD paediatric specialist also says about vaccination, the safety of this drug is not proven and to give it to children with developing brains is questionable. Scientists are also perplexed why the virus contains the original 1918 flu virus, the bird flu virus and two new virus genes from Eurasia, were these elements connected or is it possible that 'Swine Flu' virus is a 'Genetically Engineered Virus' a man-made virus to make us sick? They then sell us the vaccine through the NHS!!! She's published a book called, 'Return to healing' considering the safety of thimerosal or mercury and neuro-toxins which is a disinfectant in the vaccines.

I know all medical sectors are requested to take the flu jab, but physicians are exempt, why?

Georg Bernard Shaw once said, "Every Doctor will allow a colleague to decimate a whole countryside, sooner than violate the bond of professional etiquette by giving him away" things haven't changed. I ask on behalf of all parents in the world, "How much damage and death is enough to warrant the first INVESTIGATION into the dangers of vaccinations, I repeat the FIRST.

No other industry is allowed to operate in secrecy with no accountability and without any recall program in place!

Australia Public Health have called for an independent body to monitor the vaccines safety, after it emerged that young children and the elderly were more likely to end up in hospital because of the side effects from the flu vaccination.

Finland have already agreed to pay 79 children compensation for 'Life time medical care' after proving conclusively that there was links that Swine Flu Vaccine caused irretrievable Chronic Nervous System Damage.

In my opinion vaccination is serious business and if it's warranted, then the public deserve to know its content and that its passes vigorous independent tests to prove its safety and not administered by force, bribes or gimmick tactics such as 'Vaccines are not just kid stuff' or 'All their shots while they're tots'! No wonder Julian refused his flu vaccine when he was ill! You have to be strong to tackle its content.

Yes we want to be protected, but at what cost?

Lastly when I was looking into Julian's intolerance of most antibiotics I mentioned I discovered something called pro-drugs. To remind you again, pro-drug is a drug which has undergone chemical transformation, in other words it's a synthetic product. Pharmacy's today dispense on average 33% of pro-drugs daily, but they don't come problem free; the drugs can suffer inadequate activation when digested and unfortunately most of them lead to liver damage.

Examples of some of these synthetic prescriptions are synthetic blood pressure tablets, synthetic birth control pill, synthetic testosterone, synthetic antibiotics (such as any Cipros which not only cause liver failure but muscle and tendon damage too) synthetic statins (can cause liver, muscle and kidney damage) synthetic thyroid hormone called levothyroxine (must never be used by patients with adrenal malfunction, it can lead to adrenal crisis and fatty liver. (Sorry Julian you were right it would of made you feel worst) including patients who have suffered from myocardial infarctions should not accept it either. Synthetic sugar substitute called xylitol found on coated medication can cause liver damage and must never be given to dogs.

I wonder, who thought it might be safe for humans?

One last comment on the subject of medicines and that is vitamins and minerals. I've already worked out for myself in the 'Question of Diabetes' chapter, how important an adequate amount of vitamins can prevent us developing Type Two Diabetes but of course that is my opinion, but now to support my finding I've come across a Doctor M. Rath from Germany who unfortunately has come under criticism from such organisations as 'World Health Organisations' 'United Nations Children Fund' and 'United Nations Aids' when they all issued a joint statement ridiculing Doctor Rath's advertisement as "wrong and misleading" but don't forget all these regulators were instigated by the Rockerfell and funded by the Rothschild's, both had an added interest in selling drugs to mend us the sick population, not to mention their intention of depopulation. So can any of these regulators opinion be taken seriously, because they do have a conflict of interest here?

Doctor Rath identified 'micro-nutrient deficiency' as the primary cause of diseases; these diseases include heart attacks, high blood pressure, circulation problems, cancer, Diabetes and even immune deficiency diseases such as Aids! In my opinion this Doctor has become the Sherlock Holmes of Medical Science and between 1990-1992 he traced the real cause of the diseases, which was caused by companies deliberately hiding away from millions of people, the vital vitamins and minerals we all desperately need to stay healthy. They did this for one reason only, and that was to feed their own greed of the pharmaceutical business, by first causing the disease then profiting by pretending to heal us at great cost to our health and in some cases to our lives. Doctor M Rath is determined to face the children and grandchildren of tomorrow by saying,

"Defence is no longer an option for us; let us tackle this historical task together"

Now we've discovered their scam, the race is on between us the commoners and the Elite who help the Roth's and the Rocks of this world to fund the likes of the almighty 'Codex Alimentation Company' who intend to take over our vitamin and mineral replacement supply by classifying all 'vitamins and minerals' as illegal drugs. These are supplements we cannot survive without, after they have supplied us with substandard food containing artificial additives then destroying any goodness left in the food by microwaving it.

If every chapter in this book is true, it's not because I have tried to 'Witch hunt' the Roth's and the Rocks, it's because I became so cross about their deception of under handedness operating behind other organisations, inflicting deliberate trauma, disease, illness and even death.

But now we know what were up against, we don't have to fight our opponent the assassins in the dark like the Knight Templers had too all those years ago. The 'good' in us can fight the 'evil' they represent, so we can take back our own good health, our own entitled peace, and our own uncorrupted politics, reinstate our uncorrupted education, strengthen our own long lost Christian faith by replacing their Satanic and Lutheran practices. Then there will be no need to report shocking news in the media about illegal drugs and organised crime, the wickedness in the medicine world, and the production of pro-drugs should cease.

It seems that the Jesuits have been operating as wolves in lambs clothing since the early 1500's. Well their cover is blown; we can now see them for what they truly are. But how could I have tried to put things right for Julian when I had no idea what was wrong! It seems to me that the Rock and the Roth's have kept the world so busy with their Jesuit upside down, inside out Alice in wonderland life that we didn't have time to work out what they were up to behind our backs. Sadly I had to experience the loss of Julian and my job, to be blessed with adequate time to work out what's going on in the world.

An ancient Greek Philosopher Plato once said "We can forgive children who are frightened of the dark, the real tragedy of life is when men are afraid of the light" Are we frightened of the light?

So like a modern day Sat-nav this book has taken me 'round the Wrekin' as they say, and as the recorded voice always says "You have arrived at your destination" I was so lost and isolated at Julian's bed side when I whispered to him "Oh! Julian I think what you're suffering from is very big, but the answer might be as simple as a vitamin or mineral pills!

As the old saying goes, 'Never, a truer word spoken in gest'

I have now completed the 'Pyramid of Manipulation' which looks as if it was controlled by the Jesuits as part of the New World Order.

Francis Bacon which is speculated by some, to be Queen Elizabeth I son, wrote a book called 'The New Atlantis' but the last chapter was never printed because it contained the long range 'Great Plan' of the world, revealing the entire secret societies which they had been working for, for the last hundreds of years.

To understand the concept of the 'New World Order' there's no wonder Julian sent a message from the other side "Go back to the beginning"

The drugs might have destroyed his poor body but not his soul, his soul lives on to worn the living.

How strange I thought of the 12th century series called 'Brother Cadval' at the beginning of this book, which runs on the parallel line of modern day 'Forensic Science' programs. Who claim "They have to speak up for the dead; because the dead cannot speak for themselves"

But I'm not alone in my worry over modern day health concerns, there are many other 'Brother Cadvals' who have gone before me publishing similar books on the similar topics. One is called 'Adrenal Fatigue, the 21st century stress syndrome' by Doctor James, another is 'Sweet Poison' by Cynthia Perkins and 'Fats that heal, Fats that kill' by Udo Erasosmus, the list goes on. As regards to my book, I recall someone saying to me 'Good writing is about uncovering and discovering' but I also recall and value what Gill said to me "The best writing is always done from the heart" and this book has come from nowhere else but the heart!

May God forgive me, if I've got any part of this book, wrong!

In need of a Retreat

Exhausted, shocked and saddened at my findings at this stage of my book Gill, Gwenno and I decided to go on a retreat high into the Welsh mountains to try and rejuvenate our energy levels and to meditate, not surprisingly on worldly matters. Our chosen resting place was in a large Tipi away from home comforts and modern technology, a back to basics couple of days. Our aim was to sharpen our senses of sight and hearing and of course to quieten the mind. Before I left home I prayed for good weather, and what glorious weather we had. As soon as we arrived at our retreat we took to the mountain walking higher and higher to observe and enjoy the vista of the valley. As we admired the view the three of us felt very small and humble in this vast landscape. On our descent I realised my senses had already started to sharpen, as I became more aware of the sound of the river, the birds flowing franticly overhead and the bleating of the sheep in the distance. The quietening of my mind started with the constant flying of colourful butterfly's circling my head, teasingly greeting us into their beautiful valley.

In the twilight of the evening as the sun was setting we meditated around a log fire inside the Tipi, using drums the three of us quietly drummed away with our eyes closed each offering a different tempo. I was aware that my mind was troubled mainly over what I had recently discovered about the world we live in and the satanic leaders. We agreed that our intentions that evening would be well suited to meditate on world issues and send them much needed healing.

I was aware of four flash scenes while I meditated, the first was a village scene with a little girl who had a dirty face, dressed in rags and had matted hair. She was squatting by an old disused petrol pump; I can remember thinking this was not a safe place for a child to squat. My second flash scene was of a burning black 1940 'sit-up-and-beg' car, which appeared to be abandoned in the centre of a village. My third flash scene was of an old man in a dusty suit in the mid-day heat, sitting on a large rugged stone, all alone on the out skirts of the village. The old man was blind wearing dark glasses and was waving a very long white stick spanning the dusty road from side to side churning up clouds of dry dust. My fourth scene was of a pen, full of beautiful Palomino ponies, stampeding in an agitated state getting ready to escape. I saw myself releasing the gate and the penned up beasts burst to their freedom, like free spirits.

I interpreted this meditation as the innocent little girl represented us the vunrable people; the petrol pump represented danger and corruption in this world, the burning car represented the destruction in the world, the fact it happened to be a 'sit-up-and-beg' suggests we should do just that. The old blind man represented the Jesuits of this world who are sly, vindictive and behave like cowards and bullies, who hide behind other organisations they've created as their secret sadistic agents inflicting terror and war on law abiding citizens. Indeed they are blind; they cannot see the good and pure heart that other humans have to offer the world.

Thankfully the freed horses represented what we too could one day possess, and that is the same free spirit they experienced on the release of that open gate.

Was this a successful weekend, I'd like to think so if only to put my troubled world into perceptive, and that I was left with 'Hope' in my heart when those Palomino sprinting to their freedom. Without hope there is no point continuing with life.

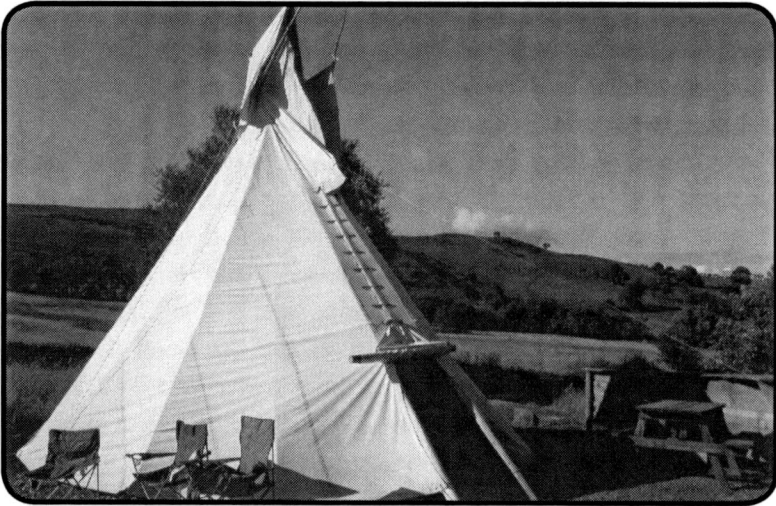

Photograph of the Tipi Gill, Gweno and I stayed in.

Unicorn's

Coincidence or not, but on my return home from my retreat the following morning I was drawn to the Crest of the Royal Family on the side of the cereal box. The white unicorn caught my eye after the discussion of the Palomino ponies the day before. It left me wondering why there was a unicorn on their crest.

No wonder this crest felt familiar to me, others use this similar icons it's found on Politics crest, the Papal crest, Canadian crest as well as the Knight Templers crest and wait for it the Rothschild's Family Crest. All of which depict two majestic beasts supporting their shield. The Lion represents strength and the golden sun, while the Unicorn represents purity, free spirit and the silver moon. The horn represents the third eye of the Illuminati. How strange that the Unicorn is depicted chained up on all the crests except on the Rothschild shield and the Papal shield. Why? Does it mean that our wild free spirit is shackled? The Canadian unicorn however depicts its chains broken, does this symbolise the unicorns resistance to oppression, captivity or bondage!

There is another familiar symbol in Banking and that's the Lloyds Black horse. Evidently it represents the 'Black Nobility' it's the same black horse that's seen on the Lord Mayor of London building, which boasts of having more than 60 Mayors, who were once 'Masters' of the Freemason Lodge. See, every day more questions than answers.

It may seem to some that through my grief, I've just dumped all my blame or reasoning on the Jesuits door step, but I'm sure there are others who have been unaware that such coordinating force has been at work, manipulating their Government, Royals and Religions. Could all this, be a load of codswallop, maybe all my findings are incorrect and the world is really flat!!!!!!

Question is; are the Jesuits in charge of our Banking through their agent Rothschild, are the Jesuits in charge of our oil through their agent Rockerfell, are the Jesuits in charge of our Religion through their agent the Pope, are the Jesuits in charge of our Food through their agent World Health Organisation, Food and Drug Administration, Genetically Modified foods and MGS foods, are the Jesuits in charge of our subduing senses by adding chlorine and phosphate to our water supply, are the Jesuits in charge of our medicines through ICI, Monsanto, Codex, GlaxoWelcome and many others, are the Jesuits in charge of our Air traffic through such agents as Richard Branson, are the Jesuits in charge of our seas through their agent Commercial Shipping companies and the Navy, are the Jesuits in charge of our land through World Wildlife Fund, are the Jesuits in charge of our World Wide Web through their agent Bill Gates, are the Jesuits in charge of our Politician's through their agent of many illegitimate-children rising them to power, are the Jesuits in charge of all World Wars through their warmongering, are the Jesuits in charge of 'Pretend Peace' through their agent United Nations, are the Jesuits in charge of the Media through their agent such as Robert Maxwell and

Rupert Murdock, are the Jesuits in charge of our Entertainment through their agent in Hollywood, Disney World and X-factor, are the Jesuits in charge of crime and illegal drugs through their Intelligence organisation agency the MI5, CIA, FBI and MI6.

And lastly are the Jesuits in charge of our prescribed medicines through the Rockerfell medical Institutes.

It has to be said the Rothschild's and the Rockerfell have been very loyal to the 'Loyola Order' the founder of the Jesuits. I'm more convinced now that all investigations lead to the house of the Rothschild and as they seem to seriously contaminate everything that is good. G. Edward Griffin once wrote "The Rothschild's dynasty has conquered the world more thoroughly, more cunningly and much more lastingly than all the Caesars before them or, all the Hitler's after them"

When I say "Deliver us from evil" in the Lord's Prayer now, suddenly it has a new meaning!

Are we now living in the last stage of the 'Big Plan' of the Illuminati, that's been designed for hundreds of years? Have they done an excellent job in deceiving us, all these years?

At last now life makes sense to me, for decades it didn't with all the evilness in this world that as been allowed to continue, how so many politicians seemed so corrupt, how some religions appeared to be at the rooted in wars, how billionaires didn't seem to help world crises, how famine is just as prevalent today as it was 100 years ago. I used to constantly ask how could God permit all these world disasters of war, famine, floods, earth quakes, volcano eruption, plains, trains and shipping disasters only to discover they were all man-made disasters!

Man has desecrated his 'Garden of Eden'.

Looking back over my private life, I couldn't understand why I couldn't bring myself to let go of the house in France? The 'my not letting go' became my stumbling block, but now I realise I had to understand, it's very foundation before I released it. What's more I had to understand what had taken place in the world while its wall remained standing.

Now in parting I will feel proud that I have contributed towards strengthening those two foot thick walls and arches, leaving it in a better condition than when I first clapped eyes on it in the millennium year of 2000. I now hope it will last another eight hundred years as a reminder to others that it once represented much needed shelter to a multitude of pilgrims, horses and the Knight Templers, who I now believe were good holy men. These mini-forts acted as a network of overnight safe sanctuary, with a bed and a meal at the end of each day throughout Europe. Strange when I first took root in this house, I had this overwhelming feeling to rename the house 'Lle Aros' when translated from Welsh means 'A place to stay'

Try as I might I couldn't find any connection between the Knight Templers and the Jesuit leader, except, Ignatius de Loyola who tried to emulate the order two hundred years later by starting with the similar number of men. To me they appear to be poles apart when Jacques de Molay's final confession at his own burning at the stake, that he had remained a loyal and faithful follower of Christ to the very end, while Ignatius de Loyal spoke of satanic oaths and constant divided loyalties between good and evil. I feel the Freemasons may have drawn from both orders, hence the use of the checker board pattern used so often in their order, representing good and evil.

We have strayed so far from what sort of life God intended us to enjoy, but I feel if there is 70,000,000,000 of us in the world, then surely there should be plenty of us to save the day.

As a teenager I used to wonder why the Jewish people couldn't say 'No' to the Nazi's, today I find myself in a similar situation. Will I, one of 700,000,000000 world population be able to say 'No' to some, not all of course, of the 1,275 Billionaires who finance such companies as Codex Aliment-ariuns Commission and Monsanto to enforce depopulation techniques on us through unscrupulous vaccination and feeding us MSG and GM food and Fluoride water to lower my IQ enough, to cause enough lethargy in me not to retaliate.

Can somebody advise us the common man in the street? Who can we trust, if we can't trust the World Health Organisation, Food Safety Association, United Nations, European Union, Codex Aliment-arian, New World Organisation, our own Government, or do we have to rely on 'our little voice of conscience?' something Julian was always in possession of?

Culling today's population is not morally ethical, by treating current population with chemical medicines and feeding them with pesticide infiltrated food, artificial additives, hoodwinking us into thinking that mechanical engine oil is edible causing untold cancer and putting fluoride into drinking water to dim their IQ into submission that the Elite know best.

It sounds more like a robot component maintenance kit to me, rather than a human diet.

The Guardian newspaper worryingly commented recently "We need to pay more attention to the gender behind the people we place in position of influential power, when it comes to culling or depopulation." And I say "Who has the right to say who can live and who should die?

It's a good job I'm no longer employed by the NHS, recalling what I was first taught at my Pupil Nurse Training, to never discus with any patient the topics of politics, money or religion. Now in my retirement I feel a sense of remorse for writing about all three forbidden subjects. But it became a necessity after the message Julian sent me after his death 'Leave no stone unturned'

In that case was it necessary to mention all the topics in the 'Pyramid of Manipulation' firstly world banking then world business, military forces, world politics, education, world organised crime, world intelligence agency, world religion, world media, world illegal drug agency, and lastly world medicine and drug companies? In my opinion "Yes" I wanted the reader to recognise how powerful the Jesuits have become, operating through all their agents.

Still living in fear that I might of got some points wrong, I beg you don't take everything I've written at face value but research everything I've mentioned yourself, then take a leaf out of Padre Poi's book "Pray, hope and don't worry"

But when shall I **pray**, shall I do it silently when I'm walking, shall I do it when I'm washing up, shall I do it when I'm standing in a queue, should I do it at the time I'm not talking? It's just I'm up against such tyranny. I always used to say when my back is against the wall and there's no fight left in me, there was always prayer. And I never, never under estimate the power of prayer that good can overpower evil without a single drop of bloodshed and **hope**fully one day the lamb will be seen to lay with the wolf and the lion will lie down with the kid. And then none of us will have to **worry** any more, just enjoy peace, perfect peace!

I wrote this book so others could see what a drug pushing end Julian endured during the last five weeks of his life and, I'm hoping I have been able to highlight that, there is something evil going on in our medical world.

I'm relying heavily on "Freedom of speech campaigners" here to protect me against the questions I'm raising about everything the Rothschild and the Rockerfell Dynasty represent, because I don't have the wealth they enjoy to drag plebs like me through the courts.

The bottom line is, no race, no nation, no man has the right to take advantage of another.

Doctor Rima Laibow MD once said "Now is the time to act, tomorrow might be too late"

I remember Julian saying similar words during the last few days of his life "Please Doc I beg you, stop this treatment right now, because tomorrow might be too late!" Shall we all wait until it's too late for us as well? Julian your right something has gone very wrong!

One might ask, why I didn't I stay focused on Julian's life, instead of meddling with all these other topics. I will tell you why, when I read that Fritz ter Mear company was so intent on destroying our immune system, I suddenly became very angry that someone had deliberately unhinged Julian's Endocrine system and in the process tried to blame me for his death. To such a degree I might have lost my job, my pension, my reputation but worst of all, my freedom. They could have been successful in imprisoning me and thrown away the key. I feel I have to tell the world his story so that his Soul, can finally find peace!

To me Julian's scenario was like treating someone with a 'gash' caused by a whip and the following day allowing him to be whipped again. The harming has to stop; Julian died after suffering from all the side effects from the synthetic world we all live in, which was created by all the organisations mentioned on the 'Pyramid of Manipulation' book marker, which I asked you to make. I don't mean to sound 'Vindictive' but these people have deliberately set out to attack our immune system.

In the words of an old Chinese philosopher called 'Confucius' who once said,

"If you understand a problem deeply enough, you will have the answer"

Thankfully at last I now feel my lose bundle is neatly tied up with a big beautiful bow, no more lose ends, no more wondering why Julian suffered like he did.

I'd forgotten about Pandora, I hope she hasn't forgotten about us and that she's got enough 'Hope' left in her box, for all Nations to wake up, to what's going on!

Questions for you

This book could go on and on, because the more I learn the less I know. So no more resurch for me but here are some questions for you to prove or disprove for your selves.

My first quirky question is; why have I always found it so difficult to accept the 100 year war between the house of York and Lancashire, giving us the symbol 'Rosette' as the English emblem? What secret was Mary Queen of Scots shown in Rosslyn Chapel when she visited, and was the English Rose or Rosette something to do with Rosslyn Chapel or did her father Henry the VIII call the Mary Rose after his sister Mary and Rose after Rosslyn Chapel. And how could Mary Queen of Scott's son, King James I have such a conflict of interest when it came to religion. If he was the 'First Official Royal Illuminati Freemason' at the same time being the same King who converted the Latin Bible into English calling it the 'King James Bible' Is it true Francis Bacon was Queen Elizabeth I son, if so why was she called the 'Virgin Queen?' Is it true Francis Bacon helped King James edit the translation of the Bible! This same King James who was subject to the Gun Powder Plot and, is it true that it was the Jesuits who was behind the conspiracy and it was they who hired Guy Fawkes to sabotage the Houses of Parliament. (Because we are well aware that the Jesuits support both sides in secret) Is it possible the Jesuits then split on Guy Fawkes in the nick of time allowing the Catholics to look bad, but gain a sympathy vote from the King! And should we consider him a hero if all he was, was a paid 'Mercenary' who's intention was to assassinate?

Another question! Why, did the St Clair's welcome the Gypsies with open arms from May through to June, annually until 1579? And why did King James the IV issue a Privy Seal to Johnnie Faa of Dunbar the leader of the Egyptians, otherwise known as the 'Gypsies' come to perform plays, with their minstrels, pipers, and fiddlers, singing, dancing and to tell fortune. The description oozes Shakespearean influence, did they also bring with them ancient playing cards, dating back to 1350 from Egypt, I don't mean the Tarot cards I mean our present day playing cards. The cards dealt with chance and fate, while the chess board game dealt with strategy and man's tactics.

Was it possible these 'Egyptians' or Gypsies could have travelled on foot from Egypt? Not impossible, they could have followed the Nile River through Egypt passing through the Holy land via Jerusalem, taking a short sea crossing from Turkey to Constantinople then over land through Bulgaria, Siberia, Romania, Hungary, Slovakia, Czech republic, Germany and lastly Belgium before taking a second short sea crossing to the shores of England, then by land to the out skirts of Edinburgh arriving at Roselyn Chapel. Although most Gypsies have experienced centuries of persecution throughout the ages, there have been some who have appreciated their talents, for example Hungary considered them to be 'Pharaohs people'

In Vienna the Queens Court once wrote "the most excellent Egyptian musicians" even in Wales we were aware of these mystic tribes. My Mother used to speak of a character called Abram Wood he was the first Gypsy family to settle in North Wales around 1730. He was a great fiddler and story teller, he became known as the King of the Welsh Gypsies. The son and grandson of Abram mastered the National instrument of Wales, the Harp.

Going back to the chess board, the chess pieces resemble the pack of cards with their Kings, Queens, Knights, Bishops and Pawns, coupled with the fact the floors to all temple buildings consisted of chequered black and white tiles. Is it true the black and white represented the difference between good and evil! Examples of this flooring can be found in Westminster Abbey, Notre Dame in Paris and masonic buildings including masonic artefacts such as certificates.

I digress, is it true that the board game depicted <u>The Crusaders pieces</u> The King represented Richard the Lion heart, the Queen Berengaria of Navarre, the Bishop the Pope, the Knight the Knight of the Holy Grail, the Castle was Jerusalem and the Pawn, the Crusader. <u>The Muslim pieces</u> was similar, the King was the Saladin, the Queen the Saladin's wife, the Bishop the Caliph, the Knight the Saracen Knight, the Castle was Jerusalem and the Pawn was the Saracen, both sides battling for Jerusalem. Is it true other organisations controlled by the Freemasons such as the Metropolitan Police Force have incorporated the chequered pattern into their uniform?

This is a wild card, is the modern day chequered flag, used in the ground prix car racing was it also used by the Saracens in the 11 century during horse racing?

St Georges Flag

I hope I haven destroyed everything you hold dear to you, I'm just learning to let go of the bad and hang on to the good of this world, my life, my health, my faith, my country, my culture and my flag. Question is; did the Knight Templers have a more lasting effect on our culture?

Because I'm left wondering, if we should be more indebted to Jacques de Molay because if the Knight Templers Head Quarters was once based in London at Westminster Abbey, is it possible that it was discussed in that very building what symbol the English should have on their national flag? My next if is; if the Knight Templers were instrumental in bringing the story of St George to the shores of England and we were willing enough to adopt him as our Patron Saint, it would make sense to me that the Templers might have some say in the design of the flag. And if their Order was first conformed by Pope Honorius II in1128 and, if he requested they wore a white vestment representing purity and, if the red cross wasn't added for another 18 years in the year 1146 by Pope Eugenius symbolising Christianity. Is it then possible to assume, that the St Georges flag evolved from the Knight Templers uniform of white vestment and their red cross? But wait there's more, in 1606 the Union Jack was formed, but why was it called Union Jack, because it was King James I that was reigning at the time, not a King John. Could the Grand Master Jacques de Molay also be involved in the formation of the Union Jack? Because Jacques was fondly called Jack amongst his friends! There's a lot of, if's, in this chapter, I will surrender the topic as food for thought for you. And one last did you know, on-land the English flag is called Union Flag but out at sea it's called a Union Jack, why?

And one last random question for you, why do the British sing 'Zadok the Priest and Nathan crowned King Solomon' during coronation of all British monarchists?

Do you remember I wrote in a confused state at the beginning of this book about Sarah Brightman, who sang at a Luna concert dedicated to political conflict? She sang "Requiem" meaning "Grant them eternal rest"

Did Julian mean, all these souls who have departed were not resting peacefully because of their final days on earth, were they worried their kin left behind might suffer like they did? Will they now rest peacefully when the world starts to question my concerns? I hope I have disturbed a hornet's nest? I wonder could it be, that is why Julian has sent me someone to help me every single day since his death, through dreams, messages, phone calls, lyrics in songs, people I've met who have guided me of what to peruse or write about the next day, but more to the point will all these signs stop, once all my concerns are resolved?

This book came about because, as time went by there appeared to be more than just Julian suffering from the treatment, I can't honestly say he ever suffered from the condition only the treatment.

My awareness was first aroused when my friends Mother died shortly after Julian in similar circumstances, same condition, same treatment, same pain, same side effects and finally the same oedema and of course same outcome her heart stopped. There are many others, whose funerals I have attended, who I consider to have suffered in the same way as Julian including another friend of mine who said about her mother "How could she have died Olwen, she died in Intensive Care Unit from multi-organ failure. How can that be Olwen, she only had Diabetes for two years, nothing else?"

I could only shrug my shoulders!

I can't believe I've managed to put Julian's story together, but none of us know what we can achieve until we aspire to our highest ability.

I hope, you the reader agree with me that we can all contribute in making this world a better place to live in. Please don't under estimate your own values and abilities and think you have nothing to offer. Remember I was once a farmer's daughter who ran bare foot on the hillside and was not introduced to the English language until I was eleven.

Yet, here I am with my poor English and a passion for justice, managing to put a few words together, hopefully to arouse the passion to change our ways.

All I had to inspire me was my Grandmother who was such a good story teller, but I assure you this book is no tall story. I like my Grandmother only have an interest in telling true stories not fables.

Nain, my Grandmother veered two people beside her Faith they were not political leaders, but they were recognised as world peace makers, one was Mother Teresa. I remember someone telling me about a widow sending Mother Teresa a letter asking if she could join her in Calcutta to help her with the needy. Evidently Mother Teresa wrote back telling her to stay at home and find her own Calcutta in her own village, town or city, that she would be needed wherever she was in life, why did she have to travel halfway across the world when she could do the same near her home. I have no proof of this incident but does it matter, it's the weight the story carries that matters.

I wonder if the saying "Charity begins at home" could it mean your own home town, if that's the case, we could all start right now by cleaning up our home town of its contamination.

Nain's other hero was Mahatma Gandhi, who once said "Be the change you want to see in the world" and that is what I hope to achieve by keeping the good ways and changing the bad, whatever they maybe, old or new.

In case anyone is wondering, if I'm a lot richer since Julian died, the answer to that question is "No" I've never been so poor financially, but in the words of the singer Enya 'Memories are more precious than gold' in which case, because he has left me with so many memories I conclude myself to be very rich. In laying him to rest, it might have left me poor, but at least I live in the knowledge that I did not abandon him in a Pauper's grave and his dying wish of getting to the root of why he suffered like he did, is now complete.

Raising Concerns

Throughout the entirety of writing this book I had been frightened of daring to go public in case the very company that has employed me since 1975 ceased my pension for going against the firm. But just as I was drawing towards the end of my career, I received in the post 'in the nick of time' as they say a copy of the Nursing and Midwifery Council guide book on "Raising concerns"

It explains; raising concerns is not the same as making a complaint. It's more of a let's not point fingers at individuals, but let's learn from the bad experience and ensure that it does not happen again. It's about speaking up on behalf of the people we care for "Doing nothing and failing to report concerns, is unacceptable."

We don't need to have all the facts to prove your concerns, but if you have a reasonable belief that a wrongdoing is either happening now, took place in the past, or is likely to happen in the future we have to speak up. Raising concerns is when we are acting as a witness to what we have observed and are taking steps to draw attention to the situation. Raising concerns externally should be done in the most extreme circumstances when all internal steps have failed.

I needed conformation what legalisation is in place, to protect me?

It stated; the Public Interest Disclosure Act (1998) (PIDA) was introduced to provide protection for those who honestly raise genuine concern about wrongdoing or malpractice in the workplace, when they do so in good faith and are acting in the public interest.

Protection is also available for disclosure to regulatory bodies and in exceptional circumstances, wider disclosure for example, to a MP or the media.

I hope the above will protect me in my hour of need, because I believe the whole book has been about "Raising concern" I never intended to be vindictive against anyone or any order. Raising concern, I think would have been a good title for Julian's book, but as Julian had chosen his own title, I will side with him. I always did during his life, I don't see why I should change now were parted. The title being, "They didn't listen, they didn't know how" I'm sure he's got a bigger picture from where he is to send me that message. I thought of two other fitting titles, 'My life became too sweet' or simply "Abandoned without a Plan B"

I feel Julian's legacy to the world is to continue the excitement he enthralled in life and to instilled it in others around you, but not just his enthusiasm but also learn from life's experience, the good and the bad ones, especially the bad ones. He used to say "We learn more from bad experience" This Diabetic drama was definitely Julian's worst experience and unfortunately his last, hopefully we have learnt from at his expence.

There must be some of you wondering, do I think Julian could have survived this last hospitalisation. The answer is most definitely 'yes' I think he could have. After all he only had an abscess. The biggest worry I had before his admission was, would they insist he had to take the insulin which may lead him to multi-organ failure for the second time.

I never dreamt he would be hounded like he was to take the concoction of drugs that he was obviously so hypersensitive to. Neither did I imagine he'd have to be involved in so many different deals and negotiations to stop the prescribed drugs pushers.

His care was nothing like holistic, when I recalled what I said at the Inquest 'we have to treat everybody in a holistic manner' and the Coroner there-after asked each Doctor in turn on the stand, did they feel they had treated Julian holistically. Each answer was woolly, but for those who are not quite ofay with the meaning of the word 'holistic care' It means to take care of someone's 'whole wellbeing' that is physically, emotionally, mentally and spiritually? In reality the body, mind and spirit are intertwined and cannot be separated. In essence it requires to be balanced not negative or positive just in balanced. Once this is achieved healing can take place, and not before.

That means physically the body requires adequate diet, adequate fluids, adequate exercise, and adequate sleep, but above all be toxic free. Hence the old saying 'you are what you eat'.

It means mentally the mind needs to be free from health worry, financial worry and emotional worry to stay healthy. Hence the old wives tale 'worry can make you sick'.

Spiritually the body needs to be free to practice own belief, according to holistic care we all need a spiritual guide to be fear free. Hence another saying 'fear is an enemy you cannot heal in'

In most professions it is recommended that the three taboo subjects are never mentioned in the work place for fear of offending others, they are money, politics and religion. At times I've thought I should apologise about mentioning Biblical quotes as often as I have, but if we all need some sort of faith to be healthy then I'm <u>not</u> sorry, I have drawn on my grandmothers teachings. How nice to think her simple childlike bible stories have healing qualities for my ailments in old age. That's something I must endeavour to draw on to stay healthy.

A Priest once said to me it does not matter what faith we have as long as we remain faithful to the faith we were born into. Every faith has good grounding, it's only when faiths are taken to the extreme it becomes a problem. It's there to soothe and heal us, not to cause distress and war.

Some of you might also be wondering if I'm harbouring the deepest of secrets 'Did I help Julian pass over by encouraging him not to take his medication" The answer to that is;

I loved Julian first and cared for him second, completely without any reservations throughout the 28 years of married life, especially during the last 5 weeks of his life. However if there are some people out there who may have any misgivings, doubts or reservations that just maybe I may have helped him on his way, as someone asked me on the phone one evening quite soon after he died. I'm telling you now in plane black and white English **"I did not"** and in writing this book I hope I am letting the caller and the world know that too.

Maybe this was another reason Julian wanted me to write this book, maybe it's the only way some people can be convinced that I didn't harm him. In harming him I had such a lot to lose.

Now, quietly in these pages, I can tell the world how I'm hurting and missing him.

Maybe I should have filed this paragraph under thank you, because without these four long years of investigating his case I would not have been able to decipher those difficulties he encountered during those last five weeks of his life. Hopefully now I can prove my innocence to his mother and his sister. Because I didn't intentionally cause his death, unfortunately I did indirectly cause him to develop a tumour on his Adrenal gland, but only as much as any other man or woman in this country who has an interest in buying, cooking and feeding their loved ones. My only crime had been to feed him pesticides, preservatives,

GM and MSG food, GM prescribed medicine, refined food, synthetic cooking oils and fats, and artificial sweeteners. Although it's too late for Julian, but now I am better informed I now intend to forbid these food substances to come over my thresh-hold and sneak into to my kitchen cupboards let alone in to my boiling pot to later grace the table to feed any guests.

Did Julian become a non-identity or in the eyes of some, an "Useless Eater"

Julian was definitely not a useless eater; in fact he was more useful than most able man. If he had been culled at the tender age of 18 when he became disabled, society would have lost a very good example of human endurance.

Julian definitely suffered injustice and as Martin Luther King Jr. once said "Injustice anywhere is a threat to justice everywhere"

So I have to tell Julian's story as it was, to avoid further injustice.

Looking back over our life together it seems to form a chain of strange coincidences, coincidence that Julian stayed at a **Freemason** public house, coincidence I changed my faith from Methodist to Roman **Catholic,** coincidence before our daughter was born I had a repetitive dream that the **Gypsies** had taken me to Rome, coincidence we renovated part of a **Knight Templers** Fort, coincidence how the house possessed a vertical shaft turning into a **tunnel** just like the one in Jerusalem Mount which was excavated by the Templers in 1124.

Coincident that Julian became a **Diabetic,** coincident that I unlike others took Julian's **drug intolerance** seriously! And finally was it a coincidence, that I had **accusations** made against me and that I may have been harming Julian, which could have resulted in me being locked up.

Were all these coincidences, or were they there to attract my attention so I could make sense of the complicated dark secret that's trying to choke the living daylight out of all of us?

I have been blessed with a companion called 'Old man time' allowing me freedom and space to look deeper into the struggle he endured at the end. And because of what I have discovered, I could never return to nursing, now I have a different understanding of medicine. I have no proof that Diabetes Type Two does not exist, but I do know if one is suffering from Adrenal malfunction then the glucose levels are affected. My belief is; that Julian was not your regular Type Two Diabetic patient, after recalling the struggles he endured attempting so fiercely and tried to make the treatment work. He might as well of tried to force a square cog into to a round hole, it just wouldn't work. Then coupled with the fact that, when the Doctor at Shrewsbury asked me behind closed doors "Was I sure I was a real nurse?" He wrenched something out of me that day. All the 'caring' came out of my heart and since that day I've started to question my-self-worth. Maybe 34 years of caring as a nurse and 29 years of caring not so much for a Tetraplegia, but for a husband which totals 63 years of caring, was not up to their standard any more. In the end it wasn't a question of giving more to nursing but my destiny is to give up on nursing. The end of my career was made easier when someone at work raised concerns about my memory issues, regarding failing to record a patients intake and output on their fluid balance chart.

To try and find out why my memory failed me in my work place I agreed to go on sick leave and undergo investigations. I took part in four memory tests, agreed to have an MRI scan, the very same scan poor Julian had to endure even though he suffered from claustrophobia. I was referred to a Dementia clinic and I was investigated for Alzheimer's, I attended several appointments with psychotherapists which lasted for four months. And lastly I was counselled by a bereavement team. The end conclusion was, I was suffering from overload due to 'The need to retain all information as it was unclear in my mind, why Julian suffered and died like he did and my constant questioning of could I have done things differently?'

The book has accomplished exactly what Julian intended it to do; it's made me delve into painful situations in order to understand why things happened as they did.

How ironic during all those years of broken sleep during our married life, with Julian's periodic illnesses, I never once forgot to check that I had updated my patients fluid balance charts at the end of every shift, but sadly during Julian's last 35 days of his life Julian's fluid balance charts were hardly ever filled in at all. It seems to me the nurses who looked after Julian, weren't even questioned for their poor documentation where as I was asked to leave and haunted by the fact Julian had to endure bullying with enforced treatment and then the humiliation of refusal of not being allowed to choose where he wanted to spend the last few days of his life.

I feel the three decades I dedicated to nursing, always trying to put my patients first by going without breaks, constantly changing shifts to accommodate the ward cover, mixing day shifts with night shifts leading to sleep deprivation, teaching students when I could, always living by my heroin Agnes Hunt's ethos, which was "Patients cannot recover without good food, fresh air and plenty of laughter" There were plenty of times when I went to work and didn't feel like laughing, but I always locked my miserable head away in my locker until the end my shift. And on the odd occasion when I felt unwell, I'd do the same because who wants to be looked after by a self-pity nurse? We often worked an hour or two over our shift, taking into account full timers couldn't claim overtime pay, we used to light-heartedly refer to it as our 'charity work' hours.

Non-medical friends would sometimes comment "Don't do it, just work to rule" I would jokingly agree and say "Ok, even when I'm looking after your Mum" They would soon back down and understand why nurses do those extra miles, because they want their kin taken care of properly.

So when the Doctor so carelessly tossed those harsh words towards me behind closed doors, when I felt all I was doing was trying to defend Julian cornor. He attacked me when I was at my most vulnerable and also insulted my very being, to which I've never recovered.

Looking back, my Manager was right to want to terminate my contract now I realise I had all these pages stored inside my head, it was hard to remember everything. The feeling of leaving my long career behind was mutual in the end, because I came to realise that once I returned back to work I couldn't achieve any life changing practice without proper research.

Although it's my belief that Type Two Diabetics do produce enough Insulin and to give them additional Insulin is like giving a Non-Diabetic person Insulin, and in the words of the pharmacist who once said to me "Do you know how dangerous it is give someone Insulin when they don't need it? My answer that day and today remains the same "Yes I do, it's very dangerous"!

To back this comment up I recall meeting a retired friend in the hospital corridor after Julian died, when she informed me her neighbour had committed suicide by taking her boyfriend's Insulin. She didn't realise what a dagger those comments were to me, they went straight through my heart. My private thoughts were; that is exactly what happens to people who take medication they know may harm them or don't need, it can prove to be fatal, just like it did in Julian's case.

Just as I knew how dangerous it is to be treated by a Doctor who can barely speak English, like the Spanish Doctor who could not understand Julian's plea when he tried to reason with him that he was allergic to Insulin.

Now at last the Government recognises; that we the public can and do sometimes suffer at the hands of poor spoken English amongst foreign Doctors.

In 2012 Andrew Lansley the Health Secretary spoke out saying "It can lead to situations where Doctors put patients safety at risk . . . the last Government knew this was a problem, but failed to change the system to protect patients"

Although I did not complete my race in nursing, I hope I've continued to contribute to the medical profession in other ways by completing this book by simply relaying Julian's message, of going back to the beginning of every topic that affected him in life. I hope I've done what Julian used to do in life, which was to think laterally and always outside the box.

What I hope I have achieved is; I've looked at Julian's diabetic problem through the eyes of a suffering man instead of looking at it through the eyes of a stubborn nurse, insisting every patient has to be slotted into either type one or type two diabetes category, regardless of how he or she is begging for mercy.

When this book started its journey it was originally intended to act as an SOS signal to others who may have been suffering similar side effects as Julian.

How ironic that the letters, SOS, represents, someone in distress "Please help me" but literary stands for 'Save Our Souls' what a heart rendering plea. How Julian would have liked it, if someone had paused for a moment to listen to his distress call, in order to Save His Soul. As far as I know his death was never filed under any statistic, such as medical misadventure, forced suicide, insulin allergy or prescribed drug abuse. Do you the reader think it should have been?

Sadly since Julian's death, Julian's father has also passed away so Julian, his father and his youngest brother are now keeping company together. And I'm sure whatever earthly issues they may have had on the earthly plain are now cancelled and I imagine they are now the best of friends.

I was glad Julian read what his father wrote in his last birthday card before he died, he expressed how, he 'admired the way Julian bore his suffering with such gallantry'. At least his Father recognised Julian's life struggles before they both passed away. His Father suffered with Rheumatoid Arthritis in his later years, and became acquainted with an unwelcomed guest called 'Pain'

After Julian died I attended a Mask Ball, where a live band entertained us called 'The lady and the Sax'. Entertaining us were three marvellous singers, one of whom was called David Lawrence whose stunning performance aroused in me a positive-ness to continue with this book for the sake of others. I can't believe how music has played such a big part in my journey of healing. On this particular night it was the lyrics yet again that made me cry, it was originally from the musical "Man of La Mancha" where Peter Ottol and Sophia Loren performed in 1959 on Broadway. The song was called

"To reach the un-reachable stars"

And the world will be better for this,
That one man, scorned and covered with scars,
Still strove with his last ounce of courage,
To reach the un-reachable star.

Each verse in this song just depicts Julian's journey, except for the fourth and fifth verse, they express my feelings. We all need to leave this world a better place; otherwise we live our lives just existing from one minute to the next waiting for death. How pointless is that, when we were given this beautiful gift of life in the first place. Julian's life I'm glad to say, passed all expectations and even in death he is still teaching us "Death does not have to be like his" Death should be like life, beautiful and graceful gliding from one world into another.

I now see my purpose in life; it is to prevent others experiencing the same struggle Julian endured at the end. Only then will I be able to lie peacefully knowing I attempted to right the wrong, when I'm laid to rest. Every man deserves to die in a peaceful way, that's why I could not bring myself to write in the obituary 'died peacefully on 12th November 2008 because he didn't. The first verse says; to dream the impossible dream, he never thought it was impossible to achieve the impossible he did on many occasions, even from wheelchair. He just thought big, and aimed high.

My sister has now adopted his Motto "Think big and aim high" just like him.

The last verse depicts how Julian strived for survival, with his struggling last breath.

I started this book in the hope that others would not suffer in the same way as Julian, but now I fear as the book come to a conclusion, the realisation I now have in publishing this book is "**The life that I might one day save, might be my own!**" Because at my hour of need I don't want to find myself whispering silently into the starry night through a vial of tears in agonising pain, wishing I had done something about this Diabetic dilemma after Julian died, only to suffer the same fate as him with no one as my advocate. (The medical profession cannot help me or others if they are not made aware of this problem)

In my mature years I see life as a wall with a thousand windows; we often miss our chance of looking through some of them for all sorts of reasons and excuses. This is where the phrase "The window of opportunity" comes from. I now feel that this was one of Julian's windows of missed opportunity. His life may have been very different, had he researched his complaint more thoroughly during those 15 months grace he was given, he didn't however rest on his laurels. Instead, as his health returned when his treatment was discontinued he was distracted by good health and excitement took over and he continued on his life's journey by enjoying the physical activities he craved for when he was so ill. With hindsight, what he should have done was to research his complaint, doing what I'm doing now in his absence. Backing up his case with facts and figures so when he was next Hospitalised he would have been fore armed with the fact that, he was firstly affected by his Adrenal tumour, then exposed to a host of other things that just aggravated his original complaint.

The clock, we cannot turn back for poor Julian but we can do something for us, the survivors! We need to be quick, the clock is ticking this book is not about the end of his life but rather, the closure to his suffering.

In the lyrics of the singer Enya "Night has come to those who sleep, only dreams they cannot keep" I hope Julian, I have lived out your dream by attempting to solve your Diabetic dilemma.

And now my task is done, I have my freedom to do what I couldn't do at your bed side and that was to retreat to a mountain top and scream my head off, to release all the psychological gagging we both endured.

A friend of mine suggested I sat in a corner and close my eyes, then visualise myself flying over the situation leaving it behind. Saying quietly to myself "This was a negative situation in my life; I will not let it destroy me, I admit I am hurting because of what happened but I am now releasing it and letting go of my pain" In the end, this book became my positive affirmation allowing me to let go of the past and look forward to the future. My frayed edged tapestry of life is now tidy and neatly rolled away; I don't need to revisit this painful place again not until I meet my Maker.

In the words of the 14th Dalai lama who once said,

> Old friend's pass away, new friends appear.
> It is just like the days.
> An old day passes and a new day arrives.
> The important thing is to make meaningful friends,
> And meaningful days.

I hope I have made meaningful days and will continually to do so every day of my life, but more importantly make meaningful friends.

Who would have thought the Jesuits was at the core of this catastrophic world we live in. Even though things seem pretty hopeless with the New World in charge, we need to remind ourselves there are only 12,000 Freemasons in the Vatican and only 1,274 billionaires in this world. There are still 700,000000 of us who make up the rest of the world population and although we have no money or weapons to fight these Anti-Christs with their evil mind controlling and satanic practices, there are two places we must not allow them to control and that is our faith and our mind. They are the two places we can find solace and refuge, we need to keep them sacred. The New World Order, New Era,

Illuminati, New Age, Global Ellite, Freemasons, Guilderberg and the remainder of the Satanic of this world. I for one don't wish to belong to this New World Order but wish to belong to the 'Old World Order' with its simple way of life.

I recently visited the 'Back to Back houses' in the Birmingham Black Country Museum and the lady on the guided tour reminded us the visitors saying "Remember, it <u>wasn't</u> the Elite of this country who made this country great, it was the true grit of the poverty stricken working class" I think between the 700,000000 of the world population and on a wing and a prayer we could make this world a better place to live once more. I found an old Chinese proverb which might help,
'If there is light in the soul, there will be beauty in the person.
If there is beauty in the person, there will be harmony in the house.
If there is harmony in the house, there will be order in the Nation.
If there is order in the Nation there will be peace in the world"
(But we need to start with the light in the soul!)

If 2011 was meant to be the 'year of the <u>truth</u>' and 2012 was meant to be the 'year for <u>listening</u>' they say 2013 is now meant to be the 'year of <u>exposure</u>' then these three small words truth, listening and exposure almost capsulate my agony over Julian's unnecessary suffering. With the book title amplifying "They didn't listen, they didn't know how" But of course if the reader disbelieves my possible theory's, then I will have to live with the two last lyrics in the song which are "They're not listening still" but my biggest dread is if I have to hear "Perhaps they never will" then sadly I will indeed not have achieved Julian's intention after all. His 'experiment' as he called it, will truly have been in vain.
Mahatma Gandhi once said "If I die, then maybe they will stop" Julian used to say similar words. "I don't think they will stop until I die" They both carried a similar massage.
I would like Julian to be remembered for 'It's so important to listen' sadly no one listed to him at the end. Just like the punishment he endured at the hands of the headmaster when he was caned, he didn't listen either. Sometimes they say, the most painful experience inspires the greatest of change and improvement in our life and, we should use our memories as a catalyst to propel ourselves into an amazing future. I hope I've made good use of my painful experience by researching why

775

Julian could no longer tolerate 'man's modern-day medicine' Now I feel confident enough to return to the Consultant, who showed us no pity at his bed side and at last let him know why Julian could not tolerate his medicine. Do you remember I called after another Doctor into the dark of night "I will find out why he can't tolerate your medicine, mark my words dead or alive, I will find out. Then I will come back to let you know why" I found a quote written by an anonymous person "There is dignity in dyeing, that Doctors should not dare to deny" Sadly they failed him on this score too!

The eighth Native American rule says "Dedicate a share of your efforts to the greater good" I hope in sharing this book with others I will have achieved that.

The book started as my battle, but now surprisingly has ended up as my peacemaker. I stress this book is based on personal experiences, living with a person who could no longer tolerate any medication at all. But had he survived this hospital incident, would he have to live in exile from the medical world, always hunted down to take their prescribed drugs? Not a one for running away he stood his ground, trying to reason with them and sort it out once and for all, sadly in the end he was like a druggy trying to go clean in a 'prescribed drug pushing environment'

I hope I won't be alienated regarding the content of this book, but instead I seek a vote of confidence to help support my theory. Is there a Specialist, a Scientist, a Doctor, a Consultant, a Good Politician or a Solicitor out there, who can further research my personal feelings about Julian's complicated Endocrine life and turn it into a test case? All I know is, this man was not ready for death his intention in life was to be a good 'God-parent', he intended to pay back a large loan, he intended to guide Llewela through University, he intended to give Llewela away on her wedding day, he intended to finish renovating our house in France, he intended to enjoy our retirement together, he intended for the first time in a long time to return to full time employment, he had such a lot to live for and a lot more to offer. Early death was not on this man's agenda.

It really doesn't matter to me anymore what they wrote on his death certificate, in my heart of hearts I now know what he died from and if anyone asks me, if I think Julian was culled by modern day drugs, what do you think I should tell them? I realise I cannot bring Julian back, but if it was possible to change his death certificate I would like it to state-:

Cause of death due to Ph. Imbalance, Drug Toxicity with Chemical and Drug reaction, resulting in Decomposition of tissue leading to death. Incidentally it's something we're all in danger of suffering from in this corrupt world. Instead it states, Cause of death due to pneumonia, diabetes and tetraplegia. I'm not concerned about being remembered for fighting against what is wrong, but I certainly don't want to be remembered for 'NOT raising concerns about his suffering '!

I invite you to agree or disagree with my questioning, but please don't sue me! All I've tried to do, is write this book through the eyes of a child, constantly asking "Why" to all aspects of life, that I felt he had been wronged. Recalling a verse in the New Testament Matthew 18 v3 "Unless you change and become like little children, you will never enter the kingdom of heaven"

Most of all, what I've come to realise is that the affection that we once shared has become a bond that cannot be broken, I realise love is an everlasting energy that cannot be disbursed and it was this love that enabled me to ride on the crest of a wave and elevate myself above my bereavement to write this book. I conclude this book with one last quote from Mother Teresa "I know God won't give me anything I can't handle; I just wish he didn't trust me so much."

My parting words to you Julian are 'Peace be with you, and I hope all the Angels and Saints did escort you through those gates as you were received into heaven. As you left our company here on earth in our parting, heaven certainly gained a good soul, while here on earth we certainly lost a very wise and clever man. Until we meet again, in the beautiful garden of reunion to commune once more. It was after all the one thing we both enjoyed and did best and that was to talk'.

In English we say, "God bless you".
In Hebrew we say, "Shalom and mighty blessings be upon you."
In French we all wish you a "Bon voyage". (Good journey)
In Welsh we bid you "Nosweth dda Julian". (Good night)
And Llewela and I wish to send you a greeting from our hearts, "Rwyn dy garu di"

Photograph of how I hope Julian was welcomed home, greeted with opened arms with a host of Angels forming his 'Guard of Honour' playing angelic music with their sweet sounding trumpets.

And if heaven is a prepared place for prepared people then I think Julian might be accepted, because he spent all our married life secretly doing good for others, asking for no praise in return. He did this hoping he was securing the prepared place Jesus had promised us. In John chapter 14 v2 Jesus says "There are many rooms in my Father's house; if there were not I should have told you. I am going now to prepare a place for you"

My Affidavit

I stated earlier in the book, that I would end it with my affidavit. I will, but what has puzzled me for some time, is when people who attend court and asked to take the stand, they are asked to swear on the Bible. As I am a Christian, I find this a strange practice, all through my growing up years my Parents and Teachers have asked me not to swear, yet when it comes to something as important as a court room or an Inquest the Judge or Coroner (the most powerful people in the land they keep telling me) ask us, not only to swear, but to do it on the Bible in front of witnesses. When I was asked to make a statement at Telford Police Station I had to sign,

"I swear that the statement I have made was true".

As this is my book, I'm going to **assure or affirm** to you the reader, that on my honour, the content of this book is true to the best of my knowledge and belief and I make it knowingly that if it is tendered in evidence I shall be liable to be prosecuted if I have wilfully stated anything in it, which I know to be false, or do not believe to be true.

The last Native American Indian rule asks "Be truthful and honest at all times" I hope I have been.

Olwen Davies signing off 3pm on the 12th November 2012, how strange exactly four years to the day Julian died.

References

Mari Carter first published in 2000 "Healing and Hope" . . . .

Anita Bean first published in 2001 "Detox for life" London by Virgin books, page 21.

Cherry Chappell first published in 2009 "Grandma's Remedies" London by Random

Say No to Diabetes by Patrick Holford, BSc, DipION, FRBANT, NTCRP published in 2011

By Piatkus.

Type 4 Diabetes by Robert Ransom in 2007 published by B.B.G media page 145.

The Fibromyalgia Relief by Chet Cunningham published in 2000 by United Research Publishers page 111.

Prescribed and Forgotten by Georges Camoussa published in 2008 by Aid to the Church in need page 82.

Healing our Hormones by Linda Crocket published 2009 by John Hunt Publishing Ltd page 10-27.

Name of the book by Doctor Brucetyle, Certified Nutritionist, Doctor in Naturopathic Medicine.

The Wall Street Journal, 7 June 1995 pB6(W) Pb6€ col 1(11colin) compiled by Darleen Bradley. (Re macular hole)

Code of Conduct 2011

www.jctonic.com/include/healingcrises/20rancid_oils.htm (2004 Dr Bruce Fife)

www.wisegee.com/is_there_a_realationship_between_macular_degener____ (re Rapeseed)

thesescreamonline.com/essays/essays5-1/vegoil.html by Mary Enig

www.wikipedia.org/wiki/canola_(re canola)

paleodietlifestyle.com/the_many_virtues_of_butter (re butter)

www.ithyroid.com/canola_oil.htm_(re-horror stories)

endthe.com/ . . . 27000-organic-farmers-fight-back-ag

www.elmhurst.edu/-chum/vchembook/549saccharin.html

www.squidoo.com>HealthyLiving

en.wikipedia.org/wiki/aspartame

www.splendaexposed.com/

articles.mercola.com/ . . . neotame—receives-fda-approval

onlinelibrary.wiley.com/doi/10.1111/1467-9523.0016/pdf.

Info.organic.org.tw/supergood/ezcatfiees/organic . . . 199627017.pdf

www.whitedragon.org.uk/photoess/p-ess2.htm

www.wrf.org/ancient-medicine/oldest-medical-books.php

www.complete-herbal.com/history.htm

www.tearea.govt.nz/en/overseas-trade-policy/4

www.organicconsumers.org/ge/pusztai.halt.cfm

saynotogmfood.blogspot.com/ . . . animal-genes-in-normal-vegetaria

www.i-sis.org.uk/GMCCHHTAL.php

www.dietmindspirit.org/category/organic/feed/

www.complete-herbal.com/history.htm

www.whale.to/w/chlorine.html

www.cassiopaea.org/cass/Fluoride.htm

www.webnd.com/biosuperfoods.php.

www.whfoods.com/genpage.php?tname=foodsspicedbid=96

www.dailymail.co.uk . . . /Britons-dont-want-GM-crops-survey.html

articles.mercola.com/sites/ . . . microwave-hazards.aspx-us

www.tpa-uk.org.uk/adrenal_thyroid_stockolim.sep09.pde

http://simplydstooday.blog

Services>Burnscentre

bestmeal.info/Monsanto/company-history.shtml (sighted1:05:12)

www.canolainfo.org/canloa/index.php.page=5 (sighted 1:05:12)

www.rense.comp/politics6/canola.htm(sighted1:05:12)

www.benbest.com/health/essfat.html

http://wikicompany.org/wiki/911;RothschildHistory

thedaysofhoah.wordpress.com/ . . . /1901-1919-thesecre

www.bibliotecapleyades.net/biggestsecret/ . . . /biggestsecret19.htm

en.wikipedia.org/wiki/History-of-the-Knight-Templers sited 13/09/12

www.answers.com.Library.Travel.Place

http://www.davidicke.com/icke/articles/hitler.html

www.whale.to/b/knox.html. (sited23/8/12

the freemanperpective.blogspot.com/ . . . / . . . mindcontroll

mountzion144:ning.com/xn/detail/2127676Topic:Topic690158?xg:

DavidNoakeshttp;//eutruth.org.uk

www.cospiracyplanet.com/channel.cfm?channelid=36 . . . 6135
www.truthistreason.net/russian-politician-wars-of-secret-weather-we
www.illuminati-news.com/nwo.htm
ww.angelfire.com/113/threehawks/images19/indextemplar.html
www.iamthewitness.com/DaryIBradfordSmith_Rothchild_ori.htm
worldtruth.tv/the_untoldtruth_behind_the_sinking_of_the_titanic/
rense.com/general77/POWERS.HTM
monroecountrydailytest.blogspot.com/2011 . . . /secret_weather_weapon
educate-yourself.org/now/brotherhoodart9.shtml
WHATPRINCESSDIANNAKNEW-THE-OFFICIALRESISTANCE
www.resistance2010.com/xn/detail/3228704:BlogPost:188205
www.naturalnews.com/033816_swine_flu_vaccines_neurol
www.wellnessresources.com/ . . . /can-high-good-cholesterol-be . . .